New Perspectives on

# MICROSOFT®
# OFFICE 2000
# VISUAL BASIC FOR
# APPLICATIONS

## Introductory

REBEKAH TIDWELL

NEIL THOMAS

COURSE
TECHNOLOGY
THOMSON LEARNING™

Australia • Canada • Mexico • Singapore • Spain • United Kingdom • United States

New Perspectives on Microsoft Office 2000 Visual Basic for Applications is published by Course Technology.

| | | | |
|---|---|---|---|
| Managing Editor | Greg Donald | Developmental Editor | Ann Shaffer |
| Senior Editor | Donna Gridley | Production Editor | Kristen Guevara |
| Series Technology Editor | Rachel A. Crapser | Text Designer | Meral Dabcovich |
| Associate Product Manager | Melissa Dezotell | Cover Designer | Douglas Goodman |
| Editorial Assistant | Rosa Maria Rogers | | |

© 2001 by Course Technology, a division of Thomson Learning

For more information contact:

**Course Technology**
25 Thomson Place
Boston, MA 02210
Or find us on the World Wide Web at: http://www.course.com

For permission to use material from this text or product, contact us by

- **Web: www.thomsonrights.com**
- **Phone: 1-800-730-2214**
- **Fax: 1-800-730-2215**

ISBN 0-619-01936-0

Printed in the United States of America

1 2 3 4 5 6 7 8 9 MZ 05 04 03 02 01

# PREFACE
## The New Perspectives Series

### About New Perspectives

Course Technology's **New Perspectives Series** is an integrated system of instruction that combines text and technology products to teach computer concepts, the Internet, and microcomputer applications. Users consistently praise this series for innovative pedagogy, use of interactive technology, creativity, accuracy, and supportive and engaging style.

### How is the New Perspectives Series different from other series?

The **New Perspectives Series** distinguishes itself by **innovative technology**, from the renowned Course Labs to the state-of-the-art multimedia that is integrated with our Concepts texts. Other distinguishing features include **sound instructional design, proven pedagogy,** and **consistent quality**. Each tutorial has students learn features in the context of solving a realistic case problem rather than simply learning a laundry list of features. With the **New Perspectives Series**, instructors report that students have a complete, integrative learning experience that stays with them. They credit this high retention and competency to the fact that this series incorporates critical thinking and problem-solving with computer skills mastery. In addition, we work hard to ensure accuracy by using a multi-step quality assurance process during all stages of development. Instructors focus on teaching and students spend more time learning.

### What course is this book appropriate for?

*New Perspectives on Microsoft Office 2000 Visual Basic for Applications* can be used in any course in which you want to introduce students to basic programming topics. It is particularly recommended for a short course on Microsoft Visual Basic for Applications. This book assumes that students have mastered using Microsoft Office 2000, but does not require programming experience.

### Proven Pedagogy

**CASE**

**Tutorial Case**  Each tutorial begins with a problem presented in a case that is meaningful to students. The case turns the task of learning how to use an application into a problem-solving process.

**45-minute Sessions**  Each tutorial is divided into sessions that can be completed in about 45 minutes to an hour. Sessions allow instructors to more accurately allocate time in their syllabus, and students to better manage their own study time.

**1.**

**2.**

**3.**

**Step-by-Step Methodology**  We make sure students can differentiate between what they are to *do* and what they are to *read*. Through numbered steps—clearly identified by a gray shaded background—students are constantly guided in solving the case problem. In addition, the numerous screen shots with callouts direct students' attention to what they should look at on the screen.

**TROUBLE?**

**TROUBLE? Paragraphs**  These paragraphs anticipate the mistakes or problems that students may have and help them continue with the tutorial.

## Tutorial Tips

**Tutorial Tips Page** This page, following the Table of Contents, offers students suggestions on how to effectively plan their study and lab time, what to do when they make a mistake, and how to use the Reference Windows, Quick Checks, and other features of the New Perspectives series.

**"Read This Before You Begin" Page** Located opposite the first tutorial's opening page, the Read This Before You Begin page helps introduce technology into the classroom. Technical considerations and assumptions about software are listed to save time and eliminate unnecessary aggravation. Notes about the Data Disks help instructors and students get the right files in the right places, so students get started on the right foot.

**Quick Check Questions** Each session concludes with Quick Check questions that test students' understanding of what they learned in the session. Answers to the Quick Check questions are provided at the end of each tutorial.

**Reference Windows** Reference Windows are succinct summaries of the step-oriented tasks covered in a tutorial and they preview actions students will perform in the steps to follow.

**Syntax Boxes** Syntax Boxes summarize the syntax for essential VBA statements. Each syntax box includes an explanation of the most important options and an illustrative example.

**Task Reference** A table at the end of the book, the Task Reference contains a summary of the most efficient method for common tasks, as well as references to pages where the task is discussed in more detail.

**End-of-Tutorial Review Assignments, Case Problems, Review Assignments** Review Assignments provide students with additional hands-on practice of the skills they learned in the tutorial using the same case presented in the tutorial. These Assignments are followed by four Case Problems that have approximately the same scope as the tutorial case but use a different scenario. In addition, some of the Review Assignments or Case Problems may include Exploration Exercises that challenge students and encourage them to explore the capabilities of VBA they are using, and further extend their knowledge.

*New Perspectives on Microsoft Office 2000 Visual Basic for Applications* Instructor's Resource Kit (IRK) contains:

- Sample Syllabus
- Data Files
- Solution Files
- Course Test Manager Testbank
- Course Test Manager Engine
- Figure Files
- Electronic Instructor's Manual in Word 97 format

These supplements come on CD-ROM. If you don't have access to a CD-ROM drive, contact your Course Technology customer service representative for more information.

### More innovative technology

### Course CBT

Enhance your students' Office 2000 classroom learning experience with self-paced computer-based training on CD-ROM. Course CBT engages students with interactive multimedia and hands-on simulations that reinforce and complement the concepts and skills covered in the textbook. All the content is aligned with the MOUS (Microsoft Office User Specialist) program, making it a great preparation tool for the certification exams. Course

CBT also includes extensive pre- and post-assessments that test students' mastery of skills. These pre- and post-assessments automatically generate a "custom learning path" through the course that highlights only the topics students need help with.

## Skills Assessment Manager (SAM)

How well do your students *really* know Microsoft Office? SAM is a performance-based testing program that measures students' proficiency in Microsoft Office 2000. SAM is available for Office 2000 in either a live or simulated environment. You can use SAM to place students into or out of courses, monitor their performance throughout a course, and help prepare them for the MOUS certification exams.

## CyberClass

CyberClass is a Web-based tool designed for on-campus or distance learning. Use it to enhance how you currently run your class by posting assignments and your course syllabus or holding online office hours. Or, use it for your distance learning course, and offer mini-lectures, conduct online discussion groups, or give your mid-term exam. For more information, visit our Web site at: **www.course.com/products/cyberclass/index.html**.

## WebCT

WebCT is a tool used to create Web-based educational environments and also uses WWW browsers as the interface for the course-building environment. The site is hosted on your school campus, allowing complete control over the information. WebCT has its own internal communication system, offering internal e-mail, a Bulletin Board, and a Chat room. Course Technology offers pre-existing supplemental information to help in your WebCT class creation, such as a suggested Syllabus, Lecture Notes, Figures in the Book, Course Presenter, Student Downloads, and Test Banks in which you can schedule an exam, create reports, and more.

## Acknowledgments

Sincere thanks to our reviewers for their excellent feedback: Lisa Brew, Arta Szathmary, ,and Mike Tarn.

We're also grateful to John Bosco, Quality Assurance Project Leader, and Ashlee Welz and Justin Rand, QA testers, for verifying the technical accuracy of every step. Many thanks also to Kristen Guevara for sheparding this book through the production process.

I want to express my appreciation to Carson Newman College for allowing me to take a semester off from my teaching responsibilities.  Many of my colleagues assumed extra responsibilities in my absence—including Dr. Millicent Sites, chair of the Business Department and Amy Reed, secretary for the department.

Finally, I would like to thank my husband Gene for his support, his encouragement, and his undying patience.

Rebekah Tidwell

I would like to thank my wife Ann for all her support. Without her support, I could never have accomplished as much.

Neil Thomas

# BRIEF CONTENTS

Preface      iii
Tutorial Tips      xvi

## Microsoft Office 2000 Visual Basic for Applications      VBA 1

**Tutorial 1**      **VBA 3**

*Introducing Microsoft Visual Basic for Applications (VBA)*

**Tutorial 2**      **VBA 45**

*Working with Objects and Properties*

**Tutorial 3**      **VBA 111**

*Using Variables, Assignment Statements, and Control Structures*

**Tutorial 4**      **VBA 167**

*Repeating Statements with Repetition Control Structures*

**Tutorial 5**      **VBA 219**

*Creating a VBA Application for Microsoft Word*

**Tutorial 6**      **VBA 257**

*Using VBA with Excel*

**Tutorial 7**      **VBA 301**

*Creating a PowerPoint VBA Application with Multiple Forms*

**Tutorial 8**      **VBA 355**

*Using VBA with Access*

**Tutorial 9**      **VBA 405**

*Integrating the Office Applications with VBA*

**Glossary**      **VBA 445**

**Index**      **VBA 451**

**Task Reference**      **VBA 460**

**File Finder**      **VBA 462**

| | |
|---|---|
| Preface | iii |
| Microsoft Office 2000 Visual Basic for Applications | 1 |
| Read this Before you Begin | 2 |

**Tutorial 1**   **VBA 3**

*Introducing Microsoft Visual Basic for Applications (VBA)*

Creating some simple programs for TnT Consulting Group

| | |
|---|---|
| **SESSION 1.1** | **VBA 4** |
| **Reviewing the Office 2000 Suite** | **VBA 4** |
| **A Brief Introduction to Programming** | **VBA 4** |
| **Introducing Visual Basic for Applications** | **VBA 5** |
| Introducing the VBA Integrated Development Environment | VBA 5 |
| Comparing Macros to VBA Programs | VBA 5 |
| The Benefits of Using VBA | VBA 6 |
| **Exploring the VBA Integrated Development Environment (VBA IDE)** | **VBA 6** |
| Opening, Sizing, and Closing Windows | VBA 7 |
| Undocking and Manipulating the VBA IDE Windows | VBA 11 |
| **Opening the VBA IDE in PowerPoint** | **VBA 15** |
| **Switching Between Two IDEs** | **VBA 18** |
| **Session 1.1 Quick Check** | **VBA 18** |
| **SESSION 1.2** | **VBA 19** |
| **Creating a VBA Program for Word** | **VBA 19** |
| Creating a Program for Word | VBA 19 |
| Executing a Program | VBA 24 |
| Understanding the Code | VBA 26 |
| Saving the Document and Associated Modules | VBA 27 |
| **Session 1.2 Quick Check** | **VBA 27** |

| | |
|---|---|
| **SESSION 1.3** | **VBA 28** |
| **Macros and the Macro Recorder** | **VBA 28** |
| Examining the VBA Code in a Macro | VBA 31 |
| Printing a Code Module | VBA 32 |
| Saving a PowerPoint Macro | VBA 33 |
| **Using the VBA Help System** | **VBA 34** |
| **Session 1.3 Quick Check** | **VBA 37** |
| **Review Assignments** | **VBA 37** |
| **Case Problems** | **VBA 40** |
| **Quick Check Answers** | **VBA 44** |

**Tutorial 2**   **VBA 45**

*Working with Objects and Properties*

Creating a Checkbook Interface for TnT Consulting Group

| | |
|---|---|
| **SESSION 2 .1** | **VBA 46** |
| **Understanding Objects** | **VBA 46** |
| Objects and Collections | VBA 46 |
| Using Properties to Define an Object | VBA 47 |
| Understanding Methods and Events | VBA 47 |
| Understanding Interfaces | VBA 48 |
| Examining Some Sample Data Objects | VBA 49 |
| **Exploring the Excel VBA IDE** | **VBA 49** |
| Opening the Excel VBA IDE | VBA 49 |
| Studying the Project Explorer | VBA 50 |
| Changing a Project Name | VBA 52 |
| **Using Forms and Control Objects to Create an Interface** | **VBA 55** |
| Understanding Interfaces | VBA 55 |

| | |
|---|---|
| Understanding Control Objects | VBA 56 |
| Planning the Checkbook Interface | VBA 57 |
| **Working with UserForms** | **VBA 58** |
| Examining the UserForm's Properties | VBA 60 |
| Changing the UserForm's Name Property | VBA 62 |
| Changing Other UserForm Properties | VBA 63 |
| Saving Your Work | VBA 66 |
| **Session 2.1 Quick Check** | **VBA 67** |
| | |
| **SESSION 2.2** | **VBA 67** |
| **Working with Control Objects** | **VBA 67** |
| Adding Control Objects to a UserForm | VBA 67 |
| Naming Objects Within a Project | VBA 69 |
| Changing a Control's Caption Property | VBA 70 |
| Changing Properties for Multiple Objects at One Time | VBA 73 |
| Sizing a Label Control | VBA 76 |
| **Session 2.2 Quick Check** | **VBA 77** |
| | |
| **SESSION 2.3** | **VBA 78** |
| **Adding More Control Objects** | **VBA 78** |
| Dragging the Pointer to Add a Control Object | VBA 78 |
| Adjusting Properties for the New Label Control | VBA 79 |
| Switching to Runtime | VBA 80 |
| Adding the Remaining Text Box and Label Controls | VBA 81 |
| Adding Command Button Controls | VBA 83 |
| Sizing Command Buttons Appropriately | VBA 85 |
| Moving Controls and Adding an Image Control | VBA 87 |
| **Session 2.3 Quick Check** | **VBA 90** |
| | |
| **SESSION 2.4** | **VBA 91** |
| **Adding VBA Code to a Command Button's Click Event** | **VBA 91** |
| Programming the Clear Command Button | VBA 92 |
| Programming the Return to Worksheet Command Button | VBA 94 |
| **Documenting VBA Code** | **VBA 95** |
| **Printing VBA Code** | **VBA 96** |
| **Session 2.4 Quick Check** | **VBA 97** |
| **Review Assignments** | **VBA 98** |
| **Case Problems** | **VBA 99** |
| **Quick Check Answers** | **VBA 108** |

# Tutorial 3     VBA 111

## *Using Variables, Assignment Statements, and Control Structures*

Creating a Salary Calculator Program

| | |
|---|---|
| **SESSION 3.1** | **VBA 112** |
| **Interpreting Syntax in This Text** | **VBA 112** |
| **Previewing the Salary Calculator Program** | **VBA 113** |
| **Storing Data Within a Program** | **VBA 114** |
| Declaring a Variable | VBA 115 |
| Assigning a Data Type | VBA 116 |
| Naming a Variable | VBA 117 |
| Preventing Undeclared Variables with `Option Explicit` | VBA 119 |
| **Assigning Values with an Assignment Statement** | **VBA 120** |
| Understanding Mathematical Expressions and Precedence | VBA 121 |
| Following the Order of Precedence in an Expression | VBA 122 |
| **Previewing the Salary Calculator Code** | **VBA 123** |
| **Entering the Code That Calculates the Salary** | **VBA 124** |
| **Using Functions in VBA** | **VBA 127** |
| Formatting a Value with the Format Function | VBA 127 |
| Adding the Format Function to the Code | VBA 128 |
| Formatting User Input | VBA 129 |

Distinguishing Between Sub Procedures
and Functions **VBA 131**

Session 3.1 Quick Check **VBA 132**

**SESSION 3.2** **VBA 133**

Validating Data **VBA 133**

Introducing the Three Basic Control Structures **VBA 134**

Understanding the Sequence Control Structure **VBA 135**

Understanding Selection Control Structures **VBA 135**

Building an If...Then...Else Statement **VBA 135**

Displaying a Message with the MsgBox
Function **VBA 137**

Using Comparison Operators in an
If...Then...Else Statement **VBA 138**

Using Multiple Comparison Operators in
Compound Conditions **VBA 138**

Adding an If...Then...Else Statement
to the Code **VBA 139**

Debugging a Program **VBA 141**

Stepping Through a Program **VBA 141**

Setting a Breakpoint in a Procedure **VBA 145**

Using the Immediate Window **VBA 148**

Starting Help From the Immediate Window **VBA 151**

Session 3.2 Quick Check **VBA 153**

**SESSION 3.3** **VBA 153**

Viewing the TnT Check Register Project **VBA 153**

Validating Data with the IsNumeric and
IsDate Functions **VBA 156**

Explaining the Validation Code **VBA 158**

Session 3.3 Quick Check **VBA 159**

Review Assignments **VBA 159**

Case Problems **VBA 161**

Quick Check Answers **VBA 165**

**Tutorial 4**     **VBA 167**

*Repeating Statements with Repetition
Control Structures*

Completing the TnT Check Register Project

**SESSION 4.1** **VBA 168**

Creating a Standard Module **VBA 168**

Repeating Statements with Repetition
Control Structures (Loops) **VBA 172**

Using the Two Kinds of Do Loops **VBA 173**

Using Do...While Loops **VBA 173**

Using Do...Until Loops **VBA 179**

Comparing Do...Until Statements and
Do...While Statements **VBA 182**

Using Iterative Loops **VBA 185**

Examining a For...Next Statement **VBA 185**

Coding and Observing a For...Next Loop **VBA 187**

Session 4.1 Quick Check **VBA 188**

**SESSION 4.2** **VBA 189**

Interacting with Object Models **VBA 189**

Working with the Excel Object Model **VBA 189**

Referring to a Specific Excel Object **VBA 190**

Altering Object Properties with Assignment
Statements **VBA 191**

Altering a Worksheet's Name Property **VBA 192**

Using Default Values in Object References **VBA 194**

Altering a Worksheet's Cell Property **VBA 195**

Activating a Worksheet with the Activate
Method **VBA 196**

Altering Other Properties of a Worksheet **VBA 197**

Session 4.2 Quick Check **VBA 199**

**SESSION 4.3**     **VBA 200**

**Testing the Completed TnT Check Register
Project**     **VBA 200**

Finding a Blank Row with a Do...Until Loop     VBA 202

Stepping Through the Do...Until Loop     VBA 203

Inserting Data in the Worksheet Via the
Cells Property     VBA 206

**Calling a Procedure**     **VBA 208**

**Session 4.3 Quick Check**     **VBA 212**

**Review Assignments**     **VBA 212**

**Case Problems**     **VBA 214**

**Quick Check Answers**     **VBA 218**


**Tutorial 5**     **VBA 219**

*Creating a VBA Application for
Microsoft Word*

Creating a Letter-Building Application

**SESSION 5.1**     **VBA 220**

**Previewing the Completed Speaker Listing
Project**     **VBA 220**

Examining the Session Listing Form     VBA 223

Using a Frame Control on a Form     VBA 224

Hiding and Displaying Frames     VBA 225

**Planning the Session Listing Project**     **VBA 228**

**Removing the Form from the Screen**     **VBA 228**

**Session 5.1 Quick Check**     **VBA 230**

**SESSION 5.2**     **VBA 230**

**Using the Word Object Model**     **VBA 230**

**Using the Windows Object Model**     **VBA 232**

**Using the Selection Object to Select Text**     **VBA 232**

**Delete and Set Tabs with the TabStops
Collection**     **VBA 233**

Clearing Tabs with the ClearAll Method     VBA 234

Adding Tabs with the Add Method     VBA 234

Using the Continuation Character     VBA 235

Viewing the Tab Code in the Project     VBA 236

**Inserting Text in a Word Document**     **VBA 237**

Using the Range Object     VBA 238

Using Some Methods of the Range Object     VBA 238

Referring to an Object Multiple Times in a
`With` Statement     VBA 239

Adding the Code to the Project     VBA 239

**Formatting Text with the Range Object**     **VBA 241**

**Session 5.2 Quick Check**     **VBA 243**

**SESSION 5.3**     **VBA 244**

**Establishing a New Range with the Collapse
Method**     **VBA 244**

**Concatenating Strings**     **VBA 245**

**Inserting a Tabbed List in a Document**     **VBA 246**

**Session 5.3 Quick Check**     **VBA 247**

**Review Assignments**     **VBA 248**

**Case Problems**     **VBA 249**

**Quick Check Answers**     **VBA 255**


**Tutorial 6**     **VBA 257**

*Using VBA with Excel*

Developing a Gradebook Application in Excel

**SESSION 6.1**     **VBA 258**

**Previewing the Gradebook Application**     **VBA 258**

**Planning the Gradebook Application**     **VBA 261**

**Examining the Partially Completed Code**     **VBA 262**

**Session 6.1 Quick Check**     **VBA 267**

**SESSION 6.2**     **VBA 267**

**Choosing from Multiple Options with the
Select Case Statement**     **VBA 267**

Studying the `Select Case`
Statement Syntax     VBA 268

Adding a `Select Case` Statement
to the Project    VBA 269

Observing a `Select Case` Statement
with Step Into    VBA 271

**Reviewing the Excel Object Model**    **VBA 273**

**Using Control Structures Appropriately**    **VBA 274**

Avoiding Null Values with an `If` Statement    VBA 275

Using a Do…Until Loop to Find the First
Empty Row    VBA 278

Examining the Do…Until Loop    VBA 279

Comparing Do…Until and Do…While Loops    VBA 280

Inserting Data into the Appropriate Row    VBA 280

Adding the Do…Until Loop to the Project    VBA 281

**Using the AutoFit Method**    **VBA 283**

**Session 6.2 Quick Check**    **VBA 285**

**SESSION 6.3**    **VBA 285**

**Altering the Appearance of a Cell**    **VBA 285**

Adding Color with the RGB Function    VBA 286

Writing the Code That Applies Red and
Boldface to a font    VBA 286

**Sorting Rows with the Sort Method**    **VBA 288**

**Session 6.3 Quick Check**    **VBA 290**

**Review Assignments**    **VBA 290**

**Case Problems**    **VBA 293**

**Quick Check Answers**    **VBA 298**

# Tutorial 7    VBA 301

## Creating a PowerPoint VBA Application with Multiple Forms

Building a Presentation from a Word Outline

**SESSION 7.1**    **VBA 302**

**Previewing the Outline Document**    **VBA 302**

**Previewing the Presentation Builder Project**    **VBA 303**

**Planning the Presentation Builder Project**    **VBA 307**

**Sharing Information Across Modules with
Public Variables**    **VBA 312**

Declaring Public Variables    VBA 312

Referring to Public Variables in VBA
Statements    VBA 313

Using Public Variables in the Project    VBA 313

**Session 7.1 Quick Check**    **VBA 318**

**SESSION 7.2**    **VBA 318**

**Working with the PowerPoint Object Model**    **VBA 318**

Referring to the Active Presentation with the
ActivePresentation Property    VBA 319

Referring to Specific Slides in the Slides
Collection    VBA 319

**Deleting Slides with the Delete Method**    **VBA 320**

**Creating a General Procedure**    **VBA 321**

Coding a General Procedure    VBA 323

Calling a Procedure    VBA 324

**Inserting Slides in a Presentation with the
InsertFromFile Method**    **VBA 327**

**Adding a Footer to the Title Master**    **VBA 329**

**Applying a Layout with the Layout Property**    **VBA 331**

**Applying a Template with the
ApplyTemplate Method**    **VBA 335**

**Session 7.2 Quick Check**    **VBA 337**

**SESSION 7.3**    **VBA 337**

**Abbreviating Object References with the
Set Statement**    **VBA 337**

**Obtaining Data from the User with the
InputBox Function**    **VBA 338**

**Obtaining the Current Date with the
InsertDateTime Method**    **VBA 339**

**Working with the Shapes Collection**    **VBA 340**

**Altering Properties of the Title Slide**    **VBA 345**

**Session 7.3 Quick Check**    **VBA 347**

**Review Assignments**    **VBA 348**

**Case Problems**    **VBA 350**

**Quick Check Answers**    **VBA 354**

## Tutorial 8     VBA 355

### Using VBA with Access

Enhancing a Library Checkout system with VBA

**SESSION 8.1**     **VBA 356**

**Using VBA with Microsoft Access**     **VBA 356**

**Understanding Objects in Access**     **VBA 356**

**Reviewing the Database**     **VBA 357**

Viewing the Main Menu Form     VBA 361

**Examining an Object's Property Sheet**     **VBA 362**

**Creating a Macro in Access**     **VBA 364**

Attaching a Macro to a Command Button     VBA 365

Testing the Attached Macro     VBA 369

Building a Macro with the Quit Action     VBA 369

**Testing the Main Menu**     **VBA 371**

**Session 8.1 Quick Check**     **VBA 371**

**SESSION 8.2**     **VBA 371**

**Creating Navigation Buttons with VBA**     **VBA 371**

Using VBA Code Instead of Macro Actions     VBA 374

Becoming Familiar with the DoCmd Object     VBA 375

Programming the Navigation Buttons     VBA 377

Disabling a Navigation Button     VBA 382

**Session 8.2 Quick Check**     **VBA 386**

**SESSION 8.3**     **VBA 386**

**Adding and Programming Controls in an Access Form**     **VBA 386**

Inserting a Label in an Access Form     VBA 387

Programming a Label     VBA 388

Conditionally Altering the Appearance of a Control     VBA 393

Conditionally Enabling and Disabling a Text Box     VBA 395

Session 8.3 Quick Check     VBA 398

Review Assignments     VBA 398

Case Problems     VBA 399

Quick Check Answers     VBA 403

## Tutorial 9     VBA 405

### Integrating the Office Applications with VBA

Creating an Integrated Application for InTouch, Inc.

**SESSION 9.1**     **VBA 406**

**Integrating the Office Applications**     **VBA 406**

**Using General Procedures**     **VBA 406**

**Setting References to Other Applications**     **VBA 406**

**Creating a New Word Document from Within Access**     **VBA 409**

Declaring a Variable as an Application Object     VBA 410

Creating an Instance of an Application     VBA 410

Setting a Reference to an Object     VBA 410

Making the Application Visible on the Screen VBA     VBA 411

**Inserting Access Data into a Word Document**     **VBA 413**

Inserting a Title into a Word Document     VBA 413

Inserting a Word Table into a Document     VBA 415

Establishing an Access Recordset     VBA 418

Adding the Recordset Data to the Word Table     VBA 421

Iterating Through the Records in the Access Data Table     VBA 425

**Session 9.1 Quick Check**     **VBA 429**

**SESSION 9.2**     **VBA 429**

**Importing Code into a Module**     **VBA 429**

**Testing Imported Code**     **VBA 430**

**Examining the Imported Code**     **VBA 431**

Declaring Excel Object Reference Variables   VBA 432

Launching Excel and Setting up the
Workbook and Worksheet         VBA 432

Adding Column Headings to the Worksheet  VBA 433

Establishing the Access Recordset        VBA 433

Inserting the Access Table Data into the
Excel Worksheet               VBA 433

**Creating an Excel Chart with VBA Statements  VBA 435**

**Session 9.2 Quick Check**       **VBA 439**

**Review Assignments**           **VBA 439**

**Case Problems**                **VBA 440**

**Quick Check Answers**          **VBA 444**

**Glossary**                     **VBA 445**

**Index**                        **VBA 451**

**Task Reference**               **VBA 460**

**File Finder**                  **VBA 462**

# Reference Window List

Opening the VBA IDE from Within Any Office
  Application                                            VBA 7

Undocking Windows in the VBA IDE                         VBA 12

Undocking Windows in the VBA IDE                         VBA 12

Running a Program from the VBA IDE                       VBA 24

Printing a Code Module                                   VBA 32

Changing a Project Name                                  VBA 52

Opening and Sizing a New UserForm                        VBA 58

Changing a Property                                      VBA 63

Inserting a Control Object into a UserForm               VBA 68

Changing Properties for Multiple Objects at One Time     VBA 73

To Add a Comment to a VBA Program                        VBA 95

To Print a Form and Code                                 VBA 97

Configuring the VBA IDE to Add an Option Explicit
  Statement                                              VBA 119

Stepping Through a Program                               VBA 141

To Set a Breakpoint                                      VBA 145

Using a Continuation Character                           VBA 235

To Attach a Macro                                        VBA 365

To Set References to Other Applications                  VBA 408

To Import a File into a Code Module                      VBA 430

# Tutorial Tips

These tutorials will help you learn how to program in VBA for Applications. The tutorials are designed to be worked through at a computer. Each tutorial is divided into sessions. Watch for the session headings, such as Session 1.1 and Session 1.2. Each session is designed to be completed in about 45 minutes, but take as much time as you need. It's also a good idea to take a break between sessions.

To use the tutorials effectively, read the following questions and answers before you begin.

### Where do I start?

Each tutorial begins with a case, which sets the scene for the tutorial and gives you background information to help you understand what you will be doing. Read the case before you go to the lab. In the lab, begin with the first session of a tutorial.

### How do I know what to do on the computer?

Each session contains steps that you will perform on the computer. Read the text that introduces each series of steps. The steps you need to do at a computer are numbered and are set against a shaded background. Read each step carefully and completely before you try it.

### How do I know if I did the step correctly?

As you work, compare your computer screen with the corresponding figure in the tutorial. You should type all the code exactly as you see it in the tutorial figures; however, the windows on your screen may be sized or positioned differently than the those in the figures.

### What if I make a mistake?

Don't worry about making mistakes—they are part of the learning process. Paragraphs labeled "TROUBLE?" identify common problems and explain how to get back on track. Follow the steps in a TROUBLE? paragraph only if you are having the problem described. If you run into other problems:

- Carefully consider the current state of your system, the position of the cursor, and any messages on the screen.

- Consult the Help system.

- If the suggestions above don't solve your problem, consult your technical support person for assistance.

### How do I use the Reference Windows and Syntax Boxes?

Reference Windows summarize the procedures you will learn in the tutorial steps. Do not complete the actions in the Reference Windows when you are working through the tutorial. Instead, refer to the Reference Windows and Syntax boxes while you are working on the assignments at the end of the tutorial.

### How can I test my understanding of the material I learned in the tutorial?

At the end of each session, you can answer the Quick Check questions. The answers for the Quick Checks are at the end of each tutorial.

After you have completed the entire tutorial, you should complete the Review Assignments and Case Problems. They are carefully structured so that you will review what you have learned and then apply your knowledge to new situations.

### What if I can't remember how to do something?

You should refer to the Task Reference at the end of the book; it summarizes how to accomplish tasks using the most efficient method.

Before you begin the tutorials, you should know the basics about your computer's operating system. You should also know how to use the Microsoft Office applications, the Office Help system, and the Windows Explorer.

Now that you've read the Tutorial Tips, you are ready to begin.

*New Perspectives on*

# MICROSOFT®
# OFFICE 2000
# VISUAL BASIC FOR
# APPLICATIONS

**TUTORIAL 1      VBA 3**
*Introducing Microsoft Visual Basic for Applications (VBA)*
Creating some simple programs for TnT Consulting Group

**TUTORIAL 2      VBA 45**
*Working with Objects and Properties*
Creating a Checkbook Interface for TnT Consulting Group

**TUTORIAL 3      VBA 111**
*Using Variables, Assignment Statements, and Control Structures*
Creating a Salary Calculator Program

**TUTORIAL 4      VBA 167**
*Repeating Statements with Repetition Control Structures*
Completing the TnT Check Register Project

**TUTORIAL 5      VBA 219**
*Creating a VBA Application for Microsoft Word*
Creating a Letter-Building Application

**TUTORIAL 6      VBA 257**
*Using VBA with Excel*
Developing a Gradebook Application in Excel

**TUTORIAL 7      VBA 301**
*Creating a PowerPoint VBA Application with Multiple Forms*
Building a Presentation from a Word Outline

**TUTORIAL 8      VBA 355**
*Using VBA with Access*
Enhancing a Library Checkout system with VBA

**TUTORIAL 9      VBA 405**
*Integrating the Office Applications with VBA*
Creating an Integrated Application for InTouch, Inc.

# Read This Before You Begin

## To the Student

### Data Disks

To complete the Tutorials, Review Assignments, and Case Problems in this book, you need the necessary data files. Your instructor may provide them, or you can download them by going to Course Technology's Web site, *www.course.com*. See the inside cover of this book for more information on downloading your data files.

From Course Technology's Web site, the data files will be downloaded to you as a single compressed executable file named 1936-0.exe. The files will be placed on your hard drive using the following general folder structure:

**C:\1936-0\Tutorial.01\data files for the tutorial**

**C:\1936-0\Tutorial.01\Review\data files for the Review Assignments**

**C:\1936-0\Tutorial.01\Cases\data files for the Case Problems**

If you prefer, you can copy the data files for Tutorials 1-7 to two floppy disks. Put the following folders on one disk: Tutorial.01, Tutorial.02, Tutorial.03, and Tutorial.04. Then put these folders on a second disk: Tutorial.05, Tutorial.06 and Tutorial.07.

Within the tutorials, the term "Data Disk" refers to either the folder named 1936-0 on your hard drive, or to the floppy disk on which the individual folders are stored.

Note that Tutorials 8 and 9 involve database files that will not fit on a single floppy. Thus, you will need to complete Tutorials 8 and 9 using a hard drive or network drive.

In Tutorials 1-7 you are instructed to save each data file with a new name before making changes to it. This allows you to reuse the data files later, in case you want to repeat the tutorial. However, it is not possible to save a database file with a new name and leave the original file intact. Thus, Tutorial 8 and 9 instruct you to make a backup copy of the data files, which you can then use later if you decide to repeat the tutorial.

If you begin working on a hard disk and then have to transport your files using floppy disks, we recommend you take advantage of WinZip™. With this utility, you can compress and archive your files within the correct folder structure. To find out more about WinZip™ go to *www.winzip.com* and click the link for Basic Information.

### Using Your Own Computer

If you are going to work through this book using your own computer, you need:

- **Computer System** Microsoft Windows 98 or higher must be installed on your computer, along with Office 2000 Professional. This book assumes a complete installation of Office 2000 Professional (including VBA Help files.) If Office has already been installed without Help files, use the Office 2000 CD to add the Help files.

- **Data Files** You will not be able to complete the tutorials or exercises in this book using your own computer until you have the data files.

### Visit Our World Wide Web Site

Additional materials designed especially for you are available on the World Wide Web. Go to **http://www.course.com**.

## To the Instructor

The data files are available on the Instructor's Resource Kit for this title. Follow the instructions in the Help file on the CD-ROM to install the data files to your network or standalone computer. For information on creating Data Disks, see the "To the Student" section above.

You are granted a license to copy the data files to any computer or computer network used by students who have purchased this book.

In this tutorial you will:

- Review the Office 2000 suite

- Learn some basic programming concepts

- Become familiar with VBA

- Explore and manipulate the VBA IDE

- Type a simple VBA program in the VBA IDE

- Create a VBA program by recording a macro

- Use the VBA Help System

# INTRODUCING
## MICROSOFT VISUAL BASIC FOR APPLICATIONS (VBA)

*Creating some simple programs for TnT Consulting Group*

CASE

## TnT Consulting Group

TnT Consulting Group is a computer consulting company that develops software applications for businesses and government agencies. Known for its ability to deliver low-cost, effective software solutions in a timely and efficient manner, TnT Consulting relies on Microsoft's Visual Basic for Applications (VBA) as its primary software development tool. Joe Tibble and Lynn Taylor, cofounders of the company, know that VBA integrates the strengths of the Microsoft Office suite with the power of the widely used programming language Visual Basic.

As a new employee of TnT Consulting Group, you have been assigned to a project development group, which is a team of people who work on many projects together. It's assumed that you are already familiar with the Microsoft Office Suite and that you are fairly proficient with Word, Excel, Outlook, PowerPoint, and Access. However, you are not expected to be familiar with VBA. Instead, you will actually learn how to use VBA on the job. Your first assignment is to become familiar with the Visual Basic for Applications Integrated Development Environment (VBA IDE), a special program that provides the commands and tools you need to create VBA applications. In this tutorial, you will learn how to use the Macro Recorder and the VBA IDE to build a simple program. Gene Cox, the team manager, will be your supervisor. His job is to guide you through the learning process and to assign projects that will help you to learn to work in VBA. You will report your progress to Gene, and he will make suggestions for improvement.

# SESSION 1.1

In this session you will review the Microsoft Office 2000 suite and its relationship to Visual Basic for Applications. You will become acquainted with the Visual Basic for Applications Integrated Development Environment (VBA IDE) and become familiar with some basic programming concepts. You will also open the VBA IDE within two different applications. Finally, you will learn to open and identify the various components of the VBA IDE.

## Reviewing the Office 2000 Suite

The Microsoft Office 2000 suite is extremely popular, and it is used all over the world. As you know, it consists mainly of five Microsoft applications: Access, Excel, Outlook, PowerPoint, and Word. The applications of the Office suite are considered **horizontal applications**, meaning that they can be employed by many different kinds of organizations for many different kinds of tasks. Using the Office applications, people in a wide variety of situations can build professional documents, sophisticated spreadsheets, interesting and effective online presentations, and powerful desktop databases.

While Microsoft Office provides a wealth of functionality (more than enough to meet the needs of many businesses), it is sometimes desirable to add additional features. For this reason, the Office suite includes a very powerful programming language, **Visual Basic for Applications**, or **VBA**. In this book you will learn to use VBA to write programs that provide custom solutions for specific business needs. These programs will interact directly with the Microsoft Office applications. Many of the programs you will develop can be used across applications—that is, used with more than one application. For example, you might use the same VBA program in both Word and Excel.

Before you can understand what VBA is, you need to become familiar with some basic concepts related to programming. The following section provides a brief introduction to the world of programming. The definitions provided in this section will be refined and expanded on throughout this book.

## A Brief Introduction to Programming

When you are working in Word, Excel, Access, or PowerPoint, you are using **software**. By contrast, the computer itself (the keyboard, the monitor, the processor, and so on) is referred to as **hardware**. Software consists of **programs**, which are instructions that tell the computer what to do. Word, for example, includes program instructions that allow you to bold text, change the format of the text, copy and move text, etc. An **application** is a program designed to perform specific tasks—for example, Word is an application that is designed for working with text. The term **functionality** is used to refer to all the tasks a specific application can perform. For example, Excel functionality includes the ability to create pie charts, while PowerPoint functionality includes the ability to generate a slideshow.

The functionality of the Office applications is sufficient for most people. However, you can customize this functionality, or add additional features, by creating your own programs. Often such programs require input from a user. For example, you could create a program for Excel that asks the user to enter financial data, and then automatically generates a 3-D pie chart illustrating that data. Alternately, you could create a program for Word that asks the user to enter a name and address, and then stores that information in a Word document.

You create such programs by writing program statements in a programming language. A **programming language** is a collection of words or commands that allows you to communicate with the computer. Just as you need to follow certain rules in order to construct an English sentence, you must follow certain rules in order to construct a program with a programming language. The rules governing a particular programming language are called its **syntax**.

You create programs by writing program statements, which are often referred to as **code**. The code must conform exactly to the language's syntax. Once you become familiar with a language's syntax, you will be able to write code fluently, and thus create sophisticated programs tailored to the needs of your users. You can write programs in many different programming languages. One very popular language is **Visual Basic for Applications (VBA)**, which is the language you will use in this book.

# Introducing Visual Basic for Applications

Visual Basic for Applications (VBA) is a version of a widely used programming language known as Visual Basic. Unlike Visual Basic, VBA is integrated with the Microsoft Office applications, allowing it to take advantage of the components of the Office suite. VBA programs are dependent on the application in which they are written. If a VBA program is written for Word, then Word is considered to be the **host** application.

Using VBA, a **developer** (a person who creates a program) can customize the Office applications to satisfy the unique needs of an organization. Applications that have been customized in this way are often referred to as **vertical market applications**. For example, a law firm might have a collection of standard paragraphs that it adds to many of its legal documents. As a developer, you could write a VBA program that would allow the user to select which paragraphs are to be used in a document, in what order they should appear, and possibly some formatting style for those paragraphs. Once the user has made these selections, your program would build the legal document using the selected paragraphs.

## Introducing the VBA Integrated Development Environment

You actually create, or develop, a program within a special program called a **programming environment**. The VBA programming environment is known as the **VBA Integrated Development Environment**, or the **VBA IDE**. (You may also hear people refer to the VBA IDE as the **Visual Basic Editor**.)

The VBA IDE provides all the tools you need to write, edit, and test VBA programs. You can open it from within any of the Office applications. You will have a chance to explore the VBA IDE later in this tutorial.

## Comparing Macros to VBA Programs

As an experienced Office 2000 user, you are probably already familiar with creating macros to automate specific tasks within an Office 2000 application. The purpose of a macro is to record actions that you want to repeat regularly. For example, you might create a macro that automates the process of formatting a range of cells in Excel. In this way, a macro is similar to a VBA program—they can both be used to automate a series of steps. However, macros differ from VBA programs in that a macro can only record commands that are already available in the application—that is, those that make use of the application's existing functionality. For example, you might create a Word macro that inserts and bolds a company's address in a document. However, you couldn't create a Word macro that displayed a customized dialog box requesting user input, because displaying such dialog boxes is not part of the basic functionality of Word.

When you need to extend the functionality of an Office application (that is, when you want to add new features to an application), you need to create a VBA program. Sometimes the easiest way to begin creating a VBA program is to start by creating a macro, and then to edit the macro in the VBA IDE to add additional functionality. You can build complicated VBA programs by incorporating and editing a series of relatively simple macros. Actually a

VBA program is a macro. Many developers use the two terms, VBA program and macro, interchangeably. Throughout this text you will see many examples of how VBA programs (macros) can be used to tailor an Office application to fit the unique needs of its users.

## The Benefits of Using VBA

As a software developer, you are free to choose from a wide variety of programming languages and environments when creating your programs. Everyone has his or her own favorites, and in your conversations with other developers or with potential TnT clients, you may be asked to explain the benefits of your chosen language. Your supervisor, Gene, explains that VBA is perfectly suited for customizing Office applications. Among other things, he explains, VBA lets you:

- **Incorporate Existing Functionality**: Each of the Office applications provides a robust set of tools that can be used to create and modify sophisticated documents, spreadsheets, presentations, and databases. You can use VBA to enhance the functionality that already exists within these programs. This is more efficient than creating an entirely new application from scratch (in, say, Visual Basic) that incorporates existing features of Word, as well as new features.

- **Develop Programs Quickly**: Writing programs in programming languages such as Visual Basic, which are not tied closely to the Office suite, can be very time-consuming. By contrast, the close relationship between VBA and the various Office applications allows you to create programs for Office much more quickly. The tools of the VBA IDE, and the fact that you can incorporate macros into a program, speed the development process considerably.

- **Share Programs Across Applications**: You can develop a program within one of the various Office applications and then, with minor adjustments, transfer that program to other applications.

- **Reduce Development Costs**: Because new programs can be developed easily, the time to develop those programs is minimized.

- **Make Users Part of the Solution**: The Office users in an organization already know the functionality of the Office applications. They can also talk knowledgeably about the additional features they require. Thus, developers can rely on users to help shape the development of a new Office application and provide important suggestions regarding its functionality.

Now that you are familiar with some background regarding VBA, you are ready to investigate the VBA programming environment—the VBA IDE.

# Exploring the VBA Integrated Development Environment (VBA IDE)

You can start the VBA IDE from any of the Office applications. In this section, you will launch the VBA IDE in Word and then again in PowerPoint. The VBA IDE for each of the applications runs in a separate window. The VBA IDE for Word is completely separate from the VBA IDE for PowerPoint. You can switch back and forth between applications and their respective VBA IDEs just as you switch between applications, by clicking a button on the taskbar.

## Opening, Sizing, and Closing Windows

In this section you will see that the VBA IDE contains several windows, which you must open and close according to what you are doing at the time. When you launch the VBA IDE, you cannot be sure which windows will be open. Nor can you be sure what size the open windows will be, or where they will be positioned on the screen. Thus, your VBA IDE screen will probably not match the figures in this book exactly. That's fine, and not something you need to worry about. Instead, you should concentrate on becoming familiar with opening, sizing, and closing windows so that you can set up the VBA IDE screen to suit your particular needs.

To open the VBA IDE from within any of the Office applications, you can use the Visual Basic Editor command on the Tools menu.

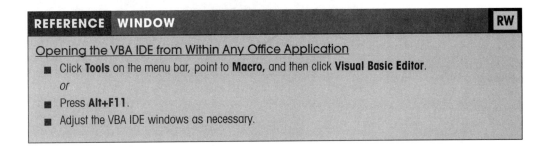

**REFERENCE  WINDOW**    **RW**

Opening the VBA IDE from Within Any Office Application
- Click **Tools** on the menu bar, point to **Macro,** and then click **Visual Basic Editor**.
  *or*
- Press **Alt+F11**.
- Adjust the VBA IDE windows as necessary.

Note that after you open the VBA IDE, you will need to manipulate the windows within it. For example, you may need to close some windows, open other windows, and then move or size the open windows. You probably already have experience with opening, closing, sizing, and moving windows. However, you may not have worked with the number of windows you will find in the VBA IDE. If you take the time now to become comfortable with manipulating these windows, you will not have to concern yourself with whether or not your screen matches the figures in this book exactly.

### *To start the VBA IDE from Within Microsoft Word:*

**1.** Close any open programs.

**2.** Start Word and, if necessary, open a new blank document. The taskbar should now contain one button, labeled "Document1 - Microsoft Word". To view the entire name of this button, place the mouse pointer over the button and read the ToolTip that appears above the button.

**3.** Click **Tools** on the menu bar, point to **Macro,** and then click **Visual Basic Editor.** The Microsoft Visual Basic – Document 1 window opens, similar to Figure 1-1. (Your window might be called "Microsoft Visual Basic – Normal," instead.) Don't be concerned if your screen looks somewhat different from Figure 1-1. For instance, you might have windows open within the Microsoft Visual Basic window, or you might see the Microsoft Word window behind the Microsoft Visual Basic window. You will have an opportunity to adjust these windows in the following steps.

**Figure 1-1**    **VBA INTEGRATED DEVELOPMENT ENVIRONMENT (IDE)**

the Project Explorer

toolbar

menu bar

VBA IDE

4. If you see windows open within the large window, click the Close button ☒ on each open window inside the VBA IDE so that your screen matches Figure 1-1. Only the Microsoft Visual Basic – Document 1 window should remain open. (Again, on your screen it might be called the Microsoft Visual Basic – Normal window.) The Microsoft Visual Basic window is the workspace for the entire VBA IDE. Notice that the taskbar now contains two buttons, one for Microsoft Word and one for Microsoft Visual Basic, as shown in Figure 1-1.

TROUBLE? If your screen is split horizontally or vertically, with the Microsoft Word window on top (or on one side) and the Microsoft Visual Basic window on the bottom (or on the other side), click the Maximize button ☐ on the Microsoft Visual Basic title bar. Your screen should then match Figure 1-1.

TROUBLE? If you have other programs running at this time, you will also see buttons for those programs on your taskbar. When you are working through these tutorials, you should close all other programs.

5. Click the **Document1-Microsoft Word** button in the taskbar. You see the Microsoft Word window again.

6. Click the **Microsoft Visual Basic** button in the taskbar. You see the Microsoft Visual Basic window again.

Now that you have opened the VBA IDE, you can practice opening some windows within the VBA IDE.

## To open windows within the VBA IDE:

1. Click the **Project Explorer** button ⬛ on the toolbar. The Project Explorer window opens, as shown in Figure 1-2. (Your Project Explorer windows may be in a different position or may be a different size from the one shown in the figure.) The Project Explorer window is used to organize the various VBA files that are associated with a VBA project. Its contents are arranged hierarchically, just as in Windows Explorer. You will learn more about the Project Explorer window later in this tutorial. For now, you simply need to notice that the ThisDocument icon is selected within the Microsoft Word Objects folder. Also, note that "ThisDocument" refers to the new blank Word document that opened when you first started Word. You will learn more about the relationship between the code you create within the VBA IDE and the Word document later in this tutorial.

| Figure 1-2 | VBA IDE WITH THE PROJECT EXPLORER WINDOW |

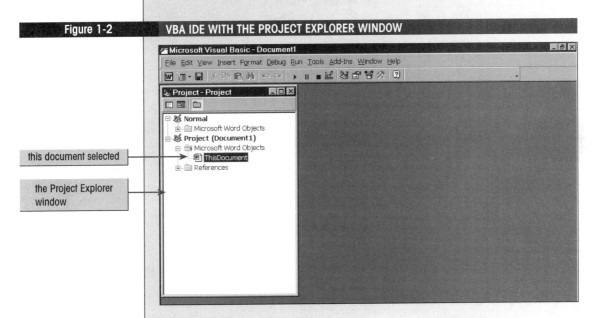

this document selected

the Project Explorer window

TROUBLE? If the Project Explorer does not include all the items shown in Figure 1-2, click the Expand button ⊞ next to Project (Document1) to expand the list. If necessary, click the Expand button ⊞ next to the Microsoft Word Objects folder. Keep in mind that anytime you see ⊞ beside a hierarchical list of files, you can click it to display a hidden list.

TROUBLE? If the Project Explorer window is maximized (i.e., if it fills up the entire Microsoft Visual Basic – Document1 window), click the Restore button 🔲 in the upper-right corner of the Project Explorer window. Don't be concerned if your Project Explorer window is longer or wider than the one shown in Figure 1-2.

2. Click the **Properties Window** button 🔲 on the toolbar. The Properties window opens. The Properties window is used to select specific settings for parts of a VBA program. You will learn more about the Properties window in Tutorial 2. But for now, you are simply learning how to open and close the various windows of the IDE. The Properties window is now the active window, as indicated by its blue title bar. To activate the Project Explorer window, you can either click the Project Explorer window, or click the Project Explorer button on the toolbar. It's often easier to use the toolbar button, especially when another window within the VBA IDE hides the Project Explorer window.

**3.** Click the **Project Explorer** button 🖼 on the toolbar. The Project Explorer window is now the active window, as indicated by its highlighted (blue) title bar. Your screen should now look like Figure 1-3.

TROUBLE? If the Properties window is maximized (i.e., if it fills up the entire VBA IDE screen), click the Restore button 🖫 in the upper-right corner of the window. Don't be concerned if your Properties window is longer or wider than the one shown in Figure 1-3. In the same vein, don't be concerned if your Properties window covers more of the Project window than the one shown in Figure 1-3.

| Figure 1-3 | VBA-IDE WITH THE PROJECT EXPLORER AND PROPERTIES WINDOWS OPEN |

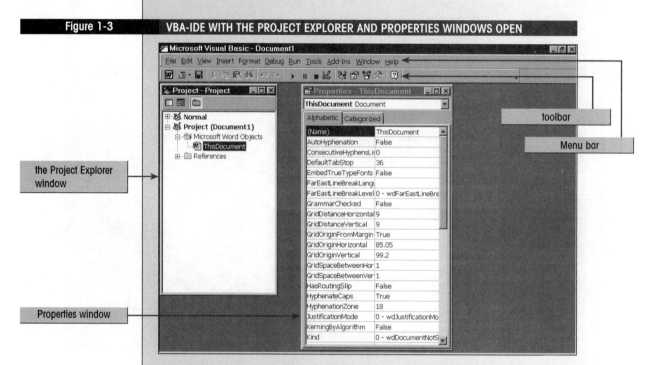

**4.** Double-click **ThisDocument** in the Project Explorer window. The Document1 - ThisDocument (Code) window opens, similar to Figure 1-4. (In this book, this window will be referred to simply as the Code window.) You actually begin creating a VBA program by typing code in the Code window. You will learn more about the Code window later in this tutorial.

TROUBLE? Depending on how your computer is set up, you may or may not see the words "**Option Explicit**" in the Code window. If you do see these words, simply ignore them.

At this point, your screen should look similar to Figure 1-4, which consists of the Microsoft Visual Basic window (the IDE that encompasses all other VBA windows), the Project Explorer window, the Properties window, and the Code window.

| Figure 1-4 | WORD VBA IDE WITH CODE WINDOW OPEN |
|---|---|

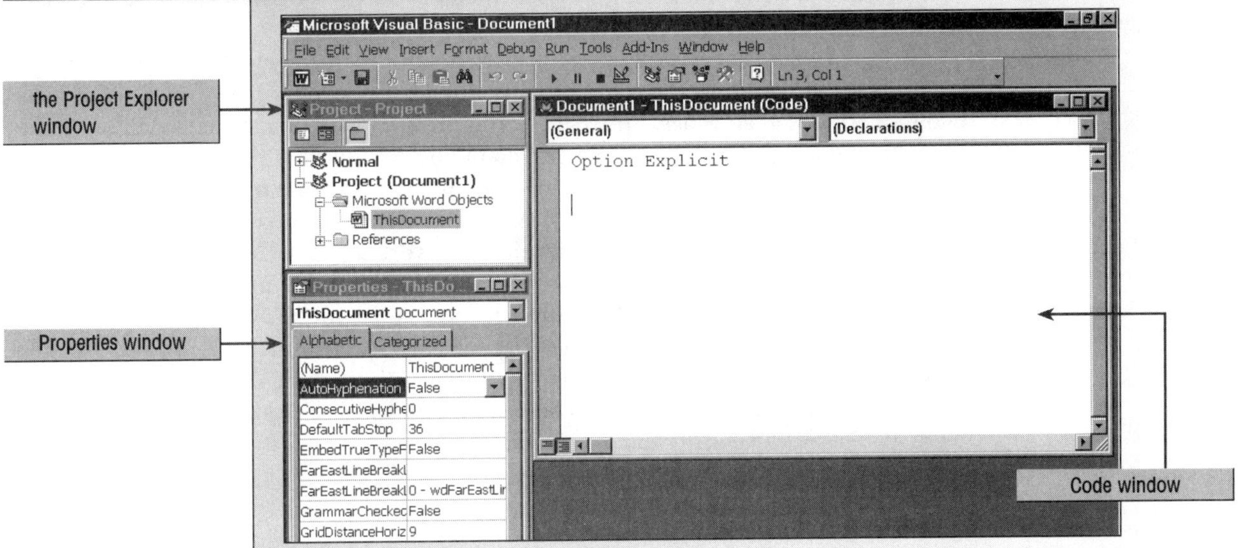

the Project Explorer window

Properties window

Code window

TROUBLE? Don't be concerned if your screen does not appear exactly as in Figure 1-4. Later in this tutorial you will learn to move and size windows to suit your personal preference.

5. Take a few moments to study the VBA IDE. You will notice that much of the screen looks very similar to other Windows-based programs you have used. Notice that each window has a title bar, a Minimize button ▬ , a Maximize button ☐ , and a Close button ☒ . If a window is maximized, it will contain a Restore button 🗗 in place of a Maximize button.

6. Click each item on the menu bar and browse through the list of options under each. At this point, you won't be able to understand what each command is used for, but you can still get a general idea of the options available through the menu system.

7. Move the mouse pointer slowly across the buttons on the toolbar. At each button, pause long enough to read the button's ToolTip. You will learn more about the toolbar buttons later.

8. Keep the Word VBA IDE open on the screen as you continue with the remainder of this session.

## Undocking and Manipulating the VBA IDE Windows

Now you are ready to practice moving and sizing the windows in the VBA IDE. As you build on your experience with VBA and the IDE, you will develop your own personal preferences for window placement. For now, just keep in mind that you can move and change the size of the VBA IDE windows just like any other window.

The VBA IDE windows can be **docked** (that is, anchored to the edge of another window) or allowed to **float** (that is, left unanchored, so that they can be moved and sized at will). The VBA IDE windows are docked by default. Alternately, you can turn off the docking option.

Once you turn off the docking option, you can size and position the windows according to your personal preferences. Most developers prefer to have the windows undocked so that they can move windows.

There is no right or wrong way to arrange the VBA IDE windows on your screen. For example, some developers like to keep the Project Explorer window docked so that they know where it is at all times. Others prefer to position windows as they open them. In this book, the figures show windows that are all undocked and then sized and positioned in the way that best illustrates the relevant concepts. However, you are free to position and size the VBA IDE windows to suit your own preferences. You should try several window arrangements until you settle on one that best suits your working habits.

The following steps give you some practice sizing and moving the IDE windows. You should practice the procedures described in these steps, so that you can easily manipulate windows on your screen. It is not necessary for your windows to have the exact same position or size as the figures in this book. Rather, it is important that you are able to open, close, size, and move windows as needed, according to what you are doing at the moment. Here, you'll start by closing the open windows.

## To practice closing the VBA IDE windows:

1. Verify that the Word VBA IDE is displayed on the screen. At this point, the Project Explorer, Properties, and Code windows should be displayed, similar to Figure 1-4.

2. Click the **Close** button ☒ on the Project Explorer window. The Project Explorer closes.

   TROUBLE? The Properties window may increase in size to fill the space formerly taken up by the Project Explorer window. Do not be concerned about this right now; you will learn how to adjust the size of the windows as you proceed through these steps.

3. Click ☒ on the Properties window. The Properties window closes.

   TROUBLE? The Code window may increase in size to fill the space formerly taken up by the Properties window. Do not be concerned about this right now; you will learn how to adjust the size of the windows as you proceed through these steps.

4. Click ☒ on the Code window. At this point, only the Microsoft Visual Basic window remains open.

Now that you have closed all the open windows (except for the larger Microsoft Visual Basic window) you can turn off docking for all windows within the VBA IDE. To do so, you need to use the Options command on the Tools menu.

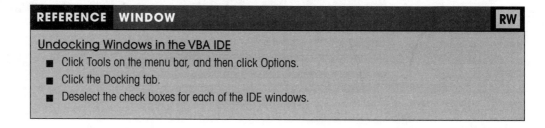

**REFERENCE    WINDOW**    **RW**

Undocking Windows in the VBA IDE
- Click Tools on the menu bar, and then click Options.
- Click the Docking tab.
- Deselect the check boxes for each of the IDE windows.

Now you are ready to turn off docking within the VBA IDE.

## To turn off docking:

**1.** Click **Tools** on the menu bar, and then click **Options**. The Options dialog box opens.

**2.** Click the **Docking** tab. This tab includes a check box for all of the IDE windows you have seen so far, and for some that you haven't seen yet. Exactly which of these check boxes are currently selected depends on how your computer is configured. See Figure 1-5.

| Figure 1-5 | OPTIONS WINDOW WITH DOCKING TAB SELECTED |

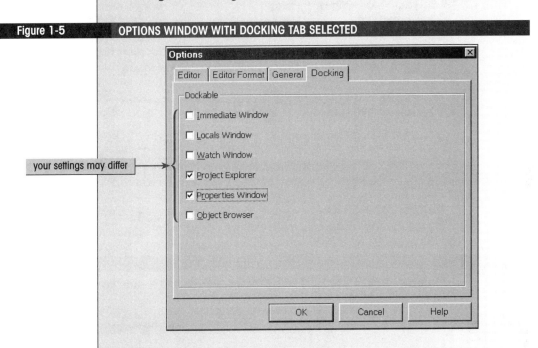

your settings may differ

**3.** Deselect all the check boxes on the Docking tab. When you are finished, none of the check boxes should be checked.

**4.** Click **OK**. The Options dialog box closes, and you return to the Microsoft Visual Basic window.

The undocked windows are no longer anchored to the edge of the screen, but are instead free to be moved around the VBA IDE window. In the next set of steps, you will practice moving and sizing the undocked windows.

## To move and size the undocked windows:

**1.** Click the **Project Explorer** button 📓 on the toolbar. The Project Explorer opens.

TROUBLE? If your Project Explorer window fills the entire screen, click the Restore button 🗗 in the top-right corner of the Project Explorer window.

**2.** Position the mouse pointer on the Project Explorer title bar, then press the mouse button and hold it down while you drag the window to a different position on the screen. When the window is in a new position, release the mouse button. Next, you will practice changing the size of this window.

**3.** Position the mouse pointer over any part of the Project Explorer window's border. The pointer changes to a double arrow ↔.

**4.** Click and drag the border until the Project Explorer window is a different size.

**5.** Click the **Properties** button 🖻 on the toolbar. The Properties window opens.

**6.** Practice moving and sizing the Properties window so that it doesn't cover any portion of the Project Explorer window.

TROUBLE? If your Properties window fills the entire screen, click the Restore button 🗗 in the top-right corner of the Project Explorer window.

**7.** Click the **Close** button ✕ on the Properties window. The Properties window closes. Next, you will practice manipulating the Code window.

**8.** Double-click **ThisDocument** in the Project Explorer. The Code window opens.

TROUBLE? If your Code window fills the entire screen, click the Restore button 🗗 in the top-right corner of the Project Explorer window.

**9.** Move and size the Code and the Project Explorer windows so that they are positioned similarly to the windows in Figure 1-6.

**Figure 1-6**     **THE PROJECT EXPLORER AND CODE WINDOWS**

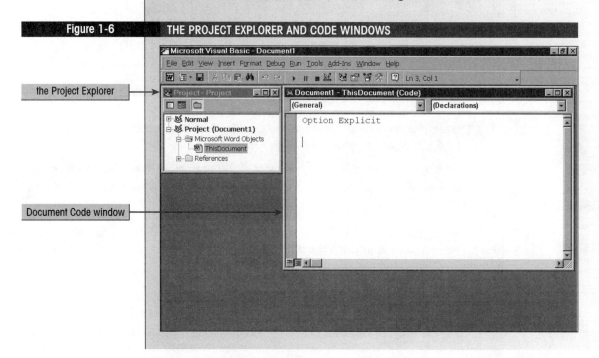

You should now be familiar with some of the windows within the VBA IDE. If necessary, take some time to practice the techniques you have just learned, until you are comfortable with opening, closing, and moving these windows. In the next section, you will practice opening the VBA IDE from within a program other than Word.

# Opening the VBA IDE in PowerPoint

As a developer at TnT Consulting, you will have to use the VBA IDE for each of the Office applications. So now that you are comfortable opening and manipulating windows within the Word VBA IDE, Gene wants you to practice using the PowerPoint VBA IDE.

You currently have the Word VBA IDE open. In the following steps, you will start PowerPoint, and then open the PowerPoint VBA IDE. Thus, you will have a separate VBA IDE for each open application. In the following steps, observe that the VBA IDE for Word remains open when the PowerPoint VBA IDE opens. Keep in mind that just as Word and PowerPoint are two totally separate applications, the Word VBA IDE and the PowerPoint VBA IDE are also totally separate.

## To start the VBA IDE from within PowerPoint:

1. Start Microsoft PowerPoint. You see the Microsoft PowerPoint window, with the PowerPoint dialog box open.

   TROUBLE? If you see the New Slide dialog box, skip to Step 3.

2. In the PowerPoint dialog box, click the **Blank presentation** option button (if necessary), and then click **OK.** The New Slide dialog box opens.

3. Click **Cancel.** You see the Microsoft PowerPoint – [Presentation1] window.

4. Look at the taskbar. Notice that it now includes an additional button, for PowerPoint. The full name for this button is "Microsoft PowerPoint – [Presentation1]." In the next step, you will open the PowerPoint VBA IDE. You could use the same procedure you used when opening the Word VBA IDE (that is, click Tools, click Macro, and then click Visual Basic Editor). However, this time you will use a shortcut, which works in all the Office applications.

5. Press **Alt+F11**. The Microsoft Visual Basic – Presentation1 window opens.

   TROUBLE? If you see the screen split vertically, with the PowerPoint window on the top and the Microsoft Visual Basic – Presentation1 window on the bottom, click the Maximize button ▣ on the Microsoft Visual Basic – Presentation 1 window.

Now that you have opened the PowerPoint VBA IDE, you can practice manipulating its windows, just as you did in the Word VBA IDE.

## To practice manipulating the PowerPoint VBA IDE windows:

1. Close any open windows within the Microsoft Visual Basic – Presentation1 window.

2. Click **Tools** on the menu bar, click **Options**, and then click the **Docking** tab. Notice that many of the check boxes are selected, even though you deselected the same check boxes within the Word VBA IDE. This illustrates the fact that one application's VBA IDE is completely separate from another application's VBA IDE. In this case, you need to undock all the PowerPoint VBA IDE windows, just as you did for the Word VBA IDE windows.

**3.** Deselect all the check boxes to remove the checks, and then click **OK**.

**4.** Click the **Project Explorer** button ⬚ . The Project Explorer opens.

**5.** Click the **Properties Window** button ⬚ and then arrange and size the windows similarly to the way they are shown in Figure 1-7. Notice that the taskbar now includes an additional Microsoft Visual Basic button, indicating that a second VBA IDE is now open.

| Figure 1-7 | POWERPOINT VBA IDE |
| --- | --- |

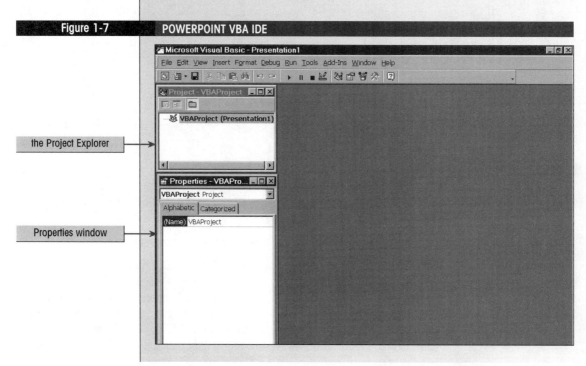

the Project Explorer

Properties window

If you seem to have "lost" one of your windows, it is probably simply hidden behind another window. You can always drag the windows around the screen until you find the misplaced window. Alternately, you can click the Window command on the menu bar and then click the name of the particular window you are seeking. You can also use commands on the Window menu to arrange the VBA IDE windows more systematically.

## To practice using the Window commands on the menu bar:

**1.** Click **Window** on the menu bar. The Window menu opens. At the bottom of the menu, you see a list of the windows currently open within the PowerPoint VBA IDE. You could activate (or select) one of these windows by clicking it on the menu. In this case, however, you will use the Cascade command to have the windows arranged automatically.

**2.** Click **Cascade**. The open windows now overlap each other, in a cascading format, as in Figure 1-8.

**Figure 1-8**          CASCADED WINDOWS

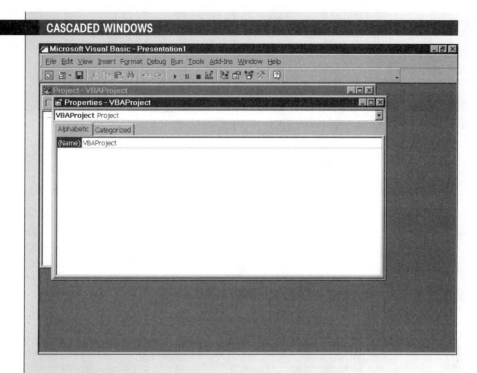

3. Click **Window** on the menu bar, then click **Tile Horizontally**. The windows are now arranged horizontally, in a tiled format, as in Figure 1-9. The Window menu contains other options for arranging windows, with which you can experiment on your own after you finish this tutorial.

**Figure 1-9**          WINDOWS TILED HORIZONTALLY

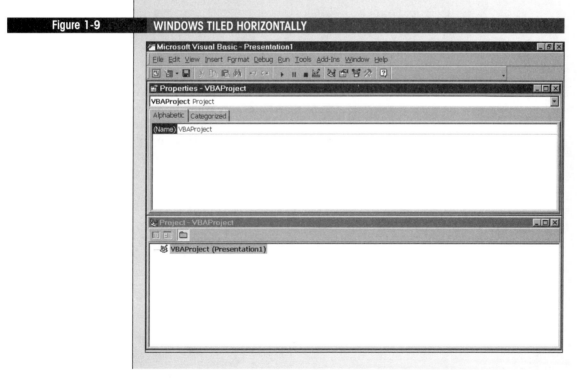

## Switching Between Two IDEs

You now have two IDEs running on the taskbar, as indicated by the two Microsoft Visual Basic buttons. You can switch between the two just as you would switch between any other applications on your taskbar. However, keep in mind that it is not immediately apparent which Microsoft Visual Basic button is associated with which program. To find out, you need to place the pointer over the button and read its complete name in the ScreenTip.

*To practice switching between two IDEs:*

1. On the taskbar, place the mouse pointer over the left Microsoft Visual Basic button and read its ScreenTip.

2. Place the mouse pointer over the right Microsoft Visual Basic button, and read its ScreenTip. The complete label for one button should read "Microsoft Visual Basic –Document1," while the other should read "Microsoft Visual Basic – Presentation1". The former is associated with Microsoft Word, while the latter is associated with PowerPoint.

3. Click the taskbar button for the Word VBA IDE. The Word VBA IDE is displayed.

4. Click the taskbar button for the PowerPoint VBA IDE.

   Notice that, although these are two separate environments running at the same time, they are exactly alike. They contain the same menu commands and tool-bar buttons. The differences are in the way you program within the two different applications. You will learn more about this as you work through this tutorial.

5. Click the taskbar button for PowerPoint and then close PowerPoint. The taskbar now contains only two buttons, one for Word, and one for the Word IDE. This indicates that the PowerPoint IDE window closed when you closed PowerPoint.

As you have worked through these steps, you have seen several of the windows contained within the VBA IDE. Gene explains that you will see additional windows as you begin your work as a TnT developer. Once you become more comfortable with the VBA IDE, you will develop a style of your own and make your own decisions regarding the placement and sizing of the windows. Throughout the book, you may find that your windows are not placed in the same position or may not be the same size as those in the figures. If you prefer to have your screen match the figures, then each time you open a window, move and size it as necessary.

## Session 1.1 QUICK CHECK

1. Each Office application provides a complete programming _____ called the _____  _____  _____.

2. Identify each of the lettered items in Figure 1-10.

   a.

   b.

   c.

   d.

   e.

**Figure 1-10**

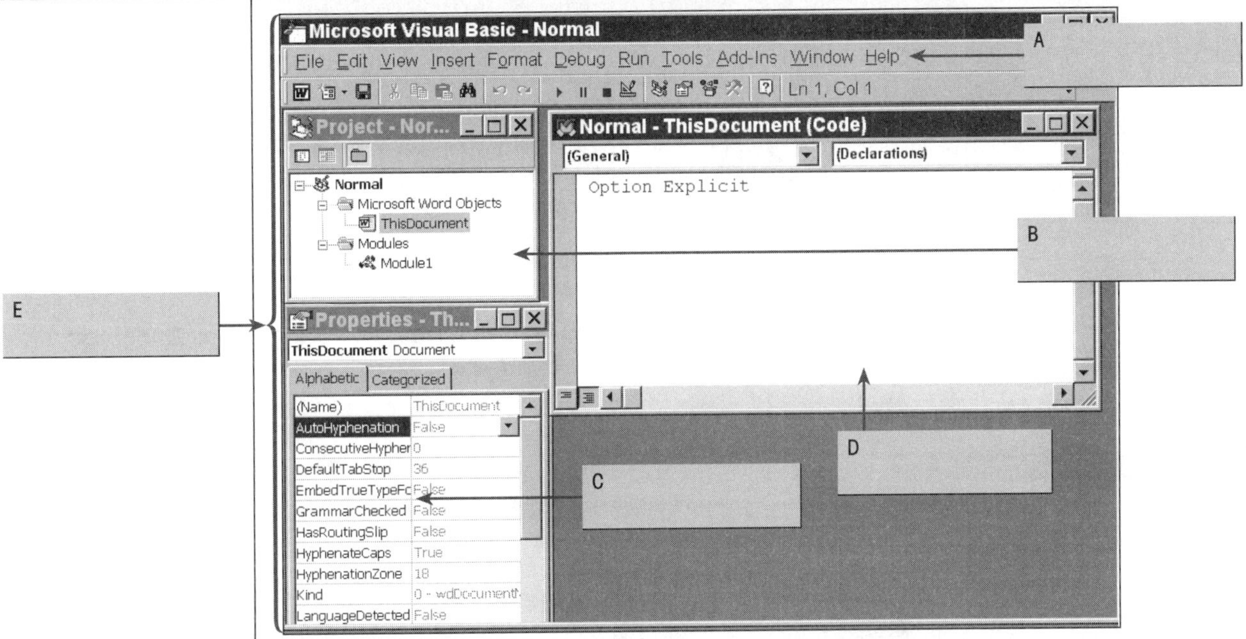

3. The _____ window displays a hierarchical list of components within a VBA project.

4. The _____ window displays settings for parts of a VBA program.

5. You actually enter VBA statements within the _____ window.

**SESSION 1.2**

In this session you will type some simple program statements. These statements will accept some data from the user, insert that data into a Word document, and format it.

## Creating a VBA Program for Word

Now that you are familiar with the VBA programming environment, you are ready to learn how to use it. Gene wants you to enter program statements, called **code**, and then test the statements to observe how they work. At this stage, you don't have to be concerned with the statements themselves but rather with the process of entering and testing a VBA program. You'll learn more about the concepts involved in creating a VBA program beginning in Tutorial 2.

### Creating a Program for Word

For your first program, you will simply type in some program statements. The program you create will provide a dialog box in which the user can type some data; the program will then insert that into a Word document. (Data provided by the user is known as **input**.) In the following steps, you will type code that you won't fully understand. However, all of the statements will be explained in later tutorials. For now, you simply need to learn how to enter program statements.

Before you can begin typing the code, you need to make sure that the VBA IDE is set up in a convenient way, to make it easy for you to type your code.

## To prepare the VBA IDE:

1. Verify that the Word VBA IDE is open, with only the Project Explorer and the "ThisDocument" Code window open. If you took a break at the end of the last session, you will need to start Word and open the IDE as described earlier.

2. If you have other open windows besides the Project Explorer and Code windows, close them now.

3. Position and size the windows to match Figure 1-11. Don't be concerned if you do not see the words "**Option Explicit**". You will learn about these words in Tutorial 3.

| Figure 1-11 | CODE WINDOW OPENED IN WORD |
|---|---|

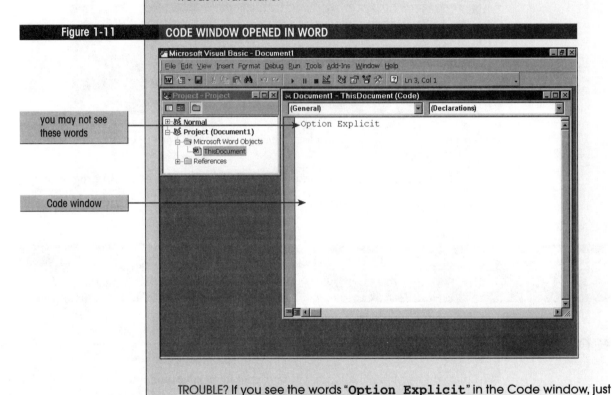

TROUBLE? If you see the words "**Option Explicit**" in the Code window, just ignore them for now. If you do not see these words, don't be concerned. You will learn more about these words in Tutorial 3.

Now you are ready to begin typing code. As you type code, the VBA IDE is in **design mode**. In design mode, the programming environment displays all the tools and menus you need to create and edit program statements.

To create your first program, follow the steps below exactly. Pay careful attention to wording and punctuation. The code you type must match the steps exactly. However, if you do make a mistake, you will have a chance to correct it later.

## To begin typing VBA code:

1. Click in the Code window, type **Sub FirstWordVBA ()** and then press **Enter**. (If you see the words "**Option Explicit**", click below those words.) Be sure to include the open and close parentheses at the end of the line, and do not add any extra spaces. Notice that when you press Enter, the cursor moves to a new line and the words End Sub appear below the pointer. You'll learn more about what this means later. For now, just continue with these steps.

2. Press the **Tab** key. The pointer moves to the right, so that it is now indented several spaces under the first statement. Note that indenting in VBA code makes the code easier for you to read, but does not affect the way the code works. Some programmers indent lines two spaces at a time, while others indent lines five spaces. Still others use no indentations at all. It is best if you decide how many spaces you prefer to indent and then consistently use the same amount of indentation.

3. Type **Dim strNewData** As and then pause.

4. Press the **Spacebar**. A pop-up window appears with a list of words, as shown in Figure 1-12. This feature of VBA, called Intellisense, is designed to help you insert the right words in the right order, within a line of code. For now, simply ignore it and continue with the next step.

| Figure 1-12 | EXAMPLE OF INTELLISENSE |

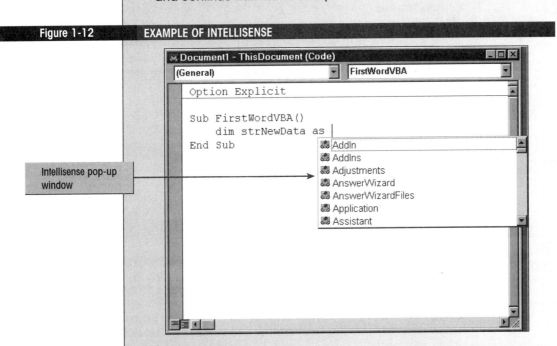

Intellisense pop-up window

5. Type **String** and then press **Enter**. The pop-up window closes, and the pointer moves to the next line, immediately below the "D" in "**Dim**". Notice that once you indent a line, as you did in Step 2, the following lines will also be indented. Indenting statements is an accepted practice among developers and makes it easier for you to read and interpret the code you type.

6. Type **strNewData = InputBox (** and then pause. Notice that after you type the opening parentheses, another Intellisense box opens on the screen, as shown in Figure 1-13. This box provides information that explains the proper rules (or syntax) for whatever code will follow the word InputBox. For now, simply ignore it and continue with the next step.

Figure 1-13    FUNCTION INTELLISENSE

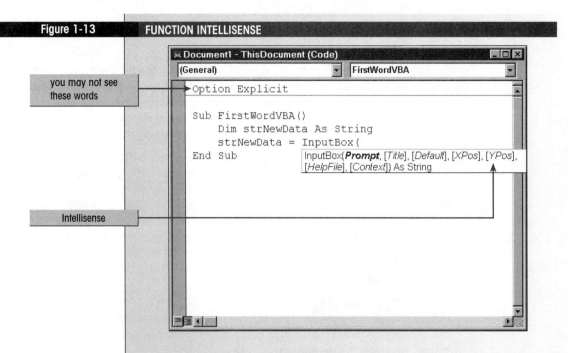

you may not see
these words

Intellisense

**7.** Type **"Enter your name")** and then review what you just typed. Make sure that you included a space on either side of the equals sign and that you typed the quotation marks as shown. If you made a mistake, you can correct it just as if you were typing a line of text in Word. Simply use the left and right arrow keys on the keyboard to move the pointer to the error. Use the Delete key to delete the error, and then retype the code.

**8.** When you are certain that the line is correct, press **Enter**. The pointer moves to the next line, immediately below the "**s**" in strNewData. If you still think you made a mistake, don't worry. You'll have a chance to correct any errors later.

As you continue with the next set of steps, you will see pop-up boxes at various points. Simply ignore these boxes for now, and type the code as shown.

*To continue typing code:*

**1.** Type **Selection.TypeText Text:=strNewData** and then press Enter. The pointer moves to the next line, below the "**S**" in Selection.

**2.** Type the following three lines, using the Enter key to complete a line and move the pointer to the next one. After you type the last line, press **Enter** twice to insert a blank line.

```
Selection.WholeStory
Selection.Font.Color = wdColorDarkBlue
Selection.Font.Name = "Arial Black"
```

3. Verify that you inserted a blank line after the last line you typed above, and then type the following three lines directly under the preceding three lines. This time, do not press Enter after you type the last line. Don't be concerned if a pop-up window remains open after you type the last line.

```
Selection.Font.Size = 24
Selection.Font.Italic = True
Selection.Collapse
```

4. Click the **Save** button 🖫 on the toolbar. The Save As dialog box opens.

5. Use the Save in list arrow to switch to the Tutorial.01 folder on your Data Disk.

6. Change the file name to **First Word VBA Program** and notice that the Save as type list box indicates that the code you just typed will be saved as a Word document. This tells you that you are actually saving a document file, and that your VBA code will be saved as part of that document file. If you were creating this code in the VBA IDE for Excel, the Save as type list box would indicate that you were saving an Excel workbook.

7. Click **Save**. Notice that the Word button on the taskbar is now labeled "First Word VBA Program – Microsoft Word," reflecting the fact that the document now has an assigned name rather than the default name of Document1.

8. Compare your screen with Figure 1-14. If you notice a mistake, you can correct it as you would text in any word processor. That is, use the Up, Down, Left, and Right arrow keys to move the pointer to the error, use the Delete key to remove the error, and then retype the code correctly. After correcting any errors, click the Save button 🖫 again.

| Figure 1-14 | CODE WINDOW WITH CODE ENTERED |
| --- | --- |

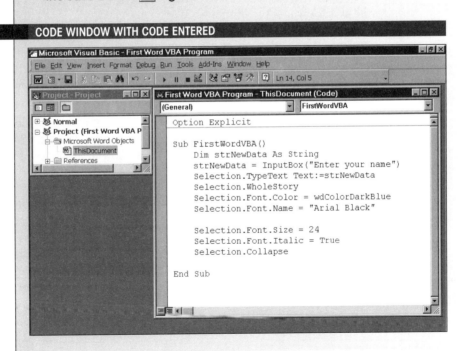

You have finished creating your first VBA program. In the next section you will actually learn how to use this program.

## Executing a Program

After you type the code for a program, you need to test the code by running, or executing, it. When you **execute** a program, the computer reads, or interprets, each line of the code and performs the action it specifies. In this case, the program will ask the user to enter a name into an input screen, place the name into the current document, and then format the name. To run a program from within the VBA IDE, you simply click the Run Sub/User Form button in the toolbar.

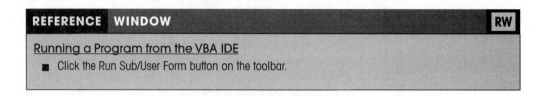

**REFERENCE WINDOW**                                                          **RW**

Running a Program from the VBA IDE
■ Click the Run Sub/User Form button on the toolbar.

When you click the Run Sub/User Form button, the VBA IDE switches from Design mode to **Run mode**. In Run mode, your program is said to be "running" or "executing." As you develop programs within the VBA environment, you will regularly switch from Design mode to Run mode. Some developers use the terms runtime and design time. These terms are used interchangeably with Run mode and Design mode. Note that the word runtime does not contain a space.

This underscores the fact that, when you become a developer of applications, you take on dual roles. In Design mode, you are the developer (or designer) of the program. Then when you test the program, you enter into Run mode, at which time you take on the role of the user. In Run mode, you can test your program, interacting with the program as if you were the user for whom the program has been designed.

*To test the code you just typed:*

1. Verify that the code is displayed in the Code window, as illustrated in Figure 1-14. Place the pointer anywhere within the code.

2. Click the **Run Sub/User Form** button ▶ on the toolbar. The Word window becomes the active window. Inside the Word window, a VBA dialog box is displayed, as shown in Figure 1-15. As you can see, this dialog box includes the instructions "Enter your name." The pointer is positioned inside a blank text box, ready for you to type your name. This kind of dialog box is known as an input box, because it allows the user to provide information, or input, for the program.

| Figure 1-15 | INPUT BOX WITH WORD IN THE BACKGROUND |
|---|---|

input box

type your name here

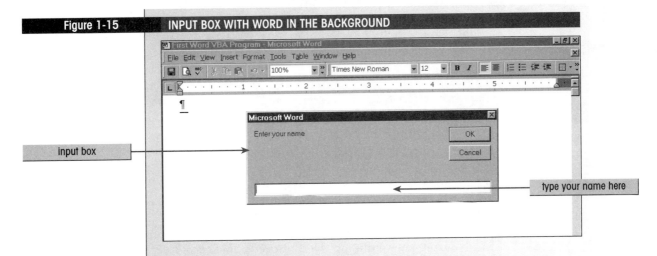

3. Type your first and last name, and then click **OK**. The VBA IDE becomes the active window again, indicating that the program has finished running. In other words, the VBA IDE has returned to Design mode. Now you can switch to the Word window to see the results of the program.

4. Click the **First Word VBA Program** button on the taskbar. Notice that your name has been inserted into the document. Notice also that your name has been formatted in 24-point italicized Arial Black and the color of the font is Dark Blue. Your screen should look similar to Figure 1-16, though of course you should see your own first and last name in the document rather than "Rebekah Tidwell."

| Figure 1-16 | WORD DOCUMENT WINDOW AFTER RUNNING VBA PROGRAM |
|---|---|

you will only see the paragraph and space symbols if nonprinting characters are displayed in your Word window

name inserted and formatted by the program

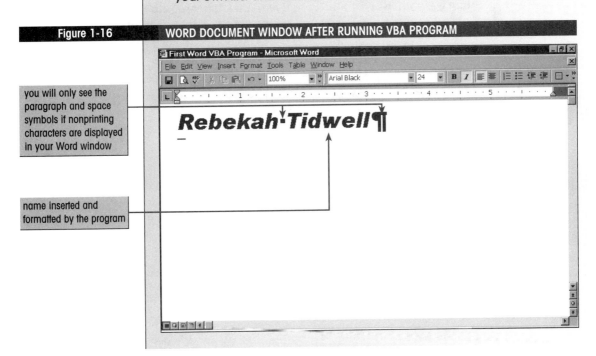

> TROUBLE? If you see an error message, click OK, then click the Reset button on the VBA IDE toolbar. Repeat Step 8 in the preceding section to correct any errors, and then repeat the steps in this section, starting with Step 1.

Now that you have practiced entering and running code, you will take a moment to learn about the basic structure of the program you created.

## Understanding the Code

Gene congratulates you on successfully creating and executing your first VBA program. Now he asks you to take a few minutes to examine the code you typed.

The following steps provide a brief explanation of each statement in the program. The explanation provided here is simply an introduction; you will learn more details as you work through the tutorials in this text. Don't expect to understand all the code at this time.

### To examine the program code:

1. Click the **Microsoft Visual Basic** button in the taskbar. The VBA IDE is displayed on the screen.

2. Click at the beginning of the following line:

```
Dim strNewData As String
```

This statement creates a temporary storage location in the computer's memory, that will store the name entered by the user. This temporary storage location is called a variable. You will learn more about variables in later tutorials.

3. Press the **Down Arrow** key ↓ to move the pointer to the following line:

```
strNewData = InputBox("Enter your name")
```

This statement creates an input box in which the user can type information, in this case a name.

4. Press ↓ to move the pointer to the following line:

```
Selection.TypeText Text:=strNewData
```

This statement takes the text the user types into the input box and inserts it into the Word document.

5. Press ↓ to move the pointer to the following line:

```
Selection.WholeStory
```

This statement selects all the text in the document—which, in this case, is the name originally entered in the input box.

6. Press ↓ to move the pointer to the following line:

```
Selection.Font.Color = wdColorDarkBlue
```

This statement sets the color of the selected text to dark blue.

7. Use ↓ to move the pointer to the following three lines:

```
Selection.Font.Name = "Arial Black"
Selection.Font.Size = 24
Selection.Font.Italic = True
```

These three statements set the font of the selected text to 24-point Italicized Arial Black.

8. Press ↓ to move the pointer to the following line:

```
Selection.Collapse
```

This last statement deselects the text in the Document window.

9. Notice the statements beginning with the words Sub and End Sub. These statements fall at the beginning and the end of the code. You can think of these as marking the beginning and ending of a section of code. As you will learn later, VBA code is organized into sections called subprograms. The Sub statement marks the beginning of a subprogram, and the End Sub statement marks the ending of a subprogram.

You have examined the code and have an understanding of how the code will work. You will now save the First Word VBA Program document (containing your name) along with the code.

## Saving the Document and Associated Modules

Earlier in this session you saved the code that you typed. The code itself is referred to as a **module**. When you saved the code, you were actually saving the Word document (which opened when you first opened Word) and the module. Whenever you save a document in Word or any of the other Office applications, you also save any VBA program associated with that document. At this point, you simply want to save changes made to the Word document. (In other words, you want to save your formatted name, which the VBA program entered into the document for you.) By saving a document, then, you are also saving the code you entered. Later you will learn how to save modules separately from a document.

*To save the document along with its code:*

1. Click the **First Word VBA Program** button on the taskbar.

2. Click the **Save** button 🖫 on the Word Standard toolbar. Any changes to the document (and the code) are saved.

3. Close Word by clicking its **Close** button ☒. Notice that when you close Word, the VBA IDE closes along with it.

## Session 1.2   Quick Check

1. When you are writing a VBA program, you take on the role of _____, and when you run the program, you become the _____.

2. A(n) _____ is a temporary storage location in memory where you can store data.

3. The statement _____ will select all the text in a document.

4. The _____ and the _____ statements mark the beginning and ending of a subprogram, respectively.

5. The statement _____ will deselect text within a Word document.

## SESSION 1.3

In this session you will learn to record a macro. You will then view the VBA code produced by the recorded macro. Finally, you will save and print the code.

## Macros and the Macro Recorder

As an experienced Office user, you know that a macro is a program that automates a commonly performed task. You have probably created macros for several of the Office applications. If so, then you know that the easiest way to create a macro is to record a series of keystrokes, using the Macro Recorder. You probably did not realize, however, that the Macro Recorder translates each step you perform into VBA code and stores it in a file known as a **macro module file**. To repeat the steps contained in a macro module file, you can then simply run, or play, the macro.

Recording macros is also a very useful way to become familiar with VBA program statements. You can also use a macro as the basis for a larger VBA program. Often, a developer will record a macro and then edit the macro code to add additional features. For example, you might record a macro that selects a section of the document and formats the text in italics. You might then edit this code so the program takes the formatted text and inserts it into another document. A recorded macro provides a good foundation on which to build a complex subprogram.

Your supervisor, Gene, has asked you to record a macro within PowerPoint. He explains that, since you are just learning to use VBA, this experience will give you some more experience working with code. The macro should create a new slide, add some text, change the fill color of the title and the bulleted list box, and change the font color and size of the title.

### To begin recording a PowerPoint macro:

1. Start PowerPoint, open a blank presentation, and close the New Slide dialog box if necessary.

2. Click **Tools** on the menu bar, point to **Macro**, and then click **Record New Macro**. You see the Record Macro dialog box, as shown in Figure 1-17.

| Figure 1-17 | RECORD MACRO DIALOG BOX |

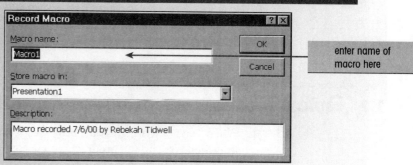

3. Replace "Macro1" in the Macro Name text box with **FirstPPMacro**, and then press **Enter**. The Record Macro dialog box closes, and the Macro Recording toolbar is displayed, indicating that you are now in recording mode. See Figure 1-18.

TROUBLE? If you see an error message when you press **Enter**, you probably mistyped the Macro name. Re-enter the name and make sure you do not add any spaces. Press **Enter**.

**Figure 1-18** | **POWERPOINT WITH MACRO RECORDER RUNNING**

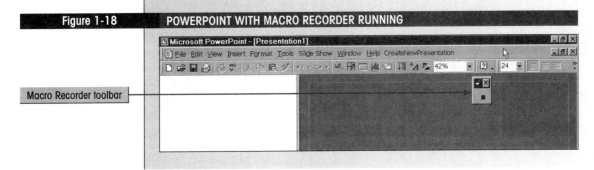

Macro Recorder toolbar

Anything you do from this point on will be recorded in your macro. You must follow the directions in the next steps carefully and in the order they are presented. If you make a mistake, the mistake will be recorded in the macro. This is similar to recording a speech or a song. If, while recording, you stumbled over a word, you would either have to edit the speech or start over again and rerecord the speech. In the same manner, if you make a mistake while recording your macro, you will either have to start over or edit the macro to fix the error.

Keep in mind that if you make a mistake when recording the macro, you can click the Stop button on the Macro Recording toolbar, close PowerPoint without saving any changes, and then begin again with Step 1 above.

Now you are ready to perform the steps you want the macro to record.

## To record the steps of the macro:

1. Click the **New Slide** button ⬚ on the PowerPoint toolbar. The New Slide dialog box opens.

2. Click the icon in the top row, second from left. The description "Bulleted List" is displayed in the lower-right corner of the dialog box.

3. Click **OK**.

4. Click on the rectangle containing the text "Click to add title" and type **Goals of TnT Consulting**. Before proceeding to the next step, make sure you typed the text correctly. If you made an error, correct it now, so that the error does not get incorporated into the macro.

5. Click the rectangle containing the text "Click to add text," type **To Provide Competent Software Solution Advice**, press **Enter**, type **To Develop Efficient, User-friendly Software**, press **Enter**, and then type **To Provide Continuing User Support**. Again, take care not to make any typing errors.

6. Click the fillcolor down arrow (on the drawing toolbar) and click any color. The box containing the three bullet points is filled with the color you selected.

TROUBLE? If you make a mistake, you can click the Stop button on the Macro Recording toolbar, close PowerPoint without saving any changes, and then begin again with Step 1 in the preceding set of steps.

7. Click the title, **Goals of TnT Consulting**.

8. Click the fillcolor down arrow (on the drawing toolbar) and click a color of your choice.

9. Select the text "Goals of TnT Consulting".

10. Click the **Bold** button **B** . The title is now formatted in bold.

11. Click the **Increase Font Size** button **A** . The title increases in size.

12. Click the **Font color** list arrow **A ·** (on the drawing toolbar) and click a color of your choice.

13. You are now finished recording your macro. Click the **Stop Recording** button on the Macro recording toolbar. The Macro Recording toolbar disappears from the screen.

You have now successfully recorded your macro for PowerPoint. In order to test the macro, you will first delete the slide you just created.

### To delete the slide you created while recording the macro:

1. Click **Edit** on the menu bar, and then click **Delete Slide**.

Now you will execute, or run, the macro you created and observe how the macro repeats the steps you recorded.

### To run the macro:

1. Click **Tools**, point to **Macro**, and then click **Macros**. The Macro dialog box opens, as shown in Figure 1-19. This dialog box lists all the macros you have recorded for the current presentation. In this case, you have only created one—FirstPPMacro. This macro is selected, as shown in Figure 1-19.

| Figure 1-19 | MACRO DIALOG BOX CONTAINS A LIST OF CURRENT MACROS |

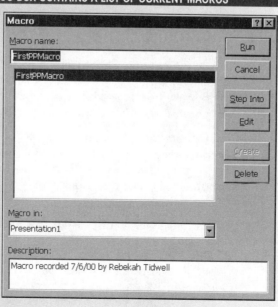

**2.** In the Macro dialog box, click **Run** and watch as the macro rebuilds the slide.

As you can see, a macro is a very valuable tool for automating steps that you need to repeat. You will find that the recording of macros is also a very useful tool when writing VBA code. In the next section, you will examine the VBA code you created when creating the macro.

## Examining the VBA Code in a Macro

As you record a macro, each step you perform is translated into VBA code. This code is stored in a macro module, which is then attached to the open document, spreadsheet, or presentation. In the following steps, you will view the code you created when you recorded the macro in the previous steps.

*To view the macro code:*

**1.** Open the PowerPoint VBA IDE.

**2.** If necessary, click the **Project Explorer** button [icon] to open the Project Explorer.

**3.** If necessary, click the **Expand** button [icon] next to VBAProject (Presentation1) to display the Modules folder. The code you just created is stored in this folder.

**4.** If necessary, click [icon] next to the Modules folder to display its contents. You see an item entitled "Module1." This is the file that contains the macro you created earlier. See Figure 1-20.

| Figure 1-20 | THE PROJECT EXPLORER IN POWERPOINT |

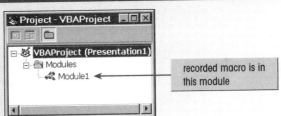

**5.** Double-click **Module1**. The macro code is displayed in the Code window, as shown in Figure 1-21.

**Figure 1-21**   CODE CREATED BY RECORDING A MACRO

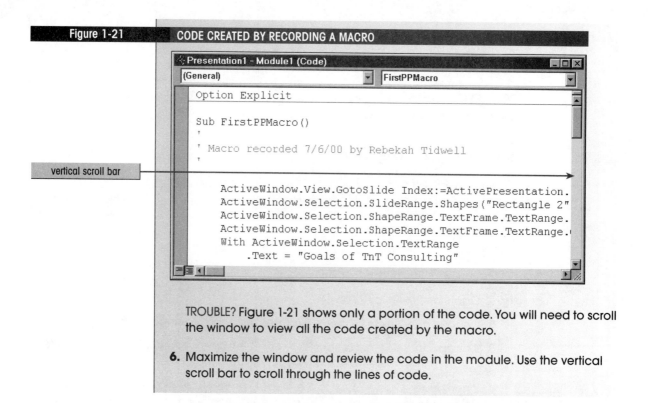

vertical scroll bar

TROUBLE? Figure 1-21 shows only a portion of the code. You will need to scroll the window to view all the code created by the macro.

**6.** Maximize the window and review the code in the module. Use the vertical scroll bar to scroll through the lines of code.

As you can see, the code you created by recording a macro is very complicated, containing numerous lines. Imagine how long it would have taken to type each of those lines. By recording the statements as a macro, you saved yourself a great deal of time and effort. And because you already know that the macro works, you know that the code is free of errors.

## Printing a Code Module

Gene doesn't have time to review your code module now, so he asks you to print it so that he can review it later. Printing a code module is as easy as printing a document in Word.

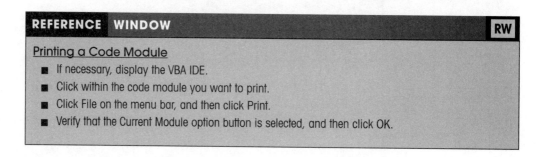

REFERENCE WINDOW   RW

Printing a Code Module
■ If necessary, display the VBA IDE.
■ Click within the code module you want to print.
■ Click File on the menu bar, and then click Print.
■ Verify that the Current Module option button is selected, and then click OK.

You are now ready to print the macro code.

## To print the code module:

1. Verify that the cursor is located anywhere within the macro code.

2. Click **File** on the menu bar, and then click **Print**. The Print - VBA Project dialog box opens, as shown in Figure 1-22. This dialog box allows you to print different items within the IDE. In this case, you only want to print the current module.

| Figure 1-22 | PRINT VBA PROJECT DIALOG BOX |

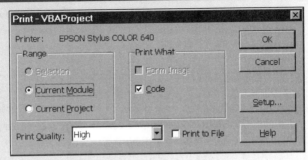

3. Verify that the Current Module option button is selected, and then click **OK**. The module prints.

By examining the printed code, you can see that it is quite detailed and contains statements with which you are unfamiliar at this point. You probably recognize the first and last statements, the Sub and End  Sub statements, which mark the beginning and end of the macro, respectively. These same words marked the beginning and end of the program for Word that you created earlier in this tutorial. Like that program, this macro is considered a VBA subprogram. You will learn more about the statements it contains as you work through the tutorials in this book. You might want to return to Word and to Excel and record a macro for each of these applications and then view the resulting VBA code.

## Saving a PowerPoint Macro

Now that you have created and printed the macro code, you need to save it. You could save the macro code by saving it from within the VBA IDE. Alternately, you can save it by saving the PowerPoint presentation. You'll try this approach in the next set of steps.

## To save the macro code:

1. Click the **Microsoft PowerPoint** button on the taskbar, and then click the **Save** button 🖫 on the toolbar. The Save As dialog box opens. Notice that this time the Save As Type list box indicates that the file will be saved as a Presentation. This makes sense, because you created the code module within a PowerPoint presentation.

2. Type **First PP Macro** in the File Name text box, use the Save in list arrow to switch to the Tutorial.01 folder on your Data Disk, and then click **Save.**

3. Close PowerPoint. The PowerPoint VBA IDE closes at the same time.

You may have noted the absence of any reference to Access in this tutorial. There are several reasons for this. First, creating VBA code for Access is more complicated than doing so for Word, Excel, and PowerPoint. Second, Access does not have a macro recorder that you can use to help you learn the VBA. For these reasons, the introductory tutorials will focus on Word, Excel, and PowerPoint. Tutorial 8 in this book will focus on writing VBA programs for Access.

After your first day on the job at TnT Consulting, you have learned that VBA provides a complete environment in which you can create custom solutions. You gained some experience in entering code and in testing the code. Finally, you learned that creating macros provides a means of creating VBA code. By now, you are probably learning the value of programming in VBA. In the next section, you will learn how to use the VBA Help system.

## Using the VBA Help System

TnT Consulting is a busy place, so it's important that all the developers know where to look for the information they need, rather than asking for help on every project. Thus, in order to make you more self-sufficient as a developer, Gene wants you to take a few minutes to explore the VBA Help system.

The VBA Help system is extensive and explains most aspects of VBA programming. You open a VBA Help window just as you do in the Office applications, via the Help menu. In the next set of steps, you will open the Excel VBA IDE and then use its Help system to find information on the various tools you have used in this tutorial. The goal of these steps is to introduce you to the VBA Help system. You'll use this rich and helpful resource as you complete the other tutorials in this book.

### To start the Help system:

1. Start Excel and open its VBA IDE, using the menu commands you used earlier for Word and PowerPoint.

2. Close any open windows within the VBA IDE.

3. Click **Help** on the menu bar and then click **Microsoft Visual Basic Help**. The Office Assistant opens.

   TROUBLE? If you see a message indicating that the Help files are missing or not installed, you need to install them from the Office 2000 installation CD before proceeding. See your instructor or technical support person for help.

4. In the Office Assistant, type **Project Explorer** and then click **Search**.

5. Click **Use the Project Explorer**. You see a window with information on the Project Explorer window, as shown in Figure 1-23.

**Figure 1-23**   "USE THE PROJECT EXPLORER" HELP TOPIC

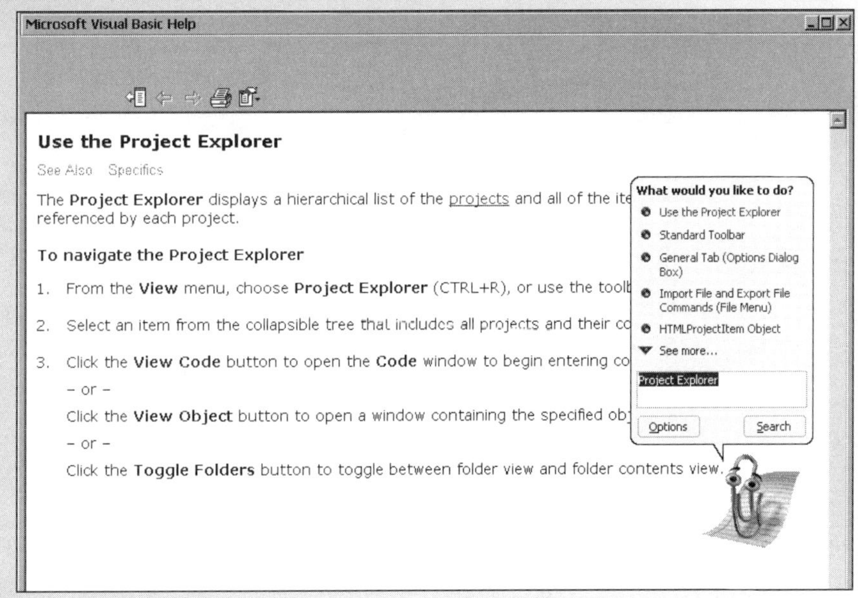

**6.** Read the material on the Project Explorer. Note the reference to projects. In this tutorial you have been working with only one project at a time. However, as you probably know, you can have multiple documents open in Word, multiple workbooks open in Excel, and multiple presentations open in PowerPoint. The Project Explorer will contain a folder for each document, spreadsheet, or presentation that is open in the application.

**7.** In the Office Assistant, type **Properties Window** and press **Enter**.

**8.** Click **Use the Properties Window**. A window opens with information on the Properties window, as shown in Figure 1-24. Recall that in this tutorial you simply opened the Properties window and then closed it. You will use the Properties window extensively in Tutorial 2. Read the information in the Help window to get a basic idea of what the Properties window is used for. You might want to return to this Help window later, when you start to use the Properties window in Tutorial 2.

**Figure 1-24**    "USE THE PROPERTIES WINDOW" HELP TOPIC

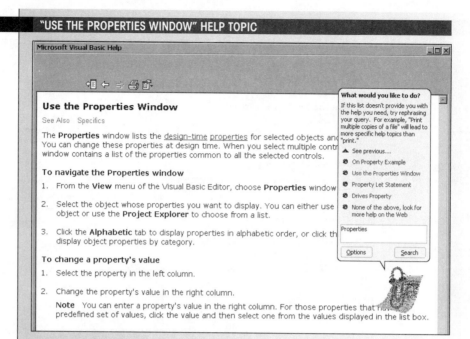

**9.** In the Office Assistant type **Sub statement** and then click **Search**.

**10.** Click **Sub Statement** and then read the information in the Help window, as shown in Figure 1-25. Again, don't worry if you don't understand every detail. You'll learn more about sub statements throughout this book.

**Figure 1-25**    SUB STATEMENT HELP TOPIC

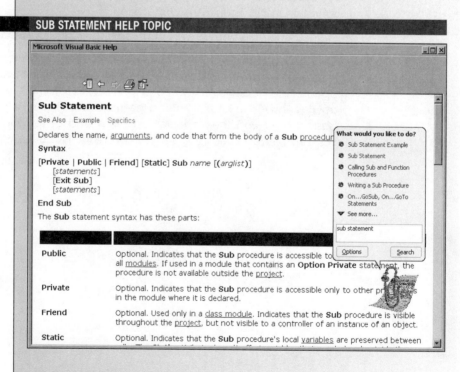

**11.** Close the Help window.

**12.** Close Excel.

Now that you know how to look for information within the VBA Help system, you can consult it on your own whenever you would like more information on a particular topic. You'll also use the Help system more extensively throughout this book.

## Session 1.3 QUICK CHECK

1. A(n) _____ is a recorded set of keystrokes that generates _____ code.

2. Once a macro has been recorded you can view and edit the resulting code within the _____.

3. Why would a developer ever choose to record a macro?

4. The _____ toolbar is displayed only when you are recording a macro.

5. If you want to alter a macro, you will need to either _____ the code produced by the macro or _____ the macro.

6. _____ does not have a macro recorder as do the other applications in the Office suite.

7. The _____ system provides answers to questions the developer might have, pertaining to programming in VBA.

## REVIEW ASSIGNMENTS

Gene, your supervisor at TnT Consulting, wants you to learn how to alter the VBA code in the program for Word that you created earlier. He would like you to alter the code so that the user is prompted to enter her company name rather than her own name. In addition, the program should format the text in red, 36-point Times New Roman.

1. Start Word and open the document **VBA Program**, which is located in the Review folder for Tutorial 1, on your Data Disk. If you see a message box asking if you want to disable or enable macros, select the Enable Macro option.

2. Save the file as **Edited VBA Program**.

3. Press ALT+F11 to open the VBA IDE.

4. Close all open windows within the VBA IDE.

5. Open the Properties window and the Project Explorer window. Size and position these windows as in Figure 1-26.

**Figure 1-26**

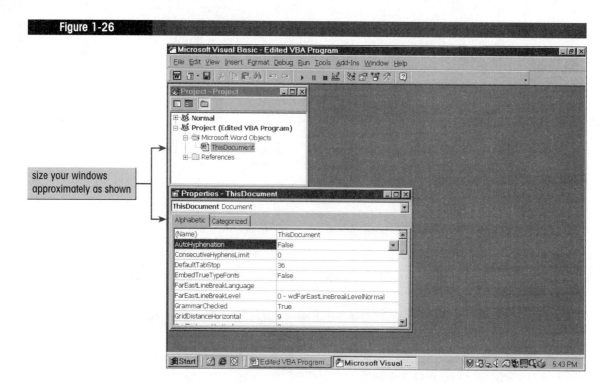

size your windows approximately as shown

6. Close the Properties window.

7. Within the Project Explorer, double-click **ThisDocument** to open the Code window. Size and position both windows to match Figure 1-27.

**Figure 1-27**

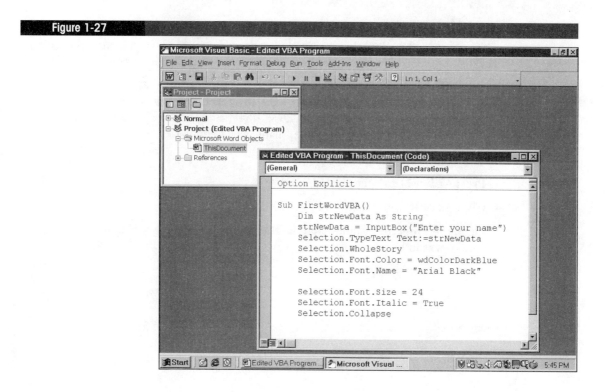

8. Click at the end of the line `Selection.Font.Color = wdColorDarkBlue`.

9. Use the backspace key to delete = `wdColorDarkBlue`. (Remember to delete the equals sign as well as the text `wdColorDarkBlue`.)

10. Type a new equals sign. The Intellisense feature displays a list of all default colors for Word documents. Scroll through the list and double-click **wdColorRed**. The color `wdColorRed` is added to the end of the line of code.

11. Locate the line `strNewData = Inputbox("Enter your name")`.

12. Click between `"your"` and `"name"` and then type **company**. The phrase should now read `"Enter your company name"`.

13. Locate the line `Selection.Font.Name = "Arial Black"` and change `Arial Black` to `Times New Roman`.

14. Locate the line `Selection.Font.Size = 24`. Change `24` to `36`. At this point, your code window should look like Figure 1-28.

---

**Figure 1-28**

```
Microsoft Visual Basic - First Word VBA Program - [ThisDocument (Code)]
File  Edit  View  Insert  Format  Debug  Run  Tools  Add-Ins  Window  Help
                                                            Ln 10, Col 29
(General)                              FirstWordVBA

Sub FirstWordVBA()
    Dim strNewData As String
    strNewData = InputBox("Enter your company name")      ◄──── change the string
                                                                to include the
                                                                word company
    Selection.TypeText Text:=strNewData
    Selection.WholeStory
    Selection.Font.Color = wdColorRed     ◄────
    Selection.Font.Name = "Times New Roman"  ◄──── change font color,
                                                   name, and size
    Selection.Font.Size = 36    ◄────
    Selection.Font.Italic = True
    Selection.Collapse

End Sub
```

---

15. Click the **Save** button 💾 on the toolbar.

16. Click the **Run Sub/User Form** button ▶ on the toolbar.

17. When prompted to enter your company name, type **TnT Consulting Group**, and then click **OK**.

18. Click the **Word** button on the taskbar and observe that the company name has been entered into the Word document and has been formatted in red, 36-point Times New Roman.

19. Switch to the VBA IDE and print the code.

20. On the printout, circle the statements that you altered in these Review Assignments.

21. Click Help and then, in the Office Assistant input window, type **change font values**. Press Enter or click Search.

22. Click "Bold, Italic, Size, StrikeThrough, Underline, Weight Properties," as shown in Figure 1-29.

**Figure 1-29**

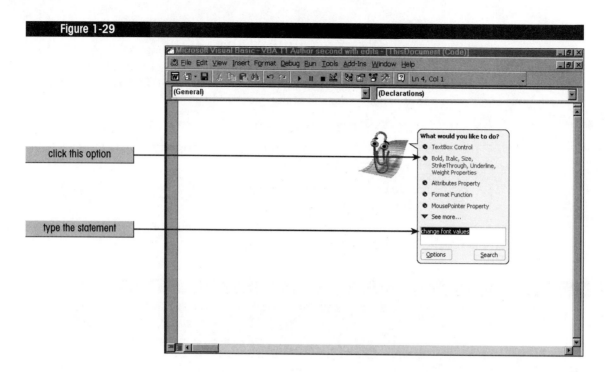

click this option

type the statement

23. Review the information provided by Help and then print it.

24. Save your work and close Word.

**Explore**

25. Start Excel and record a macro. Open the Excel VBA IDE and examine the VBA code generated by the macro recorder. Print the macro code. Save the workbook as Sample Excel Macro and then close Excel.

## CASE PROBLEMS

**Case 1. Creating a Program for Sailaway Charters**  Sailaway Charters, an excursion company based in Miami, Florida, maintains a large fleet of sailboats. While Sailaway does rent boats to individuals, the majority of its sales come from corporations, who charter day-long excursions in order to entertain clients or provide a special perk for employees. Tony Loftus, Sailaway's operations manager, tracks corporate reservations in an Excel worksheet. He asks you to create an Excel VBA program that will request a company name from the user, place the name in a worksheet, and format the name in green, 24-point Arial.

1. Start Excel and then open the VBA IDE.

2. If necessary, open the Project Explorer, but close any other windows.

3. If necessary, expand the VBA Project (Book1) item, expand the Microsoft Excel Objects folder, and then double-click Sheet1 (Sheet1), as shown in Figure 1-30. The Code window opens.

---

**Figure 1-30**

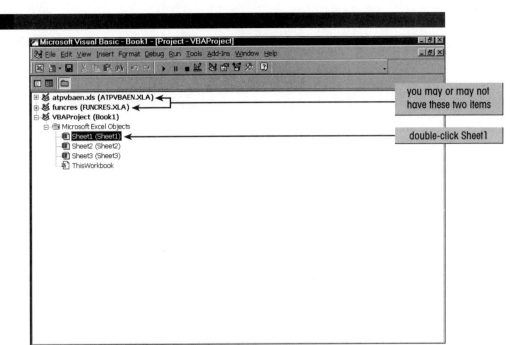

4. Type the following code into the Code window. Note that you don't have to indent the lines exactly as they appear here. You may, for instance, choose to indent the second line five spaces using the Tab key, or to press the Spacebar twice to indent the line two spaces.

```
Sub FirstExcelVBA()
   Dim strInputData As String
   strInputData = InputBox("Enter your company name")
   ActiveCell.FormulaR1C1 = strInputData
   With ActiveCell.Font
        .Name = "Arial Black"
        .FontStyle = "Italic"
        .Size = 24
        .Color = vbBlue
    End With
End Sub
```

5. Save the file in the Cases folder for Tutorial 1, using the name **FirstExcelVBA**.

6. Click the Run Sub/User Form button and, when you are prompted to enter a company name, type "Sailaway Charter Company" (without the quotation marks) and then click OK.

7. Switch to the Excel window to see the results of the program.

8. Print the code and circle the statements that format the text.

9. Write your first and last name at the top of the print out.

10. Save the file and then close Excel.

*Case 2. Creating a Macro for StoneWater Bookstore*   StoneWater BookStore is currently creating a number of promotional fliers in Word to send out to customers. The fliers will all be quite similar, but will require varying formatting options (such as different fonts, font colors, and font sizes). Bob Stewart, the store's promotions manager, has asked you to create a small program that will automatically format text in a Word document. Then he wants you to print the code and show him how to edit the code so that he can change the formatting options applied by the program. You will write the program for Bob by recording a macro. You will then print the macro and circle the items that Bob can change to suit the needs of the various fliers he plans to create.

1. Start Word and verify that a new, blank document is open.

2. Save the document file as **StoneWater Bookstore Macro** in the Cases folder for Tutorial 1.

3. Type the following, replacing YOUR NAME with your first and last name:

    This is sample text created by YOUR NAME to try out some formatting options. To test the program, Bob will select the text he wants to change, change some font options, and then view the results of the changes. This paragraph is only for testing purposes.

4. Select the second sentence in the paragraph.

5. Turn on the macro recorder. Name the macro **BookstoreMacro**. If you see a message asking if you want to replace an existing macro with the same name, click Yes.

6. Select the second sentence in the paragraph.

7. Change the text to 20-point italicized Courier, in bold.

8. Stop the macro.

*Explore*    9. Now you'll try a new method of opening the VBA IDE: Click Tools, click macro, and then click Macros. Select BookstoreMacro in the list, and then click Edit.

10. Print the macro and circle the font options Bob might want to change in the program.

11. Save your work and close Word.

*Case 3. Gateway Promotional Services*  Gateway Promotions provides promotional materials for a variety of clients who need to advertise events, such as lectures or concerts. Gateway specializes in producing high-quality fliers, posters, newspapers and advertisements. The company also creates PowerPoint presentations that clients can use to promote their products or services. Gateway has hired you to help automate the production of these PowerPoint presentations. You know that you will be able to provide some solutions, and you decide to begin with recording some macros that will help you identify statements you might use as you work on this project.

1. Start PowerPoint and open a blank presentation. Close the New Slide dialog box if it opens.

2. Start the Macro Recorder; name the macro **GatewayMacro**.

3. Insert a new slide and select the slide layout of your choice.

4. Insert several items of text of your own choosing including your first and last name.

5. Change the formatting for each of the items you entered (i.e., change the font, the font size, the font color, and the fill color). Make selections you feel would make an attractive slide.

6. Add some clipart somewhere on the slide. Alter the size and placement of the clipart.

7. Stop the Macro Recorder.

8. Delete the slide you just created.

9. Start the VBA IDE.

10. Open the Project Explorer window (if necessary), expand the VBAProject(Presentation1) item, expand the Modules folder, and then double-click Module1.

*Explore*   11. In the tutorial, you typed code in the VBA IDE, and then executed the code by clicking the Run Sub/User Form button in the VBA IDE. Since a macro is simply a VBA program, you can also run a macro from within the VBA IDE. To try running the macro now, click the Run Sub/User Form button on the toolbar. When the Macro dialog box opens, select the GatewayMacro, and click Run.

12. Switch to PowerPoint and observe that your slide has been recreated.

13. Print the slide, and then delete it.

14. Print the macro code.

15. Locate and circle a line of code that has to do with changing font size.

*Explore*   16. Referring to the line you circled, edit the code in the code window so that it formats text in a different font size. For example, if the code currently formats text in a slide in 44-point, you might edit the code so that it formats text in 32-point. (*Hint*: Make the change significant enough that you can see the difference when you run the program.) Run the macro again, and print the newly created slide. Compare the new print-out to the previous version of the slide, and note the change in font-size.

17. Print the Macro code again and circle the change you made to the code.

18. Save your work and close PowerPoint.

19. Write your name at the top of all printouts.

*Case 4. Researching the VBA Help for G&R Computer Learning Center*  Computer Learning Center provides training for people who want to expand their computing skills. Currently, G&R offers several classes on VBA development. However, after completing these classes, many students call the instructor, Jane Hamilton, with questions about VBA that she thinks are answered in the VBA online Help system. Jane asks you to explore the Help system and verify that it does indeed provide the answers the students need.

1. Start Excel, open the VBA IDE, and then open the Help window.

2. Search for information on the term "inputbox."

3. Click Inputbox Function. You used the inputbox function in this tutorial. Read through this material to see if you gain further insight into what this function does.

4. Print the information on the Inputbox Function.

5. Click the example link on the top of the Help window.

6. Examine the example of the inputbox function and then print it.

7. On the printout, circle the inputbox function along with the parentheses that follow it. Write your name at the top of the printout.

8. Search for information on "Sub statement." Print the information and any examples.

9. Close the Help window.

10. Close Excel.

# Q<small>UICK</small> | C<small>HECK</small> **ANSWERS**

*Session 1.1*

1. environment, Integrated Development Environment

2. a. VBA IDE Menu, b. the Project Explorer window, c. Properties window, d. Code window, e. VBA Integrated Development Environment

3. Project Explorer

4. Properties

5. Code

*Session 1.2*

1. developer, user

2. variable

3. `Selection.WholeStory`

4. `Sub, End Sub`

5. `Selection.Collapse`

*Session 1.3*

1. macro, VBA code

2. VBA IDE

3. The developer might record a macro to learn some new programming statement that could then be used in another VBA program. Also the developer might record a macro and then add the VBA statement to the macro to increase its functionality.

4. Macro

5. rerecord, edit

6. Access

In this tutorial you will:

- Learn about objects, collections, properties, methods, events, and interfaces

- Explore the Excel VBA IDE

- Work with a new UserForm

- Add control objects to a UserForm

- Change a control object's properties

- Program a command button control object

- Document VBA code

- Print VBA code

# WORKING WITH OBJECTS AND PROPERTIES

*Creating a Checkbook Interface for TnT Consulting Group*

CASE

## TnT Checkbook Form

Clients like the applications developed by TnT Consulting Group because they are so easy to use. No matter how complex the code at the heart of a TnT application, the interface—that is, the part that the user interacts with—is simple and easy to understand. In particular, TnT is known for making simple, customized data entry forms that mask the complexity of the underlying applications.

The forms developed by TnT Consulting organize information in a way that is familiar to users. The forms can also check data for accuracy and validity.

Gene Cox, your supervisor, has asked you to develop a simple data entry form that looks similar to a check in a checkbook. This form will ultimately be part of a larger application that will allow the user to enter data into an electronic checkbook register. (An Excel workbook will serve as the checkbook register.)

Gene explains that the check form should ensure that dates are entered in a valid format. In the same vein, the form should also verify that the user has entered the check amount in the right format. For now, however, you only need to be concerned with designing and developing a form that can serve as an interface to the Excel worksheet. Before you can begin creating this interface, you need to become familiar with the term "object" as it is used in VBA programming.

In this session you will learn about objects, collections, properties, methods, events, and interfaces. You will also examine the Excel VBA IDE, and, in the process, take a closer look at the Project Explorer and the elements that make up a project. Finally, you will begin to build an interface using a VBA UserForm and control objects.

# Understanding Objects

When writing programs in VBA, you write code that manipulates objects. Briefly, an **object** is a thing that is defined both by its characteristics and by what it can do. A Microsoft Excel worksheet is an object, as is an individual cell within a worksheet, a Microsoft Word document, or, for that matter, Microsoft Word itself. Visual Basic for Applications is an **object-based programming language**, which means that it works very closely with the objects available within an application such as Word or Excel.

For beginning programmers, getting a firm grasp on the concept of objects can be difficult. But after reading the following sections, you should have a clearer understanding of this complicated idea.

## Objects and Collections

The easiest way to understand programming objects is to begin by thinking of objects in the real world. In everyday life an object is any noun. For example, your college campus can be considered an object. The campus itself contains other objects, such as buildings, sidewalks, lawns, and people.

Figure 2-1 illustrates a campus as an object that contains other objects. In the figure, the college campus contains a variety of buildings; the buildings, in turn, contain a variety of rooms; the rooms, in turn, contain varying assortments of objects, such as chairs, desks, and so on. The objects in Figure 2-1 are arranged in a hierarchical fashion, with the college campus at the left, and the contents of the rooms on the right.

**Figure 2-1**     A COLLEGE CAMPUS AS AN EXAMPLE OF AN OBJECT MODEL

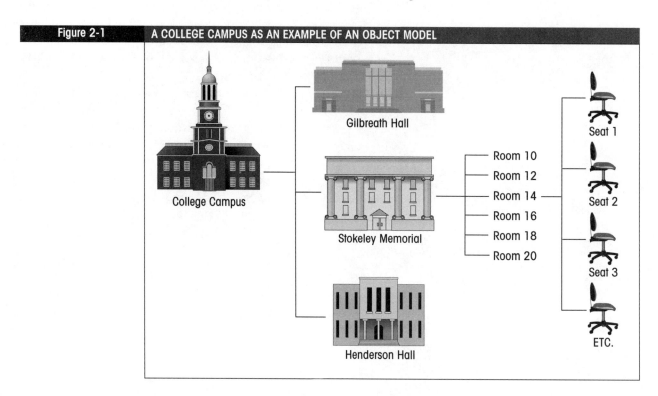

College Campus

Gilbreath Hall

Stokeley Memorial
- Room 10
- Room 12
- Room 14
- Room 16
- Room 18
- Room 20

Henderson Hall

Seat 1
Seat 2
Seat 3
ETC.

In object-based programming, a group of objects contained within another object is known as a **collection**. For example, a classroom might contain a collection of chairs, a collection of computers, a collection of erasers, and a collection of doors (though the collection would probably consist of only one door).

## Using Properties to Define an Object

In the real world, each object has certain characteristics. Among other things, the characteristics of your campus include its school name, its architectural style, and its size. The characteristics of a chair might include its size, the material from which it is made, and its color. In VBA terms, the characteristics that define a particular object are known as **properties**. Each property has a specific **value**. For example, suppose a classroom contained a red chair. The Color property for that Chair object would then have the value "red." In the same way, the Size property for a classroom might have the value "150 square feet." Figure 2-2 shows a list of properties that characterize a Chair object, along with possible values for those properties. Note that for some properties, the possible values are numerous. For other properties, such as whether or not the chair has casters, the value can only be either "Yes" or "No."

| Figure 2-2 | PROPERTIES OF A CHAIR OBJECT | |
|---|---|
| **PROPERTY** | **POSSIBLE VALUES** |
| Color | Gray, Black, Blue, Brown, etc. |
| Material type | Wood, Plastic, Upholstered, etc. |
| Number of legs | 4 or 5 |
| Casters (rollers) | Yes or No |
| Arms | Yes or No |

Notice that the chairs have properties, which in turn have specific values. A given seat might have a Color property with the value "gray," a Material Type property with a value "plastic," a Number of Legs property with a value of "5," a Caster property with a value of "Yes," and an Arms property with a value of "Yes." Of course, this is not an exhaustive list of the characteristics of any one chair, but rather a list of some possible chair properties. The important concept here is that objects have properties, and properties have specific values.

## Understanding Methods and Events

In addition to having properties, each object can perform specific actions. The set of actions that an object can perform are known as the object's **methods**. Returning again to our example of a Chair object, consider a chair with casters, which can roll around a room. You might say that one of the methods of this chair is "roll" (meaning that it can move by rolling).

The chair does not roll around by itself, however. Rather, something must happen for the chair to roll. Unless someone or something pushes the chair, it will remain stationary. In other words, an event must take place that will cause the chair to roll. In this example, the event is a "push," which triggers the method, which is "roll." In VBA terminology, then, an **event** is an action that causes an object's method to begin. To use more programming terminology, you can say that an event triggers an object's method. Only specific events can trigger a method. For instance, shouting (that is, a shouting event) will not cause a chair to roll. Only pushing (that is, a pushing event) can trigger a roll method.

One of the most common programming events is the **Click** event. The Click event happens when the user clicks the mouse button on a particular object (such as a toolbar button). Object-based programs are often said to be **event-driven** because the programs are not "triggered" until a particular event takes place, just as the chair does not move until the "push" event takes place.

VBA programs are both object-based and event-driven. In event-driven programming, the click of the mouse will often cause an action to begin. When you highlight some text in Word and click the Bold button, you are triggering an event. The event is the click, which then activates a method that bolds the selected text.

## Understanding Interfaces

In the previous section you looked at a college campus and its contents as an example of a collection of objects. This section presents a second real-world example of an object, a simple calculator. This example differs from the college campus example in that it involves the additional concept of an interface.

As shown in Figure 2-3, a calculator, which is an object itself, contains a collection of buttons, which are also objects. Each button is characterized by its appearance and, most importantly, by the number or symbol printed on top of it. For example, one button has a 5 printed on it. Of course you realize that the 5 printed on the button means that when you press this button, a 5 will appear in the window. The calculator contains a number of other buttons, including the + button. You know that when you press the + button, the calculator will perform an addition operation.

| Figure 2-3 | A CALCULATOR AS AN EXAMPLE OF A REAL-WORLD OBJECT |

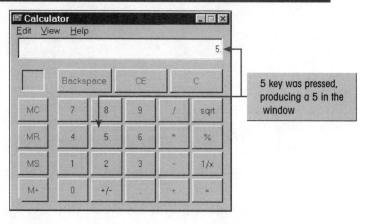

Now consider the operation of the calculator in terms of object-based programming. The calculator is dependent on its objects. That is to say, the objects (buttons) tell the calculator what to do. Until a user starts clicking buttons, the calculator does nothing.

You can think of the external components of the calculator (the buttons and the display window) as an example of an interface, which is something that lets one thing (say, the user) interact with another thing (say, the internal workings of the calculator). In programming terminology, an **interface** is the means by which the user interacts with a program. The graphical window that opens when you start Microsoft Word is one example of an interface, as is the Windows desktop that you see when you start your computer.

Events take place within the calculator interface. For example, pressing a button on the calculator is a kind of event, something that happens on the interface. The event, the pressing of a button, triggers some activity inside the calculator. If you wanted, you could assign names to the various events. For example, the event in which a 5 is pressed on the keyboard could be called Button 5 Pressed. The Button 5 Pressed event has a specific result: a 5 is displayed in the calculator window. This happens because the calculator has been programmed to display a 5 when the Button 5 Pressed event takes place. In the same way, events also take place within a VBA interface.

## Examining Some Sample Data Objects

By examining a few real-world objects, you have learned a great deal about some complicated programming topics. To summarize, an object is a thing that can be defined by its characteristics (properties) and can contain a collection of other objects. Each object has a set of characteristics, or properties, and each of these properties has a specific value. Objects can perform certain actions, which are known as methods, but those methods are only performed in response to a particular event. The user causes events to take place by interacting with the interface.

With that in mind, you are ready to learn more about how objects work in VBA. Within the world of programming, an object is sometimes referred to as a **data object**. One example of a data object is the employee database maintained by the TnT Personnel Department. This database includes one record for every employee. The database itself is an object. Likewise, each record in the database is an object. The records make up a collection of objects, which is then contained within the database object.

Now consider a single employee record. Like any other object, an employee record has properties. You already know that any record in a database is made up of fields such as Employee ID, Employee Name, Employee Address, etc. But you probably didn't realize that those fields are actually the record's properties. Each of the properties has values that identify the employee record as a unique object among the collection of employee objects (or records). For example, the property Employee Name might have a value of Rebekah Tidwell, and the property Employee ID# might have a value of 555-244-5555.

As you learned earlier in this tutorial, objects are associated with specific methods (or actions). Several methods can be associated with employee records. For example, an employee record could be added, deleted, or modified.

The user can interact with the database objects via an interface. You are already familiar with the graphical windows, tools, and menu bars that make up the Access interface. You may also have experience using the text-based SQL Query window, which advanced database users sometimes prefer to use when working with databases. Both the Access graphical window and the SQL Query window act as an interface, allowing the user to interact with the database objects.

Now that you have become more familiar with objects, you can learn how to use them when creating a VBA program. In the next section, you will open the Excel VBA IDE. Then, later, you will learn how to use a special kind of object known as a control object.

# Exploring the Excel VBA IDE

The checkbook VBA program you will work on for TnT Consulting will be integrated with an Excel workbook. Thus, you need to create the VBA application from within the Excel VBA IDE. In Tutorial 1, you took a brief look at the VBA IDE. As you open the Excel VBA IDE now, you will learn more about the elements of a VBA project.

## Opening the Excel VBA IDE

You will now launch Excel, and then the VBA IDE within Excel, so that you can view the various parts of a project.

## To launch the Excel VBA IDE:

1. Start Excel and then press **ALT+F11**. The VBA IDE for Excel opens.

2. Click the **Excel** button on the taskbar. You return to the Excel window. Next, you will save the new, blank workbook with a new name.

3. Click **File** on the menu bar, and then click **Save As**.

4. Switch to the location of your Data Disk.

5. Save the workbook as **Checkbook**. In the next step you will open a second workbook so that you can compare its IDE with the one you just opened.

6. Open a new, blank workbook.

You now have two workbooks loaded within Excel. In the next section you will compare the Project Explorer window, which will contain components of both workbooks.

## Studying the Project Explorer

A **project** consists of a collection of files. Within the Word VBA IDE, each open Word document is considered a separate project. Within the PowerPoint VBA IDE, each open presentation is considered to be a separate project. Likewise, within the Excel VBA IDE, each open workbook is considered to be a separate project. A project is made up of a number of files; for example, an Excel project would include worksheets, code modules, and other items. In Word, projects include documents, whereas in PowerPoint, projects include presentations. Projects are managed from within the Project Explorer, which you will open now.

## To view the Project Explorer:

1. Click the **Microsoft Visual Basic** button on the taskbar.

2. Close any open VBA IDE windows, except for the main VBA IDE window, as shown in Figure 2-4.

| Figure 2-4 | VBA IDE WITH ALL WINDOWS CLOSED |
|---|---|

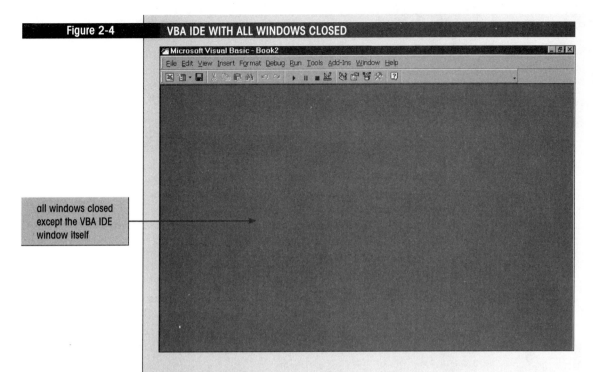

all windows closed
except the VBA IDE
window itself

**3.** Click the **Project Explorer** button on the toolbar. Remember that you should size and place the VBA IDE windows according to your own preference. If you prefer, you can arrange your Project Explorer to match the Project Explorer shown in Figure 2-5.

| Figure 2-5 | VBA IDE WITH THE PROJECT EXPLORER WINDOW |
|---|---|

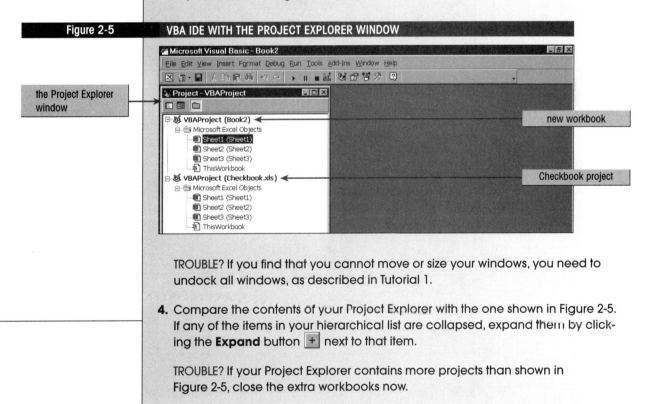

the Project Explorer
window

new workbook

Checkbook project

TROUBLE? If you find that you cannot move or size your windows, you need to undock all windows, as described in Tutorial 1.

**4.** Compare the contents of your Project Explorer with the one shown in Figure 2-5. If any of the items in your hierarchical list are collapsed, expand them by clicking the **Expand** button next to that item.

TROUBLE? If your Project Explorer contains more projects than shown in Figure 2-5, close the extra workbooks now.

You now have two projects open in the Project Explorer, one associated with the Checkbook workbook and one associated with the Book2 workbook. The Project Explorer should include two hierarchical lists, one for each project. Each list includes a number of Microsoft Excel Objects. Each workbook (or project) is considered an object, as are the worksheets they contain. Thus, each hierarchical list includes icons for three worksheets, representing the three worksheets included by default in any new Excel workbook. The ThisWorkbook icon in the list represents the entire Workbook object (including its individual worksheets).

At the top of the hierarchical list for each project, you see VBAProject, followed by the file name of the Excel workbook in parentheses. For example, at the top of the hierarchical list for the Checkbook project, you should see VBAProject (Checkbook.xls). At the top of the hierarchical list for the unsaved workbook, you should see VBAProject (Book2). If you had saved the second workbook, its filename would appear in the Project Explorer as well, next to VBAProject.

## Changing a Project Name

As you learned in Tutorial 1, when you save a project, all the files associated with it are saved within the workbook whose name appears at the top of the hierarchical list (e.g., Checkbook.xls). This might give you the impression that the workbook *contains* the VBA project. However, within the VBA IDE, the logic actually works the other way around—that is, within the VBA IDE, the workbook is considered just one part of the project. Other parts might include code modules and a program interface (which, as you will learn later, is called a UserForm in VBA). Thus, the VBA IDE actually makes a distinction between the name of the workbook file (Checkbook.xls) and the project of which the workbook is only a part. The word VBAProject, at the top of the hierarchical list, is actually the default name for the project.

You could keep the default project name (VBAProject) for each project, and then distinguish among open projects by referring to the workbook filename (e.g., Checkbook.xls). However, at TnT Consulting, developers always give their projects descriptive names in order to make them easier to identify.

You change a project name via the Properties command on the Tools menu. Within the Properties dialog box, you can type a more descriptive name for the project, and also include a general description of the project. It's a good idea to include a description of every project you create. That way you can quickly review the description later, within the project's Properties dialog box, just as you might review the Properties dialog box for a file created in an Office application.

---

**REFERENCE WINDOW** | **RW**

<u>Changing a Project Name</u>
- Select the project in the Project Explorer.
- Click Tools on the menu bar and then click the Properties command for the selected project. For example, if the project is named VBAProject, you click VBAProject Properties.
- Verify that the General tab of the Project Properties dialog box is displayed.
- In the Project Name text box, replace the current project name with a new one, and then click OK.
- In the Project Description text box, type a general description of the project.
- Click OK.

---

In the next set of steps, you will change the name of the Checkbook project.

*To change the name of a project:*

1. In the Project Explorer, click **VBAProject (Checkbook.xls)**.

2. Click **Tools** on the menu bar and then click **VBAProject Properties**. The VBA Project Properties window opens, with the General tab displayed, as in Figure 2-6. Note that the default project name, VBAProject, is displayed in the Project Name box.

---

**Figure 2-6**                    **VBAPROJECT PROPERTIES WINDOW**

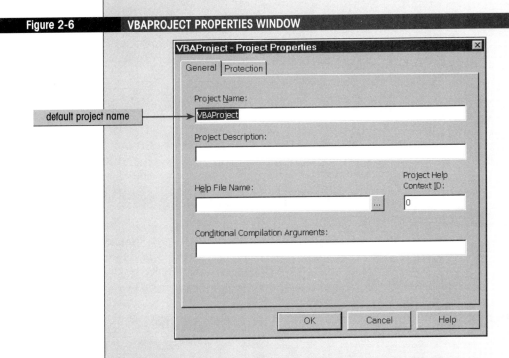

default project name

---

3. In the Project Name box, replace VBAProject with **Checkbook**. The default project name is replaced with the new one.

4. Click the **Project Description** box and type **A checkbook application for TnT Consulting Group**. Your dialog box should match Figure 2-7. As you review the project's Properties dialog box, note that you only change properties for the project itself within this dialog box. You adjust the properties for all the objects contained within the project by using the Properties window. You'll learn how to use the Properties window later in this tutorial.

| Figure 2-7 | VBA PROJECT PROPERTIES DIALOG BOX WITH NEW VALUES |
| --- | --- |

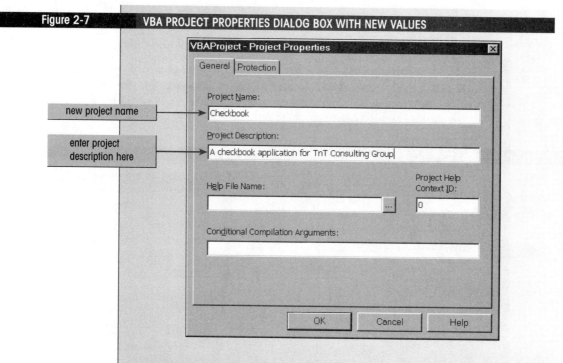

**5.** Click **OK**. The dialog box closes, and you return to the Excel VBA IDE. The new name of the project appears in the Project Explorer, as shown in Figure 2-8. Note that the Checkbook project is now the first project listed in the Project Explorer, because projects are listed alphabetically in the Project Explorer.

| Figure 2-8 | CHECKBOOK PROJECT WITH NAME CHANGE |
| --- | --- |

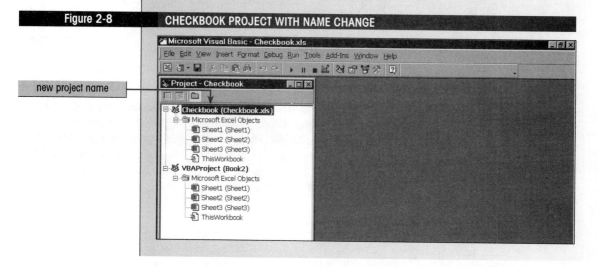

So far in this tutorial, you have learned that objects are things that can be defined and manipulated. In the preceding steps, you actually defined the Project object. You did this by altering two of its properties, the project name and the project description. This tells you that the project itself is an object and that it has properties, which, in turn, have values. Almost anything can be an object. In Excel, the project is an object, the workbook is an object, each worksheet is an object, and even each individual cell is an object. Each of the Office applications is made up of a different set of objects. For example, in Word you would not work with a Worksheet object; instead, you would work with a Document object. When creating a VBA program for an Office application, it is important that you learn which objects exist within that application. You will learn more about the objects contained in each of the Office applications throughout this book.

Before you continue with the next section, you should close the extra Excel workbook. You won't need it for the rest of this tutorial.

---

### To close the Book2 Excel workbook:

1. Click the **Book2** button on the taskbar. You return to the Excel workbook window.

2. Close the Book2 Worksheet window (but not the Excel window) without saving any changes.

---

Now you're ready to learn about some special kinds of VBA objects, UserForms and control objects.

# Using Forms and Control Objects to Create an Interface

Your manager at TnT Consulting, Gene Cox, has asked you to create a data entry form that looks similar to a check in the company checkbook. The form you will create will serve as the interface for a VBA checkbook project that will ultimately be capable of automatically entering checking data in an Excel workbook. Before you begin creating this interface, you need to learn a little more about the term "interface" in VBA.

## Understanding Interfaces

As you know, an interface is the means by which the user interacts with a program. The Windows interface is primarily made up of pictures, or graphics, and is therefore known as a **graphical user interface**. (This term is usually shortened to the acronym **GUI**, which is pronounced "gooey.") The desktop screen you see when you start Windows is part of the Windows GUI. By clicking and dragging the pictures, or **icons**, on the desktop, you can interact with Windows, thereby selecting specific settings, starting programs, and so on. The Office interface, which is based on the Windows interface, is also a GUI.

If you want users to be able to interact with a VBA program, you need to create an interface for the program. A VBA interface is by nature a GUI. A VBA interface might simply consist of a data entry form, such as you might use when entering name and address information into an Access database. In Tutorial 1, you typed some code that created another kind of interface—a dialog box, or input box, in which the user could type her name, and then click an OK button in order to close the dialog box.

In this tutorial, you will create a more extensive interface—one that includes additional GUI elements such as text boxes for entering data, labels to provide information, and command buttons that cause an action to take place (such as closing the dialog box). These various parts of a GUI are known as **control objects** (or sometimes just **controls**). In VBA, you actually create an interface by adding control objects to a UserForm (more commonly called simply a **form**). Essentially, a **UserForm** is a container for control objects; it serves as the background for the entire form. Just as you open a blank document in Word in order to begin typing a letter, you open a blank UserForm in VBA in order to begin creating an interface.

You'll learn more about how to insert control objects into a UserForm later in this tutorial. But first, take a moment to review the terminology involved in developing a program, which can be a bit tricky. For starters, keep in mind that the terms "interface" and "graphical user interface" (or "GUI") are often used interchangeably. In the same vein, within VBA, an interface is often referred to as either a "form" or a "UserForm." Note that a VBA form (that is, a UserForm) is not the same thing as a data entry form, such as you might have used in Microsoft Access or Excel. However, if you wanted to create a data entry form for one of your VBA programs, you would create that form within a VBA UserForm.

All of these terms will become clearer to you as you proceed through this tutorial. For now, just keep in mind that, within the world of VBA, the terms "interface," "GUI," "UserForm" and "form" are essentially synonymous.

## Understanding Control Objects

Now that you are familiar with the concept of an interface, you can learn more about the building blocks used to create an interface—control objects. You create an interface by placing control objects on a UserForm. Each control object has its own set of properties, events, and methods. As you work through this tutorial, you will learn how to incorporate several control objects into a VBA interface. Some of these controls will be associated with an event that triggers an action, or method. For example, an OK button (one kind of control object) might be associated with a code that closes a dialog box. That code is only executed when the user clicks the OK button. Because the code associated with a control object is only executed in response to an event, control objects are said to be event-driven.

While you may not realize it, you actually have a lot of experience interacting with control objects as a user. After all, the Office interface is made up of control objects. For example, the average Office dialog box includes many control objects, as illustrated in the Print dialog box shown in Figure 2-9 and the Find and Replace dialog box shown in Figure 2-10.

| Figure 2-9 | PRINT DIALOG BOX ILLUSTRATING THE USE OF CONTROLS |
| --- | --- |

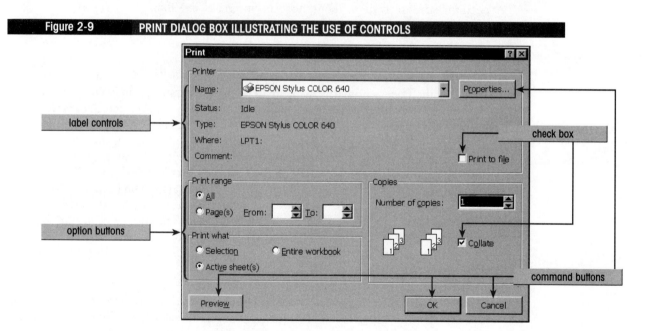

**Figure 2-10** **FIND AND REPLACE DIALOG BOX ILLUSTRATING USE OF CONTROLS**

You will learn about many kinds of controls throughout this text, as you use them. For now, you only need to concentrate on the following controls, which you will use when creating the checkbook interface. As you read this list, look for examples in Figures 2-9 and 2-10.

- **Label control**: Used to place some text on the screen for documentation (that is, descriptive) purposes. In most instances, a label is used to provide information to the user. The user does not interact with the label control, which is to say that the user usually cannot change the text that is displayed in the label control.

- **Text Box control**: Usually used to obtain data from the user. The user can enter the text in the text box, or the VBA program can place data in the text box. The program can use the data placed in the text box. The program can also insert data in the text box.

- **Command button control**: Provides a way for the user to execute some action. For example, the user can click the Find Next command button (shown in Figure 2-10) in order to find the next instance of the text entered in the Find What text box. The specific action associated with a command button depends on how the button is programmed—that is, on which program statements you write for that command button. In this tutorial, you will write some VBA statements for the Click event of one of the command buttons you place on the checkbook interface. You will write additional statements for the other command buttons in Tutorials 3 and 4.

- **Image control**: Used to place a picture or graphic on a UserForm.

Note that programmers often tend to refer to "text boxes" or "command buttons" instead of "text box controls" or "command button controls." This shorthand is often used throughout this book, as well.

## Planning the Checkbook Interface

Gene Cox explains that the checkbook program you are working on is designed to replace the standard (i.e. paper) company checkbook currently used by the Accounting Department. The same accounting assistant who currently manages the paper checkbook will use this new, electronic version of the checkbook. Thus, in order to make the electronic checkbook as easy to use as possible, you need to make its interface similar to the paper checks currently in use. In fact, the entire purpose of this interface is to provide a means for entering check data into the worksheet in a manner that is familiar to the accounting assistant.

Gene sits down at your desk with you and sketches the check interface for you on a [?] of paper. The drawing, shown in Figure 2-11, indicates which control objects you will [?] to add to the form.

| Figure 2-11 | SKETCH OF CHECK INTERFACE |
| --- | --- |

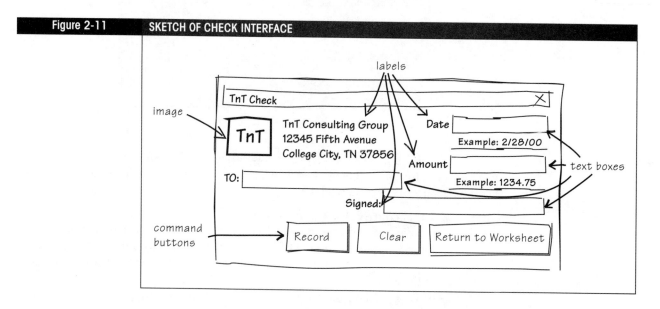

With this drawing in hand, you can begin creating the interface in VBA, a process that involves translating each element of the paper check into a VBA control object. The design of the check will be relatively simple at this point; however, in the next few tutorials you will observe additional functionality added to this application. The end product will be a fully functional checkbook register that will allow the user to fill in information regarding checks and deposits.

## Working with UserForms

To begin creating your interface for the checkbook program, you need to open a blank UserForm. Think of the UserForm as an empty canvas on which you will "draw" the check interface. Once you have displayed a new UserForm on the screen, you can add controls to the UserForm, move the controls to their appropriate positions on the UserForm, and set their properties to change their appearance. You open a new UserForm via the UserForm command on the Insert menu.

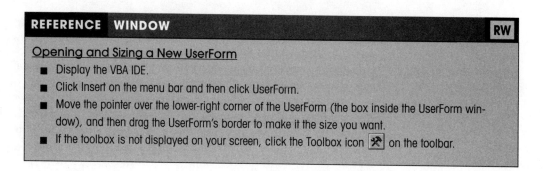

In the following steps, you will open a new, blank UserForm, and then enlarge it to make room for the necessary control objects.

## To open and enlarge a new UserForm:

1. Switch to the VBA IDE.

2. Verify that the Project Explorer is open, and that it currently displays the contents of the project you named Checkbook. Note that you should have closed the Book2 workbook earlier in this tutorial, so only one project should currently be displayed in the Project Explorer. The Project Explorer contains objects named Sheet1, Sheet2, Sheet3, and ThisWorkbook, as described earlier. You will now open a new UserForm, which will be added to the project as yet another object.

3. Click **Insert** on the menu bar and then click **UserForm**. A UserForm window opens, containing a blank UserForm. By default, the blank UserForm is named "UserForm1." In addition, you see the toolbox, which contains buttons you can use to add controls to your UserForm. Your screen should now look like Figure 2-12. Notice that the UserForm is displayed within a UserForm window, just as a document in Word is displayed within the Document window.

| Figure 2-12 | VBA IDE WITH NEW USERFORM AND TOOLBOX |
| --- | --- |

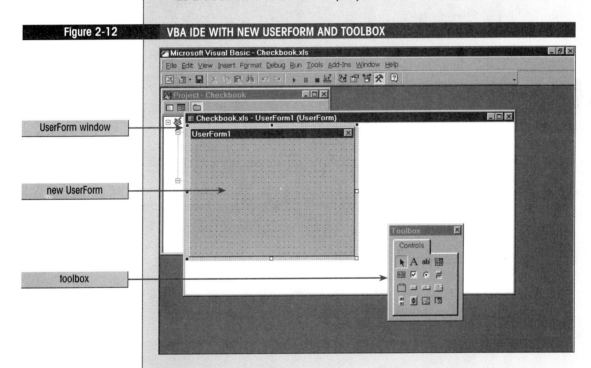

UserForm window

new UserForm

toolbox

TROUBLE? Do not be concerned if you do not see the toolbox on your screen. In Step 4 you will learn how to display the toolbox if it is not already open.

4. Compare your screen with Figure 2-12. If you see any open windows other than those shown in Figure 2-12, close them now.

5. Click within the Project Explorer to display it, and notice that a new folder, named "Forms," has been added to the Checkbook project. The Forms folder contains the new UserForm, which, like all components of a project, is an object. As mentioned earlier, the UserForm object is named "UserForm1" by default.

   Now that you have opened a new, blank UserForm, you need to enlarge it within the UserForm window. You want the shape of the UserForm to match the interface drawing shown earlier in Figure 2-11, thus making room for the necessary control objects.

**6.** Click the UserForm window to select it.

**7.** Move the pointer over the lower-right corner of the UserForm (the box inside the UserForm window). The pointer changes to ↘. Drag the UserForm's border to increase its size, until it looks approximately like Figure 2-13.

| Figure 2-13 | NEW USERFORM RESIZED TO RESEMBLE A CHECK |

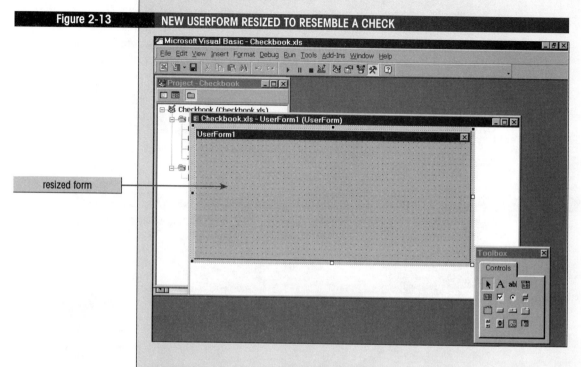

resized form

**8.** If the toolbox is not displayed on your screen, click the toolbox icon 🔨 on the toolbar. You can drag the title bar of the toolbox to move the toolbox to any position you prefer.

**9.** Place the mouse pointer over each button on the toolbox. As you pause over each button, a ToolTip appears, telling you the button's name. Note that these buttons are used to insert control objects into a UserForm.

## Examining the UserForm's Properties

Like any object in a VBA project, a UserForm has a number of properties. In this section you will familiarize yourself with the UserForm's properties. Then, in subsequent sections, you will change the UserForm's Name property and Caption property. You will also change several other properties that affect the UserForm's appearance.

You view the properties associated with an object in the Properties window. The Properties window displays the properties of the object that is currently selected within the VBA IDE window. In this case, you want to view the properties of UserForm1, so you begin the steps below by selecting the new UserForm.

*To examine the properties of the UserForm:*

**1.** If necessary, click the title bar of the UserForm to select it. Now that you have selected the object whose properties you want to view, you need to open the Properties window.

2. Click the **Properties window** button 📋 on the toolbar. The Properties window opens, displaying the properties of the currently selected object. In this case, it displays the properties of the UserForm1 object. The Properties window should look similar to Figure 2-14. (You may need to move and resize the Properties window so that it does not obscure the UserForm.) The Object list box, at the top of the Properties window, is used to display a list of all the objects contained within the UserForm1 object.

| Figure 2-14 | PROPERTIES WINDOW |

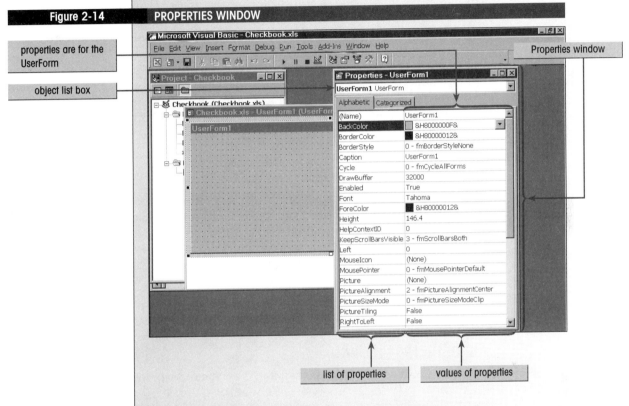

properties are for the UserForm

object list box

Properties window

list of properties

values of properties

3. Click the drop-down arrow on the Object list box. You see a list of all the objects on the UserForm. Because you haven't added any objects to the UserForm yet, at this point you only see "UserForm1 UserForm" included on the list.

4. Verify that "Userform1 Userform" is displayed in the Object list box. This tells you that the properties in the Properties window pertain to the UserForm named "UserForm1". The left column of the Properties window contains a list of properties, while the right column contains each property's value. For example, the Name property is the first property in the list, and its value is currently "Userform1." Notice that the Properties window has two tabs. The Alphabetic tab, which is currently displayed, provides an alphabetized list of all properties associated with the current object. The Categorized tab provides a categorized list of properties, arranged according to their function. The alphabetized list contains all the properties, listed in alphabetic order. Both lists contain the same properties, just in a different order.

In the next two sections, you will change three of the UserForm's properties. First, you will change its Name property, and then you will change its background color. Finally, you will change the UserForm's caption.

## Changing the UserForm's Name Property

When you opened the new UserForm, it was assigned the name `UserForm1` by default. This name is one of the UserForm's properties, and you can change it from within the Properties window. In this section, you will give the UserForm a more descriptive name by altering its Name property. To change the Name property for any object (including a UserForm), you simply select the object, click the current value of the Name property (in the Properties window), and type the new value.

It's important to assign a UserForm a name that is easy to remember, so that you can use it later when writing VBA statements that affect the UserForm. As a general rule, when naming objects, you should choose names that both indicate the object's type and describe its purpose. By convention, VBA developers begin object names with a prefix that indicates the object's type. In this case, the object is a UserForm, so you should begin the object's name with the abbreviation `frm`. Because the UserForm will mimic the functions of a check, you should include the word "check" in its name. Thus, `frmCheck` is a good descriptive name for the new UserForm. (You will learn more about naming objects later in this tutorial.)

### To alter the UserForm's Name property:

1. In the Properties window, locate the Name property at the top of the list of properties in the Alphabetic tab. Notice that the Name property is not in alphabetic order even on the alphabetic tab. The Name property always appears first because it is the single most important property in terms of identifying a particular object. You see the Name property's current value, "UserForm1," in the right-hand column.

2. Double-click **UserForm1** in the right-hand column. The property value, `UserForm1`, is highlighted. (Notice that at this point, the toolbox disappears from view. It will reappear later when you select the form or one of its objects in the UserForm window.)

3. Type **frmCheck** and then press **Enter**. The original property value (`UserForm1`) is replaced with the new one, `frmCheck`, as shown in Figure 2-15. The new UserForm name now appears in the UserForm window title bar. However, in the title bar of the UserForm itself, the text `Userform1` is still displayed. This is because the text at the top of the UserForm itself is actually controlled by a different property, the Caption property. You will change the value of the Caption property in the next section.

Figure 2-15    **USERFORM SHOWING NEW VALUE FOR THE NAME PROPERTY**

new form name

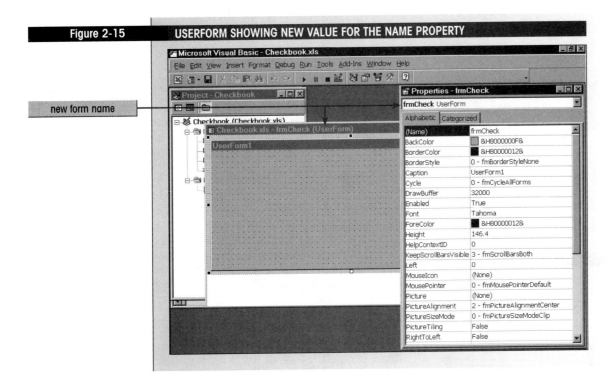

You have successfully altered the UserForm's Name property. Next, you will change some other properties of the UserForm.

## Changing Other UserForm Properties

As a rule, the VBA IDE makes it easy to select an appropriate value for a particular property. For instance, when you click the BackColor property, the right-hand column displays a list arrow, which you can use to select a color in a color palette. This ensures that you specify a color as the value for the BackColor property, and not something completely unrelated, such as "0" or "True." (The BackColor property specifies the background color for the UserForm.)

Exactly what happens when you click a property value in the Properties window varies, depending on the property. For example, as you will see later in this tutorial, when you click a property value that governs which image is displayed on a form, a dialog box opens, which you can then use to select an image file. You will learn more about how to select the right value for each property as you work through this book. In most cases, the right course of action should be intuitively obvious once you click the property value in the Properties window.

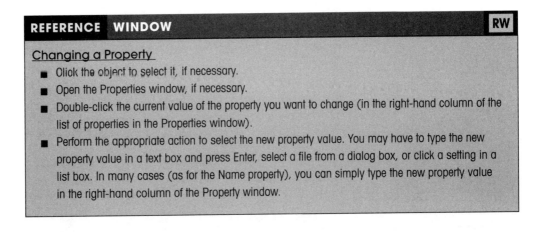

**REFERENCE   WINDOW**                                                          **RW**

### Changing a Property

- Click the object to select it, if necessary.
- Open the Properties window, if necessary.
- Double-click the current value of the property you want to change (in the right-hand column of the list of properties in the Properties window).
- Perform the appropriate action to select the new property value. You may have to type the new property value in a text box and press Enter, select a file from a dialog box, or click a setting in a list box. In many cases (as for the Name property), you can simply type the new property value in the right-hand column of the Property window.

In the next set of steps, you will change the BackColor property to a light blue.

## To change the form's BackColor property:

1. Locate the BackColor property, immediately below the Name property, in the Properties window. In the right-hand column you can see the property's current value, as indicated by a gray square. This gray matches the gray background of the UserForm itself. (The text to the right of the square is a special code associated with the gray color. You can simply ignore this code.)

2. Click the right-hand column of the BackColor property. A drop-down arrow appears in the right-hand column. You can use this drop-down arrow to select a new background color for the UserForm (that is, a new value for the BackColor property). See Figure 2-16.

| Figure 2-16 | PROPERTIES WINDOW WITH DROP-DOWN ARROW FOR BACKCOLOR PROPERTY |

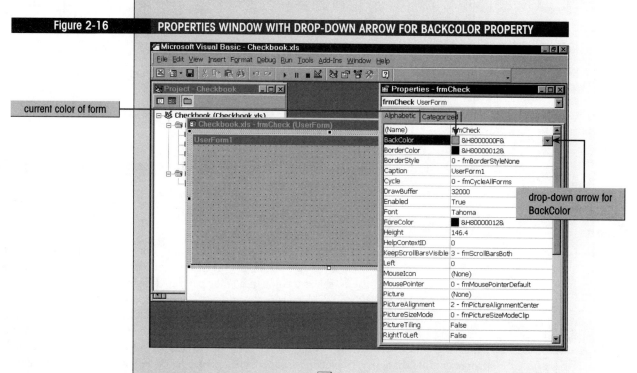

3. Click the drop-down arrow. A list box appears, as shown in Figure 2-17. This list box has two tabs, the Palette tab and the System tab. The System tab, which is displayed by default, lists standard colors for windows. The Palette tab provides a wider selection of colors.

**Figure 2-17**    **BACKCOLOR LIST BOX**

Palette tab                                                    System tab

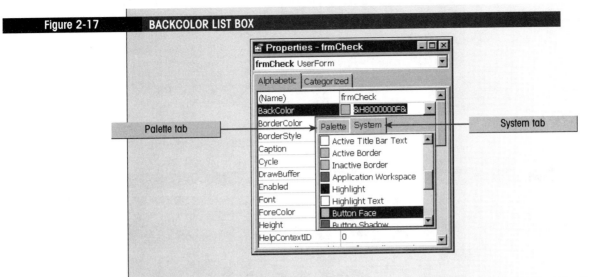

**4.** Click the **Palette** tab. The Palette tab displays an array of color options for the background color, as shown in Figure 2-18. In the next step you will select a light blue color.

**Figure 2-18**    **PALETTE TAB FOR THE BACKCOLOR PROPERTY**

colors available on the palette tab                            select this color

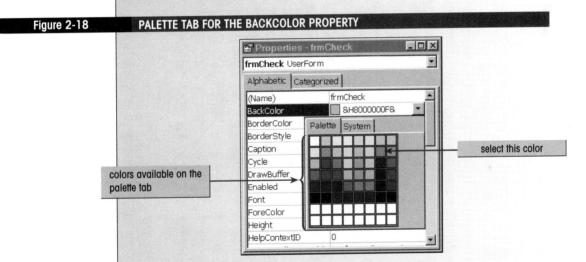

**5.** Click the light blue color in the second row, second column from the right. The form's background color changes to match the BackColor's new value.

Next, you need to change the form's Caption property. The **Caption** property specifies the text that appears in the title bar of the UserForm itself (as opposed to the title bar of the UserForm window, in which the UserForm is displayed). The UserForm caption is displayed in the UserForm's title bar at runtime (that is, when you run the program). It is easy to confuse the Caption property with the Name property. The Name property specifies the name by which you can refer to the object in program statements. The Caption property, however, only specifies the text that will appear in the UserForm's title bar.

### To change the UserForm's Caption property:

1. Locate the Caption property in the Properties window. Notice that its current value, `UserForm1`, matches the original value of the Name property.

2. Double-click **UserForm1** (the Caption property value). The property value "UserForm1" is highlighted in the right-hand column.

3. Type **TnT Check** and then press **Enter**. The new property value replaces the original one in the form's title bar, as shown in Figure 2-19.

| Figure 2-19 | CHECK FORM WITH NEW CAPTION PROPERTY |
| --- | --- |

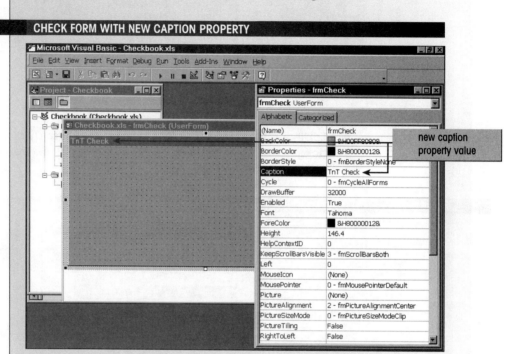

You have now finished changing the property values for the UserForm. It's time to save your work.

## Saving Your Work

After making significant changes to a project, you should take the time to save it, just as you learned to do in other applications. In fact, you should develop a habit of saving your project about every half an hour. This will prevent you from losing large amounts of work in the case of a power failure or some other interference with your work.

When you save a VBA project, you are really saving the workbook and all the files associated with the project. Later you will learn to save files separately from the workbook. For now you will save the workbook and all its files together as a project.

### To save your work:

1. Click the **Save** button 🖫 on the VBA IDE toolbar. Your changes to the project, and all its files, including the workbook, are saved in the Checkbook.xls file.

Now that you have prepared the blank UserForm, which will serve as the background for your check, you can add controls to it. You'll start by adding three labels at the top of the UserForm.

## Session 2.1 QUICK CHECK

1. _____ are things that can be identified by their properties and methods.

2. A(n) _____ is a characteristic of an object, whereas, a(n) _____ is an action an object can perform.

3. A VBA program is said to be _____-_____ because something like a mouse click must happen before an event is "triggered."

4. A(n) _____ serves as a container for other _____.

5. The acronym GUI stands for _____.

6. A(n) _____ button provides a way for the user to execute some action.

## SESSION 2.2

In this session you will begin adding controls to the checkbook form. First you will insert several label controls on the form and learn to alter the properties of the controls. You will learn to change the properties of controls one by one, as well as in a group. Finally, you will learn to adjust the size and spacing of the controls on the form.

## Working with Control Objects

To add control objects to a UserForm, you first select the control you want from the toolbox, place it on the UserForm, and finally move and size the control as needed. After you have positioned the control on the UserForm, you can adjust its properties, just as you adjusted some of the properties of the UserForm. The following sections walk you through the process of adding control objects to the UserForm and then modifying them.

### Adding Control Objects to a UserForm

After reviewing your new, blank UserForm, Gene says you are ready to add some control objects. First, you will add the label controls that will contain the name of the company and its address. As you begin adding controls to the UserForm, Gene reminds you to refer back to the interface sketch (shown earlier in Figure 2-11).

To add a control object to a UserForm, you click the button for the desired control in the toolbox. At this point, you have two options. If you prefer, you can click the location in the UserForm where you want the control object to appear. A control object inserted in this way will have a default size and shape. Alternately, you can drag the pointer in the UserForm to draw a control object in the shape and size you desire.

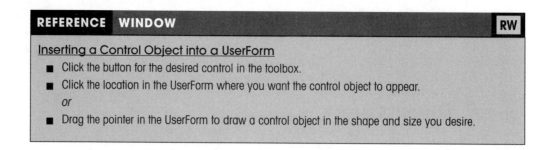

**REFERENCE WINDOW** RW

**Inserting a Control Object into a UserForm**

■ Click the button for the desired control in the toolbox.

■ Click the location in the UserForm where you want the control object to appear.

*or*

■ Drag the pointer in the UserForm to draw a control object in the shape and size you desire.

You'll try the first method in the steps below. You'll have a chance to practice dragging the mouse pointer later in this tutorial.

## To add a label control to the UserForm:

1. If you closed Excel at the end of the last session, start Excel, open the Checkbook workbook, open the VBA IDE, and display the UserForm.

2. Click the UserForm, if necessary, to display the toolbox.

3. Click the **Label** button A on the toolbox, and then move the pointer onto the top-left corner of the form. Notice that the pointer changes to $^+$A.

4. Position the pointer in the top-left corner of the form, and then click the left mouse button. A new label control appears in the upper-left corner of the form, similar to Figure 2-20. Don't worry if the placement or appearance of your label control does not match the figure exactly. You will have a chance to alter the appearance of the label control later. Notice that the control has selection handles and that it contains the text "Label1."

| Figure 2-20 | FIRST LABEL CONTROL ADDED TO THE FORM |

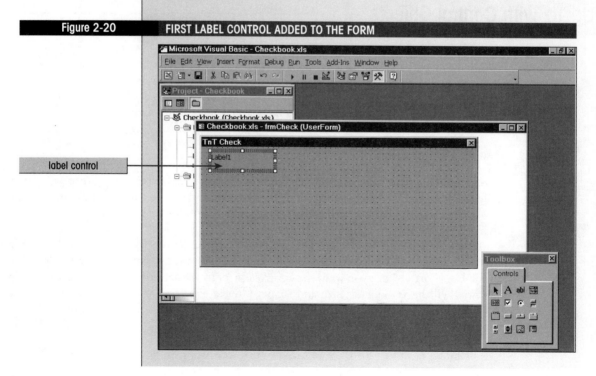

label control

TROUBLE? If you discover that you have added the wrong control (any control other than a label control), verify that the control is selected (as indicated by the white selection handles on its border), press Delete, and then begin again with Step 1.

5. Repeat Steps 1 and 2 to add two more label controls below the first label control in the UserForm. You should not be concerned if your labels do not line up exactly with each other. You will learn how to adjust their alignment in a later step. Notice that the two new labels contain the text "Label2" and "Label3".

6. Click the form anywhere off the labels so that none is selected, then compare your form with Figure 2-21.

**Figure 2-21** | **CHECK WITH THREE LABEL CONTROLS ADDED**

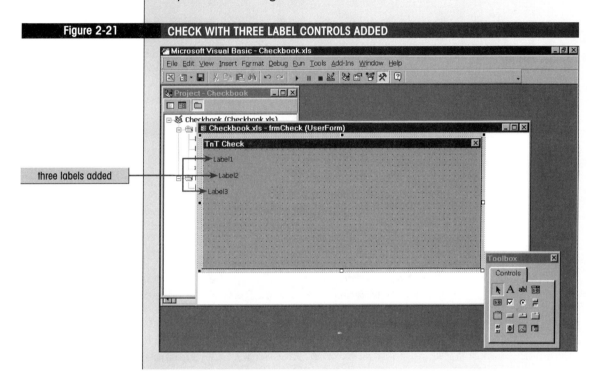

three labels added

Your form now contains three Label control objects. In a moment, you will learn how to alter the appearance, position, and size of the label controls. Note that you do *not* have to change the Name property for the Label control objects; the next section explains why.

## Naming Objects Within a Project

Earlier in this tutorial, you changed the UserForm's Name property. As explained in that section, you changed the Name property so that you could refer to the UserForm in program statements. As a general rule, you should assign a descriptive Name property to each control object that will be used in your program statements. If you do not change the Name property for a control, VBA will retain the control's default, nondescriptive name, such as Label1.

Visual Basic developers use some standard naming conventions, which provide for quick identification of objects in a project. Recall, for instance, that the UserForm name, frmCheck, includes the prefix frm. This prefix identifies the object as a UserForm. You will learn about some other standard prefixes as you continue to add objects to your

UserForm. For example, text boxes should always have a prefix of "txt", and labels should have a prefix of "lbl". VBA does not require these prefixes, but wise developers use them to ensure that other developers can easily understand their work.

While it is essential to provide descriptive names for objects that will be referred to later in your program statements, you can simply accept the default names for objects that are not altered during runtime—that is, that aren't directly affected by the VBA program statements. For example, the Label control objects that you just added to the UserForm are simply included in order to display information on the check; they will not be altered during runtime. Thus, there is no need to give the labels a more descriptive name.

## Changing a Control's Caption Property

At this point, you have three label controls on your UserForm. As explained earlier, label controls are designed to display descriptive information in a form. In this case, the labels will display the information you would normally see on the top of a check—specifically the company name, and the company address, including the city and state. The text displayed in a label at runtime is controlled by the label's Caption property. You can change text displayed in a label by changing the label's Caption property. (Remember that for the UserForm, the Caption property controls the text that appears in the UserForm's title bar at runtime. Thus, you can see that properties control different features in different objects. As you become more proficient at VBA programming, you will become familiar with the properties of each object.)

Currently, the Caption property for the first label is set to the default value, Label1. Thus, the first label displays the text Label1 within the form. In the following steps, you will change the Caption property for each of the label controls.

*To Change the Caption property for the first label:*

1. Click the **Label1** control object in the form. The Label control object is selected, as indicated by the selection handles. The toolbox appears, in case you want to add another control to the form.

   TROUBLE? If you mistakenly double-clicked the label control, the Code window opens. Close this window, and then single-click the Label1 control object.

2. If necessary, click the **Properties** button 🔲 to display the Properties window. The Properties window now displays the properties for the selected object (that is, the Label1 object.) See Figure 2-22.

| Figure 2-22 | **LABEL1 SELECTED** |

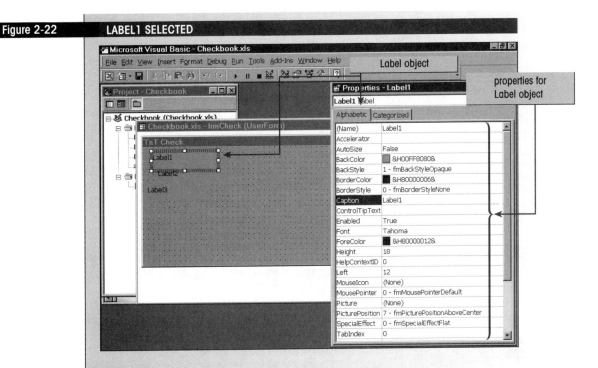

3. In the Properties window, double-click the Caption property value (that is, the right column of the Caption property), type TnT Consulting Group, and then press Enter. The original value for the Caption property, Label1, is replaced with the new caption, TnT Consulting Group. This new text is displayed in the top label, as shown in Figure 2-23. At this point the text is not attractively formatted. You'll adjust its appearance later in this tutorial.

| Figure 2-23 | **LABEL1 WITH CAPTION PROPERTY CHANGED** |

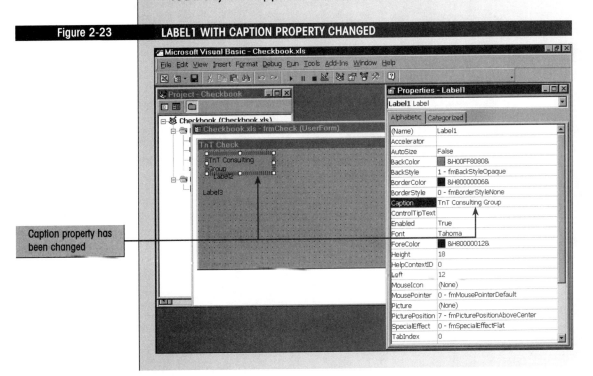

4. Click the Label2 control object. The Properties window now displays the properties for the second label.

5. Replace the default value for the Caption property with "12345 Fifth Avenue". Now you are ready to change the Caption property for the last label. You could select the Label3 caption by clicking it in the form. Alternately, you can select it using the Object list box at the top of the Properties window. You'll practice that technique in the next step.

6. Click the **Object** list arrow at the top of the Properties window. You see a list of all the objects in the project, as shown in Figure 2-24. This list specifies the object's name and type. For instance, the first item in the list, `frmCheck UserForm` is the UserForm you named earlier. In this case, you want to select the label object named Label3.

| Figure 2-24 | OBJECT LIST DISPLAYS OBJECTS IN THE FORM |
| --- | --- |

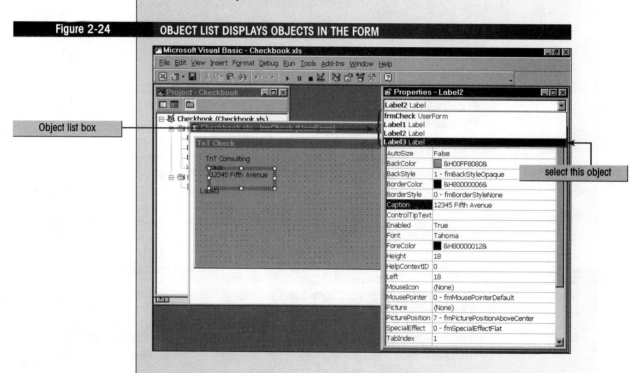

7. Click Label3 Label. The Label3 control object is selected in the UserForm, as indicated by the selection handles. The Properties window now displays the properties for the Label3 control object.

8. Change the default Caption property for this label to "College City, TN 37856", and then press Enter. Your UserForm should now look similar to the one shown in Figure 2-25.

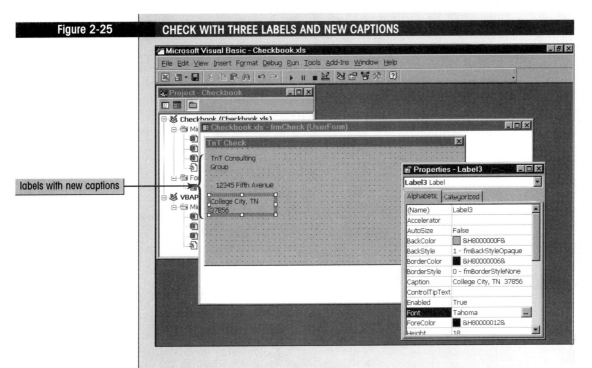

Figure 2-25 — CHECK WITH THREE LABELS AND NEW CAPTIONS

labels with new captions

As you can see, the captions do not fit on a single line within the label controls. In the next section you will change properties that control the size of the label and the way its caption is formatted.

## Changing Properties for Multiple Objects at One Time

In many cases, you will want multiple objects to have the same general appearance. For instance, in this case you want the text in all the label controls to be formatted in the same font. You could adjust the font for each of the labels by selecting each one individually, and then changing its Font property. It's more efficient, however, to select all the label controls at one time. To select multiple control objects, simply press and hold the Shift key while you click each control object. Once you have selected each of the label controls, you can adjust the Font property for all three objects at once.

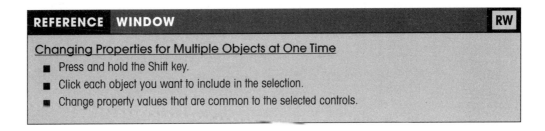

**REFERENCE  WINDOW**    **RW**

Changing Properties for Multiple Objects at One Time
- Press and hold the Shift key.
- Click each object you want to include in the selection.
- Change property values that are common to the selected controls.

In the following steps you will change the Font property for all three labels to 12-point Times New Roman. A Label's **Font** property controls the font in which the caption is displayed.

At the same time, you will change the background style of the labels by adjusting the BackStyle property, which controls whether or not the background of the label is visible on the form. The Backstyle property can be set to transparent or opaque. (It is currently set to opaque.) Usually you will want the BackStyle property of a label to be transparent so that the color of the form shows through and you only see the text of the label. In the Checkbook form, the labels you inserted have the same color as the UserForm, so it's not strictly necessary to change the BackStyle property to transparent. However, it is good practice to change the BackStyle property for all labels to transparent; that way, if you change the color of the UserForm later, you won't have to worry about changing the color of the labels to match. (For instance, if you changed the BackColor of the UserForm to yellow, the labels would remain as blue boxes on top of the yellow form, which wouldn't be very attractive.) As a general rule then, you should change the BackStyle of all labels to transparent. You will do that in the next set of steps.

## To change the properties of the label controls:

1. Click the first label, which contains the caption "TnT Consulting Group." White selection handles appear around the selected object.

2. Press and hold the **Shift** key.

3. Click the other two labels. All three labels are now selected. The label that was selected first has white selection handles, while the other two have black selection handles.

4. Click the **Properties Window** button 🗋 on the toolbar. The Properties window appears on top of the UserForm. Notice that the Properties window displays a list of properties that apply to all three labels. Notice that some of the properties, including the Caption property, have no assigned value, indicating that it is not permissible to change these properties for multiple objects at one time.

5. Click the **Font** property. An Ellipse button appears in the right-hand column, indicating that you need to select a value for this property via a dialog box.

   TROUBLE? If the Font dialog box opens, you accidentally double-clicked the Font property rather than single-clicking it. Click Cancel, and then continue with the next step.

6. Click the **Ellipse** button ... . The Font dialog box opens. This dialog box is similar to the Font dialog boxes you have used in the Office applications.

7. Click **Times New Roman** in the Font list, click **Bold** in the Font Style list, and then click **10** in the Font Size list. Your settings should now match those in Figure 2-26.

| Figure 2-26 | FONT DIALOG BOX WITH NEW SETTINGS |

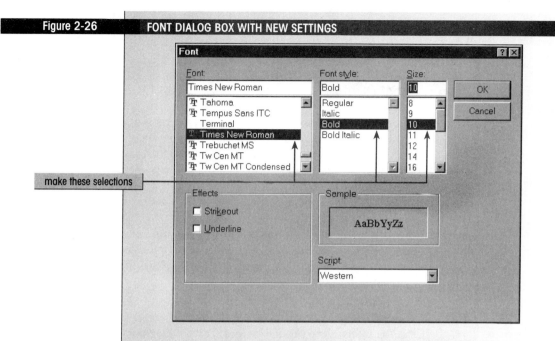

make these selections

8. Click **OK**. The Font dialog box closes. Observe the changes in the appearance of all three label controls. The label captions are now formatted in 10-point Times New Roman, bold. Don't be concerned that the captions are no longer fully visible. You'll fix this problem later, when you change the size of the label controls. Next, you're ready to change the background style for all three labels.

9. Click the **BackStyle** property value, and then click the down arrow ![down arrow] in the right-hand column. A list appears with the two possible background settings for a label control-transparent and opaque. The current selection, opaque, results in a label with the specified BackColor background. You want to select the transparent setting, so that only the label caption is visible against the form.

10. Click 0-fmBackStyleTransparent.

11. Click anywhere in the form to deselect the labels. Your screen should now look similar to Figure 2-27. For now, don't be concerned that you can't read the complete text of the label captions.

| Figure 2-27 | LABELS WITH NEW PROPERTY VALUES |

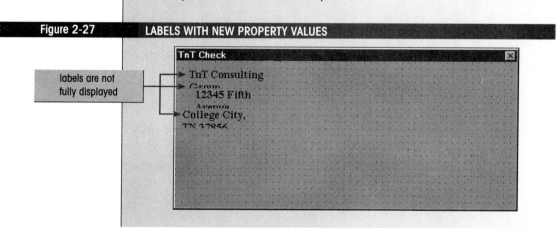

labels are not fully displayed

Now that you have the text formatted against a transparent background, you can adjust the size of the labels so that the captions are fully displayed. You'll learn how to size a label control in the next section.

## Sizing a Label Control

You can change the size of a control object by clicking its sizing handles and dragging it until the control is the desired size. Alternately, you can change the control's Height or Width property (or both). You'll probably find that the first method, dragging the sizing handles, is the easiest, because it allows you to observe the change in size.

In this section you will select the first label and size it appropriately, by dragging a sizing handle. Your goal is to make the controls uniform in appearance, so you'll want to make sure the second two labels match the first in size. The easiest way to ensure uniformity is to use the Make Same Size command on the Format menu, which automatically makes the selected control objects the same size as the first label selected in a multiple selection (as described earlier). In other words, the size of the first label controls the size of the other labels.

### To resize the labels:

**1.** Click the **TnT Consulting** label to select it, and then position the pointer over the right-middle sizing handle, as shown in Figure 2-28. The pointer changes to ↔, as shown in Figure 2-28.

Figure 2-28 | SELECTED LABEL WITH SIZING HANDLES AND RESIZING POINTER

**2.** Drag the handle to the right until all of the text within the label is displayed, without any extra space. You may need to try several times until you get the size of the label just right. For instance, you may need to drag the bottom edge of the label up, to allow just enough room for the caption in the label. Once the first label is the correct size, you can apply this same size to the other two labels.

**3.** With the first label still selected, press and hold the **Shift** key and then click the other two labels. With all three labels selected, you can use the Make Same Size command to apply the size of the first label to the other two.

**4.** Click **Format** on the Menu bar, and then point to **Make Same Size**. At this point you could choose the Width option (which would apply the same width to all three labels), the Height option (which would apply the same height to all three labels), or the Both option, which would apply the same height and width to all three labels.

**5.** Click **Both**. The last two labels are now the same size, both in width and height, as the first label.

Now that you have adjusted the size of the labels, you can adjust the vertical distance between the labels, using the Vertical Spacing command on the Format menu. This command helps you create a UserForm that is neat and orderly.

### To adjust the vertical spacing between the labels:

1. Click **Format** again, point to **Vertical Spacing**, and then click **Remove**. Your screen should now match Figure 2-29. You should not be concerned if your labels are not in the exact same position as shown in the form. You will be adjusting their placement on the UserForm later in this tutorial. However, the labels on your UserForm should be uniform in size, and the captions should be fully displayed. If they are not, then repeat the steps in this section and change the properties you missed.

| Figure 2-29 | CHECK WITH THREE LABELS COMPLETELY FORMATTED |

In this session you have learned more about objects, interfaces, and projects. You learned how to add controls to a UserForm and how to alter their appearance by setting their Property values. You learned how to change the properties of a single control and how to change properties for multiple controls. You learned how to size controls individually and how to match the size of multiple controls. Finally you learned to set vertical spacing between multiple controls so that there is equal vertical distance between the controls.

## Session 2.2 QUICK CHECK

1. To alter the appearance of the text displayed within a control, you need to change the _____ property.

2. You did not give a name to the _____ controls because you will not use them in program statements.

3. You can select several controls at one time by holding the _____ key down as you select controls.

4. The _____ property will allow you to set a control to be either transparent or opaque.

5. To set the amount of spacing between two controls, you would alter the _____ spacing or the _____ spacing.

<table>
<tr><td>SESSION<br>2.3</td><td>In this session you will add more controls to the check form, including an Image control object. You will also view the form in runtime. Finally, you will size and move control objects.</td></tr>
</table>

## Adding More Control Objects

You will now continue adding to the UserForm you started in the previous section. If you refer back to the interface design, in Figure 2-11, you will see that you need to add more label controls, several text box controls, several command button controls, and an Image control. You will begin by adding the date label and the text box in which the user will enter a date. Remember that labels are used to provide information on the UserForm, and text boxes are used to obtain data from the user or to display data for the user.

### Dragging the Pointer to Add a Control Object

Earlier in this tutorial, you inserted a Label control object by clicking the Label button in the toolbox, and then clicking in the UserForm where you wanted the control object to appear. In the following steps, you will practice drawing a Label control object, using the mouse pointer.

> *To add the date label and the date text box:*
>
> 1. Click the **Label** button Ⓐ on the toolbox.
>
> 2. Move the pointer to the form and draw a rectangle in approximately the same size and location as in Figure 2-30. Now that you have added the Label control object, you can add a Text Box control object.

| Figure 2-30 | FORM WITH NEW LABEL ADDED |

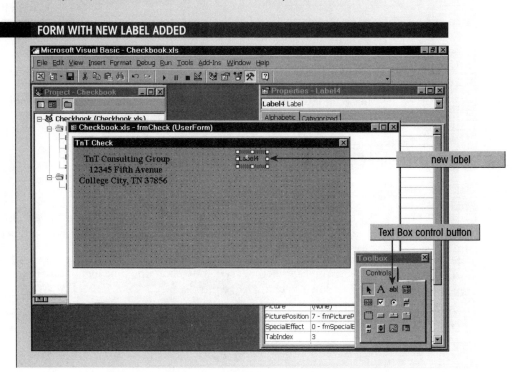

**3.** Click the **Text Box** button abl on the toolbox. Move the pointer to the right of the Label control you just inserted, and drag the pointer to create a rectangle approximately the size of the rectangle in Figure 2-31. When you are satisfied that the rectangle is the right shape, release the mouse button.

| Figure 2-31 | CHECK FORM WITH TEXT BOX ADDED |
| --- | --- |

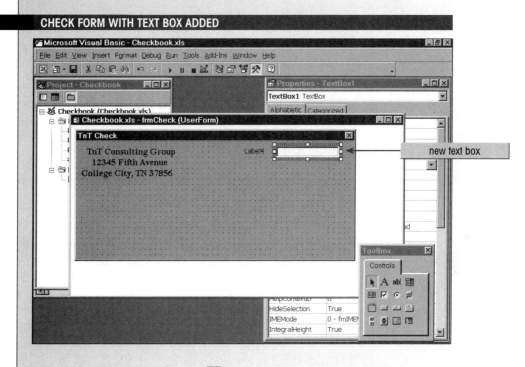

**4.** Click the **Properties** button on the toolbar and change the Name property of the new text box to `txtDate`.

You have successfully added two more control objects to the UserForm. The next step is to change their appearance by adjusting their properties.

## Adjusting Properties for the New Label Control

At this point, you should be comfortable with the process of changing a control object's properties. So from now on, the steps in this book will simply tell you which properties to change.

*To change the properties of the label control and the text box control:*

**1.** Click the Label4 control.

**2.** Verify that the Label4 control is selected, and then change its properties as indicated in Figure 2-32. (You will not change the name of the label because you will never refer to this label in your program statements.)

**Figure 2-32**    **PROPERTY VALUES FOR THE LABEL4 CONTROL OBJECT**

| PROPERTY | VALUE |
|----------|-------|
| Caption | DATE: |
| Font | Times New Roman<br>Bold<br>10 point |
| BackStyle | 0-BackStyleTransparent |

**3.** Click the **Save** button 🖫 on the toolbar.

## Switching to Runtime

The Check interface is beginning to take shape. Before you continue adding more control objects, you should take a moment to review your work so far. Up to this point, you have viewed the UserForm only in design time. As you learned in Tutorial 1, in design time a project is displayed in the VBA IDE along with all the VBA development tools, such as the VBA toolbar, the VBA menu bar, the toolbox, and so on. By switching to runtime, you can see how your program will look to the user, without the distraction of the tools actually used to create the program.

As you create a VBA program, you will periodically have to switch back and forth between design time and runtime. In design time, you assume the role of the developer. In runtime, you assume the role of the user. This is to say that when the project is in runtime, you should view the project from the perspective of the user.

In the following steps, you will view the check interface in runtime. When you view a project in runtime, you are said to be "running the project." To run a project, you simply click the Run button in the toolbar. (Note that the exact name of this button changes, depending on what is selected in the project. For example, sometimes it is called the Run Sub/Userform button, while other times it is the Run Macro button. In this book it will be referred to as the Run button.) To switch back to design time from runtime, you can either click the Stop button or simply close the form window.

### To run the Check project:

**1.** Make sure that the form is still selected, and then click the **Run** button ▶ on the toolbar. You see the check interface in the Excel window. Compare your results with Figure 2-33.

**Figure 2-33** **CHECK FORM AT RUNTIME**

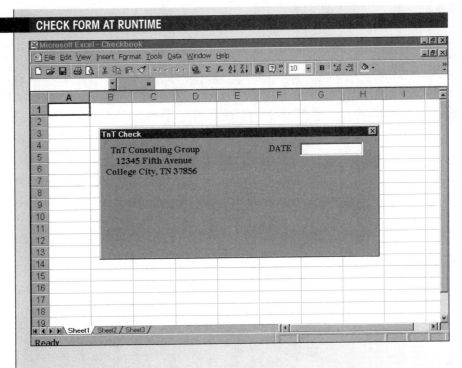

**2.** As you observe the check interface in runtime, notice that the background no longer contains the dots you see in design time. Also notice that you do not see the outline of the labels; instead, you only see the captions that you specified via the label control's Caption property.

**3.** Click the **Close** button ⊠ on the TnT Check window. You return to the Excel VBA IDE, in Design mode.

**4.** If your Check interface differed substantially from Figure 2-33, adjust the properties of the UserForm and its control objects in Design mode.

It's important to view your projects in runtime periodically, in order to verify that you have adjusted the properties of each control object appropriately. Remember to switch to runtime occasionally as you complete the Review Assignments and Case Projects at the end of each of the tutorials in this book.

Now you're ready to finish building the check interface in design time.

## Adding the Remaining Text Box and Label Controls

Now that you have become familiar with the process of adding controls to the UserForm, you should be able to add the remaining text boxes and labels without detailed directions.

## To add the remaining text box and label controls to the UserForm:

**1.** Add the text box and label controls shown in Figure 2-34. Adjust the properties for each of these control objects as specified in Figure 2-35 and 2-36.

| Figure 2-34 | CHECK FORM AFTER ALL LABELS AND TEXT BOXES HAVE BEEN ADDED |
|---|---|

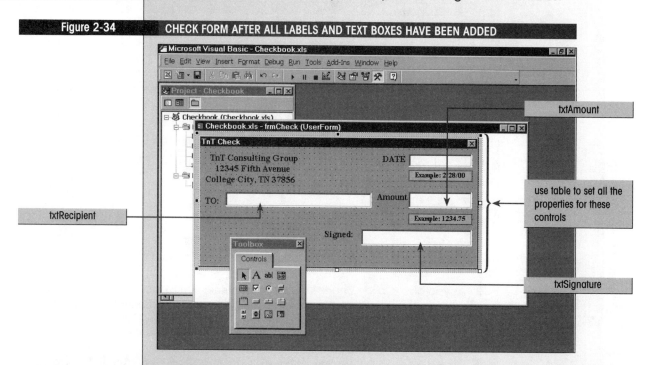

| Figure 2-35 | PROPERTY VALUES FOR REMAINING TEXT BOX CONTROLS |
|---|---|

| PURPOSE OF TEXT BOX | PROPERTY | VALUE |
|---|---|---|
| Provides a space in which the user can enter the recipient of the check. | Name | txtRecipient |
| Provides a space in which the user can type the amount of the check. | Name | txtAmount |
| Provides a space in which the user can type the name of the person who wrote the check. | Name | txtSignature |

| Figure 2-36 | PROPERTY VALUES FOR REMAINING LABEL CONTROLS |
|---|---|

| PURPOSE OF LABEL | PROPERTY | VALUE |
|---|---|---|
| Displays the text "To:" | Caption<br>Font<br><br><br>BackStyle | "TO:"<br>Times New Roman<br>Bold<br>8-pt.<br>0-BackStyleTransparent |
| Displays the text "Amount:" | Caption<br>Font | "Amount:"<br>Times New Roman<br>Bold<br>10 pt. |

| Figure 2-36 | PROPERTY VALUES FOR REMAINING LABEL CONTROLS (continued) | |
|---|---|---|
| **PURPOSE OF LABEL** | **PROPERTY** | **VALUE** |
| Displays the text "Signed:" | Caption<br>Font | "Signed:<br>Times New Roman<br>Bold<br>10 pt. |
| Displays the text "Example: 1234.75" which serves as an example of how the user should enter the check amount. | Caption<br>Font<br><br><br>BorderStyle<br>BorderColor<br>BackColor<br>TextAlign | "Example: 1234.75"<br>Times New Roman<br>Bold<br>8 pt.<br>-1FmBorderStyleSingle<br>On the System tab choose Highlight<br>On the System tab choose ButtonFace<br>2-fmTextAlignCenter |
| Displays the text "Example: 2/28/00" which serves as an example of how the user should enter the date. | Caption<br>Font<br><br><br>BorderStyle<br>BorderColor<br>BackColor<br>TextAlign | "Example: 2/28/00"<br>Times New Roman<br>Bold<br>8 pt.<br>FmBorderStyleSingle<br>On the System tab choose Highlight<br>On the System tab choose ButtonFace<br>2-fmTextAlignCenter |

2. Verify that the new control objects match those shown in Figure 2-34. Adjust the properties as necessary.

3. Save your work.

You have finally finished adding all the label controls and text box controls to the UserForm. Next, you need to add some command buttons.

## Adding Command Button Controls

The command buttons on the check interface should provide a way for the user to activate some of the program statements. Specifically, the Record button should allow the user to transfer information entered into the text boxes to the checkbook register (that is, to the Excel worksheet). The Clear button should clear the text boxes of any data that has already been entered. Finally, the Return to Worksheet button should allow the user to close the check interface and return to the Excel worksheet.

You will now add the command buttons to the UserForm. The command buttons will not actually do anything until you program them (that is, until you write program statements for them). In Session 2.4 of this tutorial you will program the Clear button and the Return to Worksheet button. You will see how the Record button is programmed in Tutorial 3 and Tutorial 4.

## To add the command buttons to your check:

**1.** Click the **CommandButton** button ▢ in the toolbox, then move the pointer to the UserForm and drag the rectangle to create the outline of the Return to Worksheet button. Place the command button in approximately the same location as it appears in Figure 2-37.

TROUBLE? If your UserForm is too small to accommodate the new command buttons, drag its lower-right corner to increase the size of the form. Then continue with Step 1, above.

| Figure 2-37 | FIRST COMMAND BUTTON HAS BEEN ADDED |
|---|---|

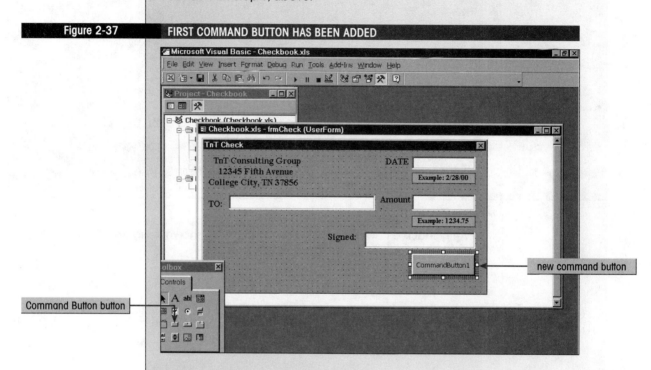

Command Button button

new command button

**2.** Repeat Step 1 to create two more command buttons, placing them in the positions you see in Figure 2-38. The buttons display the default names Command1, Command2, and Command3.

| Figure 2-38 | CHECK WITH COMMAND BUTTONS AND DEFAULT NAMES |

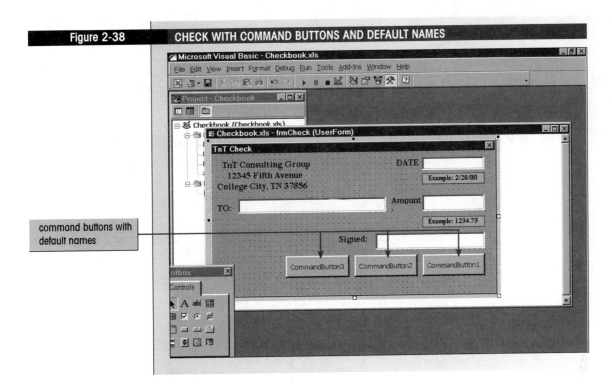

command buttons with
default names

Just as you changed the properties of the controls you already added to the check, you will now change the properties for the command buttons.

## Sizing Command Buttons Appropriately

The Caption property for a command button controls the text displayed on the Command button, so in this case you want to use Record, Clear, and Return to Worksheet as the captions. Next, you will change the command button's AutoSize property, which affects the sizing of the button in relation to the caption. Setting the AutoSize to True ensures that the command button will automatically size itself to accommodate its caption. You can double-click the AutoSize property to change its value. Alternately, you can click the list arrow on the right side of the value box for the Autosize property and then click True.

### To size the command buttons:

1. Select the rightmost command button (the one that will be the Return to Worksheet button).

2. Open the Properties window, and change the Caption property to **Return to Worksheet**.

3. Double-click the **Autosize** property. The value changes from False to True.

4. Repeat Steps 2 and 3 for the other two buttons, using **Clear** for the middle button's Caption property and **Record** for the leftmost button's Caption property.

5. Click the **Return to Worksheet** button and change the value of the Name property to **cmdReturn**.

**6.** Click the **Clear** button and change the value of the Name property to cmdClear.

**7.** Click the **Record** button and change the value of the Name property to cmdRecord, then click anywhere within the form (outside the Record button) to deselect the Record button. Your check should now look like Figure 2-39.

**Figure 2-39**    **CHECK WITH COMMAND BUTTONS AUTOSIZED**

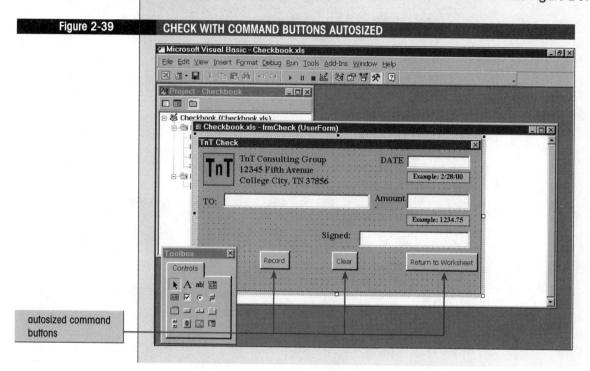

autosized command buttons

As you look at the check, you notice that the command buttons are now different sizes. This happened because you set the Autosize property to True. Recall that the Autosize property makes the command button's size conform to the button's Caption property. You decide that this makes your check look messy, and you would prefer the command buttons to be all the same size. In the next set of steps, you will select all the command buttons and then make them the same size as the Return to Worksheet button, which has the longest caption.

After sizing the three buttons, you can space them equally on the UserForm via the Horizontal Spacing command on the Format menu. Spacing an object on a UserForm is usually a two-step process. First, you use the Make Equal option in order to space the selected objects evenly. Then you use the Increase option to add space between the buttons.

Finally, you need to adjust the buttons' alignment, using the Align command on the Format menu. You can choose from Top, Bottom, Left, and Right alignment options. The Top option, which you'll use in the following steps, aligns the selected objects on their top edges.

## To size, space, and align the command buttons:

**1.** Click the **Return to Worksheet** button. You need to select this button first because you want the other controls to match it in size.

2. Press and hold the **Shift** key, then click the other two buttons. All three buttons are now selected.

3. Click **Format** on the Menu bar, point to **Make Same Size**, and then click **Both**. All three buttons are now the same size as the Return to Worksheet button. However, the buttons are too close together. You will now move the buttons apart by adding some horizontal space between them.

4. Verify that the three buttons are still selected, click **Format** on the Menu bar, point to **Horizontal Spacing**, and then click **Make Equal**. Notice that the three buttons now have the exact same horizontal space between them, thus making the form more attractive. Next, you will increase this amount of space slightly.

5. Click **Format** on the menu bar, point to **Horizontal Spacing**, and then click **Increase**. To create an attractive form, you also want to make sure that the three command buttons are in alignment with each other.

6. Click **Format** on the menu bar, point to **Align**, then click **Tops**. The upper borders of the three command buttons are now aligned.

7. Deselect the command buttons, and then compare your check interface with Figure 2-40. Make any necessary alterations so that your UserForm matches the figure.

| Figure 2-40 | CHECK WITH ALL CONTROLS, EXCLUDING THE IMAGE CONTROL |

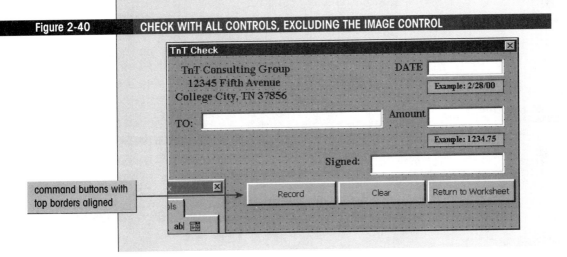

command buttons with top borders aligned

You are almost finished adding the necessary control objects to the check interface. All that remains is to reposition some of the controls and add an image control.

## Moving Controls and Adding an Image Control

The interface design (shown earlier in Figure 2-11) includes a logo image to the left of the company name and address. To add an image to the UserForm, you need to add an Image control object—which you do just as you would add any other control object—via the appropriate button in the toolbox. Note that the Image control is really just a kind of frame to contain an image. The image displayed within the Image control is governed by the Picture property.

Before you can add the Image control, you need to make room for it by moving the labels containing the company name and address. The easiest way to move a control object on a form is to select it, and then drag it using the mouse pointer. In this case, you will need to select all three label controls, and then drag them all at one time.

In the following steps, you will move three label controls, and then insert the Image control in the upper-left corner of the UserForm. Finally, you will select the actual logo image (which is saved in a separate file) by changing the image control's Picture property.

## To move three label controls and add the image control:

1. Select all three labels at the top-left corner of the UserForm, starting with the top label.

2. Click **Format** on the Menu bar, point to **Align**, and then click **Lefts**.

3. Position the pointer over the selected labels, verify that the pointer changes to ✛, then drag the labels to the right approximately one inch. The left edge of the labels should now be positioned about one inch from the left border of the UserForm. This should provide the room you need to insert the Image control.

4. Click the **Image** button 🖼 in the toolbox.

5. Click the top-left corner of the UserForm and drag the pointer to draw a square approximately 1 inch by 1 inch.

6. In the Alphabetic tab of the Properties window, click the value column for the Picture property to display the Ellipsis button, and then click the **Ellipsis** button [...] The Load Picture dialog box opens. Here you can select the image you want to appear in the Image control.

7. Use the Look in list arrow to switch to the Tutorial.02 folder on your Data Disk.

8. In the File list box, click **logo**, and then click **Open**. The Load Picture dialog box closes, and you return to the UserForm. Notice that the logo image is displayed in the Image control, but you can't see the entire image. See Figure 2-41.

| Figure 2-41 | IMAGE ADDED TO THE FORM |

image does not fit at this point

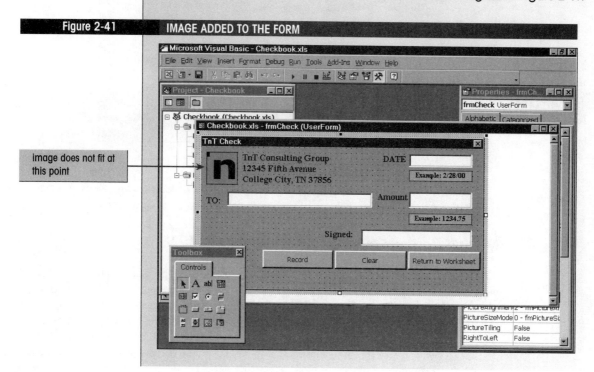

You will display the image fully in the next few steps by adjusting the control's properties. Specifically, you will adjust the PictureSizeMode property, which governs how the picture will be displayed within the control. You will also adjust the BorderStyle property, which controls whether or not the image has a border.

## To adjust the Image control and review the form in runtime:

1. In the Properties window, change the value of the PictureSizeMode property to `1-fmPictureSizeModeStretch`. The image should now be displayed correctly in the Image control.

2. Change the BorderStyle to `1-fmBorderStyleSingle`, then deselect the Image control. You have finished inserting all the necessary controls into the UserForm. Your check interface should look like Figure 2-42. Next, you should review the completed interface in runtime.

| Figure 2-42 | NEWLY SIZED IMAGE WITH A BORDER |

image is now sized properly, and a border has been added

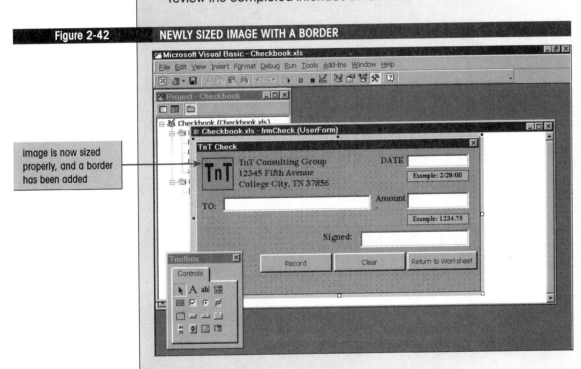

3. Verify that the form is selected and click the **Run** button ▶ on the toolbar. In runtime, your check interface should look similar to Figure 2-43.

**Figure 2-43** | **CHECK FORM DISPLAYED AT RUNTIME**

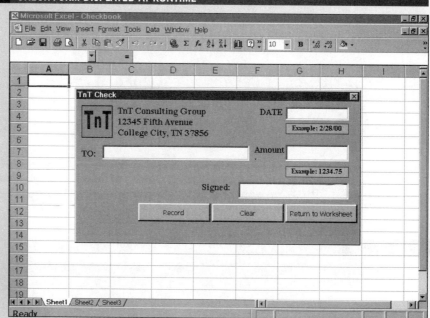

4. Compare your screen with the check in the figure. Make any alterations necessary to ensure that your UserForm matches the figure.

5. Close the form and return to the VBA IDE.

The check interface itself is now complete. You have added the necessary control objects, and you have set the properties for each of these objects. At this point, however, the check cannot do anything because you haven't yet assigned any methods to the objects in the UserForm. In the next session you will write some VBA statements for two of the command buttons that will perform specific actions.

## Session 2.3 QUICK CHECK

1. The _____ control allows you to add a graphic to a UserForm.

2. To see how your UserForm would look at runtime, click the _____ button on the toolbar.

3. The _____ property of a label control determines what will be displayed in the label.

4. Alter the _____ property of the label to change the way text appears in the label.

5. _____ refers to the time in which you are designing a form, whereas _____ refers to the time when the form is actually displayed in the way the user will see it.

In this session you will write VBA code for the Clear button. You will also write VBA code for the Return to Worksheet button. You will also learn how to add comments to your VBA program for documentation purposes. Finally, you will learn to print VBA code.

# Adding **VBA Code to a Command Button's Click Event**

As you learned earlier in this tutorial, the term "method" is used to refer to an action that an object performs. In fact, however, a method is really a set of VBA program statements that, when run, perform a particular action. A method is "triggered" (that is, the program statements begin to run) in response to a particular event.

In a program involving a GUI, one very common event occurs when the user clicks the left mouse button. For instance, in the check interface you are currently creating, you want to make it possible for the user to click the Clear button in order to erase any values that are currently in the text boxes. In other words, the Clear button's method should include statements that clear (empty) each of the text boxes on the form. The event that will trigger these statements is the Click event.

The process of assigning an event to a particular object and then writing the program statements that the event will trigger is known as **programming the object**. In the case of the Clear button, for example, you need to write statements that will clear the four text boxes.

In the previous session, you learned the necessity of assigning descriptive names to the controls that you plan to refer to in program statements. Because you will need to refer to the text boxes within the VBA code, you assigned them the following descriptive names: `txtDate`, `txtRecipient`, `txtAmount`, and `txtSigned`. You will use these names in your VBA statements.

How, exactly, will the Clear button empty (or clear) the four text boxes? You do this by changing the Text property, which governs what text is displayed within a Text Box control object.

When the program is run, users will type text into the text boxes, thereby changing the value of the Text property to specific settings such as Joe Smith or 3/15/00. The job of the Clear button, then, is to empty the text boxes by changing the value of the Text property to a null value. A **null value** is an empty value, or no value at all. In other words, the VBA statements for the Clear button must change the Text property for the text box controls to a null value.

The statements you will write for the Clear button will change the Text property of the text boxes during runtime. To refer to a specific property within a set of program statements, you must type the name of the control whose property you want the program to change, followed by a period, followed by the name of the property. For example, you might include `txtDate.text` in a program statement to refer to the Text property of a control named `txtDate`.

You specify the new value for a property (that is, the value you want the program to assign during runtime) by adding an equals sign followed by the desired value in quotation marks. For example, if you wanted a program to change the Text property of a control named `txtDate` to 2/15/00, you would include `txtDate.text = "2/15/00"` in the program statements. To indicate a null value, you type an opening and closing quotation mark, without any space between them. For example, if you wanted to set the `txtDate` text box to null, you would use the statement: `txtDate.text = ""`. Figure 2-44 describes some additional examples.

| Figure 2-44 | CODE USED TO CHANGE TEXT PROPERTY TO A SPECIFIC VALUE |
|---|---|
| **EXAMPLE** | **EXPLANATION** |
| `txtRecipient.text = "John Williams Company"` | Changes the Text property of a control named "txtRecipient" to "John Williams Company" |
| `txtSignature.text = "Thomas Southerland"` | Changes the Text property of a control named "txtSigned" to "Thomas Southerland" |
| `txtAmount.text = 1234.75` | Changes the Text property of a control named "txtAmount" to "1234.75" |
| `TxtDate.text = ""` | Changes the Text property of a control named txtDate to null |

Note that another term for a null value is "empty string." A **string** is simply a collection of alphanumeric characters. Within VBA code, a string can be anything typed within quotation marks. For example, "Hello World" is a string. The desired values for the Text property, shown in Figure 2-44 above, are all examples of strings. An **empty string** is a string that contains no characters, and is written as "". Thus, in Figure 2-44, opening and closing quotation marks, with no space in between, indicate a null value. If there were a space between the quotes, the string would not be empty, but would, rather, contain a single space.

In the following section you will actually program the Clear command button. In doing so, you will write the complete set of program statements, including code that changes the Text property of each Text Box control object to a null value.

## Programming the Clear Command Button

To program the Clear command button, you need to write a series of programming statements that will clear all the text from each text box. As explained earlier, you do this by writing code that sets the Text property for each text box to a null value, or empty string (indicated by "").

You type all of the program statements (or code) for a form and its control objects in the form's Code window. You can open the form's Code window by double-clicking the form itself, or by double-clicking any object in the form. Exactly what you see when you open the Code window depends on which object you double-click in the form. You'll see how this works in the next set of steps, when you open the Code window in order to begin programming the Clear command button.

### To open the Code window:

1. Double-click the **Clear** command button on the UserForm. The form's Code window opens, as shown in Figure 2-45. You may not see the words Option Explicit in your Code window. You'll learn more about the Option Explicit statement in Tutorial 3. For now, if you do see this statement, ignore it.

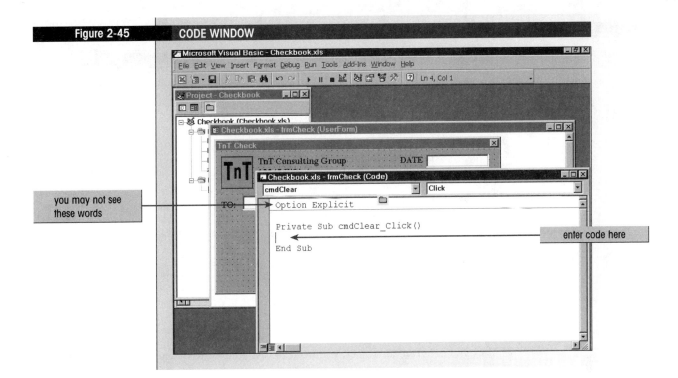

Figure 2-45     CODE WINDOW

you may not see
these words

enter code here

The first line in the Code module window is `Private sub cmdClear_Click ()`. You are already familiar with the word `Sub` which begins any set of VBA statements. The word `Private` indicates that the code can only be used within the current form. The name of the control object is followed by an underscore, which is followed by the name of the event (in this case, `Click`) that will trigger the program statements. Note that VBA provides all this information for you automatically. You only need to begin typing the actual program statements on the next line.

Think of the `Private Sub cmdClear_Click()` and `End Sub` statements as the beginning and end of the Click event. In programming terminology, the complete set of statements that you will write, beginning with `Private Sub` and ending with `End Sub`, makes up a **Click event procedure.** Notice that the `Private Sub` statement contains the name of the command button and the name of the event (in this case, the Click event). The `End Sub` statement, however, contains neither the name of the command button nor the name of the event. The `Private Sub` and the `End Sub` statements always come in pairs (that is, you must have one of each for every sub program).

### To program the Clear command button:

1. Enter the following code between the `Private` and `End` statements in the Code window, using the Tab key to indent it, as shown in Figure 2-46:

   ```
   txtDate.Text = ""

   txtRecipient.Text = ""

   txtAmount.Text = ""

   txtSignature.Text = ""
   ```

2. Compare your code with Figure 2-46 and make any necessary changes.

Figure 2-46    CODE FOR CLEAR BUTTON

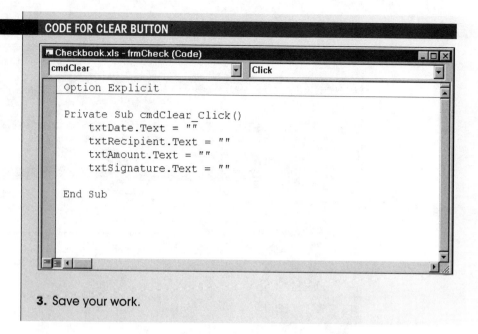

**3.** Save your work.

After you program an object, you need to test your code by running the project.

*To test the Clear command button:*

**1.** Click the **Run** button ▶ on the toolbar.

**2.** Type some sample data in each of the text boxes. It does not matter what you type because you will clear it in the next step.

**3.** Click the **Clear** command button. You should notice that all the data you entered has now disappeared, leaving room for new data.

TROUBLE? If you see an error message, or if any of the text boxes are not empty at this point, you need to return to the preceding set of steps and correct the code in the Code window. Make any necessary changes and run the project again.

**4.** Click the **Return to Worksheet** button on the form.

Assuming that the project ran successfully, you are now ready to program another object—the Return to Worksheet command button.

## Programming the Return to Worksheet Command Button

You will now write the program statement that will cause the UserForm to be removed from the screen when the user clicks the Return to Worksheet command button. This requires only one simple statement. In this case, you could use either the `Hide` statement or the `Unload` statement.

The **Hide method** removes the UserForm from the screen; once removed, the UserForm continues to reside in memory. You can also use the **Unload method** to remove the UserForm from the screen. This method actually removes the UserForm from memory and ends the program. In this case, you will use the `Unload` method. The complete statement looks like this: `Unload Me`.

*To program the Return to Worksheet button:*

1. Double-click the **Return to Worksheet** button. The Code window displays a new set of `Private Sub` and `End Sub` statements for the selected control object (cmdReturn).

2. Between the `Private Sub` and the `End Sub` statements, enter the following:
   `unload Me`

3. Save your work. Now you are ready to test your code.

4. Click the ▶ button. The check interface is displayed in runtime.

5. Click the **Return to Worksheet** button. The check is removed from the screen and you return to the VBA IDE, where the UserForm is displayed in design time.

In Tutorials 3 and 4, you will learn how to run the project directly from the worksheet. You will also learn how to make the project return to the worksheet when the user is finished working with the check interface. But for now, you are almost finished with the project. Your last job is to add some information to the code that will help other developers understand your work.

## Documenting **VBA Code**

When you write VBA code, it is usually a good idea to add some explanation, or documentation, that describes the code. The process of adding documentation is known as **documenting your work**. You document VBA code by adding **comments**—statements that only provide information and that are ignored at runtime. At the very least, for each program you should include the date you created the code and your name.

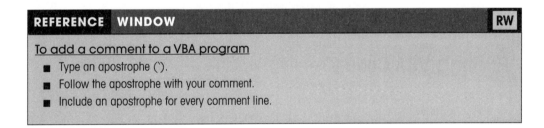

REFERENCE WINDOW ‎RW

To add a comment to a VBA program
- Type an apostrophe (').
- Follow the apostrophe with your comment.
- Include an apostrophe for every comment line.

You indicate a comment in VBA code by preceding it with an apostrophe ('). After you insert a comment, and then move the pointer to another line in the Code window, the text of the comment turns green, thus making it easier to spot comments within a long series of program statements.

*To add the date and your name to your VBA code:*

1. If necessary, use the scroll bar to display the top of the Code window.

2. Click at the beginning of the first line at the top of the window, press **Enter** to insert a blank line, press ↑ to move the pointer to the top line, and then type **'** (an apostrophe).

3. Type **Date:** followed by today's date.

4. Press **Enter**. The line turns green, indicating that it is a comment.

5. Type **'** followed by **Developer:** followed by your name.

6. Press **Enter**. Some developers prefer to add a line of asterisks after the code at the beginning of a module, to clearly distinguish between the code and the opening comments. You'll add asterisks in the next step.

7. Type an apostrophe followed by approximately 40 asterisks, then click anywhere in the code window. Your comments should look like Figure 2-47.

| Figure 2-47 | COMMENTS ADDED TO CODE WINDOW |
|---|---|

you may or may not have this statement, depending on your system settings

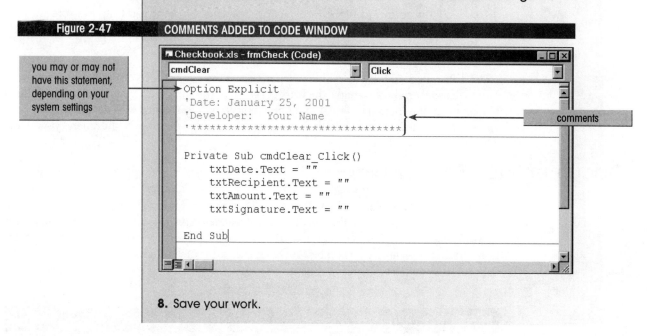

comments

8. Save your work.

## Printing **VBA Code**

Now that you are finished creating the form, you want to print it to show to Gene. He requests that you print the code you have created so far and also an image of the check form. The VBA Print dialog box allows you to indicate which portions of a project you want to print. In this case, you want to print both the UserForm (that is, the Form Image) and the Code.

---

**REFERENCE  WINDOW**    `RW`

**To print a form and code**

- Click File on the menu bar, then click Print.
- In the Print dialog box, indicate whether you want to print just the code, or the form as an image.

---

You are now ready to print your Checkbook project.

*To print your VBA code and the UserForm:*

1. Click **File** on the menu bar, and then click **Print**. The Print - Checkbook dialog box opens.

2. Verify that the Current Module check box is selected.

3. Click the **Form Image** check box to display a check.

4. Click the **Code** check box (if necessary) to display a check. Your dialog box should look like Figure 2-48.

**Figure 2-48**    **PRINT DIALOG BOX**

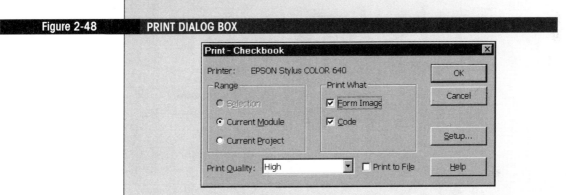

5. Click **OK**. Your code and an image of the UserForm print.

6. Switch to the Excel window and close Excel.

In this tutorial you created a new form, added controls to the form, and programmed two of the command buttons on the form. In the next two tutorials you will learn how to program the remaining command buttons.

# Session 2.4 QUICK CHECK

1. Write the statement that will place John Doc in the text box named `txtCustomer`.

2. Write the statement that will place the number 56.5 in the text box named `txtHoursWorked`.

3. Write the statement that will clear the text in the text box named `txtAddress`.

4. What character indicates that a line is a comment?

5. Write the statement that will remove the current form from the screen and from memory.

## REVIEW ASSIGNMENTS

In this tutorial, you began developing the checkbook application by creating a form for entering check data. Gene explains that the checkbook application should also allow users to record deposits. It's your job to develop a form for entering deposit data. The form should allow the user to enter: the date of the deposit, the amount of cash, the amount deposited by check, the total amount of the deposit, and the name of the person who prepared the deposit (the person who counted the money for the deposit).

Gene gives you a sketch of the form design, which is shown in Figure 2-49. The form design indicates which control objects will be used for each element of the form. It also indicates the necessary command buttons. Notice that the form should include three command buttons. The functions of the command buttons are indicated by the caption printed on them, as shown in Figure 2-49. As you create the form in the steps below, remember to save your work periodically.

| Figure 2-49 | SKETCH OF DEPOSIT FORM |
| --- | --- |

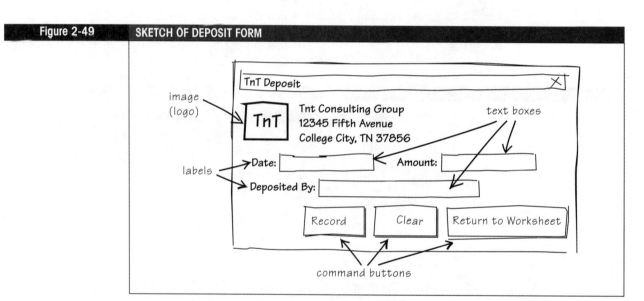

1. Study the form design in Figure 2-49, and familiarize yourself with the required control objects.

2. Start Excel.

3. Open the workbook named **Deposit** from the Review folder for Tutorial 2 on your Data Disk.

4. Save the workbook as **Deposit Form**.

5. Open the Excel VBA IDE.

6. Add a UserForm to the project.

7. Display the Project Explorer and observe the additional UserForm in the project. What is the project's default name?

8. Change the project name to `TnTDeposits` (no spaces).

9. Change the Name property of the UserForm to `frmDeposit`.

10. Change the Caption property of the UserForm to `TnT Deposit`.

11. Change the BackColor property to a color of your choosing.

12. Add all the labels and text boxes included in Figure 2-49.

13. Use the sizing and alignment techniques you learned in the tutorial to make your form attractive.

14. Change the Name property for each text box and command button to something descriptive. Be sure to include the `txt` prefix for the text boxes and the `cmd` prefix for the command buttons. Recall that it is not necessary to name the labels, since they will not be used in programming statements.

15. Alter the BackColor and BackStyle properties to suit your own preference.

16. Write the VBA code for the Clear button. (*Hint*: You can use the same code you typed in the tutorial, except that you will need to alter it to apply to the text boxes in the `frmDeposit` UserForm).

17. Write the VBA code for the Return to Worksheet button.

18. Test the UserForm in runtime. Enter data in each of the text boxes and then click the Clear button. Also test the Return to Worksheet command button.

19. Add comments to the UserForm's code module to indicate the date the project was created and to identify you as the developer. Your instructor might also request that you add other information in your comment section.

20. Print the UserForm and the code for the UserForm.

21. Save the workbook.

22. Close Excel.

## CASE PROBLEMS

*Case 1. Tracking Employees at Scott Temporary Personnel* Scott Temporary Personnel (STP) provides temporary employees for a wide range of companies. You have been hired as a software developer at STP. The Human Resources manager, Leah Hayes, tells you that she would like to use an Excel worksheet to keep track of STP's pool of temporary workers. Leah stresses that she wants the process of entering data in the worksheet to be as user-friendly as possible. It's your job to develop a UserForm that will allow for easy entry of personnel data.

1. Start Excel and verify that a new, blank workbook is displayed.

2. Save the workbook as **STP Personnel Management** in the Cases folder for Tutorial 2.

3. Open the Excel VBA IDE and rename the project **STPPersonnel** (no spaces).

4. Add a new UserForm to the project.

5. Select the new UserForm and change the UserForm properties as indicated in Figure 2-50.

| Figure 2-50 | PROPERTY VALUES FOR NEW USERFORM | |
|---|---|---|
| **PROPERTY** | **VALUE** | |
| Name | frmPersonnel | |
| BorderStyle | 1 - frmBorderStyleSingle | |
| Caption | Personnel | |

6. Save your work.

7. Add label controls, text box controls, and command button controls to the UserForm as shown in Figure 2-51. Format and align all the controls so that they are similarly placed, sized, and aligned, as the figure indicates. You will change the properties in the next step; for now, simply size and align the controls.

| Figure 2-51 | SKETCH OF FRMPERSONNEL USERFORM WITH CONTROL OBJECTS |
|---|---|

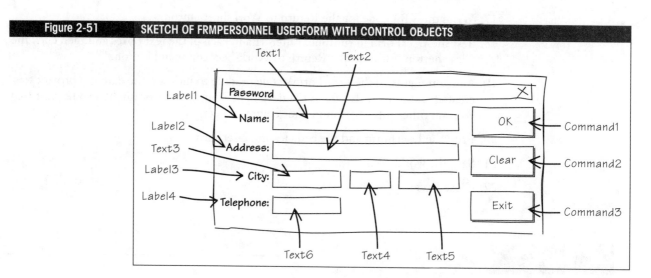

8. Use the information in Figure 2-52 to adjust the label control properties.

| Figure 2-52 | PROPERTY VALUES FOR THE LABEL CONTROL OBJECTS | |
|---|---|---|
| **CONTROL** | **PROPERTY** | **VALUE** |
| Label1 | Caption | Name |
| | TextAlign | 3 - frmTextAlignRight |
| Label2 | Caption | Address |
| | TextAlign | 3 - frmTextAlignRight |
| Label3 | Caption | City |
| | TextAlign | 3 - frmTextAlignRight |
| Label4 | Caption | Telephone |
| | TextAlign | 3 - frmTextAlignRight |

9. Use the information in Figure 2-53 to adjust the text box control properties.

| Figure 2-53 | PROPERTY VALUES FOR THE TEXT BOX CONTROL OBJECTS | | |

| CONTROL | PROPERTY | VALUE |
|---------|----------|-------|
| Text1 | Name | txtName |
| Text2 | Name | txtAddress |
| Text3 | Name | txtCity |
| Text4 | Name | txtState |
| Text5 | Name | txtZipCode |
| Text6 | Name | txtPhone |

10. Use the information in Figure 2-54 to set the properties for the Command Button control objects.

| Figure 2-54 | PROPERTY VALUES FOR THE COMMAND BUTTON CONTROL OBJECTS | | |

| CONTROL | PROPERTY | VALUE |
|---------|----------|-------|
| CommandButton1 | Name | cmdOK |
|  | Caption | OK |
| CommandButton2 | Name | cmdClear |
|  | Caption | Clear |
| CommandButton3 | Name | cmdExit |
|  | Caption | Exit |

11. Add the following code to the Click event for the Clear button.

```
txtName.text = ""

txtAddress.text = ""

txtCity.text = ""

txtState.text = ""

txtZipCode.text = ""

txtPhone.text = ""
```

12. Add the following code to the Click event for the Exit button:

```
Unload Me
```

13. Test the UserForm and its command buttons in runtime. Make any necessary corrections and save your work.

14. Add comments at the top of the code to indicate the current date and your name as the developer.

15. Print the code.

16. Save your work and close Excel.

*Case 2. Recording Tuition Payments at Cheryl's Kids*   Cheryl's Kids is a preschool and day-care center that serves a thriving urban neighborhood in downtown Chicago. Cheryl, the owner and program director, has asked you to prepare an application that would simplify the process of recording tuition payments in an Excel worksheet. Because she teaches the toddler program in addition to managing the day-care facility, Cheryl doesn't have time to learn Excel. Instead, she would rather have a simple form that would allow her to simply type information for each tuition payment, click a button, and have the information be entered into an Excel worksheet automatically. The form should allow her to record the date of the payment, the client's name, a description of the payment, and the amount of the payment. Your job is to create a form for Cheryl according to her specifications.

**Explore**

1. On a piece of paper, sketch a design for the interface. Remember to include all the necessary text boxes and command buttons.

2. Start Excel and verify that a new, blank workbook is displayed.

3. Save the workbook as **Cheryl's Kids**.

4. Open the Excel VBA IDE and rename the project **CherylsKids** (no spaces).

5. Change the description of the project to Cheryl's Kids Tuition Payments.

6. Add a new UserForm to the project.

7. Select the new UserForm and adjust the UserForm properties according to the information in Figure 2-55.

**Figure 2-55**   **PROPERTY VALUES FOR THE USERFORM**

| PROPERTY | VALUE |
| --- | --- |
| Name | frmPayments |
| BorderStyle | 1 - frmBorderStyleSingle |
| Caption | Payments |

8. Save the UserForm.

9. Add label, text box, and command button control objects to the UserForm. When you have finished adding the control objects, your UserForm should resemble the sketch you prepared earlier, except that you haven't yet named or sized any of the controls. Verify that your UserForm includes all the control objects shown in Figure 2-56; note that you may have arranged your control objects differently, depending on the choices you made in your original design. At this point you should just have the controls placed on the form, you will alter their properties in the next steps.

| Figure 2-56 | INTERFACE WITH CONTROL OBJECTS ADDED |
|---|---|

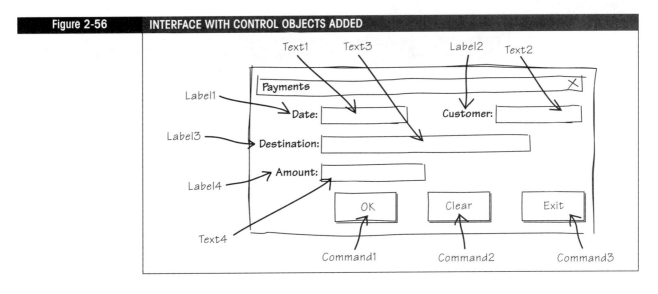

10. Use the information in Figure 2-57 to set the label control properties.

| Figure 2-57 | PROPERTY VALUES FOR THE LABEL CONTROL OBJECTS |
|---|---|

| CONTROL | PROPERTY | VALUE |
|---|---|---|
| Label1 | Caption | DATE |
|  | TextAlign | 3 - frmTextAlignRight |
| Label2 | Caption | Customer |
|  | TextAlign | 3 - frmTextAlignRight |
| Label3 | Caption | Description |
|  | TextAlign | 3 - frmTextAlignRight |
| Label4 | Caption | Amount |
|  | TextAlign | 3 - frmTextAlignRight |

11. Use the information in Figure 2-58 to set the text box control properties.

| Figure 2-58 | PROPERTY VALUES FOR THE TEXT BOX CONTROL OBJECTS |
|---|---|

| CONTROL | PROPERTY | VALUE |
|---|---|---|
| Text1 | Name | txtDate |
| Text2 | Name | txtCustomer |
| Text3 | Name | txtDescription |
| Text4 | Name | txtAmount |

12. Use the information in Figure 2-59 to set the properties for the command button control objects.

| Figure 2-59 | PROPERTY VALUES FOR THE COMMAND BUTTON CONTROL OBJECTS | | |
| --- | --- | --- | --- |
| **CONTROL** | **PROPERTY** | **VALUE** | |
| CommandButton1 | Name | cmdOK | |
| | Caption | OK | |
| CommandButton2 | Name | cmdClear | |
| | Caption | Clear | |
| CommandButton3 | Name | cmdExit | |
| | Caption | Exit | |

13. Add the following code to the Click event for the Clear command button.

```
txtDate = ""
txtCustomer = ""
txtDescription = ""
txtAmount = ""
```

14. Add the following code to the Click event for the Exit command button.

```
Unload Me
```

15. Save your work.

16. Test the UserForm and its command buttons in runtime. Make any changes necessary and save them.

17. Add comments to the top of the code, indicating today's date and your name as the developer.

18. Save your work.

19. Print the code.

20. Close Excel.

*Case 3. Managing Personal Finances for Patricia Sutherland* You run a private consulting firm that provides computerized approaches to everyday activities. Patricia Sutherland, one of your clients, wants to keep track of her expenses each month in an Excel worksheet. However, she does not want to take the time to learn Excel. Rather, she would prefer to have a simple form in which she can enter her data. In a later tutorial, you will write VBA statements that will move the data from a UserForm to an Excel worksheet. For now, you are simply creating the UserForm for Patricia's approval.

1. If necessary, start Excel and verify that a new, blank workbook is displayed.

2. Save the workbook as **Sutherland Expenses**.

3. Open the VBA IDE.

4. Add a new UserForm to the project.

5. Set the UserForm properties according to the information in Figure 2-60.

| Figure 2-60 | USERFORM PROPERTIES | |
| --- | --- | --- |
| **PROPERTY** | **VALUE** | |
| Name | frmExpenses | |
| BorderStyle | 1 - frmBorderStyleSingle | |
| Caption | Expenses | |

6. Save your work.

7. Add label controls, text box controls, and command buttons to the UserForm so that they are placed in the positions shown in Figure 2-61. At this point you should just have the controls in place with their default properties; you will alter the properties in the next steps.

| Figure 2-61 | SKETCH OF FRMEXPENSE FORM |
| --- | --- |

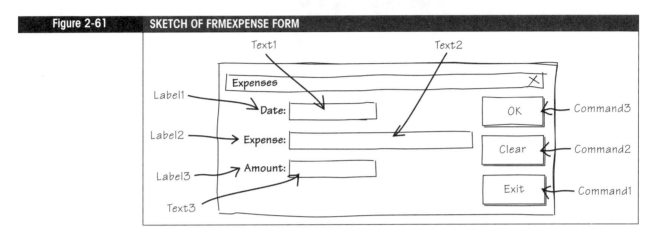

8. Use the information in Figure 2-62 to set the label control properties.

| Figure 2-62 | PROPERTIES FOR LABEL CONTROLS |
| --- | --- |

| CONTROL | PROPERTY | VALUE |
| --- | --- | --- |
| Label1 | Caption | Date |
|  | TextAlign | 3 - frmTextAlignRight |
| Label2 | Caption | Expense |
|  | TextAlign | 3 - frmTextAlignRight |
| Label3 | Caption | Amount |
|  | TextAlign | 3 - frmTextAlignRight |

9. Use the information in Figuree 2-63 to set the text box control properties.

| Figure 2-63 | TEXT BOX NAME PROPERTY VALUES |
| --- | --- |

| CONTROL | PROPERTY | VALUE |
| --- | --- | --- |
| Text1 | Name | txtDate |
| Text2 | Name | txtExpense |
| Text3 | Name | txtAmount |

10. Use the information in Figure 2-64 to set the command button control properties.

| Figure 2-64 | COMMAND BUTTON PROPERTIES | | |
| --- | --- | --- | --- |
| **CONTROL** | **PROPERTY** | **VALUE** | |
| CommandButton1 | Name | cmdOK | |
| | Caption | OK | |
| CommandButton2 | Name | cmdClear | |
| | Caption | Clear | |
| CommandButton3 | Name | cmdExit | |
| | Caption | Exit | |

11. Add the following code to the Click event for the Clear button.

```
txtDate = ""
txtExpense = ""
txtAmount = ""
```

12. Add the following code to the Click event for the Exit button.

```
Unload Me
```

13. Save your work.

14. Run the form and test both the Clear button and the Exit button. Make any changes necessary and save them.

15. Add comments to the top of the code, indicating today's date and your name as the developer.

16. Save your work.

17. Print the code

18. Close Excel.

*Case 4. Tracking Projects for C & B Construction*  C & B Construction has many projects in various stages of completion. Lee Chan, the company's project manager, explains that he needs to assign tasks to his foremen and then keep track of their progress. He asks you to create a VBA program that will help him keep track of the assigned tasks. The program should make it easy to record a task description, the start date, the end date (date of completion), and the name of the person assigned to the task. Your assignment is to develop a form that Lee can use to enter task information into an Excel worksheet.

1. Start Excel and verify that a new, blank workbook is displayed.

2. Save the workbook as **C&B Construction**.

3. Start the VBA IDE.

4. Change the name of the project to **CBConstruction** (no spaces).

5. Change the project description to C & B Construction Project Manager.

6. Add a new UserForm to the project.

7. Set the UserForm properties according to the information in Figure 2-65.

**Figure 2-65**    **USERFORM PROPERTY VALUES**

| PROPERTY | VALUE |
|----------|-------|
| Name | frmTasks |
| BorderStyle | 1 - frmBorderStyleSingle |
| Caption | Tasks |

8. Save the UserForm.

9. Add label controls, text box controls, and command buttons to the UserForm so that they are placed and sized similarly to those shown in Figure 2-66. At this point the controls retain their default values. You will alter the properties in the next steps.

**Figure 2-66**    **SKETCHES OF FRMTASKS FORM**

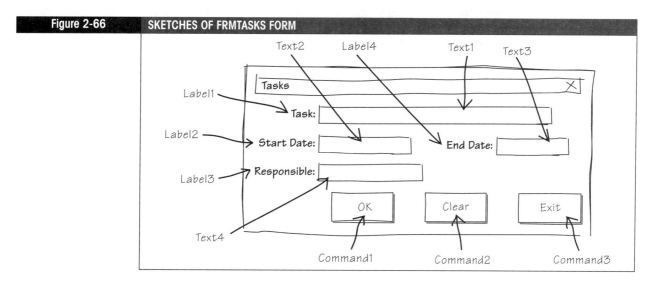

10. Use the information in Figure 2-67 to set the label control properties.

**Figure 2-67**    **LABEL CONTROL PROPERTIES**

| CONTROL | PROPERTY | VALUE |
|---------|----------|-------|
| Label1 | Caption<br>TextAlign | Task:<br>3 - frmTextAlignRight |
| Label2 | Caption<br>TextAlign | Start Date:<br>3 - frmTextAlignRight |
| Label3 | Caption<br>TextAlign | End Date:<br>3 - frmTextAlignRight |
| Label4 | Caption<br>TextAlign | Responsible:<br>3 - frmTextAlignRight |

11. Use the information in Figure 2-68 to set the text box control properties.

| Figure 2-68 | TEXT BOX PROPERTY VALUES | | |
|---|---|---|---|
| **CONTROL** | **PROPERTY** | **VALUE** | |
| Text1 | Name | txtTask | |
| Text2 | Name | txtStart | |
| Text3 | Name | txtEnd | |
| Text4 | Name | txtResponsible | |

12. Use the information in Figure 2-69 to set the command button control properties.

| Figure 2-69 | COMMAND BUTTON PROPERTY VALUES | | |
|---|---|---|---|
| **CONTROL** | **PROPERTY** | **VALUE** | |
| CommandButton1 | Name<br>Caption | cmdOK<br>OK | |
| CommandButton2 | Name<br>Caption | cmdClear<br>Clear | |
| CommandButton3 | Name<br>Caption | cmdExit<br>Exit | |

13. Add the following code to the Click event for the Clear button.

```
txtTask = ""
txtStart = ""
txtEnd = ""
txtResponsible = ""
```

14. Add the following code to the Click event for the Exit button.

```
Unload Me
```

15. Add comments to the code, indicating today's date and your name as the developer.

16. Save your work.

17. Run the form and test the Clear and Exit buttons. Make any changes necessary and save them.

18. Print the code.

19. Close Excel.

## QUICK CHECK ANSWERS

*Session 2.1*

1. Objects
2. property, method
3. event-driven
4. UserForm, control objects
5. graphical user interface
6. command

*Session 2.2*

1. font
2. label
3. Shift
4. BackStyle
5. vertical, horizontal

*Session 2.3*

1. image
2. Run
3. Caption
4. Font
5. Design time, runtime

*Session 2.4*

1. `txtCustomer.text = "John Doe"`
2. `txtHoursWorked = 56.5`
3. `txtAddress = ""`
4. apostrophe (')
5. `Unload Me`

In this tutorial you will:

- Store data temporarily in variables

- Assign values to variables and properties with assignment statements

- Incorporate functions into VBA statements

- Learn how to distinguish between functions and sub procedures

- Learn the importance of validating data

- Examine the three basic control structures

- Create a one kind of Selection control structure

- Debug a VBA program

- Examine data validation code in a completed VBA project

# USING
## VARIABLES, ASSIGNMENT STATEMENTS, AND CONTROL STRUCTURES

*Creating a Salary Calculator Program*

## TnT Consulting Group

Under the direction of your supervisor, Gene Cox, you are continuing to develop your VBA programming skills. You've already learned the basics of VBA, how to launch and use the VBA IDE, and how to develop forms by using VBA controls. Gene feels you are now ready to begin developing programs using a basic programming tool, called a control structure. In addition, he wants you to learn how to use variables to store data within a VBA program.

You will learn about these concepts as you work on two different projects. The first is an application for Potters House Gallery, a picture framing shop. Jennifer Morton, the gallery's manager, has requested a simple program for calculating employee salaries. Gene has asked you to work on the portion of this system that actually does the calculation. Other consultants will be working on some of the more complicated portions of this system. (Gene explains that software developers often divide the work on a single project among several developers. This allows work on the project to proceed at a faster pace, and gives the developers useful experience in developing a variety of different programs.)

In addition to the Salary Calculator program, Gene has asked you to work with Ashley Andrews, on the code for the Check Register program. You've already spent some time on this project (in Tutorial 2), when you helped create the form. Ashley then took your work on the form and began the fairly complicated process of coding the control objects. Gene feels that you could benefit from looking at Ashley's work, and has asked Ashley to demonstrate the Check Register program for you. In this tutorial, Ashley will demonstrate the portion of the project that checks the validity of the data entered into the check form.

Gene believes that the combination of these two projects will provide you with some valuable experience that you can apply to future projects.

**SESSION 3.1**

In this session you will learn how to interpret the syntax examples used throughout this text and then you will preview the Salary Calculator program. You will then learn how variables are used to store data temporarily within a program. Next, you will practice writing assignment statements, in order to assign a value to a variable or property. Finally, you will explore the use of functions in VBA.

## Interpreting Syntax in This Text

Before you learn how to use variables in program statements, you need to understand the typographical conventions used throughout this book to present new VBA statements. Each time a new statement is introduced, you will see a box that specifies its basic structure, or **syntax**. The box will also include an explanation of the syntax, and at least one example. The following example shows the standard format that will be used throughout this book. (This example covers a function you have already used, the InputBox function.)

| Syntax | **InputBox(**prompt[, title] [, default] [, xpos] [, ypos] [, helpfile, context]**)** |
|---|---|
| Explanation | The InputBox function displays a small form in which the user can enter a single item of data. |
| | The InputBox function returns a string containing the value the user typed in the box. |
| Example | **InputBox(**"Enter Your Name: "**)** |

Note that within the syntax of a statement, boldface and square brackets have special meaning. For example, items in bold (such as **InputBox**, above) are required. Items that are not bold represent words that will have to be supplied by the user. For instance, in the example, the InputBox is required but everything else (the unbolded words) represents items the developer will supply. Also, note that words in square brackets, such as [title], above, are optional. To summarize, when reading the syntax boxes in this book, the following conventions apply:

- **Bold:** All words in bold are required. If you do not include these parts of the statement, the statement will not work.
- Not bold: All words that are not boldface must be supplied by the user.
- [Square Brackets]: Words in square brackets are optional.

Note that within a Syntax box, the syntax for a statement will always include all available options. However, the explanations will only cover the options you will most likely use. To learn more about each new statement, consider looking up the statement in VBA Help.

Finally, the example portion of a Syntax box will show how the statement will be used at that particular point in the tutorial. The example will not include all optional portions of the statement. (You can always read more about them in VBA Help.)

# Previewing the Salary Calculator Program

Gene sits down at your computer with you to demonstrate the Potters House Salary Calculation project. The project includes a Salary Calculation form (also called a Userform) that includes text boxes in which the user can enter the number of hours worked and the rate of pay for a particular employee. When the user clicks the Calculate command button, the program should then calculate the employee's salary. Gene has already created the form, which you will review in the following steps.

## To open the form:

1. Start Excel and open the workbook named **Salary**, which is stored in the Tutorial.03 folder on your Data Disk.

2. Save the workbook as **Salary Calculator** in the Tutorial.03 folder on your Data Disk.

3. Start the VBA IDE and open the Project Explorer.

4. If necessary click the **Expand** button ⊞ to expand the Forms folder. As shown in Figure 3-1, the Forms folder includes a form entitled `frmSalaryCalculator`.

| Figure 3-1 | THE PROJECT EXPLORER WITH FORM'S SUBDIRECTORY EXPANDED |
|---|---|

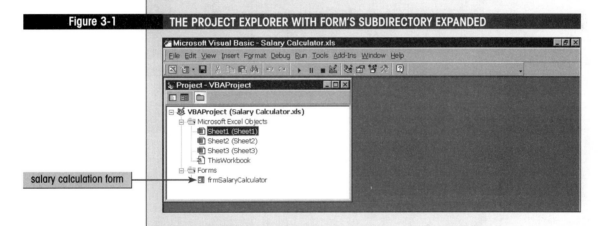

5. Double click `frmSalaryCalculator`. The form opens in Design View, as shown in Figure 3-2. (You may need to enlarge the UserForm window to display the form fully.)

| Figure 3-2 | SALARY CALCULATION FORM IN DESIGN TIME |
|---|---|

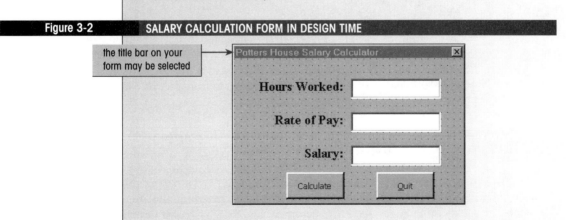

6. Click the form's title bar, if necessary, to select it (that is, to make the title bar turn blue).

7. Click the **Run Sub/UserForm** button ▶ on the toolbar. You return to the worksheet window, with the form displayed in runtime.

8. Click the **Calculate** button. Nothing happens because the Calculate button's Click event has not yet been programmed.

9. Click the **Quit** button. You return to the VBA IDE, where the form is again displayed in design time.

10. Double-click the **Quit** button. The Code window opens, as shown in Figure 3-3. Note that the code for the Quit button is identical to the code you used in Tutorial 2 for closing the Form window. Also notice that, at this point, there is no code for the Calculate button. You will write this code later in this tutorial.

| Figure 3-3 | CODE WINDOW WITH CMDQUIT_CLICK EVENT PROCEDURE |
| --- | --- |

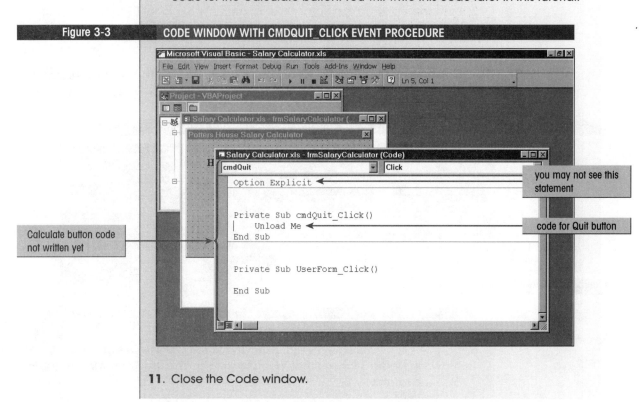

11. Close the Code window.

Notice that the Potters House Salary Calculator form is designed to allow a user to enter the hours worked and the rate of pay for a particular employee. When the user clicks the Calculate button, the program will actually calculate the employee's salary. Your job, then, is to write the necessary code for the Calculate button. Before you can do that, you need to learn about an important programming tool—variables.

## Storing Data Within a Program

In order to program the Calculate button, you need a means of temporarily storing data at runtime. To understand why, remember that any computer program is made up of a series of steps that execute one after another. The Salary Calculator program, for instance, cannot calculate the employee's salary and display it in the Salary text box instantaneously—this actually involves a series of programming statements. From the point of view of the program, this process is not at all instantaneous. First, the program must retrieve the data from the Hours Worked text box. Then the data must be stored in the computer's memory so that a subsequent statement can use it. Another program statement must do the same for the data in the Rate of Pay text box. Next, the program must retrieve these two pieces of data from memory, and then multiply them in order to determine the employee's salary. Additional statements are then responsible for displaying the salary in the Salary text box and formatting it properly.

As you can see, the Salary Calculator program cannot work properly without some means of storing data temporarily in memory. The location in memory where data is temporarily stored at runtime is called a **variable.** Once data is stored in a variable, the program can then access that storage location in order to alter the data or to use that data to perform calculations. Note that data can be stored in a variable only at runtime; once the program stops running, the data stored in the variable is no longer accessible.

Before you can use a variable in your program statements, you must first define, or **declare**, the variable. That is, you must give the variable a name and specify the type of data that will be stored in the variable. (As you will learn later in this tutorial, one type of data is best for storing numbers, another for storing text, and so on.)

You have already gained some experience with variables in Tutorial 1. There, you typed the following statements:

```
Dim strNewData As String
strNewData = InputBox("Enter your name")
Selection.TypeText Text:=strNewData
```

The first statement declares or defines a variable, giving it the name `strNewData` and assigning it the "String" data type (meaning that it will contain text and not numbers). The second statement retrieves some data entered in an input box by the user and places that data in the variable named `strNewData`. The third statement takes the data from the variable and places it into a Word document. The purpose, then, of `strNewData` is to "hold" the data so that a subsequent statement can insert the data into a Word document.

You will learn more about using variables throughout this tutorial. In the next section, you will focus on the process of declaring a variable.

## Declaring a Variable

You can declare, or define, a variable within a **Dim statement**. You could say that the `Dim` statement sets up the variable for later use. (You can also declare a variable in several other kinds of statements—specifically, the `Private`, `Public`, `ReDim`, or `Static` statements. You will learn more about these statements in a later tutorial.) The `Dim` statement's job is to indicate the name of the variable and the type of data it will store.

The `Dim` statement should always come before the statements that actually use the variable. By convention, developers usually place `Dim` statements at the beginning of a program's code. This makes it easy to see at a glance the variables that will be used in the program. The syntax of the `Dim` statement is explained below. (The conventions used in this book for indicating required words, optional words, and so on, in a statement syntax, were explained earlier in this tutorial. Review them now, if necessary, so that you can fully understand the syntax of the `Dim` statement.)

| Syntax | **Dim** variablename **As** variabletype |
|---|---|
| Explanation | The **Dim** statement declares or defines a variable by giving the variable a name and assigning it a data type. |
| Example | **Dim** strNewData **As** String |

As you learned earlier, the Dim statement in the example above specifies that the variable is named **strNewData** and that its data type is **String**, meaning it will be used to store text (not numbers). Later in this tutorial you will learn some conventions for selecting a name for a variable. The next section explains about the various data types available in VBA.

## Assigning a Data Type

As you know, one job of the Dim statement is to indicate the variable's data type—that is, it should state what type of data is stored in the variable. VBA provides an assortment of data types. Each data type is allotted a specific amount of storage space in memory, with some data types taking up a great deal more memory space than others. With the exception of the String data type (which can accommodate anything you can type on the keyboard) certain restrictions apply to the type of information that can be stored in each data type. For example, the Integer data type can accommodate only whole numbers such as the number 238 (which is an integer) but not the number 238.57 (which is not an integer). The number 238 is therefore **valid** data for an Integer variable, while the number 238.57 is **invalid**.

Figure 3-4 describes the most commonly used data types, and provides examples of valid and invalid data for each. While Figure 3-4 does not come close to including all the possible VBA data types, it does describe all the data types you will be using in this tutorial.

| Figure 3-4 | COMMONLY USED VBA DATA TYPES | | | | |
|---|---|---|---|---|---|
| **DATA TYPE** | **DESCRIPTION** | **STORAGE SIZE** | **VALID SAMPLE DATA** | **INVALID SAMPLE DATA** | |
| String | Alphanumeric characters enclosed in quotation marks | 1 byte for each character in the string | "Todd Greene" "Greeneville, SC" "The rain in Spain stays mainly on the plain" | There are no invalid strings. Anything you can type on the keyboard can be stored in a String variable. | |
| Integer | Whole numbers in the range of –32,768 to 32,767 (Commas are included here only for clarity. Integer variables cannot contain commas.) | 2 bytes | 56792 -899 | 50,000 (too large) 32,500 (contains a comma) 56.78 (contains a decimal) | |
| Long Integer | Whole numbers in the range of –2,147,483,648 to 2,147, 483,647 (Commas are included here only for clarity. Long Integer variables cannot contain commas.) | 4 bytes | 567 -2000000 | 200,000,000 (contains comas) 200000.85 (contains a decimal) | |
| Single | Numbers containing decimals, with a maximum of six decimal places | 4 bytes | 3.876 -0.876 | 8.8976345 (too many decimals) 8.897.634 (two decimal points) 8,876.89 (contains commas) | |

When defining a variable, you should consider carefully what that variable will be used for and then select a data type that is appropriate for its use. If you choose the wrong data type, the data entered by the user might be considered invalid, causing the program to display an error message. For example, suppose you need a variable to store telephone numbers. Upon first consideration, you might think Integer is the appropriate data type because the telephone number is numeric. In fact, however, Integer is not the appropriate choice. To understand why, consider two common formats for a telephone number: (909) 555-1234 and 909-555-1234.

Both formats contain other characters besides numbers; the first contains parentheses and a hyphen, and the second contains two hyphens. Now suppose you write program statements that retrieve a telephone number from a text box and store the telephone number in a variable that has been assigned the Integer data type. This would yield an error, because the non-numeric characters in a telephone number make it invalid data for an Integer variable.

Developers commonly use the **numeric data types** (e.g., Integer, Long Integer, and Single) only when the variable will be used within calculations. If the data will *not* be used in calculations, then you should use the String data type (or one of the other VBA data types that can accommodate non-numeric characters). Telephone numbers, for example, are best stored as String variables. The String data type will allow the program to store the parenthesis and the hyphens commonly used in telephone numbers. Because you would never write a program that uses a telephone number in a calculation, there's no need to use one of the numeric data types to store a telephone number.

If, on the other hand, you want to store a person's age (which is often used in calculations), you would probably choose Integer as the data type. The integer data type allows for whole numbers only. Since a person's age is usually represented as a whole number, Integer would be an appropriate choice. However, if your program requires more precise age values, you might want to include a decimal. For example, you might want to indicate that a person is 37.5—meaning 37 and a half years old. Or you might want to indicate that a person is 3.75—meaning 3 years and 9 months old. If your program requires this kind of precision, then you will need to have the ability to store decimals, in which case you would choose the Single data type rather than the Integer data type. In any case, you would not want to use the String data type, because then the age data could not be used in calculations.

For further information on data types not listed in Figure 3-4, start Help in any VBA IDE and read the information on "Declaring Variables." Also view the "Data Type Summary" for a complete list of data types. Some of these other data types will be introduced later in this text.

## Naming a Variable

When naming variables, you should follow some basic rules, which are used widely by all VBA developers. According to these rules, the first three characters of a variable name should consist of a prefix indicating the variable's data type. For example, in the variable name `strEmployeeName`, the first three characters, `str`, indicate the string data type. It is customary to follow the prefix with a descriptive name that documents how the variable will be used. In the variable name `strEmployeeName`, the text after the prefix (`EmployeeName`) indicates that the variable will be used to store an employee's name as a string. The name of the variable can be up to 255 characters in length, so you can provide as long a name as is necessary to describe the variable's use in the program. Note, however, that spaces and some special characters are *not* allowed in variable names. By convention, when the name consists of more than one word, the beginning of each word should be in upper case (as in `EmployeeName`).

The following list summarizes the rules you should follow when naming variables in your VBA programs:

- The first three characters of a variable should consist of a prefix indicating the variable's data type.
- Follow the prefix with a descriptive name that documents how the variable will be used.
- The name of the variable can be up to 255 characters in length.

The following characters are *not* allowed in a variable name: space, period, !, @, &, $, #

Figure 3-5 lists some commonly used prefixes and naming examples for the data types listed earlier in Figure 3-4. The names used in Figure 3-5 are very descriptive; just by looking at the variable name, you should have a pretty good idea of what will be stored in that variable.

**Figure 3-5**    COMMONLY USED VARIABLE PREFIXES

| DATA TYPE | PREFIX | NAME EXAMPLES |
|---|---|---|
| String | str | strName<br>strTelephoneNumber<br>strAddress |
| Integer | int | intHoursWorked<br><br>intAge<br>intStatus |
| Long | lng | lngSales<br>lngProfit |
| Single | sng | sngRateOfPay<br>sngSalary |

Figure 3-6 provides some examples of valid and invalid variable names as used within sample Dim statements.

**Figure 3-6**    VALID AND INVALID VARIABLE NAMES IN DIM STATEMENTS

| VALID DECLARATION | INVALID OR POOR DECLARATION | EXPLANATION OF INVALID OR POOR EXAMPLE |
|---|---|---|
| Dim strEmployeeName As String | Dim Employee Name As String | Variable name (Employee Name) contains a space |
| Dim strEmployeeName As String | Dim stremployeename As String | Variable name (stremployeename) is not capitalized correctly |
| Dim sngHoursWorked As Single | Dim sng HoursWorked As String | Variable name (sng HoursWorked) contains a space |
| Dim sngRateOfPay As Single | Dim sngRate.Of.Pay As Single | Variable name (sngRate.Of.Pay) contains a period |
| Dim sngSalary As Single | Dim sngS As Single | The example is not technically invalid. However, it is poor practice to assign a variable such non-descriptive name. |

## Preventing Undeclared Variables with `Option Explicit`

VBA does not require that every variable be declared. You can actually use a variable that has not been declared, and VBA will assign a data type to it. However, most developers agree that it is necessary to declare variables, select an appropriate data type, and use a descriptive variable name. Following good declaration practices will make your code easier to read. The `Dim` statement (or one of the other variable declaration statements discussed later in this text) will serve as a reminder of your original intent within the program.

As you begin to create complicated programs, however, it is sometimes easy to forget to declare a variable before you actually use it in your code. Thus, most programmers include a special statement, known as the `Option Explicit`, which prevents the use of variables that have not yet been declared. Once you have included an `Option Explicit` statement in your code, VBA requires you to declare all variables. If you try to use a variable in your code that has not been declared, VBA will display an error message in order to remind you to declare that variable.

In order to ensure that you always include an `Option Explicit` statement, you can configure the VBA IDE to add the `Option Explicit` statement to the top of every code module. This is a good practice for all developers. Because you have a separate VBA IDE for each of the Office applications, you will need to configure the VBA IDE for each application separately.

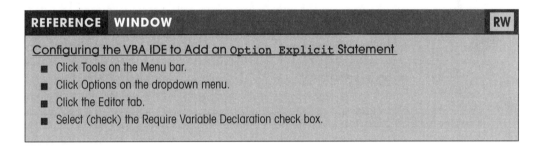

**REFERENCE WINDOW**                                                                      **RW**

Configuring the VBA IDE to Add an `Option Explicit` Statement
- Click Tools on the Menu bar.
- Click Options on the dropdown menu.
- Click the Editor tab.
- Select (check) the Require Variable Declaration check box.

You will now configure the Excel VBA IDE to add the `Option Explicit` statement to all new code modules. Then, you will repeat the steps for the other Office applications.

*To configure the Excel VBA IDE to add the `Option Explicit` statement to all modules:*

1. Verify that the VBA IDE for Excel is displayed on your screen.

2. Click **Tools** on the menu bar and then click **Options**.

3. If necessary, click the **Editor** tab to select it.

4. If necessary, click the **Require Variable Declaration** check box to select it. Compare your screen with Figure 3-7.

| Figure 3-7 | EDITOR TAB IN OPTIONS DIALOG BOX |
| --- | --- |

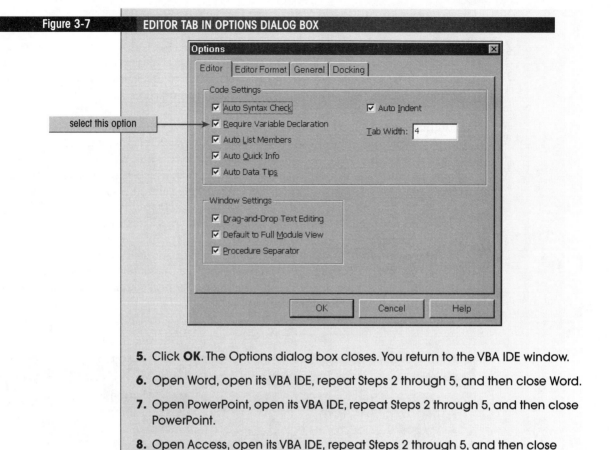

5. Click **OK**. The Options dialog box closes. You return to the VBA IDE window.

6. Open Word, open its VBA IDE, repeat Steps 2 through 5, and then close Word.

7. Open PowerPoint, open its VBA IDE, repeat Steps 2 through 5, and then close PowerPoint.

8. Open Access, open its VBA IDE, repeat Steps 2 through 5, and then close Access. You return to the Excel VBA IDE.

Now that you have set up the VBA IDE for the various Microsoft Office applications to require the declaration of variables, you will see an error message if you try to use a variable that has not yet been declared.

# Assigning **Values with an Assignment Statement**

Using a variable's name within a program statement is known as **referring** to the variable. For instance, you might write a program statement that multiplied a variable named sngHoursWorked by an hourly wage of, say, $12.00. That program statement would then refer to the variable sngHoursWorked. When you use a variable in a program statement, you are actually referring to the value stored in the variable—that is, to the value assigned to the variable. But how do you assign a specific value to a variable in the first place?

For instance, suppose you have created an interface that requires the user to enter a number in a text box named txtHoursWorked. Now suppose that your next job is to write a program statement that will take the value entered by the user in the text box and assign it to the variable named sngHoursWorked. To do this, you need to use an assignment **statement,** which is a special kind of program statement that assigns a single value to a variable. Assignment statements are also used to assign property values to objects.

The syntax of the assignment statement is explained below. Note that, within the syntax, the variable or property to which you want to assign a value is known as the **target.** The value to be assigned is known as the **expression.**

| **Syntax** | `target = expression` |
|---|---|
| **Explanation** | An assignment statement assigns a value to the target. The target can be a variable or an object's property. An expression can be almost anything that results in a single value. The expression must result in a value that has the same data type as the target. Often, expressions consist of calculations involving other variables. |
| **Examples with Variables** | `sngHoursWorked = 39.5`<br>`sngRateOfPay = 10.85`<br>`sngSalary = sngHoursWorked * sngRateOfPay`<br>`strEmployeeName = "Smith, Robert"` |
| **Examples with Properties** | `txtName.Text = "Smith, Robert"`<br>`frmWages.Caption = "Salary Calculator"` |

An assignment statement assigns a single value to the variable or property. In its simplest form then, the expression itself is a single value such as 39.5 (in the first example) or 10.85 (in the second). However, an expression can also be a mathematical expression as you see in the third example, which multiplies one variable (`sngHoursWorked`) by another (`sngRateOfPay`) to calculate the value that will be assigned to the variable named `sngSalary`. In this case, the mathematical expression must evaluate to a single value—that is, after all the calculations specified in the expression are performed, the result should be a single value. A very simple way of saying this is that whatever is on the right of the equal sign must first be evaluated to a single value; then that single value is stored in the variable.

Take a closer look at the third example above (`sngSalary = sngHoursWorked * sngRateOfPay`), which involves one variable multiplied by another. To be more precise, the expression takes the value assigned to one variable (`sngHoursWorked`) and multiples it by the value assigned to another variable (`sngRateOfPay`). Before you could actually use this third example in a program, you would have to write the two example assignment statements that assign values to the variables `sngHoursWorked` and `sngRateOfPay`. Suppose, for example that the value 39.5 was assigned to the variable `sngHoursWorked` and that the value 10.85 was assigned to the variable `sngRateOfPay`. Then the assignment statement `sngSalary = sngHoursWorked * sngRateOfPay` actually says the following: Take the value of `sngHoursWorked` (that is, 39.5) and multiply it by the value of `sngRateOfPay` (that is, 10.85) and assign the value of that calculation to the variable `sngSalary`. After the assignment statement had been processed, the value of `sngSalary` would be 428.575.

Figure 3-7 also includes examples of assigning values to properties. In the first example, the value "Smith, Robert" is assigned to the Text property of a text box control called `txtName`. The second example assigns "Salary Calculator" to the Caption property of the form named `frmWages`.

## Understanding Mathematical Expressions and Precedence

The expressions used in assignment statements can be simple or complicated, depending on the requirements of the program. In any case, VBA evaluates, or processes, expressions following the same basic rules you learned when studying algebra. To begin with, expressions often include mathematical operators, such as the plus sign (+) or the subtraction sign (-). Note that in programming, the asterisk (*) is used to indicate multiplication. The slash mark (/) indicates division.

When two or more operators are included in an expression, they are processed according to the rules governing the **order of precedence** (some programmers might use the term "order of operators" instead). The operator with the highest precedence is evaluated first, followed by the operator with the next highest precedence, and so on. Operators on the same level of precedence are evaluated from left to right. Parentheses can be used to override the order of precedence; any part of the expression enclosed in parentheses is evaluated first. (You'll learn more about the use of parentheses in the next section.)

Figure 3-8 summarizes the mathematical operators and their order of precedence in VBA.

| Figure 3-8 | MATHEMATICAL OPERATORS AND ORDER OF PRECEDENCE | | | |
|---|---|---|---|---|
| LEVEL | OPERATOR (SYMBOL) | DESCRIPTION | EXAMPLE | RESULT |
| 1 | ^ | Exponentiation. The number to the left of the ^ is raised to the power of the number following the ^. | 3 ^ 3 | 27 |
| 2 | * | Multiplication. The number to the left of the * is multiplied by the number to the right of the *. | 5 * 10 | 50 |
| 2 | / | Division. The number to the left of the / is divided by the number to the right of the /. | 20 / 6 | 3.33... |
| 3 | \ | Integer division. Same as division, only the result is always an integer (and not a decimal). | 10 \ 3 | 3 |
| 4 | Mod | Modulus arithmetic. Returns the remainder portion of a division operation. | 8 Mod 5 | 3 |
| 5 | + | Addition | 5 + 6 | 11 |
| 5 | – | Subtraction | 10-5 | 5 |

While you will be working with a very simple expression in this tutorial, keep in mind that expressions can become very complicated. In these more elaborate expressions, the use of parentheses can be critical. You'll learn more about this in the next section.

## Following the Order of Precedence in an Expression

Expressions can be long and include various combinations of operators. As you build such an expression, you must keep the order of precedence in mind. You can always use parentheses to override the order of precedence or to simply make the expression easier to read. For example, Figure 3-9 shows two expressions that yield two entirely different results. Assume that the variable intX equals 5, intY equals 3, and intZ equals 4.

| Figure 3-9 | EVALUATING EXPRESSIONS WHEN INTX=5, INTY=3, AND INTZ=4 |
|---|---|
| EXPRESSION | RESULT |
| intX + intY + intZ / 3 | 9.33 |
| (intX + intY + intZ) / 3 | 4 |

In the first expression, the order of precedence dictates that intZ be divided by 3 first; the result is then added to the value of intX and intY. In the second expression, the order of precedence is overridden by the parentheses; that is, the first three variables are summed, and then the result is divided by 3. These expressions are still relatively simple expressions, yet the use of parentheses created completely different results.

Figure 3-10 graphically illustrates the calculation of a more complicated expression. Pay careful attention to the order of precedence, as it is critical to the outcome. Again, assume that `intX=5`, `intY=3`, and `intZ=4`.

| Figure 3-10 | ORDER OF PRECEDENCE IN A CALCULATION |
| --- | --- |

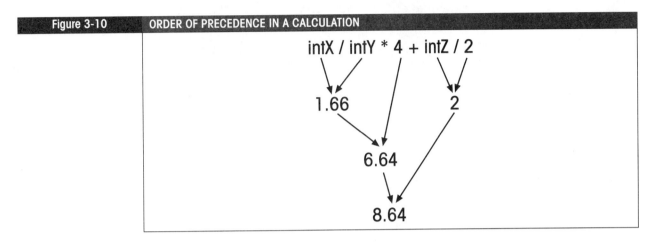

Figure 3-11 provides another illustration of the expression shown in Figure 3-10, except that parentheses have been added to the expression. As you can see, the parentheses affect the outcome by altering the order of calculation. When creating expressions, you must be mindful of the order of precedence to ensure that you get the results that you are expecting.

| Figure 3-11 | ORDER OF PRECEDENCE WITH PARENTHESES |
| --- | --- |

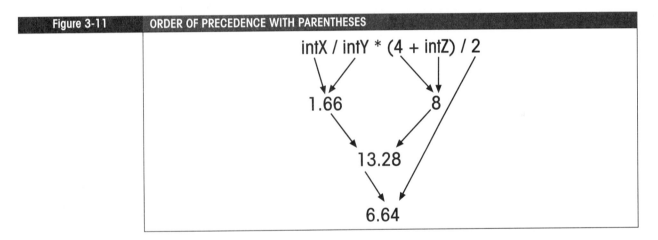

## Previewing the Salary Calculator Code

At this point, you should have a basic understanding of how variables and assignment statements work in VBA. Now you are ready to put that knowledge to work in the Salary Calculator program. Gene explains that your job, as the developer, is to write statements that: 1) declare the variables that will be used in the calculations; 2) retrieve the values entered by the user on the UserForm and store them in the appropriate variables; 3) calculate the salary; and 4) display the salary in the appropriate text box on the form. Before you actually type the necessary statements, Gene takes a moment to walk you through them, line by line.

First, you need to declare the variables. In this case, you need to declare three variables to be used in the calculation of the salary. The three declaration statements are as follows:

```
Dim sngHoursWorked As Single
Dim sngRateOfPay As Single
Dim sngSalary As Single
```

The first `Dim` statement declares a variable, `sngHoursWorked`, that will contain the number of hours the employee has worked. The second declares a variable, `sngRateOfPay`, that will contain the rate at which the employee is paid. Finally, the third declaration is for a variable, `sngSalary`, which will contain the results of calculating the salary. All of the variables have the single data type, which, as you learned earlier, is used for numbers containing decimals, with a maximum of six decimal places.

After declaring the variables, the next task within the program is to retrieve the values entered into the form by the user. The user will enter values into the `txtHours` text box and the `txtRate` text box, and then the program must assign those values to the appropriate variables. Whatever the user enters into a text box becomes the current value of that text box's **Text property**. So to retrieve those values, you need to write an assignment statement that assigns the Text property of the `txtHours` text box to the `sngHoursWorked` variable. Then, you need to write an assignment statement that assigns the Text property of the `txtRate` text box to the `sngRateOfPay` variable. This results in the following two assignment statements:

```
sngHoursWorked = txtHours.Text
sngRateOfPay = txtRate.Text
```

Next, you need to write a statement that assigns a value to the `sngSalary` variable. The expression portion of the `Assignment` statement (the part on the right of the equals sign) actually performs the salary calculation, as follows:

```
sngSalary = sngRateOfPay * sngHoursWorked.
```

Finally, you need to display the calculated salary in the `txtSalary` text box. In other words, you need to assign the value of the `sngSalary` variable to the Text property of the `txtSalary` text box, as follows:

```
txtSalary.Text = sngSalary
```

Now that you have previewed the code and understand what each line of code does, you are ready to enter the code into the Code window. Recall that you must enter the code in the event procedure that you want to trigger the code. In this case, you want this code to be triggered when the user clicks the Calculate button. So you will place the code in the Click event of the Calculate button.

## Entering the Code That Calculates the Salary

You are now ready to enter code into the Calculate button's Click event. When you are finished, Gene asks you to test the Calculate button to make sure you have entered the code correctly.

### To program the Calculate button:

1. Double-click the **Calculate** button on the form. The code module window opens with the cursor in the Calculate button's Click event, as shown in Figure 3-12.

**Figure 3-12**    **CODE MODULE WITH CURSOR IN THE CALCULATE BUTTON'S CLICK EVENT**

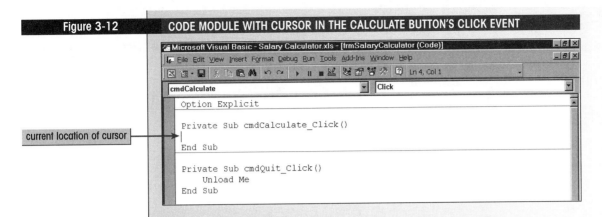

current location of cursor

2. Maximize the Code window.

3. Now type the code exactly as you see it below, indenting one tab stop below
   the opening `Private` Sub statement. Notice that each VBA statement is followed by a comment (on the same line) describing the statement, including
   line breaks. Type the comments just as they appear below, aligning them (when
   possible) on the same tab. Don't forget to include the apostrophes. Notice that
   some of the comments are broken into two lines. To type the second line of a
   two-line comment, you'll need to press Enter at the end of a line. Use the Tab key
   to align the cursor below the first line of the comment, type a second apostrophe, and then type the rest of the comment. Remember that the purpose of
   comments is to document the program so that you and others can understand
   the code later. When you finish typing the code, carefully read through the
   statements and the comments so that you understand what this program does.

```vba
Dim sngHoursWorked As Single      'declares a variable for Hours Worked
Dim sngRateOfPay As Single        'declares a variable for Rate of Pay
Dim sngSalary As Single           'declares a variable for Salary

sngHoursWorked = txtHours.Text    'assign the value of txtHours
                                  'to sngHoursWorked
sngRateOfPay = txtRate.Text       'assign the value of txtRate
                                  'to the sngRateOfPay

sngSalary = sngRateOfPay * sngHoursWorked 'calculates the salary

txtSalary.Text = sngSalary        'assign the value of sngSalary
                                  'to txtSalary
```

After you have typed the code, compare it to the code shown in Figure 3-13.

**Figure 3-13**    CODE FOR THE CALCULATE BUTTON ENTERED IN CODE WINDOW

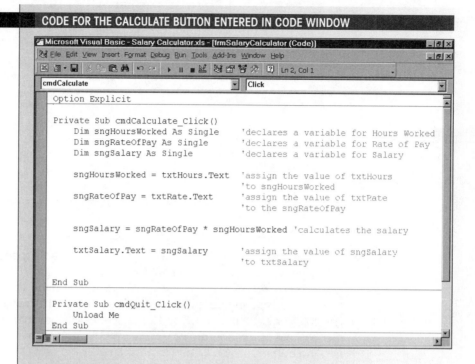

```
Microsoft Visual Basic - Salary Calculator.xls - [frmSalaryCalculator (Code)]
File  Edit  View  Insert  Format  Debug  Run  Tools  Add-Ins  Window  Help
                                                        Ln 2, Col 1

cmdCalculate                              Click

    Option Explicit

    Private Sub cmdCalculate_Click()
        Dim sngHoursWorked As Single      'declares a variable for Hours Worked
        Dim sngRateOfPay As Single        'declares a variable for Rate of Pay
        Dim sngSalary As Single           'declares a variable for Salary

        sngHoursWorked = txtHours.Text    'assign the value of txtHours
                                          'to sngHoursWorked
        sngRateOfPay = txtRate.Text        'assign the value of txtRate
                                          'to the sngRateOfPay

        sngSalary = sngRateOfPay * sngHoursWorked 'calculates the salary

        txtSalary.Text = sngSalary        'assign the value of sngSalary
                                          'to txtSalary

    End Sub

    Private Sub cmdQuit_Click()
        Unload Me
    End Sub
```

**4.** Check your code carefully for accuracy. Make any necessary corrections.

**5.** Save your work.

**6.** With the cursor located anywhere in the **cmdCalculate_Click** procedure, run the program.

TROUBLE? If you see an error message, your code contains a mistake. Click OK and return to the Code window. Make any necessary corrections and run the program again.

**7.** Verify that the cursor is displayed in the Hours Worked text box, type **39.5,** press **Tab**, type **10.85** in the Rate of Pay text box, and then click the **Calculate** button. The program calculates the salary and displays the result, 428.575, in the Salary text box, as shown in Figure 3-14.

**Figure 3-14**    FORM AFTER CLICKING CALCULATE BUTTON

```
Microsoft Excel - Salary Calculator
File  Edit  View  Insert  Format  Tools  Data  Window  Help

        A       B       C       D       E       F       G       H       I
1
2
3          Potters House Salary Calculator
4
5
6          Hours Worked:   39.5
7
8          Rate of Pay:    10.85
9
10         Salary:         428.575  ◄──────────────  salary has been
11                                                   calculated
12         Calculate        Quit
13
14
15
```

> TROUBLE? If your results are incorrect, click Quit in the form, review the code you typed, make any necessary changes, and run the program again.
>
> **8.** Test the program again by entering any numbers you choose and then clicking the Calculate button.
>
> **9.** Click the **Quit** button on the form. You return to the VBA IDE.

As you just saw, the form now receives data from the user and uses that data to calculate the salary. However, the salary is displayed with three decimal places, rather than as currency, which would be more appropriate. In the next section you will learn how to use a function to change the way values are displayed on the screen at runtime.

# Using Functions in VBA

When you worked in Excel worksheets, you used several functions such as Sum, Average, Min, and Max. These functions work by receiving one or more values and then producing a result. For example, suppose you entered the function SUM(A1:F10) in cell F11. As a result, Excel would add the values in cells A1 through F10 and then display the result of this calculation in the cell containing the function (that is, cell F11). Figure 3-15 graphically illustrates how the function SUM produces a single result.

| Figure 3-15 | THE EXCEL SUM FUNCTION |
|---|---|

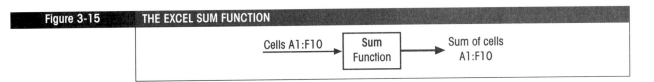

Functions work similarly in VBA. Throughout this book you will encounter a wide variety of functions available in VBA, all of which work in the same way: they take one or more values and produce a result. The next section introduces you to a very useful example, the Format function.

## Formatting a Value with the Format Function

In Excel, you can format a value in a cell by using a formatting button on the toolbar or a formatting command on the menu bar. For example, you might add boldface to a value displayed in a cell, or display it with fewer decimal places. In programming, you also need to apply various kinds of formatting, but rather than formatting a value in a cell, you need to format input entered by the user or output produced by the program.

The term **input** (or **user input**) refers to the values or text that the user types in a text box. The term **output** (or **program output**) refers to the result of one or more statements displayed either on the screen or on a printed page. For example, in the Salary Calculator program, the salary amount, which is calculated by an assignment statement, is considered output. Once you have ensured that your statements produce the output you want (in this case, the salary figure), and once you have ensured that your statements allow the user to type the input you want (in this case, the hours worked and the rate of pay), you can turn your attention to the way the output and input are displayed—that is, to the way it appears on the screen at runtime. You do this by applying some kind of formatting.

Just as in Excel, the term **formatting** in VBA refers to how a value or string appears on the screen. Also, as in Excel, the formatting of a value in VBA does not affect the number that is actually used in calculations. For example, you might format a value to display only two decimal places on the screen, when in fact the actual value contains seven decimal places.

In VBA, you format program output or user input by using the **Format function**, which converts a numeric value into a specified format. Figure 3-16 illustrates how the Format function works.

**Figure 3-16** · **THE VBA FORMAT FUNCTION**

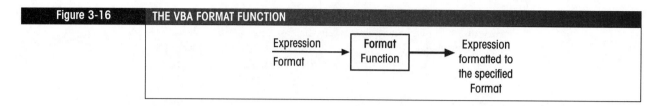

| Syntax | `Format(Expression, Format)` |
|---|---|
| Explanation | **Expression** can be a variable, a value, or any valid arithmetic expression.<br>**Format** is a string that describes how you want the value formatted. VBA offers several formatting options, but for now, you only need to be concerned with the currency format. |
| Example | `txtSalary.Text = Format(sngSalary, "currency")` |

In the example above, the Format function (`Format(sngSalary, "Currency")`) is located to the right of the equals sign. In this case, the function will format the value assigned to the variable `sngSalary` as currency (including the dollar sign, a decimal point, and commas). The complete example (including the part to the left of the equals sign) is an assignment statement that assigns the formatted value (that is, the result of the Format function) as the Text property of the text box named `txtSalary`.

This example illustrates an important point about functions—a function always returns a single value. As you learned earlier, an assignment statement is used to assign a value (on the right of the equals sign) to a variable or property (on the left of the equals sign). When a function appears on the right side of the equals sign, this means that the function will perform its work and return its single value to the variable or property on the left side of the equals sign. In the example above, the Format function formats a value as currency; the formatted value is then assigned to the Text property of the `txtSalary` text box.

## Adding the Format Function to the Code

Now that you understand how the Format function works, you are ready to add it to the program code. You want to use the Format function to change the way the salary amount is displayed in the Salary text box at runtime.

*To format the salary value as currency:*

**1.** Make sure the cursor is positioned in the Calculate button's Click event.

**2.** Locate the following statement, which assigns the salary value to the Text property of the `txtSalary` text box: `txtSalary.Text=sngSalary`.

**3.** Edit the statement so that it includes the Format function , as follows:

```
txtSalary.Text = Format(sngSalary, "currency")
```

TROUBLE? Don't be concerned if the comments for this line scroll out of view.

**4.** Save your work

**5.** Run the program.

**6.** Enter **45.75** for the hours worked and **15.75** for the rate of pay.

**7.** Click the **Calculate** button. The formatted salary ($720.56) appears as in Figure 3-17.

| Figure 3-17 | CALCULATED AND FORMATTED SALARY |
|---|---|

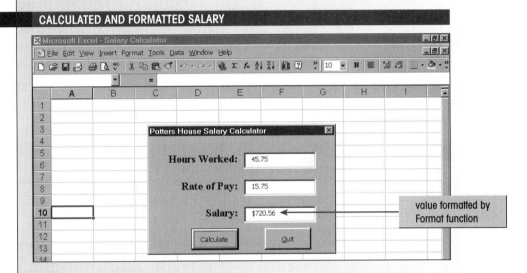

**8.** Test the form a few times using your own data, and observe the format of the salary each time.

**9.** Click the **Quit** button on the form.

## Formatting User Input

Gene is happy with the way you used the Format function to format the program's output. Next, he explains that you can also use the Format function to format user input—that is, to change the way data entered by the user is displayed in the form. For example, in the Salary Calculator program, it makes sense to format the value entered into the Rate of Pay text box as currency. You could write a statement that would apply this formatting as soon as the user entered the value, but that would involve more complications than you are prepared for at this point. To simplify matters, Gene wants to show you how to write a statement that will format the value displayed in the Rate of Pay text box at the same time that the salary is calculated and formatted (that is, after the user clicks the Calculate button)

This requires writing an entirely new statement, rather than simply modifying an existing one, as you did in the last section. To understand what the necessary statement should consist of, take a moment to recall the relationship between a text box and its Text property. Simply put, the value displayed within a text box becomes the value of the text box's Text property. In other words, whatever value the user enters in the `txtRate` text box automatically *becomes* the value of the text box's Text property. So to format the value displayed in the text box, you really need to format the text box's Text property. Essentially, then, you need to create an assignment statement that assigns the Text property of the `txtRate` text box (that is, `txtRate.Text`) to a formatted version of itself. Figure 3-18 illustrates this process.

| Figure 3-18 | FORMATTING THE TXTRATE VALUE AS CURRENCY |
| --- | --- |

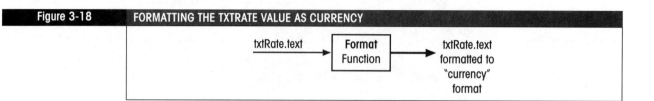

In the complete statement, `txtRate` appears on both sides of the equals sign, as follows:

```
txtRate.Text = Format(txtRate.Text, "currency")
```

This statement will format the contents of the `txtRate` text box (that is, `txtRate.Text`) as currency, and then store the results of the function in the Text property of the `txtRate` text box. You will enter this statement into the Code window now.

### To format the user input displayed in the Rate of Pay text box:

1. In the `cmdCalculate_Click` procedure, click the blank line just above the `End Sub` statement. Note that this is just below the following statement, which formats the salary amount: `txtSalary.Text = Format(sngSalary, "currency")`.

2. Type this statement:

```
txtRate.Text = Format(txtRate.Text, "currency")
```

3. Your code should now look like Figure 3-19.

| Figure 3-19 | CODE WINDOW WITH NEW STATEMENT ADDED |
| --- | --- |

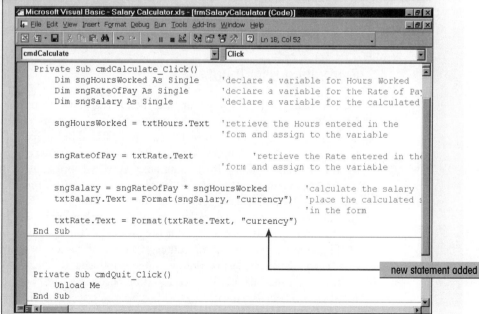

4. Save your work and run the program.

5. Enter **40** for the number of hours worked and **18.65** for the rate of pay.

6. Click the **Calculate** button. Compare your results to Figure 3-20, noting that the rate of pay is now formatted with a dollar sign.

| Figure 3-20 | SALARY CALCULATOR FORM |

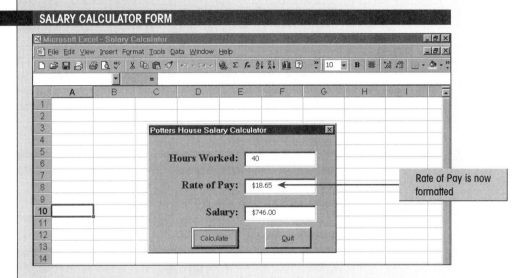

7. Click the **Quit** button on the form.

8. If you are going to take a break before the next session, switch back to the Excel workbook window and close the workbook. If asked if you want to save the workbook, click Yes.

This completes your work with the Format function. Gene congratulates you on mastering the concept of VBA functions, and is pleased with the way the two examples of the Format function work within the Salary Calculator program. But before you move on to other topics, he wants you to take a moment to learn about an important distinction within VBA—the difference between a function and sub procedure.

## Distinguishing **Between Sub Procedures and Functions**

As you learned in Tutorial 1, a procedure is a collection of statements. You can use two kinds of procedures in VBA—functions and sub procedures (sometimes called subroutines). The difference between the two is that the sub procedure performs a series of statements and might or might not return a value. A **function**, on the other hand, performs a series of statements and returns a single value.

In Tutorial 1 and Tutorial 2 you entered VBA code into the Code window between the `Private Sub` and `End Sub` statements. You learned to think of these two statements as the beginning and the end of a procedure. But in fact the `Private Sub` statement does more work than simply mark the beginning of a procedure. This statement actually states which of the two common types of procedures is being defined—specifically, a sub procedure.

In addition to creating your own procedures by typing the individual steps, you can use one of VBA's intrinsic functions, such as the Format function that you used earlier in this tutorial. You can think of an **intrinsic function** as a procedure that is provided along with VBA. The steps are essentially *built in* to VBA, which is why an intrinsic function is sometimes called a **built-in function**. You can incorporate intrinsic functions within a sub procedure, just as you did earlier in the Salary Calculator program. To use an intrinsic function, you must type the function statement, taking care to use its predefined syntax. (For example, in the Salary Calculator program, you used the following syntax for the Format function: `Format(Expression, Format)syntax`.) As you can see, then, intrinsic functions are useful programming shortcuts; they make it unnecessary to type all the steps involved in producing the function's output, because VBA already knows those steps and will perform them automatically as a result of the single function statement.

Although you were not aware of it, you have already used several intrinsic functions within the code you wrote in the previous two tutorials. For example, you used the **InputBox** function, which is a function that provides an easy way to retrieve a single item of data from the user of the program. The statement you used previously is as follows:

```
strNewData = InputBox("Enter your name")
```

The function displays a form with a single text box and the prompt specified in the function statement (in this case the prompt is "Enter your name:"). Like any function, the InputBox function produces a result, which in this case is the text or value entered by the user in the text box. In this example, the InputBox function is incorporated into an assignment statement. Essentially, this statement says "Take the result of the InputBox function and assign it to the variable named `strNewData`."

You might wonder why the developers of the VBA language would have created the intrinsic function InputBox in the first place. The reason is that programs often need to retrieve a single item of data from the user. If it were not for the intrinsic function InputBox, you would need to create a form to receive the data from the user and then write code to accept the data and place it in a variable. Since this is such a common task, the developers of VBA created the InputBox function as a handy tool for you to use whenever you need it.

While VBA provides a rich set of intrinsic functions, often a developer will want to create a new function to perform an action specific to the application currently being developed. Thus, VBA also allows you to create your own functions. Throughout the text you will be developing both sub procedures and functions. For now, the important difference is that a function returns a single value, whereas, the sub procedure does not necessarily return a value.

## Session 3.1 QUICK CHECK

1. Name the four data types described in this tutorial.

   a. _____

   b. _____

   c. _____

   d. _____

2. The _____ statement declares a variable and assigns it a _____ and a _____.

3. The _____ function will alter the way a value is displayed on the screen at runtime. For instance, it might display a value as currency.

4. The _____ statement prevents the use of undeclared variables.

**5.** For the following data items, name the appropriate data type and provide an appropriate name for the variable:

| DATA ITEM | DATA TYPE | VARIABLE NAME (INCLUDING THE PREFIX) |
| --- | --- | --- |
| telephone number | | |
| age | | |
| salary | | |
| hours worked | | |
| number of members in a household | | |
| average grade | | |

**6.** Briefly explain the difference between a sub procedure and a function.

## SESSION 3.2

In this session you will learn about the importance of validating data and be introduced to the three basic control structures of programming (sequence, selection, and repetition). You will review the control structure you have already used, which is the selection control structure. You will then learn to implement one kind of selection control structure in VBA by creating an If...Then...Else statement. Finally, you will learn to use the tools available for finding errors in (debugging) your programs.

# Validating Data

You've done a lot of work on the Salary Calculator program. It can now calculate a salary and display values in a currency format. Your next job, Gene explains, is to write some statements that will verify that the user has typed valid data in the txtHours and txtRate text boxes. In other words, you need to write statements that can check, or **validate**, the data, before the program uses the data in any calculations.

When creating a program that receives numeric values from the user, it is good practice to verify that the data provided by the user is a valid numeric value. This prevents the program from attempting to use data that could produce inaccurate results or possibly an error message that causes your program to stop running. For example, you wouldn't want the Salary Calculator program to attempt to use the value "ABC" in its calculation, because this would result in an inaccurate salary calculation. Seasoned programmers know how to anticipate the possibility that the user might attempt to enter invalid data, by including statements that validate the data, before actually using it in a calculation. Anticipating and attempting to prevent errors in this way is known as **defensive programming**.

So what kind of data validation is required in the Salary Calculator program? Gene explains that Potters House employees can work up to 60 hours in any given week. Thus, you can assume that if a user enters a value greater than 60 in the txtHours text box, then the value is invalid. Therefore, Gene would like you to add statements that will ensure that a valid value is entered into the txtHours text box. If the value is greater than 60, then your program should display a message that tells the user that an invalid value has been entered. If, however, the value is valid, the program should simply calculate the salary.

In order to validate data, a program needs to make some decisions. That is, it requires some means of evaluating a piece of data and then determining whether or not it is valid. When your program needs to make decisions like this, you need to use a special arrangement of statements, known as a control structure. The next section introduces you to the three basic control structures, which are used in all programming languages.

## Introducing the Three Basic Control Structures

Visual Basic for Applications is only one of the many programming languages you could use to develop applications. All of these programming languages make use of control structures (often referred to as **programming constructs**) to govern the order in which program statements are executed. A **control structure** is simply a logical arrangement of statements. There are three basic control structures used in programming: sequence, selection, and repetition.

Briefly, the **Sequence control structure** processes one statement after another. The **Selection control structure** "decides" between two alternatives based on the results of a condition. (This type of structure is sometimes called a **Decision control structure**.) If the condition in a Selection control structure is true, one set of statements is executed; if the condition is false, another set of statements is executed. Finally, the **Repetition control structure** continually repeats a series of statements based on the value of a particular condition. (Note that a Repetition control structure is sometimes referred to as a **loop**.) You will learn about the Sequence and Selection control structures, in detail, in this tutorial. The Repetition control structure will be explained in Tutorial 4.

Figure 3-21 illustrates these three control structures.

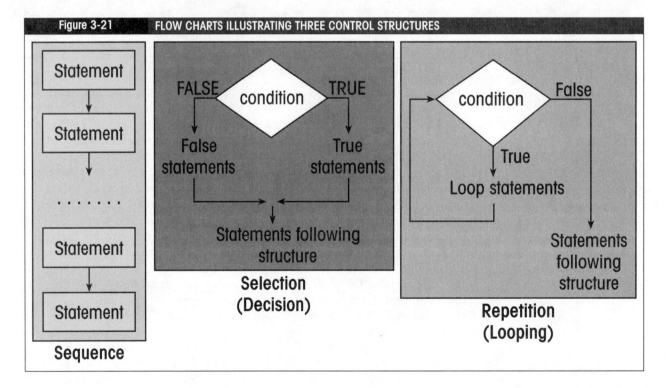

**Figure 3-21   FLOW CHARTS ILLUSTRATING THREE CONTROL STRUCTURES**

Diagrams like those in Figure 3-21 are called **flowcharts.** Flowcharts are often used in programming to illustrate the order in which statements are processed. As you look at the flowcharts, follow the arrows to see which statement will be processed next. Recall that the arrows in a flowchart illustrate the **flow of control**, which is to say the order in which statements are processed.

# Understanding the Sequence Control Structure

You have already used the Sequence control structure. As you can see in Figure 3-21, in a Sequence control structure, each statement is processed after the one before it, in the order they appear in the Code window. All the VBA code that you have entered so far takes the form of a Sequence control structure. For example, when executing the code you wrote for the salary calculator program, the computer begins by executing the first statement, then the next, then the next, and so on until the statements are complete.

When you want the statements to be executed one right after the other, you should use a Sequence control structure. When you need to execute one set of statements in one situation, and another set of statements in a different situation, you need to use a Selection control structure, as described in the next section.

# Understanding Selection Control Structures

The Selection control structure is used when a program needs to choose between multiple sets of statements. There are two different kinds of selection control structures—the `If...Then...Else` statement, and the `Select Case` statement. The following section focuses on the `If...Then...Else` statement. You will learn about the `Select Case` statement in Tutorial 6.

## Building an `If...Then...Else` Statement

Within an `If...Then...Else` statement, the choice of which statements to execute depends on the value of the **condition**. The condition is a special expression, known as a **Boolean expression**, which can only evaluate to true or false.

You make real-world selections involving Boolean expressions every day of your life. For example:

> **If** Today is a weekday **then**
> > Go to school
>
> **Otherwise**
> > Stay home

> **If** you are on a diet **then**
> > order a lowfat meal
>
> **Otherwise**
> > order a hamburger and fries

> **If** it is raining **then**
> > Carry an umbrella
> > Wear galoshes
>
> **Otherwise**
> > Wear sandals

Looking at the selection flowchart in Figure 3-21, you can see that if the result of the condition is true, then the flow of control goes down the right side of the flowchart, but if the condition is false, the flow of control goes down the left side of the flowchart. In other words, *if* the condition is true, *then* the set of statements on the right are executed; *otherwise* (if the condition is false), the statements on the left are executed. Notice that only one or the other set of statements is executed, never both. Also, notice the use of italics on the words *if*, *then*, and *otherwise*. These three words are crucial in an `If...Then...Else` statement.

An `If...Then...Else` statement is designed to make similar selections. For example, you know that at Potters House Gallery, employees cannot work more than 60 hours a week. This means you need to write statements that evaluate the value entered in the `txtHours` text box and determine if it falls in the appropriate range. *If* the value is less than or equal to 60, *then* the program should calculate the salary; *otherwise* (if the value is greater than 60), the program should display a message indicating that an invalid value was entered. The flowchart for this example is shown in Figure 3-22.

| Figure 3-22 | FLOWCHART FOR SALARY CALCULATION |
| --- | --- |

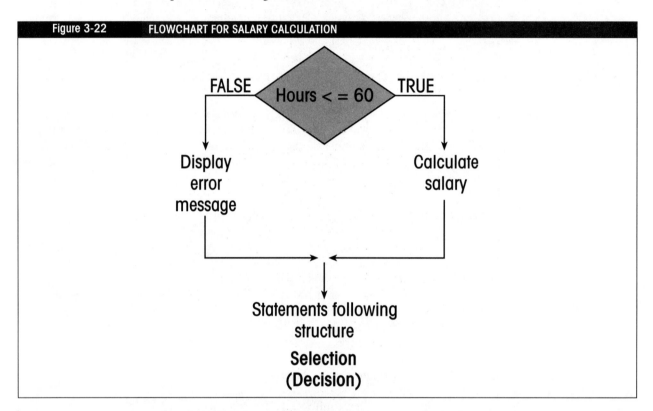

In the preceding explanations, the words *if*, *then*, and *otherwise* were italicized to draw your attention to them within the control structure. In programming, `If...Then...Else` statements are built around a variation of these three words: if, then, and else. (Note that "else" is a shorthand way of saying "otherwise.") The syntax of the `If...Then...Else` statement is explained below.

| Syntax | If condition **Then**<br>        True Statements<br>**Else**<br>**End If** False Statements |
|---|---|
| Explanation | The **If** statement checks the condition. If the result is true then the True statements are executed, otherwise the False statements are executed. The True portion of the structure can be one statement or many statements. Likewise, the False statements can be one statement or many statements. Notice the words End If at the end of the structure. This is a VBA syntax requirement. Not all programming languages require End If. |
| Example | IF sngHoursWorked <= 60 **Then**<br>        sngSalary = sngHoursWorked * sngRateOfPay<br>**Else**<br>        MsgBox ("Hours Worked must be 60 or less")<br>**End If** |

In this example, `sngHoursWorked` <= 60 is the Boolean expression. When it evaluates to true (that is, when the value of the `sngHoursWorked` variable is less than or equal to 60), the salary is calculated via an assignment statement. However, when the expression evaluates to false (that is, when the value of the `sngHoursWorked` variable is greater than 60) a statement containing the MsgBox function is executed. This function (which is explained in the next section) displays a message (in this case `"Hours Worked must be 60 or less"`) in a small dialog box.

The next section sets aside the discussion of Selection control structures momentarily in order to explain more about the MsgBox function. You will use the MsgBox function within the Salary Calculation Selection control structure, so you should take time to become familiar with it.

## Displaying a Message with the MsgBox Function

The **MsgBox function** is an intrinsic function that you can use to display a message to the user in a special form. The simplest version of this form contains both the message and an OK button. The user must click the OK button before the program will proceed, thus ensuring that the user has read the message. The syntax of the MsgBox function is explained below.

| Syntax | MsgBox(*prompt*[, *buttons*] [, *title*] [, *helpfile*, *context*]) |
|---|---|
| Explanation | Notice that the prompt (the message displayed in the message box) is required. If you do not enter a value for a button the message box will display the default button, which is the OK button. |
| Example | MsgBox("Hours worked must be 60 or less.") |

This example produces a small dialog box containing the message ("Hours worked must be 60 or less.") This dialog box will remain on the screen until the user clicks its OK button. All other processing is suspended until the user clicks the OK button.

## Using Comparison Operators in an `If...Then...Else` Statement

Now that you understand how to use the MsgBox function, you are ready to return to the main topic: Using an `If...Then...Else` statement. As you know, the "If" part of an `If...Then...Else` statement consists of a condition that evaluates either to true or false. If the condition is true, then the True statements are executed. If the condition is false, then the False statements will be executed. To create a condition you must use a comparison operator, which is a symbol used to indicate the relationship between two values. Figure 3-23 lists the comparison operators you can use to create a condition.

| Figure 3-23 | COMPARISON OPERATORS | |
| --- | --- | --- |
| **COMPARISON OPERATOR** | | **DESCRIPTION** |
| = | | Equal to |
| > | | Greater than |
| < | | Less than |
| >= | | Greater than or equal to |
| <= | | Less than or equal to |
| <> | | Not equal to |

A comparison operator can be used to compare two expressions, which might contain variables, values, and operators. For example, assume that a variable named `intGrade` has a value of 95, and a variable named `sngHoursWorked` has a value of 50. Some sample conditions and the resulting values for these variables are shown in Figure 3-24.

| Figure 3-24 | SAMPLE CONDITIONS | |
| --- | --- | --- |
| **SAMPLE CONDITION** | | **RESULT WHEN INTGRADE= 95 AND SNGHOURSWORKED= 50** |
| `intGrade > 80` | | True |
| `intGrade = 95` | | True |
| `sngHoursWorked > 65` | | False |
| `sngHoursWorked = intGrade` | | False |
| `sngHoursWorked <> 65` | | True |

## Using Multiple Comparison Operators in Compound Conditions

In some situations, you will need to create a condition involving two or more comparison operators. For example, you might want to determine if a value is between 10 and 15. In other words, you want to determine if the number is greater than or equal to 10 *and* if the number is less than or equal to 15. As you can see, this is actually two conditions. You join conditions, to make a **compound condition**, using special words called **logical operators**.

In the current example, the conditions are joined by the logical operator "and." You are also familiar with the logical operator "or." In everyday English, the difference between "or" and "and" is crucial. For example, if you say that "Bob *and* Mary are going to the store", you know that both Bob and Mary are going to the store. However if you say "Bob *or* Mary is going to the store," you know that either Bob or Mary will go to the store.

In programming, you can use logical operators to combine conditions into compound conditions. Figure 3-25 contains the three most widely used logical operators; it also provides an example of each and shows the result of the example. (In the examples, `intX = 5`, `intY=10`, and `intZ = 3`.) Like mathematical operators, logical operators are evaluated according to a specific order of precedence. The operators in Figure 3-25 are listed in their order of precedence, with NOT having the highest precedence, AND the next highest, and so on. Note also that in programming the logical operators are all uppercase.

| Figure 3-25 | LOGICAL OPERATORS | | |
| --- | --- | --- | --- |
| **LOGICAL OPERATOR** | **DESCRIPTION** | **EXAMPLES** (NOTE: INTX = 5, INTY=10, AND INTZ= 3) | **RESULT** |
| NOT | Reverses the condition, a process known as **logical negation**. If the condition results in true, the NOT operator makes it false. If the condition is false, the NOT operator makes it true. | `NOT (intX > intY)`<br>`NOT (intX < intY)`<br>`NOT (intZ = 3)` | True<br>False<br>False |
| AND | Combines two conditions through a process called **logical conjunction**. If both conditions are true, then the combined condition is true but if only one is true then the entire condition is false. | `intX > intY AND intX = 5`<br>`intY = intX AND intX > intZ`<br>`intX > intZ AND intY > intZ` | False<br>False<br>True |
| OR | Combines two conditions through a process called **logical disjunction**. If one or the other of the conditions is true then the entire condition is true. | `intX > intY OR intX = 5`<br>`intY = intX OR intX > intZ`<br>`intX > intZ OR intY > intZ`<br>`intX = 8 OR intX < intZ` | True<br>True<br>True<br>False |
| | The logical operators can be combined to develop quite complicated compound conditions. | `intX > intY Or intX = 5 AND`<br>`intY = 10 AND NOT intX = 5` | False |

# Adding an If...Then...Else Statement to the Code

Now that you are familiar with all the elements of an `If...Then...Else` statement, you are ready to add one to the Salary Calculator application.  Recall that Figure 3-22 presented a flowchart for the data validation statements in the Salary Calculator program. The statements include the following condition: Hours<=60. The program should check to see if the value entered for hours worked is less then or equal to 60; in other words, it should check to see if the condition is true. *If* the condition is true, *then* the program will calculate the salary. *Otherwise*, if it is not true, a message box should inform the user that an invalid value has been entered. You will now incorporate an `If...Then...Else` statement into the Salary Calculator program.

*To add the `If...Then...Else` statement:*

1. If you took a break after the last session, open the workbook **Salary Calculator** from the Tutorial.03 folder on your Data Disk, switch to the VBA IDE, and open the Code window.

2. Position the cursor within the Calculate button's Click event.

**3.** Edit the code to add the statements shown below in bold. Indent the code as shown here to make the structure of the `If...Then...Else` statement easier to see. (Remember to add only the statements in bold below. The rest of the code is provided to make it easier for you to see where the new code belongs.)

```
Private Sub cmdCalculate_Click()
    Dim sngHoursWorked As Single    'declare a variable for Hours Worked
    Dim sngRateOfPay As Single      'declare a variable for the Rate of Pay
    Dim sngSalary As Single         'declare a variable for the calculated Salary

    sngHoursWorked = txtHours.Text  'retrieve the Hours entered in the
                                    'form and assign to the variable

    sngRateOfPay = txtRate          'retrieve the Rate entered in the
                                    'form and assign to the variable

    If sngHoursWorked <= 60 Then
      sngSalary = sngRateOfPay * sngHoursWorked          'calculate the salary
      txtSalary.Text = Format(sngSalary, "currency")     'place the calculated salary
                                                         'in the form
      txtRate.Text = Format(txtRate.Text, "currency")
    Else
      MsgBox ("Hours worked must be 60 or less")
    End If
End Sub
```

**4.** Save your work.

**5.** Run the program, and then type **65** in the Hours Worked text box and **10** in the Rate of Pay text box.

**6.** Click the **Calculate** button. You see a message box that tells you that you must enter a value less than or equal to 60. See Figure 3-26.

| Figure 3-26 | MESSAGE BOX |

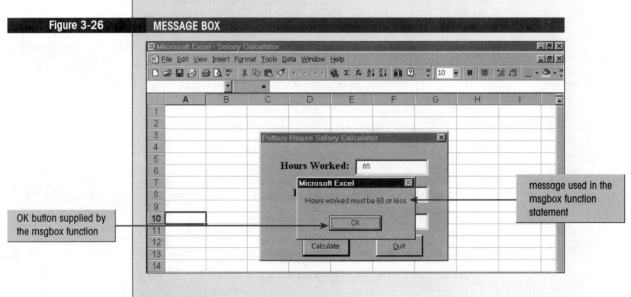

OK button supplied by the msgbox function

message used in the msgbox function statement

**7.** Click **OK**.

**8.** Change the value in the Hours Worked text box to **55**.

**9.** Click the **Calculate** button. The form displays a salary of $550.00.

**10.** Click the **Quit** button.

In the Salary Calculator example, the program had only two options, either the Hours worked value was within the acceptable range or it was not. When you show your work to Gene, he explains he wanted you to work on this fairly simple example in order to learn how a selection construct works. But as you can probably imagine, decision-making in a program can get much more complicated. Sometimes a program must decide between numerous options rather than just two. Later on, you will demonstrate the Check Register program, which involves several options. But first, Gene wants to show you how to find errors in your code.

# Debugging a Program

Gene explains that, at this stage in your VBA education, you are beginning to write fairly complicated code. If you make a mistake, your program will probably not work properly, and may generate error messages. So in addition to learning how to write complicated code, you must also learn to handle errors in a program—a process known as **debugging** a program.

VBA provides a rich set of **debugging tools**, which are designed to make the process of finding errors as simple as possible. Learning to use these tools will free you from having to run to an expert every time you encounter a problem with your program. Instead you will be able to examine your code, find problems, and resolve those problems on your own. It takes practice to learn to use these tools well, but it is worth the effort because these techniques will ultimately save you a great deal of time.

In the following sections, you will look at each tool separately; however, as you work with your own programs you will need to select the tool that best suits your needs. You can combine the tools to give you a clear understanding of what is going wrong in your program and, thus, make fixing the program easier.

## Stepping Through a Program

So far, your only means of testing a program has been to run the entire program and observe the results. However, sometimes it is beneficial to step through the program, one statement at a time. This allows you to observe both the flow of control (which statements are being processed and in what order) and the current value of variables at runtime.

To step through a program, you press F8 continually as the program progresses, one line of code at a time. Each time you press F8, the program control moves to the next line.

---

**REFERENCE WINDOW** **RW**

Stepping through a program
- Position the cursor inside the program you want to debug.
- Click Debug on the menu bar, and then click Step Into. (You can also press F8).
- Press F8 to step from one line of code to the next.
- Continue to press F8 until you reach the end of the program.
- Click the Reset button on the toolbar to end the program.

You will now step through the Salary Calculator procedure. As you do this, work slowly, taking time to observe all the values of the variables. Pay very close attention to the order of statements. These kinds of observations often reveal errors that you may have not recognized previously.

## To step through the program:

1. Verify that the cursor is located anywhere within the procedure.

2. Click **Debug** on the menu bar, and then click **Step Into**. (You can also simply press F8). The form is displayed in the Excel window.

3. Type **40** for Hours Worked and **15.0** for Rate of Pay.

4. Click the **Calculate** button. You see the Code window displayed in the IDE. Even though you are looking at the code, VBA is still in runtime; the program is running and you are watching it run. The first statement of the Calculate button's Click event, the Sub statement, is highlighted in yellow. Also, an arrow in the left-hand margin indicates that the highlighted line is currently being executed. Compare your screen with Figure 3-27.

| Figure 3-27 | THE PROGRAM IS RUNNING IN STEP INTO MODE |
| --- | --- |

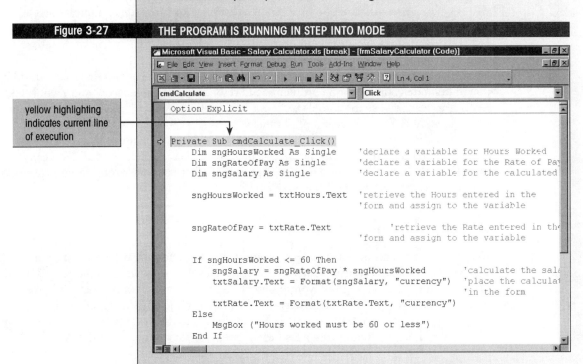

yellow highlighting indicates current line of execution

5. Press **F8** to execute the next line. Notice that the yellow highlighting jumps past the Dim statements to the first assignment statement in the module: sngHoursWorked = txtHours.Text, as shown in Figure 3-28. A Dim statement is a variable declaration and not an executable statement, so the yellow highlighting will not stop on a Dim statement.

**Figure 3-28**   **THE PROGRAM STILL IN STEP INTO MODE**

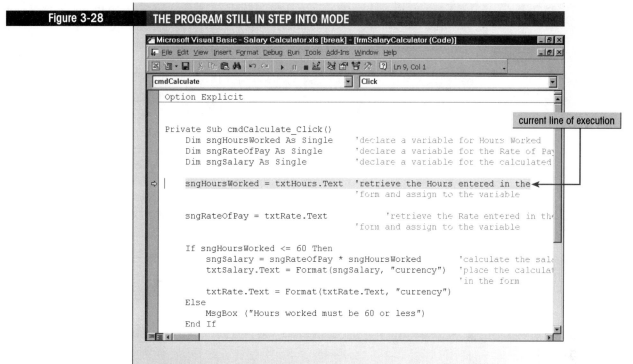

6. Position the mouse pointer over the variable name, `sngHoursWorked`. A
ToolTip appears, indicating that the value of `sngHoursWorked` at this time is 0.

7. Position the mouse pointer over `txtHours.Text`. The ToolTip indicates that the
value of the `txtHours.Text` property is 40. Compare your screen with Figure 3-29.

**Figure 3-29**   **CURRENT VALUE OF VARIABLE DISPLAYED IN TOOLTIP**

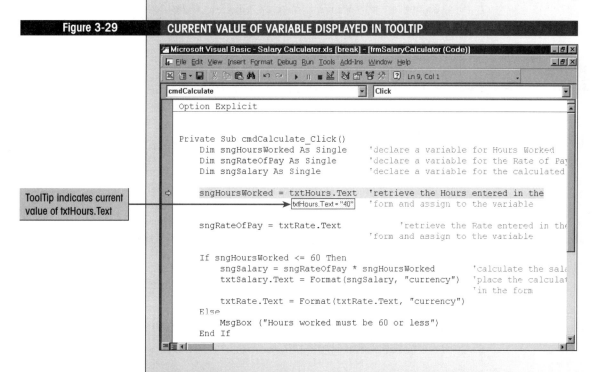

8. Press **F8** and then position the mouse pointer over `sngHoursWorked` in the
previous line of code. Notice that the value of `sngHoursWorked` is now 40.

9. Position the mouse pointer over `sngRateOfPay`. The value of `sngRateOfPay` is 0.

VBA is now ready to execute the `If` statement. As you move through the code, you will see how the value of the variables affects which statements are executed within the selection structure.

## To continue stepping through the program:

1. Press **F8**. The `If` statement is now highlighted.

2. In the preceding line, place the mouse pointer over `sngRateOfPay`. Notice that the value of `sngRateOfPay` is now 15. This should illustrate to you the before and after results of a statement. With the `If` statement highlighted, ask yourself this question: "What statement will be executed next?" You should know the answer to that question based on the value of `sngHoursWorked`. It is less than 60, so the next statement executed will be the first statement in the "true" part of the `If` control structure.

3. Press **F8**. The cursor moves to the first line within the `If` control structure.

4. Continue to press **F8** until you reach the `End Sub` statement. Because this completes the Calculate button's Click event, your program will now just wait for another event to take place on the form.

5. Press **F8** again. It will appear to you that your program has stopped, but it has not.

6. Click the **Microsoft Excel** button on the taskbar. The form appears in the workbook window, where it is waiting for the next event to take place. This is a good illustration of the concept of Event-driven programming. Nothing will happen until an event takes place.

7. Type **65** in the Hours Worked text box, click the **Calculate** button, and press **F8**. Again, the highlighting returns to the beginning of the Calculate button's Click event.

This time through the procedure, the program will run a little differently. You can probably guess what is going to happen as you step through it this time.

## To step through the procedure a second time:

1. Press **F8** continuously until you reach the `If` statement, and then position the mouse pointer over the `sngHoursWorked` variable within the `If` statement. At this point, the value is 65. Once again, ask yourself the question: "What statement will be executed next?" You probably know the answer. The next statement will be the `Else` statement since the condition in the `If` statement will be false.

2. Press **F8**. The highlighting moves to the `Else` statement.

3. Press **F8** twice. The message box appears indicating that the Hours Worked must be less than 60.

4. Click **OK** in the message box. You have completed testing this program.

5. Click the **Reset** button on the VBA toolbar to end the program.

Gene explains that the experience of "walking through" a program one statement at a time provides a very valuable lesson. No matter how much you read about the Selection control structure, nothing can replace the actual experience of observing how one executes in a program. But keep in mind that the debugging tools, such as the Step Into command, are more often used to find and fix problems in a program.

By using the Step Into technique, you can examine a program one statement at a time. At any point in the program, you can stop and check the value of the variables. This technique often shows where a variable has obtained an incorrect value. The Step Into technique also allows you to observe the flow of control. If you observe that the flow of control is not correct, you can then change the statement that is causing the problem. In the next section, you will learn about another debugging tool, breakpoints.

## Setting a Breakpoint in a Procedure

Stepping through a program is very helpful in that it allows you to observe which statements are being processed and in what order. This can help you figure out which statements are causing problems. However, sometimes, you may already suspect which statement is problematic, in which case it is helpful to set a breakpoint in your program. When you insert a **breakpoint**, you mark a statement in a way that tells VBA to execute all of the statements in the procedure up to (but not including) that statement. The breakpoint tells VBA to suspend execution at that statement. When the breakpoint is reached, execution will cease and will only continue when you click the Run Sub/UserForm button again. Setting a breakpoint is less time-consuming than stepping through a program, because processing continues as usual until VBA reaches the statement that has been set as the breakpoint.

To mark a statement as a breakpoint, click the left-hand border of the Code window immediately to the left of the statement and then press Enter. A brown line will appear in the code, marking the statement as a breakpoint. A brown dot is also displayed in the code window border, next to the statement.

| REFERENCE WINDOW | RW |
|---|---|

**To Set a Breakpoint**
- Locate the line where you want to set the breakpoint.
- Click the left-hand border of the Code window immediately to the left of the line. (The left-hand border is a gray bar.)
- To remove the breakpoint, click the brown dot in the code window border.

Suppose that when you test the Salary Calculator program, you find that it displays the wrong salary value. For example, when you enter 10 for the number of hours worked and 8.76 for the rate of pay, you know that the result should be $87.60. However, instead you see $18.76 as the Salary. You suspect that the problem has to do with assigning the right value to the `sngHoursWorked` variable, but you want to check to see if that is really the case.

In the following steps, you will first alter the program to cause this error. You will change the asterisk (*), which represents multiplication, to a plus sign (+), which represents addition. (Of course, this would cause quite an error in calculation that is supposed to involve multiplication.) You will then set a breakpoint that you can use to pinpoint the error.

## *To create an intentional error and then set a breakpoint:*

1. In the `cmdCalculate_Click` procedure, locate the following line: `sngSalary = sngRateOfPay * sngHoursWorked`.

2. Create an intentional error in the code by changing the asterisk (*) to a plus sign (+). The revised statement should read as follows: `sngSalary = sngRateOfPay + sngHoursWorked`.

3. Run the program using 10 as the number of hours worked and 8.76 for the rate of pay, and then click the **Calculate** button and observe that the incorrect result is $18.76.

4. Click the **Quit** button. You return to the VBA IDE.

5. In the Code window, click in the gray border to the left of the statement that calculates the salary. The line is now highlighted in brown and a brown circle appears in the left margin, indicating that the line has been set as a breakpoint. Compare your screen to Figure 3-30.

| Figure 3-30 | CODE WINDOW WITH BREAKPOINT SET |
| --- | --- |

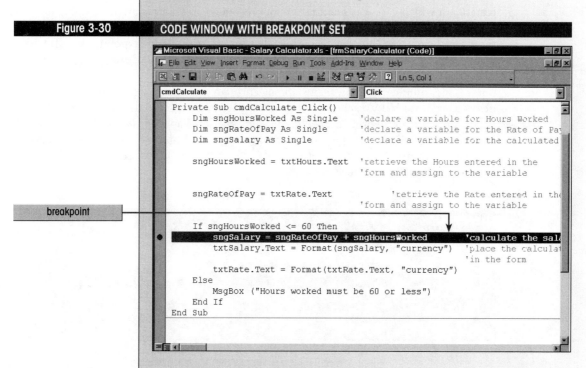

6. Click the **Run button** ▶ on the toolbar.

7. When the form appears, enter the same values that you entered before (10 for Hours worked and 8.76 for rate of pay) and then click the **Calculate** button. The program runs through the procedure but stops when it encounters the statement that calculates the salary. The salary calculation statement is highlighted in yellow in the Code window.

8. Position the mouse pointer over each variable to determine if the right values are being used—that is, the values you entered in the text boxes. Assuming that the right values are being used, you still haven't pinpointed the problem, so you must continue.

**9.** Press **F8**. The program executes the next statement, which is now highlighted in yellow.

**10.** Position the mouse pointer on the variable `sngSalary` and read the ToolTip stating the value of the variable is 18.76.

You have now determined that the variables being used in the calculation contain the right values but that the results are incorrect. So now you decide there must be something else wrong. As you examine the Salary Calculator program you realize that you have mistakenly used a "+" sign where you intended to use a "*" sign. You realize that this is what is causing the problem. You will now correct the problem and then you can "back up" the program to re-execute the revised statement. You do this by dragging the yellow arrow in the margin.

## To correct the error and re-execute the revised program:

**1.** Replace the + sign with an *.

**2.** Click and drag the yellow arrow (in the Code window border) up to the statement that calculates the salary, as shown in Figure 3-31.

| Figure 3-31 | CODE WINDOW WITH BREAKPOINT AND CURRENT LINE OF EXECUTION |

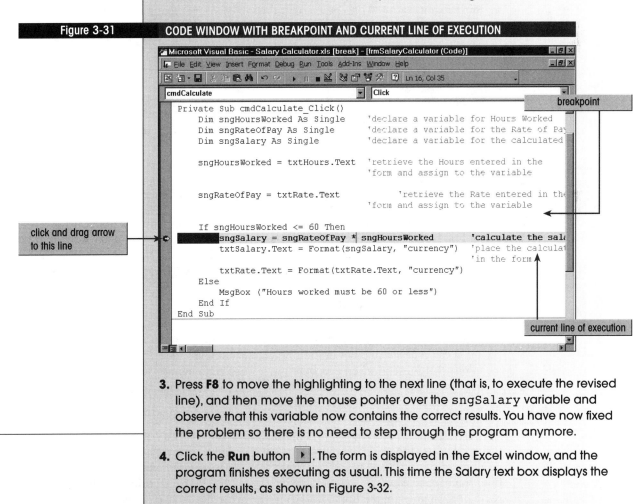

**3.** Press **F8** to move the highlighting to the next line (that is, to execute the revised line), and then move the mouse pointer over the `sngSalary` variable and observe that this variable now contains the correct results. You have now fixed the problem so there is no need to step through the program anymore.

**4.** Click the **Run** button ▶ . The form is displayed in the Excel window, and the program finishes executing as usual. This time the Salary text box displays the correct results, as shown in Figure 3-32.

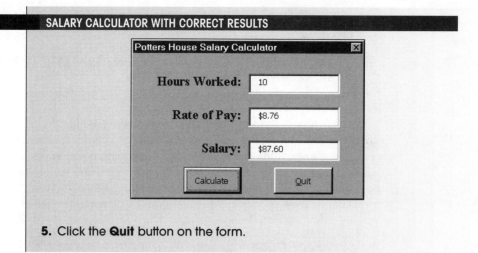

**Figure 3-32    SALARY CALCULATOR WITH CORRECT RESULTS**

**5.** Click the **Quit** button on the form.

Now that you have detected and fixed the error, you can remove the breakpoint so that it doesn't stop the program every time you run it. To remove a breakpoint, you simply click on the statement that is marked as a breakpoint, and then press F9. The breakpoint is a **toggle**, meaning that it is turned off and on with the same keystroke.

### To remove the breakpoint:

**1.** Return to the Code window in the VBA IDE.

**2.** Click the brown circle in the Code window border. The brown line disappears, indicating that the breakpoint is no longer set.

**3.** Save your work.

You can set as many breakpoints as you want in your programs. Each breakpoint will cause execution to stop at that point so that you can observe what is happening in your program. You will find as you write large programs that it is sometimes difficult to determine which line is causing the problem. Setting several breakpoints will allow you to stop your program and observe the current value of the variables. In the next section you will learn about yet another debugging tool, the Immediate window.

## Using the Immediate Window

Within the **Immediate window**, you can see the value of any variable at runtime. In addition, you can type a statement in the Immediate window and see it executed immediately, a technique that is useful when you want to try out a statement to see what it will do.

Gene has just learned that Potters House management is considering a 5% pay increase for all employees. He wants to observe the effect of this raise on the salary of employees who work 40 hours at $15.75 an hour. Gene asks you to set a breakpoint on the statement just after the statement that calculates the salary. Then he wants you to test the results of a new statement that recalculates the salary by multiplying the rate of pay times the hours worked times 1.05, resulting in a 5% increase in salary. Instead of using an assignment statement for this calculation, you need to use a special statement known as the **Print statement**, which displays the result of a statement in the Immediate window. To use the `Print` statement, you type `Print` followed by the statement whose results you want to see displayed in the Immediate window. For example: `Print sngRateOfPay * 1.05 * sngHoursWorked`.

The example above multiplies the rate of pay times 1.05, times the hours worked. If instead of this `Print` statement, you actually typed an assignment statement that assigned the new salary value to the `sngSalary` variable, the value would be altered in your program and the new results would be displayed in the form.

You will test this `Print` statement in the Immediate window.

## To test a new statement in the Immediate window:

**1.** In the Code window, set a breakpoint on the statement *after* the statement that calculates the salary. Your breakpoint should look like the one in Figure 3-33.

| Figure 3-33 | CODE WINDOW WITH BREAKPOINT SET |
| --- | --- |

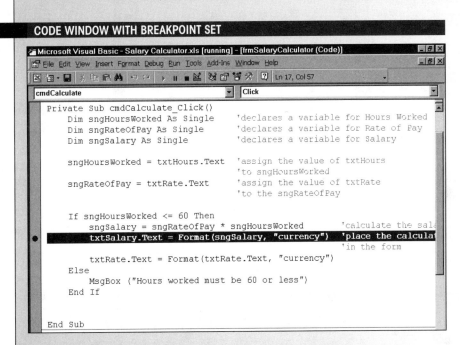

```
Microsoft Visual Basic - Salary Calculator.xls [running] - [frmSalaryCalculator (Code)]
File  Edit  View  Insert  Format  Debug  Run  Tools  Add-Ins  Window  Help
                                                               Ln 17, Col 57

cmdCalculate                              Click

Private Sub cmdCalculate_Click()
    Dim sngHoursWorked As Single      'declares a variable for Hours Worked
    Dim sngRateOfPay As Single        'declares a variable for Rate of Pay
    Dim sngSalary As Single           'declares a variable for Salary

    sngHoursWorked = txtHours.Text    'assign the value of txtHours
                                      'to sngHoursWorked
    sngRateOfPay = txtRate.Text       'assign the value of txtRate
                                      'to the sngRateOfPay

    If sngHoursWorked <= 60 Then
        sngSalary = sngRateOfPay * sngHoursWorked       'calculate the sal
        txtSalary.Text = Format(sngSalary, "currency")  'place the calcula
                                                        'in the form
        txtRate.Text = Format(txtRate.Text, "currency")
    Else
        MsgBox ("Hours worked must be 60 or less")
    End If

End Sub
```

**2.** Run the program, enter **40** for the hours worked, enter **15.75** for the rate of pay, and then click the **Calculate** button. The program stops running, and you see the Code window on the screen, with the breakpoint statement highlighted in yellow.

**3.** Place the mouse pointer on the `sngSalary` variable in the highlighted line and observe that the calculated salary is 630. Now you will test a statement that will calculate the salary with a 5% increase.

**4.** Click **View** on the menu bar and click **Immediate Window**.

TROUBLE? If you do not see the Immediate window, it is probably hidden behind one of the other open windows. Click Window on the menu bar, then click Immediate.

**5.** Size the window similarly to the one shown in Figure 3-34.

**Figure 3-34**    **VBA IDE WITH IMMEDIATE WINDOW DISPLAYED**

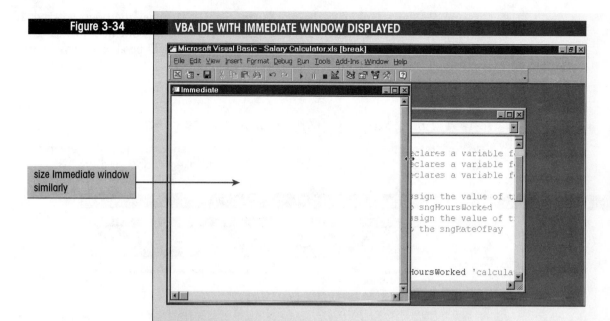

size Immediate window similarly

TROUBLE? Remember that you can move and size your windows as you wish. The important thing here is that you can see the Immediate window on your screen.

6. Click in the Immediate window and type the following statement
   **Print sngRateOfPay * 1.05 * sngHoursWorked**

7. Press **Enter.** The result of the new calculation is displayed in the Immediate window, as shown in Figure 3-35.

**Figure 3-35**    **RESULTS OF NEW CALCULATION IN THE IMMEDIATE WINDOW**

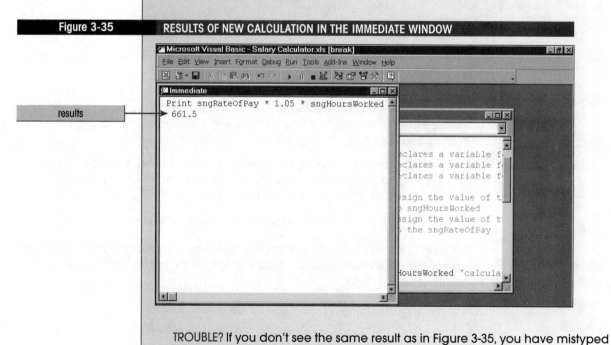

results

TROUBLE? If you don't see the same result as in Figure 3-35, you have mistyped the statement. Retype the statement correctly and press Enter again.

Note that the execution of the `Print` statement you typed in the Immediate window has no effect on the program in the Code window. For instance, the new calculation does not change the original value of the `sngSalary` variable, which still contains the calculated value at the current rate of pay. You can verify this by checking the variables in the Code window.

---

*To check the variables in the Code window:*

1. Close the Immediate window.

2. Position the mouse pointer over the `sngSalary` variable in the line above the highlighted line, and observe that the value is still 630. Now you will remove the breakpoint. Note that, because the breakpoint is also highlighted in yellow, you need to press F9 (rather than clicking the brown circle) to remove the breakpoint.

3. Click the line with the breakpoint, and press **F9**. The breakpoint is removed, although the line is still highlighted in yellow.

4. Click the **Reset** button ■ on the toolbar to stop the program.

5. Close the Code window and save your work.

---

When you use the Immediate window in the future, keep in mind that a `Print` statement simply displays results in the Immediate window. If, instead of the `Print` statement, you actually typed an assignment statement, the assignment statement would be executed, thereby changing the values of variables in the program and changing values displayed in the form.

## Starting Help From the Immediate Window

You can also use the Immediate window when you want to use a statement but you are not sure how it works or what its correct syntax might be. In that case, you simply need to type a command, and then, with the cursor in or next to that command, press F1. Pressing F1 displays a Help window containing information about that particular statement. Gene suggests you experiment with the Immediate window, by looking up the syntax of the MsgBox function that you used earlier.

---

*To use the Immediate window to find information on the MsgBox function:*

1. Click **View** on the menu bar and then click **Immediate Window**. The Immediate window opens, still displaying the test statement and its result.

2. In the line below the result of the test statement, type: **MsgBox**

3. Verify that the cursor is next to the command you just typed, and then press **F1**. A Help window opens, containing information on the MsgBox function, as shown in Figure 3-36.

**Figure 3-36**     **HELP WINDOW FOR THE MSGBOX FUNCTION**

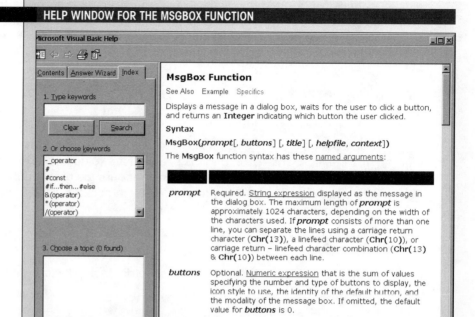

TROUBLE? If you receive a message indicating that Help is not installed, check with your instructor about installing Help files on your computer.

**4.** Use the same technique to look up information on the following statements: **InputBox**, **Format**, and **If**.

**5.** Close the Help window and the Immediate window.

**6.** Switch to the Excel workbook window and close the Salary Calculator workbook

**7.** If you are going to take a break before the next session, close Excel.

In this session you have been introduced to the debugging tools provided by the VBA IDE. You learned to step through your program one statement at a time, and you learned to set a breakpoint in your program. You also learned to use the Immediate window to test some program statements to see how they would affect the outcome of your program.

You have now completed the Salary Calculator project for Potters House Gallery. Gene Cox is pleased with what you have done and encourages you to expand your experience with data validation and decision structures. To help you learn more, Gene has asked Ashley Andrews, another consultant at TnT Consulting, to show you a project that she is working on. In the next session, you will view Ashley's project and learn the statements she used to complete part of the project.

## Session 3.2 QUICK CHECK

1. The three control structures of programming are:

   a. _____

   b. _____

   c. _____

2. The _____ function displays a small form containing a message to the user.

3. The _____ statement is used when the program needs to choose between two options.

4. The _____ option on the Debug menu allows you to execute code one line at a time.

5. The _____ window allows you to try out statements to determine the result of the statements without actually changing your program.

## SESSION 3.3

In this session you will study the TnT Check Register project, and observe how the concepts you learned earlier in this tutorial apply to that program. In particular, you will study examples of statements that validate dates. You will also learn about the isNumeric and isDate functions.

# Viewing the TnT Check Register Project

In Tutorial 2, you developed a form for recording checks in an Excel worksheet. The completed check form looked similar to the one in Figure 3-37.

| Figure 3-37 | CHECK FORM FOR THE CHECK REGISTER PROJECT |

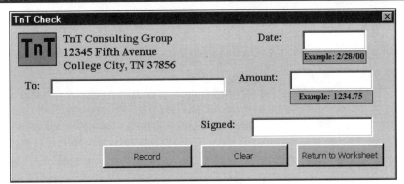

Recall that in Tutorial 2 you wrote some code for the Clear command button and also for the Return to Worksheet button. After you completed the check form, Gene assigned the remainder of the project to Ashley. Ashley has completed a portion of the project and is ready to show you the new code. She has started the code for the Record button. She explains that, because you want to make sure the data is accurate, the code must ensure that a valid date has been entered into the Date text box and in the Amount text box. If either of these items is invalid, a message box should appear, notifying the user that an error has been made.

Ashley has already written the code that performs these validity checks. You will now observe the program as it runs. Then Ashley will show you the code she used to accomplish the validity checks.

## To test the TnT Check Register form with both valid and invalid values:

1. If you took a break after the last session, start Excel.

2. Open the **TnTChk** workbook located in the Tutorial.03 folder of your Data Disk.

3. Save the workbook as **TnT Checkbook**.

4. Examine the Checkbook worksheet, and notice that the worksheet itself has been prepared for the check entries as shown in Figure 3-38. Also notice that the worksheet contains a command button labeled "Record a Check."

| Figure 3-38 | TNT CHECKBOOK WORKSHEET |

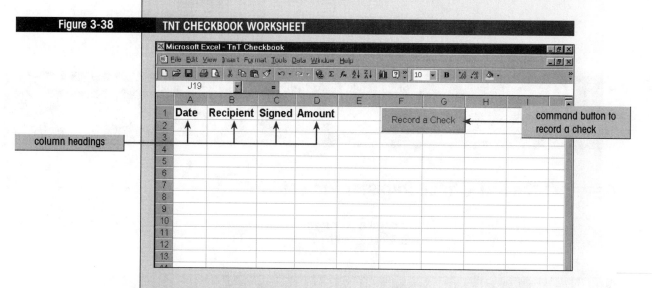

5. Click the **Record a Check** command button on the worksheet. The TnT Check form is displayed on top of the worksheet.

6. Type **ABC** in each of the text boxes. Of course, this is an intentional error that will illustrate how the project works when invalid data is entered.

7. Click the **Record** button on the form. You see a message box telling you to enter a valid date, as shown in Figure 3-39.

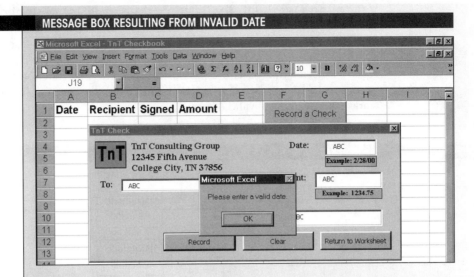

**Figure 3-39**

**MESSAGE BOX RESULTING FROM INVALID DATE**

8. Click the **OK** button in the message box and notice that the entry "ABC" in the Date text box is now highlighted.

Now you can replace the invalid date with a valid one.

*To test the program with valid data:*

1. Type **01/10/03** in the Date text box. This is a valid date.

2. Click the **Record** button. A new message box appears, telling you to enter a valid amount.

3. Click **OK** on the message box. The Amount text box is highlighted.

4. Enter **1234.56** in the Amount text box.

5. Click the **Record** button. Because you entered all valid data, no more messages are displayed. Instead, the check is cleared, and the program waits for the next entry.

6. Click the **Return to Worksheet** button on the form and observe that the check form is removed from the screen. You see the Excel worksheet on the screen.

Ashley explains that so far she only programmed the Record button to check for invalid date and amount values. She has not yet programmed the portion that actually records the data in the worksheet. Instead, Ashley has placed a comment in place of the code she will need to add later. This comment serves as a "place holder" so that she will know what she still needs to add to the code later. She will be working on this later while you are working on other projects; you will have a chance to see the finished Check Register project at the end of Tutorial 4.

Ashley tells you that she used two functions in the Check Register project, the IsNumeric function and the IsDate function. You'll learn about these functions in the next section.

## Validating Data with the IsNumeric and IsDate Functions

The **IsNumeric** function receives a value and determines whether it is a valid number. Valid numbers consist of the digits 0–9. If you wish, you can also use the IsNumeric function to require a decimal place, and a plus or minus sign. The function will return "true" if the value is valid and "false" if it is not. Figure 3-40 illustrates how the IsNumeric function works with invalid and valid data.

| Figure 3-40 | ISNUMERIC FUNCTION |
| --- | --- |

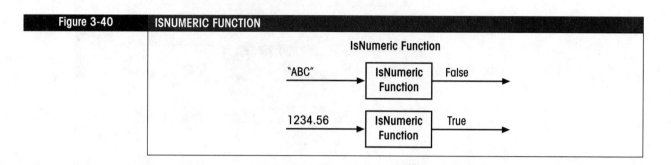

In the Checkbook project, Ashley used the IsNumeric function to evaluate the amount in the `txtAmount` text box.

The second validation function that Ashley used in the Checkbook project is the IsDate function. The **IsDate** function works in the same manner as the IsNumeric function, except that it checks a value to determine if it is a valid date. Figure 3-41 illustrates how the function works with valid and invalid data.

| Figure 3-41 | ISDATE FUNCTION |
| --- | --- |

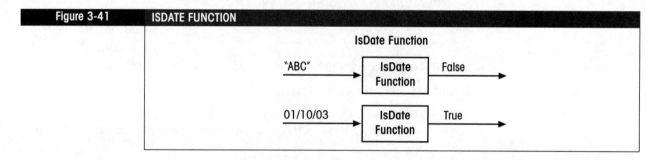

Ashley explains that she has already coded the project to use the IsNumeric and the IsDate function to validate these fields. As she created this code, she used the flowcharts in Figure 3-42 as a guide.

**Figure 3-42** FLOWCHARTS FOR THE CHECKBOOK VALIDATION CODE

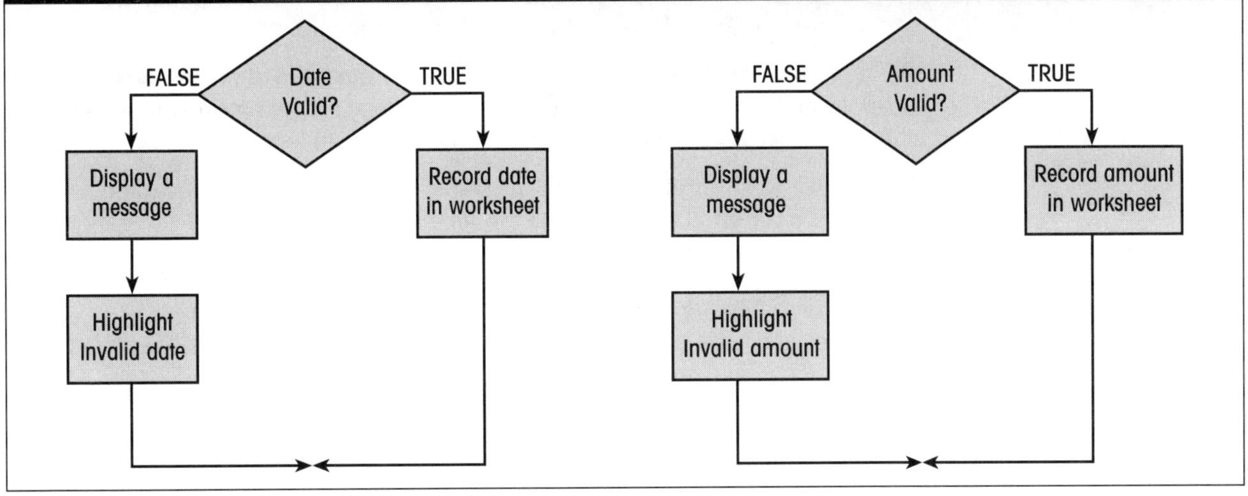
Date Valid?
FALSE
TRUE
Display a message
Highlight Invalid date
Record date in worksheet
Amount Valid?
FALSE
TRUE
Display a message
Highlight Invalid amount
Record amount in worksheet

You will now open the Code window and look at this code. Don't expect to understand every single element of this code. But after all that you have learned by working on the Salary Calculator project, you should be able to understand roughly how this code works.

## *To view the validation code in the TnT Checkbook project:*

1. Start the VBA IDE and then, if necessary, open the Project Explorer window.
2. If necessary, expand the **Forms** subdirectory and then double-click **`frmCheck`**.
3. Double-click anywhere on the form to open the Code window. Scroll the Code window so that you can view the top of the `cmdRecord_Click` procedure, as shown in Figure 3-43.

**Figure 3-43** CODE WINDOW WITH THE RECORD BUTTON

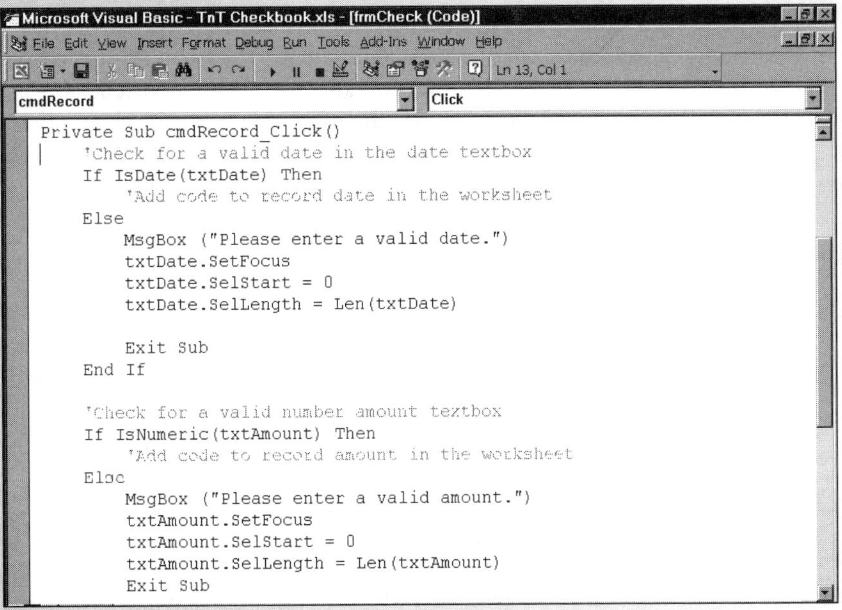
Microsoft Visual Basic - TnT Checkbook.xls - [frmCheck (Code)]
File Edit View Insert Format Debug Run Tools Add-Ins Window Help
Ln 13, Col 1
cmdRecord
Click
Private Sub cmdRecord_Click()
'Check for a valid date in the date textbox
If IsDate(txtDate) Then
'Add code to record date in the worksheet
Else
MsgBox ("Please enter a valid date.")
txtDate.SetFocus
txtDate.SelStart = 0
txtDate.SelLength = Len(txtDate)
Exit Sub
End If
'Check for a valid number amount textbox
If IsNumeric(txtAmount) Then
'Add code to record amount in the worksheet
Else
MsgBox ("Please enter a valid amount.")
txtAmount.SetFocus
txtAmount.SelStart = 0
txtAmount.SelLength = Len(txtAmount)
Exit Sub

**4.** Observe that the first section of code uses the IsDate function within an `If...Then...Else` statement to check the date for validity.

**5.** If necessary, scroll the window so that you can see the rest of the code for the Record button. Observe that the next section uses the IsNumeric function to check for validity of the value entered in the Amount text box.

**6.** Locate the following line: `txtDate.SetFocus`. This statement uses the SetFocus method, as explained in the next section.

**7.** Locate the following line: `txtDate.SelStart = 0`. You will also learn about this statement in the next section.

**8.** Leave the code on your screen so that you can examine it in the next section.

## Explaining the Validation Code

If the user has entered an invalid date or amount, Ashley wants the user to return to the appropriate text box and enter correct data. To make this as easy as possible for the user, she included a statement (`txtDate.SetFocus`) that moves the cursor automatically to the text box containing invalid data, as soon as the error message box is closed. This statement involves the **SetFocus method,** which will move the cursor to the specified object. Its syntax is as follows:

| Syntax | `Object.SetFocus` |
|---|---|
| Explanation | The SetFocus method moves the cursor to the specified Object. |
| Example | `txtAmount.SetFocus` |

The example statement will cause the cursor to move to the `txtAmount` text box. Once the cursor is positioned in the correct text box, the user can delete its current entry and replace it with the correct value.

In order to make it easier for the user to delete the current entry, Ashley included some code that automatically selects the contents of the text box. As you know, once text is selected, the user can simply start typing, thus replacing the selected text with new text. In VBA, it actually takes two statements to accomplish this, one involving the SelStart method, and the other involving the SelLength property and the Len function. In the Check Register project, these two statements look like this:

```
txtDate.SelStart = 0
txtDate.SelLength = Len(txtDate)
```

In the example statements, **SelStart** specifies where the highlighting (selection) in the `txtDate` text box should begin. Because Ashley wanted the highlighting to begin at the left edge of the text box, she used the number zero (0). The **Len** function used in the second statement determines the length of the text stored in the text box. The value returned by the Len function is then stored in the SelLength property of the `txtDate` text box. The **SelLength** property value specifies how long a selection will be and, in this case, it is the length of the date entered in the `txtDate` text box.

While this might seem complicated, the concept is really rather simple. To summarize the explanations above, the two statements in the example above select all the text in the `txtDate` text box. Thus, when the user starts typing in the text box, the next text replaces all of the old text. You have used this type of select and replace concept throughout your use of Windows applications, now you know how it is programmed. To reuse these two statements in a different program, simply replace "txtDate" with the name of the text box whose contents you want to select.

Note that the code for validating the Amount text box is exactly the same as that for the Date text box with the exception of the actual object being referred to. Finally, Ashley explains that she added an ExitSub statement at the end of each of these sections of code. The ExitSub statement causes the procedure to end so that none of the remaining statements in the procedure will be executed. Ashley can remove this ExitSub statement later, after she actually writes the code that records data in the worksheet.

This completes the view of the Check Register at this point. You can close it now.

### To close the Check Register project:

1. Switch to the Excel workbook window.

2. Close the workbook without making any changes.

3. Exit Excel.

Ashley will demonstrate the project again when it is completed. Gene explains that studying the work of a more experienced developer is an important part of your training. After reviewing this project, while you might not fully understand all the statements, you should have a general idea of how the program works. Hopefully, you have also gained some new ideas that you may want to implement in your own programs.

## Session 3.3 QUICK CHECK

1. The _____ function checks to see if a value is a valid number. If the value is invalid, it will return a value of _____.

2. The _____ function checks to see if a value is a valid date. If the value is valid, this function will return a value of _____.

3. The _____ method will move the cursor to the specified object.

4. The _____ function will determine the length of a value.

## REVIEW ASSIGNMENTS

The Magnolia Playhouse has recently contracted with TnT Consulting to create a VBA program. The Playhouse, a regional theater company, offers performances throughout the year, charging $20 a ticket. Patrons purchasing more than five tickets receive a 10% discount. Your job is to design a program that will calculate the amount the customer owes, depending on the number of tickets. Gene has already begun creating the form for you. You should familiarize yourself with the form before you begin.

1. Start Excel and open the workbook named **Tickets**, which is located in the Review folder for Tutorial 3.

2. Save the workbook as **Magnolia Playhouse**.

3. Start the VBA IDE.

4. Open the form named `UserForm1`. (*Hint*: Open the Project Explorer, expand the form subdirectory, and double-click on the form).

5. Look at the properties of each text box and command button. Be sure to familiarize yourself with the names of each control since you will need to use their names in programming statements.

6. Change the caption on the form to "Magnolia Playhouse Tickets."

7. Name the form "`frmTickets`."

8. Open the Click event procedure for the Calculate button, and enter the following code. This code will validate the data entered into the Number of Tickets text box. If the data is not valid, the program should highlight the Number of Tickets text box. It should also display a message box telling the user to enter a valid number.

```
If IsNumeric(txtTickets) Then
        'Add code to calculate the amount owed here
Else
        MsgBox("Please enter a valid number of tickets")
        txtTicket.SetFocus
        txtTicket.SelStart = 0
        txtTicket.SelLength = Len(txtTicket)
End If
```

***Explore***

9. Write code that will calculate the amount the customer owes and place the amount in the Amount text box. Remember to have the program check to see if the customer will receive the 10% discount. Be sure to use the right variable types and descriptive variable names. Be sure to format the amount as "currency". This code should replace the following comment: "Add code to calculate the amount owed here." Use an `If` statement to calculate the amount owed, followed by another `If` statement that checks to see if the patron should receive a 10% discount.

10. Use the debugging techniques you used in the tutorial to step through this code. Run the project first with correct data and then again with incorrect data. As you go through the program step by step try to guess which statement the program will execute next.

11. Open the Clear button's Click event procedure and write the code that will clear the text boxes.

12. Open the Click event procedure for the Quit button and write the code that will remove the form from the screen.

13. Test the form with several different numbers (including an invalid number) to make sure that it works properly.

14. Place comments at the top of the code that include your name and today's date.

15. Save your work.

16. Print the `frmTickets` code module.

17. Close Excel.

## CASE PROBLEMS

*Case 1. Bristol High School* Serena Potter teaches at Bristol High School. She uses Excel to track student grades on assignments and exams. She grades every assignment or exam on a scale from 0 to 100 points. She records the students' scores in a worksheet and then uses Excel to determine the students' average score. Currently, she has to convert the average score (a numeric figure) to a letter grade by hand. She has hired you to create a VBA program that will convert the numeric score to a letter grade.

1. Start Microsoft Excel, and open the workbook named **Potter** located in the Cases folder for Tutorial 3.

2. Save the workbook as **Potters Grades**.

3. Open the VBA IDE.

4. Open the form named `frmGradeCalc`.

5. Familiarize yourself with the form. Check the name of each control in the Properties window.

*Explore*　6. Before proceeding with the case study, look up "Using If Then Else Statements" in the VBA Help system. Scroll the Help description to the "Testing a Second Condition if the First Condition is False" and review the help information. You will use the `ElseIf` statement in the next step.

7. In the Click event procedure for the OK button, add the following code:

```
If txtAvgGrade.Text > 89 Then
   txtLetterGrade.Text = "A"
ElseIf txtAvgGrade.Text > 79 Then
   txtLetterGrade.Text = "B"
ElseIf txtAvgGrade.Text > 69 Then
   txtLetterGrade.Text = "C"
ElseIf txtAvgGrade.Text > 59 Then
   txtLetterGrade.Text = "D"
Else
   txtLetterGrade.Text = "F"
End If
   txtAvgGrade.SetFocus
```

8. Save your work.

9. Run the program.

10. Test the form by entering the following number grades 75, 91, 43, and 82. Click the OK button after entering each number grade. Notice how the grade is displayed in the Letter Grade text box.

11. Click the Exit button to close the form.

12. Print the project's code and close the workbook.

*Case 2. Peshtigo, Inc.* You have been using Excel to record the number of hours that you work on each project at Peshtigo, Inc. Sometimes the total number of hours for all the projects exceeds 40 hours, but you are supposed to get approval from your supervisor when you work more than 40 hours per week. To help ensure that you don't work too many hours in a particular week, your supervisor asks you to create a program that notifies you when the number of hours recorded is greater than 40 hours.

1. Start Microsoft Excel, and open the workbook named **Hours** located in the Cases folder for Tutorial 3.

2. Save the workbook as **Hours Recorder** in the Cases folder for Tutorial 3.

3. Open the VBA IDE.

4. Open the form named `frmHours`.

5. Familiarize yourself with the form. Look at each control in the Properties window to see the name of the control.

**Explore**

6. Open the Click event procedure for the OK button and add the following code. Note that the underscore in the first line (_) tells VBA that the code on the second line is actually part of the first line. The underscore is a continuation character. The continuation character tells VBA that the following line is part of the current line. Using a continuation character makes your code easier to read on the screen, by breaking up long lines of code into short segments.

```
txtTotal.Text = txtProject1.Text + _
        txtProject2.Text + txtProject3.Text
```

**Explore**

7. Notice that this statement adds the values in the Text properties of the three text boxes (that is, the values entered into the text boxes). The code you saw in the tutorial used assignment statements to set a variable equal to the Text property, and then added the variables. Note that, in a simple program like this one, it's easier to simply add the Text properties. However, in a longer program, you could use variables instead of the text box values to improve the clarity of your code.

8. Now add an `If` statement that displays a message box with the note "Total exceeds 40 hours" when the total hours exceed 40.

9. Save your work.

10. Run the project.

11. Enter 20 for Project 1 hours, 10 for Project 2 hours, and 15 for Project 3 hours. Click the OK button after entering each line of data. Notice how the sum of the hours is displayed in the Total Hours text box. When you click OK the last time, you see a message box indicating that the Total exceeds 40 hours.

12. Close the message box, and retest the program using 10 for Project 1 hours, 10 for Project 2 hours, and 10 for Project 3 hours.

13. Set a breakpoint at the line beginning with `txtTotal.Text`. (*Hint:* Position the cursor on the line and press the F9 key to set the breakpoint.)

14. Run the form using the values from Step 13.

15. Position the cursor over the variables on the right side of the equals sign and examine their values.

16. Continue to execute the code by pressing the F5 key.

17. Switch to the Excel window and close the workbook.

18. Print the code for the project. Circle and label the part of the code that checks the total number of hours.

*Case 3. Whitman's Lumber*  Whitman's Lumber supplies many different types of wood. Each type is assigned a unique inventory code. However, most of the sales associates find it much easier to refer to the type of lumber by name rather than by inventory number. John Lieberman, the company's inventory manager, would like you to develop a VBA program that allows the user to type in an inventory code and then display the name of that type of wood. The codes and their associated types are listed in Figure 3-44.

**Figure 3-44**   **INVENTORY CODES AND WOOD TYPES**

| CODE | WOOD TYPE |
|------|-----------|
| 100  | Pine      |
| 200  | Oak       |
| 300  | Maple     |
| 400  | Redwood   |

1. Start Microsoft Excel, and open the workbook named **Whitman** located in the Cases folder for Tutorial 3.

2. Save the Workbook as **Whitman Lumber**.

3. Open the VBA IDE.

4. Open the form named `frmInventory`.

5. Familiarize yourself with the form. Look up each control's name in the Properties window.

**Explore**

6. Look up "Using If Then Else Statements" in the VBA Help system. Scroll the Help description to the "Testing a Second Condition If the First Condition Is False" and review the Help information. You will use the `ElseIf` statement in the next step. As you review this material become familiar with this statement.

7. Add the following code to the OK button's Click event procedure.

```
If txtCode.Text = 100 Then
   txtLumber.Text = "Pine"
ElseIf txtCode.Text = 200 Then
   txtLumber.Text = "Oak"
ElseIf txtCode.Text = 300 Then
   txtLumber.Text = "Maple"
ElseIf txtCode.Text = 400 Then
   txtLumber.Text = "Redwood"
Else
   txtLumber.Text = ""
   MsgBox "Inventory code not found"
End If
'Add code for selecting the entry in the txtCode text box.
txtCode.SelLength = Len(txtCode.Text)
```

8. Replace the comment in the second to last line with two statements that select the code in the `txtCode` text box.

9. Save your work.

10. Run the program.

11. Use the form to display the wood type for the following inventory codes: 200, 400, and 300. Click the OK button after entering each number. Notice how the lumber type is displayed in the Lumber Type text box when you enter a valid lumber type.

12. Enter 500 for the Inventory code. Note that the program displays a message when you enter an invalid lumber type.

13. Click the Exit button to close the form when you've finished testing.

14. Print the project code.

**Case 4. OnTrack Bicycles** OnTrack Bicycles makes a variety of different bikes for the recreational market. The bicycles are sold in many different states, and each state has a different sales tax rate. The OnTrack sales staff would like to have a form that calculates the total price of a bicycle, including the appropriate state sales tax.

1. Start Microsoft Excel, and open the workbook named **OnTrack** located in the Cases folder for Tutorial 3.

2. Save the workbook as **OnTrack Bicycles**.

3. Open the VBA IDE.

4. Open the form named `frmSalesTax`.

5. Familiarize yourself with the form. Look up the names of each control in the Properties window.

**Explore**

6. Double-click on the OK button and add the following code. Note that this code uses a new variable type—the Double type. The Double data type is identical to the Single data type, except that it allows for larger numbers.

```
Dim dblPrice As Double
Dim dblTax as Double
Dim dblTotal as Double

If IsNumeric(txtPrice.Text) And IsNumeric(txtTax.Text) Then
   dblPrice = txtPrice.Text
   dblTax = txtTax.Text
   dblTotal = (dblPrice * dblTax / 100) + dblPrice
   txtTotal.Text = Format(dblTotal, "Currency")
End If
```

7. Save your work

8. Run the form by clicking on the Run button on the Visual Basic IDE toolbar.

9. Enter the first two rows of data shown in Figure 3-45. Click the OK button after you enter each row.

| Figure 3-45 | PRICE AND SALES TAX DATA |
| --- | --- |

| PRICE | SALES TAX |
| --- | --- |
| 100 | 8.5 |
| 27.50 | 4.5 |
| 49.99 | 0 |

10. Notice how the cost is displayed in the total cost field.

11. Click the Exit button to close the form when you've finished testing.

12. Set a breakpoint at the line beginning with `If IsNumeric`. (*Hint*: Position the cursor on the line and press the F9 key to set the breakpoint.)

13. Run the program and enter the information from the last row in Figure 3-45.

14. Step through the code by pressing the F8 key.

15. At each line, position the cursor over the variable on the right side of the equals sign and review its value.

16. When you reach the line that begins `txtTotal.Text`, use the Immediate window to change the value of `dblTotal` to 107.935.

17. Continue executing the program. Notice how the cost value is displayed on the form.

18. Print the code for the form.

19. On a piece of paper, sketch a flowchart that shows how the `If` statement works in this program.

# QUICK | CHECK ANSWERS

## Session 3.1

1. a. string, b. integer, c. long integer, d. single
2. `Dim`, name, data type
3. format
4. `Option Explicit`
5. See Figure 3-46.

| Figure 3-46 | DATATYPES AND VARIABLE NAMES | | |
|---|---|---|---|
| **DATA ITEM** | | **DATA TYPE** | **VARIABLE NAME (INCLUDING THE PREFIX)** |
| telephone number | | String | `strTelephNumber` |
| age | | Integer | `intAge` |
| salary | | Single | `sngSalary` |
| hours worked | | Single | `sngHoursWorked` |
| number of members in a household | | Integer | `intNumHousehold` |
| average grade | | Single | `sngAverageGrade` |

6. A function returns a single value, whereas, the procedure does not return a single value.

## Session 3.2

1. a. Sequence b. Selection (Decision) c. Repetition (looping)
2. MsgBox
3. `If...Then...Else`
4. StepInto
5. Immediate

## Session 3.3

1. IsNumeric, false
2. IsDate, true
3. SetFocus
4. Len

In this tutorial you will:

- Create a standard module

- Become familiar with the repetition construct (or, loops)

- Use Do...While, Do...Until, and Iterative loops

- Work with the Excel object model

- Examine an advanced VBA program containing loops

- Examine code that calls a procedure

# REPEATING STATEMENTS WITH REPETITION CONTROL STRUCTURES

*Completing the TnT Check Register Project*

CASE

## TnT Consulting Group

Gene Cox is pleased with your progress so far on the projects that have been assigned to you. You've already learned enough to understand how Ashley used the If statement in the TnT Check Register program. Now she'd like to demonstrate the completed project, which includes the code that inserts the check data into an Excel worksheet. Before she can do that, though, you need to learn how to create a Repetition control structure and about some basic Excel objects. According to Ashley, it would be difficult to explain the remainder of the Check Register project unless you understood these concepts.

Once you understand each type, you will be free to choose the one that suits your needs. You have already learned about two control structures: Sequence and Selection (Decision). In this tutorial, you will learn about the third control structure: Repetition (Looping).

## SESSION 4 .1

In this session you will create a standard code module in which you will insert several procedures. You will also observe the behavior of the Repetition control structure. You will learn three different statements that can be used to implement the Repetition control structure in VBA. Throughout, you will use the debugging tools to demonstrate the steps of a Repetition control structure.

## Creating a Standard Module

By now you should be comfortable typing VBA code in the Code window. So far, you have focused on code associated with particular control objects in a form. For example, in Tutorial 2, you learned to write program statements for the command button Click events in the Check Register project. Recall that you wrote code for the Record button, the Clear button, and the Quit button. That is, you typed the code for the Record button within the Record button's Click event; you typed the code for the Clear button within its Click event, and so on. Figure 4-1 shows the basic structure of the code you created for the Check Register form. For illustration purposes, Figure 4-1 only includes the `Private Sub` and `End Sub` statements, along with some explanatory comments. The point of this figure is to illustrate the essential structure of a series of procedures associated with a particular form. Note that the name of a procedure is found on the first line of the procedure, immediately after the words "Private Sub."

| Figure 4-1 | FORM MODULE FOR THE FRMCHECK FORM IN THE TNT CHECK REGISTER PROJECT |

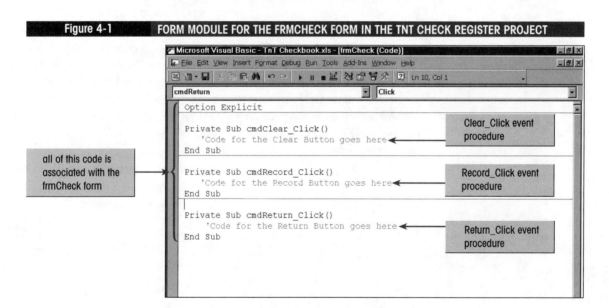

Collectively, all of the code written for a particular form is known as a **form module**. You can scroll the Code window to display the various procedures in a form module, but from VBA's point of view, each of the procedures is distinct. That is, an individual procedure will only run when that procedure's Click event is activated. For example, the Clear button's procedure will only run when the user clicks the Clear button.

In some cases, you will need to write VBA code that is not associated with a form. In that case, you can use a **standard module** (called a code module in previous versions of VBA), which is a module that contains only procedures and variable declarations. You should use a standard module when you need VBA to perform some task that does not require intervention on the part of the user—that is, when the program doesn't require any input from the user. Gene wants you to use a standard module while you practice writing looping statements.

In the first two sessions of this tutorial, you will write some simple procedures in a standard module. The goal of these procedures is to help you understand the concept of loops in VBA. The procedures you write will be named; "TryDoWhileLoop", "TryDoUntilLoop", and "TryForNextLoop". When you have completed this tutorial, your standard module will be structured as in Figure 4-2.

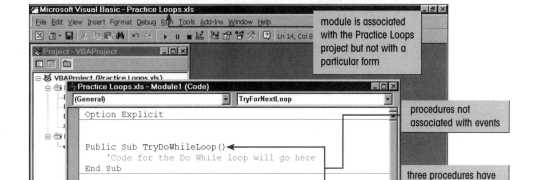

**Figure 4-2** | **STANDARD MODULE WITHIN THE CHECK REGISTER PROJECT**

To insert a standard module into a project, you use the Module command on the Insert menu. (By contrast, to create a form module, you use the UserForm command on the Insert menu.) This opens a Code window where you can then insert the procedures that will make up the module.

You will now create the module and add the three procedures to the module. You will actually add the code to the three procedures later in this tutorial. Note that, normally, it is not necessary to create all procedures for a standard module at one time. But Gene wants you to do it now to help you understand the structure of a standard module.

## To create the module and add the three procedures:

**1.** Start Excel and open a new workbook.

**2.** Save the workbook as **Practice Loops** in the Tutorial.04 folder on your Data Disk.

**3.** Start the VBA IDE.

**4.** Open the Project Explorer window.

**5.** Click **Insert** on the menu bar, and then click **Module**. A Code window opens, as shown in Figure 4-3. Now you can add the three procedures that will make up the complete module.

| Figure 4-3 | NEW STANDARD MODULE PRIOR TO ADDING ANY CODE |
| --- | --- |

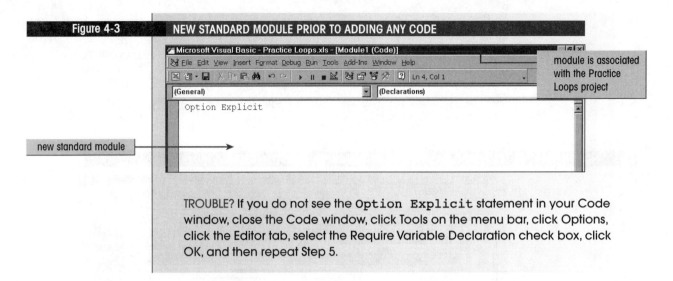

new standard module

module is associated with the Practice Loops project

TROUBLE? If you do not see the `Option Explicit` statement in your Code window, close the Code window, click Tools on the menu bar, click Options, click the Editor tab, select the Require Variable Declaration check box, click OK, and then repeat Step 5.

Now that you have inserted the standard module into the project, you can insert the three procedures into the module. You insert procedures by using the Procedure command on the Insert menu.

## To insert the procedures into the standard module:

1. Click **Insert** on the menu bar and then click **Procedure**. The Add Procedure dialog box opens, as shown in Figure 4-4. Next, you will type the name of the first procedure in the Name text box. Procedure names must follow the same rules used for naming variables.

| Figure 4-4 | ADD PROCEDURE DIALOG BOX |
| --- | --- |

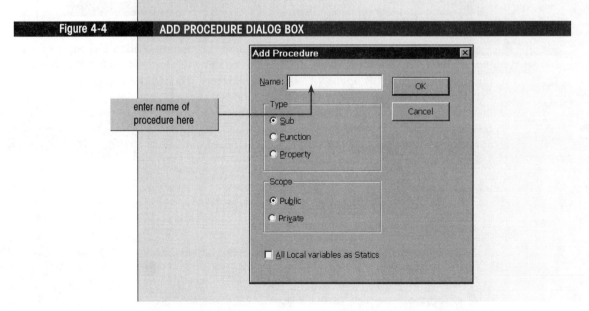

enter name of procedure here

2. Type `TryDoWhileLoop` in the Name text box, and then click **OK**. The procedure's opening statement (`Public Sub`) and ending statement (`End Sub`) are added to the code module, as shown in Figure 4-5. Note that the procedure's name "`TryDoWhileLoop`" is included on the same line as the `Public Sub` statement. The cursor is positioned between the opening and closing statements, ready for you to begin typing the procedure's code. However, you will not actually type the code for the procedure right now. Instead, you will insert a second procedure.

| Figure 4-5 | STANDARD MODULE WITH FIRST PROCEDURE ADDED |
| --- | --- |

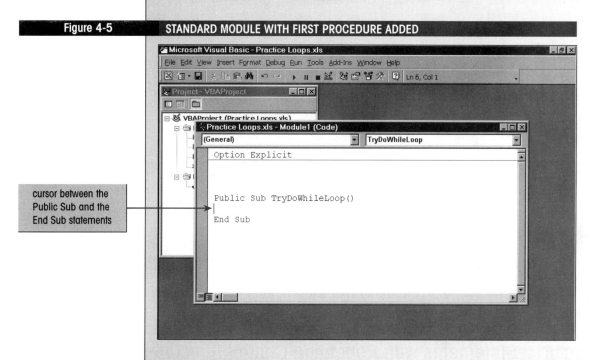

cursor between the Public Sub and the End Sub statements

3. Repeat Steps 1 and 2 to insert a procedure named `TryDoUntilLoop`. The new procedure is inserted into the Code window. VBA also inserts a horizontal line to separate the `TryDoWhileLoop` procedure from the `TryDoUntilLoop` procedure. Note that you did not have to move the cursor below the first procedure in order to insert the second procedure.

4. Insert a procedure named **`TryForNextLoop`**. The new procedure, along with a horizontal line, is added to the module. Your Code window should now look like Figure 4-6.

Figure 4-6 | **STANDARD MODULE WITH THREE PROCEDURES ADDED**

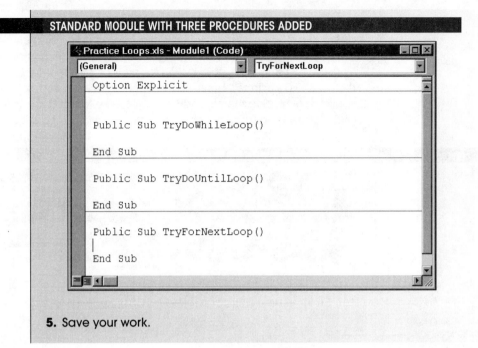

**5.** Save your work.

You have just created a standard module with three procedures. You will add code to these procedures later in this tutorial. In the next sections you will learn to write three different kinds of Repetition control structures, or loops. You will start by learning about the concept of repetition, and then you will learn the Do…While loop, the Do…Until loop, and the For…Next loop.

## Repeating Statements with Repetition Control Structures (Loops)

In Tutorial 3, you learned about the Sequence control structure, which processes statements one after the other until each statement has been completed. You also learned about one kind of Selection control structure, which allows a program to decide between two alternatives based on a condition you specify. Then you wrote some code that incorporated a Selection structure in the form of an If…Then…Else statement.

In this tutorial you will learn about the Repetition control structure, which is sometimes called a **looping mechanism** (or simply a **loop**). As its name implies, a **Repetition control structure** is used to repeat one or more statements.

To understand why loops can be helpful, suppose you were asked to create a program that calculates total wages for each of 90 employees. Rather than writing a long series of statements consisting of 90 separate salary calculations, you could write a loop that would repeat the same few salary calculation statements for each employee.

Depending on your needs, you can choose from two types of Repetition structures—Do loops, and Iterative loops. A **Do loop** continually processes one or more statements until a condition results in either true or false as specified. An **Iterative loop** processes a series of statements a certain number of times. As a developer, you will have to learn how to select the type of loop that is most appropriate for your application. You will learn more about this as you work through the remaining tutorials in this text. After you have observed the different kinds of loops and how they look, you will begin to understand when to use each kind of loop.

In the next several sections, you will write some very simple loops. Once you have become acquainted with the looping mechanisms, you will select the appropriate looping mechanism to use in the Check Register project.

# Using the Two Kinds of Do Loops

The Do loop actually has two forms—the Do…While loop and the Do…Until loop. Like the Selection structures you studied in Tutorial 3, both Do…While loops and Do…Until loops include a condition. Within a Do loop, the condition tells VBA when to stop processing a set of statements. (By contrast, the condition in a selection structure tells VBA which two sets of statements should be processed.) As in a Selection structure, the condition in a Do loop evaluates to either true or false. (Recall that such an expression is known as a Boolean expression.) As you learned in Tutorial 3, such a condition is known as a Boolean expression. The two types of Do loops (Do…While and Do…Until) are distinguished by how they respond to the condition. A **Do…While loop** continues repeating statements *while* the condition *remains* true. By contrast, a **Do…Until loop** repeats statements *until* a condition *becomes* true.

In VBA, you create a Do…While loop by writing a `Do…While` statement. Likewise, you create a Do…Until loop by writing a `Do…Until` statement. You will look at these two options separately, beginning with the Do…While loop

## Using Do…While Loops

As explained earlier, the Do…While loop repeats statements while a condition is true. When the condition becomes false, the Do…While loop stops repeating the statements. The flowchart in Figure 4-7 illustrates the Do…While loop.

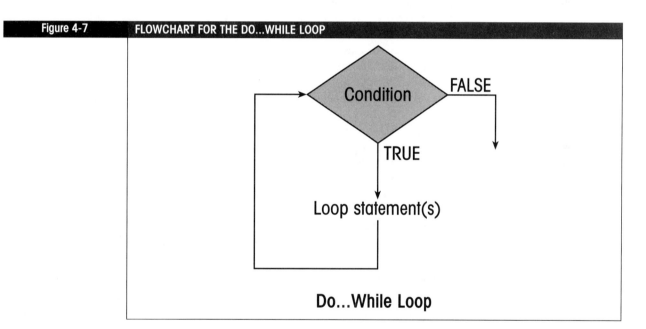

| Figure 4-7 | FLOWCHART FOR THE DO…WHILE LOOP |
|---|---|

**Do…While Loop**

The condition is tested, or evaluated, at the top of the loop, before the set of statements. As long as the condition result is true, the statements are repeated. When the condition becomes false, the loop discontinues, and VBA begins processing the statement immediately following the loop structure.

### Examining a `Do…While` Statement

All programming languages include statements that you can use to implement a Do…While loop. The syntax might be a little different from language to language, but the Do…While loop performs the same basic way in all programming languages. The following is the VBA syntax for the Do…While loop.

| Syntax | ```
Do While condition
        Statement(s)
Loop
``` |
|---|---|
| Explanation | The condition is evaluated at the top of the loop. If the condition is true, the statements are repeated. (Note that the loop may contain one statement or multiple statements.) If the condition is false the loop stops. The Loop statement tells VBA to return to the top of the loop and test the condition again. |
| Example | ```
Dim intLoopNumber as Integer
intLoopNumber = 1
Do While intLoopNumber <= 25
        intLoopNumber = intLoopNumber + 2
        Debug.Print intLoopNumber
Loop
Debug.Print "Loop has ended!"
``` |

In the example, the first statement declares a variable named `intLoopNumber`. The second line (`intLoopNumber = 1`) is an assignment statement that sets the variable equal to 1. You learned about variable declarations and assignment statements in Tutorial 3. If these statements don't seem familiar to you, review the relevant sections in Tutorial 3 now.

The loop itself actually begins with the line: `Do While intLoopNumber <= 25`. This line evaluates the condition (`intLoopNumber <= 25`). If the value of `intLoopNumber` is less than or equal to 25 (that is, if the result of the condition is true), then the statement in the next line is executed. This statement (`intLoopNumber = intLoopNumber + 2`) is an assignment statement that sets the variable `intLoopNumber` equal to 2 more than its original value. Because the `intLoopNumber` variable was initially set to 1, the first time through the loop, this assignment statement would make the variable equal to 3. The next statement (`Debug.Print intLoopNumber`) prints the value of `intLoopNumber` to the Immediate window (which you learned about in Tutorial 3). The next statement, the `Loop` statement, then sends control of the program back to the first line of the loop, to evaluate the condition again. Because 3 *is* less than or equal to 25 (in other words, because the condition is still true) the loop begins again. The second time through the loop, the assignment statement would make the variable equal to 5, the next time 7, and so on, until finally the variable is equal to 27. At that point, the condition would result in false, because 27 is *not* less than or equal to 25. The loop then ends, and the line after the `Loop` statement (`Debug.Print "Loop has ended!"`) is executed, displaying the sentence "The Loop has ended!" in the Immediate window.

## Coding a Do...While Statement

Now that you are familiar with the structure of the Do...While statement, you can practice creating one in VBA. In this section you will create the Do...While statement example described in the preceding section. You'll actually type the Do...While statement within the TryDoWhileLoop procedure you created earlier. Because the example Do...While loop involves the Debug. Print method, you'll need to open the Immediate window within the VBA IDE before running the program.

## *To create and run a Do...While loop:*

1. Click on the blank line between the Public Sub and End Sub statements in the **TryDoWhileLoop** procedure.

2. Type the code shown below.

```
Dim intLoopNumber as Integer
intLoopNumber = 1
Do While intLoopNumber <= 25
      intLoopNumber = intLoopNumber + 2
      Debug.Print intLoopNumber
Loop
Debug.Print "Loop has ended!"
```

3. Compare your screen with Figure 4-8 and make any necessary corrections.

**Figure 4-8**   STANDARD MODULE WITH TRYDOWHILELOOP STATEMENTS ADDED

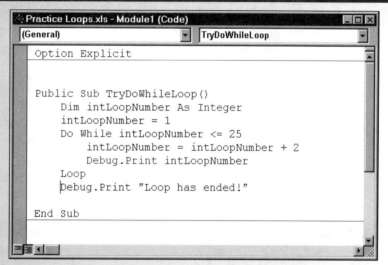

4. Click **View** on the menu bar, click **Immediate window**, and then arrange the Immediate window and the Code window so they are displayed side-by-side, as in Figure 4-9.

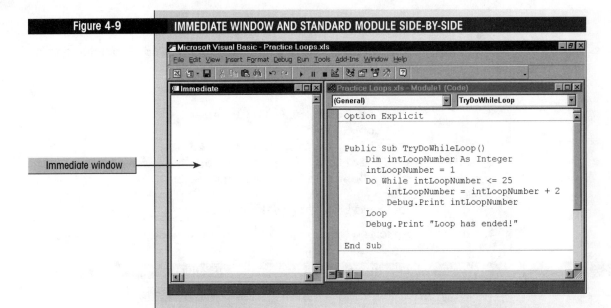

Figure 4-9    IMMEDIATE WINDOW AND STANDARD MODULE SIDE-BY-SIDE

**5.** Verify that the cursor is positioned anywhere inside the `TryDoWhileLoop` procedure.

Now you are ready to run the program. In the next step, you'll use a method you haven't tried before. Instead of using the Run button on the toolbar, you will use the F5 key. In the future, when told to run your program, you can choose from either the F5 key or the Run button.

**6.** Press **F5**. The program runs, and the procedure prints the value of the variable `intLoopNumber` in the Immediate window each time the loop executes. Your screen should look like Figure 4-10.

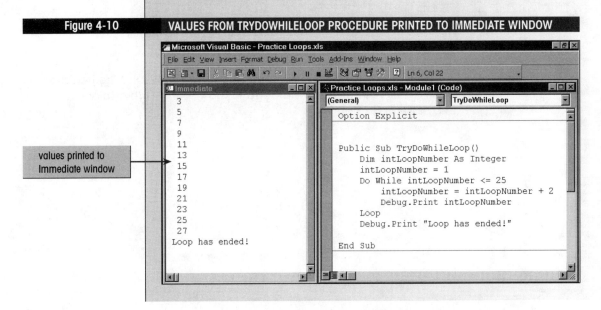

Figure 4-10    VALUES FROM TRYDOWHILELOOP PROCEDURE PRINTED TO IMMEDIATE WINDOW

The procedure printed the values in the Immediate window so quickly that you couldn't possibly observe the loop's progress. To actually observe the operation of the loop, you can use the Step Into debugging tool, described earlier in Tutorial 3.

## Observing a Do...While Statement with Step Into

As you learned in Tutorial 3, the Step Into feature of the debugging tools allows you to observe a program as each line is executed. By using this feature with the Do...While statement, you will be able to observe how statements are repeated within the loop. You'll try using the Step Into feature now.

### To observe the Do...While Statement with Step Into:

1. Verify that the cursor is positioned anywhere in the TryDoWhileLoop procedure, click **Debug** on the menu bar, and then click **Step Into**. The Step Into feature highlights the first line of code, the Public Sub statement, as shown in Figure 4-11.

**Figure 4-11**   **CODE WINDOW IN STEP INTO MODE, SHOWING CURRENT LINE OF EXECUTION**

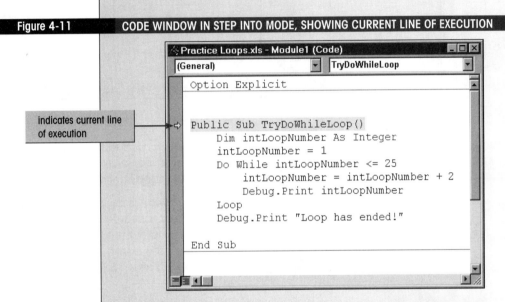

indicates current line of execution

```
Practice Loops.xls - Module1 (Code)
(General)                              TryDoWhileLoop

Option Explicit


Public Sub TryDoWhileLoop()
     Dim intLoopNumber As Integer
     intLoopNumber = 1
     Do While intLoopNumber <= 25
         intLoopNumber = intLoopNumber + 2
         Debug.Print intLoopNumber
     Loop
     Debug.Print "Loop has ended!"

End Sub
```

2. Press **F8** twice. The Do...While statement is now highlighted.

3. Position the cursor over the intLoopNumber variable to check its value. At this point, the value of the variable is 1.

4. Press **F8** twice. The Debug.Print statement is now highlighted. Place the cursor on the inLoopNumber variable. The value of the variable is now 3, because the preceding statement added 2 to the variable's initial value.

5. Press **F8**. The Loop statement is now highlighted. A 3 appears in the Immediate window, immediately below the phrase "Loop has ended!" See Figure 4-12.

| Figure 4-12 | CODE WINDOW AND IMMEDIATE WINDOW |
|---|---|

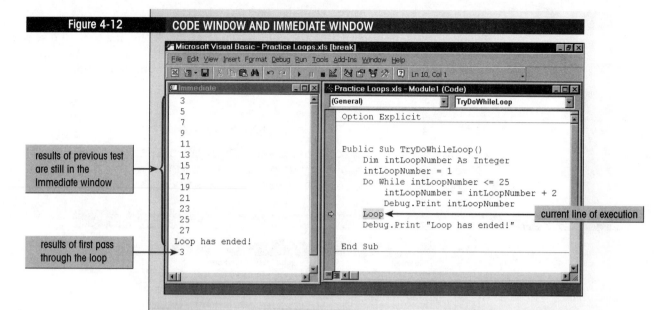

results of previous test are still in the Immediate window

results of first pass through the loop

current line of execution

6. Press **F8** again. The highlighting returns to the top of the loop. The `Do...While` statement will now test the condition. If the condition is true, the loop will continue. If the condition is false, the loop will stop. Because the value of `intLoopCounter` is currently equal to 3 (which is less than 25), the condition results in true.

7. Continue to press **F8** until the line "Loop as ended!" is displayed in the Immediate window. As you go through the loop, observe the Immediate window. Each time the highlighting returns to the top of the loop ask yourself if the loop will continue or if the loop will stop. When the complete procedure has been executed, your screen should look like Figure 4-13. The procedure has now terminated.

| Figure 4-13 | IMMEDIATE WINDOW AFTER LOOP HAS BEEN COMPLETED |
|---|---|

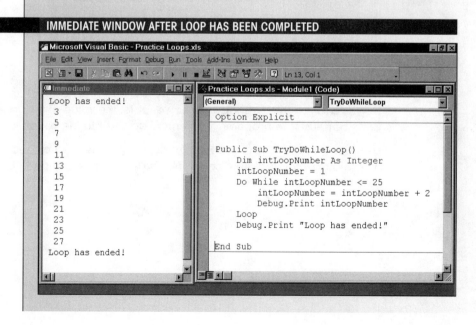

In the previous steps you tried one form of the looping mechanism. You observed that a test of the condition was performed at the top of the loop and if the condition result was true, the loop continued. The loop ended when the condition result became false. Now that you are familiar with a Do...While loop, you can learn about another kind of Do loop, the Do...Until loop.

## Using Do...Until Loops

The Do...Until loop works similarly to the Do...While loop in that the result of a condition determines whether the loop will continue. The difference has to do with when the condition is tested and the value that stops the loop. In a Do...While loop, the condition is positioned at the top of the loop, and the loop continues to execute *while* the condition result is true. As soon as the condition result becomes false, the Do...While loop stops. By contrast, the condition in the Do...Until loop is positioned at the bottom of the loop, and the loop continues to execute *until* the condition result becomes true. The flowchart in Figure 4-14 illustrates the Do...Until loop. Comparing Figure 4-14 with Figure 4-7 will help you understand the differences between the two loops.

| Figure 4-14 | FLOWCHART ILLUSTRATING THE DO...UNTIL LOOP |
| --- | --- |

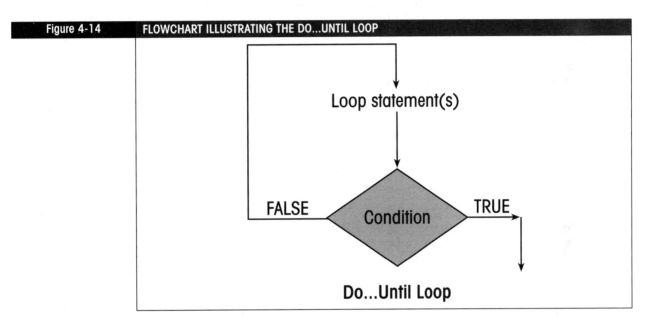

### Examining a Do...Until Statement

You create a Do...Until loop in VBA by writing a Do...Until statement. The syntax of the Do...Until statement is shown below.

| Syntax | Do |
| --- | --- |
| | `        Statement(s)`<br>`Loop Until condition` |
| **Explanation** | After the statement (or statements) in the loop are executed, the condition (which is at the bottom of the loop) is evaluated. If the condition results in *true*, the loop stops. If the condition results in *false*, the loop is repeated. |
| **Example** | `Dim intLoopNumber as Integer`<br>`intLoopNumber = 1`<br>`Do`<br>`        intLoopNumber = intLoopNumber + 2`<br>`        Debug.Print intLoopNumber`<br>`Loop Until intLoopNumber > 25`<br>`Debug.Print "Loop has ended!"` |

In the example above, the first line declares a variable named `intLoopNumber`. The second line sets the variable, `intLoopNumber` to 1. The third line marks the beginning of the Do...Until loop. The fourth line (`intLoopNumber = intLoopNumber + 2`) adds 2 to the variable, `intLoopNumber`. The fifth line, (`Debug.PrintintLoop Number`) prints the value of the variable `intLoopNumber` to the Immediate window. The sixth line (`Loop Until intLoopNumber > 25`), at the bottom of the loop, checks to see if the value of `intLoopNumber` is greater than 25, if it is, the loop stops; if it is not, the loop repeats.

### Coding a `Do...Until` Statement

You will now enter and test the `Do...Until` statement shown in the preceding section. As you test the `Do...Until` statement, pay attention to when the condition is tested and what result of the condition causes the loop to discontinue.

---

### *To enter and test the Do...Until loop:*

1. Scroll the Code window so that you can see the `TryDoUntilLoop` procedure you inserted earlier. Increase the length of the window, if necessary, so that you can see more of the module.

2. Click the blank line between the procedure's `Public Sub` and `End Sub` statements.

3. Type the following:

   ```
   Dim intLoopNumber as Integer
   intLoopNumber = 1
   Do
        intLoopNumber = intLoopNumber + 2
        Debug.Print intLoopNumber
   Loop Until intLoopNumber > 25
   Debug.Print "Loop has ended!"
   ```

4. Compare your procedure with Figure 4-15 and make any necessary changes.

| Figure 4-15 | CODE ADDED TO TRYDOUNTILLOOP PROCEDURE |

results of previous tests

new code

```
Microsoft Visual Basic - Practice Loops.xls
File  Edit  View  Insert  Format  Debug  Run  Tools  Add-Ins  Window  Help
                                                          Ln 23, Col 1

Immediate
Loop has ended!
3
5
7
9
11
13
15
17
19
21
23
25
27
Loop has ended!
```

```
Practice Loops.xls - Module1 (Code)
(General)                    TryDoUntilLoop

Public Sub TryDoWhileLoop()
    Dim intLoopNumber As Integer
    intLoopNumber = 1
    Do While intLoopNumber <= 25
        intLoopNumber = intLoopNumber + 2
        Debug.Print intLoopNumber
    Loop
    Debug.Print "Loop has ended!"

End Sub

Public Sub TryDoUntilLoop()
    Dim intLoopNumber As Integer
    intLoopNumber = 1
    Do
        intLoopNumber = intLoopNumber + 2
        Debug.Print intLoopNumber
    Loop Until intLoopNumber > 25
    Debug.Print "Loop has ended!"
End Sub
```

The code is now ready to test. But before you run the program, you should erase the contents of the Immediate Window so that you can start with a fresh, blank window. To erase the Immediate window, you simply select its contents, and then use the Clear command on the Edit menu. You'll try that technique now.

### To erase the Immediate window and run the Do...Until loop:

1. Click anywhere in the Immediate window.

2. Click **Edit** on the menu bar and then click **Select All**. All the values are now highlighted, ready to be deleted.

3. Click **Edit** again, and then click **Clear**. Now that the results of the Do-While loop are gone, you can test the Do...Until statement.

4. Click anywhere inside the TryDoUntilLoop procedure.

5. Run the procedure. The procedure prints the value of intLoopNumber in the Immediate window each time it executes the loop.

Because your computer executes the statements in the Do...Until loop so quickly, the multiple values of the variable appear almost instantaneously in the Immediate window. As with the Do...While loop, in order to actually see the Do...Until loop execute, line by line, you need to use the Step Into feature of the debugging tools.

### Observing a Do...Until Statement with Step Into

The Step Into feature will help you observe the Do...Until loop in action. Gene suggests that you take your time as you run the loop again with Step Into. Carefully observe the value of the variable each time through the loop, and try to determine whether the loop will continue or stop.

## To observe the Do...Until loop using Step Into:

1. With the cursor positioned anywhere in the `TryDoUntilLoop` procedure, click **Debug** on the menu bar and then click **Step Into**. The `Public Sub` statement is highlighted.

2. Press **F8** twice. The `Do` statement is now highlighted.

3. Check the value of the variable, `intLoopNumber`. At this point, the value is 1.

4. Continue to press **F8** until "Loop has ended!" is displayed in the Immediate window. Pause at each step and check the value of the variable. As the loop is executed, observe the Immediate window. Each time the highlighting returns to the bottom of the loop, ask yourself if the loop will continue or if the loop will stop. Remember that, in the case of the Do...Until loop, the loop will terminate when the condition becomes true. In other words, the loop will terminate once the value of `intLoopNumber` becomes greater than 25.

As you finish testing the Do...Until loop with Step Into, Gene stops by to observe your work. He explains that beginning programmers are sometimes confused by the differences between the two types of Do loops. To ensure that you fully grasp the distinction, he suggests you take some time to compare Do...While loops with Do...Until loops.

## Comparing `Do...Until` Statements and `Do...While` Statements

Figure 4-16 presents the examples of the two Do loops side by side. As you examine the two examples, notice the differences in the way they are processed.

| Figure 4-16 | COMPARISON OF THE DO...WHILE LOOP AND THE DO...UNTIL LOOP |
|---|---|

| DO...WHILE LOOP | DO...UNTIL LOOP |
|---|---|
| `Dim intLoopNumber as Integer` | `Dim intLoopNumber as Integer` |
| `IntLoopNumber = 1` | `IntLoopNumber = 1` |
| `Do While  intLoopNumber <= 25` | `Do` |
| `    IntLoopNumber = intLoopNumber + 2` | `    IntLoopNumber = intLoopNumber + 2` |
| `    Debug.Print intLoopNumber` | `    Debug.Print intLoopNumber` |
| `Loop` | `Loop Until intLoopNumber > 25` |
| `Debug.Print "Loop has ended!"` | `Debug.Print "Loop has ended!"` |

Because the condition is tested at the bottom of the Do...Until loop, the statement (or statements) will necessarily be processed at least one time (until the condition is tested the first time). The Do...While loop, however, tests the condition at the top of the loop, which means that the condition could be false from the very beginning, in which case the loop would never be processed at all.

The structural difference between the two types of Do loops means that the two will behave differently in certain circumstances. In the next set of steps, you will observe what happens in both loops if the value of the `intLoopNumber` is greater than 25 at the very beginning. As you will see, the two loops respond very differently.

*To observe the difference between the Do...Until loop and the Do...While loop:*

**1.** Clear the Immediate Window.

**2.** In the `TryDoWhileLoop` procedure, edit the statement that sets the initial value of `intLoopNumber` so that the initial value is equal to 26, as seen in Figure 4-17.

| Figure 4-17 | VALUE OF INTLOOPNUMBER |
| --- | --- |

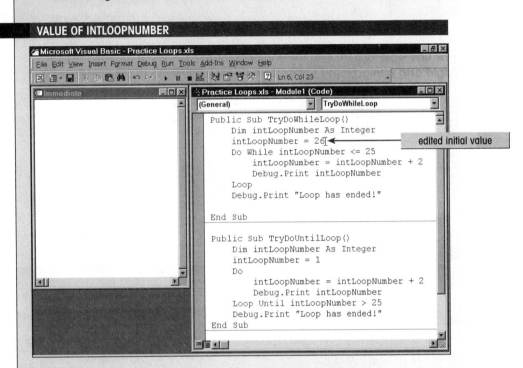

**3.** Now test the loop as you did earlier, using Step Into. Continue to press **F8** until your procedure has reached the `End Sub` statement. Notice that the statements in loop are not processed at all because the condition is false at the beginning of the loop. Thus, the procedure only prints "Loop has ended!" in the Immediate window. See Figure 4-18.

| Figure 4-18 | RESULTS OF TRYDOWHILELOOP PROCEDURE |

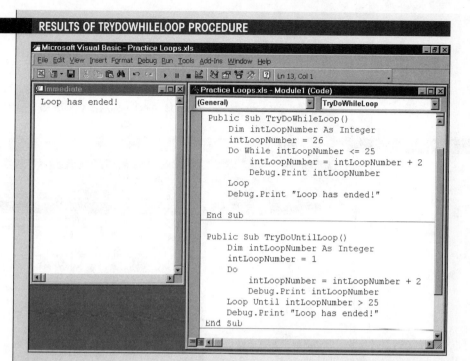

**4.** In the `TryDoUntilLoop` procedure, edit the statement that sets the initial value of `intLoopNumber` so that the initial value is equal to 26, as seen in Figure 4-19.

| Figure 4-19 | EDITED INITIAL VALUE IN TRYDOUNTILLOOP PROCEDURE |

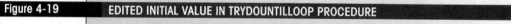
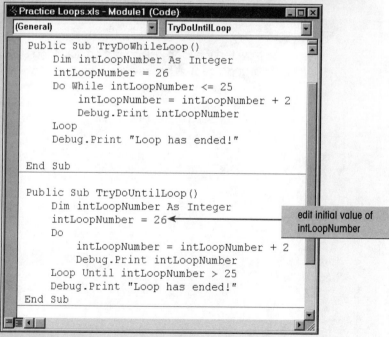

**5.** Now test the Do...Until loop using Step Into. The Do...Until loop processes one time and then discontinues. This is because the condition is tested at the bottom of the Do...Until loop, rather than at the top, as it is with the Do...While loop.

6. Compare your Immediate window with Figure 4-20. As you can see, the procedure containing the Do...While loop only printed the line "Loop has ended" in the Immediate window. It did not change the value of the variable. When the Do...While loop ended, the variable still had the same value, 26. By contrast, the procedure containing the Do...Until loop increased the value of the variable to 28 before it terminated.

| Figure 4-20 | RESULTS OF CHANGING THE INITIAL VALUE OF INTLOOPNUMBER |
| --- | --- |

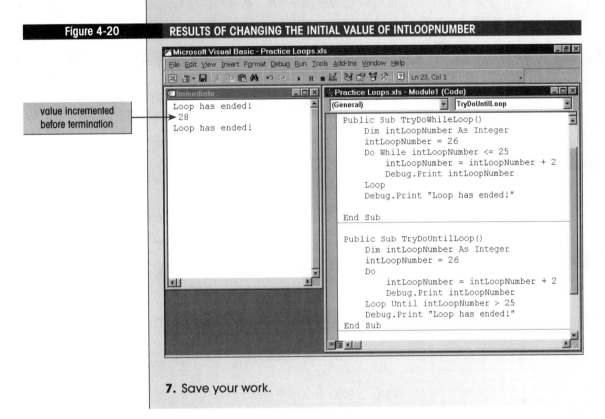

value incremented
before termination

```
Microsoft Visual Basic - Practice Loops.xls
File  Edit  View  Insert  Format  Debug  Run  Tools  Add-Ins  Window  Help
                                                        Ln 23, Col 1

Immediate
Loop has ended!
28
Loop has ended!

Practice Loops.xls - Module1 (Code)
(General)                          TryDoUntilLoop

Public Sub TryDoWhileLoop()
    Dim intLoopNumber As Integer
    intLoopNumber = 26
    Do While intLoopNumber <= 25
        intLoopNumber = intLoopNumber + 2
        Debug.Print intLoopNumber
    Loop
    Debug.Print "Loop has ended!"

End Sub

Public Sub TryDoUntilLoop()
    Dim intLoopNumber As Integer
    intLoopNumber = 26
    Do
        intLoopNumber = intLoopNumber + 2
        Debug.Print intLoopNumber
    Loop Until intLoopNumber > 25
    Debug.Print "Loop has ended!"
End Sub
```

7. Save your work.

You have finished observing the two versions of the Do loop. Now Gene wants you to learn about the other kind of looping mechanism—an Iterative loop.

# Using **Iterative Loops**

As explained earlier, the Iterative loop is a repetition structure that repeats a series of statements a specified number of times. An Iterative loop is useful when you know how many times you want to execute the statements in the loop. For example, suppose you need to calculate weekly wages for exactly 20 employees each week. You know, then, that you want to go through the loop 20 times—so an Iterative loop would be a good choice. (Don't be concerned if, at this point, you do not completely understand which loop is best in any given situation. As you continue to work through the tutorials, you will see each of the different types of loops used, and you will begin to develop a feel for the appropriate loop to use.)

## Examining a `For...Next` Statement

Most programming languages provide a set of statements that can be used to implement an Iterative loop. In VBA, you create an iterative loop by writing a **For...Next** statement. Recall that, with the Do...While and the Do...Until statements, a condition controls whether the loop continues or stops. By contrast, a For…Next loop begins with a special variable called a **control variable**, which is responsible for counting the number of times that VBA processes the loop. Thus, a control variable is also referred to as the loop's **counter**. At the beginning of the For…Next statement, the control variable is set to a beginning value. This value automatically increments the value each time through the loop, and stops when the value reaches an ending value that you specify. For example, you might specify that the loop should stop when the control variable reaches 15. The flowchart in Figure 4-21 illustrates how the For…Next statement works.

| Figure 4-21 | FLOWCHART ILLUSTRATING FOR…NEXT LOOP |
| --- | --- |

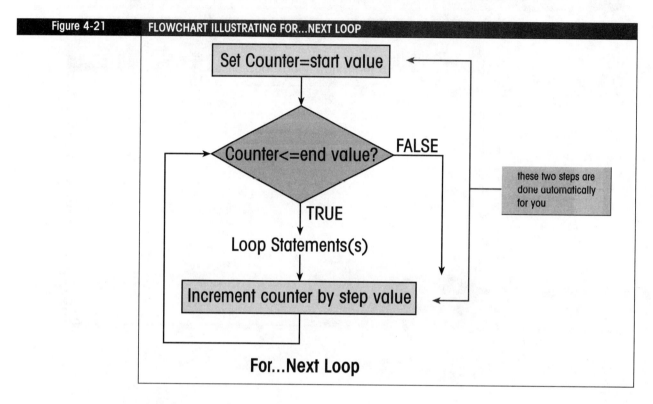

| Syntax | For counter = start To end [Step step]<br>    [statement(s)]<br>Next [counter] |
| --- | --- |
| Explanation | The control variable, or counter, is simply an integer variable that will be increased or decreased as the loop is executed. The Start value specifies the value of the counter before the loop is executed for the first time. When the counter becomes greater than the End value, the loop will stop. The optional step value represents the amount by which the counter should be incremented or decremented (i.e., the step value can actually be a negative number) at each pass through the loop. If you do not include a step value, the counter will increase by one each time through the loop. |
| Example | For intLoopCounter = 1 To 10<br>    debug.print intLoopCounter<br>Next intLoopCounter |

In the example above, the first statement (For intLoopCounter = 1 To 10) is used to control the loop. The first time through the loop, the variable, intLoopCounter is set to 1. It is then compared to the end value (10). If it is not greater than the end value, then the loop is processed. The second statement (debug.print intLoopCounter) prints the value of intLoopCounter to the Immediate window. The third statement (next intLoopCounter) increases the value of intLoopCounter by 1. (Note that 1 is the default increment—this For...Next statement does not include a step option.) This last statement also sends control back to the top of the loop. When the control returns to the first statement (For intLoopCounter = 1 To 10), the value of the intLoopCounter variable is compared to the ending value (10); if it is greater than 10, the loop terminates, if not, the loop is repeated.

## Coding and Observing a For...Next Loop

Next, Gene asks you to enter the example For...Next statement into a procedure, just as you did with the other two loops. You will test the loop using the same debugging tools you used in the previous examples.

*To test the For...Next loop:*

1. Click between the Public Sub and End Sub statements in the TryForNextLoop procedure.

2. Type the following:

```
Dim intLoopCounter as Integer
For intLoopCounter = 1 to 10
    Debug.Print intLoopCounter
Next intLoopCounter
Debug.Print "Loop has ended!"
```

3. Run the TryForNextLoop procedure. The loop executes and displays its results in the Immediate window, as in Figure 4-22.

| Figure 4-22 | CODE WINDOW AND IMMEDIATE WINDOW DISPLAYED |

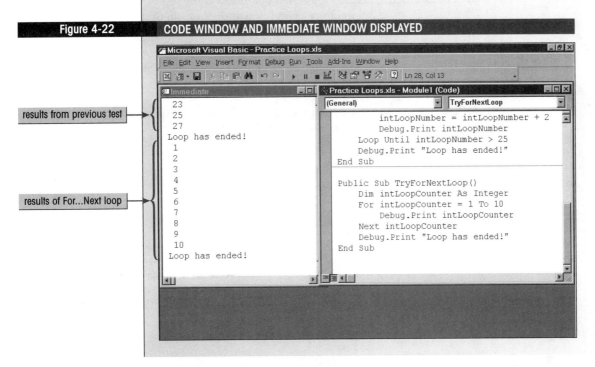

results from previous test

results of For...Next loop

**4.** Run the loop again, this time using Step Into. As you make your passes through the loop, observe that the value of `intLoopCounter` is printed to the immediate window. After the loop ends, the code prints "Loop has ended!" in the Immediate window.

**5.** Save your work, switch back to the Excel workbook window, and close the Practice Loops workbook.

**6.** If you are going to take a break, close Excel

You have finished creating samples of the two major types of Repetition structures, or loops. As you begin to incorporate looping into your programs, keep in mind that you should use the Do...Until loop when you want to process a loop at least one time and you do not know how many times you want to process the loop. If you want to create a loop that is never processed under certain conditions, use the Do...While loop. If you know how many times you want the loop to process, use the For...Next loop.

Gene explains that Ashley used Repetition structures in her code for the Check Register program. In Session 4.3, you will have a chance to examine that code. But before you can fully understand the loops Ashley wrote, you need to learn about some of the Excel objects she used in her program.

## Session 4.1 QUICK CHECK

**1.** List the three types of loops examined in this session:

a. _____

b. _____

c. _____

**2.** The _____ loop tests a condition at the top of the loop, whereas the _____ loop tests a condition at the bottom of the loop.

**3.** The _____ loop will always be processed at least one time.

**4.** The _____ loop increments the loop counter automatically.

**5.** A(n) _____ loop counts the number of times a loop is processed.

**6.** The _____ option of the For...Next loop specifies how much to increase or decrease the control variable.

**SESSION 4.2**

In this session you will study parts of the Excel object model and then you will learn how to write VBA statements that interact with Excel objects. You will write VBA statements to alter the names of the workbook's worksheets, place data into a worksheet, and alter some of the formatting properties of Excel objects.

## Interacting with Object Models

So far, you have worked with forms and their associated objects and events. You have learned that you can place an object on a form, alter its properties, and then write code that will respond to events that take place on that object. You have also learned that VBA projects always run in conjunction with one of the Office applications—for example, the TnT checking program will run in conjunction with Microsoft Excel. Projects written in VBA are dependent on the application for which they were written. For example, if a VBA project is written to work in conjunction with Word, then that application can run only in Word.

In order to write programs that interact with a particular Office application, you need to learn about that application's **object model**—that is, about the various objects included in the application. In the case of the TnT Check Register project, which is designed to interact with Excel, you need to learn about the objects included in Excel, such as workbooks, worksheets, cells, charts, etc. If, on the other hand, you were writing a program that was to operate in Word, you would need to learn to write statements that interact with Word objects, such as documents, paragraphs, sentences, characters, tables, etc. The same is true of PowerPoint, Outlook, and Access.

In the remainder of this tutorial, you will become familiar with the Excel object model in general, and then investigate a few specific Excel objects. You will learn more about the Excel object model, and about the object models of the other Office applications, in later tutorials.

## Working with the Excel Object Model

In Tutorial 2 you learned about objects through the analogy of a college campus. You learned that an object (such as the college campus) could contain a collection of other objects (such as buildings). Furthermore, objects are arranged in a hierarchy, with one object containing others, which in turn contain others, which in turn contain others, and so on. (For example, the college campus contains a collection of buildings, the buildings contain a collection of rooms, and the rooms contain a collection of seats.)

The diagram in Figure 4-23 represents the top few levels of the hierarchy of the Excel object model. The complete Excel model is actually quite detailed and contains many more collections and objects. Figure 4-23 only contains those collections and objects pertinent to the Check Register project. In other words, Figure 4-23 shows only a portion of the Excel object model. In the diagram, notice that some of the rectangles have shadows. These shadowed rectangles represent collections of objects. Rectangles without shadows are objects.

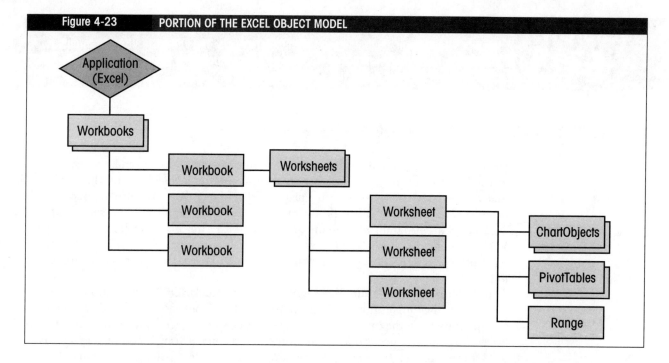

**Figure 4-23** **PORTION OF THE EXCEL OBJECT MODEL**

The object at the highest level is the application object. The **application object** is the Office application itself, in this case, Excel. The second level in the Excel object model is the **Workbooks collection**. You are probably aware that you can have more than one workbook open in Excel at any given time. Thus, the Workbook collection is a collection of all open workbooks. The **Workbook object**, on the next level, is a particular workbook—that is, the workbook object is one workbook within the Workbook collection. You are probably also aware that any workbook can contain more than one worksheet. In fact, when you open a new workbook, it automatically opens with three worksheets. Each workbook, then, contains a collection of worksheet objects.

## Referring to a Specific Excel Object

The position of an object within the object model hierarchy is important because in order to refer to an object within VBA code, you need to give the object's precise location within the hierarchy. To help you understand the importance of the hierarchy of objects, recall the object model for the college campus. Suppose a chair in a particular classroom needs a new wheel. The work order for the repair would have to include the building, the classroom within the building, the chair number in the classroom, and perhaps even which leg needs the replacement wheel.

Writing code that accesses particular Office objects requires similar precision. For example, to specify a particular worksheet, you need to specify the Excel application object, followed by a specific workbook within the Workbooks collection, followed by a specific worksheet within the Worksheets collection, followed by the object itself (such as "Sheet1"). To understand how this all works, look at the following reference to an Excel worksheet named Sheet2:

```
Application.Workbooks(1).Worksheets(1)
```

The first part (`Application`) is the top-level of the object model hierarchy. If you are writing code for Excel, `Application` represents Excel. If you are writing code for Word, `Application` represents Word, and so on. Note that you do not have to actually specify the name of the application; rather, VBA automatically assumes that within Word VBA programs, the application object is Word, that within Excel VBA programs, the application object is Excel, and so on.

The next part of the notation—Workbooks(1)—refers to the first workbook in the Workbook collection. Specifically, the word Workbooks specifies the Workbooks collection, and the number in parentheses (1) indicates the first workbook in that collection. The next part of the notation specifies the first worksheet in the Worksheets collection. Specifically, the word Worksheets specifies the Worksheet collection, and the number in parentheses (1) indicates the first worksheet in that collection.

The worksheet numbers refer to the order, from left to right, of the worksheet's tabs in the lower-left corner of the Excel window. The worksheet with the leftmost tab would be worksheets(1), the worksheet with the next tab over would be worksheets(2), and so on. Thus, if you were writing a program for a workbook that contained the three default worksheets, named "Sheet1," "Sheet2," and "Sheet3," then Sheet1 would be the first worksheet—that is, worksheets(1). Likewise, Sheet2 would be worksheets(2), and so on. Figure 4-24 illustrates this concept by indicating the number of the worksheet in the Worksheets collection.

| Figure 4-24 | DEFAULT WORKSHEETS AND THEIR VBA NAMES |
| --- | --- |

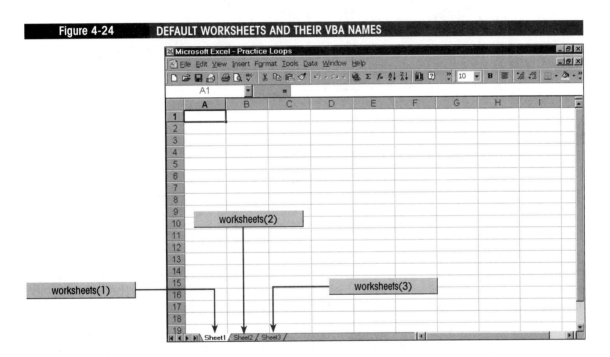

While this example refers to specific workbooks and worksheets by number, you can also refer to workbooks and worksheets by name. (The name of a worksheet is the name that is displayed on the worksheet tab, within the Excel workbook. The name of the workbook is the name of the .xls file itself.) For example, to refer a worksheet named "Expenses" within a workbook named "Report," you would use the following reference:

```
Application.Workbooks("Report").Worksheets("Expenses")
```

Note that the workbook and worksheet names must be enclosed in quotation marks.

## Altering Object Properties with Assignment Statements

Like all other objects, the objects in the Excel object model have specific properties. Once you understand how to refer to a specific object within an Office application, you can write statements that alter the value of the object's properties. For example, you might write a statement that changes a worksheet's Name property—thus changing the name displayed on the worksheet's tab within the Workbook window.

Changing any property of a worksheet **programmatically** (that is, with VBA program statements) requires an assignment statement. (You learned about assignment statements in Tutorial 3.) Within the assignment statement, the complete reference to the object belongs on the left of the equals sign. The name of the property you want to change follows the object reference, on the left side of the equals sign. The new value for the property you want to change belongs on the right of the equals sign. The following is an assignment statement that changes the Name property of worksheets (2), the second worksheet in the Worksheets collection, to "Deposits":

```
Application.Workbooks(1).Worksheets(2).Name = "Deposits"
```

To understand this statement, you might find it easier to read it backwards. The statement above would then read: "Assign the value 'Deposits' to the name property of the second worksheet in the Worksheet collection, which is in the first workbook of the Workbooks collection in the Excel application."

## Altering a Worksheet's Name Property

In the following steps you will have a chance to implement statements such as the one discussed above. Specifically, you will write statements that will change the default names of the three worksheets in an Excel workbook.

### To change the Name properties of three worksheets:

1. Start Excel (if you closed it after the last session).

2. Verify that the Excel Workbook window (and not the VBA IDE) is displayed, and open a new workbook if you do not have one open already. (You should only have *one* workbook open.) This workbook contains three default worksheets, named "Sheet1", "Sheet2", and "Sheet3."

3. Save the workbook as **Excel Objects** in the Tutorial.04 folder on your Data Disk.

4. Switch to the Excel VBA IDE, and, if the Immediate window is still open, close it. If necessary, open the Project Explorer window. In the next step, you will open the Code window associated with the current workbook.

5. In the Project Explorer, expand the Microsoft Excel Object folder (if necessary), and then double-click **ThisWorkbook**. The Code window opens. See Figure 4-25. Now you can insert a new procedure into the Code window.

**Figure 4-25** CODE WINDOW FOR THIS WORKBOOK

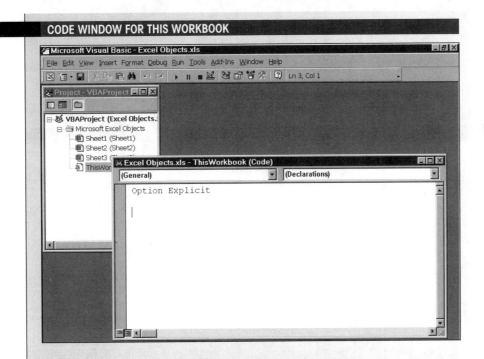

6. Click **Insert** on the menu bar, click **Procedure**, type **TryExcelObjects** in the Name text box, and then click **OK**. Now you are ready to type the statements that will change the Name property for each of the three worksheets in the current workbook. Specifically, you will change the Name property of Sheet1 to "Checks," the Name property of Sheet2 to "Deposits," and the Name property of Sheet3 to "Summary."

7. With the cursor within the **TryExcelObjects** procedure, type the following statements:

```
Application.Workbooks(1).Worksheets(1).Name = "Checks"
Application.Workbooks(1).Worksheets(2).Name = "Deposits"
Application.Workbooks(1).Worksheets(3).Name = "Summary"
```

When you are finished, your screen should match Figure 4-26.

**Figure 4-26** CODE WINDOW WITH NEW STATEMENTS ADDED

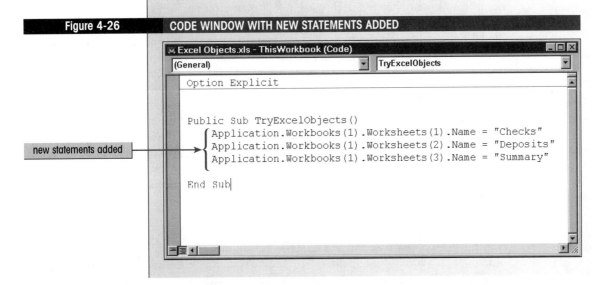

new statements added

8. With the cursor positioned anywhere within the **TryExcelObjects** procedure, press **F5**. The procedure runs.

9. Switch to the Excel workbook window. The new worksheet names, which were assigned by your VBA program, are displayed in the worksheet tabs. See Figure 4-27.

**Figure 4-27**  **WORKSHEET WITH NEW WORKSHEET NAMES**

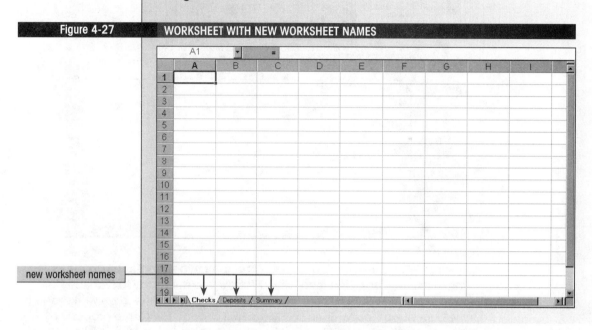

new worksheet names

The assignment statements you used to change the worksheet's Name properties are rather long. Thus, as you might imagine, changing properties for many objects could involve quite a bit of typing. To save time, you can employ a useful shortcut, which is explained in the next section.

## Using Default Values in Object References

In the preceding section you wrote statements in which you referenced each worksheet by number and then changed each worksheet's Name property. The statements were rather long, because they included the complete reference to the object within the Excel object model hierarchy. It's important to know how to refer to an object completely. However, when writing your statements you can often take some shortcuts.

Each VBA object has one default property. If you do not include a property in an assignment statement, VBA assumes you are referring to the default property. Likewise, within an object reference, VBA will assume certain values by default, unless you specify otherwise. For example, if you do not state the application object, VBA assumes you mean the current application—that is, the application in whose VBA IDE you are writing the code. In the preceding section, you were writing the code in the Excel VBA IDE, so Excel is the current application. Also, unless you state explicitly otherwise, VBA assumes you are referring to the current workbook—that is, to the workbook selected in the Project Explorer. The following two statements, then, are equivalent.

```
Application.Workbooks(1).Worksheets(1).Name = "Checks"
Worksheets(1).Name = "Checks"
```

Ashley, and the other developers at TnT Consulting, routinely accept these defaults. In other words, they do not include **Application.Workbooks(1)** in their assignment statements. To save time, Gene suggests that you follow the same practice. Next, Gene wants you to become familiar with another worksheet property—the Cells property.

## Altering a Worksheet's Cell Property

The **Cells** property of a worksheet controls the contents of a single cell. Within a statement, the Cells property is always followed by parentheses containing the row number and the column number of a specific cell, as follows: `Cells (row number, column number)`. Notice that, when using the Cells property, you must refer to *both* rows and columns by number. This differs from cell references in the Excel workbook window, where columns are referred to by letter (A,B,C, etc.). Within VBA statements, you must refer to columns by number. Column "A" is referred to as Column 1, Column B is referred to as Column 2, and so on. Thus, to reference cell C5 in a VBA statement, you would use the following Cells property:

```
Cells(5,3)
```

In this reference, 5 is the row number and 3 is the column number.

The Cells property is very useful, because you can use it to control what is displayed in a particular cell. In fact, in the TnT Check Register project, Ashley used the Cells property to insert the checking data into the worksheet.

As when changing the Name property, in order to change the Cells property you need to write an assignment statement. If you wanted to place the string "Example One" in the cell C5 in the worksheet named "Checks", you would use the following statement:

```
Worksheets("Checks").Cells(3,5) = "Example One"
```

Note that this statement does not include any mention of the application or workbook objects. As mentioned earlier, the current application (Excel) and the current workbook are assumed by default, so you do not actually have to include them in your assignment statements.

Now Gene asks you to write a few statements that will insert some simple strings in three different worksheets. Later you will see how Ashley used similar statements to transfer checkbook data from the form to the worksheet.

---

### *To write statements that change the Cells property of the active worksheet:*

1. Switch back to the Excel VBA IDE and make sure the cursor is positioned just below the statements you entered previously, then press **Enter** to add a blank line. When you run this procedure, the statements that name the sheets will be executed again, but since the worksheets have already been renamed, you will see no results of these statements. In this case, you are only interested in demonstrating the various statements in this procedure. In a real application, you would probably separate the two sets of statements into two procedures.

2. Type the following statements

```
Worksheets("Checks").Cells(3, 5) = "Example One"
Worksheets("Deposits").Cells(2, 3) = "Example Two"
Worksheets("Summary").Cells(4, 4) = "Example Three"
```

3. Compare your Code window with Figure 4-28 and make any necessary corrections.

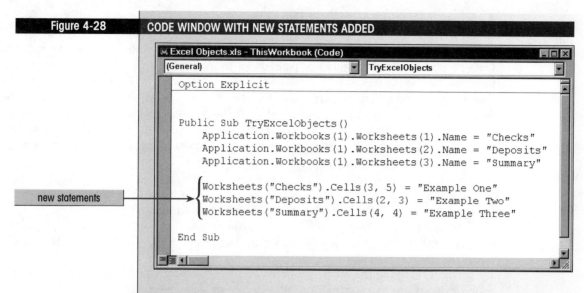

**Figure 4-28**    CODE WINDOW WITH NEW STATEMENTS ADDED

new statements

```
Excel Objects.xls - ThisWorkbook (Code)
(General)                              TryExcelObjects

    Option Explicit


    Public Sub TryExcelObjects()
        Application.Workbooks(1).Worksheets(1).Name = "Checks"
        Application.Workbooks(1).Worksheets(2).Name = "Deposits"
        Application.Workbooks(1).Worksheets(3).Name = "Summary"

        Worksheets("Checks").Cells(3, 5) = "Example One"
        Worksheets("Deposits").Cells(2, 3) = "Example Two"
        Worksheets("Summary").Cells(4, 4) = "Example Three"

    End Sub
```

4. With the cursor positioned anywhere within the procedure, press **F5**. The procedure runs.

5. Switch to the Excel workbook window.

6. Examine each worksheet, and observe the string inserted into it. As you look through the worksheets, look back at the code in Step 2. Compare each statement with the results you see in the worksheets. Notice how each reference to the cells property selected a particular cell and placed a string at the cell's location in the specified worksheet.

In the previous steps you learned how to access a worksheet by specifying its name in the statement. As you can imagine, this could become quite tedious if you wanted to place many items on the same worksheet since you would have to include the name of the worksheet in each statement. An alternate method is to make a particular worksheet the active worksheet. You will learn how to do this in the next section.

## Activating a Worksheet with the Activate Method

Writing statements that specifically refer to a particular worksheet can be time-consuming in a long program. Instead of typing the worksheet name in each statement, it's easier to begin by writing one statement that selects, or activates, a particular worksheet. That worksheet then becomes the **active worksheet**. Once a a worksheet is activated, VBA assumes that any subsequent statements refer to that active worksheet.

To activate a worksheet, you need to use the **Activate method**. The syntax of the Activate method is as follows:

| Syntax | `object.`**`Activate`** |
|---|---|
| **Explanation** | This statement makes the specified object active. Any references following the activate statement do not have to reference the activated object. |
| **Examples** | `Worksheets("Checks").Activate`<br>`Worksheets(1).Activate` |

Once a worksheet has been activated, a reference to the Cells property will, by default, refer to the active worksheet. Consider, for example, the following:

```
Worksheets("Summary").Activate
Cells(1, 2) = "Example Four"
```

The first statement in this example makes the worksheet named "Summary" the active worksheet. The second statement uses the Cells property and, since it contains no reference to a particular worksheet, the Cells property applies to the active worksheet. You could then make as many references as you would like to the Cells property, and it will continue to apply to the "Summary" worksheet.

## Altering Other Properties of a Worksheet

In the preceding section you simply placed a string of characters in a particular cell. The Cells property controls the contents of a particular cell in the worksheet. You can also write statements that change other properties of a cell, such as its font name, font size, italics, bold, etc.

For example, suppose you wanted to place the heading "TnT Check Register Summary Report" in the first row and first column of the worksheet named "Summary." Also, suppose you wanted to alter the appearance of the heading so that the font was 14-point Times New Roman bold. Finally, suppose you also wanted to place the date in row 2, by inserting the label "Date:" in the first column, and the current date (from your computer system) in the second column. The following code would accomplish all these tasks:

```
Worksheets("Summary").Activate
Cells(1, 1) = "TnT Check Register Summary Report"
Cells(1, 1).Font.Name = "Times New Roman"
Cells(1, 1).Font.Size = 16
Cells(1, 1).Font.Bold = True
Cells(2, 1) = "Date:"
Cells(2, 2) = Date
```

The first line activates the worksheet named "Summary." The second line places the string "TnT Check Register Summary Report" in the first row and first column of the worksheets (in Excel terms this would be cell A1). The third line uses the `Font.Name` property to set the font to "Times New Roman." The fourth line uses the `Font.Size` property to set the font size to 16-points. The fifth line sets the `Font.Bold` property to true—meaning that the text should be bold. (Note that you can use the Font property to set other font characteristics, such as italics and underlining.)

The sixth line in the code places the string `Date` in the second row, first column of the worksheet (in Excel terms this would be cell A2). Finally, the seventh line uses the Date function to place the current date in the second row and second column (in Excel terms this would be cell B2).

Now that you are familiar with this code, Gene wants you to enter it into the `TryExcelObjects` procedure. Your goal here is just to try out these statements, in order to observe how they work. In the next session, Ashley will show you how she actually incorporated them into the Check Register project.

## To write code that will place some data in the active worksheet:

1. Return to the Excel VBA IDE, and click below the last line of code you entered earlier, just above the End Sub statement. Maximize the window so that you can see your code more clearly.

2. Press **Enter** to insert a blank line, and then type the following statements:

```
Worksheets(3).Name = "Summary"
Worksheets("Summary").Activate

Cells(1, 1) = "TnT Check Register Summary Report"
Cells(1, 1).Font.Name = "Times New Roman"
Cells(1, 1).Font.Size = 16
Cells(1, 1).Font.Bold = True

Cells(2, 1) = "Date:"
Cells(2, 2) = Date
```

3. Compare your screen with Figure 4-29, checking your code for accuracy. Make any necessary corrections.

| Figure 4-29 | CODE THAT WILL RECORD DATA IN WORKSHEET |
| --- | --- |

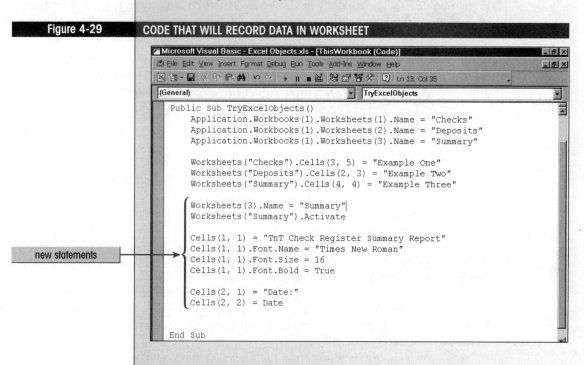

new statements

4. Press **F5** to run the procedure.

5. Switch to the Excel worksheet window. Notice that worksheet "Summary" is the current worksheet and that the headings have been added and formatted as shown in Figure 4-30.

**Figure 4-30**    **HEADINGS HAVE BEEN ADDED TO THE "SUMMARY" WORKSHEET**

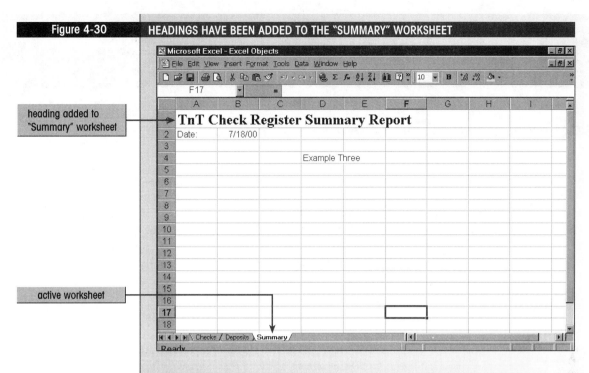

heading added to "Summary" worksheet

active worksheet

TROUBLE? Depending on how your computer is set up to display dates, the dates on your screen may be formatted differently from the ones in the figure. If the dates on your system are too large for the column, increase the width of the column to accommodate the size of the date.

**6.** Save your work.

**7.** Close the workbook, and if you are going to take a break, also close Excel.

In these steps you learned to activate a particular worksheet, to place data into a cell, and to format the appearance of a range of cells. You also learned how to place the current date in a cell. In the next session you will once again look at the Check Register project that Ashley has developed. She will show you how she used the concepts you learned in the first two sessions of this tutorial in the Check Register project.

# Session 4.2 QUICK CHECK

1. The _____ collection refers to all open worksheets in the current workbook.

2. The _____ property refers to a single cell within the current worksheet.

3. The reference `cells(3,4)` refers to cell _____ (in Excel terms).

4. Write the statement that will make the sheet name "My Sheet" the active sheet.

5. Write the statements that will place your name in cell C8 of the active worksheet, change the font to "Arial", change the font size to 22-points, and change the Bold property to "false".

**SESSION 4.3**

In this session you will retrieve the TnT Consulting Group Check Register program. You will observe some VBA statements that locate the first available row in the worksheet and then insert data in that row. Finally, you will learn how to call a procedure.

# Testing the Completed TnT Check Register Project

Ashley is ready to show you the rest of her work on the Check Register program. When you meet in her office, she reminds you that she already demonstrated the code she wrote to validate the data. The goal of that code is to verify that the date entered in the Date text box is a valid date. The code also checks to see if the data entered into the amount field is a valid numeric amount. Finally, the code highlights an invalid date or amount, so that the user can easily replace it with a valid one.

Take a moment to review this code, which you examined in Tutorial 3:

```
'Check for a valid date in the date textbox
If IsDate(txtDate) Then
    'This code will be added in Tutorial 4
Else
    MsgBox ("Please enter a valid date.")
    txtDate.SetFocus
    txtDate.SelStart = 0
    txtDate.SelLength = Len(txtDate)

End If


'Check for a valid number amount textbox
If IsNumeric(txtAmount) Then
    'This code will be added in Tutorial 4
Else
    MsgBox ("Please enter a valid amount.")
    txtAmount.SetFocus
    txtAmount.SelStart = 0
    txtAmount.SelLength = Len(txtAmount)

End If
```

Notice that the "true" part of the `If` statement contains the comment "`This code will be added in Tutorial 4`". Since you last looked at that code, Ashley has replaced the comment with code that will actually insert the checking data in the worksheet. To understand how this code works, she asks you to take some time to observe the Check Register program in action. Ashley reminds you that the program is designed to do the following:

- Display a form in which the user can enter checking data.
- Transfer the data from the form to a blank row in the worksheet. Each successive check should be entered on the next blank row in the worksheet.

You will now open the Check Register project and observe how it works. Then Ashley will explain the statements she used to get the program to perform the tasks listed above.

## To test the Check Register project:

**1.** If necessary, start Excel.

**2.** Open the workbook **TnTChk** from the Tutorial.04 folder on your Data Disk.

TROUBLE? If you see a dialog box alerting you to the fact that the workbook contains macros, then your system is configured to check all files for macros. This is a means of protecting your computer from macro viruses. Click Enable Macros and continue with Step 3.

**3.** Save the workbook as **TnT Check Register** in the Tutorial.04 folder on your Data Disk. The workbook already contains data for several checks that were previously entered. Observe that the entries are in successive rows, as shown in Figure 4-31. Also, notice the Record Checks command button, in the upper-right portion of the worksheet.

| Figure 4-31 | CHECK REGISTER PROJECT |

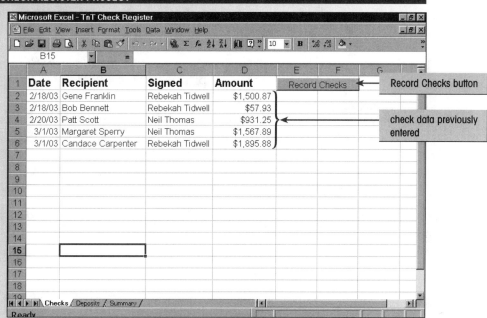

TROUBLE? If you find that the data in the worksheet is too wide for any of the columns, widen the columns now.

**4.** Click the **Record Checks** button on the worksheet. The TnT Check form appears.

**5.** Enter the data shown in Figure 4-32.

| Figure 4-32 | CHECK FORM WITH DATA ENTERED |
| --- | --- |

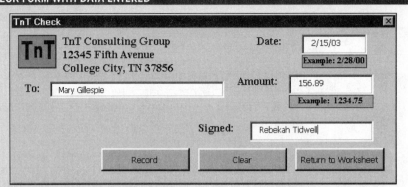

6. Click the **Record** button on the check form. The data is added to the worksheet. If necessary, move the form out of your way so that you can see the data entered in the worksheet.

7. In the check form, enter the data you see in Figure 4-33. Be sure to click the **Record** button after each entry. Notice that the data for each check is entered on the next blank line in the worksheet. Also notice that each time you enter a check the previous check's data is deleted from the form, thus preparing the check form to accept the next check's data.

| Figure 4-33 | DATA TO BE ENTERED INTO THE CHECK FORM |
| --- | --- |

| DATE | TO | AMOUNT | SIGNED |
| --- | --- | --- | --- |
| 03/15/03 | Carla Stockman | 345.67 | Rebekah Tidwell |
| 03/18/03 | Pamela Soderman | 1234.98 | Neil Thomas |
| 03/20/03 | Gordon Bales | 4376.88 | Neil Thomas |

8. Click the **Return to Worksheet** button. The form is removed from the screen. You return to the worksheet window.

Now that you understand what the Check Register project does, you are ready to learn how it works.

## Finding a Blank Row with a Do...Until Loop

Ashley's first challenge in writing the code for the Check Register Project was finding some way for the program to locate the next blank row in which to insert the data. To accomplish this task, she used a Repetition structure. Specifically, she chose to use a Do...Until loop—one that contains the following condition: `Cells(intRowCount, 1) = ""`. This condition examines the first column of each row to determine if it is empty (that is, to determine if it contains a null string, ""). Specifically, it checks to see if the Cells property is blank.

To understand how this works, notice the parentheses after the Cells property. Normally, in these parentheses, you would expect to see the row number followed by the column number. But in this case you see a variable name (`intRowCount`) followed by a column number. This variable (which Ashley declared earlier in the code as an integer) is a counter. This counter increases by one each time the loop is processed. So the first time through the loop, the condition checks the Cells property of the cell at the intersection of row 1 and column 1; if that cell already contains data (that is, if the Cells property is *not* equal to ""), then the loop processes again. The second time, it checks the Cells property of the cell at the intersection of row 2, column 1, and so on through the loop. When the loop finally encounters a blank cell—that is, a cell whose cells property is a null value—the loop stops. This is then the row in which the new check data will be inserted.

The complete loop is as follows:

```
Worksheets("Checks").Activate
Do
        intRowCounter = intRowCounter + 1
Loop Until Cells(intRowCounter, 1) = ""
```

Notice that the Activate method statement before the loop ensures that the Checks worksheet is active. The only statement within the loop is the assignment statement that increases the value of intRowCounter by 1 each pass through the loop. The Until condition checks to see if the cell in column 1 of the row represented by `intRowCounter` is empty (indicated by ""). If the cell has any value in it at all, the loop continues. The loop will continue until a cell is located that has no data in it. When the loop is complete, the variable, `intRowcounter`, contains the number of the first row that has no data. The program then uses the value of that variable to determine where to insert the check data.

## Stepping Through the Do...Until Loop

In the next set of steps you will first view the code in the Code window and then you will use the Step Into debugging feature to walk through the code that locates the next available row in the worksheet. This should help you to understand how the code works.

*To observe the loop in action:*

1. Switch to the Excel VBA IDE.

2. Open the Project Explorer, if necessary.

3. Expand the Forms folder if necessary by clicking its expand button ⊞ .

4. Double-click **frmCheck** in the Forms folder. The form appears.

5. Double-click the **Record** button on the form. The Code window opens with the code for the Record button, as shown in Figure 4-34.

| Figure 4-34 | CODE WINDOW WITH CMDRECORD_CLICK PROCEDURE SHOWING |
|---|---|

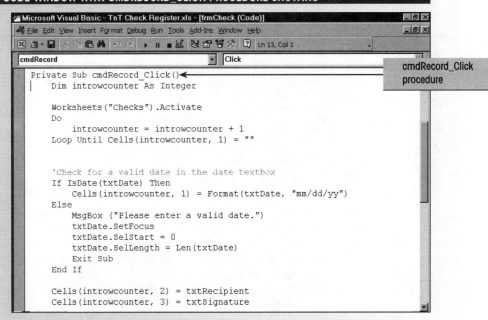

**6.** Focus your attention on the first several lines of the code in this procedure. Notice that the loop checks for an empty row. See Figure 4-35.

| Figure 4-35 | CODE WINDOW |
|---|---|

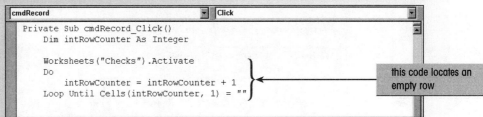

**7.** Switch to the Excel window. You should see that the row number for the next check is row 11.

In the next set of steps you will step through the loop using Step Into. Keep in mind that the next set of check data should be inserted into row 11.

**1.** Switch to the VBA IDE, and verify that the cursor is positioned within the `cmdRecord_Click` procedure.

**2.** Click **Debug** on the menu bar and then click **Step Into**. The check form is displayed.

**3.** Enter the following data:

Date: **3/22/03**

Recipient: **Steve Smith**

Amount: **1345.67**

Signed: **Rebekah Tidwell**

4. Click the **Record** button on the check form. The first line in the cmdRecord_Click procedure is highlighted, as shown in Figure 4-36.

**BEGINNING STEP INTO MODE**

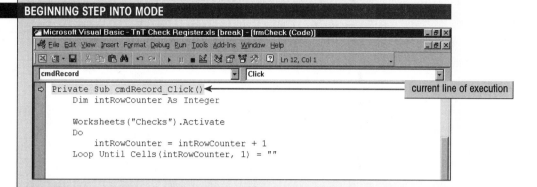

5. Press **F8** twice. The first statement within the loop, the Do statement, is highlighted.

6. Press **F8** and check the value of the variable intRowCounter. Its value is currently 0.

7. Press **F8** again and check the value of the variable, intRowCounter. This time, the value is 1. At this point, the Loop Until statement is highlighted, as shown in Figure 4-37. Stop and think about the condition in the Loop Until statement. Because the value of intLoopCounter is 1, in effect, the condition is: cells(1,1) = "".

**CODE WINDOW IN STEP INTO MODE**

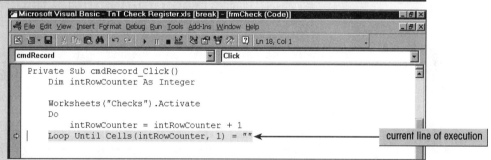

8. Press **F8** continually until the loop stops and the next statement (If IsDate (txtDate) Then) is highlighted. Each time through the loop ask yourself if the loop should stop. Remember that earlier you determined that the new data should be placed in row 11. This means the loop should terminate when intRowCounter is equal to 11.

9. When the first statement after the loop (If IsDate (txtDate) Then) is highlighted, check the value of intRowCounter again. The value is 11, as shown in Figure 4-38.

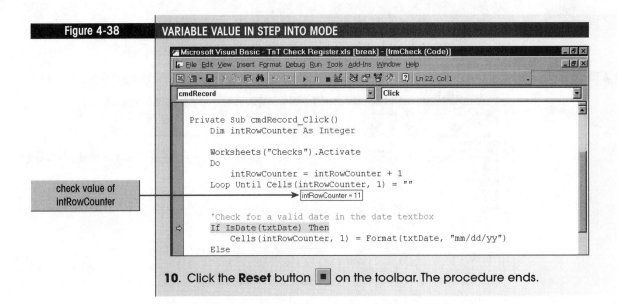

**Figure 4-38**   VARIABLE VALUE IN STEP INTO MODE

check value of intRowCounter

**10.** Click the **Reset** button ■ on the toolbar. The procedure ends.

The new check data was not recorded because you stopped the procedure before the data was actually recorded. You will return to the recording of the check later. But first, you need to understand the remainder of the code.

## Inserting Data in the Worksheet Via the Cells Property

After Ashley wrote the code that found a blank row in the worksheet, she had to write the code that actually inserted the data into that row. Specifically, she had to write code that would insert the date in column 1, the recipient in column 2, the name of the person who signed the check in column 3, and the amount in column 4.

The first statement she wrote places the date in column one. Recall that the loop you observed in the last steps determined in which row the check data should be placed by setting the variable `intRowCounter` to the number of the first empty row. So to place the date in the first column of the row indicated by `intRowCounter`, Ashley used the following statement:

```
Cells(intRowCounter, 1) = Format(txtDate, "mm/dd/yy")
```

This is an assignment statement that assigns the value of the `txtDate` text box to the specified cell in the worksheet. Notice that the statement uses the Format function (presented in Tutorial 2) to format the date in an appropriate date format.

The statements for inserting the remaining data into the worksheet are similar to the statement above. You will now examine these statements and observe their behavior.

*To view the VBA code that inserts data into the worksheet:*

**1.** Position the cursor within the Record button's Click event.

**2.** Maximize the Code window, if necessary, and then adjust your screen so you can see all the code shown in figure 4-39.

**Figure 4-39** | CODE WINDOW WITH CMDRECORD_CLICK EVENT DISPLAYED

```
Microsoft Visual Basic - TnT Check Register.xls - [frmCheck (Code)]

File Edit View Insert Format Debug Run Tools Add-Ins Window Help

Ln 13, Col 1

cmdRecord                                    Click

    'Check for a valid date in the date textbox
    If IsDate(txtDate) Then
        Cells(intRowCounter, 1) = Format(txtDate, "mm/dd/yy")
    Else
        MsgBox ("Please enter a valid date.")
        txtDate.SetFocus
        txtDate.SelStart = 0
        txtDate.SelLength = Len(txtDate)
        Exit Sub
    End If

    Cells(intRowCounter, 2) = txtRecipient
    Cells(intRowCounter, 3) = txtSignature

    'Check for a valid number amount textbox
    If IsNumeric(txtAmount) Then
        Cells(intRowCounter, 4) = Format(txtAmount, "currency")
    Else
        MsgBox ("Please enter a valid amount.")
        txtAmount.SetFocus
        txtAmount.SelStart = 0
        txtAmount.SelLength = Len(txtAmount)
```

> statements that format data and place in worksheet

3. Examine the statements indicated in Figure 4-39. These statements are responsible for formatting the contents of the text boxes and then assigning their contents to the specified cell.

4. When you have finished observing the code, run the program and reenter the data shown in Figure 4-40.

**Figure 4-40** | ADDITIONAL DATA TO BE ENTERED INTO THE CHECK FORM

| DATE | RECIPIENT | AMOUNT | SIGNED |
|------|-----------|--------|--------|
| 03/22/03 | Steve Smith | 1345.67 | Rebekah Tidwell |

5. Click the **Record** button on the Check form and notice that the data is placed in the worksheet in the next blank row, as indicated in Figure 4-41.

**Figure 4-41** | EXCEL WINDOW WITH CHECK FORM RUNNING

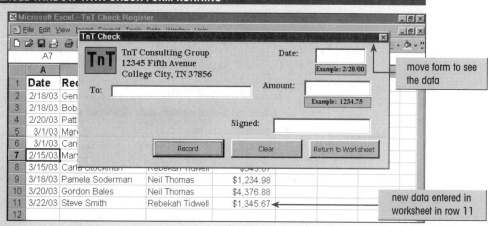

> move form to see the data

> new data entered in worksheet in row 11

**6.** Click the **Return to Worksheet** button. Because you originally ran this program from the VBA IDE, you return to the VBA IDE rather than to the worksheet. (If, however, you ran the program from the command button on the worksheet, you see the worksheet itself.)

In these steps you have seen how the data is actually recorded in the worksheet. First, the data in the text box is formatted, and then it is moved to the specified cell. In the next section you will learn how to clear the form of data to provide a clean slate in which the user can enter the next check's data.

# Calling a Procedure

Ashley wants the user to be able to enter as many checks as desired, and she wants to make it as easy for the user as possible. It would be helpful, then, if the data from a check that has already been recorded is deleted from the text boxes in preparation for the next check's data. As you may recall, the form's code module already contains code that clears all the text boxes on the form. This code can be found in the Clear button's Click event procedure. As you know, an event procedure is only executed when the associated event takes place—in this case, when the user clicks the Clear button.

However, you can also write a statement that **calls,** or invokes, an event procedure. Essentially, a **Call statement** serves as a substitute for an actual event. A `Call` statement triggers an event procedure, just like an actual event. The `Call` statement is very useful because it allows you to transfer control from the current procedure to a different procedure. The syntax of the `Call` statement is as follows:

| Syntax | `Call procedure name [argument list]` |
|---|---|
| **Explanation** | The call statement causes program control to "jump" to the procedure specified in the Call statement. The "called" procedure will then execute. When the "called" procedure has finished, program control will be returned to the original procedure (the one that made the call), to the statement immediately following the call statement. |
| **Example** | `Call cmdClear_Click` |

In the example, the `Call` statement involves the `cmdClear_Click` procedure (i.e., the Click event procedure for the `cmdClear` button). As a result, the statement in `cmdClear_Click` procedure will execute. When the procedure is finished, program control will be returned to the statement following the `Call` statement.

In the next steps you will view the call to (that is the statement that calls) the `cmdClear_Click` procedure and then you will enter some data to observe the `Call` statement in action. You will use the Step Into method to once again observe the behavior of the program. Because stepping through the whole program would take a great deal of time, you will set a breakpoint at the statement that calls the `cmdClear` procedure. As you learned in Tutorial 3, a breakpoint causes a program to stop at that particular line of code. You will then use the Step Into feature from the breakpoint on, to see how control passes to the `cmdClear_Click` procedure and then back to the `cmdRecord_Click` procedure.

*To view the call to* `cmdClear` *procedure and observe how it works:*

1. Switch to the Code window, and scroll until you see the call statement at the bottom of the `cmdRecord_Click` procedure, as indicated in Figure 4-42. This statement calls the `cmdClear_Click` event procedure.

| Figure 4-42 | CODE WINDOW FOR CMDRECORD_CLICK PROCEDURE |
| --- | --- |

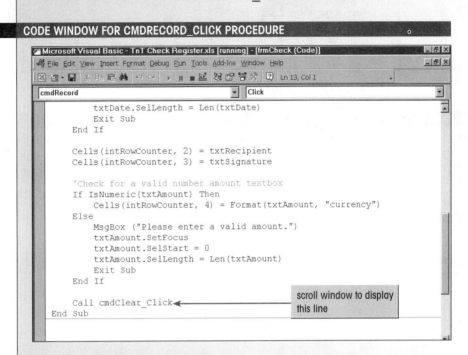

2. Click in the gray border of the Code window, to the left of the statement `Call cmdClear_Click`. The line is highlighted in brown, indicating that it is a breakpoint, as shown in Figure 4-43.

| Figure 4-43 | CODE WINDOW WITH BREAKPOINT SET |
| --- | --- |

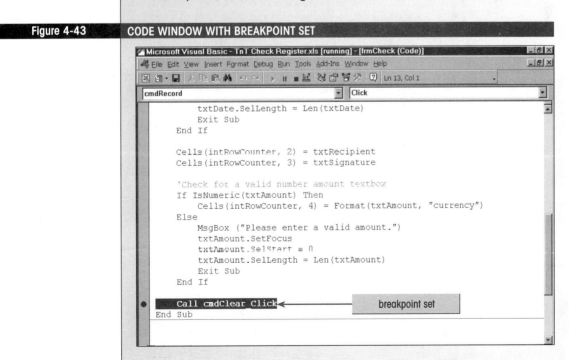

**3.** Run the procedure.

**4.** Enter the following valid data into each of the text boxes.

Date: **2/18/03**

Recipient: **Bob Bennett**

Amount: **57.93**

Signed: **Rebekah Tidwell**

**5.** Click the **Record** button on the form. The Call statement is highlighted in yellow in the VBA IDE, as shown in Figure 4-44.

**Figure 4-44** **HIGHLIGHTED CALL STATEMENT**

```
            txtDate.SelLength = Len(txtDate)
            Exit Sub
        End If

        Cells(intRowCounter, 2) = txtRecipient
        Cells(intRowCounter, 3) = txtSignature

        'Check for a valid number amount textbox
        If IsNumeric(txtAmount) Then
            Cells(intRowCounter, 4) = Format(txtAmount, "currency")
        Else
            MsgBox ("Please enter a valid amount.")
            txtAmount.SetFocus
            txtAmount.SelStart = 0
            txtAmount.SelLength = Len(txtAmount)
            Exit Sub
        End If

        Call cmdClear_Click          breakpoint and current line
    End Sub                          of execution are the same
```

The program is still running but it has temporarily stopped at this point because of the breakpoint you placed in the procedure. You can now Step Into the procedure from this point on, to observe how the program passes control to the cmdClear_Click procedure.

## To step through the procedure:

**1.** Press **F8** to start the Step Into feature. The yellow highlighting "jumps" to the cmdClear_click procedure, as shown in Figure 4-45.

**Figure 4-45** | CODE WINDOW IN STEP INTO MODE SHOWING CURRENT LINE OF EXECUTION

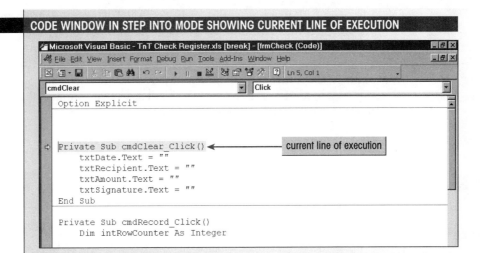

2. Press **F8** continuously until the current line of execution is the End Sub statement in the cmdClear_Click procedure.

3. Press **F8** one more time. Notice that the program returns to the statement following the call to the cmdClear_click event, in the cmdRecord_Click procedure, as shown in Figure 4-46.

**Figure 4-46** | CODE WINDOW WITH CURRENT LINE OF EXECUTION

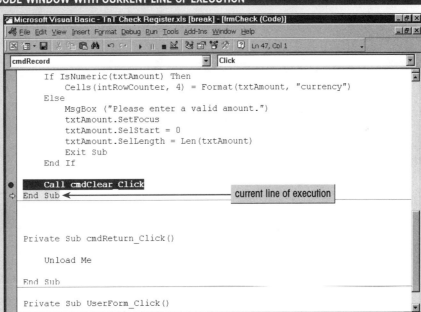

4. Click **F8** one more time to end the procedure.

5. Click the brown circle in the margin of the Code window (next to the call statement). The breakpoint is removed.

6. Save your work.

7. Close the workbook and Excel.

In these steps you viewed the process of calling a procedure from another procedure. You used the Step Into technique so that you could observe that the procedure is called, then that procedure completes all of its steps, and then finally the program returns to the procedure that made the call.

Ashley states that she has now shown you all the code she has placed in the Worksheet project up to this point. She also tells you that she will continue to work on the project. Later she will be adding code to process deposits and to create a summary of the checkbook data.

## Session 4.3 QUICK CHECK

1. Write the statements that will locate the first row that has the word "Dog" in the second column.

2. Write the statement that will take the data in the text box named `txtStudent` and insert it into cell C8 (*Hint*: Remember that in VBA, columns are referred to by number rather than by letter).

3. The _____ statement will cause the remainder of a sub procedure to be skipped and will end the procedure.

4. Write the statement that would execute the procedure `cmdCalculate_Click` from within another procedure.

5. Write the statement that will activate the worksheet named "Deposits."

## REVIEW ASSIGNMENTS

Ashley has created a Deposits form, which will ultimately be part of the Check Register project. The code for this form should automate the process of inserting deposit information into an Excel worksheet. Your job is to write statements that will take data from the deposit form and place it on the deposit worksheet. Your code should also clear the form when the data has been transferred to the worksheet.

1. Start Excel and open the workbook named **ChkBk** located in the Review folder for Tutorial 4.

2. Save the workbook as **TnT Deposit** in the Review folder for Tutorial 4.

3. Start the VBA IDE.

4. Open the form named `frmDeposit`. Notice that there is also a `frmCheck` form. This form is the one that Ashley demonstrated in the tutorial.

5. Use the Properties window to look up the properties of each text box and command button. Be sure to familiarize yourself with the names of each control since you will need to use their names in programming statements.

6. Add the code necessary to record the form data in the worksheet. Be sure to include code that validates the date and amount fields. When invalid data is entered, the program should display a message box that tells the user to enter valid data. Also, if invalid data is found, end the procedure so that the data is not recorded in the worksheet. (*Hint*: This is exactly what Ashley did with her checkbook project, so you can use her program as a guide.)

7. Thoroughly test the deposit form for accuracy by recording several deposits in the worksheet.

8. Create a new form for the project and give it the name `frmMenu`. On this form place a caption of "TnT Check Register Menu". Add three command buttons, as specified in the Figure 4-47.

| Figure 4-47 | COMMAND BUTTONS FOR THE MENU FORM | |
| --- | --- | --- |

| BUTTON NAME | CAPTION | FUNCTION |
| --- | --- | --- |
| `cmdChecks` | Record Checks | Activate the Checks worksheet<br>Load the frmCheck form |
| `cmdDeposit` | Record Deposits | Activate the Deposits worksheet<br>Load the frmDeposits form |
| `cmdQuit` | Quit | Unload the frmMenu |

9. These three new command buttons should load the appropriate form so that the user can record check data, record deposit data, or exit the program. Write the code for each of the command buttons so that the appropriate worksheet is activated and the appropriate form is opened. The Quit button should simply unload the `frmMenu` form. Figure 4-48 provides the code you will need to add to each command button's Click event.

| Figure 4-48 | CODE FOR NEW COMMAND BUTTONS |
| --- | --- |

| NAME OF BUTTON | CODE |
| --- | --- |
| CmdChecks | `Worksheets ("Checks").Activate`<br>`frmCheck.Show` |
| CmdDeposit | `Worksheets ("Deposits").Activate`<br>`frmDeposit.Show` |
| CmdQuit | `Unload Me` |

10. Test the form to make sure that each form opens correctly. Record data of your choosing in each of the forms as they are displayed, and then close them with the Close button on the form.

11. Add comments to the Code module of each of the three forms, which indicate that you are the developer and the date you developed the program.

12. Save your work.

13. Print the Project code only.

## CASE PROBLEMS

*Case 1. Gradebook Application for Bristol High School*  Serena Potter teaches at Bristol High School. She uses Excel to record her students' grades. Each semester, she creates a new Gradebook workbook, with a separate worksheet for each class. She enters the student names into the worksheet for each class. She asks if you could help automate the procedure for entering student names.

1. Start Excel and open the workbook named **Grdbk** located in the Cases folder for Tutorial 4.

2. Save the workbook as **Potter Gradebook** in the Cases folder for Tutorial 4.

3. Open the VBA IDE.

4. Open the form named `frmAddStudent`.

5. Familiarize yourself with the form. Check the names of each control in the Properties window.

6. Add the code to the Quit button that will remove the form from the screen. (*Hint*: You have done this before. It involves only one statement. )

7. Add code to the OK button that will locate the first empty row and then move the name in the text box to the first column in that row. (*Hint*: To find the next available row use the same code that was used to find the first available row in the Checkbook project.)

8. Save the form.

9. Run the program.

10. To test the form enter the names: "Smith, Margaret", "Boxer, Amanda", "Pepper, Felix", and "Dante, Miguel". Click the OK button after entering each name. Notice how each name is displayed in the worksheet.

11. Click the Quit button to close the form when you've finished testing.

12. Run the program once again and add your name to the student list. Click the Quit button.

13. Add comments to the Code window that identify you as the developer and indicate the current date.

14. Save your work.

15. Print the project's code. On the printed code, circle and label the code that finds the next available row. In your own words, write a short paragraph that explains how this works.

*Case 2. Flower Inventory Application for Ann's Flower Shoppe*  Ann Woodhouse is the owner and manager of a small flower and gardening store called Ann's Flower Shoppe. She receives a shipment of fresh flowers every day. Each day she has to enter the flower names and the quantity received into an Excel worksheet so she can record the daily sales. She has hired you to create a VBA application that will simplify the process of adding the flower names and quantities to the worksheet. The application should also place the current date at the top of the worksheet.

1. Start Excel and open the workbook named **Flower** located in the Cases folder for Tutorial 4.

2. Save the workbook as **Flower List** in the Cases folder for Tutorial 4. Notice that the column headings have already been placed in the worksheet for you.

3. Open the VBA IDE.

4. Open the form named `frmFlowers`.

5. Familiarize yourself with the form. Check the names of each control in the Properties window.

6. Add code for the Quit button that will remove the form from the screen.

7. Add code for the OK button that will locate the first empty row in the worksheet and then place the flower name and quantity in the first two columns of that row. (*Hint*: This is exactly the same code that was used in the Checkbook project to locate the row and place the data in the worksheet.)

*Explore*

8. A good location for the date in the worksheet is just to the right of the column headings, in the fourth column. The necessary VBA statement belongs in the Userform's Initialize event procedure, which is triggered each time the form is run. Open the UserForm's Initialize event procedure. (*Hint*: In the Code window, click the Object list arrow and select Userform, and then click the Procedure list arrow and select Initialize.) Now type the following code:

```
Cells(1, 4) = Date
```

9. Save your work and run the program.

10. To test the form, enter the following names (and quantities) of flowers: "Roses" (Quantity: 150), "Carnations" (Quantity: 75), "Daisies" (Quantity: 80), "Irises" (Quantity: 200), and "Lilies" (Quantity: 25). Click the OK button after entering each set of data. Notice how the flowers' names and quantities are displayed in the worksheet. Also notice that today's date is placed in the fourth column and first row of the worksheet.

11. Click the Quit button to close the form.

12. Add comments at the top of the code that include your name and the current date.

13. Save your work.

14. Print the code for the project and the worksheet.

15. On the printed code, circle and label the statement that actually adds the flower names and quantities to the worksheet.

**Case 3. Whitman's Lumber**  Lucy Cheng, the Accounts Manager for Whitman's Lumber, uses Microsoft Excel to keep track of the company's invoices. For each invoice, she needs to enter the invoice number, amount, and payment type. Whitman's only accepts cash (prepaid) or COD (cash on delivery) orders. She has already created the necessary worksheet, including the column headings. She has hired you to develop the VBA code that will insert the data into the worksheet as it is entered into a form. Before the data is entered in the worksheet, the program should make sure that a valid date has been entered into the Date text box and that a valid numeric value has been placed in the Amount text box. In case of invalid data, the program should display a message box that asks the user to enter valid data. Finally, whenever "COD" is entered for the payment type, this item should be displayed in red to call attention to the fact that cash will need to be collected at the time of delivery.

1. Start Microsoft Excel and open the workbook named **Invoice** located in the Cases folder for Tutorial 4.

2. Save the workbook as **Whitman Invoices.** Notice that the column headings have already been placed in the worksheet for you.

3. Open the VBA IDE.

4. Open the form named `frmInvoice` Open the Code window for the form. Notice that the code for the Quit button and the Clear button has already been completed. A series of comments indicate the major sections of code that you must complete.

5. Familiarize yourself with the form. Check the names of each control in the Properties window.

6. Create the code for the OK button that will check for a valid amount in the Amount text box. If the amount is invalid, display a message box that indicates that a valid amount must be entered (*Hint*: This is the same code used in Tutorial 3 to check for a valid amount.) The code should then place the data in the worksheet in the next available row. (*Hint*: The code to find the next available row is exactly the same as the code for the Check Register project.)

*Explore*

7. Now you need to complete the code that will check to see if the payment type is COD. (*Hint*: Use just COD rather than C.O.D). Whenever the payment type is COD, the program should format the worksheet cell in a red font. The `cmdOK_Click` procedure already contains this code, but it is written as comments. Remove the comment marks in order for the statements to be executed.

8. Save your work and run the program.

9. To test the form, enter the data shown in Figure 4-49. Be sure to click OK between each entry.

| Figure 4-49 | DATA FOR INVOICE FORM | |
|---|---|---|
| **INVOICE #** | **AMOUNT** | **PAYMENT TYPE** |
| 67898 | 1234.98 | COD |
| 67899 | 23409.99 | Cash |
| 701890 | 12567.90 | COD |
| 701891 | 567.00 | COD |

10. Click the Quit button to close the form when you've finished testing.

11. Add comments to the code that include your name and the current date.

12. Save your work.

13. Print the code and the worksheet. On the printed code, circle and label the code that checks for COD orders and changes them to red. Write a brief paragraph explaining how the RGB function works.

14. Close the VBA IDE

15. Close Excel.

*Case 4. C & B Construction*   Todd Greene, a manager at C & B Construction, is responsible for tracking construction projects for the company. He uses Microsoft Excel to record each project and the tasks associated with the project. Each task in the project should have a description of the task, the date when the task is scheduled to start, and the date when the task is finished. He would like you to provide a VBA application that builds a new project worksheet. He wants the application to add the correct headings for the worksheet and set the worksheet name to the project title.

1.  Start Excel and open the workbook named **Project** located in the Cases folder for Tutorial 4.

2.  Save the workbook as **C&B Projects**.

3.  Open the VBA IDE.

4.  Open the form named `frmProjects`.

5.  Familiarize yourself with the form. Check the names of each control in the Properties window.

6.  Add code to the Quit button that will remove the form from the screen.

7.  Add code to the Clear button that will clear all the text boxes when it is clicked.

8.  Add code to the OK button's Click event that will record the data in the worksheet. The code should also check to see if each of the two dates is valid. In the case of invalid data, the program should require the user to reenter the data. Make sure your code clears all text boxes once the data is entered into the worksheet.

**Explore**

9.  Add a statement to the OK button that will "Autofit" the columns each time project data is entered. You can do this by adding the statement:

```
Columns("A:D").Autofit
```

10.  Save your work and run the program.

11.  Test the form by entering the data in Figure 4-50. Be sure to click the OK button between each entry.

| Figure 4-50 | DATA FOR NEW PROJECT FORM | | |
|---|---|---|---|
| **PROJECT NAME** | **DESCRIPTION** | **START DATE** | **END DATE** |
| Baker Building | Rebuild front stairwell | 03/15/03 | 06/01/03 |
| Franklin Addition | Add restroom | 05/20/03 | 06/15/03 |
| Downtown Offices | Build office complex | 06/20/03 | 12/30/03 |
| Vinces Spaghetti House | Rebuild kitchen and dining area | 06/01/03 | 01/15/04 |

12.  Click the Quit button to close the form when you've finished testing.

13.  Add comments to the top of the code that include your name and the current date.

14.  Save your work.

15.  Print the workbook.

16.  On the printed code, circle and label the code that actually places the headings in the worksheet.

# QUICK CHECK ANSWERS

*Session 4.1*

1. a. Do...While     b. Do...Until    c. For...Next
2. Do...While, Do...Until
3. Do...Until
4. For...Next
5. For...Next
6. Step

*Session 4.2*

1. worksheets
2. cells
3. D3
4. `sheets("My Sheet").activate`
5. `cells(8,3) = "student name"`
   `cells(8,3).font.name = "Arial"`
   `cells(8,3).font.size = 22`
   `cells(8,3).font.bold = false`

*Session 4.3*

1. `intRowcounter = 1`
   `Do`
   `IntRowcounter = introwCounter + 1`
   `Until Cells(intRowcounter, 2) = "Dog"`
2. `Cells(8,3) = txtStudent`
3. `Exit Sub`
4. `Call cmdCalculate_click`
5. `Worksheets("Deposits").Activate`

In this tutorial you will:

- Preview an application that inserts text into a Word document

- Learn how to use a frame in a UserForm

- Interact with the Word object model

- Interact with the Windows object model

- Select text in a Word document by using the Selection object

- Delete and set tabs by using the TabStops collection

- Insert text in a document by using the Range object

- Establish a new Range object with the Collapse method

- Write a `With` statement and concatenate strings

# CREATING A VBA APPLICATION FOR MICROSOFT WORD

*Creating a Letter-Building Application*

CASE

## TnT Consulting Group and Sutherland Event Planners

Patricia Sutherland, of Sutherland Event Planners, recently contacted TnT Consulting about creating an application for Microsoft Word. Sutherland Event Planners organizes events for college-related conferences. Among her other responsibilities, Patricia is responsible for preparing a list of speakers for each event. She uses the same basic style for each list, with the same organization, formatting, and tabs. In each list, the session title and date appear at the top of the page in a fairly large font. The title and date are then followed by the list of speakers. For each, she includes the speaker's name, the title of the speech, and the speaker's college affiliation.

To save time, Patricia has hired TnT Consulting to create a VBA application that will automate the process of creating these lists. Gene Cox has assigned this project to you. He has asked another consultant, Ricardo Juarez, to do some of the preliminary work on the project. Ricardo will then pass the project to you to complete. As you work on this project, you will learn how to write applications that interact with Microsoft Word.

## SESSION 5.1

In this session you will preview the completed Speaker Listing project. You will run the project and, in the process, create a list of speakers for a particular session. You will also learn how to use the frame control object to hide and display portions of a form. You will then view the code that initializes the document in preparation for creating a new speaker list.

# Previewing the Completed Speaker Listing Project

In this section, you will preview the completed Speaker Listing project. Testing the project in this way will give you a good grasp of how it should work, and make it easier for you to understand the tasks you will perform in this tutorial.

As you will see, the Speaker Listing program displays a form where the user can enter the title and date for a group of related speeches (called a session). After the user enters a title and date for a particular session, the program allows the user to enter information about individual speakers. Finally, the program takes all the data entered by the user, formats it, and inserts it into a Word document. At that point, the user is free to save, edit, or print the newly created document.

You will now open the Speaker Listing project and observe how it works.

### To test the completed application:

1. Start Word and open the document named **Speaker** from the Tutorial.05 folder on your Data Disk.

2. Save the document as **Speaker Listing Preview** in the Tutorial.05 folder on your Data Disk.

3. If necessary, display nonprinting characters, and then make absolutely certain you don't have any other Word documents open on your computer. At this stage, only the Speaker Listing Preview document should be open.

4. Start the VBA IDE, open the Project Explorer window (if necessary), expand the **Project (Speaker Listing Preview)** folder, expand the **Forms** folder, and double-click **UserForm1**. The Session Listing form is displayed on the screen in design time. Note that the form is made up of two sets of text boxes. The top set of text boxes (labeled Session Title and Session Date) have to do with recording information regarding a specific session. The bottom set (Speaker Name, Speech Title, and College) have to do with recording information for an individual talk within a session.

5. Run the project. The Session Listing form is displayed in runtime, as shown in Figure 5-1. At this stage, only the top set of text boxes (containing the Session Title and Session Date text boxes) is visible in the form.

**Figure 5-1** | **SESSION LISTING FORM DISPLAYED WITH WORD IN THE BACKGROUND**

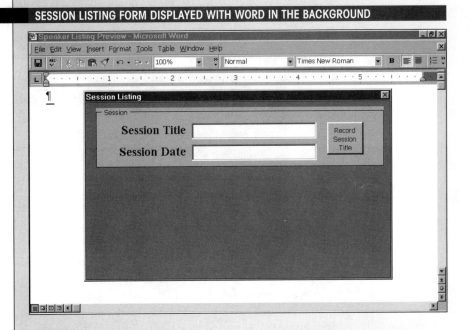

6. Click the Session Title text box, type **Session 1: World Wide Web Retail**, press **Tab** to move the cursor to the Session Date text box, type **January 15, 2003**, and then click the **Record Session Title** button on the form. The title (Session1: World Wide Web Retail) and the date (January 15, 2003) are inserted into the current Word document. (You may need to drag the Session Listing form to the lower-right corner of the Word window in order to see the complete title and date.) Also notice that the Session Title and Session Date text boxes are no longer displayed in the form. Instead, they are replaced with the bottom set of text boxes (containing the Speaker Name, Speech Title, and College text boxes). You can use these text boxes to insert the name of a speaker, the speech's title, and the speaker's college affiliation into the Word document. See Figure 5-2. Note that a session normally includes multiple speeches, so in the next step you will record information for several speakers.

**Figure 5-2** | **SESSION LISTING FORM WITH SPEAKER PORTION DISPLAYED**

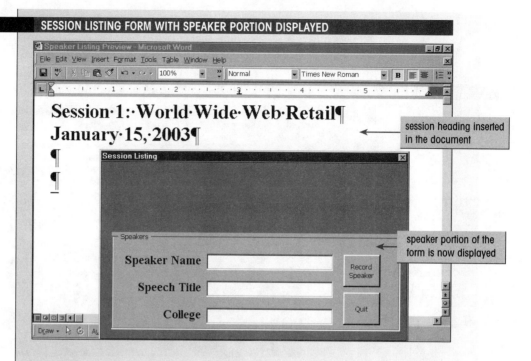

7. Enter the speaker data listed in Figure 5-3. Be sure to click the **Record Speaker** button after each entry. Notice that after you click the Record Speaker button, the information for a speaker is inserted into the Word document. At the same time, the form is cleared in order to allow you to enter data on the next speaker.

**Figure 5-3** | **SPEAKER DATA**

| SPEAKER | TITLE | AFFILIATION |
|---|---|---|
| Franklin Graham | Creating an Effective Order Form | Cryton University |
| Suzanne Shavinsky | Setting up a Business Online | Starklin College |
| William Charles | Web Development Tools | Augustine University |
| Sarah Frankmire | Storing Data Received on the Web | Frank Jones University |

8. Click the **Quit** button on the form. You return to the VBA IDE.

9. Switch to the Word window. Your document looks like Figure 5-4.

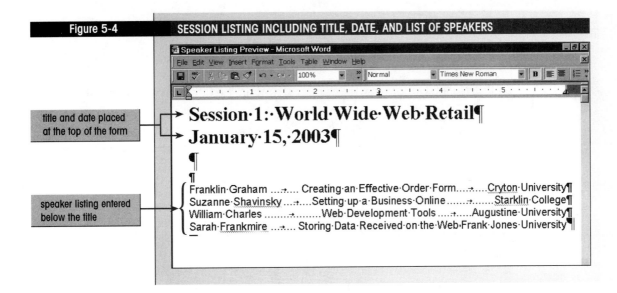

**Figure 5-4**     SESSION LISTING INCLUDING TITLE, DATE, AND LIST OF SPEAKERS

title and date placed at the top of the form

speaker listing entered below the title

At this point, the user could save, print, or edit the document created by the Speaker Listing project. Because you are only testing the project, you will not do anything to the document now. Instead, you'll run the project again to see what happens to the existing document when you do.

## To run the project again:

1. Return to the VBA IDE, verify that the form is still selected, and run the project. The Session Listing form is displayed in the Word window, on top of a blank Word document. The information you inserted earlier has been deleted from the document, in preparation for a new list.

2. Click the **Close** button ☒ on the top of the Session Listing form. You return to the VBA IDE.

3. Close the form, close the VBA IDE, and then close the document without saving it.

You are now finished previewing the Speaker Listing project. Of course, normally, you can't examine a VBA project before you actually create it. But you may sometimes have the opportunity to examine the work of a more experienced programmer. In doing so, you can learn a great deal about how to design and code a VBA program. Studying another developer's VBA code will expand your familiarity with VBA objects and properties, and give you new ideas that you can try out on your own.

Now that you have a clear idea of how the Speaker Listing project should work from the user's point of view, you can start work on it as a developer, as if you were designing it from scratch. Gene tells you that Ricardo has already developed the Session Listing form. It's your job to complete parts of the project by adding the necessary code. But before you can start writing this code, you need to examine the form.

## Examining the Session Listing Form

Gene suggests you start by taking a close look at the various control objects in the Session Listing form.

*To examine the Session Listing form:*

1. Open the document named **Listing** from the Tutorial.05 folder on your Data Disk.

2. Save the document as **Speaker Listing** in the Tutorial.05 folder on your Data Disk.

3. Verify that the Speaker Listing document is the only one open on your computer at this time. *Make sure you do not have any other documents open during this tutorial.*

4. Open the VBA IDE.

5. Double-click **frmListing** in the Project Explorer window.

6. Examine the form, and note the various control objects it contains. Figure 5-5 indicates the name of each control object in the form.

| Figure 5-5 | SESSION LISTING FORM INDICATING NAMES OF CONTROLS |
|---|---|

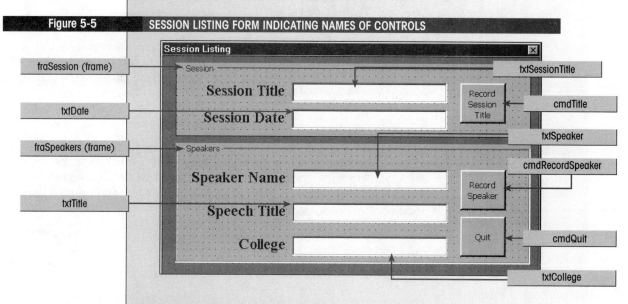

3. Take a few minutes to become familiar with the names of these control objects. This will help you understand the VBA code that will be presented in the next session.

Most of the control objects on the Session Listing form should be familiar to you. In particular, you are familiar with labels, text boxes, and command buttons. However, the form does include one new control object, called a frame control that requires some explanation.

## Using a Frame Control on a Form

When you examined the Session Listing form in design time, you saw that it contained five text boxes. However, in runtime, the form only displayed the text boxes required for the particular task at hand. When you first ran the program, the Session Title and Session Date text boxes appeared, allowing you to enter information related to an individual session. After you completed that task, session text boxes disappeared, and the text boxes related to entering information for a specific speaker (Speaker Name, Speech Title and College) became visible.

Hiding portions of a form like this is useful when you want to focus the user's attention on a specific task. You accomplish this in VBA by using a frame control.

A **frame control object** is a kind of container into which you can insert other control objects in a form, thereby separating one part of a form from another. In its most basic form, a frame simply serves as a visible divider, similar to a border in a Word document. However, a frame can be more sophisticated than a simple border. Because controls placed inside a frame function as a single unit, you can use a frame to control which portion of a form is available to a user at any given time.

For example, in the Speaker Listing project, frames are used to hide one part of the form and make another visible. To understand how this works, you first need to review the position of the frames in the Session Listing form. Figure 5-6 shows the frames used in the Session listing form, as they appear in design time.

---

**Figure 5-6** **SESSION LISTING FORM SHOWING FRAMES WITHIN THE FORM**

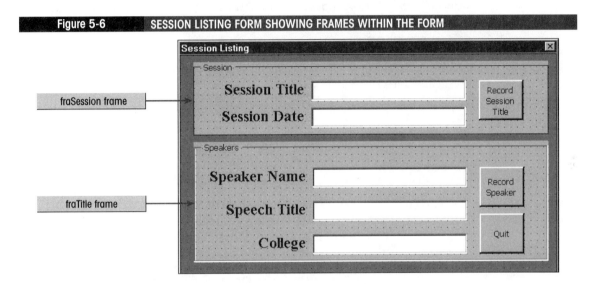

Within the Session Listing form, the Session Title and Session Date text boxes are grouped inside a frame named `fraSession`. The Caption property for the `fraSession` frame is set to "Session," which is why you see the word session in the top-left corner of the frame. At the same time, the Speaker Name, Speech Title, and College text boxes are grouped inside a frame named `fraSpeakers`. The caption for this frame is "Speakers."

Now that you understand how Ricardo incorporated frames into the Session Listing form, you are ready to learn about the statements he used to display and hide the frames at runtime.

## Hiding and Displaying Frames

Once you group controls inside a frame, you can then use its **Visible property** to either display or hide the frame. If the Visible property is set to true, then the control is displayed. If the Visible property is set to false then the control is hidden. Controls inside the frame are also hidden when the frame, itself is hidden. Likewise, when the frame is displayed, the controls inside the frame are also displayed.

The following statement, then, will hide the `fraSpeakers` frame:

```
fraSpeakers.Visible = False
```

The following statement will display the `fraSpeakers` frame:

```
fraSpeakers.Visible = True
```

You will now look at these statements in the Code window. First, you will examine a statement in the Userform's **Initialize event**, which is triggered when the form is loaded. As you look at this code, do not be concerned about the other statements in the project. You shouldn't expect to understand this code until you finish the next session. For now you are simply interested in how the frames are made visible and invisible.

## To examine the statement that makes the `fraSpeakers` frame invisible:

1. Verify that the form is displayed within the VBA IDE in design time.

2. Double-click anywhere on the form. The Code window opens.

   TROUBLE? If you find that a new procedure has been added to your Code window just ignore it. This happens sometimes when you click within an object because VBA assumes that you want to write a procedure associated with the object you clicked on. The new procedure should be empty and will not cause you any problems.

3. Within the Code window, click in the Object list arrow, scroll down the list, and then click **UserForm**.

4. Maximize the Code window.

5. Verify that Initialize is displayed in the Procedure box. (If it is not, select Initialize now.) This confirms that you are currently viewing the Initialize event procedure associated with the UserForm. The statements in this procedure are executed when the form is first displayed on the screen at runtime.

6. Scroll down to observe the final line of code in this procedure, as shown in Figure 5-7. This statement (`fraSpeakers.Visible = False`) makes the `fraSpeakers` frame invisible when the form is initialized.

| Figure 5-7 | CODE WINDOW WITH USERFORM INITIALIZE PROCEDURE SHOWING |

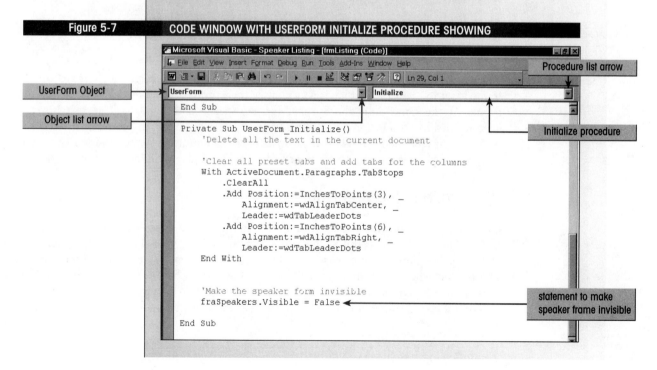

Next, you will view the statements that hide the `fraSessions` frame and display the `fraSpeakers` frame. Where do you think you would find them? When you tested the project, you entered the session title and date in the Session frame, and then clicked the Record Title button. After you clicked the Record Title button, the `fraSession` frame disappeared; at the same time, the `fraSpeakers` frame appeared. Thus, to find the statements that control the two frames' Visible property, you need to look in the code for the Record Title button. In VBA terminology, you need to look in the Click event procedure for the command button named `cmdTitle`.

### To examine the statements that make the frames visible and invisible:

1. Click the **Object** box list arrow, scroll up, and click **cmdTitle**.

2. Verify that **Click** is displayed in the Procedure box.

3. If necessary, scroll down to display the last two lines of code in this procedure, as shown in Figure 5-8. These two lines hide the session portion of the form and display the speaker portion.

| Figure 5-8 | CODE WINDOW WITH CMDTITLE CLICK EVENT PROCEDURE SHOWING |
|---|---|

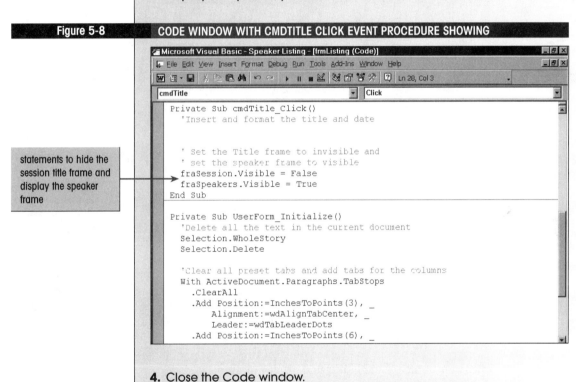

statements to hide the session title frame and display the speaker frame

```
Private Sub cmdTitle_Click()
   'Insert and format the title and date


   ' Set the Title frame to invisible and
   ' set the speaker frame to visible
   fraSession.Visible = False
   fraSpeakers.Visible = True
End Sub

Private Sub UserForm_Initialize()
   'Delete all the text in the current document
   Selection.WholeStory
   Selection.Delete

   'Clear all preset tabs and add tabs for the columns
   With ActiveDocument.Paragraphs.TabStops
      .ClearAll
      .Add Position:=InchesToPoints(3), _
         Alignment:=wdAlignTabCenter, _
         Leader:=wdTabLeaderDots
      .Add Position:=InchesToPoints(6), _
```

4. Close the Code window.

At this point, you should be familiar with the basic design of the Session Listing form. You should also understand the code Ricardo used to display and hide parts of the form at runtime. Next, you are ready to work on other aspects of the project. You'll begin by studying the overall plan for the Session Listing project.

## Planning **the Session Listing Project**

Gene stops by your desk with the plan he created for the Speaker Listing project. His plan consists of a list of tasks that the program should be able to perform. Figure 5-9 contains the written list of tasks for the Speaker Listing project.

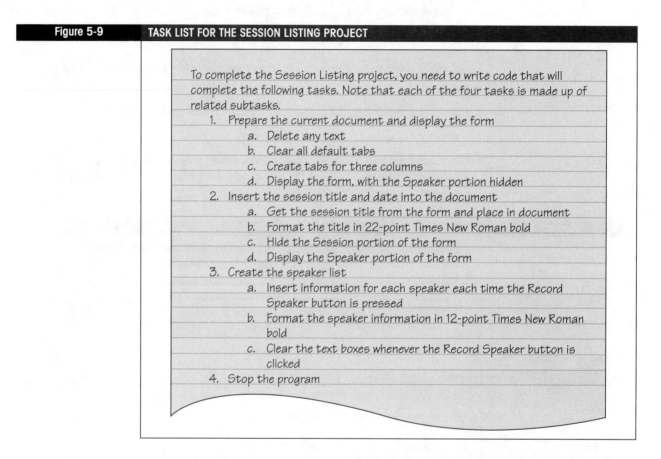

**Figure 5-9**    **TASK LIST FOR THE SESSION LISTING PROJECT**

To complete the Session Listing project, you need to write code that will complete the following tasks. Note that each of the four tasks is made up of related subtasks.
1. Prepare the current document and display the form
   a. Delete any text
   b. Clear all default tabs
   c. Create tabs for three columns
   d. Display the form, with the Speaker portion hidden
2. Insert the session title and date into the document
   a. Get the session title from the form and place in document
   b. Format the title in 22-point Times New Roman bold
   c. Hide the Session portion of the form
   d. Display the Speaker portion of the form
3. Create the speaker list
   a. Insert information for each speaker each time the Record Speaker button is pressed
   b. Format the speaker information in 12-point Times New Roman bold
   c. Clear the text boxes whenever the Record Speaker button is clicked
4. Stop the program

You can think of the plan as an outline for approaching the project. Often a project will seem overwhelming if you look at it in its entirety. By examining a project one piece at a time, you'll soon begin to see the project as a series of manageable tasks. For example, notice that the first task (Prepare the current document and display the form) consists of four subtasks. The last of these subtasks (Display the form with the Speaker portion hidden) has already been completed for you; you reviewed these fairly simple statements earlier, when you learned about hiding and displaying frames.

Likewise, the last step in the plan (Stop the program) is really a minor task—and one you already know how to perform. You'll complete that step in the next section. The important point here is that once you break a project down into its component tasks, the project will seem less intimidating and be easier for you to complete.

## Removing **the Form from the Screen**

Because the last task in the project plan is so simple, Gene wants you to begin there. Specifically, he wants you to program the Quit button. As you saw when you previewed the project, the Quit button (that is, the `cmdQuit` button) on the Session Listing form removes the entire form from the screen and ends the program. As you learned in Tutorial 1, this requires only the following statement:

```
Unload Me
```

This statement will remove the form from the screen and, thus, end the program. You will enter that statement now.

---

### To program the `cmdQuit` command button:

**1.** If necessary, display the form in the VBA IDE in design time.

**2.** Double-click the **Quit** button. The Code window opens, displaying the `cmdQuit_Click` procedure. The cursor is positioned between the `Private Sub` and `End Sub` statements.

**3.** Press **Tab,** and then type `Unload Me.`

**4.** Save your work.

---

You have programmed the Quit button, thus completing Task 4 in the project plan. You can't test the Quit button yet, because you haven't programmed the Record Session Title button yet, which will ultimately display the frame that contains the Quit button. Some of the other subtasks have already been completed for you. In the next steps you will view the code that has already been placed in the project. You will also look for the comments that identify the code you need to add.

---

### To view the existing code:

**1.** Display the Code window, scroll through the code and notice that some of the code has already been inserted into the project. Ricardo has inserted comments to indicate the code you need to add, as shown in Figure 5-10.

| Figure 5-10 | COMMENTS INDICATING CODE YOU WILL ADD |

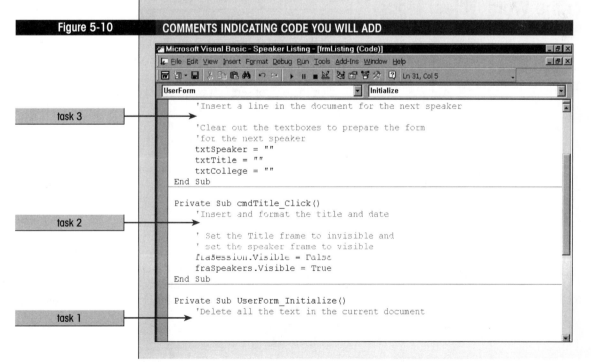

> **2.** Spend some time comparing the comments in the Code window with the plan for the project shown earlier in figure 5-9.

In order to work on the first three tasks, you must learn about the objects, properties, and methods associated with the Word object model. In the next session you will become familiar with the Word object model and learn how to access parts of the object model with VBA code.

## Session 5.1 QUICK CHECK

1. A(n) _____ control is used to separate portions of a form.

2. Write the statement that will make the frame named `fraEmployeeData` invisible.

3. Write the statement that will remove the current form from the screen.

4. The _____ event of a form is triggered when the form is loaded.

5. Suppose you want some statements to be executed when the user clicks the command button named `cmdEnterData`. You should place these statements in the `cmdEnterData` _____ event procedure.

## SESSION 5.2

In this session you will learn about the Word object model. You will use the Selection object (which is part of the Windows object model) to delete all text in the document. You will also learn to set tabs in a document with VBA statements. Finally, you will learn how to add text to a Word document.

## Using the Word Object Model

In the last session, you completed the fourth and simplest task in Gene's project plan—coding the Quit button to remove the form from the screen. Next, Gene asks you to turn your attention to the first task in the project plan—writing the code that prepares the Word document for the list of speakers. As discussed earlier, the task of setting up the Word document actually consists of four subtasks: (1) delete any existing text in the document, (2) clear all default tabs in the document, (3) create new tabs, and (4) hide the session portion of the form. You already examined the code for the last subtask, hiding the speaker portion of the form. Now you need to add the remainder of the code in the Initialize event.

The first subtask is to delete all the text in the document. When you previewed the project, you saw that the Speaker Listing program should delete any text in the current Word document before inserting new text. You want the task of deleting existing text to be performed when the form is loaded (or initialized), so you must enter the necessary statements in the form's Initialize event procedure.

Before you can delete a block of text in Word, you first need to select the text. In order to write VBA statements that select text, you need to use the Word selection object, which is just one part of the Word object model. As you learned in Tutorial 2, an application's object model consists of all the objects (and collections of objects) in that application. You are already familiar with parts of the Excel object model. The Word model is made up of a similar hierarchy of collections and objects. A portion of the Word object model is presented in Figure 5-11. Because the model is very large and intricate, only the most commonly used objects are included in the figure.

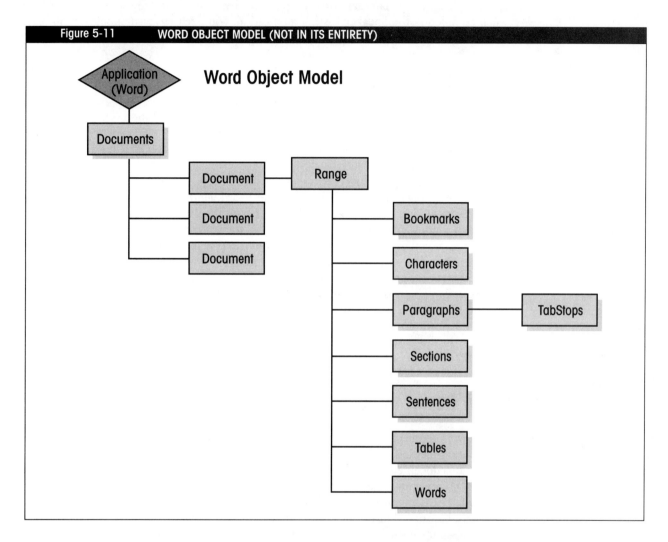

**Figure 5-11   WORD OBJECT MODEL (NOT IN ITS ENTIRETY)**

As you know, the application object—that is, Word itself—is the highest level of all the objects in the object model. The next level in the hierarchy is the **Documents collection**. As you probably know, in Word, you can have several documents open. The documents collection, then, includes all open documents. Within that collection is the **ActiveDocument**, which, at this stage in your VBA education, you can think of as the active document within the Word window. (In programming terminology, the active document is said to be the document that has **focus**.)

The next level down in the object model shown in Figure 5-11 is the range object. You'll learn how to use the Range object later in this tutorial, but for now just keep in mind that the Range object consists of a contiguous portion of a document. Below the Range object, you see a number of different objects—one of these is the **Paragraphs collection,** which consists of all the paragraphs in the document. To reference the fifth paragraph in the collection you would use `Paragraphs(5)`. Each paragraph, in turn, has a **TabStops collection**, which includes every tab that is set for that paragraph. When a new document is started, tabs are automatically set every one-half inch along the horizontal ruler. If you want to reference the first tab in the TabStops collection you would use `TabStop(1)` in your statement. As you may recall from your work with Word, you can set tabs for the whole document or you can set tabs for a selected paragraph. You have these same options when setting the tabs through VBA statements.

Now that you are familiar with the parts of the Word object model that you will use when completing the Speaker Listing application, you need to learn about a small part of the Windows object model.

# Using the Windows Object Model

Just as each application has its own object model, Microsoft Windows itself also has an object model. The Windows object model is extremely large, but in order to complete the Speaker Listing project, you only need to learn about two of its objects, the Active Window object and the Selection object.

The **Active Window** object represents the window that is currently active. For example, if you were typing a letter in Word, then the Word window would be the active window. However, if you were editing a worksheet in Excel, then the Worksheet window would be the active window (that is, the window that has focus). Only one window at a time can be active, even if you have other applications running. When you have an application running, but it is minimized to the task bar, it is considered inactive.

The **Selection** object consists of whatever items are selected within the active window. The Selection object is important in VBA for Word, because it is often necessary to select a portion of text in a document in order to manipulate it in some way. For example, the Speaker Listing program must select any and all text in the active document, and then delete it. In the next section, you will learn how to use two methods associated with the Selection object in order to do just that.

# Using the Selection Object to Select Text

The Selection object has many methods. For this application two methods are used—the WholeStory method, and the Delete method—which are useful when you need to select all the text in a document and then delete it.

In VBA, you can select all of the text in a Word document by using the **WholeStory method**. The name of the method comes from the fact that, in VBA, a Word document is considered a **story**. Thus, to select all the text in the document, you need to select the *whole story*. The following statement, then, will select all the text in the document.

```
Selection.WholeStory
```

You could use a different method to select portions of a document. However, since in this case you want to select the whole document, you need to use the WholeStory method. The WholeStory method works exactly as if you had clicked Edit on the menu bar in Word and then clicked Select All.

Once all of the text in the document is selected, you can delete all the text within the selection by using the Selection object's **Delete method**. The following statement would delete all the text in the Selection object:

```
Selection.Delete
```

You will now add these two statements to your project. You will enter the statement in the form's Initialize procedure because you want any text currently in the document to be deleted as soon as the form is loaded.

*To add the code that deletes all text in the document:*

1. Verify that the Code window for the `frmListing` form is still open in the VBA IDE.

2. Position the cursor in the `UserForm_Initialize` procedure, just below the first comment, as indicated in Figure 5-12.

| Figure 5-12 | **USEFORM INITIALIZE PROCEDURE** |
| --- | --- |

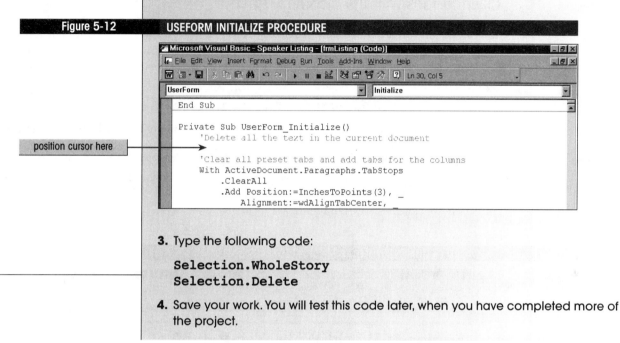

position cursor here

3. Type the following code:

```
Selection.WholeStory
Selection.Delete
```

4. Save your work. You will test this code later, when you have completed more of the project.

The next part of the first task in the project plan has to do with clearing tabs and adding new ones. To perform these tasks in VBA, you need to use the TabStops collection.

# Delete **and Set Tabs with the TabStops Collection**

When you previewed the Speaker Listing application, you saw it create a speakers list consisting of three items (the speaker's name, the title of the speech, and the speaker's college) all aligned as columns in the document. You could create these columns several different ways in Word. However, the simplest way is to use tabs. Recall that a new Word document has default tabs set at every one-half inch. Thus, before the Speaker Listing program can set the tabs for the speakers list, it must first delete all the default tabs.

Within VBA, you manipulate tabs by manipulating the TabStops collection. When you first reviewed the Word object model, you saw that the TabStops collection is part of the paragraph collection, which is in turn part of the documents collection. As mentioned earlier, the paragraphs collection includes all paragraphs in a document. The TabStops collection consists of each tab in a paragraph. The TabStops collection has a number of useful methods, which you can use to manipulate the tabs in a document. In the next two sections, you will learn how to use the ClearAll method and the Add method.

## Clearing Tabs with the ClearAll Method

You can use the **ClearAll method** to delete all tabs in a paragraph or document. The following statement selects all the tabs in the active document because no particular paragraph was specified. (If, on the other hand, you wanted to set tabs for a particular paragraph you would specify which paragraphs.)

```
ActiveDocument.Paragraphs.TabStops.ClearAll
```

Once your program has cleared all the tabs in the active document, it can add new tabs. In the case of the Speaker Listing project, there is no need to set a tab for the first column because you want the first column aligned on the left margin. The first tab, then, should be at the three-inch mark, and should be a center-aligned tab. The second tab should be on the six-inch mark, and it should be a right-aligned tab. Using these tabs would result in a document formatted like the one shown in Figure 5-13.

| Figure 5-13 | WORD DOCUMENT WITH TABS INDICATED |

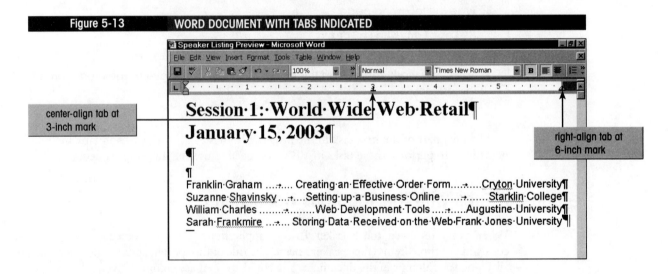

## Adding Tabs with the Add Method

You add tabs by using the **Add method** of the TabStops collection. This method requires a little more explanation then the ClearAll method. Its complete syntax is explained on the following page. Note that the Add method includes a number of arguments, which you can use to specify the desired position for a tab.

| Syntax | *expression*.**Add**(*Position, Alignment, Leader*) |
| --- | --- |
| **Explanation** | The Add method adds a tab at the position stated in the arguments. |
| | Expression: Consists of a reference to a particular TabStops object. |
| | Position: Specifies the desired location of the tab, in points. If you prefer, however, you can apply the InchesToPoints function, which allows you to specify the position in inches instead. For example, to set the tab position to three inches you would use `InchesToPoints(3)`. |
| | Alignment: Specifies the desired alignment of the tab. The two that pertain to the Speaker Listing project are `wdAlignTabCenter` (center-alignment) and `wdAlignTabRight` (right-alignment) |
| | Leader: Specifies the type of leader between the tabs. For the Speaker Listing project, you want to insert dots between the tabs. This type of leader is specified as `wdTabLeaderDots`. To learn about other types of tab leaders, consult VBA Help. |
| **Example** | ```
ActiveDocument.Paragraphs.TabStops. Add _
        Position:=InchesToPoints(3), _
        Alignment:=wdAlignTabCenter, _
        Leader:=wdTabLeaderDots
``` |

The example above sets a tab at the 3-inch mark on the Word ruler. It formats the tab with center alignment and with leader dots. Notice that three lines in the example end with an underscore character. You'll learn the meaning of this character in the next section.

## Using the Continuation Character

The underscore at the end of each line in the example is called a continuation character. The **continuation character** tells VBA that the code on the second line is a continuation of the first line. Likewise, the continuation character on the second line tells VBA that the code on the third line is a continuation of the code on the second line. In order to work properly, the underscore must be preceded by a blank space.

The continuation character is useful whenever you need to type a long statement that would otherwise scroll off the right edge of the Code window. The continuation character doesn't change the meaning of your code; it's a device designed for the convenience of the developer. In VBA, the results are the same whether you let a long, one-line statement scroll off the right edge of the Code window or use the continuation character to break a statement into multiple lines. Most developers find it easier to use the continuation character, so they can see all their code in the Code window at a glance, without having to scroll to the right to read the ends of especially long statements.

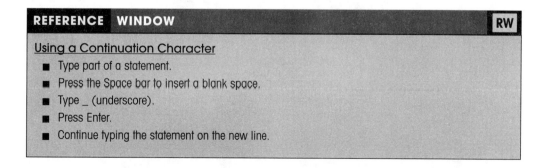

**REFERENCE WINDOW**                                                          **RW**

Using a Continuation Character
- Type part of a statement.
- Press the Space bar to insert a blank space.
- Type _ (underscore).
- Press Enter.
- Continue typing the statement on the new line.
```

Now that you understand how to use continuation characters, you should feel free to use them in any of the code you write for TnT Consulting.

## Viewing the Tab Code in the Project

To save typing time, Ricardo has already added code that will create the tabs. He put this code in the form's Initialize procedure because you want the program to clear default tabs and set new ones as soon as the form is displayed on the screen. You will view and test these statements now.

### To view and test the tab code:

1. Switch to the Word window, and look at the default tabs in the document.

   TROUBLE? If you see three tabs in your document, rather than the default tabs, you ran the Speaker Listing project at some point earlier in this tutorial. Click the horizontal ruler several times to insert additional tabs. Repeat several times to add multiple tabs, and then continue with Step 3.

| Figure 5-14 | WORD WINDOW SHOWING DEFAULT TABS |
| --- | --- |

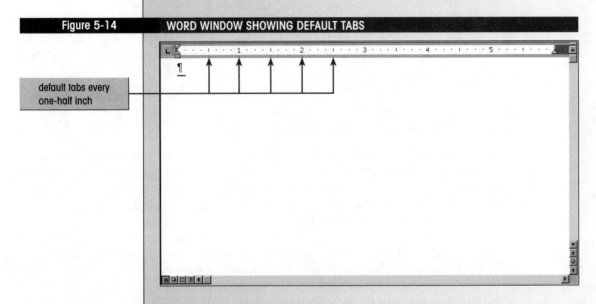

default tabs every one-half inch

2. Press **Tab** repeatedly. The cursor jumps from one tab to the next. Stop pressing Tab when the cursor reaches the second line of the document.

3. Type the following: **I am testing the Speaker Listing project**. If the form's Initialize procedure runs properly, it should delete this sentence when you run the program.

4. Switch to the VBA IDE and scroll down the Code window to display the code for setting tabs, as shown in Figure 5-15.

**Figure 5-15**   **THE CMDTITLE CLICK EVENT PROCEDURE WITH TITLE CODE ADDED**

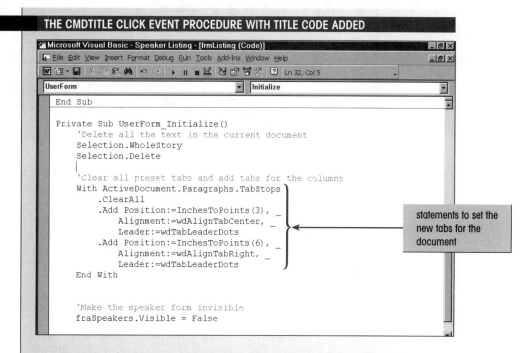

statements to set the new tabs for the document

**5.** Run the procedure. The form appears in the Word window—that is, the form initializes. This means that the Initialize procedure has finished executing. Because you are only testing the User_Form Initialize event, you don't need to test the program any further.

**6.** Click the **Close** button ☒ on the top of the form. You return to the VBA IDE, in design time. In the next step, you will confirm that the Initialize procedure worked according to plan.

**7.** Switch to the Word window. You see a blank Word document on the screen. The sentence you typed earlier has been deleted. Also, the default tabs have been cleared and new ones inserted.

**8.** Press **Tab**. The cursor jumps to the 3-inch mark. A line of dots (the tab leader) extends from the left margin to the first tab.

**9.** Press **Tab** again. The cursor jumps to the 6-inch mark. The tab leader now extends all the way across the page. This tells you that the tabs have been correctly set.

This completes the first task in Gene's project plan—preparing the document for the speaker list. The next task in the project plan has to do with inserting the session title and the session date into the document.

## Inserting Text in a Word Document

Your next task is to write the code that will place the session title and the date of the session at the top of the document. The title and date should be formatted in 22-point Times New Roman bold. In order to write the necessary statements, you need to learn about the Word Range object. Then you need to learn how to refer to one object multiple times in a series of statements, by using a `With` statement.

## Using the Range Object

As mentioned earlier, in Word the **Range object** consists of a contiguous portion (or block) of a document. The block might contain a sentence, a word, a character, or even an insertion point (a location between characters). The most important property of the Range object is the **Text property**, which contains the actual text included in the range. Since most VBA applications for Word revolve around manipulating text, VBA programming for Word centers around the Range object.

As you learned in Tutorial 4, in order to refer to an object in a VBA statement, you need to specify the object's exact position within the object model. For some Office objects, this means you can use rather formulaic, or repetitious, statements to refer to a particular object. For example, to refer to a particular sheet in Excel, you would use a reference like: `Workbooks(1).Sheets(1)`. However, referring to a specific Range object in Word requires a little more care. The difficulty lies in the fact that the Text property of the Range object can be text in the main body of the document, in the header or footer, or even in a table. For example, if you wanted to access all the text in a document's main body, you would use the statement:

```
ActiveDocument.Range.Text
```

The first part of the statement refers to the active document—that is, the one that has focus. The next element in the statement is the Range object, which in this case represents the entire main body of the document. The final element in the statement is the Text property, which returns the text that falls within the range. Taken as a whole, this example statement refers to all of the text in the current document.

If, instead of the whole document, you wanted to refer to a range consisting of the third paragraph, you could use the statement:

```
ActiveDocument.Paragraphs(3).Range.Text
```

Since `Text` is the default property of the Range object in Word, you don't actually have to include the Text property. Thus, the following statement is equivalent to the previous statement.

```
ActiveDocument.Paragraphs(3).Range
```

Both of these statements refer to the third paragraph in the document.

The Range object has a rich set of properties and methods that you can use to manipulate text in a Word document. You will learn about a few important methods in the next section. VBA Help contains a lot of useful information on the others if you want to explore more.

## Using Some Methods of the Range Object

In order to complete the Speaker Listing project, you are most interested in the InsertAfter method and the InsertParagraphAfter method. You use the first of these—the **InsertAfter method**—to insert text into a document. The InsertAfter method will insert text you specify at the end of a particular range. The range then expands to include the newly inserted text. You use the second method, **InsertParagraphAfter**, to add a paragraph mark (that is, a new, blank line) at the end of a range. (This is similar to pressing Enter in Word.)

Now you are ready to examine the statements that will take the session title (which the user will enter in a text box named `txtSessionTitle`) and the session date (which the user will enter in a text box named `txtSessionDate`) and insert them into the document. The following five statements will take the text entered in the `txtSessionTitle` text box and insert it in the first line of the document. These statements will then take the text entered in `txtSessionDate` and insert it in to the second line of the document. Notice that the date will also be followed by two paragraph marks, thus providing a blank line in the document following the date, and a new line in which to insert the speaker information that will follow the session title and date.

```
ActiveDocument.Paragraphs(1).Range.InsertAfter txtSessionTitle
ActiveDocument.Paragraphs(1).Range.InsertParagraphAfter
ActiveDocument.Paragraphs(1).Range.InsertAfter txtSessionDate
ActiveDocument.Paragraphs(1).Range.InsertParagraphAfter
ActiveDocument.Paragraphs(1).Range.InsertParagraphAfter
```

As you can see, `ActiveDocument.Paragraphs(1).Range` occurs in each statement because each statement applies a method to the same range. To avoid this kind of repetitious notation, you can use the shortcut described in the next section.

## Referring to an Object Multiple Times in a `With` Statement

Often you will want to write several statements that affect a single object. In the code above, for example, several statements referred to the same Range object. In order to avoid retyping a reference to a particular object, you can use the **With statement**. The syntax of the `With` statement is shown below:

| | |
|---|---|
| **Syntax** | `With Object`<br>　　　`[statements]`<br>`End With` |
| **Explanation** | The word **With** marks the beginning of the **With** statement. Any statement between the **With** and **End With** statements are assumed to refer to the Object specified in the **With** statement. |
| **Example** | `With ActiveDocument.Paragraphs(1).Range`<br>　　　`.InsertAfter txtSessionTitle`<br>　　　`.InsertParagraphAfter`<br>　　　`.InsertAfter txtSessionDate`<br>　　　`.InsertParagraphAfter`<br>　　　`.InsertParagraphAfter`<br>`End With` |

The example above performs identically to the statements in the preceding section. The `With` statement, then, is simply a shortcut that you can use when you want to apply several statements to the same object.

## Adding the Code to the Project

You are now ready to type the statements that will insert and format the session title and date. Then you can test these statements with some sample input. You will enter these statements in the Click event procedure for the Record Session Title button—that is, the `cmdTitle` button. (As you'll recall, this is the button the user clicks in order to enter the session information into the document.)

### To insert the code that will add the title and date to the document:

1. Switch back to the VBA IDE.

2. Scroll up in the Code window, and then click in the **cmdTitle_Click** procedure, just below the comment, as shown in Figure 5-16.

| Figure 5-16 | CODE WINDOW WITH CMDTITLE_CLICK PROCEDURE SHOWING |
| --- | --- |

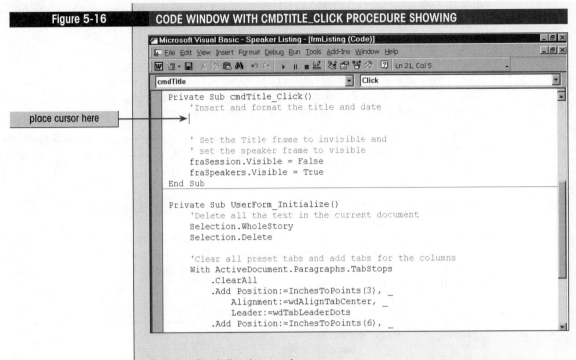

3. Type the following code:

```
With ActiveDocument.Paragraphs(1).Range
    .InsertAfter txtSessionTitle
    .InsertParagraphAfter
    .InsertAfter txtSessionDate
    .InsertParagraphAfter
    .InsertParagraphAfter
End With
```

4. Compare your screen with Figure 5-17.

| Figure 5-17 | THE CMDTITLE CLICK EVENT PROCEDURE AFTER ADDING STATEMENTS |
| --- | --- |

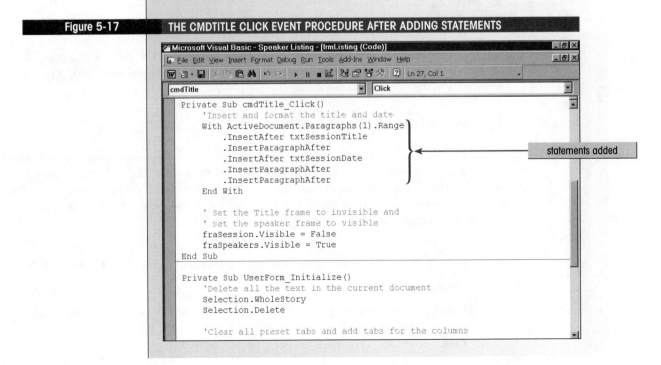

5. Save your work and run the project. The Session Listing form is displayed in the Word window. At this stage, only the top frame (the Session portion of the form) is visible.

6. Click the **Session Title** text box, type **Session 2: VBA Programming**, click the **Session Date** text box, and then type **February 18, 2003**. Now you can test the statements you just wrote to see if they do actually insert the title and date into the document when you click the Record Session Title button.

7. Click the **Record Session Title** button. The Session frame is removed from the screen, and the Speakers frame is displayed. You're not interested in the rest of the program right now, so you can stop testing.

8. Click the **Quit** button on the form. You return to the VBA IDE.

9. Switch back to the Word window and observe that the title and date are displayed in the document as shown in Figure 5-18.

| Figure 5-18 | DOCUMENT WITH TITLE AND DATE INSERTED |
| --- | --- |

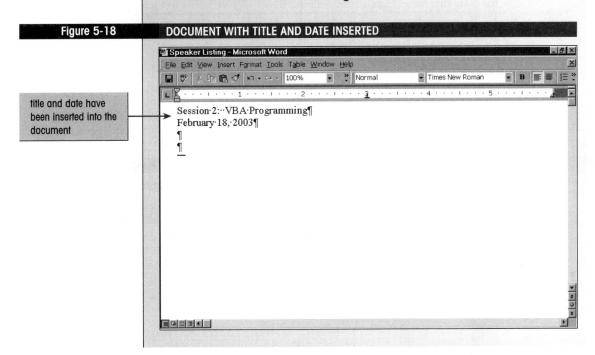

title and date have been inserted into the document

As you learned earlier, the InsertAfter method automatically expands the range to include the newly added text. Thus, at the beginning of the `With` statement (when the Word document is still blank) the Range object includes only the blank first line. But after the last line within the `With` statement is executed, the Range object includes the two paragraphs you added to the range. Your next job, then, is to add the code that will format these two paragraphs.

## Formatting **Text with the Range Object**

You alter the font of text in a range by using the **Font property**. The Font property, in turn, is associated with several other properties. The three font-related properties that you will use in the Speaker Listing project are the Name property, the Size property, and the Bold property. You use the **Name property** to specify the name of a font, such as "Times New

Roman" or "Arial". The **Size property** will set the point size of the font. Finally, you can add boldface by setting the **Bold property** to True. (Alternately, you can turn boldface off by setting the Bold property to False.)

Recall that Gene has asked you to write statements that will format the session title and date as 22-point Times New Roman bold. The following three statements will accomplish this.

```
.Font.Name = "Times New Roman"
.Font.Size = 22
.Font.Bold = True
```

You can add these statements to the bottom of the With statement you started earlier. By including them in the With statement, you ensure that VBA will apply these property settings to the Range object (which, by the end of the existing lines in the With statement, has grown to encompass the newly inserted date and title).

You will now add these statements to your project. When you test the project this time, notice that the title you entered the last time is replaced with the next text. This is a result of the code that clears the current document, which you placed in the form's Initialize procedure.

### To enter the statements to alter the font properties of the title and date:

**1.** Switch back to the Code window in the VBA IDE.

**2.** In the `cmdTitle_Click` procedure, insert a blank line just before the End With statement, as shown in Figure 5-19.

| Figure 5-19 | THE CMDTITLE_CLICK EVENT PROCEDURE WITH NEW LINE ADDED |
| --- | --- |

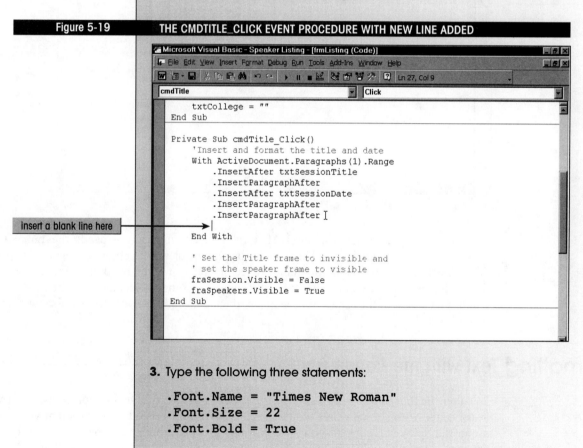

**3.** Type the following three statements:

```
.Font.Name = "Times New Roman"
.Font.Size = 22
.Font.Bold = True
```

**4.** Save your work, and then run the program.

**5.** Enter **Session 3: Using VBA with Office 2000** for the title and **January 18, 2003** for the date.

**6.** Click the **Record Session Title** button on the form.

**7.** Move the form so that you can observe that the new title has been inserted into the document and formatted according to your specifications, as shown in Figure 5-20.

| Figure 5-20 | DOCUMENT WITH TITLE AND DATE FORMATTED |
|---|---|

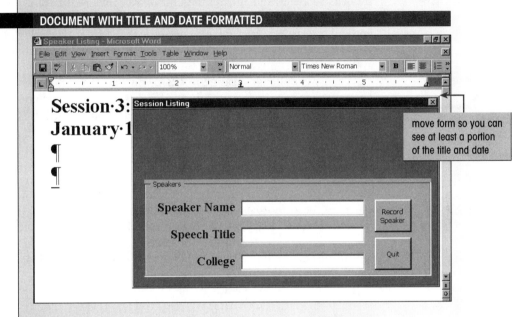

**8.** Click the **Quit** button on the form. You return to the VBA IDE.

You have now completed the second task in your project plan. The only remaining task is to write the code that will insert the list of speakers into the document. You will do this in the next session.

## Session 5.2 QUICK CHECK

1. The highest level of the Word object model is the _____ object.

2. The second level in the Word object model is the _____ object.

3. The _____ object is an object associated with Windows rather than Word, and represents anything selected in a window.

4. The _____ object represents the window that currently has focus, whereas the _____ object represents the document that currently has focus.

5. You would use the _____ method of the Range object to insert a paragraph mark at the end of the range.

6. Write the statements that will set the text in the Range object to 15-point Arial, with no boldface.

**In this session you will create the speaker list. You will learn to collapse a range and establish a new range. You will also learn to concatenate strings into a single string.**

# Establishing a New Range with the Collapse Method

The final task in the Speaker Listing project is to write the code that will add the list of speakers to the document, and then format the list in a different font and font size from the session title and date. In order to format the speaker section differently from the title section, you will need to establish a new range—one that does not include the session title or the date. You can establish a new range in several ways, the simplest of which is to collapse the range at the end of the current range.

When you **collapse a range** in VBA, you "wipe out" the selection within the range. To conceptualize this process, imagine a Word document containing only one sentence. If you select that sentence and then delete it, the selection no longer exists, and the end of document mark moves back to the beginning of the document. You do this in VBA by employing the Collapse method, which is a method of the Range object.

The **Collapse method** will collapse a range to the beginning or end of the text in the current range. This results in a new range that is essentially an insertion point in the document, a place to insert new text. In other words, the new range contains no characters. This is useful when you need to establish an insertion point at the beginning or ending of a range. For instance, at the end of the `With` statement you just created, the Range object consists of the session title and the date and an extra blank line. In order to insert even more text into the document (that is, the list of speakers) you need to establish a new insertion point for that text. You'll do that by collapsing the current range.

The syntax of the Collapse method is shown below:

| Syntax | `expression.Collapse [Direction:= constant]` |
|---|---|
| Explanation | The Collapse method will collapse a range to the beginning or ending of the current range. After the Collapse method, the starting and ending point of the new range are the same. In other words, the new range contains no characters. The Direction argument specifies the direction in which you want to collapse the range. Use the constant `wdCollapseEnd` to collapse to the end of the range. Alternately, you can use `wdCollapseStart` to collapse to the beginning of the range. If you do not include a direction, the default is to collapse to the beginning of the range. |
| Example | `ActiveDocument.Range.Collapse Direction:= wdCollapseEnd` |
| | This example will collapse the range (the selected text) to the end of the current range. |

In the Speaker Listing project, you want to establish a new range at the end of the range specified in the `With` statement (that is, at the end of the session title and date). To do this, you will use the following statement:

```
ActiveDocument.Range.Collapse Direction:=wdCollapseEnd
```

Once the new range is established (thanks to the Collapse method) you can insert text in this range and format it, just as you did for the session title and date.

Note that if you wanted to add text prior to the title, you could collapse the range to the beginning using `wdCollapseStart` as the Direction argument.

# Concatenating **Strings**

Now that you know how to establish a new range in which to insert the speaker information, you need to learn the statements that will actually insert the information. In order to understand these statements, first recall that the user will enter the speaker's name in a text box named `txtSpeaker`, the title of the speech in the text box named `txtTitle`, and the speaker's college affiliation in the text box named `txtCollege`. Each time the user clicks the Record Speaker button on the form, the program should insert a new paragraph in the document and then insert the speaker information into that one-line paragraph. Recall, also, that the speaker list must be aligned in columns, based on the tabs specified in the form's Initialize event procedure.

Now think about what you would do if you were typing the speaker list directly into the document. You would set up the tabs and then you would type the speaker's name, press Tab, type the speech title, press Tab, type the college, and then press Enter. In VBA, what you really want to do is combine one string (the speaker's name) with another string (the speech title). You then want to combine the resulting string with yet another string (the college affiliation). You merge, or combine, strings through a process known as **concatenation**. In VBA, you concatenate strings by typing an ampersand (&) between the strings you want to concatenate. (As you'll recall, a string is a contiguous collection of characters.)

You can use concatenation to write statements that join simple strings ("Mary" & "Smith"). However, you will more commonly use concatenation to join variables that have been assigned string values. Consider the following code:

```
strFirstName = "Mary"
strLastName = "Smith"
strFullName = strFirstName & strLastName
```

The first statement sets the variable `strFirstName` equal to the string "Mary." The second statement sets the variable `strLastName` equal to the string "Smith." The third statement sets the variable `strFullName` equal to a combination of the first two variables—that is, it sets it equal to a concatenation of the string "Mary" and "Smith," or MarySmith. In order to include a blank (" ") between the first and last name, you would have to concatenate a blank space between "Mary" and "Smith." Thus, to assign the string "Mary Smith" (rather than MarySmith) to the variable `strFullName`, you would use this statement:

```
strFullName = strFirstName & " " & strLastName
```

To expand this example, suppose you wanted to concatenate the first and last name with a comma in between so that the variable `strFullName` contains "Last Name, First Name". The following statement would accomplish this:

```
strFullName = strLastName & ", " & strFirstName
```

In the same vein, you can concatenate strings (or string variables) with the VBA constant, **vbTab**, which represents a tab. For example, in the Speaker Listing project, you want to insert the speaker name, followed by a tab, followed by the speech title, followed by another tab, followed by the college affiliation. The following statement will concatenate the text and tabs into a single string:

```
txtSpeaker & vbTab & txtTitle & vbTab & txtCollege
```

You can combine this statement with the InsertAfter method in order to add the concatenated string to the document. You'll learn how to do that in the next section.

# Inserting a Tabbed List in a Document

You are now ready to add the code that will create the speaker list. Recall that the user will enter the speaker information and then click the Record Speaker button on the form. Therefore, you will add the code that creates the speaker list to the `cmdRecordSpeaker` button's Click event procedure. Gene wants you to format the speaker list in 12-point Arial, without boldface. Again, you will use the `With` statement to shorten the code by cutting down repetitive references to the range object. Thus, the code for the `cmdRecordSpeaker` button is as follows:

```
With ActiveDocument.Range
    .Collapse direction:=wdCollapseEnd
    .InsertParagraphAfter
    .InsertAfter txtSpeaker & vbTab & txtTitle & vbTab & txtCollege
    .Font.Name = "Arial"
    .Font.Size = 12
    .Font.Bold = False
End With
```

You will now add this code to the project and then test it.

### To enter the code that creates the speaker list:

1. Scroll up in the Code window, and position the cursor within the `cmdRecordSpeaker` button's Click event, as shown in Figure 5-21.

Figure 5-21 | CODE WINDOW

place cursor here

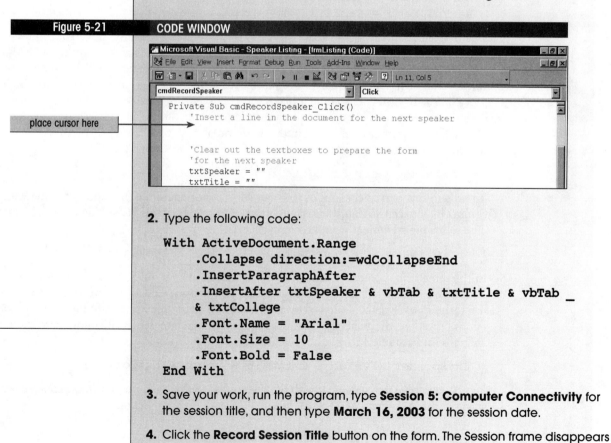

2. Type the following code:

```
With ActiveDocument.Range
    .Collapse direction:=wdCollapseEnd
    .InsertParagraphAfter
    .InsertAfter txtSpeaker & vbTab & txtTitle & vbTab _
    & txtCollege
    .Font.Name = "Arial"
    .Font.Size = 10
    .Font.Bold = False
End With
```

3. Save your work, run the program, type **Session 5: Computer Connectivity** for the session title, and then type **March 16, 2003** for the session date.

4. Click the **Record Session Title** button on the form. The Session frame disappears and the Speakers frame appears.

5. Enter the data shown in Figure 5-22. Be sure to click the **Record Speaker** button after each entry.

| Figure 5-22 | DATA FOR SPEAKERS FRAME | | |
| --- | --- | --- | --- |
| **SPEAKER** | **TITLE** | | **COLLEGE** |
| Gary Brown | Notebook Computers in Year 2003 | | Carlton-Wilson University |
| Felicia Hall | Hand-held Computers and the WWW | | Romano College |
| Douglas Fairchild | Wireless Connectivity | | Sinclair University |

6. Verify that you clicked the **Record Speaker** button after the last entry. All the text boxes in the Speakers frame are now empty.

7. Click the **Quit** button on the form. You return to the VBA IDE.

8. Switch to the Word window and view the document. Your document should look like Figure 5-23.

| Figure 5-23 | DOCUMENT WITH ALL DATA INSERTED |
| --- | --- |

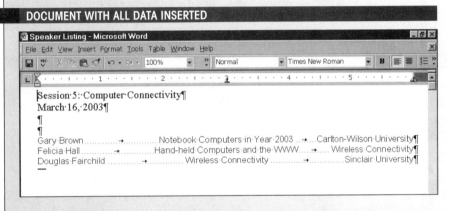

9. Save the document and close Word.

You have now completed the project and you are ready to demonstrate it for Patricia Sutherland at Sutherland Event Planners.

# Session 5.3 QUICK CHECK

1. To start a new range at the end of a current range, you would use the _____ method. To start the new range at the end of the old range, you would use the _____ constant.

2. You use the _____ character to concatenate strings in VBA.

3. Write a statement that will collapse a range to the beginning of the current range.

4. Write a statement that will concatenate `strAuthor`, a tab, and `strBookTitle`.

5. Write the statements that would concatenate `strMonth`, `strDay`, and `strYear` with a comma and a space between `strDay` and `strYear`.

## REVIEW ASSIGNMENTS

The TnT account representatives frequently make lists of potential clients that they plan to contact in the coming month. For your next project, Gene asks you to apply what you have learned in the Speaker Listing project in order to help automate the process of making these lists. The list created by the program should have a title, indicating the type of clients included in the list. (For example, some clients might be drawn from the local university, while others are drawn from the service industry.) Gene has already created the form for this project and programmed some of the controls. Your job is to write the remaining code. Gene tells you that you should be able to adapt much of the code from the Speaker Listing project in order to complete this one.

1. Start Word and open the document named **Phone**, located in the Review folder for Tutorial 5.

2. Save the file on your Data Disk as **Phone List** in the Review folder for Tutorial 5.

3. Open the VBA IDE, and open the form named **frmPhoneList**. Figure 5-24 shows the names of all the control objects in this form. The form is designed to function just like the Speaker Listing form. The title and name are visible in the form when the form is first launched. Once the title and name of the representative are entered, the lower portion of the form is displayed and the upper portion is hidden.

**Figure 5-24**     **THE FRMPHONELIST FORM IN DESIGN VIEW**

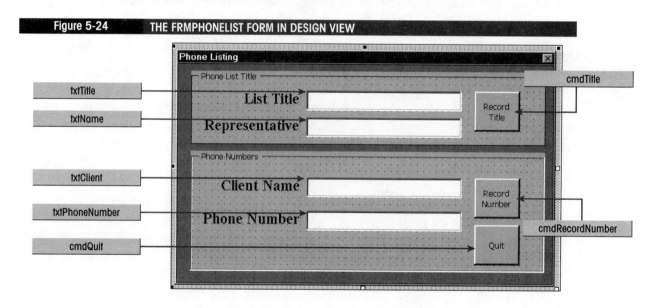

4. Run the program. Enter "University Clients" for the list title and your name for the account representative. Click Record Title button. Nothing happens in the document. However, the Phone List Title frame disappears and the Phone Numbers frame appears.

5. Enter data of your choice in the text boxes, and click the Record Number button on the form. Again, nothing happens in the document because the code that will record the data has not been entered yet.

6. Click the Quit button on the form.

7. Double-click anywhere on the form and examine the form's Initialize event procedure. Locate the code that inserts tabs in the document. Add a comment that indicates where the tabs will be positioned on the ruler, the tab style, and whether or not they include a leader. Add the code that deletes text in the document.

8. Locate the code that displays and hides the appropriate portions of the form. (*Hint*: You should find two occurrences of this code in the project.) Add comments before these lines, describing their purpose.

9. Code the Record Title button. When the user clicks this button, it should place the title and the account representative name at the top of the document. The program should format these items in 24-point Arial bold. (*Hint*: You can modify the code you used in the Speaker Listing project to insert the Session Title and Date in the document. You need only modify the names of the text boxes and the font information.)

10. Test the project to make sure it works properly.

11. Verify that a title and name were entered into the document. If this did not work properly, return to the Code window and make any necessary corrections.

12. Code the Record Number button. The statements for this button should place a contact's name and phone number in the document. (*Hint*: Again, you can modify code you used in the Speaker Listing project to write this code.)

13. Insert comments at the top of the Code window that include your name and the date.

14. Save your work.

15. Run the program and test it by entering the names and phone numbers of five fictitious clients.

16. Print the document and print the project's code.

17. Close Word.

## CASE PROBLEMS

**Case 1.** *Valley Community College*  At Valley Community College, students submit essays for Alesandra Ruffolo's Expository Writing class as Microsoft Word files. Sometimes the students forget to put their names on their disks when they turn in their assignments, making it difficult for Ms. Ruffolo to identify the author of these essays. She would like you to develop a VBA program that will prompt the student for his or her name and class number. The program should then insert the student's name and class number into the document.

1. Start Word and open the document named **Valley**, located in the Cases folder for Tutorial 5.

2. Save the file as **Valley Community College** in the Cases folder for Tutorial 5.

3. Open the VBA IDE.

4. Use the Insert menu to add UserForm to the project.

5. Add two label controls, two text box controls and two command buttons to the form.

6. Set the properties for the form and controls using the information in Figure 5-25.

**Figure 5-25**       **TEST DATA**

| CONTROL | PROPERTY | VALUE |
|---|---|---|
| Userform1 | Name | frmStudent |
| | Caption | Student Information |
| Label1 | Name | lblName |
| | Caption | Name |
| Label2 | Name | lblClass |
| | Caption | Class |
| Textbox1 | Name | txtName |
| Textbox2 | Name | txtClass |
| CommandButton1 | Name | cmdOK |
| | Caption | OK |
| CommandButton2 | Name | cmdQuit |
| | Caption | Quit |

7. Arrange the controls on the form similarly to those shown in Figure 5-26. Use a font of your choice for the text displayed on the form. Be creative but make sure that the form is attractive when you are finished with it.

**Figure 5-26**       **THE NEW USER FORM, FRMSTUDENT, WITH NAMES OF CONTROL OBJECTS**

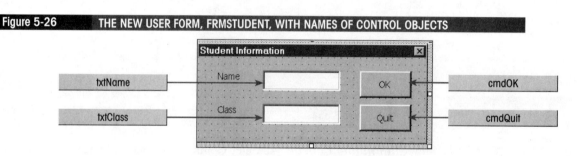

8. Double-click the OK button and add code that does the following:

   ■ Takes the value entered into the `txtName` text box and inserts it into the first paragraph of the document

   ■ Inserts a paragraph mark after the `txtName` value

   ■ Takes the value entered into the `txtClass` text box and inserts it into the second paragraph of the document

   ■ Inserts a paragraph mark after the `txtClass` value

   ■ Formats the inserted text in 22-point italicized Arial, bold

9. Save your work.

10. Run the form.

11. Enter your name and a class number of your choice into the appropriate text boxes. Click the OK button. End the program and observe the results of your test.

12. Print the code and print the document. On the printed code, circle the code that actually places the text in the document.

13. Alter the code so that the headings are formatted in a different font and a different size.

14. Run the program, again entering your name and a class number.

15. Print the code and the document. On this printout, circle the statements that you altered to change the format of the headings.

16. Save the document.

*Case 2. Whitman's Lumber*  Many clients of Whitman's Lumber order special shipments of materials. Alan Marker is responsible for notifying the clients when their shipments have arrived from the supplier. He has hired you to develop a VBA form that prompts him to enter the name of the client and the client's company. The program should then automatically insert the client information into a document, which he can then use as the basis for a notification letter to the client.

1. Start Word and open the document named **Whitman**, located in the Cases folder for Tutorial 5.

2. Save the file as **Whitman Client Heading** in the Cases folder for Tutorial 5.

3. Open the VBA IDE.

4. Use the Insert menu to add a UserForm to the project.

5. Add a frame control to the form.

6. Insert two label controls and two text box controls into the frame.

7. Add two command buttons outside of the frame.

8. Set the properties for the form and controls using the information in Figure 5-27.

| Figure 5-27 | PROPERTIES FOR FORM CONTROLS | | |
|---|---|---|---|
| **CONTROL** | **PROPERTY** | **VALUE** | |
| Userform1 | Name | frmClient | |
| | Caption | Whitman Client Information | |
| Frame1 | Name | fraClient | |
| | Caption | Client Information | |
| | BorderStyle | 1 - fmBorderStyleSingle | |
| Label1 | Name | lblCompany | |
| | Caption | Company Name | |
| Label2 | Name | lblClient | |
| | Caption | Client Name | |
| Textbox1 | Name | txtCompany | |
| Textbox2 | Name | txtClient | |
| CommandButton1 | Name | cmdOK | |
| | Caption | OK | |
| CommandButton2 | Name | cmdQuit | |
| | Caption | Quit | |

9. Arrange the controls on the form similarly to those shown in Figure 5-28. Use a font of your choice for the text displayed on the form. Be creative but make sure that the form is attractive when you are finished with it.

Figure 5-28      NEW FORM, FRMCLIENT, WITH NAMES OF CONTROL OBJECTS

10. Double-click the OK button and add code that will do the following:

- Take the company name (entered in the `txtCompany` text box) and insert it into the first paragraph of the document
- Insert a paragraph mark
- Take the client's name (entered in the `txtClient` text box) and insert it into the document
- Insert a paragraph mark
- Format the text in a font of your choice

11. At the top of the code add comments that include your name and today's date.

12. Save your work.

13. Run the form and enter "Carson Construction" into the company text box and "Paul Carson, CEO" into the client text box. Click the OK button.

14. Print the document and the project code. On the printed code, circle the statements that format the headings in a particular font.

**Explore**

15. When Alan reviews your work, he asks if you could also provide a place on the form where he can enter the items that are ready for shipment, along with the quantity. He doesn't want this part of the form to be visible until after the client name and company name have been placed in the document. Increase the size of the form and add a new frame. In the frame, insert appropriate text box, label, and command button controls that will make it possible for the user to enter the item and quantity. Use the techniques you learned in the tutorial to display this frame only after the headings have been entered into the document. Also use the techniques you learned in this tutorial to place the item name at the left margin and the quantity at the 5-inch mark (aligned right). Save and test the form, entering the items in Figure 5-29 to test the form.

Figure 5-29      TEST DATA

| ITEM NAME | QUANTITY |
| --- | --- |
| ¾ inch Plywood | 15 |
| ¾ inch drywall | 25 |
| 2½ inch drywall screws | 1000 |

16. Print the code and the document.

17. Save your work.

18. Close the document.

**Case 3.** **Write Word, Inc.**  Write Word, Inc. specializes in word processing for the publishing industry. Each of Write Word's clients employs numerous word processing firms (besides Write Word) so it's important that every file sent out from Write Word be clearly labeled as a Write Word product. Each file should also contain information indicating which typist worked on the project, and the document's official title.

Katie Chi, the Project Coordinator, knows that she could simply ask her typists to use the File Properties dialog box in Word, which contains text boxes for recording a variety of information about a document, including title, author, and company. However, she's found that, when up against a deadline, many typists fail to enter all the required information. She has asked you to develop a VBA program that would automate the process of entering this information. You decide to create a program that will prompt for the author's name, the company name, and the title of the document.

1. Start Word and open the document named **Write**, located in the Cases folder for Tutorial 5.

2. Save the file as **Write Word** in the Cases folder for Tutorial 5.

3. In the VBA IDE, open the form named `frmDocInfo`. Figure 5-30 shows the names of each control object in the form.

| Figure 5-30 | THE FRMDOCINFO FORM, SHOWING NAMES OF CONTROL OBJECTS |
| --- | --- |

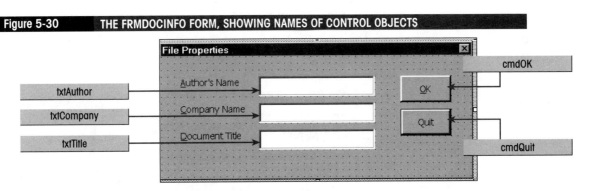

4. Write the statement for the Quit button that will remove the form from the screen.

**Explore**

5. In VBA Help, look up BuiltInDocumentProperties. Be sure to look at the sample code on these pages. Print any information you think might be useful to you later, as you develop other VBA programs.

6. Double-click the OK button and enter the code that will do the following:

- Take the value entered into the `txtAuthor` text box and place it in the document's Author property

- Take the value entered in the `txtCompany` text box and place it in the document's Company property

- Take the value entered in the `txtTitle` text box and place it in the document's Title property

Use a `With` statement to write this code, the first line of which is shown below. (Note: Be sure to replace the comments below with the necessary code.)

```
With ActiveDocument
    .BuiltInDocumentProperties(wdPropertyAuthor) = txtAuthor
    'Statement that assigns a value to the company property
    'Statement that assigns a value to the title property
End With
```

7. In comments, add your name and the date at the top of the code module.

8. Save your work and test the program, using your name as the author name, "Write Word, Inc." as the company name, and "Author Information" as the title. Click the OK button on the form to add the data to the document.

**Explore**    9. In the Word window, check the document properties dialog box to verify that the new properties have been added to the Summary tab. (*Hint*: Click File on the menu bar and then click Properties.)

10. Save your work, print the form's code.

11. Close and save the document.

*Case 4. C & B Construction*    When bidding on new construction projects, C & B Construction must submit proposal estimates. A proposal has many sections, and different authors may work on each section. In addition, a proposal may go through several drafts before the final version is submitted. C & B Construction would like you to develop a VBA program that will insert text into the document footer that indicates the draft number of the document.

1. Start Word and open the document named **C&B**, located in the Cases folder for Tutorial 5.

2. Save the file as **Construction Footer** in the Cases folder for Tutorial 5.

3. In the VBA IDE, open the form named `frmFooter`. Figure 5-31 shows the names of the control objects in the form.

**Figure 5-31      THE FRMFOOTER FORM WITH NAMES OF CONTROL OBJECTS**

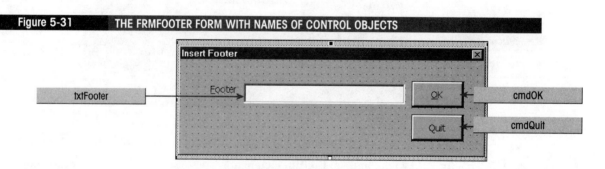

**Explore**    4. In VBA Help, look up information on the footer object. In particular, focus on the code example. Print the code example topic.

5. Open the Click event procedure for the OK button and add the following code between the `Private Sub` and `End Sub` statements. This code will place the draft number (entered in the `txtFooter` text box) into the document's footer.

```
With ActiveDocument.Sections(1).Footers(wdHeaderFooterPrimary)
    .Range.Delete
    .Range.InsertBefore txtFooter
End With
```

**Explore**    6. Add a statement to the code you used in Step 5 that will place your name in the footer on the right-hand side. You will need to use the information from VBA Help files in order to learn how to do this. Your name should appear in the right side of the footer and the draft number should appear on the left.

7. Code the Quit button.

8. Save your work and run the project. Enter "Draft #5" in the `txtFooter` text box, and then click OK.

9. Verify that the footer (which includes the draft number and your name) was added to the document.

10. Save the document and close Word.

## QUICK CHECK ANSWERS

### Session 5.1

1. frame
2. `fraEmployeeData.Visible = false`
3. `Unload Me`
4. Initialize
5. Click

### Session 5.2

1. Application
2. Document
3. Selection
4. `ActiveWindow, ActiveDocument`
5. `InsertParagraphAfter`
6. 
```
With ActiveDocument.Range
    .Font.name = "Arial"
    .Font.size = 15
    .Font.bold = False
End With
```

### Session 5.3

1. `collapse, wdCollapseEnd`
2. `&`
3. `ActiveDocument.Range.Collapse Direction:=wdCollapseStart`
4. `strAuthor & vbTab & strBookTitle`
5. `strMonth & strDay & ", " & strYear`

OBJECTIVES

In this tutorial you will:

- Plan an Excel application

- Choose from multiple options with a `Case Select` statement

- Review the Excel object model

- Learn how to choose the right control structure for a particular situation

- Size columns with the AutoFit method

- Apply color and boldface to a cell

- Sort rows with the Sort method

# USING VBA WITH EXCEL

*Developing a Gradebook Application in Excel*

CASE

## Pemberly Country Day School

Wanda Pollack, a teacher at Pemberly Country Day School, has hired TnT Consulting to create an application that will help her record grades for the three major tests she gives at the end of each six-week term. She would like to have the data recorded in an Excel worksheet, but she would rather not work directly with Excel. Instead she would like to enter the data into a form and have the VBA program insert the data in the appropriate cells. Wanda has also requested that the application determine the letter grade on the basis of the student's average for the three tests.

Gene thinks you are ready to expand your experience working with Excel, and asks you to work on part of this project. He explains that another consultant, Tim Richards, will complete the more advanced parts of the Gradebook application. It will be your job to complete the rest of the application.

## SESSION 6.1

In this session you will preview a gradebook application and observe how it works. You will then review a plan for developing your own gradebook application. Finally, you will view the code in a partially completed gradebook application.

## Previewing the Gradebook Application

In this section you will view a complete version of the Gradebook project so that you can see how it should work. First, the program should display a form for entering three test grades. The application should then calculate the average grade and the letter grade. Once the grade is calculated, the data should be inserted into a worksheet.

### To preview the application:

1. Start Excel and open the workbook named **GrdPrev**, located in the Tutorial.06 folder on your Data Disk.

2. Rename the file **Gradebook Preview** and save it in the Tutorial.06 folder on your Data Disk.

3. The workbook opens as in Figure 6-1. Notice that some student records have already been entered into the worksheet named "GradeSheet." Rows 1–6 are filled with column headers and data. The next available blank row is row 7. Note that the data in the Letter Grade column is in boldface. When Tim set up the worksheet, he formatted the entire Letter Grade column in bold. Alternately, he could have included a program statement that formatted each grade individually in bold. But formatting the entire column within the worksheet was much simpler.

**Figure 6-1** **GRADEBOOK PREVIEW WORKBOOK**

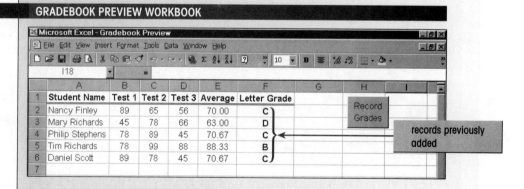

4. Click the **Record Grades** button on the worksheet. The Calculate Grade form appears, as shown in Figure 6-2.

| Figure 6-2 | THE CALCULATE GRADE FORM IN THE GRADEBOOK PREVIEW WORKBOOK |

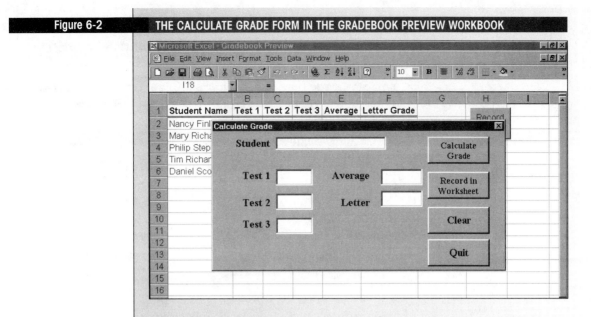

5. In the Student Name text box, type **Michael Turner**, then enter **65** for Test 1, **89** for Test 2, and **76** for Test 3.

6. Click the **Calculate Grade** button on the form. Both the average grade and the letter grade are calculated, as shown in Figure 6-3.

| Figure 6-3 | CALCULATE GRADE FORM WITH DATA ENTERED AND GRADE CALCULATED |

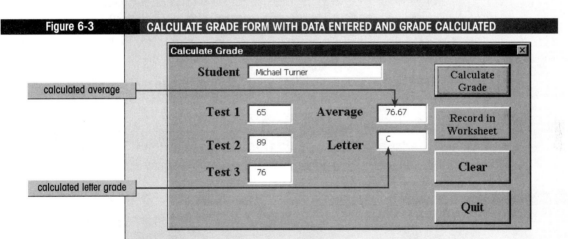

calculated average

calculated letter grade

7. Click the **Record in Worksheet** button on the form. The new data is recorded in the worksheet in row 7 (i.e., the first row that does not already have data stored in it). As in the TnT Check Register project you examined in Tutorial 4, notice that this program must find a blank row in which to insert the data. Notice that all the text boxes are now empty and the form is ready to receive the next student's data.

You have seen how the program performs when you enter valid data. Now take a moment to test its behavior when you enter invalid data.

*To test the program with invalid data:*

1. Enter **Edward Cutshall** for the student name, then enter **ABC** for each of the test grades.

2. Click the **Calculate Grade** button on the form. You see a message box telling you that you must enter a valid grade for Test 1, as shown in Figure 6-4.

Figure 6-4    **GRADEBOOK PREVIEW WITH VALIDATION MESSAGE**

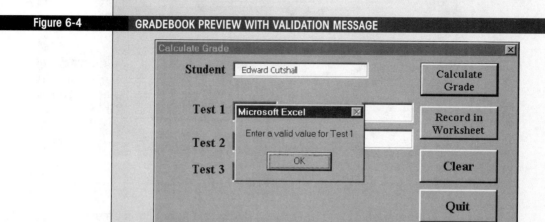

3. Click **OK** on the message box.

4. Enter **98** for Test 1 and then click **Calculate Grade** on the form. This time you will receive a message telling you to enter a valid grade for Test 2.

5. Click **OK**. The message box closes and you return to the form, where the entry in the Test 2 text box (ABC) is selected.

6. Enter **88** for Test 2 and click **Calculate Grade**. Again, you see a message, this time for Test 3.

7. Click the **OK** button and then enter **75** for Test 3.

8. Click **Calculate Grade** once again. This time the numeric and letter grades are calculated, as shown in Figure 6-5.

Figure 6-5    **GRADEBOOK PREVIEW WITH CALCULATED GRADE**

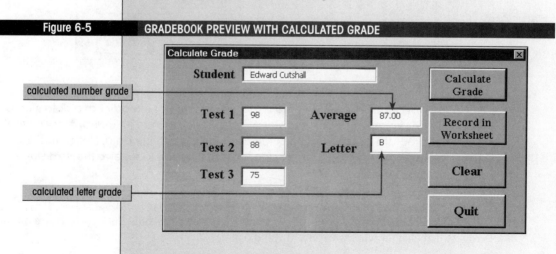

9. Click the **Record in Worksheet** button on the form.

Next, you can test the Clear button and the Quit button.

### To test the last two buttons:

1. Enter **Bobby Suarez** in the Student Name text box. Now suppose that you made an error entering the name, and would like to start over. You could delete the characters, but it's faster to use the Clear button.

2. Click the **Clear** button on the form. The form is cleared and is ready for you to enter new data.

3. Click the **Record in Worksheet** button on the form. Notice that you see a message box telling you that you must enter a student name. This button is programmed in such a way that the user is forced to enter a name for the student in order to have the test grades recorded in the worksheet. You will learn how to do this in the tutorial.

4. Click **OK**.

5. Click the **Quit** button on the form. The form is removed from the screen. You return to the worksheet, which now contains the new data, as shown in Figure 6-6.

| Figure 6-6 | GRADEBOOK PREVIEW WITH NEW DATA ADDED |

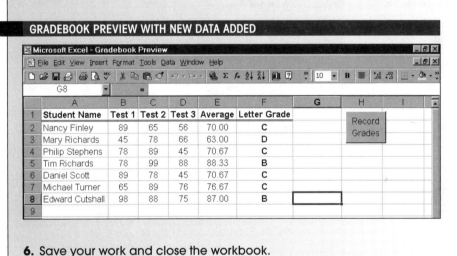

6. Save your work and close the workbook.

Now that you understand how the Gradebook project should work, you can begin developing it. As mentioned earlier, Gene has asked Tim Richards to start the project for you. In the next section, you will examine the interface for this project, the Calculate Grade from. Then you will study the project plan, which lists the tasks the program should perform.

## Planning the Gradebook Application

Tim Richards asks you to sit down with him and design the form. Together, you decide what control objects to place on the form and what to name each control object. This kind of planning will make it easier to write the VBA program statements that will refer to these objects. Recall that labels are rarely, if ever, accessed with program statements, so they do not require a name. However, all text boxes and command buttons should be named. Figure 6-7 shows the final form design, including the name of each object. As you examine this form, pay careful attention to the name of each control object.

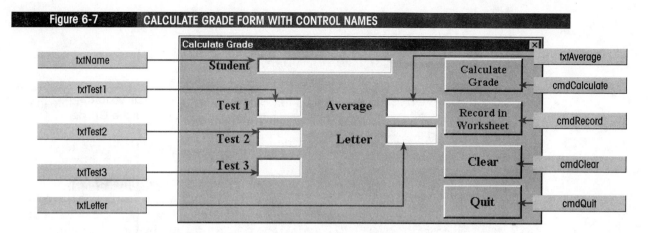

**Figure 6-7**    **CALCULATE GRADE FORM WITH CONTROL NAMES**

The plan for this project, shown in Figure 6-8, consists of a list of tasks and subtasks that the program should be able to perform. Study this plan carefully and keep it in mind as you develop the project.

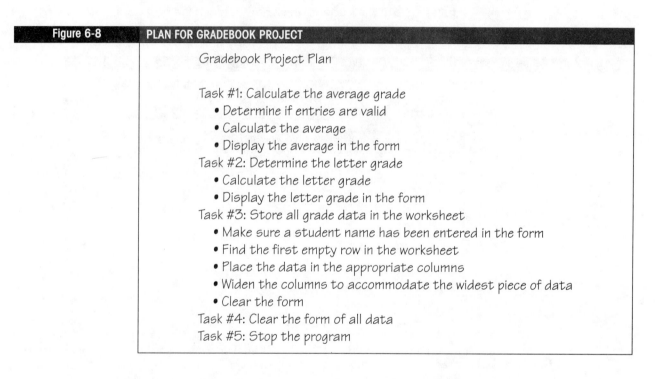

**Figure 6-8**    **PLAN FOR GRADEBOOK PROJECT**

Gradebook Project Plan

Task #1: Calculate the average grade
• Determine if entries are valid
• Calculate the average
• Display the average in the form
Task #2: Determine the letter grade
• Calculate the letter grade
• Display the letter grade in the form
Task #3: Store all grade data in the worksheet
• Make sure a student name has been entered in the form
• Find the first empty row in the worksheet
• Place the data in the appropriate columns
• Widen the columns to accommodate the widest piece of data
• Clear the form
Task #4: Clear the form of all data
Task #5: Stop the program

Tim is responsible for Tasks 4 and 5. Your job is to write the code for Tasks 1–3. In the next few sections, you will open the partially completed project and examine the code (for Tasks 4 and 5) that Tim has already completed.

## Examining the Partially Completed Code

Tim e-mails you the workbook file, and asks you to spend some time studying the code he has started for you. He suggests that you test the program in its current state to get an idea of what it can and cannot do right now.

## To explore the partially completed project:

1. Open the workbook named **GdStart** located in the Tutorial .06 folder on your Data Disk.

2. Save the workbook as **Gradebook Complete** in the Tutorial .06 folder on your Data Disk. Compare your screen with Figure 6-9. Notice that the GradeSheet worksheet contains column headings and a Record Grades command button, but no student records. This is because the workbook is not yet complete.

| Figure 6-9 | GRADEBOOK COMPLETE WITHOUT ANY RECORDS |
|---|---|

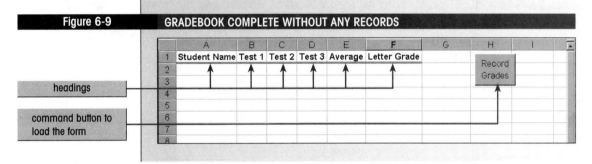

You will now view the code that Tim has written.

## To view the project code:

1. Open the VBA IDE and display the Project Explorer window.

2. Open the **frmGrade** form and then open the Code window.

3. Scroll to the top of the Code window to display the code for the Clear button, as shown in Figure 6-10. You have written similar procedures before. Briefly, this procedure clears any values currently in any of the text boxes on the form.

| Figure 6-10 | CODE WINDOW WITH CLEAR BUTTON CODE SHOWING |
|---|---|

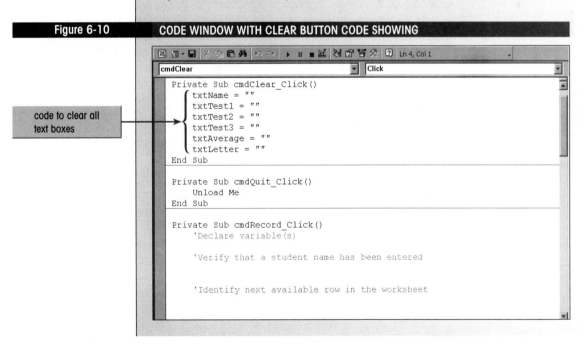

**4.** Scroll down in the Code window to display the code for the Quit button. This code is also shown in Figure 6-10. As you know, a Quit button requires only a single statement, the `Unload Me` statement. This statement removes the form from the screen and stops the processing of that form.

**5.** Scroll down to the `cmdRecord_Click` procedure. As the comments indicate, the code for the Record in Worksheet button is not completed yet. You will be working on this code in this tutorial. See Figure 6-11.

| Figure 6-11 | THE FRMGRADE CODE WINDOW |
|---|---|

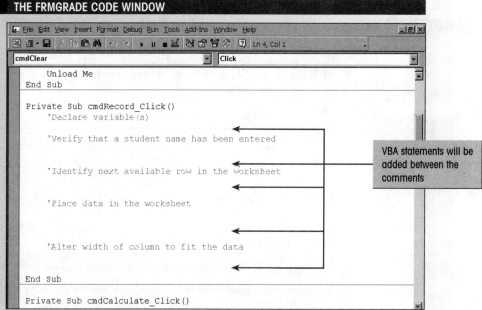

**6.** Scroll down in the Code window to display the `cmdCalculate_Click` procedure. At this stage, this procedure contains only the code that validates the data entered by the user and calculates the numeric grade average. As indicated by the comment at the bottom of the procedure, it does not yet contain the code that calculates the letter grade. See Figure 6-12.

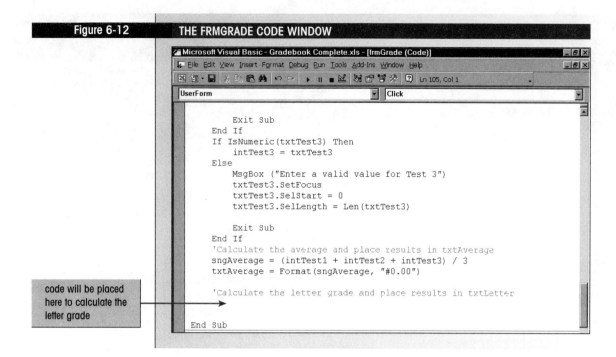

Figure 6-12 THE FRMGRADE CODE WINDOW

```
        Exit Sub
    End If
    If IsNumeric(txtTest3) Then
        intTest3 = txtTest3
    Else
        MsgBox ("Enter a valid value for Test 3")
        txtTest3.SetFocus
        txtTest3.SelStart = 0
        txtTest3.SelLength = Len(txtTest3)

        Exit Sub
    End If
    'Calculate the average and place results in txtAverage
    sngAverage = (intTest1 + intTest2 + intTest3) / 3
    txtAverage = Format(sngAverage, "#0.00")

    'Calculate the letter grade and place results in txtLetter


End Sub
```

code will be placed here to calculate the letter grade

The code that calculates the grade average and the corresponding letter grade is more complicated than the code for the Quit and Clear buttons, and requires some explanation. Tim stops by your desk to check on your progress. He sees that you are looking at the code for the Calculate button, and sits down to discuss it with you.

The code for the Calculate button performs the first and second tasks in the Gradebook project plan (shown earlier in Figure 6-8). That is, this code takes the test grades entered by the user, validates this data, calculates the average numeric grade, and displays the numeric average in the form.

Actually calculating the average is a simple process of adding the three grades together and then dividing the sum by three. The three test grades are in the text boxes named **txtTest1**, **txtTest2**, and **txtTest3**. Likewise, the average will be placed in a text box named **txtAverage**. Tim decided to validate the test scores using the IsNumeric function discussed in Tutorial 3. Recall that the IsNumeric function receives a value and checks to see if it is a valid number. If the value is valid, then a *true* is returned. If the value is not valid, a *false* value is returned. Tim decided that he would check each value for validity; in the case of invalid data, the program should stop the calculation. He used the **Exit Sub** statement to end the procedure, as described in Tutorial 3.

Figure 6-13 shows the complete procedure code and some general explanations.

| Figure 6-13 | GRADE AVERAGE CODE AND EXPLANATIONS |
| --- | --- |

| CODE SECTION | EXPLANATION |
| --- | --- |
| `Dim intTest1 As Integer`<br>`Dim intTest2 As Integer`<br>`Dim intTest3 As Integer`<br>`Dim sngAverage As Single` | Declares the variables that will be used to store the three test scores and the average after it is calculated. |
| `' Check each test grade for valid values`<br>`If IsNumeric(txtTest1) Then`<br>`    intTest1 = txtTest1`<br>`Else`<br>`    MsgBox ("Enter a valid value for Test 1")`<br>`    txtTest1.SetFocus`<br>`    txtTest1.SelStart = 0`<br>`    txtTest1.SelLength = Len(txtTest1)`<br>`    Exit Sub`<br>`End If` | Determines if a valid entry has been entered for Test 1. If the entry is valid, the value is placed in a variable to be used later in calculating the average. If the entry is invalid (not numeric), then this code displays a message box (advising the user to enter a valid value), sets the focus to the text box with the invalid entry, selects the entry that is invalid, and finally stops the procedure. |
| `If IsNumeric(txtTest2) Then`<br>`    intTest2 = txtTest2`<br>`Else`<br>`    MsgBox ("Enter a valid value for Test 2")`<br>`    txtTest2.SetFocus`<br>`    txtTest2.SelStart = 0`<br>`    txtTest2.SelLength = Len(txtTest2)`<br>`    Exit Sub`<br>`End If` | This repeats the code above except that it applies to the Test 2 entry. |
| `If IsNumeric(txtTest3) Then`<br>`    intTest3 = txtTest3`<br>`Else`<br>`    MsgBox ("Enter a valid value for Test 3")`<br>`    txtTest3.SetFocus`<br>`    txtTest3.SelStart = 0`<br>`    txtTest3.SelLength = Len(txtTest3)`<br>`    Exit Sub`<br>`End If` | This repeats the code above except that it applies to the Test 3 entry. |
| `'Calculate the average and place results in txtAverage`<br>`    sngAverage = (intTest1 + intTest2 + intTest3) / 3`<br>`    txtAverage = Format(sngAverage, "#0.00")` | Calculates the average grade by adding the three test scores together and then dividing by 3. After calculating the average, this code places the average in the `txtAverage` text box formatted as a numeric value with two decimal places. |

Every statement used within this segment of code has been explained in previous tutorials. In summary, each text box is checked for validity. If the value is valid, the value is then stored in a variable. If the value is not valid, the text box is highlighted and the procedure is ended. When all three tests for validity are successful, then the average grade is calculated by adding the three values together and dividing by three. Finally, the calculated average is placed in the **txtAverage** text box. This value is formatted as a number with two decimal places, using the Format function (which was explained in Tutorial 3).

You are finished reviewing the code provided by Tim Richards. It is your responsibility to add the remaining code to calculate the letter grade and to place the data in the worksheet. In the next section you will add the remaining code.

# Session 6.1 QUICK CHECK

1. Write the statement that will remove the form `frmStudent` from the screen.

2. Suppose you want a form to be removed when the user clicks a command button named `cmdQuit`. Where would you place the necessary statement?

3. Assume that you have three text boxes on a form, named `txtName`, `txtAddress`, and `txtPhone`. Write the statements that would clear these three text boxes.

4. Assume that you have four variables, `intNumberOne`, `intNumberTwo`, `intNumberThree`, and `sngAverage`. Write the statement that would calculate the average of the first three variables and place the average in the variable `sngAverage`.

5. Write the statements that would do the following: (1) check to see if the text box `txtNumberOne` contains a valid number, (2) if it is valid, assign the value to `intNumberOne`, (3) if it is not valid, then display a message box telling the user the number is invalid, highlight the text, and set the focus to that text box.

## SESSION 6.2

In this session you will learn how to use the `Select Case` statement to choose from multiple options. You will also view the Excel object model and learn how to choose the appropriate control structure for various situations. You will activate the worksheet and place the data records in the worksheet. Finally you will learn how to use the AutoFit method to adjust column widths.

# Choosing from Multiple Options with the Select Case Statement

Your first task is to add the code that will calculate the letter grade. Specifically, you must write code that evaluates the average grade, and then makes a choice among letter grades of A, B, C, D, and F. Figure 6-14 shows the range of numeric grades associated with each letter grade:

| Figure 6-14 | NUMERIC GRADES AND THEIR LETTER GRADE EQUIVALENTS |
|---|---|

| NUMERIC GRADES | LETTER GRADE |
|---|---|
| 90–100 | A |
| 80–89 | B |
| 70–79 | C |
| 60–69 | D |
| Below 60 | F |

As you learned in Tutorial 3, whenever you need a program to choose among options, you need to use a selection control structure. You've already practiced using a simple form of the Selection control structure—the `If...Then...Else` statement, which allows a program to choose between two options.

However, the Gradebook application must choose among five options—that is, among the grades A, B, C, D, and E. To allow for choices among multiple options in VBA (and in most other programming languages), you need to use the `Select Case` statement.

## Studying the `Select Case` Statement Syntax

The `Select Case` statement allows you to write code that will make a selection from as many different conditions as you choose to include in the statement. Its syntax is explained below.

| | |
|---|---|
| **Syntax** | `Select Case Expression`<br>`    Case condition`<br>`        Statement(s)`<br>`    Case condition`<br>`        Statement(s)`<br>`    Case Else`<br>`        Statement(s)`<br>`End Select` |
| **Explanation** | The `Select Case` statement executes one of several groups of statements, depending on the value of the expression. (The expression can be a complicated mathematical expression, with calculations involving variables, or it can be as simple as a single variable.) The value of the expression is compared to the first case condition. If the condition results in true, then the statements that follow the case condition are executed. When those statements have been completed, the flow of control moves to the `End Select` statement. If the condition results in false, then the expression is compared to the second condition. This process continues until all conditions have been checked. If none of the conditions result in true, then the statements following the `Case Else` statement are executed. |
| **Example** | `Select Case sngAverage`<br>`    Case is >= 90`<br>`        txtLetter = "A"`<br>`    Case is >= 80`<br>`        txtLetter = "B"`<br>`    Case is >= 70`<br>`        txtLetter = "C"`<br>`    Case is >= 60`<br>`        txtLetter = "D"`<br>`    Case Else`<br>`        txtLetter = "F"`<br>`End Select` |

In the example above, the variable `sngAverage` contains the numeric grade average. This variable makes up the expression portion of the `Select Case` statement. You can interpret the rest of the example as follows: If the value of `sngAverage` is greater than or equal to 90, then place an "A" in the `txtLetter` text box and go to the `End Select` statement. If the value of `sngAverage` is greater than or equal to 80, then place a "B" in the `txtLetter` text box and go to the `End Select` statement. If the value of `sngAverage` is greater than or equal to 70, then place a "C" in the `txtLetter` text box and go to the `End Select` statement. If the value of `sngAverage` is greater than or equal to 60, then place a "D" in the `txtLetter` text box and go to the `End Select` statement. If the value is anything else (i.e., below 60), place an "F" in the `txtLetter` text box.

The flowchart in Figure 6-15 illustrates this example. After your experience reviewing flowcharts for Selection and Repetition structures in Tutorials 3 and 4, you should be able to understand this flowchart too. Remember to follow the arrows to observe the flow of control. You might find it helpful to assign a value (say, 75) to the `sngAverage` variable, and then trace the flow of control through the flowchart.

| Figure 6-15 | SELECT CASE FLOWCHART |

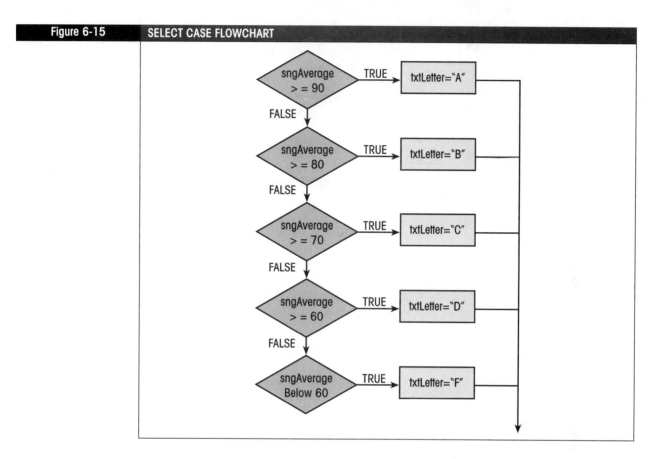

To summarize, then, you can use the `Select Case` statement when you need to write code that will select among multiple options. When you need to select between only two options, use the `If...Then...Else` statement.

## Adding a `Select Case` Statement to the Project

Now that you understand the `Select Case` statement, you can add one to the Gradebook project. As you'll recall, Tim already completed the code that calculates the numeric grade average. In the following steps you will add the `Select Case` statement that calculates the letter grade.

*To add a* `Select Case` *statement to the Gradebook project:*

**1.** Click in the **omdCalculate_Click** procedure, just above the `End Sub` statement, as shown in Figure 6-16.

Figure 6-16 | CMDCALCULATE PROCEDURE

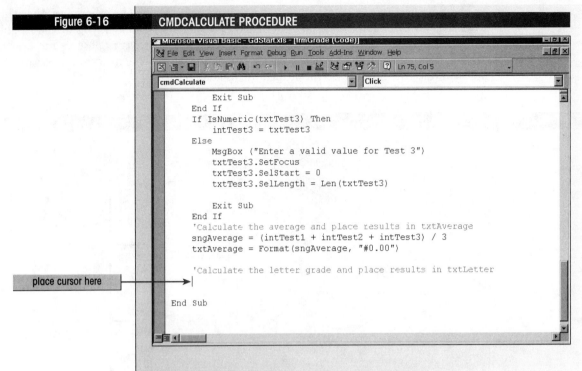

2. Type the following Select Case statement:

```
Select Case sngAverage
  Case is >= 90
        txtLetter = "A"
  Case is >= 80
        txtLetter = "B"
  Case is >= 70
        txtLetter = "C"
  Case is >= 60
        txtLetter = "D"
  Case Else
        txtLetter = "F"
End Select
```

3. Save your work and run the program.

4. Enter **David Allen** as the student name, and then enter **67**, **56**, and **80** as the three test scores.

5. Click the **Calculate Grade** button on the form. The average is calculated and displayed in the txtAverage text box; the letter grade is displayed in the txtLetter text box, as shown in Figure 6-17.

Figure 6-17

**CALCULATE GRADE FORM WITH CALCULATED LETTER GRADE**

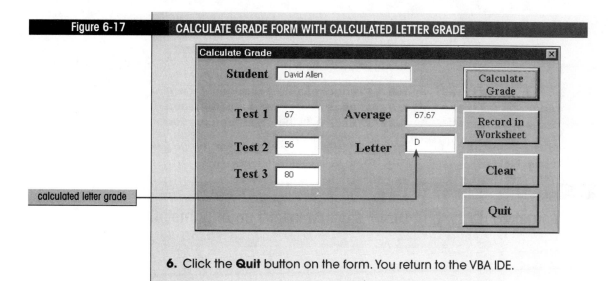

**6.** Click the **Quit** button on the form. You return to the VBA IDE.

You demonstrate the code to Gene, and he agrees with you that the calculations are working correctly. Even so, he suggests that you step through the program using Step Into.

## Observing a `Select Case` Statement with Step Into

Gene explains that, by observing the behavior of the `Select Case` statement using Step Into, you'll gain a better understanding of how it works. In the following steps, you will set a breakpoint in the project and then step through the `Select Case` statement. As you complete these steps, try to think ahead and determine on your own which steps will be executed next.

### To step through the `Select Case` statement:

**1.** In the Code window, scroll down until you see the statement that calculates the numeric average, then click the gray border of the Code window, to the left of this statement. This inserts a breakpoint, as shown in Figure 6-18.

Figure 6-18

**CMDCALCULATE PROCEDURE WITH BREAKPOINT**

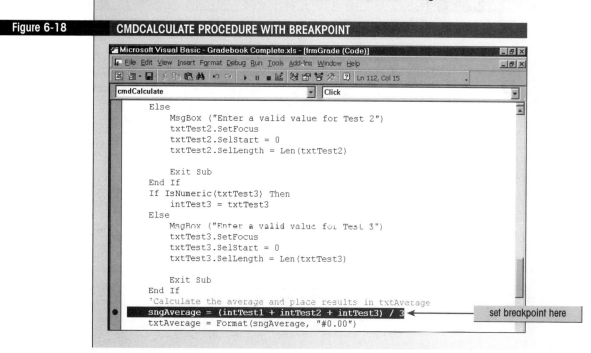

**2.** Run the program, and again enter **David Allen** as the student name and **67**, **56**, and **80** as the test grades.

**3.** Click the **Calculate Grade** button on the form. The program stops on the statement where you set the breakpoint. This statement is highlighted in yellow in the Code window.

**4.** Position the mouse pointer over the **sngAverage** variable. Its current value should be 0, because this statement (which calculates the average and assigns a value to sngAverage) has not yet executed. See Figure 6-19.

| Figure 6-19 | CMDCALCULATE WITH SCREENTIP ON SNGAVERAGE |
|---|---|

place cursor over sngAverage here

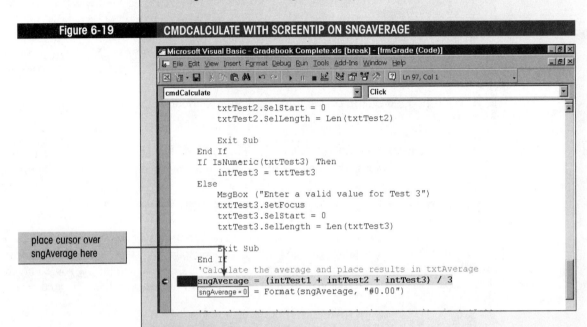

**5.** Press **F8** to execute the next line and then check the value of sngAverage. Its new value is shown in Figure 6-20.

| Figure 6-20 | CMDCALCULATE WITH SCREENTIP ON SNGAVERAGE |
|---|---|

place cursor over sngAverage here

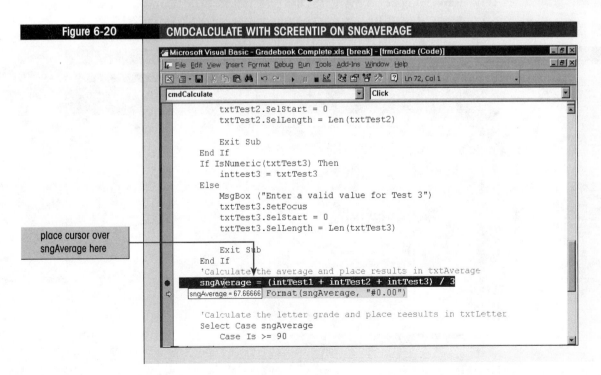

**6.** Look at the `Select Case` statement and try to determine which statement will be executed next. Remember that the program will check each condition in the `Select Case` statement until it finds a condition that is true.

**7.** Press **F8** as many times as necessary to reach a condition that is true. Since the result of the calculation is 67.66, the letter grade will be "D".

**8.** Press **F8** continually until the `End Sub` statement is highlighted, then switch to the Excel window and verify that a D is displayed in the Letter text box.

**9.** Return to the VBA IDE and then click the **Reset** ■ button on the toolbar.

Now you will step through the program using grades that average more than 90. The `Select Case` statement should assign a different letter grade this time.

### To step through the program again:

**1.** With the breakpoint still in place, run the program.

**2.** Enter **David Allen** for the student name and **88**, **90**, and **92** for the test scores.

**3.** Click the **Calculate Grade** button. The breakpoint statement is highlighted in yellow, in the Code window.

**4.** Repeat the process of stepping through the statements. Notice that this time, because the numeric average is in the A range, the `Select Case` statement ends much sooner than when the grade was in the D range.

**5.** When you reach the End Sub statement, click on the **Excel** button on the taskbar. Notice that the "A" has been placed in the letter grade text box.

**6.** Return to the VBA IDE window and then click the **Reset** ■ button. The program ends.

**7.** Remove the breakpoint.

Now that you have completed calculating the letter grade, the next task is to write the code that inserts the data into the worksheet. In Tutorial 4, you used VBA statements to interact with Excel. You were also introduced to the Excel object model. The next section reviews the Excel object model, focusing especially on the specific objects you will alter in order to insert data into the worksheet.

## Reviewing the Excel Object Model

You should already be familiar with the Excel object model from your work with the salary calculation project and the TnT Check Register program in Tutorials 3 and 4. Figure 6-21 shows the portions of the object model that you will use in the Gradebook project.

**Figure 6-21    EXCEL OBJECT MODEL (PARTIAL VIEW)**

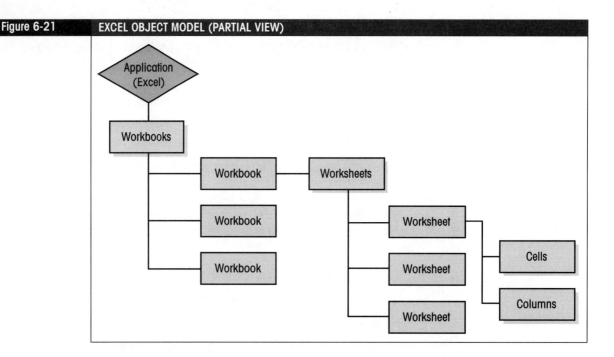

As in the Word object model, the application itself is on the highest level in the hierarchy of objects. Next is the Workbooks collection. As you know, you can have multiple workbooks open at one time; the Workbooks collection, then, contains all currently open workbooks. Next is the Worksheets collection, which contains all the worksheets in the workbook. In Tutorial 3, you learned how to alter the name of a worksheet. You also learned that you can refer to a worksheet by name or by its number in the collection. As you'll recall, the following statement would change the name of "Sheet1" to "Gradesheet".

```
Worksheets("Sheet1").Name = "Gradesheet"
```

As you can see in Figure 6-21, each worksheet contains a **Cells collection**. In Tutorial 4 you learned that you can access a cell by row number and column number. (Remember that in VBA, the columns are represented by numbers rather than letters, as they are in the workbook window.) For instance, you would refer to cell C5 as Cells(5, 3).

In addition to the Cells collection, each worksheet contains a **Columns collection**, which consists of all the columns in a worksheet. You will work with the Columns collection in this tutorial when you write code that widens a column to accommodate the data inserted into it.

The complete Excel object model is quite large and includes a multitude of collections and objects. To be a successful VBA developer in Excel, you would need to learn more about the object model and how to access the different collections in the model. But in order to complete the Gradebook project, you need only be concerned with the Worksheets collection, the Cells collection, and the Columns collection.

# Using Control Structures Appropriately

In the first session of this tutorial, you studied the project plan for the Gradebook project. So far, you have completed Tasks 1, 2, 4, and 5 in that plan. All that remains is Task 3, which is highlighted in Figure 6-22. Gene asks you to review this portion of the project plan once again, so you have a clear idea of what actions your code should perform.

| Figure 6-22 | PROJECT TASK LIST WITH TASK #3 HIGHLIGHTED |
| --- | --- |

Gradebook Project Plan

Task #1: Calculate the average grade
  • Determine if entries are valid
  • Calculate the average
  • Display the average in the form
Task #2: Determine the letter grade
  • Calculate the letter grade
  • Display the letter grade in the form
Task #3: Store all grade data in the worksheet
  • Make sure a student name has been entered in the form
  • Find the first empty row in the worksheet
  • Place the data in the appropriate columns
  • Widen the columns to accommodate the widest piece of data
  • Clear the form
Task #4: Clear the form of all data
Task #5: Stop the program

The code required to complete this task involves a number of control structures. As you learned in Tutorial 3, there are three major kinds of control structures—Sequence (which performs one step after another), Selection (which makes a selection based on some condition), and Repetition (which repeats a group of statements based on some condition). In the Gradebook project, the two statements that calculate the average and then place the average in the **txtAverage** text box make up a Sequence control structure. The two statement are executed one after the other, in the order in which they appear in the Code window. When Tim wrote the code to validate the test scores, he used the Decision control structure. You will see later in this tutorial some variations of the Decision control structure. You will use the Repetition control structure when you place the data in the worksheet.

Every programming language, including VBA, has its own syntax for implementing these control structures. As you will see in this tutorial, there are also variations of these control structures to choose from. In the next section, you will learn a variation of the **If...Then...Else** statement. Earlier in this tutorial you learned about a whole new form of the Selection control structure, the **Select Case** statement.

A new developer often struggles with choosing the right control structure and the right variation of the control structure. In this text, these decisions are mostly made for you. With practice and experience you will eventually learn how to make these decisions for yourself. In the next several sections, you will learn why a particular construct is used in a project and how a particular variation of that control structure was selected.

## Avoiding Null Values with an `If` Statement

Before the program inserts data into the worksheet, it should ensure that the user has entered a student's name in the **txtName** text box. If the text box is empty, the program should display a message box that reminds the user to enter a student name. How do you think you might implement this in VBA? The word "If" in the sentence that begins "If the text box is empty" should tell you everything you need to know—you need to use an **If** statement. Next, you need to ask what to do if the condition is true (that is, if the **txtName** text box is empty) and what to do if the condition is false (that is, if the text box is *not* empty). In the Gradebook project, if the text box is empty, you want to display a message box, set the focus to the text box, and end the procedure. However, if the condition is false (that is, if the text box is *not* empty), then the program doesn't have to do anything. This requires the following variation of the If...Then...Else statement, known as a Null...Else statement:

```
If condition then
      True statements here
End If
```

Once again, with practice you will learn to select the right control structure and the right variation of that control structure. In general when you need to choose between two conditions, and you want to do something when the condition is true and something else when the condition is false, choose the If...Then...Else statement. If, on the other hand, you only want to execute statements when the condition is true (i.e., you don't have anything you want to do when the condition is false), then you should use a Null...Else variation of the If...Then...Else statement.

Now that you understand what control structure to use when checking to make sure the user enters a name in the txtName text box, you need to learn what statements to use within that control structure. That is, you need to learn how to write the statements that will execute when the condition is true (i.e. the txtName text box is empty).

In the Gradebook project, the cursor should move to the txtName text box when the user closes the message box, so that the user can easily type a student name. In order to place the cursor in the txtName text box, you need to use the SetFocus method. You'll learn how to use this method in the next section.

### Moving the Cursor with the SetFocus Method

In the Windows environment, only one object can have focus at any given time. When you click on your form in design time, the form has focus. If you then click on the Workbook button on the taskbar, the workbook and the currently displayed worksheet have focus. When an object has focus, it has the ability to receive mouse clicks or keyboard input. Also, when an object has focus, its title bar (if it has one) is highlighted. The user can set focus just by clicking on an object. As a developer, sometimes you need to set the focus with VBA statements.

After your program displays the message reminding the user to enter a name, you want the txtName text box to have focus. You can give focus to an object by using the **SetFocus method**. This method applies to almost any object, including controls on your form. The following statement will set the focus to the txtName text box:

```
txtName.SetFocus
```

### Ending a Procedure with the Exit Sub Statement

If the user has failed to enter a student name along with the test grades, you do not want to record the test grades. To avoid entering test grades without a student name, you need to use the Exit Sub statement. You used this statement in Tutorials 3 and 4 to avoid entering invalid data into a workbook. The Exit Sub statement will cause the procedure in which the statement appears to end. You will place this statement in the cmdRecord_click event procedure, so this procedure will terminate when the Exit Sub statement is encountered.

The code to utilize these two statements when checking for the student name is as follows:

```
If txtName = "" Then
      MsgBox ("You must enter a student name")
      txtName.SetFocus
      Exit Sub
End If
```

Notice that the expression in the `If` statement checks to see if the `txtName` text box is empty. If the result is *true* then the message box is displayed, focus is set to the `txtName` text box, and the procedure is ended. This is to say that the remaining statements in the procedure are not executed.

You will now enter this code in the Gradebook project and test it.

### To enter the code in the project:

**1.** In the Code window, move the cursor just below the second comment in the `cmdRecord_Click` event procedure, as shown in Figure 6-23. (Note that you will write the code related to the first comment—"Declare variable(s)"—later in this tutorial.)

| Figure 6-23 | CMDRECORD_CLICK PROCEDURE |

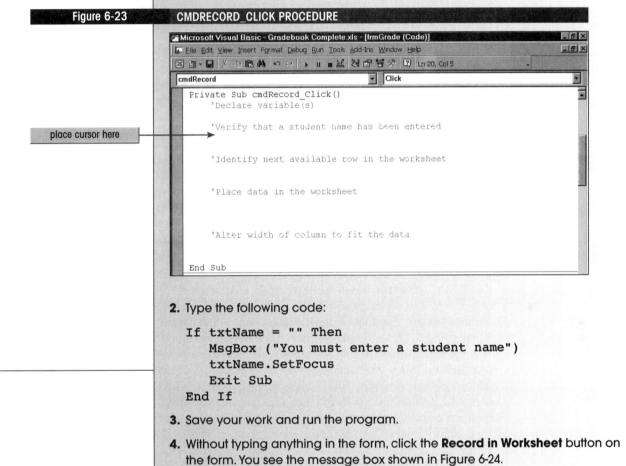

**2.** Type the following code:

```
If txtName = "" Then
    MsgBox ("You must enter a student name")
    txtName.SetFocus
    Exit Sub
End If
```

**3.** Save your work and run the program.

**4.** Without typing anything in the form, click the **Record in Worksheet** button on the form. You see the message box shown in Figure 6-24.

Figure 6-24    CALCULATE GRADE FORM WITH MESSAGE BOX

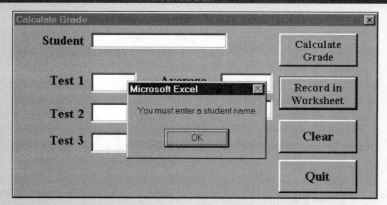

**5.** Click **OK** in the message box. The cursor blinks in the `txtName` text box, ready for you to enter a name.

**6.** Type your own name into the text box and then click the **Record in Worksheet** button. This time nothing happens because you still need to write the code that actually inserts data into the worksheet.

**7.** Click the **Quit** button on the form. You return to the VBA IDE.

## Using a Do...Until Loop to Find the First Empty Row

Referring back to Figure 6-8, you can see that you have completed the first part of Task 3—verifying that the user enters a name in the `txtName` text box. Now you're ready for the second part of Task 3—determining the first available (empty) row in the worksheet. You can accomplish this in VBA by examining the first column in each row to see if it is empty—that is, if the row contains a null string (""). If it is *not* empty, then the program should look at the next row, and the next row, until it finally finds an empty row. Now take a moment to think about how to implement this process in VBA. What control structure should you use?

When trying to decide on the appropriate control structure, it's helpful to determine first if any condition is involved. In this situation, the statement "the row contains a null string" is the condition. Since the situation does indeed involve a condition, you know that the Sequence control structure (in which statements are executed sequentially one after another, with no options involved) is not appropriate. This means you can choose between a Repetition control structure and a Selection control structure. To locate the first row, you want a condition that checks to see if a row is empty; if it is not, you want to check to see if the next row is empty, and so on until an empty row has been found. In other words, your program should repeatedly ask the question, "Is this row empty?" until an empty row is found. Any time you need to repeat a group of statements based on a condition, you should choose a Repetition control structure.

Once you have decided to use a Repetition control structure, you must next decide which of the three repetition statements you will use (`Do...While`, `Do...Until`, or `For...Next`). All of these statements were covered in detail in Tutorial 4. Your challenge, as a developer, is to choose the right statement for the current situation. You can immediately rule out the For...Next loop because you do not know exactly how many times the program should repeat the loop (i.e., you cannot predict, when you write the program, which row will be the next empty row when the user runs the program). So you must choose between the Do...While and Do...Until loops. Often this choice is simply a matter of personal preference. You can actually write any Do...Until loop as a Do...While loop. In this tutorial you will use a Do...Until loop that stops when the condition is true (that is, when an empty row has been found). Note, however, that you could use a Do...While loop instead.

The complete loop requires you to use both the Activate method and the Cells collection. You should be familiar with both of these after your work in Tutorial 4. The following sections quickly review these topics. You will learn more about choosing among the three types of loops later in this tutorial.

### Activating a Worksheet

The **Activate method** makes the specified worksheet the active worksheet. Once the sheet is active, any references to the Worksheets collections will apply to the active worksheet. Before you can write the Do...Until loop that finds the first available row in the worksheet, you must write a statement that activates the Gradesheet worksheet.

You refer to the worksheet you want to activate by using either the worksheet's index (the number of the worksheet in the Worksheets collection) or the name of the worksheet. For example, the worksheet named "Gradesheet" is the first worksheet in the Gradebook Complete workbook, which you currently have open on your computer. Thus, either of the following references would be valid.

```
Worksheets(1).Activate
or
Worksheets("Gradesheet").Activate
```

So you might ask, why would you choose one statement over the other? Using the reference that includes the worksheet's name ensures that the code will always refer to the Gradesheet worksheet, even if the user inserts new worksheets into the workbook. If you give each worksheet a name and then refer to the worksheet by name in your VBA statement, it will not matter how the worksheets are ordered in the workbook. For example, the user might insert a new worksheet prior to the "Gradesheet" worksheet. Thus, the reference "Worksheets(1)" would then refer to the new worksheet rather than to the Gradesheet worksheet. By using the reference "Worksheets"("Gradesheet"), you ensure that the reference would always be correct no matter how many other worksheets were inserted.

### Working with the Cells Collection

Once the Gradesheet worksheet is activated, the Do...Until loop (which will perform the task of finding the next available blank row) comes into play. To understand how this Do...Until loop works, recall that cells are referenced by their row number and column number. For example, a reference to cell C5 would require the VBA reference "Cells(5,3)".

In some cases, however, you may choose to replace the column or row number in a cell reference with a variable name. As the value of the variable changes, so would the specific cell referred to in your VBA code. You already used this technique in Tutorial 4, when you used a counter variable for the row number. You will use this technique in the Gradebook project, as explained in the next section.

## Examining the Do...Until Loop

The actual Do loop required to find the first available blank row is identical to the code you used in Tutorial 4 in order to locate the first empty row in the worksheet. This code is as follows:

```
Do
        intRowCounter = intRowCounter + 1
Loop Until Cells(intRowCounter, 1) = ""
```

The condition in the `Loop Until` statement is this: `Cells(intRowCounter, 1) = ""`. This condition contains a cell reference, which in turn includes a counter variable, `intRowCounter`. The first time through the loop, the condition will examine Cell (1, 1)—that is, the first column in the first row—to see if it is empty. Each time through the loop, the counter is increased by 1 (making it equal to 2 the second time through the loop). Thus, the second time through the loop, the condition checks the second row in the first column. The loop terminates when the condition is true—that is, when it encounters a cell that contains a null string (indicating the location of the first empty row).

Notice that the loop doesn't check an entire row, but only the first column in each row. If you look at the worksheet, you'll see that this column contains the student names. You've already added code that requires the user to enter a student name, so you can be sure that a row is empty if the first column of that row is empty.

When the loop terminates, the variable `intRowCounter` will contain the number of the first available row. You can make use of this fact when you write the statements that actually insert the data into the appropriate row, as explained in the next section.

## Comparing Do...Until and Do...While Loops

As explained earlier, nearly every Do...Until loop can be rewritten as a Do...While loop. Often, as in this case, the choice is a matter of personal preference. The Do...Until loop shown earlier could be rewritten as a Do...While loop as follows:

```
Do While Cells(intRowCounter, 1) <> ""
        IntRowCounter = intRowCounter + 1
Loop
```

Recall that, in a Do...While loop, the loop continues while the condition is true. By contrast, the Do...Until loop continues *until* a condition becomes true. So with the Do...While loop, the condition must be `Cells(intRowcounter, 1) <> ""` (where the "<>" means "not equal to"). This condition then will remain true until there is data in the row, at which time the loop will terminate. In this project the choice of whether to use the Do...Until or the Do...While loop is simply a matter of personal preference. Both loops will have the same effect.

## Inserting Data into the Appropriate Row

Writing the code that actually inserts the data into the worksheet is a fairly simple matter. You simply need to write a series of assignment statements that assign the Text property of each of the text boxes to the appropriate cell. To write the cell references, you use the value stored in `intRowCounter` for the row number. As for the column numbers, you know that the data from `txtName` should be placed in column 1 (which is labeled "Student Name"), the data from `txtTest1` should be placed in column 2 (which is labeled "Test 1"), the data from `txtTest2` should be placed in column 3 (which is labeled "Test 3"), the data from `txtTest3` should be placed in column 4 (which is labeled "Test 4"), the data from `txtAverage` should be placed in column 5 (which is labeled "Average"), and the data from `txtLetter` should be placed in column 6 (which is labeled "Letter Grade").

The following statements, then, will correctly place the data in the worksheet.

```
Cells(intRowCounter, 1) = txtName
Cells(intRowCounter, 2) = txtTest1
Cells(intRowCounter, 3) = txtTest2
Cells(intRowCounter, 4) = txtTest3
Cells(intRowCounter, 5) = txtAverage
Cells(intRowCounter, 6) = txtLetter
```

## Adding the Do...Until Loop to the Project

You will now enter the code in your project and then test it. Specifically, you will add the code that activates the Gradesheet worksheet, finds a blank row, and inserts data into the blank row. You must also declare the counter variable that you will use in the Do...While loop.

> *To add the code that finds a blank row and inserts data into the worksheet:*
>
> 1. In the `cmdRecord_Click` procedure, place the cursor just below the comment that reads "Identify next available row in the worksheet." See Figure 6-25.

**Figure 6-25**   **CMDRECORD PROCEDURE**

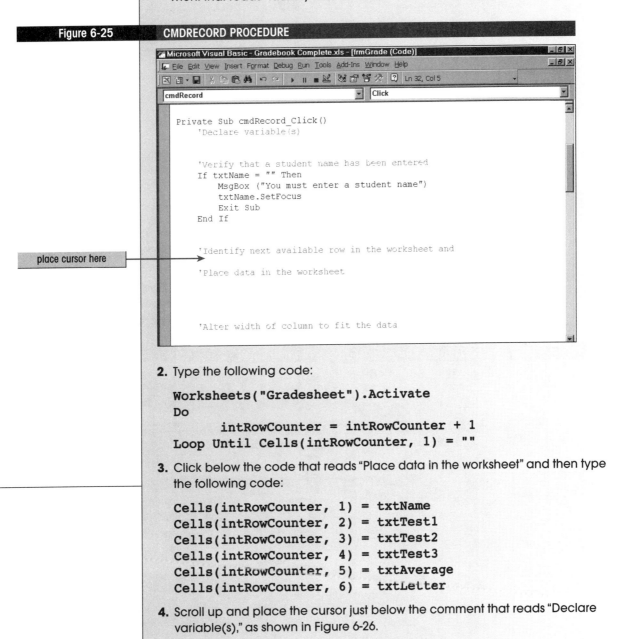

place cursor here

> 2. Type the following code:
>
> ```
> Worksheets("Gradesheet").Activate
> Do
>         intRowCounter = intRowCounter + 1
> Loop Until Cells(intRowCounter, 1) = ""
> ```
>
> 3. Click below the code that reads "Place data in the worksheet" and then type the following code:
>
> ```
> Cells(intRowCounter, 1) = txtName
> Cells(intRowCounter, 2) = txtTest1
> Cells(intRowCounter, 3) = txtTest2
> Cells(intRowCounter, 4) = txtTest3
> Cells(intRowCounter, 5) = txtAverage
> Cells(intRowCounter, 6) = txtLetter
> ```
>
> 4. Scroll up and place the cursor just below the comment that reads "Declare variable(s)," as shown in Figure 6-26.

Figure 6-26

**CMDRECORD PROCEDURE**

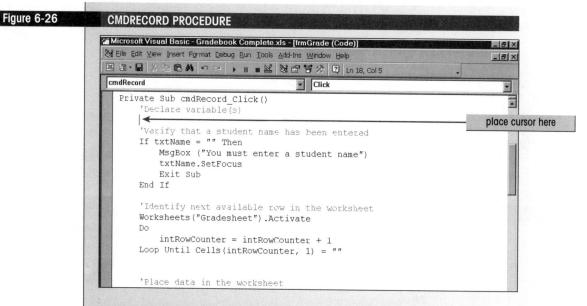

5. Type the following statement

   **Dim intRowCounter As Integer**

6. Save your work and run the program.

7. In the Name text box type **Catherine Worthington** for the student name. Also type **89**, **67**, and **75** for the three test scores.

8. Click the **Calculate Grade** button. Observe the calculated number and letter grades.

9. Click the **Record in Worksheet** button. The data is placed in the worksheet just under the column headings (the first empty row), as shown in Figure 6-27. You may need to move the form to see the records in the worksheet.

Figure 6-27

**CALCULATE GRADE FORM ON TOP OF WORKSHEET**

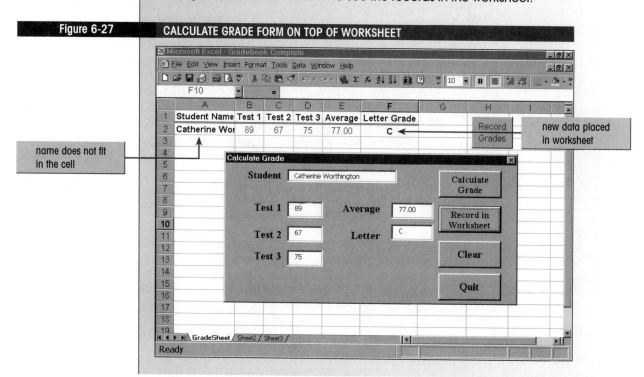

As you placed the data in the worksheet, you probably noticed that the Student Name column is not wide enough to accommodate the student's name. To ensure that the worksheet always displays data properly, it's a good idea to include code that resizes the columns each time new data is inserted. This will insure that your columns are always wide enough to hold the newly inserted data. You'll learn how to use the AutoFit method to accomplish this in the next section.

## Using the AutoFit Method

You may recall that within the Excel workbook window, you can size columns by double-clicking a column border. When you do this, Excel's **AutoFit** feature automatically widens or shrinks the column to accommodate the longest piece of data stored in that column. You can perform this same function in VBA by using the AutoFit method. When applied to one or more columns, the **AutoFit method** will increase or decrease the width of the column to match the data stored in that column.

To use the AutoFit method in VBA, simply type a reference to the columns you want to size, followed by a period and the word "AutoFit." Your Gradebook project involves columns A through F in the Gradesheet worksheet. Thus, you need to use the following statement:

```
Columns("A:F").AutoFit
```

Notice that the "A:F" is in quotes. Using quotes allows you to reference the columns in the same manner as if you were referencing columns directly in the worksheet. This is to say that you can use the column names "A", "B", "C", and so on if you enclose the reference in quotes.

Since you are placing this statement after the Activate method has been used, it will be unnecessary for you to include the name of the worksheet in this statement.

You will now add and test this statement in your project.

> *To add the AutoFit statement to your project:*
>
> **1.** Place the cursor after the comment that reads "Alter width of column to fit the data." See Figure 6-28.

| Figure 6-28 | **CMDRECORD PROCEDURE** |

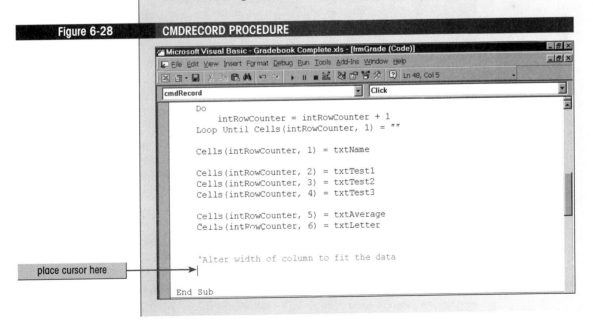

place cursor here

**2.** Type the following statement:

```
Columns("A:F").AutoFit
```

**3.** Save your work and run the program.

**4.** In the Student name text box enter **Raymond McFarland**. For the test grades, enter **78**, **87**, and **56**.

**5.** Click the **Calculate Grade** button on the form.

**6.** Click the **Record in Worksheet** button on the form. The new data is added to your worksheet, and the columns are sized to fit. In particular, column A has been expanded to fit the names of the students, as shown in Figure 6-29. (You may have to move your form so that you can see column A.)

| Figure 6-29 | CALCULATE GRADE FORM ON TOP OF GRADEBOOK COMPLETE WORKSHEET |
| --- | --- |

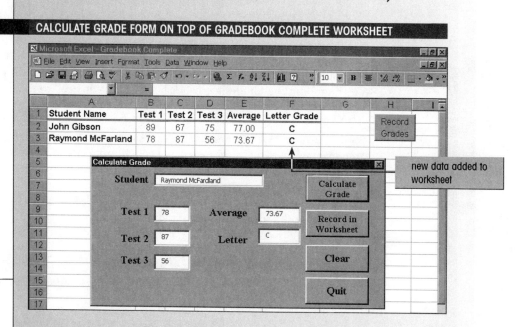

**7.** Click the **Quit** button on the form.

You have completed all the tasks listed on your original plan for the Gradebook project. When you demonstrate the project for your supervisor, Gene Cox, he is quite pleased with what you have developed. He suggests that you demonstrate the project for Wanda Pollack, the project's end user. He explains that, often, when you first demonstrate a project for a client, the client will think of additional features that would make the application easier to use.

You take Gene's advice and demonstrate the project for Wanda. She is very pleased with the project. However, when she views the results in the worksheet, she requests two additional features. Wanda tells you that she would like to have some way of easily identifying students who are not doing well. She asks you if there is some way to identify those students whose performance is at less than a "C" level. You ask her if she would like to have those grades appear in a different color, red perhaps. She likes that idea, and you suggest that you make the grade boldface as well. You tell her that you will add this feature to the project and return with a demonstration later.

Wanda's second request pertains to the sorting of the worksheet. She noticed that the student information is entered into the worksheet in the order in which it is entered into the form. It would make more sense to sort the data by student name. In the next session you will add these two features to your project. These are rather simple enhancements that will greatly increase the project's usefulness.

## Session 6.2 QUICK CHECK

1. The _____ statement allows you to choose from multiple selections.

2. Write the statement that will make the width in columns C through F automatically adjust to the size of the data.

3. Suppose you want to reference the cell represented by C5 in the worksheet. How would you reference this cell in a VBA statement using the Cells property?

4. Write the statement that will activate the worksheet named "Invoices".

5. The _____ statement will end the procedure in which it appears.

6. Write a Do...Until loop that looks in the second column of each row for an empty ("") value. Use the variable intRowCounter to keep track of which row you are currently examining.

---

## SESSION 6.3

In this session you will write statements that change the color of text in certain cells. You will also sort the data in the worksheet using the Sort method.

## Altering the Appearance of a Cell

Following your meeting with Wanda Pollack, you are ready to add the two requested features to the project. You will start by writing the code that applies a red and boldface font to the average grade and letter grade when a student's average is less than 70. To put it another way, *if* the contents of the txtAverage text box are less than 70, the numeric and letter grades should be changed to a red and boldface font. Now take a moment to decide what kind of control structure is necessary here.

You want to apply some formatting to the grade when the grade is less than 70, but you do not need to apply any formatting when the grade is 70 or above. In other words, you have a condition to test. If the condition results in true, then you want a certain set of statements to be executed. However, if the condition is false, the program doesn't have to do anything. As you learned earlier in this tutorial, when there are no statements to execute in response to a false condition, you can use an If statement with the Null Else variation described earlier.

Your If statement should include the following condition. Note that the statement relies on the default property, text, which represents the value entered into the text box.

```
If txtAverage < 70 Then
```

To complete the next part of the If statement, you need to use the **RGB function**, an intrinsic VBA function that applies color to a cell or most other objects whose color can be altered. (If you completed Case Problem 3 in Tutorial 4, you've already had experience with this function.) You'll learn more about this function in the next section.

## Adding Color with the RGB Function

As you probably know, all colors are made up of a mix of red, green, and blue. For this reason, the RGB function has three arguments. The first represents the red component of the color, the second represents the green component, and the third represents the blue component. (The function takes its name from the first letter of each of these colors—"R" for red, "G" for green, and "B" for blue.) For each argument, you include a number from 0 through 255, with 255 being the darkest version of that color possible. If you include the zero for an argument, RGB will not include any of that particular color. The syntax of the RGB function is very simple, and requires little explanation:

```
RGB(red component, green component, blue component)
```

For your project, you want to make both the average grade and the letter grade red. This is an easy combination; you want all red, with no green or blue. So to represent the color red with the RGB function, you would use the following:

```
RGB(255, 0, 0)
```

To set cell C5's font color to red, you would use this assignment statement:

```
Cells(5, 3).Font.Color = RGB(255, 0, 0)
```

As you can probably guess, the color green would be represented as RGB (0, 255, 0), and the color blue would be represented as RGB (0, 0, 255). You can specify a wide variety of other colors by varying any of the three arguments.

## Writing the Code That Applies Red and Boldface to a Font

You are ready to begin constructing the `If` statement that will apply the color red and boldface to the cell's contents. You already know what the condition looks like. Now you just need to construct the statements that will actually apply red and boldface font when the condition is true.

Recall that the average grade is in column 5 and that the letter grade is in column 6. Also recall that `intRowCounter` (the counter variable in the Do...Until loop you created earlier) contains the number of the current row. Thus, the following code will check to see if the average is less than 70 and, if so, will change the color to red and turn bold on.

```
If txtAverage < 70 Then
     Cells(intRowCounter, 5).Font.Color = RGB(255, 0, 0)
     Cells(intRowCounter, 5).Font.Bold = True
     Cells(intRowCounter, 6).Font.Color = RGB(255, 0, 0)
     Cells(intRowCounter, 6).Font.Bold = True
End If
```

When the worksheet was originally set up, the column that contains the letter grade was formatted in bold. However, the last statement in the `If...Then` control structure above will ensure that the letter grade is converted to bold, just in case a user changes the formatting in the worksheet.

You will now add these statements to your project and observe how they alter the data recorded in the worksheet.

### To enter and test the code:

1. In the `cmdRecord_Click` procedure, place the cursor right after the statement that places the letter grade into the worksheet, as shown in Figure 6-30.

| Figure 6-30 | CMDRECORD PROCEDURE |

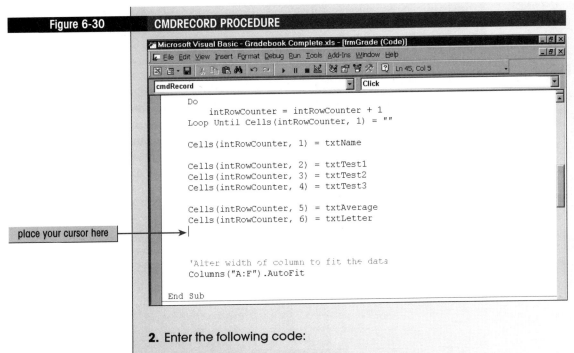

place your cursor here

2. Enter the following code:

```
If txtAverage < 70 Then
    Cells(intRowCounter, 5).Font.Color = RGB(255, 0, 0)
    Cells(intRowCounter, 5).Font.Bold = True
    Cells(intRowCounter, 6).Font.Color = RGB(255, 0, 0)
    Cells(intRowCounter, 6).Font.Bold = True
End If
```

3. Save your work and run the program.

4. In the Student Name text box enter **Thomas Vandergriff**. For the three test scores, enter **56**, **67**, and **45**.

5. Click the **Calculate Grade** button on the form.

6. Click the **Record in Worksheet** button on the form.

7. Click the **Quit** button on the form.

8. Switch to the Excel workbook window. Observe the new data added to the worksheet and notice that the average grade and the letter grade are red and bold, as indicated in Figure 6-31.

| Figure 6-31 | WORKSHEET WITH FORMATTED DATA |

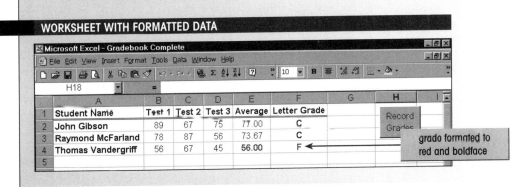

You have one remaining feature to add to your project. Wanda wants the program to sort the data by student name each time new test data is added to the worksheet.

# Sorting Rows with the Sort Method

You have most likely sorted the data in a worksheet on many occasions. So you probably realize that there are several different ways of doing this. The same is true when you write code designed to sort rows. You have many options for sorting data in VBA. However, you'll find it easiest to use a simple version of the Sort method. You can use the **Sort method**, a method of the Range object to sort data according to your specifications. Its syntax is explained below.

| Syntax | *expression*.Sort(*Key1, Header*)<br>The syntax here has been simplified to include only the portions necessary for your project. For the full syntax look up "sort" in VBA Help. |
|---|---|
| **Explanation** | The expression specifies the range of data to be sorted. Key1 specifies the column you want to sort by (that is, the sort key). The header specifies whether or not the range of data includes a header row (which you would not want sorted along with the rest of the data). To indicate a header, use the constant xlYes. |
| **Example** | Worksheets("Gradesheet").Range("A1").Sort _<br>    Key1:=Worksheets("Gradesheet").Columns("A"), _<br>    Header:=xlYes |

As you examine the example above, remember that the underscore is a continuation character that allows you to continue the statement on the next line. You should already be familiar with continuation characters after reading about them in Tutorial 5.

The example begins with a reference to the worksheet to be sorted (the worksheet named "Gradesheet"). The range to be sorted contains cell "A1". (Note that you can refer to any cell within the range that you want to sort.) In this example, the sort will be based on column "A" in the worksheet named "Gradesheet". The last part of the statement states that the data does include a header. The argument "Header:=xlYes" ensures that the header row will not be sorted along with the rest of the data; that is, the header row will remain at the top of the data range, where it belongs.

The Example statement is the very statement you need for your project. You can use this same statement any time you need to sort a worksheet with a header. To apply this statement to another worksheet, you would only need to change the name of the worksheet and include any cell within the range you want to sort.

## To add this statement to your project:

**1.** In the cmdRecord_Click procedure, place the cursor just below the statement that alters the column widths, as shown in Figure 6-32.

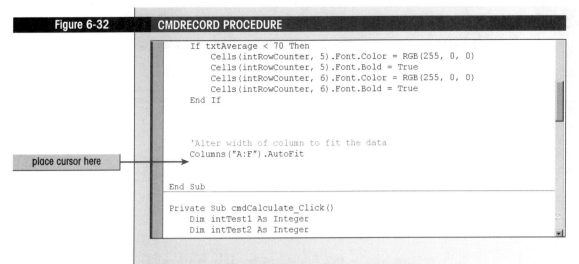

| Figure 6-32 | CMDRECORD PROCEDURE |

place cursor here

```
    If txtAverage < 70 Then
        Cells(intRowCounter, 5).Font.Color = RGB(255, 0, 0)
        Cells(intRowCounter, 5).Font.Bold = True
        Cells(intRowCounter, 6).Font.Color = RGB(255, 0, 0)
        Cells(intRowCounter, 6).Font.Bold = True
    End If



    'Alter width of column to fit the data
    Columns("A:F").AutoFit


End Sub

Private Sub cmdCalculate_Click()
    Dim intTest1 As Integer
    Dim intTest2 As Integer
```

2. Type the following code:

```
Worksheets("Gradesheet").Range("A1").Sort _
        Key1:=Worksheets("Gradesheet").Columns("A"), _
        Header:=xlYes
```

3. Review the code and correct any mistakes. This statement is unusually long, and even the slightest error will result in an error.

4. Save your work and then run the project.

5. Enter **Adam Simerly** as the student name. For the test grades, enter **87**, **67**, and **90**.

6. Click the **Calculate Grade** button on the form.

7. Click the **Record in Worksheet** button on the form.

8. Click the **Quit** button on the form.

9. Return to the Excel workbook window. The worksheet with new data has been sorted, as shown in Figure 6-33. In a more elaborate version of this project, you would probably want to include two different name columns, one for first names and one for last names, and then sort first by last name and then by first name. You will have an opportunity to try this in the Review Assignments at the end of this tutorial.

| Figure 6-33 | **WORKSHEET WITH DATA SORTED** |

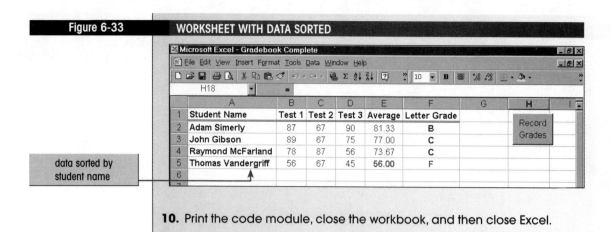

data sorted by
student name

**10.** Print the code module, close the workbook, and then close Excel.

This completes your project. Both Gene and Wanda are quite pleased with the results.

## Session 6.3 QUICK CHECK

1. The _____ function allows you to assign a color to an object that can receive color.

2. Write the function that would apply the color blue.

3. Write the `If` statement that would make the cell "C7" green and boldface *only* if the value of the variable `intQuantity` is less than 10.

4. The _____ method allows you to change the order of data in a range of cells.

5. Write a statement that will sort the data in the worksheet named "Invoices" by the values in column "B." Assume that the data range includes a header. Also, assume that the range includes the cell "A1."

## REVIEW ASSIGNMENTS

Emily Woodhouse, business manager for Martindale Homeowners Association, is responsible for collecting yearly dues for the community swimming pool. She has hired TnT Consulting to create an Excel application to automate the process of entering information about each family, calculating dues owed, and recording which families have paid their pool dues and which have not. The program should record the information about pool dues in an Excel worksheet. Paid dues should be displayed in green, with unpaid dues displayed in red. The schedule for pool dues is shown in Figure 6-34.

| Figure 6-34 | POOL DUES FOR MARTINDALE HOMEOWNERS ASSOCIATION |
| --- | --- |

| NUMBER IN FAMILY | DUES |
| --- | --- |
| 1 | $250 |
| 2 | $270 |
| 3 | $285 |
| 4 | $295 |
| 5 or more | $300 |

1. Start Excel and open the workbook named **Pool**, located in the Review folder for Tutorial 6.

2. Save the workbook as **Martindale** in the Review folder for Tutorial 6.

3. Start the VBA IDE and open the `frmPoolDues` form.

4. Look up the name of each control in the Properties window. Note that the form includes a new control, a check box. You'll learn more about the check box later in these review assignments.

5. Program the Clear button and the Quit button.

6. Program the Calculate button so that it does the following:

   ■ Check to see if the number of family members is a valid number. If it is, place the value in a variable named `intNumFamily`. If it is not valid, display an appropriate message in a message box, set the focus to the appropriate text box and highlight its current entry.

   ■ Calculate the dues according to the dues schedule in Figure 6-34 (using a `Select Case` statement) and place the value in the appropriate text box.

   The first three lines of the `Case` statement should look like this:

   ```
   Select Case intNumFamily
        Case 1
              txtDues = Format(250, "currency")
   ```

   ■ Format the value in the Total Dues text box to a currency format

7. Save and test the project to make sure it calculates dues correctly.

8. Code the `cmdRecord` button so that the data is recorded in the next available (empty) row. Your statements should check to make sure that a family name has been entered. If not, the procedure should display a message box telling the user to enter a name.

*Explore*

9. Notice that the form includes a control you haven't used before, a checkbox control. A checkbox control is used when you want the user to indicate whether something is true or false. The user selects (checks) the check box to indicate true, or leaves it unselected (unchecked) to indicate false. In this case, the user will click the check box if the dues have been paid, if the dues are unpaid, the user should leave the check box unselected. Within VBA, you can determine the current value of the check box by using an `If` statement. Write the code that will check to see if the current value of the check box is

true (that is, if the dues have been paid). In the case of paid dues, the program should set the color of the dues in the worksheet to green. If the check box is false (that is, if the dues are not paid), the program should set the color of the dues to red and boldface.

The first part of the If statement should look like this:

```
If chkPaid = True then
cells(intRowCounter, 4).Font.Color = RGB(0,255,0)
        Cells(intRowCounter,3).Font.Bold = False
    Else.... (you write the rest)
```

10. Use the AutoFit method to set the column widths.

*Explore*    11. Sort the data in the worksheet by two keys, the last name (column "A") and then the first name (column "B"). You can use the same statement you used in the tutorial, except that you should add a second key. Use VBA Help to learn how to add the second key to the sort.

12. Write the statements that clear the form each time data is recorded in the worksheet.

13. Add comments to the top of the Code window that include your name and the date.

14. Save your work.

15. Test the project by entering the data shown in Figure 6-35.

**Figure 6-35**

| FAMILY NAME | FIRST NAME | NUMBER IN FAMILY | DUES | PAID? |
| --- | --- | --- | --- | --- |
| Bryant | Mary | 1 | $250.00 | Yes |
| Brinkley | Chris | 3 | $285.00 | No |
| Francois | Pierre | 5 | $300.00 | No |
| Stonewall | Bryan | 3 | $285.00 | Yes |
| Smith | Sharon | 3 | $285.00 | Yes |
| Cutshall | Walter | 1 | $250.00 | No |
| Smith | Allen | 3 | $285.00 | Yes |
| Smith | Kevin | 1 | $250.00 | Yes |

16. Save your work.

17. Print the worksheet and the project code.

18. Close the workbook.

## CASE PROBLEMS

*Case 1. Laurel Nursery*   Laurel Plant Nursery sells indoor and outdoor plants. The store's master gardener, Kent Williams, is not always available to answer customers' questions about the ideal growing conditions for each plant. So Kent has hired you to create an Excel application that he can use to create a list of information for each plant. His store clerks will then be able to look up information in this list. The program should include a VBA form that Kent can use to enter information about each plant into an Excel worksheet. In addition, the program should sort the plant information by plant name. For starters, Kent has asked you to create a sample application that only allows him to enter information about sunlight requirements. After he reviews the application, you can expand the form (and the accompanying code) to allow him to enter more information.

1. Start Excel and open the workbook named **Nursery** located in the Cases folder for Tutorial 6.

2. Save the workbook as **Laurel Nursery Plant Information**. Notice that the column headings have already been inserted into the worksheet for you.

3. Open the VBA IDE.

4. Open the form named `frmPlants`.

5. Familiarize yourself with the form. Check the name of each control in the Properties window.

6. Code the Exit button to remove the form from the screen.

7. Add code for the OK button that will do the following:

   ■ Locate the first empty row in the worksheet
   ■ Place the plant name and the sunlight requirements in the first two columns of that row
   ■ Use the AutoFit method to make sure that the columns are large enough to display the information

8. Add additional code to the OK button to sort the worksheet information by plant name.

9. Add code that clears the text boxes and positions the cursor at the start of the name field once the data has been entered in the worksheet.

10. Save the form.

11. Run the form.

12. Use the following data to test the form. Click the OK button after entering each line of data.

**Figure 6-36**

| PLANT NAME | SUNLIGHT REQUIREMENTS |
|---|---|
| Impatiens | Partial shade to shade |
| Sunflower | Sun |
| Pansy | Sun to partial shade |
| Coleus | Partial shade to shade |

13. Click the Exit button to close the form when you've finished testing.

14. Add comments at the top of the code that include your name and today's date.

15. Print the code for the project. Also print the worksheet.

16. Save the workbook.

*Case 2. Dynamic Relations*  Dana McGuire is an associate at Dynamic Relations, a small public relations firm. Dana would like to use Excel to keep track of her accounts. She has hired you to build a form that will allow her to enter a company name, contact name, telephone number, fax number, and e-mail address. The program should store this information in an Excel worksheet, and sort it by company name.

1. Start Excel and open the workbook named **Dynamic** located in the Cases folder for Tutorial 6.

2. Save the workbook as **Dynamic Accounts**. Notice that the column headings have already been placed in the worksheet for you.

3. Open the VBA IDE.

4. Open the form named `frmAccount`.

5. Familiarize yourself with the form. Check the name of each control in the Properties window.

6. Add code for the Exit button that will remove the form from the screen.

7. Add code for the OK button that will do the following:

   ■ Locate the first empty row in the worksheet
   ■ Place the account information into that row
   ■ Use the AutoFit method to make sure that the columns are large enough to display the information

8. Add additional code to the OK button to sort the worksheet information by company name.

9. Add code that clears the text boxes and positions the cursor at the start of the company name field once the data has been entered in the worksheet.

10. Save the form.

11. Run the form.

12. Use the data in Figure 6-37 to test the form. Click the OK button after entering each line of data.

**Figure 6-37**

| COMPANY | LAST NAME | FIRST NAME | TELEPHONE | FAX | E-MAIL |
|---|---|---|---|---|---|
| Jack's Motors | Jackson | James | 555 8888 | 555 9898 | jjackson@jmotors.com |
| Zebra Stripes | Johnson | Mike | 999 1234 | 999 5678 | mj@zebra.com |
| Able Enterprise | Able | Max | 765 4321 | 765 0987 | max@able.com |

13. Click the Exit button to close the form when you've finished testing.

14. Add comments at the top of the code that include your name and today's date.

15. Print the code for the project and the worksheet.

16. Save the workbook.

*Case 3. Griffith Bookstore*   Frank Wilson manages Griffith Bookstore. The bookstore employs part-time and full-time staff. Some employees work 20 hours per week, some work 30 hours per week, and others work 40 hours per week. Every employee must record the hours worked each day on a timecard. Frank totals each employee's hours at the end of the week. He needs to compare the hours worked for each employee with the number of hours allowed for each employee. Frank would like you to develop a form that he can use to enter the employee information into an Excel worksheet. Furthermore, he would like the VBA application to change the colors of the Hours Worked cell so that he can easily distinguish among the employees who worked 20 hours, 30 hours, and 40 hours.

1. Start Excel and open the workbook named **BKStore** located in the Cases folder for Tutorial 6.

2. Save the workbook as **Griffith Bookstore Hours**. Notice that the column headings have already been placed in the worksheet for you.

3. Open the VBA IDE.

4. Open the form named `frmHours`.

5. Familiarize yourself with the form. Check the name of each control in the Properties window.

6. Add code for the Exit button that will remove the form from the screen.

7. Add code for the OK button that will do the following:

   ■ Locate the first empty row in the worksheet and then place the employee's name and hours worked into that row

   ■ Use the AutoFit method to make sure that the columns are large enough to display the information

8. Add a `Case` statement to the OK button code that changes the employee hours cell color so that 20 hours is blue, 30 hours is red, and 40 hours is green.

9. Add code to the OK button to sort the worksheet information by employee name.

10. Add code that clears the text boxes and positions the cursor at the start of the company name field once the data has been entered in the worksheet.

11. Save the form.

12. Run the form.

13. Use the data in Figure 6-38 to test the form. Click the OK button after entering each line of data.

**Figure 6-38**

| FIRST NAME | LAST NAME | HOURS |
|---|---|---|
| Darlene | Nichols | 40 |
| Jack | Francis | 20 |
| Jane | Dawkins | 30 |
| Paul | Michaels | 40 |
| Alex | Boothe | 20 |

14. Click the Exit button to close the form when you've finished testing.

15. Add comments at the top of the code that include your name and today's date.

16. Print the code for the project and the worksheet.

17. Save the workbook.

**Case 4. Jane's After School Program**   Jane Dixon runs an after school program for first, second, and third grade students. She has nearly 50 students in the program. Frequently, she will send announcements and other information to the parents of the students. Currently, she has the parents' addresses written in an address book. However, she wants to store the names and addresses of the parents in Microsoft Excel. Jane knows that she could use the address information from Excel when she sends announcements to the parents.

1. Start Excel and open the workbook named **AftSchl** located in the Cases folder for Tutorial 6.

2. Save the workbook as **Jane's After School Program**. Notice that the column headings have already been placed in the worksheet for you.

3. Examine the form shown in Figure 6-39. You will create this form in the following steps.

**Figure 6-39    THE AFTER SCHOOL FORM**

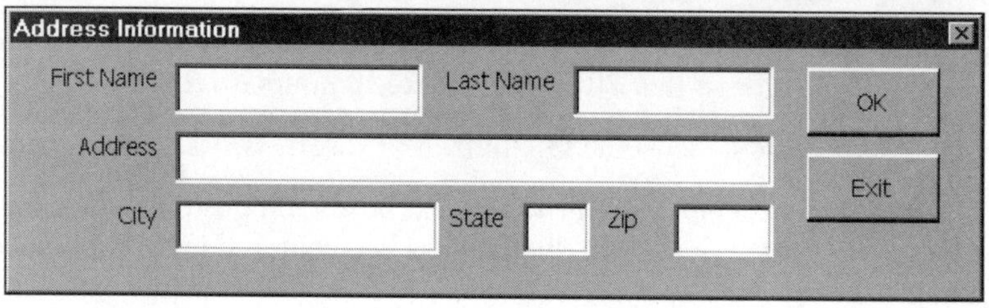

4. Open the VBA IDE.

5. Add a User form to the project from the insert menu.

6. Add six label controls, six text box controls, and two command buttons to the form.

7. Set the properties for the form and controls using the information in the Figure 6-40.

| Figure 6-40 |
| --- |

| CONTROL | PROPERTY | VALUE |
| --- | --- | --- |
| Userform1 | Name | frmAddress |
| Userform1 | Caption | Address Information |
| Label1 | Caption | First Name |
| Label2 | Caption | Last Name |
| Label3 | Caption | Address |
| Label4 | Caption | City |
| Label5 | Caption | State |
| Label6 | Caption | Zip |
| Textbox1 | Name | txtFirstName |
| Textbox2 | Name | txtLastName |
| Textbox3 | Name | txtAddress |
| Textbox4 | Name | txtCity |
| Textbox5 | Name | txtState |
| Textbox6 | Name | txtZipcode |
| CommandButton1 | Name | cmdOK |
| CommandButton1 | Caption | OK |
| CommandButton2 | Name | cmdExit |
| CommandButton2 | Caption | Exit |

8. Add code for the Exit button that will remove the form from the screen.

9. Add code for the OK button that will do the following:

   ■ Locate the first empty row in the worksheet and then place the parent's name and address information into that row

   ■ Use the AutoFit method to make sure that the columns are large enough to display the information

10. Look up the Sort method in the Help. Notice how to sort by more than one key field.

11. Add code to the OK button to sort the parent information by last name and first name.

12. Add code that clears the text boxes and positions the cursor at the start of the last name field once the data has been entered in the worksheet.

13. Save the form.

14. Run the form.

15. Use the data in Figure 6-41 to test the form. Click the OK button after entering each line of data.

Figure 6-41

| FIRST NAME | LAST NAME | ADDRESS | CITY | STATE | ZIP CODE |
|---|---|---|---|---|---|
| Dan | Jenkins | 123 May St. | College Town | NY | 09097 |
| Mary | Dawkins | 9344 Apple Dr. | Newton | NJ | 08911 |
| Carole | Hearst | 233 Poplar Deer | Park | NY | 09111 |
| Gary | White | 8988 Douglas | Newton | NJ | 08911 |

16. Click the Exit button to close the form when you've finished testing.

17. Add comments at the top of the code that include your name and today's date.

18. Print the code for the project and print the worksheet.

19. Save the workbook.

## QUICK CHECK ANSWERS

### Session 6.1

1. `Unload frmStudent`

2. In the `cmdQuit_Click` event procedure

3. ```
   txtName = ""
   txtAddress = ""
   txtPhone = ""
   ```

4. ```
   sngAverage = (intNumberOne + intNumberTwo + _
   intNumberThree) / 3
   ```
   (Don't forget the parentheses.)

5. ```
   If IsNumeric(txtNumberOne) then
       intNumberOne = txtNumberOne
   Else
       MsgBox("Enter a valid number")
       txtNumberOne.SetFocus
       txtNumberOne.SelStart = 0
       txtNumberOne.SelLength = Len(txtNumberOne)
       Exit Sub
   End If
   ```

### Session 6.2

1. `Select Case`

2. `Columns("C:F").AutoFit`

3. `Cells(5,3)`

4. `Worksheets("Invoices").Activate`

5. `Exit Sub`

6. ```
   Do
       IntRowCounter = intRowCounter + 1
   Loop Until Cells(intRowCounter, 2) = ""
   ```

*Session 6.3*

1. RGB

2. RGB(0, 0, 255)

3. 
```
If intQuantity < 10 then
    Cells(7, 3).Font.Color = RGB(0, 255, 0)
    Cells(7, 3).Font.Bold = True
End If
```

4. Sort

5. 
```
Worksheets("Invoices").Range("A1").Sort _
    Key1:=worksheets("Invoices").Columns("B"), _
    Header:=xlYes
```

OBJECTIVES

In this tutorial you will:

- Use public variables

- Work with the PowerPoint object model

- Delete slides with the Delete method

- Create a general procedure

- Insert slides with the InsertFromSlide method

- Write code that will add a footer, apply a layout, apply a template, and insert the current date

- Abbreviate object references with the `Set` statement

- Use the InputBox function

# CREATING
## A POWERPOINT VBA APPLICATION WITH MULTIPLE FORMS

*Building a Presentation from a Word Outline*

CASE

## TnT Consulting Group

Gene Cox, your supervisor at TnT Consulting, would like you to expand your experience to include VBA for PowerPoint. To help you get started, he has assigned you an in-house project that will ultimately be used by TnT account representatives as they create sales presentations for potential clients. Typically, the account representatives begin by creating a Word outline that lists the major points to be covered in a sales presentation. Your job is to create a VBA application that will transform such a Word outline into a PowerPoint presentation.

Frank Fulchez, another consultant at TnT Consulting, has already completed portions of the project, including the forms that will ask the user to select the outline file and also the template file to be used in the presentation. Frank also started a main form for the project that will guide the user step by step through the process of creating the presentation. You will collaborate with Frank throughout the project.

**SESSION
7.1**

In this session you will review the Word document that will be used as the source for the presentation. Then you will preview a completed application that converts the document into a PowerPoint presentation. Next, you will review the project plan for the Presentation Builder application. Finally, you will learn how to use public variables in the Presentation Builder project.

## Previewing the Outline Document

The Presentation Builder project is designed to take an outline from a Word document and transform it into a PowerPoint presentation. The Presentation Builder project should work with any Word outline, as long as it is prepared according to the following guidelines:

- The first heading in the outline will become the title in the title slide.
- The first subpoint will become the subtitle in the title slide.
- Each subsequent main point will become a separate slide in the presentation, and its subpoints will become the subpoints on the slide

In this section, you will preview the sample outline in order to familiarize yourself with it. Remember that this document is only being used as an example. The completed Presentation Builder project should work the same way with any outline prepared according to the guidelines listed above.

*To review the Word document:*

**1.** Start Word.

**2.** Open the file named **Outline**, located in the Tutorial.07 folder on your Data Disk. The outline appears as shown in Figure 7-1. Notice that the document is displayed in Outline View and that it contains points that will form the foundation of a PowerPoint presentation. As explained earlier, the first point contains a title, and the first subpoint contains a subtitle, both of which will be included on the title slide. All subsequent main points will become separate slides.

Figure 7-1 | OUTLINE FILE

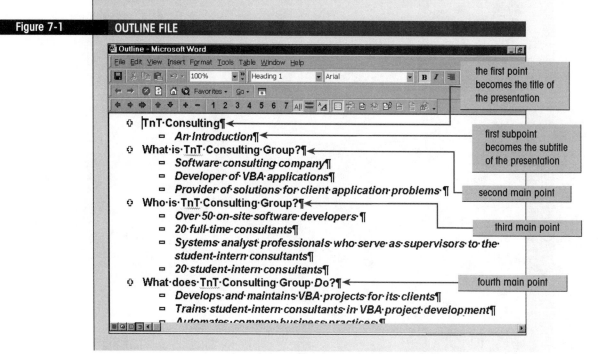

**3.** Close Word without saving any changes.

You will use the outline you just previewed as the basis of a PowerPoint presentation, when you run the Presentation Builder application in the next section.

## Previewing **the Presentation Builder Project**

Before you begin developing your own Presentation Builder project, you will preview a finished version. As you preview the project, note the major tasks it performs. In the next section you will examine a project plan that includes all of these tasks.

In order to ensure that the project runs properly, you need to verify that both the PowerPoint file named Preview and the Word document named Outline are stored in the same folder. You'll do that in the steps below.

### To check the location of the Preview file and the Outline file:

**1.** Open Windows Explorer and verify that the PowerPoint file named Preview and the Word document named Outline are stored in the same folder—that is, in the Tutorial.07 folder. If they are not in the same folder, move the files as necessary now.

**2.** Close Windows Explorer.

In order for this project to work correctly, PowerPoint should be configured to allow you to open a Word document as a presentation. In the next steps, you will verify that your installation of PowerPoint is configured properly.

### To check your configuration of PowerPoint:

**1.** Start PowerPoint.

**2.** In the PowerPoint dialog box, verify that the **Open an existing presentation** button is selected, click **More Files** (if necessary) in the list box, and then click **OK**.

**3.** Use the Look in list box to switch to the Tutotial.07 folder.

**4.** Click the **Files of type** list arrow, and then click **All Files**.

**5.** In the list of files, click **Outline**, and then click **Open**. If your installation of PowerPoint is configured to open Word files, the Word outline will open in the Presentation window. If not, you will see a message box asking if you would like to install the necessary feature. Follow the directions in this message box to install the feature, then repeat these steps again, beginning again with Step 2, to verify that the Outline file does indeed open in PowerPoint without saving it.

**6.** Close the open presentation without saving it.

You can now preview the Presentation Builder project.

*To preview the Presentation Builder project:*

1. Open the presentation named **Preview**, which is located in the Tutorial.07 folder on your Data Disk.

2. Save the presentation as **Presentation Preview** in the Tutorial.07 folder on your Data Disk. It is important that this file be in the same folder as the Outline file you looked at in the preceding section. If you are saving your files somewhere other than the Data Disk, make sure you copy the Outline file to that same directory.

3. Start the VBA IDE.

4. Open the form named `frmPresentationBuilder` in the Project Explorer. The form looks like Figure 7-2.

| Figure 7-2 | THE FRMPRESENTATIONBUILDER FORM IN DESIGN VIEW |
| --- | --- |

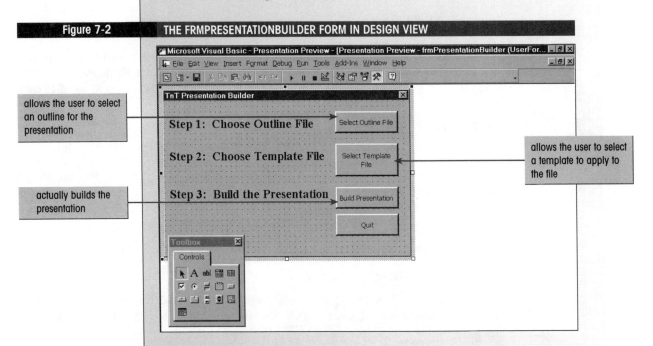

allows the user to select an outline for the presentation

allows the user to select a template to apply to the file

actually builds the presentation

5. Run the program. The TnT Presentation Builder form is displayed in the PowerPoint window. As you can see in the form, the first step in building the presentation is choosing an outline file to use as the basis of the presentation.

6. Click the **Select Outline File** button in the form. The Select Outline File form appears, as in Figure 7-3. This form contains a list of all Word documents in the current folder (the Tutorial.07 folder). This list could offer a number of Word documents from which to choose. For demonstration purposes, however, it only includes the document you previewed earlier.

**Figure 7-3**  **SELECT OUTLINE FILE FORM**

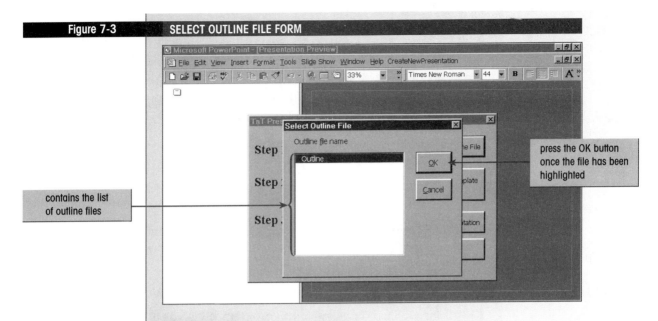

contains the list of outline files

press the OK button once the file has been highlighted

7. Verify that the file **Outline** is selected, and then click **OK** on the form. The Select Outline File form is removed from the screen, and you return to the TnT Presentation Builder form. As you can see on this form, Step 2 in building the presentation is choosing a template file.

8. Click the **Select Template File** button on the form. The Select Template File form appears, as in Figure 7-4. This form contains a list of all the template files stored on your computer. (The list of templates on your computer may differ from the one shown in Figure 7-4.)

**Figure 7-4**  **SELECT TEMPLATE FILE FORM**

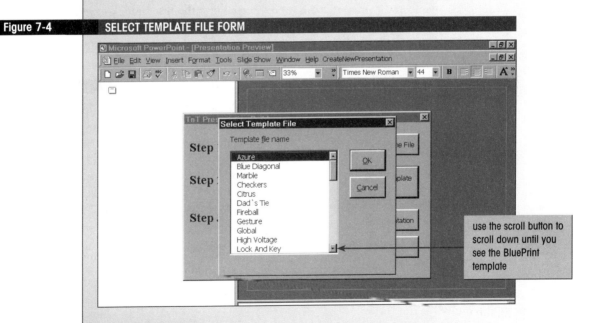

use the scroll button to scroll down until you see the BluePrint template

9. Click the **BluePrint** template in the Template file name list and then click **OK** on the Select Template File form. The form is removed from the screen, and you return to the TnT Presentation Builder form. As you can see in this form, the third and final step is building the presentation.

TROUBLE? If you do not see BluePrint in the list of template files, choose a different template. Note that if you do choose a different template file, your screen will look slightly different from the figures in this book. This is not a problem.

TROUBLE? If you do not have any files listed in the list of template files, the PowerPoint templates have not been installed on your computer. You will need to consult your instructor about installing the template files. However, the project will still run without errors. Simply click OK in the Select Template File form without selecting a template file and continue with Step 10. The presentation will be built with no template applied.

10. Click the **Build Presentation** button in the form. After a few moments, the project builds your presentation. You see a form that asks for the Presenter's name.

TROUBLE? If you see an error message, then your installation of PowerPoint is not configured to open Word documents. See the preceding set of steps for instructions.

11. Enter **Gene Cox** as the name of the presenter, and then click **OK**.

12. Click the **Quit** button on the form. You return to the VBA IDE.

As you will see in the next set of steps, the presentation has now been built according to your specifications. Before you examine the presentation, take a moment to think about the major steps that were performed as the project ran. In the first step, you selected an outline file to be used as the source for the presentation. In the second step, you selected a template from the list of all templates installed on your computer. In the final step, you actually created the presentation, based on the selections in Steps 1 and 2. During the final step, you were asked to specify the name of the presenter. As you will see in the next set of steps, the name of the presenter was then inserted into the title slide. You will also see that the current date has been inserted into the title slide.

You will now view the presentation created by the Presentation Builder project.

### To view the presentation built by the Presentation Builder project:

1. Switch to the PowerPoint window. The presentation is formatted with the template you selected. Notice that the presenter's name, Gene Cox, was inserted on the first slide. Notice also that the current date was inserted on the title slide as well. Your title slide should look like Figure 7-5. If you selected a template other than BluePrint, the formatting of your slide will differ from the figure, according to the template you selected.

| Figure 7-5 | FIRST SLIDE BUILT BY THE PRESENTATION BUILDER |

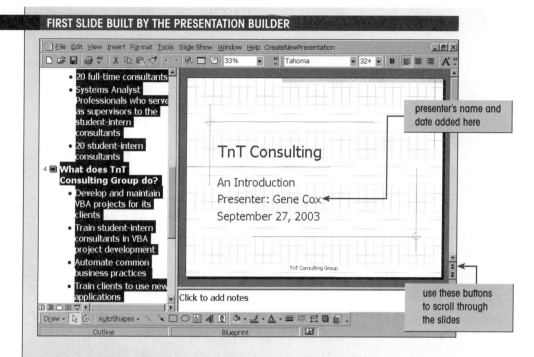

2. Scroll through the slides in the presentation, using the vertical scroll bar. Notice that the text of each slide corresponds to the text of the outline document you previewed earlier in Word. Each slide corresponds to one major point in the Word outline.

3. Close the presentation without making any changes. Keep the PowerPoint window open.

Now that you have previewed the project, you are ready to develop it on your own. As you should know by now, the first step in the development process is putting together a detailed project plan.

# Planning the Presentation Builder Project

Before you begin working on the application, Gene reminds you of the importance of planning any VBA project. To help you plan your work, he gives you a list of the major tasks involved in turning the outline into a presentation. This task list is shown in Figure 7-6.

| Figure 7-6 | PLAN FOR PRESENTATION BUILDER PROJECT |
| --- | --- |

Task 1: Display a form that walks the user through the three steps of building a presentation

Task 2: Display a form in which the user can complete the first step, selecting a Word file to be used as the basis of the presentation. (Assigned to Frank Fulchez)
- Present a list of Word files
- Allow the user to select one of the files
- Store the filename in a way that makes it available to all the modules in the project

Task 3: Display a form in which the user can complete the second step, selecting a template with which to format the presentation. (Assigned to Frank Fulchez)
- Present a list of template names
- Allow the user to select one of the templates
- Store the template name in a way that makes it available to all the modules in the project

Task 4: Allow the user to complete the third step, actually creating the presentation
- Delete any existing slides
- Create the presentation from the Word document
- Format the slides
- Apply the specified template to the presentation

Task 5: Finish the presentation
- Display a form that allows the user to enter presenter's name
- Add the presenter's name and the current date to the title slide
- Format the title slide

Gene assigned most of Tasks 1 and 2 to Frank Fulchez. Among other things, Frank has already created the necessary forms. You will now open the project begun by Frank. Then, you can begin work on your part of the project.

## To open the partially completed project:

1. In PowerPoint, open the file named **Builder**, which is located in the Tutorial.07 folder on your Data Disk. Notice that the presentation does not contain any slides.

2. Save the presentation as **Presentation Builder** in the Tutorial.07 folder on your Data Disk.

3. Switch to the VBA IDE.

4. Open the Project Explorer. If necessary expand the Forms subdirectory so that you can see the forms Frank has already created, as shown in Figure 7-7.

| Figure 7-7 | THE PROJECTOR EXPLORER SHOWING THE FORMS SUBDIRECTORY |
| --- | --- |

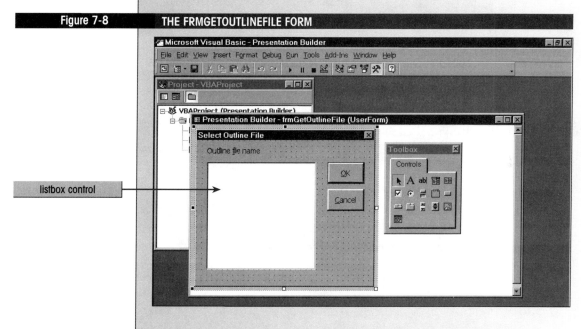

**5.** Double-click **frmGetOutlineFile** and view the form as shown in Figure 7-8. Notice that the form includes a control you haven't used before, the listbox control. Frank has already written some code for this form. You will learn more about this code later.

| Figure 7-8 | THE FRMGETOUTLINEFILE FORM |
| --- | --- |

**6.** Close the frmGetOutlineFile form.

**7.** Open the **frmGetTemplateFile** form. As shown in Figure 7-9, this form also has a listbox control. Frank has already written some code for this form too. You will learn more about this code later.

Figure 7-9    **THE FRMGETTEMPLATEFILE FORM**

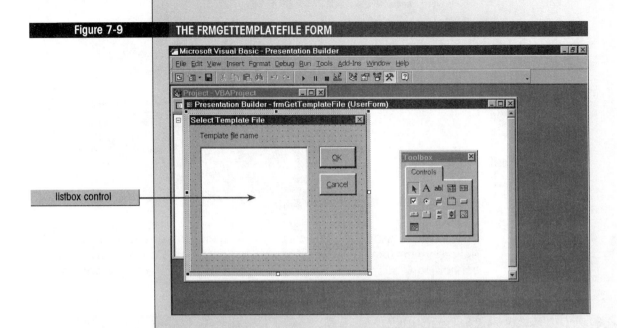

listbox control

**8.** Close the form.

**9.** Open the **frmPresentationBuilder** form, which is shown in Figure 7-10. You will write code for the command buttons in this form.

Figure 7-10    **THE FRMPRESENTATIONBUILDER FORM**

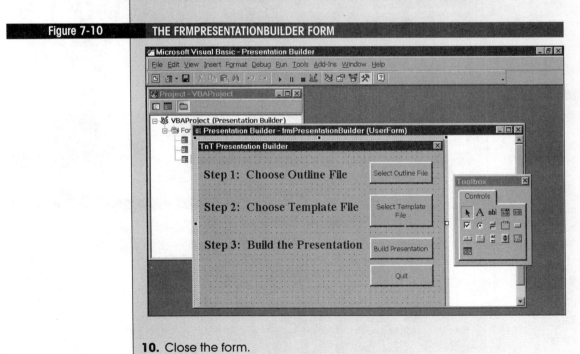

**10.** Close the form.

In addition to creating the forms named `frmGetOutlineFile` and `frmGetTemplateFile,` Frank has already written the VBA code for these forms. In this code, he used the `DIR` statement, which is a special VBA statement that allows you to list files in a specified directory according to certain criteria. The `DIR` statement is beyond the scope of this book. At this stage in your VBA education, all you need to know is that Frank used the `DIR` statement in order to provide the list of Word files and the list of template files. Also, it is important to note that, when writing this code, Frank assumed the outline file would be located in the same folder as the Presentation Builder file. If you want to learn more about the `DIR` statement, look it up in VBA Help. You might also consider browsing through Frank's code and looking up any additional statements that are unfamiliar to you. Reading through another developer's code is actually a very useful way to learn new programming techniques.

To summarize, then, Frank has completed the code that allows the user to select a Word document and a template to be used as the basis for the presentation. Now, you need to write the code that will take the Word file and template selected by the user and use them to build the presentation. This involves some interaction between the three forms in the project. Figure 7-11 illustrates how the main form (`frmPresentationBuilder`) interacts with the other two forms (`frmGetOutlineFile` and `frmGetTemplateFile`).

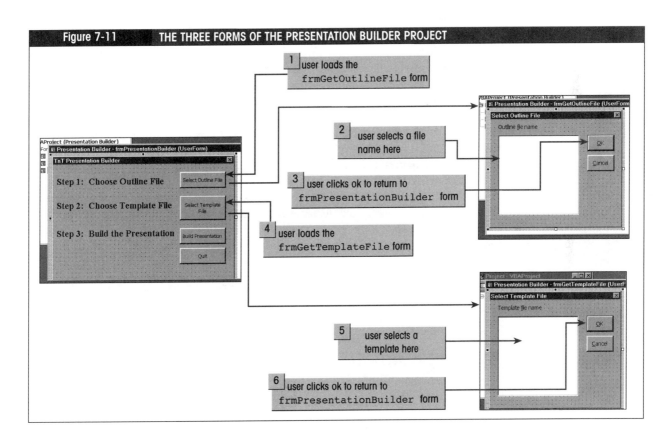

**Figure 7-11     THE THREE FORMS OF THE PRESENTATION BUILDER PROJECT**

Looked at from VBA's perspective, your portion of the project needs some way to obtain the name of the Word document and template selected by the user. In order to facilitate this process, Frank's code stores the names of the Word document and the template in a public variable. You'll learn how to use public variables in the next section.

# Sharing Information Across Modules with Public Variables

You have used variables many times in the projects you have created for TnT Consulting. But you probably aren't yet aware that there are actually two kinds of variables—private and public. So far, you have only used **private variables**, meaning that these variables are available only to the module or procedure in which they are declared. The **Dim** statement, which you have already used many times, declares a private variable. **Public variables**, by contrast, are available to all modules and procedures in a project. (Some programmers prefer the term **global variable**.) In the following sections, you will learn how to declare a public variable, and then how to refer to a public variable in your code (after it has been declared).

## Declaring Public Variables

You declare a public variable in a one-line statement, just as you declare a private variable. The only difference is that you need to replace Dim with Public. For example, to declare the variable strOutlineFile as a public variable, you would use this statement:

```
Public strOutlineFileName as String
```

Public variables are useful when you have multiple modules in a project and need to transfer data from one module to another. Recall that each form is associated with a module, which in turn can contain several procedures. The Presentation Builder project, for instance, contains multiple forms—the two forms that Frank coded (frmGetOutlineFile and frmGetTemplateFile) and the frmPresentationBuilder form, which you will be coding. As you know, the frmGetOutlineFile form and the frmGetTemplateFile form obtain information from the user—that is, the name of the Word document to be used as the foundation for the presentation, and the name of the template to be applied to the presentation. As you write the code for the frmPresentationBuilder form, you need to access those filenames. If Frank stored the file and template names in private variables (created with the Dim statement), you would not be able to access them in your portion of the project (i.e. in the Presentation Builder form). In order to ensure that you can indeed access them, Frank chose to store the filename and template name in public variables.

Frank suggests that you take a moment to examine these two public variable declarations and compare them to some private variable declarations.

> *To view the public variable declarations:*
>
> **1.** Open the form **frmGetOutlineFile**.
>
> **2.** Double-click anywhere on the form to open the Code window.
>
> **3.** Scroll to the very top of the form's code to observe the declaration of the public variable strOutlineFile, as shown in Figure 7-12.

| Figure 7-12 | CODE WINDOW FOR THE FRMGETOUTLINEFILE FORM |
|---|---|

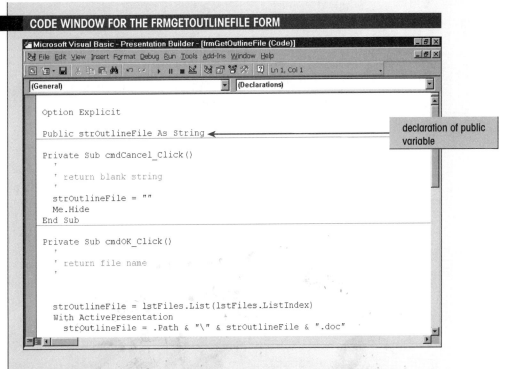

4. Scroll down until you can see the two `Dim` statements that declare the variables `strFileSearch` and `strFileFound` in the `UserForm_Initialize` procedure. Note that these variables are only available to the `UserForm_Initialize` procedure, while the public variable `strOutlineFile` can be used by all the procedures in this project.

5. Close the Code window, close the form, and then open the form named **frmGetTemplateFile**.

6. Double-click anywhere on the form to open the Code window.

7. Scroll to the very top of the form's code to observe the declaration of the public variable `strTemplateFile`.

8. Scan the rest of the code in the form module. This is a good way of learning new programming statements. However, with the exception of knowing the name of the public variables, it is not necessary that you understand how Frank coded his portion of the project.

9. Close the Code window and close the form.

## Referring to Public Variables in VBA Statements

To refer to a public variable after it has been declared, you must provide the name of the form (or module) followed by a period and the variable name. (This is similar to referring to the property of an object.) As you saw when you examined the code for the `frmGetOutlineFile` form, Frank used a public variable named `strOutlineFile` to store the name of the Word file. So to refer to this public variable in your code, you would use the following code:

```
frmGetOutlineFile.strOutlineFile
```

Within the code for the `frmGetTemplateFile` form, Frank declared another public variable, `strTemplateFile`, to store the name of the template file. To refer to this public variable in your code, you would use the following code:

```
frmGetTemplateFile.strTemplateFile
```

Now that you know how to refer to a public variable in VBA statements, you can begin programming your portion of the project.

## Using Public Variables in the Project

Frank has already completed part of the first task in the project plan. That is, he has created the form that will appear when the user clicks the Select Outline File button on the `frmPresentationBuilder` form. This form presents a list of filenames from which the user can make a selection. Then, his code stores the name of the file (selected by the user) in the form's public variable, `strOutlineFile`. Your job is to write the statements that will display the form in the first place—that is, you will write the code for the `Click` event procedure for the Select Outline File button. You also need to write statements that will retrieve the filename from the form's public variable `strOutlineFile` so that you can use it later in the code for the Build Presentation button. All of this code belongs in the module for the `frmPresentationBuilder` form.

First, turn your attention to the statements that display the `frmGetOutlineFile` form. As you'll recall from Tutorial 4, you use the Show method to display a form. You want the `frmGetOutlineFile` form to appear when the user clicks the Select Outline File button (that is the `cmdSelectOutlineFile` button). Thus, you need to include the following statement in the `cmdSelectOutlineFile_Click` event procedure within the `frmPresentationBuilder` form module:

```
frmGetOutlineFile.Show
```

Once the form is displayed on the screen, the project will wait for the user to select a file name from the list. Then, after the user clicks on a filename and clicks the OK button, the name of the file is stored in the public variable `strOutlineFile`. In the code for the Select Outline File button, you only need to include a line that takes the value stored in that public variable and assigns it to a private variable within the `frmPresentationBuilder` form module. This requires a `Dim` statement that declares a new private variable named `strOutlineFileName`. Then, you need to include an assignment statement that assigns the value of the public variable (`strOutlineFile`) to this new private variable (`strOutlineFileName`). Keeping in mind the correct way to refer to a public variable (using both the name of the form in which the variable is declared and the name of the variable itself), this results in the following assignment statement:

```
strOutlineFileName = frmGetOutlineFile.strOutlineFile
```

Finally, you need to include a statement that removes the `frmGetOutlineFile` from the screen. As you know by now, the Unload method does this job, as follows:

```
Unload frmGetOutlineFile
```

The code for the Select Template File button is identical, except that it must refer to a different form, public variable, and private variable, as follows:

```
frmGetTemplateFile.Show
strTemplateFileName = frmGetTemplateFile.strTemplateFile
Unload frmGetTemplateFile
```

You will now add these statements to your project.

*To code the Select Outline File button in the*
`frmPresentationBuilder` *form:*

1. Open the **frmPresentationBuilder** form.

2. Double-click the **Select Outline File** button and maximize the Code window.

3. In the `cmdSelectOutline_Click` event procedure, click in the blank line below the comment and then type the following code:

```
frmGetOutlineFile.Show
strOutlineFileName = frmGetOutlineFile.strOutlineFile
Unload frmGetOutlineFile
```

4. Compare your code with Figure 7-13. Correct any errors.

| Figure 7-13 | NEW CODE ADDED TO FRMPRESENTATIONBUILDER |
|---|---|

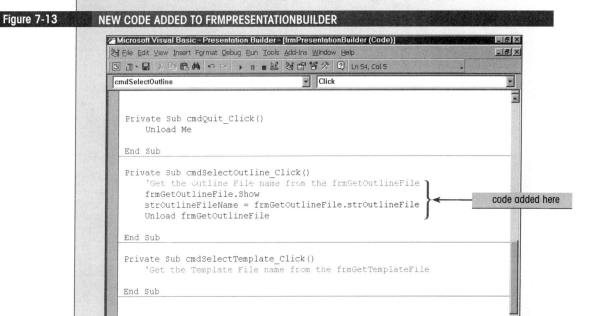

5. Save your work and close the Code window.

You have finished writing the code for the Select Outline File button. Now you can write similar code for the Select Template File button.

*To code the Select Template File button in the*
`frmPresentationBuilder` *form:*

1. In the `frmPresentationBuilder` form, double-click the **Select Template File** button. The code window reopens, this time with the cursor positioned in the `Click` event procedure for the Select Template File button (that is, the `cmdSelectTemplate` button). You could have simply moved the cursor down to this procedure at the end of the last set of steps. Instead, you reopened the Code window by double-clicking the Select Template File button in order to help you keep track of where you are in the project at this point.

**2.** Click below the comment in the `cmdSelectTemplate_Click` event procedure.

**3.** Type the following code.

```
frmGetTemplateFile.Show
strTemplateFileName = frmGetTemplateFile.strTemplateFile
Unload frmGetTemplateFile
```

**4.** Compare your code with Figure 7-14. Check your work carefully for accuracy.

Figure 7-14 — CODED ADDED FROM THE CMDSELECTTEMPLATE COMMAND BUTTON

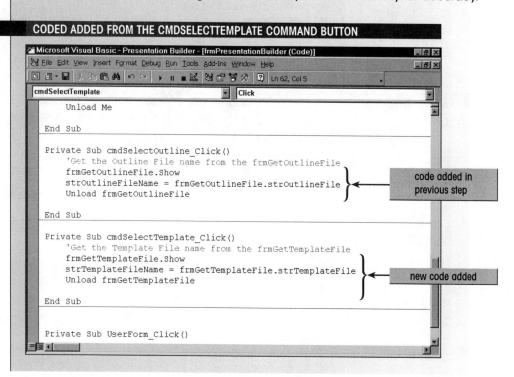

You have finished most of the code for the two buttons. All that remains is to declare the private variables for the module.

## To declare the private variables in the frmPresentationBuilder form module:

**1.** Click the **Object** list arrow at the top left corner of the Code window, and then click **(General)**. The cursor moves to the top of the module, immediately to the left of the `Option Explicit` statement. You also see a comment indicating that you need to declare variables for this module. (Later in this tutorial, you will learn the meaning of the word "General" in the Object list box.)

**2.** Click at the end of the comment, and then press **Enter** to insert a blank line.

**3.** Type the following declarations below the comment:

```
Dim strOutlineFileName As String
Dim strTemplateFileName As String
```

**4.** Compare your Code window with Figure 7-15. Correct any errors.

**Figure 7-15**          **DECLARATION ADDED TO CODE WINDOW**

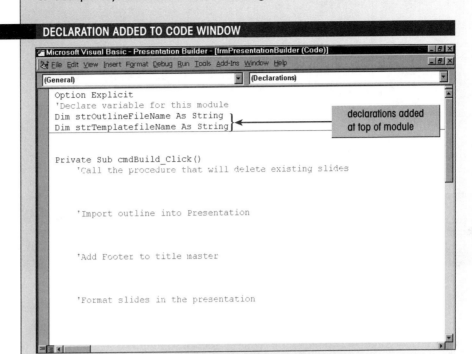

Finally, you are ready to test the new code.

## To test the new code:

**1.** Save your work and run the program.

**2.** Click the **Select Outline File** button on the form. The Select Outline File form appears.

**3.** Click **Outline** (the name of the sample Word outline you previewed earlier), and click **OK**.

**4.** Click the **Select Template File** button the form. The Select Template File form appears.

**5.** Click any template in the list and then click **OK**.

**6.** Click the **Quit** button on the form.

At this point, your project doesn't do anything except allow the user to choose the outline file and the template file. Therefore, you can't yet see any results from running your project. But even though you can't see the results of your work, the simple fact that the project runs without errors tells you that you have, most likely, coded it correctly so far.

You should make a practice of completing a small part of a project and then testing that part. Depending on where you are in the project, you may or may not see results. But if the project runs without errors, at least you know you have probably not made any typing errors or errors in syntax.

## Session 7.1 QUICK | CHECK

1. A variable declared as _____ can be used by other modules in the application.

2. Suppose that the form `frmGetNumber` declares a public variable `intNumber`. Write the statements that will display the form, and then place the value stored in its public variable in a variable `intNumberEmployees`.

3. You use the _____ statement to remove a form from the screen.

4. The _____ statement creates a private variable.

---

## SESSION 7.2

In this session you will learn about the PowerPoint object model. You will also write code that will delete and insert slides. In addition, you will create and call a general procedure. Finally, you will write code that will add a footer to the title master, apply a layout, and apply a template.

---

## Working with the PowerPoint Object Model

Tasks 1 through 3 of your project plan are now complete. Now, Gene asks you to turn your attention to Task 4, building the presentation. In other words, you need to code the Build Presentation button in the `frmPresentationBuilder` form. To refresh your memory, all of Task 4 is listed below:

Task 4: Allow the user to complete the third step, actually creating the presentation

- Delete any existing slides
- Create the presentation from the Word document
- Format the slides
- Apply the specified template to the presentation

Before you can work on Task 4, you need to learn something about the PowerPoint object model. Figure 7-16 provides an abbreviated view of the PowerPoint object model. You will need to use portions of this model to complete the Presentation Builder application. Spend some time reviewing the object model. Remember that the rectangles with shadows are collections and those without shadows are objects.

| Figure 7-16 | HIGH-LEVEL POWERPOINT OBJECT MODEL |

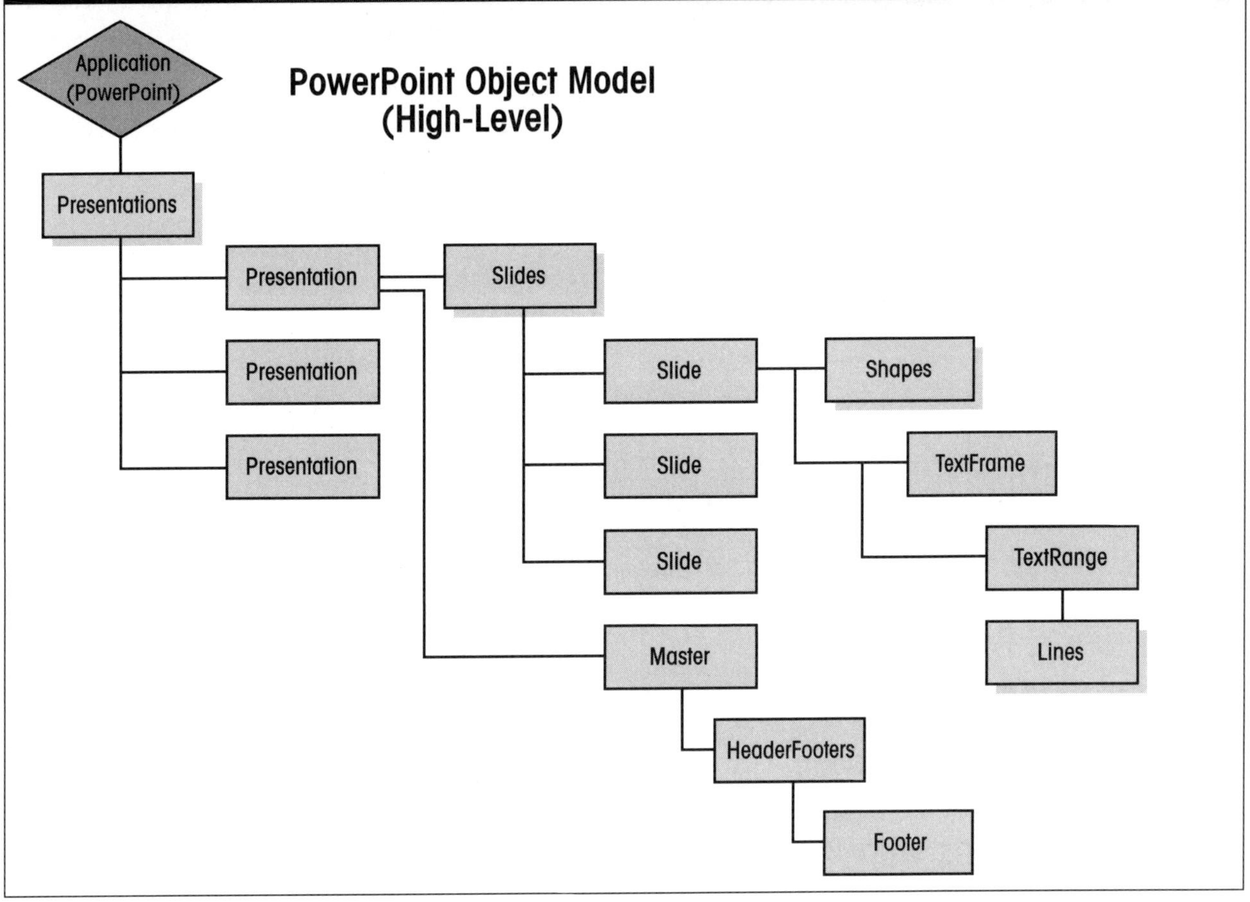

At the top of the object model is the application. In this case, "application" refers to PowerPoint itself. Below this level, is the **Presentations collection**, which consists of all open presentations. (As you know, you can have multiple presentations open at any given time.) The **Slides collection** is, as you might expect, the collection of all slides in the presentation. Other portions of the object model will be explained throughout the remainder of this tutorial.

### Referring to the Active Presentation with the ActivePresentation Property

One of the most widely used properties of the PowerPoint application object is the ActivePresentation property. The **ActivePresentation property** refers to the presentation currently open in the active window (i.e., the presentation that has focus). Anytime you want your code to refer to the presentation you are currently working on, you can use the ActivePresentation property. You will see several references to the ActivePresentation property in the following sections.

### Referring to Specific Slides in the Slides Collection

The next level in the object model hierarchy is the Slides collection. You refer to a specific slide in the Slides collection by typing the name of the Slides collection (that is, `slides`), followed by the slide's index number in parentheses. The **index number** is the number of the slide within the Slides collection. The first slide would have an index of 1, the second slide would have an index of 2, and so on. For example, the first slide would be `slides(1)`, the second slide would be `slides(2)`, and so on.

In addition to being able to refer to specific slides in your code, you need a way to determine how many slides are currently in the Slides collection. (You'll need this information in order to control the For...Next loop that will format the slides in the presentation. You'll learn more about this For...Next loop later.) To determine the number of slides in the Slides collection, you can use the **Count property** of the slides collection; its value is always the number of slides currently in the Slides collection. To refer to the current number of slides in the active presentation, you would use the following reference:

```
ActivePresentation.Slides.Count
```

Using this reference, you could write a For...Next loop that would iterate through the slides from the first slide to the last slide (the last slide being represented by the count property). The first part of this loop would look like this:

```
For intSlideCounter = 1 to ActivePresentation.Slides.Count
    ActivePresentation.Slides(intSlideCounter)…

    'Additional statements here
```

Recall that a For...Next loop will increment the control variable (`intSlideCounter`) from the start value (1) to the end value (`ActivePresentation.Slides.Count`). For example, if there were currently 10 slides in the Slides collection, the loop would be repeated 10 times. The first time through the loop, the value of `intSlidecounter` would be 1. Therefore, the statement inside the loop would be referring to the first slide in the Slides collection. The second time through the loop, the value of `intSlideCounter` would be 2. Therefore, the statement in the loop would be referring to the second slide in the Slides collection, and so on. Of course, you could add other statements to the loop that perform some additional tasks, such as formatting each slide, or inserting text into each slide.

## Deleting Slides with the Delete Method

You are now ready to start work on Task 4 in your project plan, actually building the presentation. The first subtask in this plan is deleting any existing slides in the active presentation. It's important to delete all existing slides each time the user clicks the Build Presentation button. That way, if the user runs the Presentation Builder program twice in a row, you can be certain that the first set of slides created by the first use of the Presentation Builder program will be deleted before the second set is created.

To accomplish this, you can use the Delete method of the slides collection. The **Delete method** will delete a specific slide. The following statement would delete the third slide in the Slides collection of the active presentation.

```
ActivePresentation.Slides(3).Delete
```

In the Presentation Builder application, you will delete all of the slides one by one, with a For...Next loop. Each time the loop is repeated, the first slide in the slides collection will be deleted. Of course, once you delete the first slide, the next slide then becomes the first slide. In this way, the loop will ultimately delete all the slides. After your work with For...Next loops in Tutorial 4, the code for this loop should be easy to interpret:

```
Dim intSlideCounter as Integer
'Remove existing slides
With ActivePresentation
    For intSlideCounter = 1 To .Slides.Count
        .Slides(1).Delete
    Next
End With
```

By way of reminder, this segment of code could have been written without the **With** statement. If you elected to do this, the code would look like this:

```
For intSlideCounter = 1 To ActivePresentation.Slides.Count
      ActivePresentation.Slides(1).Delete
Next
```

As you can see, without the **With** statement, you would have to refer to **ActivePresentation** at each point it is required in the code.

You want this code to execute whenever the user clicks the Build Presentation button in the **frmBuildPresentation** form. You might expect, therefore, that you would write this code in the Click event procedure for the Build Presentation button. In the next section, however, you will learn about an alternative to an event procedure—a general procedure.

# Creating a General Procedure

So far, you have entered all your code in event procedures because your code was associated with particular events—usually a click of a button. In this case, however, you will write the code that deletes all existing slides in a general procedure. A **general procedure** is a procedure that is not associated with a particular object's event. They are useful when you want to group related statements into smaller units that are easier to read and edit.

You could put all the code related to building the presentation into the Click event procedure for the Build Presentation button, but the resulting procedure would be quite lengthy. Instead, you will place some of the code for the Build Presentation button in general procedures. This will help divide the code into smaller units that you can handle more easily. For starters, you will write the several statements involved in the task of clearing the presentation of existing slides as one general procedure. To add a general procedure to a module, you use the Procedure command on the Insert menu.

At this point, you might wonder what triggers the code in a general procedure. After all, you know that a particular event triggers the code in an event procedure. For example, a mouse click makes the code in a Click event procedure execute. How then, can you make the code in a general procedure execute? You do this by inserting a **Call** statement. This statement is explained later in this tutorial.

You are now ready to add a general procedure to the project.

*To insert a general procedure:*

1. Double-click anywhere on the **frmPresentationBuilder** form to open its Code window.

2. Click **Insert** on the menu bar and then click **Procedure** on the drop-down menu. The Add Procedure dialog box opens, as shown in Figure 7-17.

| Figure 7-17 | THE ADD PROCEDURE DIALOG BOX |

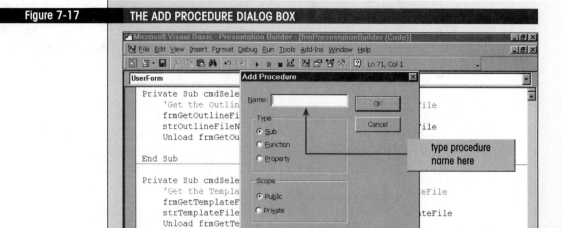

**3.** In the Procedure Name box type **ClearPresentation**, and then click **OK**. (Do not include a space between "Clear" and "Presentation.") The Add Procedure dialog box closes, and a `Public Sub ClearPresentation()` statement is inserted into the Code window, followed by an `End Sub` statement, as shown in Figure 7-18. Note that (General) is displayed in the Object list box, and the name of the procedure (`ClearPresentation`) is displayed in the Procedure list box.

When working with event procedures, you normally see the name of an object (such as a command button or a text box) in the Object box. In the Procedure box, you normally see the name of some event procedure (such as `Click`). However, because a general procedure is not associated with a specific object or event, you see only the name of the procedure itself in the Procedure box and (General) in the Object box. In the next few steps, you will examine the Procedure list box for a general procedure.

| Figure 7-18 | CODE WINDOW WITH NEW PROCEDURE ADDED |
| --- | --- |

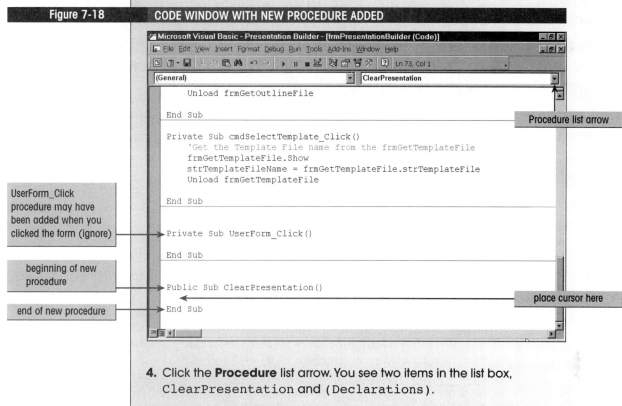

4. Click the **Procedure** list arrow. You see two items in the list box, `ClearPresentation` and `(Declarations)`.

5. Click `(Declarations)`. The cursor moves to the variable declarations portion of the form's Code module. You declared these variables earlier in this tutorial.

6. Click the **Procedure** list arrow again, and then click **ClearPresentation**. The cursor returns to the general procedure named `ClearPresentation`.

7. Verify that your cursor is positioned between the `Public Sub` and `End Sub` statements in the `ClearPresentation` procedure, just as in Figure 7-18, above.

Now that you have created the new general procedure, you need to add the code to the procedure.

## Coding a General Procedure

You are now ready to enter the code that will delete any existing slides in the active presentation.

### To code the general procedure:

1. Type the following code in the procedure:

```
Dim intSlideCounter As Integer

'Remove existing slides

With ActivePresentation
    For intSlideCounter = 1 To .Slides.Count
        .Slides(1).Delete
    Next
End With
```

**2.** Compare your code with Figure 7-19 and make any necessary corrections.

| Figure 7-19 | THE CLEARPRESENTATION PROCEDURE WITH CODE ADDED |
|---|---|

new code added here

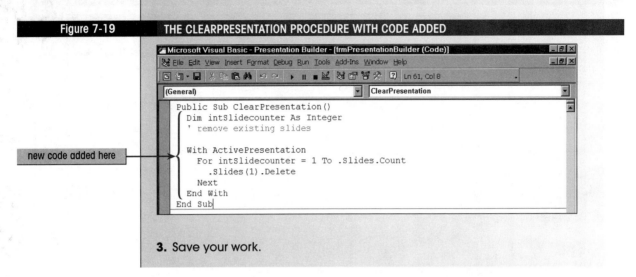

```
Public Sub ClearPresentation()
  Dim intSlidecounter As Integer
  ' remove existing slides

  With ActivePresentation
    For intSlidecounter = 1 To .Slides.Count
      .Slides(1).Delete
    Next
  End With
End Sub
```

**3.** Save your work.

In these steps, you created a general procedure that will delete any slides currently in the presentation. Now, you need to think about what in the program will make this code execute. If you had placed this code in an event procedure (such as a Click event procedure), then the associated event (such as a click) would trigger the code. However, a general procedure cannot respond to an event. Instead, a general procedure must be called into action, or invoked, by some other statement in the program. You invoke a procedure by using the `Call` statement.

## Calling a Procedure

The **Call statement** simply transfers control to the procedure specified in the `Call` statement. If you wanted to transfer control to the `ClearPresentation` procedure, you would use the `Call` statement as follows:

```
Call ClearPresentation
```

Figure 7-20 illustrates the flow of control that results from a `Call` statement. In this figure, the **cmdBuild_Click** procedure is "calling" the `ClearPresentation` procedure. In this figure, the screen has been split so that you can see both the `Call` statement and the procedure itself. Notice the flow of control in the figure. First, the call is made to the `ClearPresentation` procedure. Second, the procedure is invoked. Third, the statements in the `ClearPresentation` procedure are completed. Fourth, the control returns to whatever statement follows the call to the `ClearPresentation` procedure.

| Figure 7-20 | FLOW OF CONTROL WHEN A PROCEDURE IS CALLED |
|---|---|

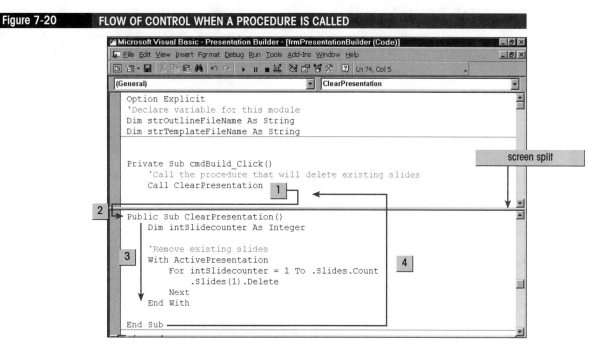

Since clearing (deleting) the slides from the presentation is the first step in the Build Presentation task, the statement to call the ClearPresentation procedure will be the first statement in the cmdBuild_Click event procedure (that is, in the code for the Build Presentation button in the frmPresentationBuilder form).

You are now ready to add the Call statement to your procedure.

### *To add the statement that will invoke the* ClearPresentation *procedure:*

**1.** Scroll up to the top of the Code window, just below the variable declarations.

**2.** Click in the cmdBuild_Click procedure directly below the following comment: "Call the procedure that will delete existing slides."

**3.** Type the following:

```
Call ClearPresentation
```

**4.** Compare your code with Figure 7-21 and make any necessary corrections.

Figure 7-21 | THE CMDBUILD_CLICK EVENT PROCEDURE WITH CALL STATEMENT ADDED

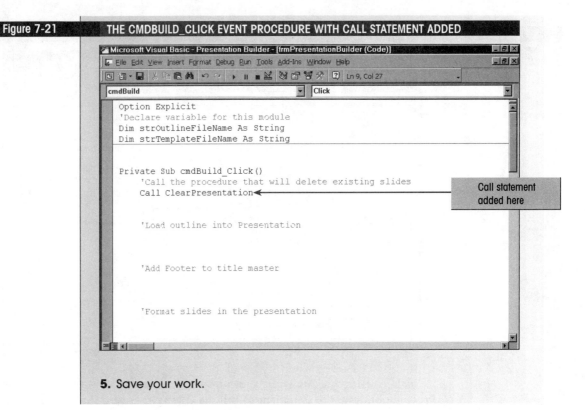

**5.** Save your work.

You can now test the `ClearPresentation` procedure (which deletes any existing slides) as well as the `Call` statement that invokes the `ClearPresentation` procedure. In order to verify that the `ClearPresentation` procedure does indeed delete any existing slides, you will first add some slides to the presentation. You will then run the program and observe that it successfully deletes any existing slides.

### To test the `ClearPresentation` procedure:

**1.** Switch to the PowerPoint window.

**2.** Click **Insert** on the menu bar, click slide **New Slide,** click any layout, and then click **OK**.

**3.** Add three more slides. The presentation now contains four slides.

**4.** Switch to the VBA IDE.

**5.** Position the cursor anywhere in the `frmPresentationBuilder` procedure in the code module.

**6.** Run the program, click the **Select Outline File** button, select **Outline** in the file list, and then click **OK**. You won't test the Select Template File button, because you haven't yet written the code that will apply a template. You may recall from your previous work with PowerPoint that if you don't select a template, a default template will be applied.

**7.** Click the **Build Presentation** button on the form. All the slides you inserted earlier are deleted from the PowerPoint window.

**8.** Click the **Quit** button on the form. You return to the VBA IDE.

At this point, the Presentation Builder application allows the user to select a Word document to use as the basis for the application, allows the user to select a template file, and then clears the current presentation of any slides. Next, you need to write the code that will build the presentation from the Word document selected by the user.

## Inserting Slides in a Presentation with the InsertFromFile Method

To create a new presentation from a Word file, you need to write code that incorporates the InsertFromFile method. The **InsertFromFile** method is a method of the Slides collection that inserts slides from a previously saved file into a presentation. The file must be a file that can be converted to slides. In your project, you are using a Word outline file that easily converts to a PowerPoint presentation. You could also use the InsertFromFile method to import a PowerPoint presentation into your current presentation. In your project, you will use the InsertFromFile method to insert one new slide for each main point in the Word outline file. The code you write will insert slides at the beginning of the active presentation. However, you could use this method to insert slides anywhere within an existing presentation.

| | |
|---|---|
| **Syntax** | `expression.InsertFromFile(FileName, Index, [ SlideStart, SlideEnd])` |
| **Explanation** | The first part of the syntax, `expression`, is the Slides collection you want to import the file into. As you probably guessed, `FileName` is the name of the file that contains the text you want to insert as new slides in the presentation. In many cases, the filename will have already been stored in the program as a variable, in which case you need to use the variable name in the `FileName` argument, as follows: `FileName:=variable`. `Index` specifies the slide after which you want to begin inserting new slides. `SlideStart` and `SlideEnd` are optional and are beyond the scope of this tutorial. |
| **Example** | `ActivePresentation.Slides.InsertFromFile _`<br>`        FileName:=strOutlineFileName, Index:= 0` |

In the example, new slides are created from the file whose name is stored in the variable `strOutlineFileName`. Alternately, you could actually place the name of a file in the statement, like this:

```
ActivePresentation.Slides.InsertFromFile _
        FileName:="c:/My Files/My Outline.ppt", Index:= 0
```

However, this makes the statement very static, meaning that VBA will *always* insert this file; your program will be more flexible if you allow the user to choose a file.

The new slides will be placed in `ActivePresentation`, at the beginning of the presentation (that is, after slide 0). In the Presentation Builder project, you need to insert slides after slide 0, or at the beginning of the presentation. (If, for some reason, you wanted to insert new slides after, say, the third slide, you would set `Index` to 3.) You should recognize the underscore character at the end of the first line of the example as a continuation character.

You will now add the statement that will insert the Word outline into the presentation. Each main point in the outline will make up one slide in the presentation. Since this task can be accomplished with just one statement, you will not place it in a general procedure. Rather, you will add the statement to the `cmdBuild_Click` procedure, along with an explanatory comment.

## To add the statement to insert slides from the outline file:

1. Place the cursor in the cmdBuild_Click procedure, just after the following comment: "Import outline into Presentation."

2. Type the following, taking care to type a space before the continuation character (that is, the underscore):

```
ActivePresentation.Slides.InsertFromFile _
        FileName:=strOutlineFileName, Index:=0
```

3. Compare your code with Figure 7-22 and make any necessary changes.

| Figure 7-22 | THE CMDBUILD_CLICK EVENT PROCEDURE WITH NEW STATEMENT ADDED |
|---|---|

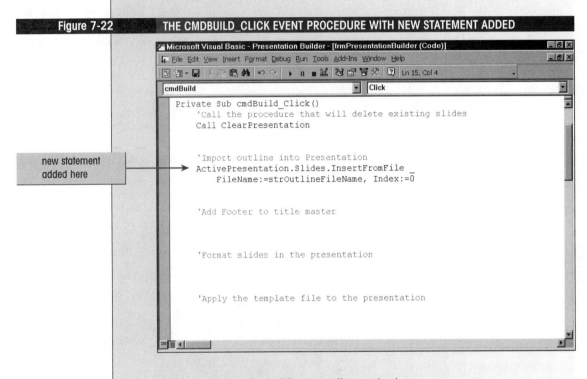

new statement added here

4. Save your work and then run the project.

5. Use the **Select Outline File** button to select an outline file.

6. Use the **Select Template File** button to select a template.

7. Click the **Build Presentation** button on the form.

8. Click the **Quit** button on the form.

9. Switch to the PowerPoint window and notice that the slides have been added to your presentation as shown in Figure 7-23. Notice that the presentation contains one slide for each main point in the outline. Also notice that a default template has been applied to the presentation. You will change this later.

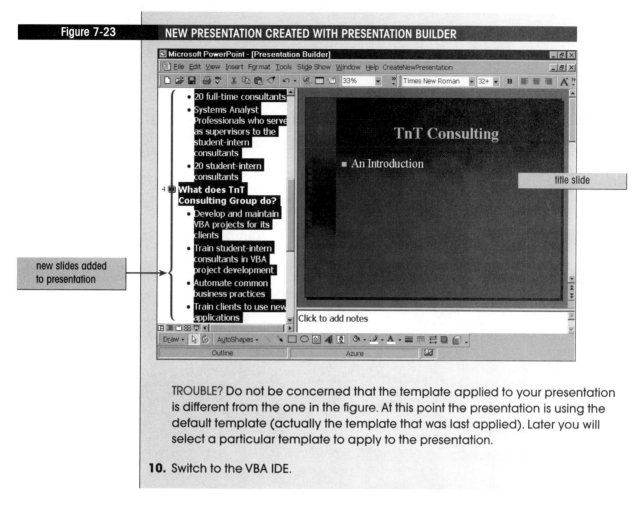

Figure 7-23    NEW PRESENTATION CREATED WITH PRESENTATION BUILDER

TROUBLE? Do not be concerned that the template applied to your presentation is different from the one in the figure. At this point the presentation is using the default template (actually the template that was last applied). Later you will select a particular template to apply to the presentation.

**10.** Switch to the VBA IDE.

So far, the project builds the body of the presentation. When you demonstrate the project for Gene, he suggests that you add "TnT Consulting" as a footer on each slide.

# Adding a Footer to the Title Master

As you probably know from your experience with PowerPoint, each presentation is associated with a **title master**, which maintains such things as the presentation's header and footer, as well as other elements common to all slides in a presentation. To insert a footer onto each of the slides in a presentation, you actually insert the footer text into the title master; the title master then ensures that the footer is displayed on the bottom of each slide.

The title master is an object within the PowerPoint object model. One collection of the title master is the **HeadersFooters** collection, which contains all headers and footers associated with the title master.  To insert the text "TnT Consulting Group" into the `HeadersFooters` collection, you would use the following statement:.

```
ActivePresentation.TitleMaster.HeadersFooters.Footer.Text = "TnT Consulting Group"
```

You will add this statement just below the statement that created the presentation from the outline file.

## To add the footer to the title master

1. Position your cursor in the cmdBuild_Click event procedure, just below the following comment: "Add Footer to title master."

2. Type the following code:

```
ActivePresentation.TitleMaster.HeadersFooters.Footer.Text = _
    "TnT Consulting Group"
```

3. Save your work and run the program. Once again, select an outline file and then click the **Build Presentation** button on the form.

4. Click the **Quit** button on the form. You return to the VBA IDE.

5. Switch to the PowerPoint window. Your presentation has been rebuilt. This time, it includes the footer indicated in Figure 7-24.

| Figure 7-24 | POWERPOINT SLIDES WITH FOOTER ADDED TO TO THE SLIDES |
| --- | --- |

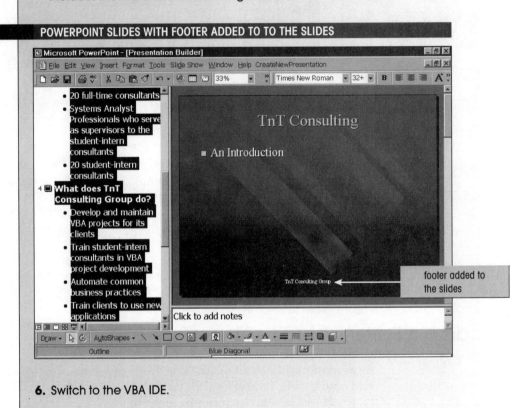

6. Switch to the VBA IDE.

Take a moment to review what you have accomplished so far. At this stage, the Presentation Builder allows the user to select an outline file and a template file. However, the project does not yet apply the template to the presentation.

The project also deletes all preexisting slides, builds the presentation from a Word outline, and, finally, adds a footer to the presentation. Your next task is to write the code that formats the slides by applying one of several predefined layouts. Then you will write the code that applies the template selected by the user.

# Applying a Layout with the Layout Property

As you know from your work with PowerPoint, slides can be formatted using a variety of different layouts. You can select a layout for a slide in the New Slide dialog box (shown earlier in Figure 7-3) or you can apply a template after you have finished creating a slide. The Presentation Builder application you are developing creates one slide for each major point in the outline selected by the user. By default, all of the slides in the presentation have the Bulleted List format, which includes a heading and a bulleted list. This is the second layout in the New Slide dialog box, as shown in Figure 7-25.

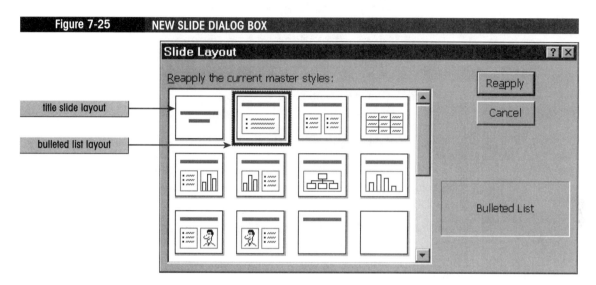

Figure 7-25    NEW SLIDE DIALOG BOX

This default layout is fine for most of the slides in the presentation, but Gene wants the first slide in the presentation to be formatted as a title slide. In other words, it should be formatted using the Title Slide format, which is the first option in the New Slide dialog box, as shown in Figure 7-25.

Within a VBA program, you can specify a layout for a slide using the **Layout property** of the Slides collection. You can choose from numerous possible values for the Layout property, each of which will result in a different slide format. In the Presentation Builder application, however, you only need to use the following values for the Layout property: **ppLayoutTitle** (Title Slide Layout) and the **ppLayoutText** (Bulleted List Layout). For example, the following statement would set the third slide to the **ppLayoutText** layout.

```
ActivePresentation.Slides(3).Layout = ppLayoutText
```

You will now write a general procedure that will apply the appropriate layouts to the slides in the presentation. First, you will use a `With` statement to indicate that all the layout statements should apply to the active presentation. Then your code will apply the **ppLayoutTitle** property value to the first slide in the Slides collection. Finally, you will use a For...Next loop to iterate through the remainder of the slides, assigning the property value **ppLayoutText** to each of them. (In order for this loop to work, you will need to declare a counter variable.) You will also need to call this procedure from the cmdBuild_Click procedure. The following code will format the slides with the right layouts:

```
Dim intSlidecounter As Integer

With ActivePresentation
    ' Set the format of the title slide
    .Slides(1).Layout = ppLayoutTitle

    ' Set the format of the body slides
    For intSlidecounter = 2 To .Slides.Count
        .Slides(intSlidecounter).Layout = ppLayoutText
    Next
End With
```

You are now ready to enter this code into your project.

### To create and call the FormatSlides procedure:

1. Click anywhere in the Code window.

2. Click **Insert** on the menu bar and then click **Procedure**. The Add Procedure dialog box opens.

3. In the Name text box, type **FormatSlides** (do not add a blank between format and slides) and then click **OK**.

4. Within the procedure type the following code:

```
Dim intSlidecounter As Integer

With ActivePresentation
    ' Set the format of the title slide
    .Slides(1).Layout = ppLayoutTitle

    ' Set the format of the body slides
    For intSlidecounter = 2 To .Slides.Count
        .Slides(intSlidecounter).Layout = ppLayoutText
    Next
End With
```

5. Compare your procedure with Figure 7-26 and make any necessary changes.

| Figure 7-26 | CODE WINDOW SHOWING THE FORMATSLIDES PROCEDURE |
| --- | --- |

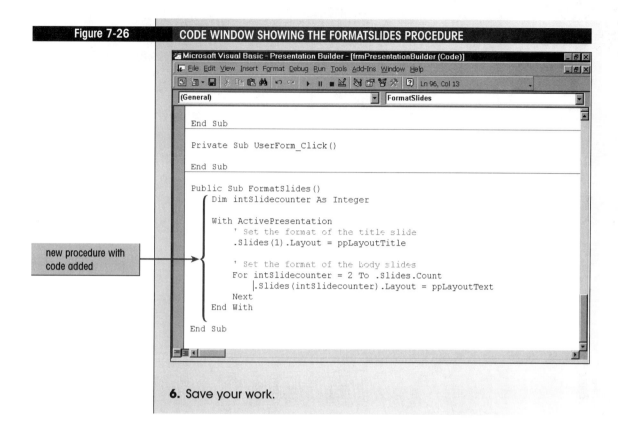

new procedure with
code added

**6.** Save your work.

As you recall, the `FormatSlides` procedure is a general procedure—not an event procedure. Thus, to make the code execute when the program is run, you must include a `Call` statement within an event procedure. You'll do that now.

---

### To add a statement that will call the `FormatSlides` procedure:

**1.** Click in the `cmdBuild_Click` procedure, and just below the following comment: "Format slides in the presentation."

**2.** Type the following statement:

```
Call FormatSlides
```

**3.** Compare your procedure with Figure 7-27 and make any necessary changes.

Figure 7-27    THE CMDBUILD_CLICK EVENT PROCEDURE WITH NEW STATEMENT ADDED

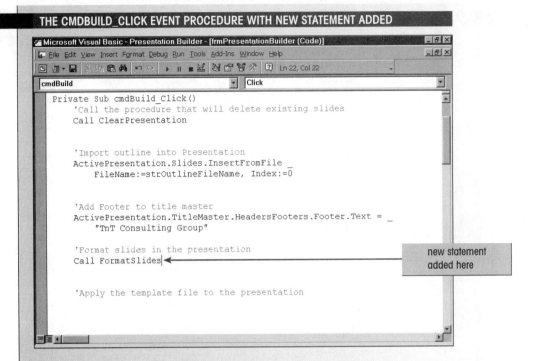

4. Save your work and run the program.

5. Again choose the **Outline** file, and then click the **Build Presentation** button on the form.

6. Click the **Quit** button on the form.

7. Switch to the PowerPoint window. Notice that the first slide has been formatted in the Title Slide format, as shown in Figure 7-28. The main difference between this version of the title slide and those you saw earlier, is that the subtitle ("An Introduction") is no longer formatted as a bullet. Instead, it is centered below the title ("TnT Consulting").

Figure 7-28    FIRST SLIDE OF PRESENTATION IN TITLE LAYOUT

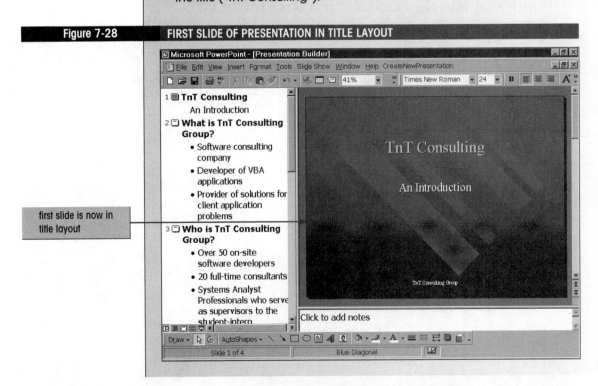

**8.** Switch to the VBA IDE.

Gene stops by to review your work so far. He is pleased to see that the application now formats the first slide as a title slide, and the remaining slides as text slides. Your next job, he says, is to write the code that will apply a template to the presentation.

# Applying a Template with the ApplyTemplate Method

You know from your experience with PowerPoint that you can make a presentation more stylish by applying any one of a wide variety of templates. A template can make a presentation more attractive and, at the same time, ensure uniformity among the slides.

Recall that Frank has already written the code for the `frmGetTemplateFile` form, which allows the user to select a template, and then stores the name of the selected template in a public variable. And you have already coded the Select Template File button (in the `frmBuildPresentation` form) to display the `frmGetTemplateFile` form and then store the value of the global, or public, variable (containing the name of the selected template) in a private variable (named `strTemplateFileName`). Now you need to write the code that actually takes the template specified in the `strTemplateFileName` variable and applies it to the active presentation.

To do this, you need to use the **ApplyTemplate method**, which is a method of the active presentation. Its syntax is explained below:

| Syntax | `expression.ApplyTemplate(FileName)` |
|---|---|
| **Explanation** | The ApplyTemplate method applies the template specified in the `FileName` argument to the active presentation. The `expression` must be a presentation, such as `ActivePresentation`. The `FileName` must be the name of a template file. |
| **Example** | `ActivePresentation.ApplyTemplate strTemplateFileName` |

In this example, the variable `strTemplateFileName` contains the name of the template to apply to `ActivePresentation`.  Recall that you have already added the code that displays the `frmGetTemplateFile` form and retrieves the name of the template file from a global variable named `strTemplateFileName`. Since you already have the filename in the variable, all you have to do now is apply the template to the presentation. The statement that will apply the template is placed within an `If` statement that checks to see if the filename is empty. Using an `If` statement in this way ensures that, if the user neglects to select a template, the program will not fail. When the user neglects to select a template, the program will simply not apply a template. The complete code is as follows:

```
If strTemplateFileName <> "" Then
   ActivePresentation.ApplyTemplate strTemplateFileName
End If
```

You will now add these statements to the project:

### To add the code that applies a template to the active presentation:

1. Place the cursor in the cmdBuild_Click event procedure, just below the following comment: "Apply the template file to the presentation."

2. Type the following:

```
If strTemplateFileName <> "" Then
   ActivePresentation.ApplyTemplate strTemplateFileName
End If
```

3. Save your work and run the program.

4. Click the **Select Outline File** button on the form, select **Outline**, and then click **OK.**

5. Click the **Select Template File** button on the form, select **Azure** in the list, and then click **OK.**

   TROUBLE? If you do not have the Azure template, choose a template of your choice.

   TROUBLE? If you do not have any templates in the list at all, then the templates have not been properly installed on your computer. Check with your instructor about installing the template files. In the meantime, click OK and then continue with Step 6.

6. Click the **Build Presentation** button on the form.

7. Click the **Quit** button on the form.

8. Switch to the PowerPoint window. Observe that the Azure template has been applied to your presentation, as shown in Figure 7-29.

| Figure 7-29 | PRESENTATION WITH AZURE TEMPLATE APPLIED |

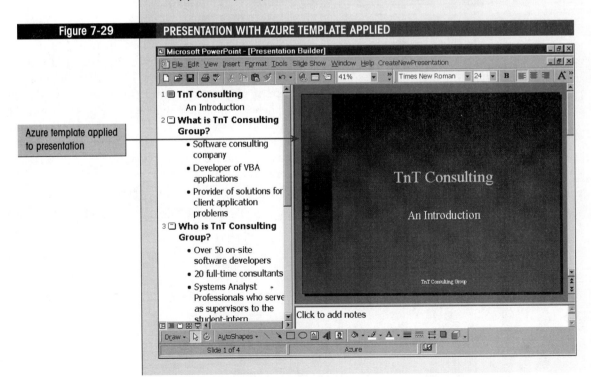

Azure template applied to presentation

**9.** Print the code for the `frmPresentationBuilder` form.

You have just about completed the entire application. Now Gene suggests adding a couple of enhancements to the presentation. He would like for you to add a feature that will allow the user to enter the name of the presenter. When the presenter's name has been obtained, it should be added to the title slide of the presentation. Also, Gene suggests that you add the current date to the title slide as well. Finally, Gene suggests that you increase the size of the title on the title slide and make it boldface. You'll learn how to make these changes in the next session.

## Session 7.2 QUICK CHECK

1. The top level of the PowerPoint object model (after the application level) is the _____ collection.

2. To refer to the third slide in a presentation you would use the reference _____.

3. Write the statement that would delete the fifth slide from the active presentation.

4. A(n) _____ procedure is a procedure that is not associated with any particular object.

5. The _____ method inserts slides from a previously saved file into a presentation.

6. Write the statement that will apply the `ppLayoutText` layout to the fourth slide in the active presentation.

7. The _____ property of the Slides collection will return the number of slides in the presentation.

## SESSION 7.3

In this session you will learn how to abbreviate references to objects in your code by using the `Set` statement. You will also learn how to use the InputBox function and the InsertDateTime method. Finally, you will learn how to work with the Shapes collection, and how to write code that will alter properties of the title slide.

## Abbreviating **Object References** with the **Set Statement**

Your final task is to write the code that will add the presenter's name and the current date to the title slide. Gene wants these items inserted into the title slide, which, because the title slide is the first slide, is referred to as `ActivePresentation.Slides(1)`. Rather than repeating this rather long reference throughout the code, you can assign this object reference to a variable in a `Set` statement. The **Set statement** assigns a reference to an object variable. In the syntax box on the next page, only the simplest form of the `Set` statement is represented. For a more complete view of the `Set` statement, look it up in VBA Help.

| Syntax | `Set objectvar = objectexpression`<br>(*Note*: some options for this statement have been left out for the sake of simplicity) |
|---|---|
| Explanation | The Set statement assigns an object reference to a variable or property.<br><br>`Objectvar` the (object variable) must be declared to be an object.<br><br>The `objectexpression` consists of the name of an object, another variable that is the same type as the **objectvar**, or a function or method that returns an object of the same object type as `objectvar`. |
| Example | `Dim sldTitle As Slide`<br><br>`Set sldTitle = ActivePresentation.Slides(1)` |

Once you assign an object reference to a variable, you can use the variable name, rather than the longer object reference, in your code. You will use the example above in the Presentation Builder project.

In the example, the first sentence declares the variable `sldTitle` as a slide type. This means that `sldTitle` is declared as a Slide object. Then you can assign `sldTitle` to a particular slide using the `Set` statement. In the example, once the `Set` statement has been executed, from that point on any reference to `sldTitle` will actually be a reference to `ActivePresentation.Slides(1)`.

## Obtaining **Data from the User with the InputBox Function**

Now you are ready to think about writing the code that will add the presenter's name to the title slide. In order to obtain the name of the presenter from the user, you can use the **InputBox** function, which displays a small default-style form. You actually used the InputBox function in Tutorial 1 to create a form in which you could enter your name. Its complete syntax is explained below.

| Syntax | `InputBox(prompt[, title] [, default] [, xpos] [, ypos]`<br>`[, helpfile, context])` |
|---|---|
| Explanation | The InputBox function displays a small form that prompts the user to enter a single item of data in a text box. When the user clicks the OK button, the string entered by the user is returned by the function. You can incorporate the InputBox function into an assignment statement that assigns the string entered by the user to a variable . The only required argument is the prompt, which consists of the directions you want displayed in the input box (such as "Type your name here"). The remainder of the arguments are beyond the scope of this text. |
| Example | `strPresenter = InputBox("Enter Presenter Name: ")` |

The example above will display a form containing the prompt "Enter Presenter Name:". When the user enters a value and clicks OK, the value entered will be stored in the variable `strPresenter`.

VBA provides the InputBox function to make it easy for the developer to obtain a single item of data from the user. If you needed to get more than one item of data, you would probably develop a form instead of using the Inputbox function. Now that you know how to get the presenter's name from the user, you need to learn how to obtain the current date from the computer's system clock.

# Obtaining the Current Date with the InsertDateTime Method

To insert the date into the title slide, you need to use the InsertDateTime method, which is a method of the TextRange object. The **InsertDateTime method** inserts the system date (the current date set on your computer) in a specified format. You can also use it to insert the current date. Its basic syntax is as follows:

```
InsertDateTime format
```

When you actually type the statement in the Code window, you will see the many date and time formats available with this method. Figure 7-30 lists just a few of those formats. For additional formats see VBA Help.

| Figure 7-30 | DATE AND TIME FORMATS AVAILABLE WITH THE INSERTDATETIME METHOD |

| FORMAT: | RESULTS IF THE DATE AND TIME WERE JANUARY 15, 2003 AT 10:45 A.M.: |
| --- | --- |
| ppDateTimedddMMMMddyyyy | Monday, January 15, 2003 |
| ppDateTimedMMMMyyyy | 15 January 2003 |
| PpDateTimeHmm | 10:45 |
| ppDateTimehmmAMPM | 10:45 AM |
| ppDateTimeMMMMdyyyy | January 15, 2003 |
| ppDateTimeMMddyyHmm | 1/15/03 10:45 AM |
| ppDateTimeMMyy | Jan-15 |

In order to insert the current date in the Presentation Builder project, you will use the following code:

```
InsertDateTime ppDateTimeMMMMdyyyy
```

At this point, you should understand how your program will obtain the name of the presenter from the user, and how it will obtain the current date. The part of the code that actually inserts the date and name is fairly simple. However, the part of the code that specifies *where* the date and name should be inserted in a slide requires more explanation. To understand how it works, you need to learn about an important part of the PowerPoint object model, the Shapes collection.

# Working with the Shapes Collection

Figure 7-31 illustrates the PowerPoint object model once again. Notice that within this model, each slide has a Shapes collection. The **Shapes collection** consists of all *Shape objects* on a particular slide. A **Shape object** is an object on the drawing layer of a slide, such as a rectangle, an Autoshape, a picture, etc. When programming in PowerPoint, the Shapes collection is very important because every part of a slide is contained within a shape.

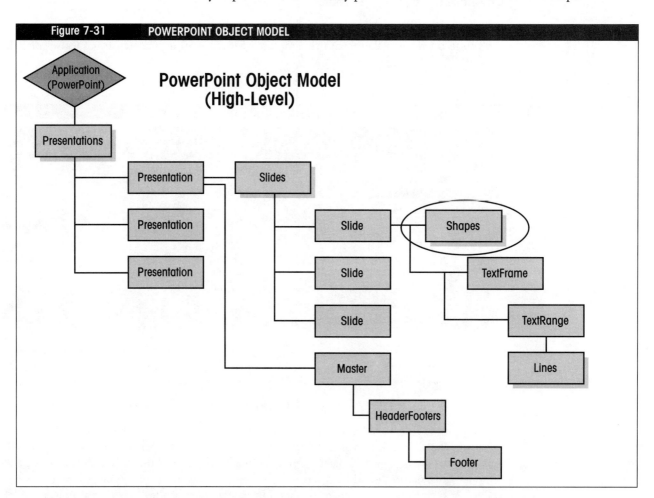

**Figure 7-31      POWERPOINT OBJECT MODEL**

Figure 7-32 illustrates a slide that contains three shapes. The names of the shapes reflect the order in which they were placed on the slide. You could also give each shape a name so that you could refer to a particular shape by its name rather than by its number. (You name shapes in the same manner that you name objects on a form.)

**Figure 7-32**    **EXAMPLE OF A SLIDE WITH SHAPES EMPHASIZED**

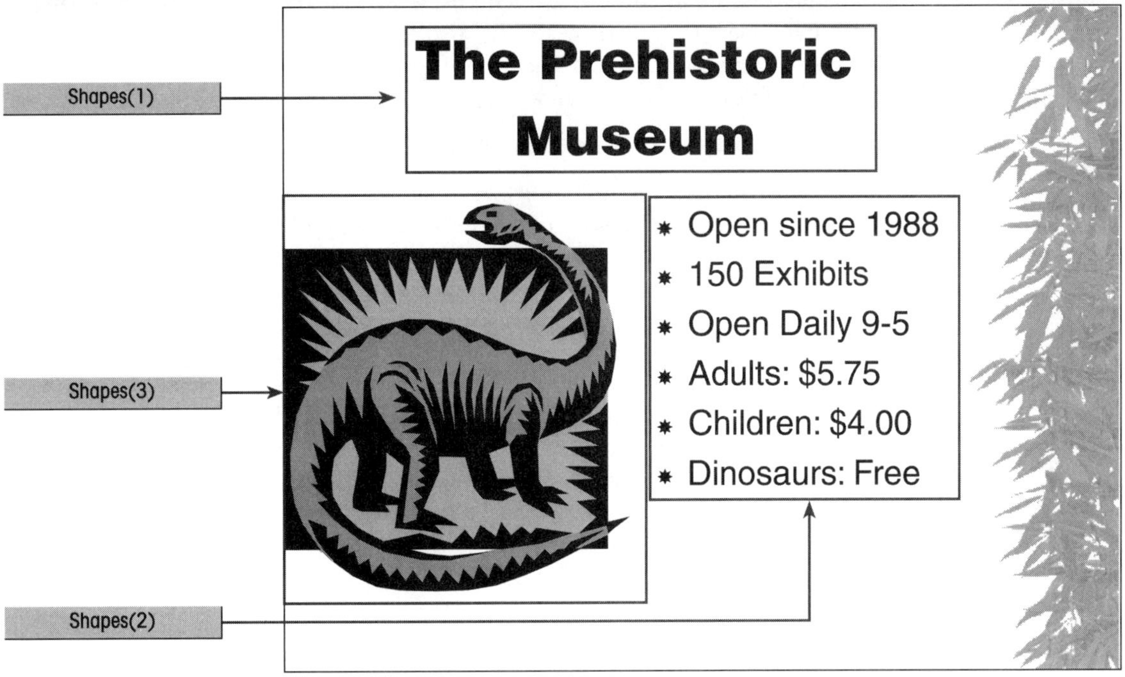

To refer to a particular line or piece of text within a presentation, you must first refer to the shape containing the text. Unless you assign names to your shapes, you must refer to shapes by index number—Shapes(1), Shapes(2), and so on. As you can see in Figure 7-33, the title slide has two shapes, the title and the subtitle. Within the title slide, Gene wants the presenter's name and the current date to be placed in the subtitle rectangle, or Shapes(2). Gene tells you that the index number of this shape is 2, so you would refer to it as Shapes(2).

**Figure 7-33**    **PRESENTATION TITLE SLIDE SHOWING SHAPES**

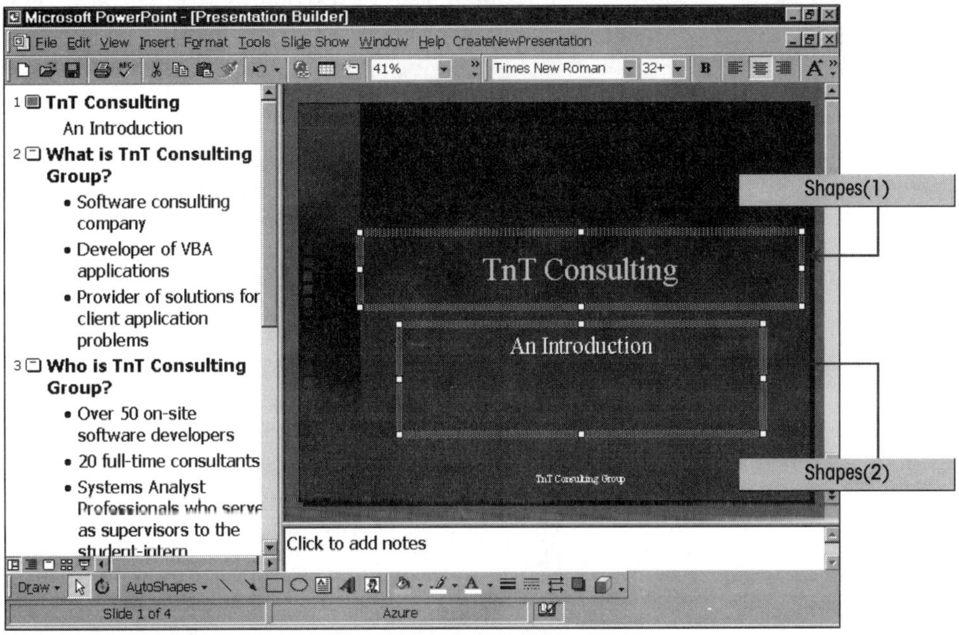

You refer to a specific piece of text within a shape by referring to the TextRange object. The **TextRange** object contains the text within a shape. Finally, you use the **Text property** of the TextRange object to actually access the text itself. The **TextFrame** object is the portion of a shape that can contain text. The following is a reference to the text in the first slide and second shape in the ActivePresentation.

```
ActivePresentation.Slides(1).Shapes(2).TextFrame.TextRange.Text
```

It is important to understand the object model pertaining to slides, shapes, and the TextRange object. Every slide has a collection of shapes, and all shapes have a TextRange object. You can alter properties of shapes, such as the font used in the shape, its border, its fillcolor, and so on. As you work through this section, you will see how to incorporate this hierarchy of objects into your statements.

Now that you know what shape to insert the current date into, you need to specify into which part of the TextRange object you want to insert the date. You refer to a specific part of a TextRange object by referring to its Lines collection. The **Lines collection** represents the lines of text within a TextRange object. Thus, in order to add the current date and the presenter's name to the slide, you need to refer to a specific line within the particular TextRange object. You refer to specific lines by index numbers, with the first line being Lines(1), the second Lines(2), and so on. Thus, the complete reference to the first line in the second shape in the title slide would look like this:

```
ActivePresentation.Slides(1).Shapes(2).TextFrame.TextRange.
Lines(1)
```

If you look back at Figure 7-33, you'll see that the second shape in the title slide (where you want to insert the date and name) already contains a single line. Gene wants the name and current date to be inserted on a new line, after this existing line. So before you can actually insert the name and date, you need to add a new line. That is, you need to add a paragraph break, or a paragraph mark (sometimes called an end-of-line marker). To do this, you can use the VBA constant **vbCrLf**, which represents a paragraph mark or an end-of-line mark. (Actually **vbCrLf** stands for "carriage return – line feed.") You can use **vbCrLf** anywhere you want to insert a new line.

To insert the carriage return at the end of the first line, you will need to concatenate the text you want to insert with the constant **vbCrLf**. In the code below you can see how this constant is used to add a paragraph break after the first line in Shape(2), and then to insert two new lines. Line(1) already consists of the subtitle; the code below concatenates this text with a paragraph break, in order to create Line(2). Line(2) is then assigned the string "Presenter:" concatenated with the presenter's name (taken from the **strPresenter** variable), and concatenated with another paragraph break. Finally, Line(3) is assigned the current date, as obtained from the InsertDateTime method.

The complete code, then, is as follows:

```
Dim strPresenter As String
Dim sldTitle As Slide

strPresenter = InputBox("Enter Presenter Name: ")
Set sldTitle = ActivePresentation.Slides(1)
With sldTitle.Shapes(2).TextFrame.TextRange
    .Lines(1) = .Lines(1) & vbCrLf
    .Lines(2) = "Presenter: " & strPresenter & vbCrLf
    .Lines(3).InsertDateTime ppDateTimeMMMMdyyyy
End With
```

At this point, you should be prepared to understand all of this code. Notice that in this code a variable, `sldTitle`, is declared as a slide type. The `Set` statement then assigns the reference `ActivePresentation.Slides(1)` to the variable `sldTitle`. After the `Set` statement, `sldTitle` references `ActivePresentation.Slides(1)`. Therefore, when it is used in the `With` statement, the reference has already been established.

You will now enter this code in a general procedure, named `AddPresenterAndDate`.

---

*To add the* `AddPresenterAndDate` *procedure:*

**1.** Place your cursor anywhere in the form's Code window.

**2.** Insert a new general procedure named `AddPresenterAndDate`.

**3.** Add the following code to the procedure. As you type the line that inserts the date, pause just after you type **InsertDateTime** and observe the list of formats that you can use with this method.

```
Dim strPresenter As String
Dim sldTitle As Slide

strPresenter = InputBox("Enter Presenter Name: ")
Set sldTitle = ActivePresentation.Slides(1)
With sldTitle.Shapes(2).TextFrame.TextRange
    .Lines(1) = .Lines(1) & vbCrLf
    .Lines(2) = "Presenter: " & strPresenter & vbCrLf
    .Lines(3).InsertDateTime ppDateTimeMMMMdyyyy
End With
```

**4.** Compare your screen with Figure 7-34 and make any necessary changes.

---

| Figure 7-34 | CODE WINDOW SHOWING ADDPRESENTERANDDATE PROCEDURE |

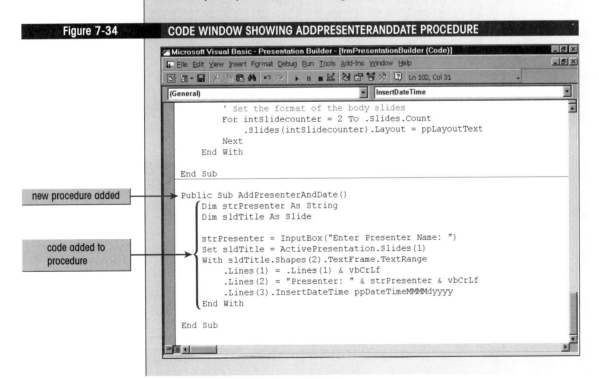

new procedure added

code added to procedure

Now you need to enter a statement (in the `cmdBuild_Click` event procedure ) that calls the `AddPresenterAndDate` procedure. Finally, you need to test the new code.

### To add a `Call` statement and test the code:

1. Place your cursor in the `cmdBuild_Click` event procedure just below the following comment: "Add Name and Date to Title slide."

2. Type the following statement:

   `Call AddPresenterAndDate`

3. Compare your screen with Figure 7-35 and make any necessary changes.

| Figure 7-35 | CODE WINDOW WITH CALL STATEMENT ADDED |
|---|---|

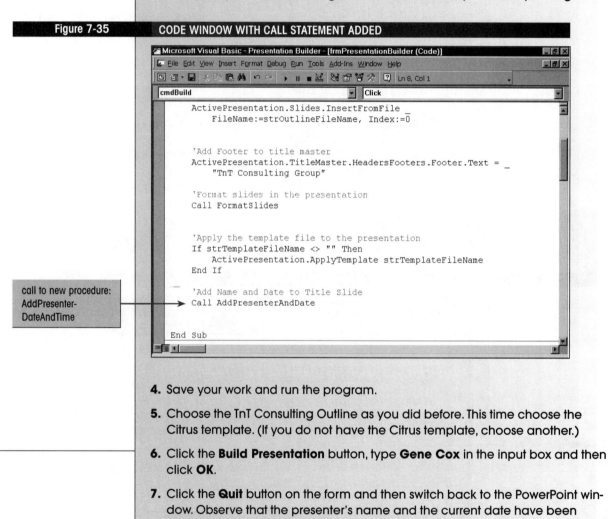

call to new procedure:
AddPresenter-
DateAndTime

4. Save your work and run the program.

5. Choose the TnT Consulting Outline as you did before. This time choose the Citrus template. (If you do not have the Citrus template, choose another.)

6. Click the **Build Presentation** button, type **Gene Cox** in the input box and then click **OK**.

7. Click the **Quit** button on the form and then switch back to the PowerPoint window. Observe that the presenter's name and the current date have been entered on the title slide, as shown in figure 7-36.

| Figure 7-36 | PRESENTATION WITH PRESENTER AND DATE ADDED |
| --- | --- |

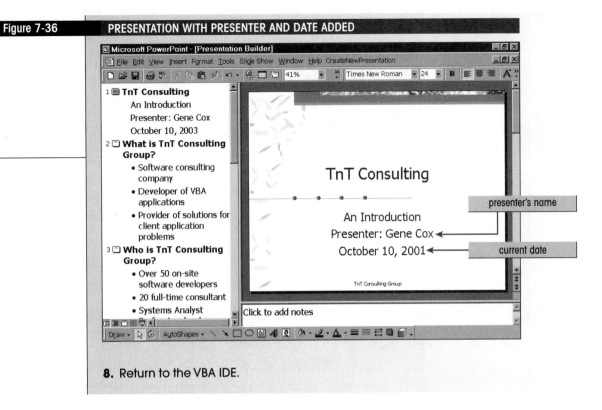

**8.** Return to the VBA IDE.

You have now responded to the first of Gene's requests for enhancing the title slide; you have added the presenter's name and the current date. Gene also asked that you format the title on the title slide so that the font is larger and bold. This is a very easy process, given what you have already learned.

## Altering Properties of the Title Slide

The title is on the first slide and is in the first shape. In order to change the font of the text in the title, you simply need to alter the font properties of Shapes(1). You have altered font properties previously in this text so this should not be new to you. The following code will change the font to 66-point Times New Roman bold:

```
Dim sldTitle As Slide

Set sldTitle = ActivePresentation.Slides(1)
With sldTitle.Shapes(1).TextFrame.TextRange
    .Font.Name = "Times New Roman"
    .Font.Size = 66
    .Font.Bold = True
End With
```

You will now enter this code in a general procedure and then program the Build Presentation button to call the new procedure.

## To add code that will format the title:

1. Place your cursor anywhere in the Code window.

2. Insert a new general procedure named FormatTitle.

3. Type the following code into the procedure:

```
Dim sldTitle As Slide

Set sldTitle = ActivePresentation.Slides(1)
With sldTitle.Shapes(1).TextFrame.TextRange
    .Font.Name = "Times New Roman"
    .Font.Size = 66
    .Font.Bold = True
End With
```

4. Place your cursor at the end of the cmdBuild_Click event procedure, as shown in Figure 7-37.

| Figure 7-37 | CODE WINDOW SHOWING CMDBUILD_CLICK EVENT PROCEDURE |
|---|---|

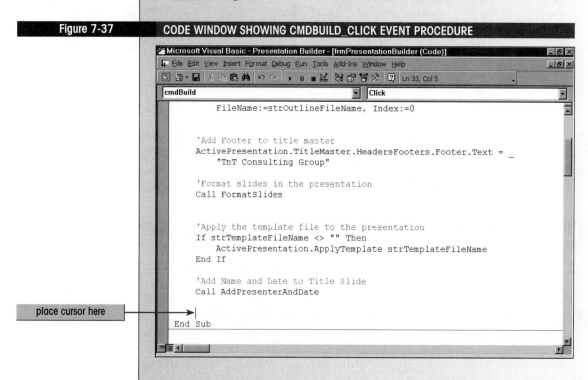

place cursor here

5. Type the following:

```
'Format the title on the title slide
Call FormatTitle
```

6. Save your work and run the program.

7. Test the program just as you did before, selecting the **Outline** document and the **Citrus** template. Again type **Gene Cox** as the presenter's name.

8. Click **Quit** on the form.

9. Return to the PowerPoint window. The title has been formatted according to your specifications, as shown in Figure 7-38.

**Figure 7-38**   **TITLE SLIDE WITH FORMATTED TITLE**

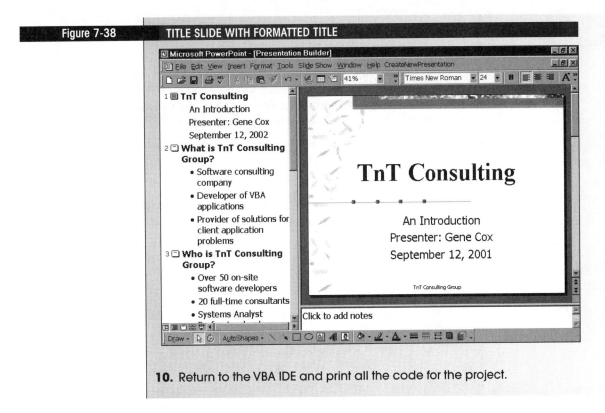

**10.** Return to the VBA IDE and print all the code for the project.

This completes the Presentation Builder project. You demonstrate the project once again for Gene, and he is satisfied with the enhancements you have made to the project. Gene explains that this project will allow the TnT account representatives to create presentations that are all formatted in the same way. This project will be a valuable asset to TnT Consulting.

# Session 7.3 QUICK CHECK

1. Each element on a slide is contained with a(n) _____ object.

2. The _____ object contains the text within a shape.

3. The _____ can be used to place the current date in an existing slide.

4. _____ is a constant value that represents a paragraph break.

5. The _____ statement assigns an object reference to a variable or property.

## REVIEW ASSIGNMENTS

After the TnT account representatives use the Presentation Builder application for a few weeks, they request some changes. Gene has assigned you the job of making enhancements to this project. As you revisit this project, Gene suggests that you take a closer look at the DIR command, which makes it possible for the user to select a filename.

Gene also asks that you make the following changes to the Presentation Builder:

- For the main title on the title slide, change the font size to 80 and also make the title italicized.

- Instead of adding the footer "TnT Consulting", the program should ask the user for the name that should appear in the footer and then use this input for the footer.

- Add a new slide at the end of the presentation that contains contact information for the presenter. In particular, provide the presenter's e-mail address and phone number.

1. Start PowerPoint and open the presentation named **Build,** located in the Review folder for Tutorial 7.

2. Save the file as **TnT Presentation Builder Final** in the Review folder for Tutorial 7. (*Note*: It is important that the Word file named **Outline2** be stored in the same folder as the file named TnT Presentation Builder Final.)

3. Open the Code window for the frmGetOutlineFile form. Locate the statement that uses the DIR function. (*Hint*: This is the statement after the comment "Search for files".) Close the Code window.

*Explore*  4. Look up "DIR function" in VBA Help. Click the Example link and read the examples. Don't be concerned if you don't understand all of this material. Close Help when you are finished.

5. Open the Code window for the frmPresentationBuilder form and then change the font size for the title slide to 80 and add a statement to make the title italicized. (*Hint*: You will need to add .Font.Italic = True to the other font specifications in the FormatTitle procedure.)

6. Insert a new procedure into the Code window and give it the name "CreateFooter". In this procedure, type the code that will display an input box with the prompt "Enter name to be placed in footer: ". Store the result of the InputBox function in a variable named strFooterText. (Don't forget to declare this variable.) When you are finished creating this procedure, the code should consist of the following:

```
Public Sub CreateFooter()
    Dim strFooterText As String

    strFooterText = InputBox("Enter name to be placed in
footer:")

ActivePresentation.TitleMaster.HeadersFooters.Footer.Text = _
        strFooterText
End Sub
```

7. Add a statement that will call the CreateFooter procedure. This statement should replace the statement that originally inserted "TnT Consulting" in the footer.

*Explore*  8. Look up the Add method in VBA Help. Close Help when you are finished learning about this topic.

*Explore*

9. Now you are ready to add the slide that will contain the contact information for the presenter. Create a new procedure called **AddContactSlide**. In the procedure, type the following code. As you enter the code, you will notice many statements you have used before, plus the new Add method. Try to determine how each statement helps to create the contact slide.

```vba
Public Sub AddContactSlide()
    Dim sldContactSlide As Slide
    Dim intNumSlides as Integer
    Dim strEmail As String
    Dim strPhone As String

    'Add a slide to the end of the presentation
    With ActivePresentation.Slides
        .Add .Count + 1, ppLayoutText
    End With

    'Add the title to the new slide
    intNumSlides = ActivePresentation.Slides.Count
    Set sldContactSlide =
ActivePresentation.Slides(intNumSlides)
    With sldContactSlide.Shapes(1).TextFrame.TextRange
        .Text = "Contact Information"
        .Font.Size = 44
    End With

    'Get the e-mail address and phone number from the user
    strEmail = InputBox("Enter email address: ")
    strPhone = InputBox("Enter phone number: ")

    'Add the e-mail address and phone number to the slide
    'and set the font size
    With sldContactSlide.Shapes(2).TextFrame.TextRange
        .Text = strEmail & vbCrLf & strPhone
        .Font.Size = 44
    End With
End Sub
```

10. Save your work and then run the project. Select the Word file named Outline 2 and the Checkers template (if you do not have this template, choose another one). As you test the project, enter your own name as the presenter, along with your own e-mail address and phone number.

11. At the top of the code, add comments that identify you as the developer and today's date.

12. Save your work and print the code for the entire project.

## CASE PROBLEMS

**Case 1. Seminar Services, Inc.** Mary Ann Andrews, owner of Seminar Services, Inc., is coordinating a training seminar for nurses from regional hospitals. There will be a variety of sessions during the seminar with many different presenters. Mary Ann is asking presenters to develop their presentation using Microsoft PowerPoint. She wants each presenter to have a standard title slide. The title slide should contain the title of the presentation, the presenter's name, and the date. She has hired you to create a VBA macro that will make it easy for the presenters to create their title slides.

1. Start PowerPoint and open the presentation named **Nurses** located in the Cases folder for Tutorial 7.

2. Save the presentation as **Nurses Training Seminar** in the Cases folder for Tutorial 7.

3. Open the VBA IDE.

4. Open the form named `frmTitle`.

5. Familiarize yourself with the form. Check the names of each control in the Properties window.

6. Add code for the Exit button that will remove the form from the screen.

7. Add code for the OK button that will insert a Title page into the presentation. (Be sure that the form layout is set to Title.)

8. Also add code for the OK button that will insert the title, author's name, and date into the title page.

9. Add code that clears the text boxes and positions the cursor at the start of the Title text box once the data has been entered in the worksheet.

10. Save the form.

11. Run the form.

12. Test the form by entering "Nurses Training Seminar" into the Title text box. Enter your name into the Author text box and today's date into the Date text box.

13. Click the OK button and review the title slide.

14. Click the Exit button to close the form when you've finished testing it.

15. Add comments at the top of the code that include your name and today's date.

16. Print the code for the project. Also print the title slide.

17. Save the presentation.

**Case 2. Delightful Treats** Daniel Sharpe is the marketing agent for Delightful Treats, a small company that produces specialty food items. He is responsible for selling the company's products to supermarkets. Dan develops a custom PowerPoint presentation for each new potential customer. Each presentation must have a title slide that contains the name of the client. In addition, each slide must have a footer that is customized for every client. Dan does not want to have to develop a new presentation format for each client. He asks you to design a VBA form that will allow him to easily enter a customer's name and any footer information for his presentations.

1. Start PowerPoint and open the presentation named **Treats** located in the Cases folder for Tutorial 7.

2. Save the presentation as **Delightful Treats**.

3. Open the VBA IDE.

4. Open the form named `frmTitle`.

5. Familiarize yourself with the form. Check the names of each control in the Properties window.

6. Add code for the Exit button that will remove the form from the screen.

7. Add code for the OK button that will insert a title page into the presentation. Set the slide layout to Title.

8. Also add code for the OK button that will insert the customer's name into the title slide.

9. Add code that will insert the footer information from the form into the presentation footer.

10. Add code that clears the text boxes and positions the cursor at the start of the customer field once the data has been entered in the worksheet.

11. Save the form.

12. Run the form.

13. Test the form by entering "Delightful Treats" into the Customer text box. Enter your name and today's date into the Footer text box.

14. Click the OK button and review the title slide.

15. Click the Exit button to close the form when you've finished testing it.

16. Add comments at the top of the code that include your name and today's date.

17. Print the code for the project. Also print the title slide.

18. Save the presentation.

**Case 3. Century Brokers**   Erin Kelley is an account executive at Century Brokers. Each month she researches a different company and presents the information she gathers to the company president. Her presentation has a title page containing the name of the company and the date and time of the presentation. She uses the slides following the title slide to describe the company she has researched. She asks you to design a VBA form that will enter a company name, as well as date and time information, into a presentation. In addition, she asks that the application add a blank slide after the title slide so she can add the company information.

1. Start PowerPoint and open the presentation named **Century** located in the Cases folder for Tutorial 7.

2. Save the presentation as **Century Brokers** in the Cases folder for Tutorial 7.

3. Open the VBA IDE.

4. Open the form named `frmCompany`.

5. Familiarize yourself with the form. Check the names of each control in the Properties window.

6. Add code for the Exit button that will remove the form from the screen.

7. Add code for the OK button to clear the existing presentation.

8. Add code for the OK button that will insert a title page into the presentation. Set the layout to Title

9. Add code for the OK button that will insert the presentation title into the title page.

10. Use the InsertDateTime method to add the date and time information into the subtitle.

11. Add code that will add a new slide to the presentation and set the layout for the new slide to Text.

12. Add code that selects the text inside the company text box and positions the cursor at the start of the text box once the data has been entered in the worksheet.

13. Save the form.

14. Run the form.

15. Test the form by entering "Century Brokers" into the Customer text box.

16. Click the OK button and review the title slide.

17. Click the Exit button to close the form when you've finished testing it.

18. Add comments at the top of the code that include your name and today's date.

19. Print the code for the project. Also print the title slide.

20. Save the presentation.

*Case 4. Newman State College*   Casey Michaels, who works in the Student Affairs office for Newman State College, has asked you to prepare a PowerPoint macro that will help her build presentations containing information about student organizations. Each year, the Student Affairs office makes a presentation to the administration about all of the student organizations on campus. The yearly presentation requires a separate slide for each organization and the names of each of the officers. Each slide should have the name of the organization and the names of the organization president, vice president, secretary, and project chairperson. Your application will provide a form wherein the Student Affairs office can enter the appropriate data and have the slides built for them automatically.

1. Start PowerPoint and open the presentation named **Newman** located in the Cases folder for Tutorial 7.

2. Save the presentation as **Newman Student Organizations** in the Cases folder for Tutorial 7.

3. Examine the form in Figure 7-39.

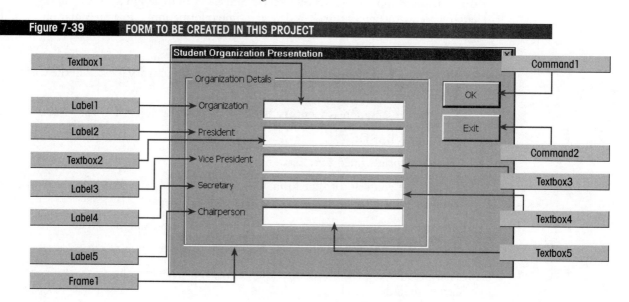

**Figure 7-39**   **FORM TO BE CREATED IN THIS PROJECT**

4. Open the VBA IDE.

5. Add a form to the project.

6. Add a frame control, five label controls, five text box controls, and two command buttons to the form.

7. Set the properties for the form and controls using the information in Figure 7-40.

| Figure 7-40 | PROPERTIES FOR FORM AND CONTROLS | | |
|---|---|---|---|

| CONTROL | PROPERTY | VALUE |
|---|---|---|
| Userform1 | Name | frmOrganization |
| | Caption | Student Organizations |
| Frame1 | Name | fraDetails |
| | Caption | Organization Details |
| Label1 | Name | lblName |
| | Caption | Organization |
| Label2 | Name | lblPres |
| | Caption | President |
| Label3 | Name | lblVice |
| | Caption | Vice President |
| Label4 | Name | lblSec |
| | Caption | Secretary |
| Label5 | Name | lblChair |
| | Caption | Chairperson |
| Textbox1 | Name | txtName |
| Textbox2 | Name | txtPres |
| Textbox3 | Name | txtVice |
| Textbox4 | Name | txtSec |
| Textbox5 | Name | txtChair |
| CommandButton1 | Name | cmdOK |
| | Caption | OK |
| CommandButton2 | Name | cmdExit |
| | Caption | Exit |

8. Add code for the Exit button that will remove the form from the screen.

9. Add code for the OK button that will insert a new slide at the end of the presentation. Set the slide layout to Text.

10. Add code for the OK button that will insert the student organization name into the title section of the slide.

11. Add code that will insert the names of the student officers into the text section of the slide.

12. Add code that clears the text boxes and positions the cursor at the start of the organization text box once the data has been entered in the worksheet.

13. Save the form.

14. Run the form.

15. Add student organization information into the active presentation.

16. Enter "Animal Friends Group" into the Organization text box.

17. Enter "Rex" into the President text box.

18. Enter "Leo" into the Vice President text box.

19. Enter "Dino" into the Secretary text box.

20. Enter "Kitty" into the Chairperson text box.

21. Click the OK button and review the slide.

22. Click the Exit button to close the form when you've finished testing it.

23. Add comments at the top of the code that include your name and today's date.

24. Print the code for the project. Also print the slide with the organization data on it.

25. Save the presentation.

## QUICK | CHECK ANSWERS

### Session 7.1

1. public

2. ```
   frmGetNumber.Show
   intNumberEmployees = frmGetNumber.intNumber
   ```

3. Unload

4. Dim

### Session 7.2

1. Presentations

2. Slides(3)

3. ActivePresentation.Slides(5).Delete

4. General

5. InsertFromFile

6. ActivePresentation.Slides(4).Layout = ppLayoutText

7. count

### Session 7.3

1. Shape

2. TextRange

3. InsertDateTime

4. vbCrLF

5. Set
   ```

## OBJECTIVES

In this tutorial you will:

■ Learn about the Access object model

■ Examine an object's property sheet

■ Create an Access macro

■ Create navigation buttons with VBA

■ Add and program controls in an Access form

# USING VBA WITH ACCESS

*Enhancing a Library Checkout system with VBA*

CASE

## Carson County Library Checkout Application

During your past several weeks of employment with TnT Consulting, you have learned about developing VBA applications for Word, Excel, and PowerPoint. Now, Gene Cox, your supervisor, wants you to get acquainted with working with VBA for Access. Access, as you know, is a database management system (DBMS) that you can use to store and retrieve data. To give you some experience with Access, Gene asks you to help create a program for the Carson County Library System that automates the process of checking out books. The program will involve a database of information used to track books checked out, borrowers, due dates, and so on. The tables for the data have already been created and the system works fairly well, but Gene believes that the system could be enhanced with some VBA code.

Your first task on this project is to create an interface that the library employees can use to choose which forms, queries, or reports they want to see on the screen. At the current time, employees have to work directly in Access, and some of them feel intimidated with having to work in this environment. Gene believes the staff at the library would be more comfortable with a menu-driven system. He has suggested that you create a menu form that will open each of the library's forms, queries, and reports. Gene explains that with the menu system, the staff will not have to interact directly with Access at all.

Once you have completed this part of the project, you will then need to enhance some of the forms displayed by the program. Also, you will use VBA code to increase the functionality of the current system. For instance, you will add code that automatically calculates when a book is due. Your new system should also calculate whether a book is overdue and, it it is, calculate the fee.

Gene explains that there are other consultants working on enhancing other parts of the library system. Later, when all consultants have completed their work, the systems will be combined into one fully operational system.

## SESSION 8.1

In this session you will learn how to use VBA with Microsoft Access, and learn about the Access object model. You will review the database you will use in this tutorial, and then learn how to examine an object's property sheet. Finally, you will learn how to create an Access macro and attach one to a command button.

## Using VBA with Microsoft Access

Access differs somewhat from the other Office applications in that Access is actually a development environment—that is, you can use it to create an entire database including tables, forms, queries, reports, and programs. You are already comfortable using Access to develop data tables, create queries, and design forms and reports. However, the Access environment intimidates many users. To alleviate that anxiety, Access developers often create a user interface (and underlying code) that provides a more user-friendly way to access the data in the database. You'll create just such an interface in this tutorial.

## Understanding Objects in Access

You are already familiar with the object models of Excel, Word, and PowerPoint. As you might expect, Access has its own object model. Figure 8-1 contains a very limited view of the Access object model.

| Figure 8-1 | LIMITED VIEW OF THE ACCESS OBJECT MODEL |

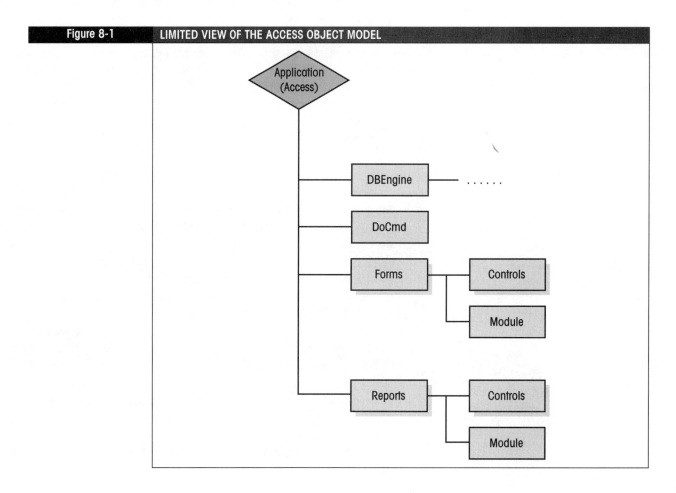

The Access model is actually much more extensive than that shown in Figure 8-1 and contains far more objects than you are prepared to use at this point. Notice that the dbEngine object is followed by a series of periods. These periods indicate that there is much more to this object than is shown in the figure (including table definitions, query definitions, etc.). Further discussion of the dbEngine is outside the scope of this text. At this stage, just keep in mind that all of the information about your database tables, queries, relations, etc. is encased in the dbEngine object.

The rest of the model shown in the figure includes the objects that you will be using in this tutorial. The DoCmd object is probably the object of most interest. Briefly, the DoCmd object contains all the methods that the VBA developer needs to interact with the database. You'll learn more about this object later in this tutorial.

# Reviewing **the Database**

Your first task is to review the Access database currently used by the Carson County Library to see what tables, forms, queries, and reports it contains. In the following steps, it is assumed that you are already familiar with using Access. In particular, you should be able to create and use tables, queries, forms, and reports. While you may not have realized it, tables, queries, and so on are all objects within the Access object model.

The library's database consists of the following tables:

- **Books Table**: Contains information on all the books in the library. Note that the database you will be working with in this tutorial contains only a sampling of the library's collection. The table includes the following fields: `BookCode`, `Title`, `Author`, `Publisher`, `DatePublished`, `NumberPage`, and `Keyword`. The key field is `BookCode`.

- **Borrowers Table**: Contains information on all library card holders (known as borrowers). The borrower's ID is automatically created as an Autonumber. The table includes the following fields: `BorrowerNumber`, `FirstName`, `LastName`, `MiddleInitial`, `Address`, `City`, `State`, `Zip`, `Minor`, and `ParentName`. The key field is `BorrowerNumber`. The `Minor` field is a Yes/No field that indicates whether or not the borrower is a minor. If the borrower is a minor, the name of the parent must also be entered into the borrower's record.

- **CheckOuts Table**: Contains information on all books currently checked out. The table consists of the following fields: `BorrowerNumber`, `BookCode`, `CheckOutDate`, `DueDate`, `PastDue`, `Fee`. The `BorrowerNumber` field is actually a "lookup" on the Borrower's name. Likewise the `BookCode` field is actually a "lookup" on the Book Title. The key field is a combination of the `BorrowNumber` and the `BookCode`.

The relationships between the tables have already been created, and are illustrated in Figure 8-2. The CheckOuts table forms a many-to-many relationship with the Books table and the Borrowers table. By way of review, a many-to-many relationship in this example means that a borrower can check out many books, and a book can be checked out by many borrowers. Further explanation of relationships between tables is beyond the scope of this book.

Figure 8-2         **RELATIONSHIP BETWEEN TABLES**

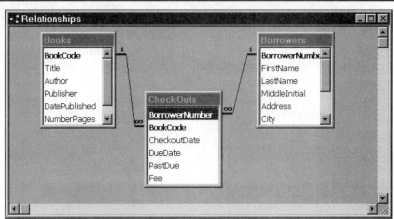

In addition to the three tables, the database also contains several forms, queries, and reports. You will open the database and look at the all of these items now. Because the files for this tutorial are so large, you'll need to store the Tutorial.08 folder on your computer's hard drive (or network drive). If you're not sure where to store the folder, see your instructor for specific instructions. Make sure the Tutorial.08 folder is already stored on your computer's hard drive (or network drive) before beginning the following steps. In the first step you will make a copy of the Tutorial.08 folder. Keep the copy as a backup, in case you want to repeat this tutorial later.

### To open the database and view its contents:

1. Use Windows Explorer to make a copy of the Tutorial.08 folder, and store that folder on your hard drive or network drive.

2. Start Microsoft Access and open the file named **Library** from the Tutorial.08 folder on your hard drive or network drive. If necessary, click **Tables** on the Objects bar. Compare your screen with Figure 8-3.

Figure 8-3        **CCLS DATABASE TABLES**

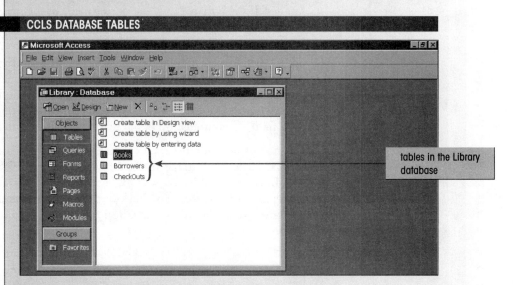

tables in the Library database

3. Open each table and examine its design and content. When you are finished, close all tables.

**4.** In the Objects bar, click **Queries**. The database's one query, Past Due, is displayed in the Database window. Compare your screen with Figure 8-4.

| Figure 8-4 | CCLS DATABASE QUERY |

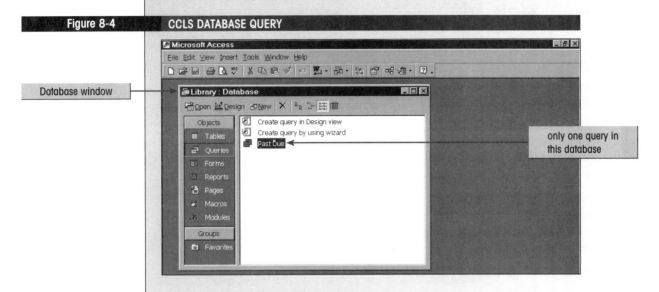

Database window

only one query in this database

**5.** Open the **Past Due query** and review its results. When you are finished, close the Query window.

**6.** In the Objects bar, click **Forms**. The database forms are displayed in the Database window. Compare your screen with Figure 8-5.

| Figure 8-5 | CCLS DATABASE FORMS |

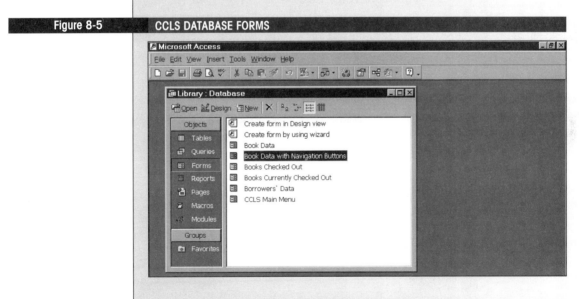

**7.** Open each form and examine its design and content. Pay particular attention to the form named **Books Currently Checked Out**, which is shown in Figure 8-6. This form contains a main form and a subform. The main form contains information about a particular borrower, and the subform (that is, the lower portion of the form) contains information about the books checked out by this borrower. In Figure 8-6, the form shows information about books checked out by Mary Cutshall. You will review the Main Menu form more closely in the next section.

**Figure 8-6** **BOOKS CHECKED OUT TO MARY CUTSHALL**

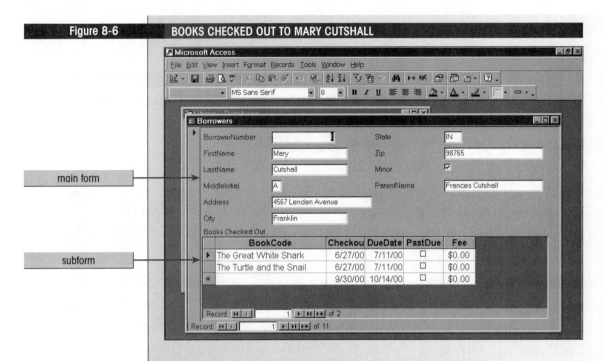

8. Close any open forms.

9. In the Objects bar, click **Reports**. The four reports in the database are displayed in the Database window, as shown in Figure 8-7. Open each report and review its design and contents. Close each report after you view it.

**Figure 8-7** **CCLS DATABASE REPORTS**

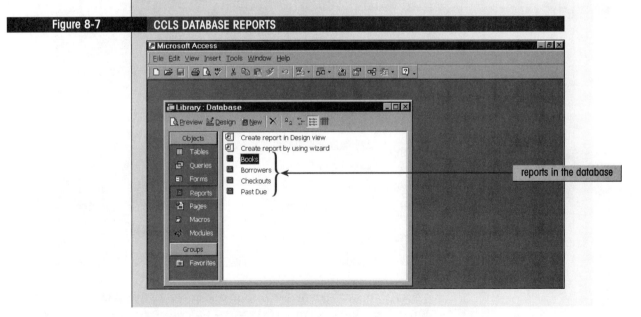

Now that you have viewed the Library database, you can probably see why navigating around such an extensive database might be a little intimidating to the novice user. In the next section you will examine a special form that Gene created in order to help library employees manipulate the database quickly and easily. The form contains a command button for each object (forms, reports, and so on) contained in the database.

## Viewing the Main Menu Form

Considering your previous experience with Access, Gene assumes that you are already familiar with creating Access forms. So he doesn't take time to discuss the process with you now. He explains that if you need some reminders about how to go about creating a form in Access, you can always review the steps in Access Help. To save time, he went ahead and created the CCLS Main Menu form for you. The form includes a number of command buttons, but at this point the form doesn't do anything except display the options available within the database. Later in this tutorial you will program some of the form's command buttons by creating a few simple macros.

### To review the CCLS Main Menu form:

1. In the Objects bar, click **Forms** and then double-click **CCLS Main Menu**. Note that when you open a form by double-clicking its name in the Database window, the form begins running. (This is in contrast to running a VBA form in one of the other Office applications, where you have usually opened the VBA IDE, opened the form, and then clicked the Run button on the VBA IDE toolbar.)

2. Take several minutes to familiarize yourself with the Main Menu form. Your form should match the one shown in Figure 8-8. Notice that each button is designed to open a form, a query, or a report. Also notice that the Main Menu form contains two Quit options, which will be explained later in this tutorial.

| Figure 8-8 | CCLS MAIN MENU FORM PLAN |

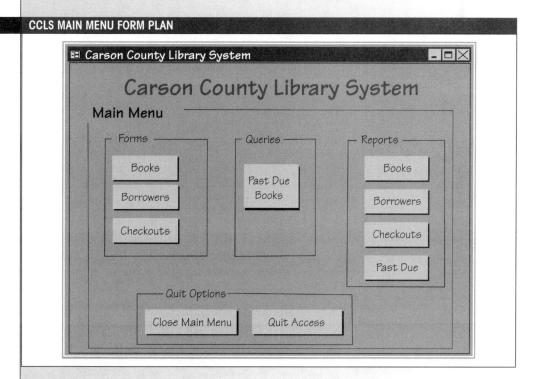

3. Click the **Close Main Menu** button on the form. Nothing happens because the button has not been programmed yet.

4. Click the **Quit Access** button on the form. Nothing happens again, for the same reason.

5. Close the form.

You have viewed all the objects in the CCLS Library System, and in particular, you have focused on the main menu. You observed that the main menu provides buttons for opening every object in the database. In the next several sections, you will learn how to make the buttons perform as intended.

# Examining an Object's Property Sheet

Earlier in this tutorial, you learned about the various objects included in the Access object model. Now you need to learn how to interact with these objects as you create VBA code. In Word, Excel, and PowerPoint, you set properties for various objects within the Properties window. In Access you also need to specify properties for each object; however, in Access, an object's properties are not displayed in a Properties window within a VBA IDE. Instead, the properties are displayed in a dialog box that contains a number of tabs. The exact name of this dialog box varies, depending on the selected object, but by convention the dialog box for a particular object is referred to as the object's **property sheet**. To open an object's properties sheet, you simply right-click the object, and then click Properties.

The property sheet for a typical Access object includes the following tabs:

- **All**: Contains a complete list of all the object's properties
- **Other**: Contains a miscellaneous list of properties that do not fit into any of the other categories
- **Event**: Contains the events that can take place on this particular object
- **Format**: Contains properties pertaining to the format of the object such as the font, alignment, size, etc.
- **Data**: Contains properties pertaining to the data itself such as the source of the data, default values to be used, etc.

In the next set of steps you will examine the property sheet for the Close Main Menu command button in the main menu. It is important to become familiar with this property sheet, because you will use them to alter the appearance and behavior of the objects in the main menu. Note that to open the property sheet for an object, you must first open the form in Design View.

---

*To review the property sheet for the Close Menu command buttons:*

1. Make sure that the CCLS Main Menu form is still selected in the Database window, and then click the Design button ⬛ in the Database window. The form opens in Design mode; the form is not actually running at this time.

2. Right-click the **Close Main Menu** command button in the form and then click **Properties**.

3. The property sheet for the cmdCloseMenu command button is displayed.

4. Click the Format tab, if necessary. The properties of the cmdCloseMenu command button that relate to how the command button looks on the screen is displayed, as shown in Figure 8-9. (The property sheet on your screen may be sized differently from the one in the figure.)

**Figure 8-9**   **PROPERTY SHEET FOR THE CMDCLOSEMENU BUTTON**

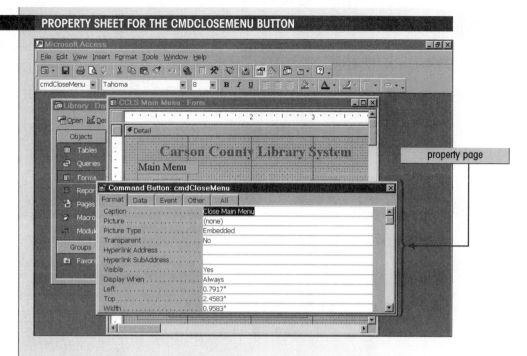

5. If necessary, click the **All** tab. All the properties applicable to the cmdCloseMenu command button are displayed, as shown in Figure 8-10. You can select property values in the All tab just as you would select property values in the Properties window for Word, Excel, or PowerPoint.

**Figure 8-10**   **THE ALL TAB ON THE PROPERTY SHEET**

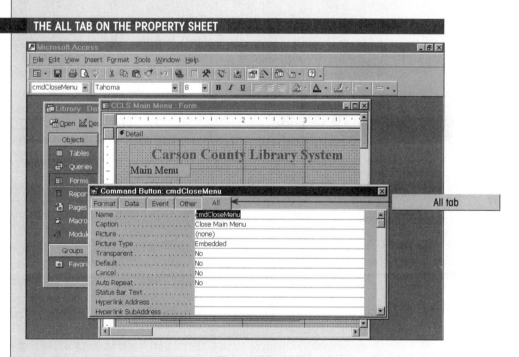

6. Click the **Event** tab. A list of events associated with a command button appears, as shown in Figure 8-11.

| Figure 8-11 | THE EVENT TAB OF THE PROPERTY SHEET |
| --- | --- |

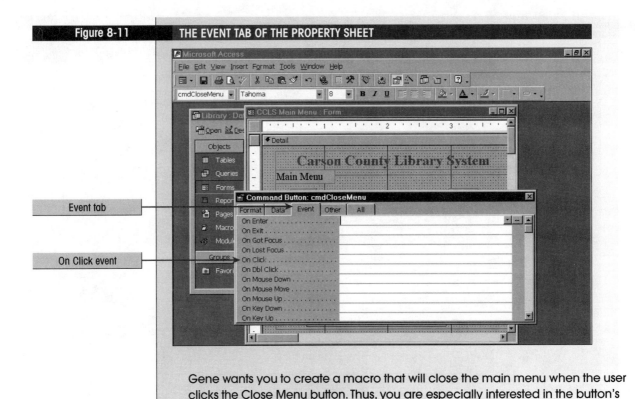

Event tab

On Click event

Gene wants you to create a macro that will close the main menu when the user clicks the Close Menu button. Thus, you are especially interested in the button's Click event. Within the Event tab, the Click event is listed as "On Click."

In the next section you will learn how to use the Macro Builder to create the necessary actions for the Close Main Menu button's Click event. When programming in VBA for Access, developers often choose to attach a macro to a button in order to perform common actions, such as closing a form.

## Creating a Macro in Access

In Tutorial 1 you recorded a macro by starting the Macro Recorder, carrying out some steps within PowerPoint, and then stopping the Macro Recorder. You saw that the process actually created VBA code. Developers often record macros in this way, and then edit the resulting VBA code in order to create a full-blown VBA program. However, unlike the other Office applications, Access does not provide a Macro Recorder. To create macros in Access, you need to use the Macro Builder, which allows you to create a macro by selecting actions commonly performed in Access (such as opening a table, opening a query, or closing a form) from a predefined list. Alternately, you could write your own VBA code. In this session, you will learn to use Access macros. Then, in the following two sessions, you will write your own VBA code.

In Access, a macro might consist of a single action or a collection of actions. Figure 8-12 contains a partial list of some commonly used macro actions, including the ones that you will use in this session. Keep in mind that Access offers a great many more macros than those listed in the table. When you look at the Macro Builder, you will have an opportunity to scan a complete list of available macro actions.

| Figure 8-12 | COMMONLY USED MACRO ACTIONS |
| --- | --- |

| ACTION NAME | DESCRIPTION |
| --- | --- |
| Close | Closes the specified window |
| OpenForm | Opens a form in Form view, Design View, Print Preview, or Datasheet View |
| OpenQuery | Opens a query in Design View, Datasheet View, or Print Preview |
| OpenReport | Opens a report in Design View or Print Preview, or prints the report immediately |
| OpenTable | Opens a table in Datasheet View, Design View, or Print Preview |
| Quit | Quits Microsoft Access |

When the user clicks the Close Main Menu button, you want the Main Menu form to close; thus, you need to use a Close action. The **Close action** is equivalent to the unload method that you have used in previous tutorials. You can use it to close any open window. You can use the Close action to close a window you specify, or simply to close whatever window happens to be active. In the case of the Close Main Menu button, you will specify that you want to close the Main Menu window.

In the next section, you will learn how to attach this macro action to a command button.

## Attaching a Macro to a Command Button

Gene explains that the process of programming an object by building a macro is sometimes referred to as **attaching a macro**. In this case, you need to attach a macro to the Close Main Menu command button. To attach a macro to a command button, you need to locate the event to which you want to attach the macro, open the Macro Builder, and then select the actions you want to use. After you select the arguments, you need to select some settings related to those arguments. (These settings are called action arguments.) In this case, you need to attach a macro to the Close Main Menu button's Click event.

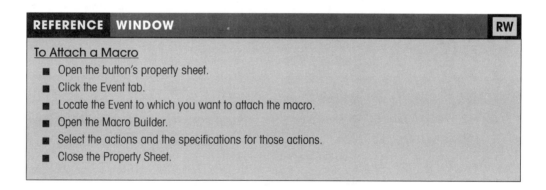

**REFERENCE WINDOW** **RW**

To Attach a Macro
- Open the button's property sheet.
- Click the Event tab.
- Locate the Event to which you want to attach the macro.
- Open the Macro Builder.
- Select the actions and the specifications for those actions.
- Close the Property Sheet.

Since you already have the Event tab for the Close Main Menu button open on your screen, you are ready to start attaching a macro.

*To attach a macro to the Close Main Menu button:*

1. Locate **On Click** in the Event tab, and then click the white box to the right of On Click. Both a list arrow and an ellipse button appear, as shown in Figure 8-13.

**Figure 8-13**    **LIST ARROW AND ELLIPSE FOR THE CLICK EVENT**

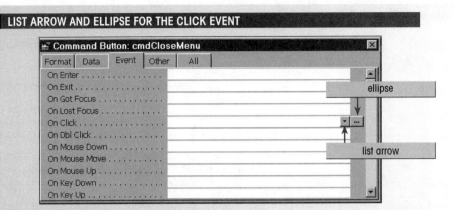

2. Click the **ellipse** button ![...]. The Choose Builder dialog box opens. You want to build a macro, so you will click Macro Builder in the next step.

3. Click **Macro Builder** and then click **OK**. The Save As dialog box opens. Here, you must supply a name for your macro.

4. In the Macro Name box type **Close Macro**, and then click **OK**. The Macro window opens. In this window you can select which of Access's predefined actions you want to attach to the Close Main Menu button.

5. Click the list arrow in the Action column. A list of predefined actions is displayed, as shown in Figure 8-14. Take a few minutes to scroll through this list of actions, the names of which are fairly self-explanatory.

**Figure 8-14**    **MACRO BUILDER WINDOW WITH ACTION LIST DISPLAYED**

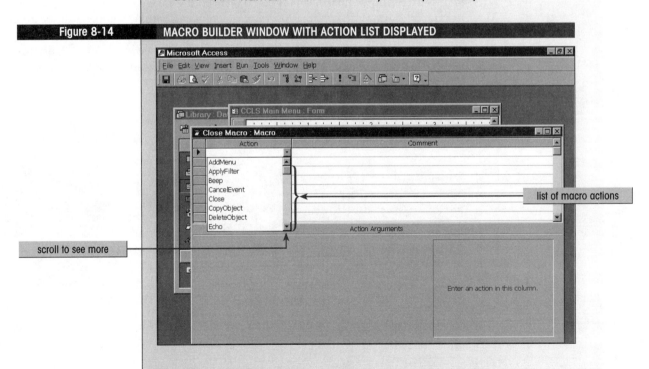

6. In the Action list, click **Close**. Some new text boxes appear in the lower portion of the Macro window, as shown in Figure 8-15. Also, a description of the selection action is displayed in the lower-right corner of the Macro window.

| Figure 8-15 | **MACRO BUILDER WITH CLOSE MACRO SELECTED** |

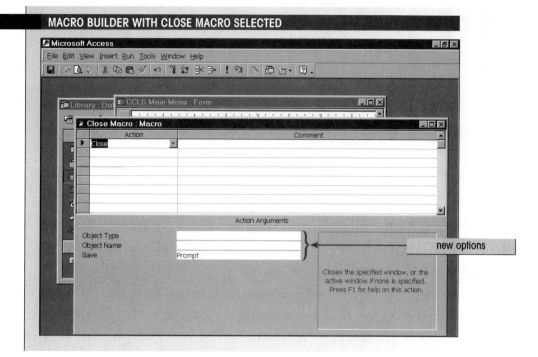

If you only wanted the macro to close the window currently open in Access, you could leave these text boxes blank. However, Gene wants you to specify a particular window (the CCLS Main Menu form) just for practice.

## To specify which window you want the macro to close:

1. Click the **Object Type** box. A list arrow appears.

2. Click the **Object Type** list arrow, and then click **Form**.

3. Click the **Object Name** box, click the list arrow that appears, and then click **CCLS Main Menu**. The final specification has to do with whether or not you want to save values on the form. In this case, there are no values, so you do not need to make any changes.

4. Locate the Comment column (next to the Action column at the top of the Macro Builder window).

5. Click at the top of the Comment column (next to the Close action) and type **Close the main menu and return to Access**. Compare your screen with Figure 8-16. The macro you have just built contains one action, the Close action. Note that you could add additional actions to your macro, in order to automate a series of actions. But in this case, you only need to add one.

**Figure 8-16**  **MACRO BUILDER WINDOW FOR THE CLOSE MACRO**

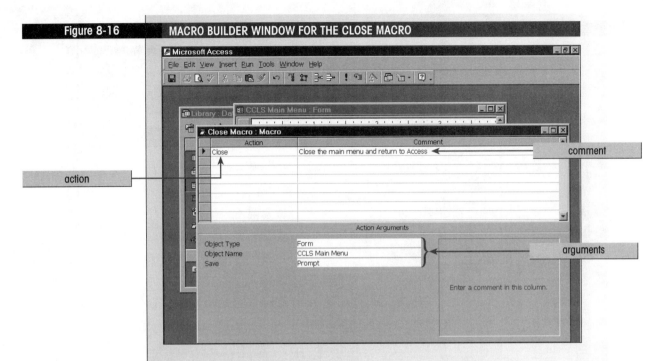

6. Click the **Close** button ☒ in the Macro window. A Microsoft Access dialog box appears, asking if you want to save your changes. Click **Yes**. You return to the Event tab of the property sheet. Notice that the name of the newly attached macro now appears in the On Click row, as shown in Figure 8-17.

**Figure 8-17**  **MACRO NAME ON EVENT TAB**

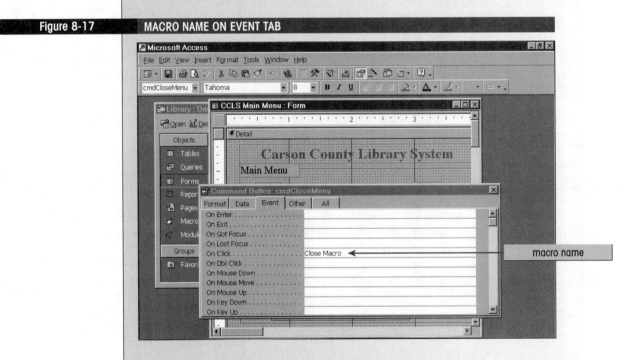

7. Close the property sheet and close the Main Menu form. When asked if you want to save your changes, click **Yes**.

Now when the Main Menu form is open, users can click the Close Main Menu button to remove the Main Menu form from the screen. In the next section, you will test the macro.

## Testing the Attached Macro

You already know from your experience with Office that it's important to test a macro right away to make sure it works properly. You will now test the Close Main Menu button to verify that the macro you attached works the way it should.

### To test the Close Main Menu button:

1. In the Database window, double-click **CCLS Main Menu**.

2. Click the **Close Main Menu** button on the form. The main menu is removed from the screen, and you see the Database window.

The macro you just created closes the Main Menu form and returns you to the Database window. However, there are times when you might want not only to close the form but also to close Access as well. For example, Gene wants the Quit Access button to close all open forms and close Access. This means that you need to attach a different macro to the Quit Access button—one that incorporates the Quit action, as explained in the next section.

## Building a Macro with the Quit Action

Gene explains that you should incorporate the **Quit action** into your macros whenever you need to close all open forms *and* close Access. You will now attach a macro to the Quit Access button. The process is just the same as in the preceding section, except that you will select the Quit action rather than the Close action.

### To attach a macro to the Quit Access button:

1. Open the **CCLS Main Menu** form in Design View.

2. Right-click the **Quit Access** button, click **Properties,** and then (if necessary) click the **Event tab**.

3. Click the right side of the On Click row (if necessary) and then click the **Ellipse button** . The Choose Builder dialog box opens.

4. Click **Macro Builder**, click **OK**, in the Save As dialog box type **Quit Access**, and then click **OK**.

5. In the Action column, click the list arrow, scroll through the list, and then click **Quit**. The Quit options are displayed in the lower portion of the window as shown in Figure 8-18. Notice that the only option associated with the Quit action is the Save All option. This option ensures that Access will save any changes to the database before closing.

| Figure 8-18 | MACRO BUILDER WITH QUIT ACTION SELECTED |
|---|---|

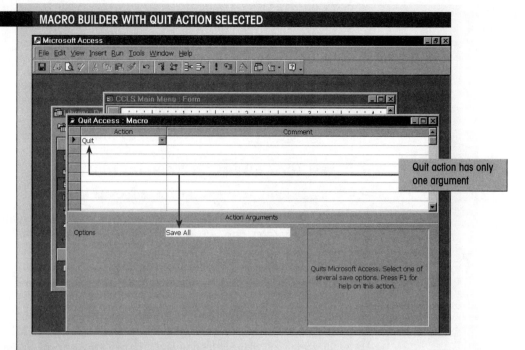

**6.** Type the comment **Close the database and quit Access** in the comment column next to the Quit action, and then close the Macro Builder window. A dialog box appears asking if you would like to save your changes to the macro.

**7.** Click **Yes**. You return to the property sheet window for the Quit Access button.

**8.** Close the property sheet window. You return to the Main Menu form.

**9.** Close the form. Click **Yes** when asked if you want to save your changes.

Next, you need to test the Quit Access button.

## To test the Quit Access button:

**1.** Double-click **CCLS Main Menu** in the Database window.

**2.** Click the **Quit Access** button on the form.

**3.** The Main Menu form closes, and Access closes as well.

**4.** Start Access again so that you can continue working.

**5.** Open the library system database.

Now that you have learned to attach a macro to a command button, you could do the same with each of the other buttons. To save time, however, all the macros for the rest of the form have been created and attached for you. In the next section, you will test these macros.

# Testing **the Main Menu**

Each of the remaining command buttons on the Main Menu form has a macro attached to them. Next, Gene asks you to test the main menu to make sure that it performs as you would expect.

*To test the Main Menu form:*

1. In the Database window, double-click **CCLS Main Menu**.

2. Click the **Books** button in the Forms frame. The Books form opens.

3. Close the Books form.

4. Test the remaining buttons to make sure they display the appropriate form, query, or report.

5. Close the Main Menu form.

You have just observed that the main menu works properly as it displays forms, queries, and reports for the Library project.

In the next session, you will add some additional functionality to some of the forms you just displayed. You will do this by adding some command buttons and then programming those buttons with VBA rather than using macros.

## Session 8.1 QUICK CHECK

1. While Word, Excel, and PowerPoint have a(n) _____, Access does not.

2. The _____ action will display a specified form on the screen.

3. The _____ action will display a specified query on the screen.

4. The _____ action will display a specified report on the screen.

5. The _____ action will close the currently open window.

6. The _____ action will close any open window and close Access as well.

---

## SESSION 8.2

In this session you will use VBA to code navigation buttons. In the process, you will use the DoCmd object. You will also learn how to write code that will disable a navigation button under certain circumstances.

---

# Creating **Navigation Buttons with VBA**

As you know, when you create a form that is based on a table or query, Access automatically adds a navigation bar to the form. This bar contains buttons (such as the First, Previous, and Next buttons) designed to help you display the records you want in the form. Figure 8-19 shows the navigation bar for the Book Data form.

**Figure 8-19**     **BOOKS FORM WITH NAVIGATION BAR**

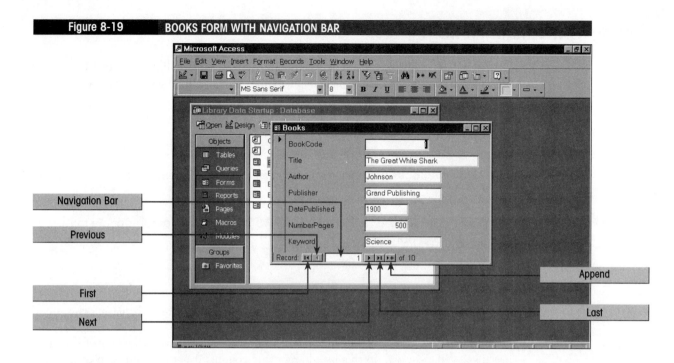

As an experienced Access user, you can probably use these buttons with ease, but some Access novices find the buttons hard to use. For this reason, developers at TnT Consulting routinely insert command buttons that users can click to move from one record to another, rather than requiring users to rely on a form's navigation bar. Command buttons used to navigate through the records in a database are often referred to as **navigation buttons**.

Gene explains that your next task is to remove the navigation bar from the Book Data form and replace it with navigation buttons. Specifically, you will add command buttons that display the first record in the database, the next record, the previous record, and the last record. In addition, he wants you to add a button that automatically displays a blank form, so that the user can add a new record. Gene sketches the new version of the form to show you where to insert the navigation buttons. This sketch is shown in Figure 8-20.

**Figure 8-20**     **FORM DESIGN WITH NAVIGATION BUTTONS**

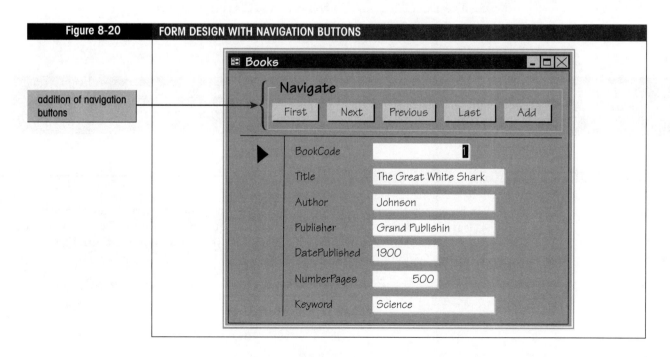

Before you alter the Book Data form, Gene suggests that you practice using its navigation bar in order to remind yourself of how it works. The command buttons you will add to the form will perform essentially the same functions as the buttons in the navigation bar.

## To practice using the navigation bar:

1. Open the **Book Data** form. The form appears as shown in Figure 8-21, displaying the first record, which contains information about a book named *The Great White Shark*.

**Figure 8-21**     **BOOK DATA FORM WITH NAVIGATION BAR**

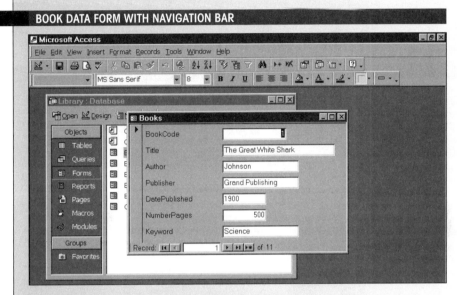

2. Click the **Last Record** button ▶︎❙. The form displays the last record in the database, containing information about a book named *Programming in VBA*.

3. Click the **First Record** ❙◀︎ button. The form displays the first record again.

4. Click the **Previous Record** ◀︎ button. The form continues to display the first record, because there is no "previous record" when the first record is displayed.

5. Click the **Next Record** ▶︎ button. The form displays the second record in the database, which contains information about a book entitled *My First Book*.

6. Click the **Last Record** ▶︎❙ button, and then click the Next Record button. The form displays blank text boxes, and is now ready for you to enter a new record. Notice that you could also click the Append Record button to add a new record.

7. Click the **Previous** button. Again, the form displays the last record in the database, which contains information on *Programming in VBA*.

8. Click the **Append** ▶︎✱ button. Again, the form displays blank text boxes, and is ready for you to enter a new record.

9. Click the **Next Record** ▶︎ button. The form does not change, because there is no "next record" at this point. You have already reached the end of the records in the database. When you are finished reviewing the form, close it.

As stated earlier, it is standard policy at TnT Consulting to replace the navigation bar with navigation buttons. Once again, Gene has assigned another consultant to help you with the preliminary work on this task. Ashley Andrews, a consultant you have worked with before, has prepared a new version of the Book Data form in which the navigation bar has been replaced with navigation buttons. Ashley stored this form in your database as "Book Data with Navigation Buttons." Ashley only placed the buttons on the form; it is your job to program them to respond to the user's click. You will now view the form that Ashley has prepared.

### To view the Book Data with Navigation Buttons form:

1. In the Database window, double-click **Book Data with Navigation Buttons**.

2. Compare the form with Figure 8-22.

**Figure 8-22**     **BOOK DATA FORM WITH NAVIGATION BUTTONS**

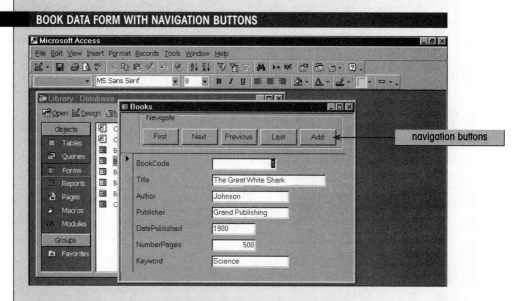

3. Click each navigation button on the form and notice that nothing happens. This is because you have not yet programmed these buttons. In the next steps you will learn to attach VBA code to the buttons.

4. Close the form.

You will program the navigation buttons by attaching some VBA code to them.

## Using VBA Code Instead of Macro Actions

In order to program the Close Main Menu and the Quit Access buttons, you attached a macro action. This is a fairly simple process and provides a quick implementation of a limited set of action. If you only wanted to program the navigation buttons to move to the first record, to the next record, etc., you could use the same technique, and simply attach macro actions to the buttons. However, you want to do more. You want to program the buttons to prevent any unnecessary confusion on the part of the user.

For example, when the user clicks the Last button, you want the last record in the database to be displayed in the form. If the user happens to click the Next button after clicking the Last button, this would normally result in an error—because there is no "next" record after the last record. Likewise, when the user clicks the First button, you want the database to display the first record in the database. If the user happened to click the Previous button after clicking the First button, Access would normally display an error, because there is no "previous" record before the first record.

Such error messages can be confusing for an Access novice. So you will "protect" your user by disabling buttons that should not be available to the user under certain situations. Figure 8-23 includes a list of situations and their appropriate actions:

| Figure 8-23 | SITUATIONS AND THE APPROPRIATE ACTIONS |

| SITUATION | ACTION |
| --- | --- |
| User has clicked the First button | Display the first record in the form<br>Disable the Previous button<br>Enable the Next button |
| User has clicked the Last button | Display the last record in the form<br>Disable the Next button<br>Enable the Previous button |
| User has clicked the Next button | If the current record is the last record then:<br>    Disable the next button<br>Otherwise:<br>    Display the next record in the form<br>    Enable the Previous button |
| User has clicked the Previous button | If the current record is the first record then:<br>    Disable the previous button<br>Otherwise:<br>    Display the previous record<br>    Enable the previous record |
| User has clicked the Add Record button | Display a blank record to be appended<br>Disable the Next button |

There are no macro actions that will perform the enabling and disabling of buttons. In order to get your navigation buttons to perform in this manner, you will need to write VBA code instead of simply using macro actions. In order to write this code, you need to learn to work with the DoCmd object, as explained in the next section.

## Becoming Familiar with the DoCmd Object

The main object in Access is the **DoCmd object**. This object is used to run Access actions, which, as you learned earlier in this tutorial, are the building blocks of macros. An action performs tasks such as opening or closing windows, navigating through the records in a database, closing Access, etc. When building a macro in Access, you simply select actions from the actions list. However, you can do all those same things, and more, with the DoCmd object and its associated methods.

Most of the methods associated with the DoCmd object have a matching macro action. For example, when Ashley programmed the command buttons on the main menu, she used macro actions to open the forms, queries, and reports. Alternately, she could have written VBA code to perform exactly the same tasks. Figure 8-24 compares the macro actions you used in Session one of this tutorial with its corresponding DoCmd methods. Note that there are many more actions and even more DoCmd methods available to you.

**Figure 8-24**   **MACRO ACTIONS COMPARED TO DOCMD METHODS**

| MACRO ACTION | DOCMD METHOD |
|---|---|
| Close | Close |
| OpenForm | OpenForm |
| OpenQuery | OpenQuery |
| OpenReport | OpenReport |
| Quit | Quit |

To get a better sense of the variety of methods associated with the DoCmd object, it's useful to look up the object in Access Help. In the next set of steps, you will do just that. In the process, you will focus on the GoToRecord method, which you will use in the CCLS project.

## View the DoCmd methods in the Help files:

1. Click **Help** on the menu bar and then click **Microsoft Access Help**.

2. In the input box type **DoCmd**.

3. Click **DoCmd Property**.

4. Click **Example** and view the example that shows the format for using the DoCmd object.

5. Click the **Back** button.

6. Click **DoCmd** in the first paragraph, as shown in Figure 8-25.

**Figure 8-25**   **DOCMD PROPERTY HELP FILE**

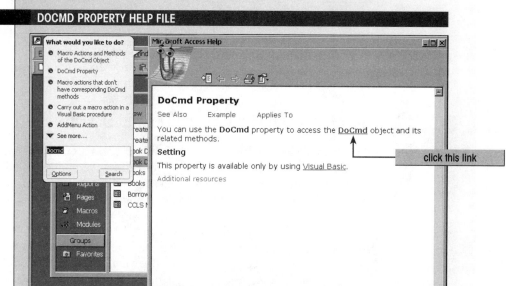

7. Click **Methods** at the top of the Help window. The Topics Found dialog box opens.

8. Scroll through the list until you see GoToRecord method, then double-click **GoToRecord method**.

**9.** Read the information on the GoToRecord method. Don't worry if you don't totally understand this material. For now you are only learning how to look up these commands in the Help files. You will learn how to use this method in the next sessions as you finish the CCLS application.

**10.** Close Access Help.

As you learned in Access Help, the **GoToRecord method** will move the current display to a particular record according to the specification on the DoCmd statement.

| | |
|---|---|
| **Syntax** | `DoCmd.GoToRecord [objecttype, objectname]` `[, record][, offset]` |
| **Explanation** | GoToRecord makes the specified record the current record. **Objecttype** refers to the type of object you want to work with. The default is `AcDatabaseObject`, which indicates that you want to display a database object. The **objectname** argument must be a valid name for an object that exists within the database. The **record** argument specifies which record you want to go to. The **record** argument can be any one of the following constants: **AcFirst** Navigate to the first record. **AcGoTo** Navigate to a specific record. **AcLast** Navigate to the last record. **AcNewRec** Append a new record. **AcNext(default)** Navigate to the next record. **AcPrevious** Navigate to the previous record. For now, ignore the final optional argument, the Offset argument |
| **Example** | `DoCmd GoToRecord AcActiveDataObject, "Book Data",` `acFirst` |

The example above will display the first record in the Book Data form. However, you do not need to include the first and second arguments because they are default values (i.e., you will be referencing the object and form in which you write the code). Since you will be writing your statement within the Book Data form, you don't need to include the second argument. Thus, the statement can be shortened to:

`DoCmd GoToRecord , "", acFirst`

Notice that a comma is required in the place of the missing arguments.

You will now use the DoCmd object and the GoToRecord method to program the navigation buttons on the Books Data form.

## Programming the Navigation Buttons

You now have all the information you need to begin programming the navigation buttons. You will start with the First button. Recall from Figure 8-23 that, when the user clicks the First button, you want to display the first record, disable the Previous button, and enable the Next button. You might wonder why that third step (enabling the Next button) is necessary. If the user had previously clicked the Last button, then the Next button would have been disabled. Now that the user has clicked the First button, you want to make sure that the Next button is reinstated, or enabled.

You have used the `Enable` property in a previous tutorial. Recall that you can set the `Enable` property to true if you want the object to be available, and to false if you do not want the object to be available. So, for example, if you want to disable the Next button (that is, the `cmdNext` button) you would use this statement:

```
cmdNext.Enabled = false
```

As you've seen, to create a macro in Access you use the Macro Builder. To write VBA code for Access, you must use the **Code Builder**. In the next set of steps you will open the Code Builder. As you will see, it is identical to the VBA IDE you have used in Word, Excel, and PowerPoint.

## To program the First button:

1. Make sure that the **Book Data with Navigation Buttons** form is selected in the Database window, and then click the Design button 🔲. The form opens in Design View.

2. Double-click the **First** button. The property sheet for the First button opens.

3. Click the **Event** tab, click the right side of the **On  Click** event, and then click the ellipse ⬚. The Choose Builder dialog box opens. Instead of the Macro Builder, this time you will use the Code Builder.

4. Click **Code Builder** and then click **OK**. The Code window opens. It looks identical to the Code windows you have used in previous tutorials. Notice that the cursor is positioned between the Sub and End  Sub statements in the `cmdFirst` button's Click event procedure, as shown in Figure 8-26.

| Figure 8-26 | FIRST BUTTON'S CLICK EVENT IN CODE WINDOW |

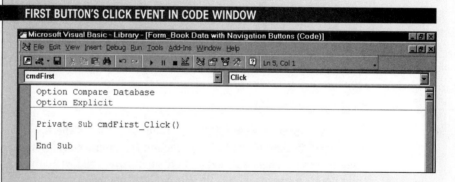

5. Type the following code:

```
DoCmd.GoToRecord , "", acFirst
cmdPrevious.Enabled = False
cmdNext.Enabled = True
```

6. Compare your screen with Figure 8-27 and make any necessary changes.

**Figure 8-27**   **CMDFIRST WITH VBA STATEMENTS ENTERED**

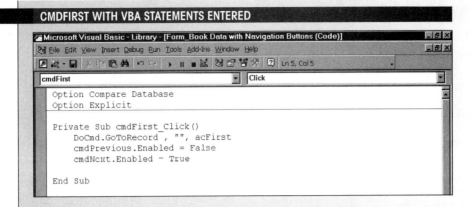

```
Microsoft Visual Basic - Library - [Form_Book Data with Navigation Buttons (Code)]
File  Edit  View  Insert  Debug  Run  Tools  Add-Ins  Window  Help                    Ln 5, Col 5

cmdFirst                                        Click

    Option Compare Database
    Option Explicit

Private Sub cmdFirst_Click()
    DoCmd.GoToRecord , "", acFirst
    cmdPrevious.Enabled = False
    cmdNext.Enabled - True

End Sub
```

**7.** Close the Code Builder window (that is, the Microsoft Visual Basic – Library window) and notice that [Event Procedure] is displayed in the Click Event on the Event tab of the property sheet. This indicates that a procedure is associated with this event. Close the property sheet making sure to save your changes.

**8.** Open the form and click the **First** button. At this stage, you can't actually perceive any activity since the first record is always displayed when you open a form. But you will have a chance to retest this button later.

You have now programmed the First button. You will repeat this process for each of the other buttons. In the next steps you will program the remainder of the buttons and then test the form to make sure it performs properly.

## To program the remainder of the navigation buttons:

**1.** Switch the **Book Data with Navigation Buttons** form to Design View.

**2.** Double-click the **Next** button, click the Event tab (if necessary), open the Code Builder for the On Click event, and type the following code in the cmdNext_Click event procedure:

```
DoCmd.GoToRecord , "", acNext
cmdPrevious.Enabled = True
```

**3.** Compare your screen with Figure 8-28 and make any necessary changes. Now you are ready to program the cmdLast button. Instead of going back to the form and re-opening the Command Builder, you can use the Object list arrow in the Code window to select this object.

**Figure 8-28**    **CMDNEXT CLICK EVENT**

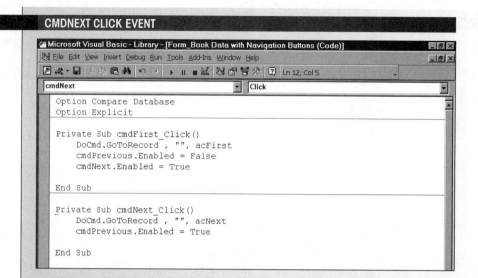

4. Click the Object list arrow, and then click **cmdLast**. The cursor moves to the Click event procedure for the cmdLast button, as shown in Figure 8-29.

**Figure 8-29**    **CMDLAST CLICK EVENT**

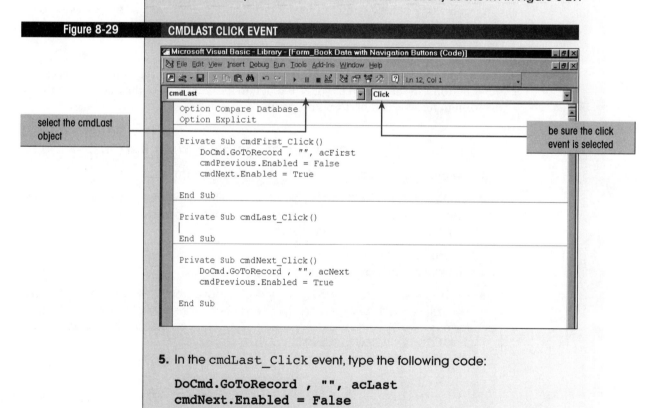

5. In the cmdLast_Click event, type the following code:

```
DoCmd.GoToRecord , "", acLast
cmdNext.Enabled = False
cmdPrevious.Enabled = True
```

6. Compare your screen with Figure 8-30 and make any necessary changes.

Figure 8-30        CMDLAST WITH VBA STATEMENTS ADDED

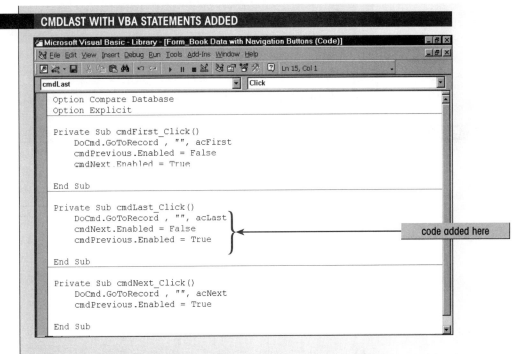

7. Click the **Object** list arrow and select the **cmdPrevious** object. Make sure your cursor is in the Click event for the cmdPrevious button and type the following:

```
DoCmd.GoToRecord , "", acPrevious
cmdNext.Enabled = True
```

8. Compare your screen with Figure 8-31 and make any necessary changes.

Figure 8-31        CMDPREVIOUS CLICK EVENT WITH VBA STATEMENTS ADDED

Microsoft Visual Basic - Library - [Form_Book Data with Navigation Buttons (Code)]

File  Edit  View  Insert  Debug  Run  Tools  Add-Ins  Window  Help

cmdPrevious          Click

Ln 25, Col 5

```
        cmdNext.Enabled = True

    End Sub

    Private Sub cmdLast_Click()
        DoCmd.GoToRecord , "", acLast
        cmdNext.Enabled = False
        cmdPrevious.Enabled = True

    End Sub

    Private Sub cmdNext_Click()
        DoCmd.GoToRecord , "", acNext
        cmdPrevious.Enabled = True

    End Sub

    Private Sub cmdPrevious_Click()
        DoCmd.GoToRecord , "", acPrevious
        cmdNext.Enabled = True

    End Sub
```

9. Click the **Object** list box and select the **cmdAdd** object. Make sure your cursor is in the Click event for the cmdAdd button and type the following:

```
DoCmd.GoToRecord , "", acNewRec
cmdNext.Enabled = False
```

10. Compare your screen with Figure 8-32 and make any necessary changes.

| Figure 8-32 | CMDADD CLICK EVENT WITH VBA STATEMENTS ADDED |
|---|---|

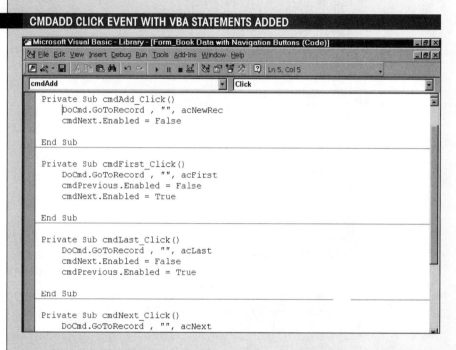

11. Close the Code Builder window, close the property sheet, and then close the Book Data form's Design window. Save your changes to the form.

12. In the Database window, double-click **Book Data with Navigation Buttons**, and test each of the navigation buttons. Verify that the buttons are enabled and disabled as Gene requested.

TROUBLE? If you click the Next button continually, you will eventually see an error message due to the fact that it is impossible to proceed past the last record (the empty record) in the database. You will fix these errors in the next set of steps. Note that you will see an error if you click the Previous button after you have reached the first record. However, if you see any other errors, then you made a mistake when typing the code. Make any necessary corrections and run the form again.

## Disabling a Navigation Button

You have programmed the navigation buttons and observed that they function correctly. One problem remains, however. Recall that Access always provides an empty record (sometimes called an Append record) at the end of table, which you can use to add (append) additional records. This is the final record in the database. If the Next button is clicked again, an error will occur because it is impossible to move past the last record.

In the next steps you will first test the Next button to observe the error. You will then alter the code to repair the problem.

## To test the Next button and cause an intentional error:

**1.** Verify that the Book Data with Navigation Buttons form is still running.

**2.** Click the **Next** button continually until you see the empty record.

**3.** Click the **Next** button once more. You see an error, as shown in Figure 8-33.

| Figure 8-33 | ERROR MESSAGE RECEIVED WHEN TRYING TO GO PAST LAST RECORD |
| --- | --- |

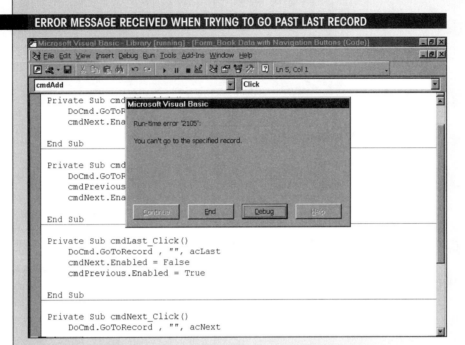

**4.** Read the error message, which indicates that you can't go to the specified record—that is, to the next record. It's impossible to display the next record because there is no next record.

**5.** In the Microsoft Visual Basic dialog box, click the **Debug** button. The problematic line of code is highlighted in yellow.

**6.** Click the **Reset** button on the toolbar.

You need to write some code for the Next button that will check to see if the next record in the database is blank. One way to do this is to write code that will check to see if the BookCode field contains a null value. (Only the BookCode field in the blank record should have a null value.) To write the necessary code, you need to use the **IsNull function,** an intrinsic VBA function that will check to see if a value is null. If the value is null, the function returns a True value, and if not it will return a False value.

To summarize, you want to determine if the BookCode field is null (that is, if it contains no value). If this field is null, then you need to disable the Next button. You cannot disable an object that currently has focus, so you must first change the focus to another object. Therefore, you will set the focus to the Last button, using the SetFocus method.

Thus, the necessary code is as follows:

```
If IsNull(Me.BookCode) Then
    cmdLast.SetFocus
    cmdNext.Enabled = False
Else
```

```
        DoCmd.GoToRecord , "", acNext
        cmdPrevious.Enabled = True
    End If
```

You will now alter the code for the Next button.

---

## To alter the Next button code:

**1.** In the Code window for the form, place your cursor in the `cmdNext_Click` event procedure.

**2.** Highlight all of the current code and replace it with the following code:

```
If IsNull(Me.BookCode) Then
    cmdLast.SetFocus
    cmdNext.Enabled = False
Else
    DoCmd.GoToRecord , "", acNext
    cmdPrevious.Enabled = True
End If
```

**3.** Compare your screen to Figure 8-34 and make any necessary changes.

---

| Figure 8-34 | NEW CODE ADDED TO THE CMDNEXT CLICK EVENT |
|---|---|

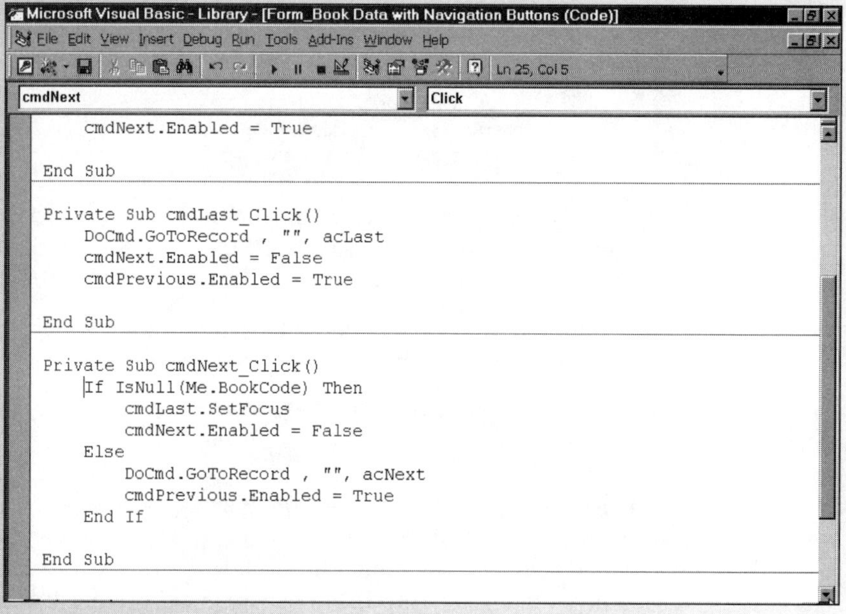

**4.** Close the Code Builder, and return to the Database window. Close the form and save your changes.

**5.** Open the **Books Data with Navigation Buttons** form once again and test the Next button. It is no longer possible to move past the last record.

**6.** Close the form.

You may have foreseen a similar problem with the Previous button: if the user continues to click the Previous button past the first record, an error will occur. The code that will take care of this problem is almost identical to the code for the Next button. The only difference is that the code must check to see if the first record has been reached. (This requires the following condition: `Me.CurrentRecord = 1`). If the first record has been reached, the Previous button should be disabled, and the focus moved to the Next button. Thus, the necessary code is as follows:

```
If Me.CurrentRecord = 1 Then
    cmdNext.SetFocus
    cmdPrevious.Enabled = False
Else
    DoCmd.GoToRecord , "", acPrevious
    CmdPrevious.Enabled = True
End If
cmdNext.Enabled = True
```

You will now alter the code for the Previous button.

---

### To alter the Previous button code:

1. In the Code window for the form, place the cursor in the `cmdPrevious_Click` event procedure.

2. Highlight all of the current code and replace it with the following code:

```
If Me.CurrentRecord = 1 Then
    cmdNext.SetFocus
    cmdPrevious.Enabled = False
Else
    DoCmd.GoToRecord , " ", acPrevious
    cmdPrevious.Enabled = True
End If
cmdNext.Enabled = True
```

3. Close the Code Builder and return to the Database window. Close the form and save your changes.

4. Open the form named **Books Data with Navigation Buttons**.

5. Click the **Next** button once to move forward in the database.

6. Click the Previous button twice. Notice that you are unable to move past the first record.

---

You are finished creating the navigation buttons. When you show your work to Gene, he is pleased with the results and recommends that you repeat this process for each of the forms in the library system. (In order to save time, you won't actually do that in this tutorial.)

In the next session, you will learn to write some VBA code that will alter the appearance of some of the objects on a form, and also use VBA to perform some calculations.

## Session 8.2 QUICK CHECK

1. The _____ object provides a collection of methods that you will use to program in Access.

2. The _____ method makes it possible to move to a particular record in the specified form or table.

3. The _____ function will return a True value if an argument's value is null and a False value if an argument's value is not null.

4. Almost every macro action has a matching VBA _____.

5. If you want to add a macro action to a control object you use the _____, but if you want to write your own VBA statements and add them to a control you use the _____.

---

## SESSION 8.3

In this session you will add some VBA programs to the Library project. You will write some code that will alter the appearance of data in a form according to the content of a particular control. You will write code that will display a label on the form when a particular condition arises. Finally, you will print all the code associated with the Library project.

## Adding and Programming Controls in an Access Form

Gene has asked you to add some simple formatting to the Book Data form and to the Borrowers Data form. He explains that most of the forms will require some formatting and other enhancements to make the system useful to the library. However, he has assigned most of the remainder of the updates to other members of the consulting team. The following are the items he would like you to work on:

- When a new book is added to the Books table, the program should check to see if it was published before 1900. If it was, it is considered antique, and a label containing the text "Caution: Antique" should be displayed. Otherwise the label should not be seen at all. Gene suggests that you use the label control's Visible property to achieve this.

- When a keyword is added to the new book record, the program should check to see if the keyword is "adult" (uppercase or lowercase). If the keyword is "adult," the program should format the keyword field in boldface red, and all uppercase. This will prevent the librarians from accidentally checking out adult books to minors. Another TnT consultant will be programming this enhancement on the Checkout form. You will only need to add the necessary code to the Book Data form.

- When a new borrower is added to the Borrowers table, the program should check to see if the Minor field has been checked. If it has been checked, indicating that the borrower is a minor, display a message box that tells the user that a parent's name must be entered. After the message box is displayed, the program should enable the Parent's Name field and set the focus to this field.

You will start by adding the requested changes to the Book Data form, which is based on the Books table. Recall that the Books table contains a field named `DatePublished`. First, you will add a label to the form with the caption "Caution! Antique." Then you will write a VBA procedure that will display the label when a book is an antique and hide the label when a book is not antique.

## Inserting a Label in an Access Form

You add labels to Access forms just as you add labels to forms created in VBA for Word, Excel, or PowerPoint—by clicking the Label button on the toolbox and drawing the button on the form. After you insert the label into the form, you need to set its properties. You want the label to display the text "Caution! Antique," so you should use that text as the label's Caption property. In addition, Gene explains that he wants you to use Old English for the label's Font property, in keeping with the fact that the book is an antique. In Old English font, the label text would look like this: Caution! Antique.

You will now add the label to the form.

### To add the label to the form:

1. Open the form named "**Book Data with Navigation Buttons**" in Design view. Maximize the form.

2. Using the appropriate Toolbox button, draw a label on the form in the approximate position shown below in figure 8-35. When you add a label to a form, you can type the caption directly into the label.

| Figure 8-35 | BOOKS DATA FORM WITH ANTIQUE LABEL |

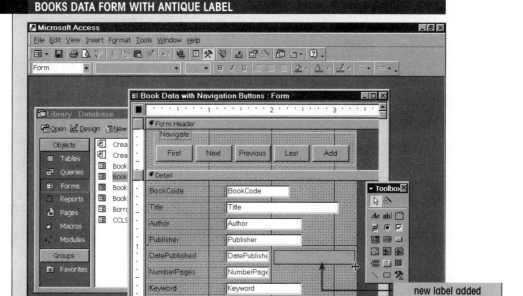

TROUBLE? If you do not see the toolbox displayed, click the Toolbox button on the toolbar.

3. Type **Caution! Antique** and then press **Enter**. The new caption is displayed in the label. If necessary, increase the width of the label so that it fits on one line.

4. With the label still selected, click the **Properties** button 📋 on the toolbar.

5. Click the **All** tab. Notice that the Caption property is already set to Caution! Antique, the text you typed directly into the label.

**6.** Make the following changes to the label's properties. If you don't have the Old English font on your computer, choose another font.

| | |
|---|---|
| Name | **lblAntique** |
| ForeColor | **Dark Green** |
| FontName | **Old English** |
| FontSize | **10** |
| FontWeight | **Bold** |

**7.** Close the property sheet and then observe the label. Adjust its size, if necessary, to display the text as shown in figure 8-36.

| Figure 8-36 | BOOK DATA FORM WITH LABEL ADDED |
|---|---|

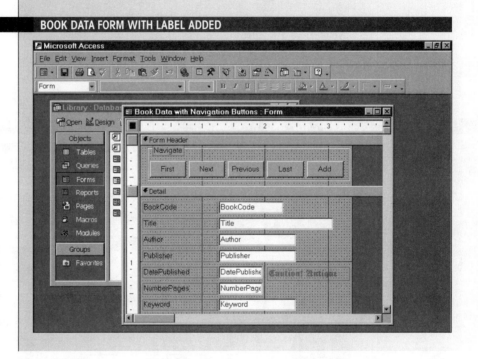

## Programming a Label

Now that you have the label on the form, you need to write VBA code that will control when the label is displayed. As you'll recall, you want the label to be displayed in the form whenever the date in the `DatePublished` field is before 1900. The VBA code to do this is shown below and should be fairly self-explanatory, given what you have learned in previous chapters.

```
If [DatePublished] < 1900 Then
    lblAntique.Visible = True
Else
    lblAntique.Visible = False
End If
```

Note that, in this code, the name of the field ([`DatePublished`]) is enclosed in square brackets. When you want to refer to the name of a field in VBA code for Access, you must enclose the name in brackets ( [] ). The code then checks to see if the value of the `DatePublished` field is earlier than 1900. If it is, then the `lblAntique` label is made visible. If, however, it is not earlier than 1900, then the label is made invisible.

The next thing you must decide is where to place this code. You want the program to check the `DatePublished` field after a date has been entered—in other words, after the user moves the cursor to the next text box. A text box (in this case, the `DatePublished` text box) has an event, **LostFocus**, that is triggered whenever the cursor has been on the field and then leaves the field. So if, for example, the user moves the cursor from the `DatePublished` text box to another text box, the `LostFocus` event will be triggered. Thus, you should insert the code in the text box's `LostFocus` event.

Gene explains that you also want the label to appear whenever the user displays a previously entered record in which the `DatePublished` field is earlier than 1900. In other words, you want the program to check the `DatePublished` field each time a new record is displayed, and then display the label if the date in that field is earlier than 1900. To make this happen, you can take advantage of a VBA event associated with an Access form, the **Current event**, which is triggered each time a new record is displayed in the form. In this particular situation, you need to place the code that checks the value of the `DatePublished` field in the Book Data form's `Current` event.

This means that you need to use the same code twice in the program, once in the `DatePublished` field's `LostFocus` event, and again in the form's `Current` event. Since you are going to use the same code in two places, it makes sense to write the code once in a general procedure. (You learned about creating and calling general procedures in Tutorial 7.) You will now create this general procedure, and then call it from within two different event procedures.

### To write the code that controls the display of the label:

**1.** Verify that the form is still displayed in Design mode. Next, you will open the Code window for the form.

**2.** Click anywhere on the form and then click the **Code** button  in the Access toolbar. The Code window for the form opens, displaying the code that you created in the previous session. Maximize the Code window, as shown in Figure 8-37. Now you will add a procedure to the Code window.

| Figure 8-37 | CODE WINDOW WITH PREVIOUS CODE DISPLAYED |
|---|---|

```
Microsoft Visual Basic - Library - [Form_Book Data with Navigation Buttons (Code)]
File  Edit  View  Insert  Debug  Run  Tools  Add-Ins  Window  Help                    Ln 25, Col 5
cmdNext                                          Click

        cmdNext.Enabled = True

    End Sub

    Private Sub cmdLast_Click()
        DoCmd.GoToRecord , "", acLast
        cmdNext.Enabled = False
        cmdPrevious.Enabled = True

    End Sub

    Private Sub cmdNext_Click()
        If IsNull(Me.BookCode) Then
            cmdLast.SetFocus
            cmdNext.Enabled = False
        Else
            DoCmd.GoToRecord , "", acNext
            cmdPrevious.Enabled = True
        End If

    End Sub
```

**3.** Click **Insert** on the menu bar and then click **Procedure**.

**4.** In the name box type **OldBooks** and then click **OK**.

**5.** Within the Sub and End Sub statements type the following code:

```
If [DatePublished] < 1900 Then
    lblAntique.Visible = True
Else
    lblAntique.Visible = False
End If
```

**6.** Compare your screen with Figure 8-38 and make any necessary corrections.

| Figure 8-38 | CODE WINDOW WITH OLDBOOKS PROCEDURE DISPLAYED |
| --- | --- |

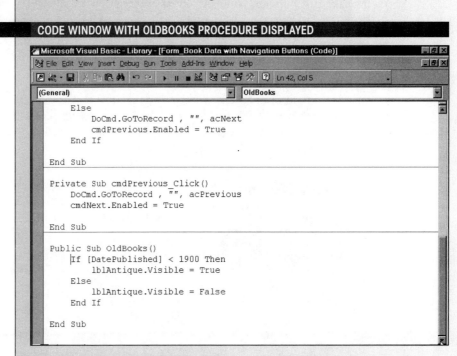

Now that you have created the general procedure, you can call this procedure from the DatePublished event procedure and from the form's Current event procedure.

### To add the Call statement to your code:

**1.** At the top of the Code window, click the **Object** list arrow, click **DatePublished**, click the **Procedure** list arrow, and then click **LostFocus**. See Figure 8-39. Now you need to call the OldBooks procedure from within the LostFocus event procedure.

| Figure 8-39 | CODE WINDOW WITH DATEPUBLISHED_LOSTFOCUS EVENT DISPLAYED |
|---|---|

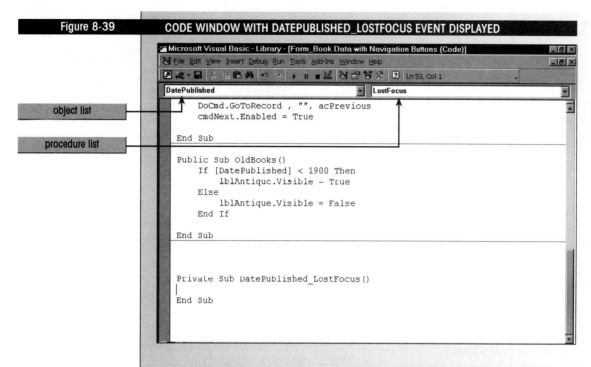

object list

procedure list

```
       DoCmd.GoToRecord , "", acPrevious
       cmdNext.Enabled = True

End Sub

Public Sub OldBooks()
    If [DatePublished] < 1900 Then
        lblAntique.Visible = True
    Else
        lblAntique.Visible = False
    End If

End Sub


Private Sub DatePublished_LostFocus()
|
End Sub
```

TROUBLE? Throughout these steps, you might find extra procedures added to the code. Just ignore these procedures as long as there is no code in them. These are created whenever you click on a procedure in the Procedure list box, which is sometimes unavoidable when you are selecting a procedure.

2. Type the following code:

**Call OldBooks**

Next you need to add the `Call` statement to the form's `Current` event.

3. Click the **Object** list arrow, click **Form**, and then select the `Current` event in the Procedure list box, as shown in Figure 8-40.

Figure 8-40 | LOSTFOCUS EVENT CALL TO OLDBOOKS PROCEDURE

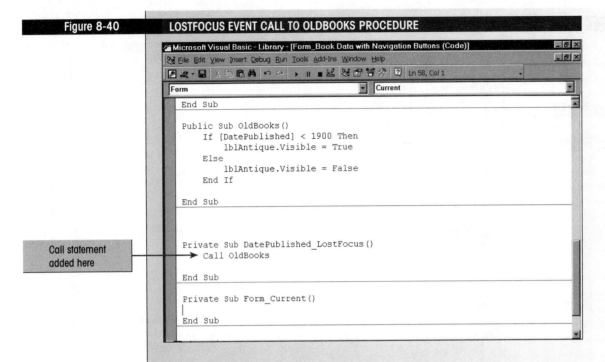

Call statement added here

**4.** In the Current event, type the following code:

```
Call OldBooks
```

**5.** Compare your screen with Figure 8-41 and make any necessary corrections.

Figure 8-41 | OLDBOOKS CALLED FROM LOSTFOCUS AND CURRENT EVENTS

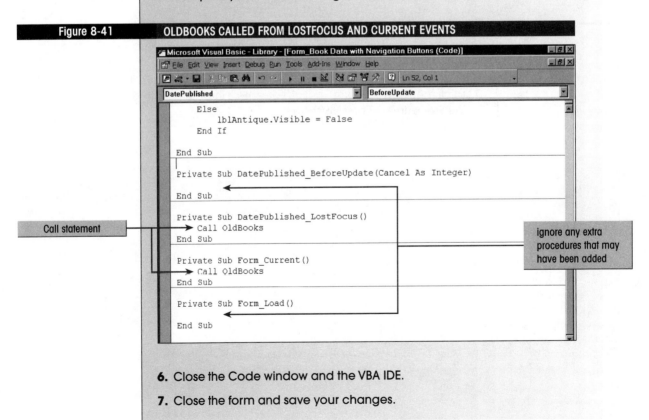

Call statement

ignore any extra procedures that may have been added

**6.** Close the Code window and the VBA IDE.

**7.** Close the form and save your changes.

Now that you have added the code, you need to test it to make sure it works as expected. Remember that the code you just added checks to see if a new book is an antique. If so, the "Caution! Antique" label should be displayed.

---

### To test the code:

**1.** In the Database window, double-click **Book Data with Navigation Buttons**.

**2.** Click the **Add** button and enter the following data for a new book:

| | |
|---|---|
| Title: | **The Life and Times of the 1850s** |
| Author: | **Bradley** |
| Publisher: | **Franklin Publishers** |
| Date Published: | **1888** |
| Pages: | **500** |
| Keyword: | **History** |

**3.** Notice that when you moved the cursor from the Data Published field to the Pages field, the label appeared on the form.

**4.** Close the form.

---

You have added the label and programmed the form to display the label only under certain conditions. Now you need to add code that will check the `Keyword` field to determine if the book is an adult book. In the case of adult books, the `Keyword` field should be formatted in red letters, all uppercase, and bold.

## Conditionally Altering the Appearance of a Control

The code you write must check the user's input for a particular value. This is problematic in that you can't assume that every user will be entering a string in exactly the same way. One user might enter the value in all uppercase, while another might capitalize just the first letter, while another might use all lowercase. These possible variations make it hard to write code that will compare the string entered by the user with a value that you specify.

In this case, you need to write an `If` statement that will compare the string entered by the user with the string "ADULT." You want to make it possible for the `If` statement to work correctly, even if the user types "adult" or "Adult." You can accomplish this by using the predefined function **Ucase,** which will convert a string to all uppercase. For example, the following will convert the string "Adult" to "ADULT":

```
Ucase("Adult")
```

The following `If...Then` statement contains an expression that will first convert the string stored in the field `Keyword` to all uppercase and then compare the result to the string "ADULT".

```
If Ucase([Keyword]) = "ADULT" Then
```

Recall that in Access, when you want to refer to a field name in code, the field name must be enclosed in brackets. Since the syntax for the UCase function requires parentheses, the field name in this case is enclosed in brackets and parentheses.

In the case of an adult book, you want to format the `Keyword` field in red, change the value to all uppercase, and make the font bold. If the book does not have a keyword of "Adult", then the field should be formatted in blue. You can accomplish this via the RGB function. As you learned in Tutorial 3, the following code represents the color red:

```
RGB( 255, 0, 0)
```

And the following code represents the color blue:

```
RGB( 0, 0, 255)
```

The following code, then, will format the `Keyword` field:

```
If UCase([Keyword]) = "ADULT" Then
        [Keyword].ForeColor = RGB(255, 0, 0)
        [Keyword].FontBold = True
        [Keyword] = UCase([Keyword])
    Else
        [Keyword].ForeColor = RGB(0, 0, 255)
    End If
```

Again, you will need to write your code in such a way that the code is executed when the form changes records (that is, in the form's `Current` event) and when the `Keyword` field loses focus. This requires a general procedure, which you can then call from the form's `Current` event and from the `Keyword` field's `LostFocus` event.

You now add this code to the Book Data with Navigation Buttons form's code module.

## To add the code that will format the `Keyword` field:

1. With the cursor on the **Book Data with Navigation Buttons** form, click the **Code** button 📇.

2. When the Code window opens, click **Insert** on the menu bar, and then click **Procedure** in the drop-down menu.

3. In the Name box, type **AdultBooks** and then click **OK**.

4. Within the `AdultBooks` procedure, type the following code:

```
If UCase([Keyword]) = "ADULT" Then
    [Keyword].ForeColor = RGB(255, 0, 0)
    [Keyword].FontBold = True
    [Keyword] = UCase([Keyword])
Else
    [Keyword].ForeColor = RGB(0, 0, 255)
End If
```

5. Click the **Objects** list arrow, click **Form**, click the **Procedure** list arrow, click **Current**, and then add this statement:

```
Call AdultBooks
```

6. Click the **Objects** list arrow, click **Keyword**, click the **Procedure** list arrow, click **LostFocus**, and then type the statement you typed in Step 5.

7. Compare your screen with Figure 8-42 and make any necessary changes.

| Figure 8-42 | ADULTBOOKS CALLED FROM KEYWORD_LOSTFOCUS EVENT |

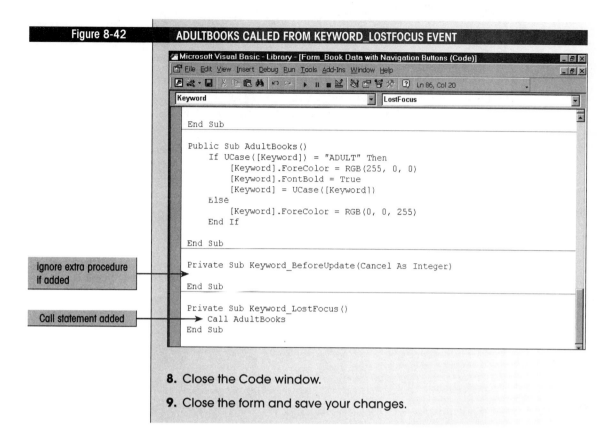

```
Microsoft Visual Basic - Library - [Form_Book Data with Navigation Buttons (Code)]
File  Edit  View  Insert  Debug  Run  Tools  Add-Ins  Window  Help
                                                        Ln 86, Col 20
Keyword                                    LostFocus

    End Sub

Public Sub AdultBooks()
    If UCase([Keyword]) = "ADULT" Then
        [Keyword].ForeColor = RGB(255, 0, 0)
        [Keyword].FontBold = True
        [Keyword] = UCase([Keyword])
    Else
        [Keyword].ForeColor = RGB(0, 0, 255)
    End If

End Sub

Private Sub Keyword_BeforeUpdate(Cancel As Integer)

End Sub

Private Sub Keyword_LostFocus()
    Call AdultBooks
End Sub
```

**ignore extra procedure if added** →

**Call statement added** →

8. Close the Code window.

9. Close the form and save your changes.

Now that you have written the program statement to perform the check for "Adult Books," you need to test the form to verify that it works properly.

## To test the form:

1. Open the form and move the cursor to the last record (the record for the book named *The Life and Times of the 1850s*).

2. Replace the value in the Keyword field with the word **adult** (in lowercase).

3. Press the **Tab** key. The string is converted to "ADULT," and is formatted in bold-face red.

4. Close the form.

Your last task involves writing the code that will check to see if the borrower is a minor.

## Conditionally Enabling and Disabling a Text Box

Gene wants you to add a procedure to the form that will determine if the user has checked the Minor field. If the Minor field is checked, then the program should display a message indicating that a parent's name is required. Once the user has read the message, the ParentName text box should then be enabled and then the ParentName text box should receive focus (i.e. the cursor will move to the ParentName text box).

However, if the `Minor` field has not been checked, then the `ParentName` text box should be disabled. The Value property of the check box will indicate whether it has been checked (True) or has not been checked (False).

The code that will perform this task is as follows:

```
If Minor.Value = True Then
    MsgBox ("Minors Must have a parent name")
    [ParentName].Enabled = True
    [ParentName].SetFocus
Else
    [ParentName].Enabled = False
End If
```

You need to insert this code in the `LostFocus` event of the Minor text box. You will now add this code to the Borrowers Data form.

### To enter the code to check the `Minors` *field:*

1. Open the **Borrowers Data** form in Design View.

2. Click the **Code** button 📖 on the toolbar.

3. Click the **Objects** list arrow, click **Minor**, click the **Procedure** list box, and then click **LostFocus**.

4. Between the Sub and End Sub statements type the following code:

```
If Minor.Value = True Then
    MsgBox ("Minors Must have a parent name")
    [ParentName].Enabled = True
    [ParentName].SetFocus
Else
    [ParentName].Enabled = False
End If
```

5. Compare your screen with Figure 8-43 and make any changes necessary.

| Figure 8-43 | MINOR_LOSTFOCUS EVENT PROCEDURE |
| --- | --- |

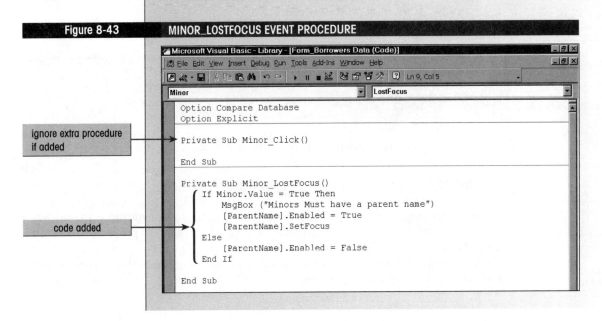

**6.** Close the Code window.

**7.** Close the form and save your changes.

**8.** Run the form, click the Append button on the navigation bar, and add the following record:

| | |
|---|---|
| First name: | **Austin** |
| Last name: | **Brooks** |
| Middle: | **D** |
| Address: | **5219 Hunter Village Dr.** |
| City: | **Carson City** |
| State: | **TN** |
| Zip: | **37363** |
| Minor: | **check** |

**9.** Press the **Tab** key. You see a message box telling you to enter a parent's name.

**10.** Click **OK**, enter **Lori Michal Brooks** as the parent's name, and then close the form.

You are satisfied that your code performs as requested. You decide to print out the code for the project so that when you show your work to Gene, he can easily view the code.

## To print the code for the project:

**1.** Place your pointer on the **Book Data with Navigation Buttons** form and then click the Code button 🔲 on the toolbar.

**2.** Click **File** on the menu bar and then click **Print**. The Print – Library Data dialog box opens. You want to print all the code in the project.

**3.** Click the **Current Project** option button.

**4.** Click **OK**. The code prints.

**5.** Close the Code Builder.

**6.** Close the form.

**7.** Close Access.

You show your work to Gene, and he explains that you have completed the portion that has been assigned to you and that he is satisfied with what you have done. He will be collecting the remainder of the changes from the other consultants and delivering a complete product to the library. Gene feels that you have made a good start on using VBA in all applications and encourages you to continue trying things and expanding your knowledge of VBA.

# Session 8.3 QUICK CHECK

1. When referencing a table field in VBA code, you must enclose the field name in _____.

2. The _____ event is "triggered" when the cursor is moved off a control.

3. The _____ event is "triggered" when a form displays a new record.

4. The _____ function converts a string to uppercase.

5. The _____ method will give the focus to a specified control.

## REVIEW ASSIGNMENTS

Sheila Seigel, the office manager at Potters House Gallery, uses an Access database to maintain employee records. Sheila is not comfortable working directly in Access, and so the gallery owner has hired TnT Consulting to create a main menu form that Sheila can use to select the form she needs. Gene assigns you the task of creating this form, and reminds you to include navigation buttons on it. In addition to creating the form, you need to add a label to the Employees form that will display the caption "High Pay Rate" whenever a pay rate greater than $25 is entered.

1. If you haven't done so already, use Windows Explorer to make a copy of the Tutorial.08 folder on your hard drive or network drive.

2. Open the database named **Potters** from the Review folder for Tutorial 8.

3. Create a Main Menu form in the database, similar to the one in the tutorial. Attach macro actions to the Close Main Menu button and the Quit Access button.

*Explore*
4. Assign macro actions to each button so that every form, query, and report can be opened from the main menu. Be sure to program each of the report buttons using the OpenReport macro action. (In the lower section of the Macro Builder, you will need to specify which report should be opened. Also, assign an action so that each report opens in Print Preview.)

5. Open the Employee Data form and write the necessary statements for the navigation buttons. Take care to enable and disable these buttons in certain situations, as you did in the tutorial.

6. Test the form to make sure that the buttons allow you to move through the records correctly. Be sure to address all the issues related to navigation buttons discussed in the tutorial.

7. Add a label to the Employee Data form that displays "High Pay Rate" whenever the value entered in the `PayRate` field is greater than $25. When the rate of pay is less than $10, the text in the `PayRate` field should be displayed in red.

8. Add your name and the current date to the top of the code.

9. Print all of the code for the database.

## CASE PROBLEMS

**Case 1.** *Mountain Valley Plants*  Mountain Valley Plants provides outdoor plants to landscape companies. The company's inventory manager, Rachel Summers, is responsible for ensuring that Mountain Valley always has a sufficient plant inventory. She uses Microsoft Access to track her plant inventory. The database is automatically updated each time a landscape company makes a purchase. However, Rachel must check the database herself to determine when quantities are running low. She would like you to develop a VBA procedure that will notify her when the quantity of a specific plant is less than 50.

1. If you haven't already, use Windows Explorer to make a copy of the Tutorial.08 folder on your hard drive or network drive.

2. Start Microsoft Access.

3. Open the database file named **MVPlants** from the Cases folder for Tutorial 8.

4. Open the form named Plants in Design mode.

5. Familiarize yourself with the form. Open the Code Builder for the form, and check the names of each control in the Properties window.

6. Select the form, display its property sheet, and click the Event tab.

7. Open the Code Builder for the `OnCurrent` event, and add code that will do the following:

   - If the `txtPlantName` field contains no value, end the procedure. (*Hint*: Use the `Exit Sub` statement.)

   - If the `txtAmtOnHand` field contains a value that is less than 50, display a message box stating that it is time to order more of this particular plant, and include the name of the plant in the message. To write this code, use a statement similar to this:

   ```
   MsgBox "Time to order more " & txtPlantName & ".", _
          vbInformation, "Order Information"
   ```

8. Save the procedure, close the Code Builder, close the property sheet, and return to the form in Design View.

9. Add a command button that will close the form. (*Hint*: Add the button to the form and then select Form Operations from the Command Button Wizard.) Set the caption property for the button to "Close" and name the button `cmdClose`.

10. Review the code created for the Close button.

11. Add comments at the top of the code that include your name and today's date.

12. Close the form and when asked if you want to save your changes, say Yes.

13. Run the form and test the code.

14. Use the buttons at the base of the form to move through the database records.

15. Print the project's code.

**Case 2. Skates and Boards** Skates and Boards, a sporting goods store, sells inline skates and skateboards to skating enthusiasts of all ages. Donnie Grahs manages the store and determines when an item will go on sale. He uses an Access data form to maintain the store inventory. The table consists of the product ID, serial number, product description, number of units in stock, and the unit price. Donnie would like the system to display a message to the sales staff whenever a particular item is on sale. He hires you to add a label to the data form that will appear only when an item is on sale. There is already a label on the inventory form named `lblOnSale`, which should be visible when an item is on sale and invisible when it is not on sale.

1. If you haven't already, used Windows Explorer to make a copy of the Tutorial.08 folder on your hard drive or network drive.

2. Start Microsoft Access and open the database named **Skates** from the Cases folder for Tutorial 8.

3. Open the form named Inventory in Design mode.

4. Familiarize yourself with the form. Check the names of each control in the Properties window.

5. In the Code Builder for the `OnCurrent` event, add code that will do the following:

   ■ If the `txtProductID` field contains no value, end the procedure. (*Hint*: Use the `Exit Sub` statement.)
   ■ If the `txtSerialNumber field` equals IS-300, then make the label named `lblOnSale` visible; otherwise make the label invisible.

6. Save the procedure, close the Code Builder, close the Properties pages, and return to the form.

**Explore**

7. In Design View add a command button to close the form. (*Hint*: Add the button to the form and then select Form Operations from the Command Button Wizard.) Set the caption property of the button to `Close` and name the button `cmdClose`.

8. Review the code for the Close button.

9. Add comments at the top of the code that include your name and today's date.

10. Close the form, and when asked if you want to save your changes, click Yes.

11. Run the form and test the code.

12. Use the buttons at the base of the form to move through the database records.

13. Print the project's code.

**Case 3. Dublin College** Dr. Karl Masters is an instructor at Dublin College. He uses Microsoft Access to record the midterm and final grades for his students. For security, he records the grades in the database using a student identification number instead of the student's name. He averages the midterm and final grades to calculate the student's grade for the course. He asks you to develop a VBA program that will calculate the average of the two grades and then convert the average grade to a letter grade equivalent.

1. If you haven't already, use Windows Explorer to make a copy of the Tutorial.08 folder on your hard drive or network drive.

2. Start Microsoft Access and open the database named **Masters** from the Cases folder for Tutorial 8.

3. Open the form named Grades in Design mode.

4. Familiarize yourself with the form. Check the names of each control in the Properties window.

5. Select the Grade button. Use the Code Builder for the `OnClick` event to add code that will do the following:

   ■ Calculate the average of the midterm and final grade.

   ■ Calculate the letter grade that corresponds to the average of the midterm and final grade.

   ■ Display the average score and display the letter grade on the form.

6. Save the procedure. Switch to the Design mode.

7. Add a command button to close the form. (*Hint*: Add the button to the form and then select Form Operations from the Command Button Wizard.) Set the button text to "Close" and name the button `cmdClose`.

8. Review the code for the Close button.

9. Add comments at the top of the code that include your name and today's date.

10. Close the form and save your changes.

11. Run the form and test the code.

12. Use the buttons at the base of the form to move through the database records.

13. Use the Grade button to calculate and display the student's average score and final letter grade.

14. Print the project's code.

*Case 4. EZClean* Maggie Townsend owns and operates a cleaning business called EZClean Home Cleaning Service. She keeps a list of her clients in a Microsoft Access database. However, she doesn't like using the standard data entry form created by the Form Wizard. Specifically, she doesn't like the default data navigation toolbar, and she wants to have a Close button on the form. She asks you to modify the form so that it includes a custom set of navigation buttons along the base of the form and a Close button along the right side of the form.

1. If you haven't already, use Windows Explorer to make a copy of the Tutorial.08 folder on your hard drive or network drive.

2. Start Microsoft Access and open the database named **EZClean** from the Cases folder for Tutorial 8.

3. Open the form named Clients in Design mode.

4. Familiarize yourself with the form. Check the names of each control in the Properties window.

5. Add controls to the form as shown in Figure 8-44.

| Figure 8-44 | EZCLEAN FORM |

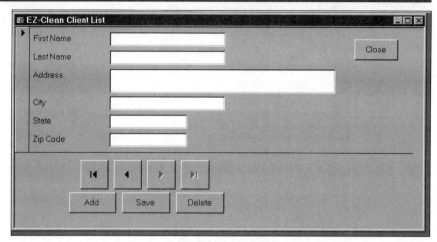

**Explore** 6. Use the Record Navigation category in the Command Button Wizard to add navigation buttons to the form. The navigation buttons should allow the user to move to the first record, move to the previous record, move to the next record, and move to the last record. Within the Command Button Wizard, select the appropriate image for each button. Name the buttons cmdFirst, cmdPrevious, cmdNext, and cmdLast, respectively.

7. Review the code that the Wizard created for each of the navigation buttons.

8. Modify the code for the OnCurrent event to set the Enable property of the Next and Last buttons to False if the Last Name field is Null. Otherwise, set the Enable property of the Next and Last buttons to True. (*Hint*: Remember that you cannot disable an object when it has the focus. Consider setting the focus to the cmdPrevious button.)

9. Close the form and save your changes. Switch to the form view and look at the form.

**Explore** 10. Use the Record Operations category in the Command Button Wizard to add database buttons to the form. The database buttons should allow the user to add a record to the database, save a record to the database, and delete a record from the database. Use the text option to display the appropriate text for each database button. Name the buttons cmdAdd, cmdSave, and cmdDelete respectively.

11. Review the code created by the Wizard for each of the database buttons.

12. Add comments at the top of the code that include your name and today's date.

13. Close the form and save your changes. Switch to Form View and look at the form.

14. Switch to Design mode and add a command button to close the form. (*Hint*: Use the Form Operations category from the Command Button Wizard.) Set the caption property of the button to "Close" and name the button cmdClose.

15. Review the code for the Close button.

16. Close the form and save your changes.

17. Run the form and test the application.

18. Add your name and address to the database using the buttons that you created.

19. Add a second record using your instructor's name and your school address.

20. Use the navigation buttons to move through the database records.

21. Print the project's code.

# QUICK CHECK ANSWERS

*Session 8.1*

1. Macro Recorder
2. openForm
3. openQuery
4. openReport
5. Close
6. Quit

*Session 8.2*

1. DoCmd
2. GoToRecord
3. IsNull
4. method
5. Macro Builder, Code Builder

*Session 8.3*

1. brackets ( [] )
2. LostFocus
3. Current
4. UCase
5. SetFocus

## OBJECTIVES

In this tutorial you will:

- Learn about integrating Office applications with VBA

- Set references to other applications

- Create a new Word document from within an Access code module

- Write code that will insert Access data into a Word Document

- Import code into a module

- Create a new Excel workbook from within an Access code module

- Create an Excel chart from within an Access code module

# INTEGRATING THE OFFICE APPLICATIONS WITH VBA

*Creating an Integrated Application for InTouch, Inc.*

CASE

## InTouch, Inc.

InTouch, Inc. sells prepaid telephone calling cards throughout the United States. The company has a large sales staff that works in four different regions: North, South, West, and East. Each month, Alexander Knight, the sales manager for InTouch Inc., prepares a Word document presenting the quarterly sales figures for sales representatives.

Samantha Chl, the company's data analyst, compiles the quarterly sales data in an Access data table, but Alexander himself is not completely comfortable working in Access. He is, however, very proficient in Word. For this reason, he has hired TnT Consulting to create an application that will take the sales data from the Access table and insert it into a new Word document as a Word table. Once the application creates the new document with the Word table, Alexander can easily complete the rest of the sales report by modifying the table as necessary. In addition to creating this Word table, Alexander wants the application to transfer the Access data to an Excel workbook, and then illustrate the data in an Excel chart.

Gene Cox, your supervisor at TnT Consulting, has asked you to work on this project, which will integrate three Office applications: Access, Excel, and Word.

## SESSION 9.1

In this session you will write code that will start Word, create a new document and add text and a table to the new document. Finally, you will write code that will transfer data from an Access table to the newly created Word table.

## Integrating the Office Applications

As you know, the Microsoft Office suite contains a collection of tools: Word (for word processing), Excel (for manipulating data, performing calculations, and creating charts), PowerPoint (for creating presentations), and Access (for storing and retrieving data). These tools are powerful within themselves; however, each fulfills only a few specific needs. One of the most powerful aspects of the Microsoft Office suite is the way the individual applications can interact with each other, to fulfill a variety of needs at one time.

Access, as you know, is very useful for working with data in a multitude of formats (i.e., forms, queries, and reports). However, Access is not very useful for creating documents. Very often, you will want to use data stored in an Access table within a Word document. You must, then, be able to transfer the data from Access to Word, which is much more suited for writing such a document.

Now, suppose you want to illustrate the data in a chart (perhaps to show how the sales staff is performing or to compare sales of various products). Because you can't produce such a chart in Access, you need some way to transfer the data from Access to Excel, which offers several charting options.

In your studies of the Office suite, you have already learned how to import and export data and graphics between the applications. You can do the same thing in your VBA programs, without ever making the user aware of the complicated interactions taking place. You'll learn how to do this as you create the application for InTouch, Inc.

## Using General Procedures

In your previous work for TnT Consulting, you have done most of your programming in event procedures. That is, you programmed the various control objects in a form to perform certain tasks. In some cases, you added a few general procedures and then called them from one of the event procedures. Gene explains that in the InTouch project, you will write all of your code as general procedures. The project itself will not include an interface. He explains that not every VBA project requires an interface. Only programs that require information from the user need an interface. The InTouch project will not require any input from the user, and so does not require a user interface. The program will simply move data from a database to Word and to Excel, without any intervention or input from the user. Thus, it is possible to write the entire project using general procedures, which you will run directly from within the VBA IDE. (Note that in the Case Problems at the end of this tutorial, you will have a chance to work on some integrated VBA applications that do involve interfaces.)

## Setting References to Other Applications

Samantha has finished compiling the sales data for the first quarter. She has stored it in an Access table named QuarterOneSales, as shown in Figure 9-1.

**Figure 9-1** **QUARTERONESALES TABLE IN THE INTOUCH DATABASE**

| Employee ID | Last | First | Region | January | February | March |
|---|---|---|---|---|---|---|
| 78909 | Stockman | Bruce | East | $87,654 | $76,345 | $55,678 |
| 89765 | Sanchez | Frances | East | $78,987 | $67,890 | $55,876 |
| 56438 | Fuller | Steven | East | $89,765 | $56,987 | $67,543 |
| 45321 | Soderman | Pamela | North | $19,087 | $27,890 | $56,888 |
| 56456 | Carpenter | Candace | North | $18,907 | $19,098 | $78,986 |
| 90876 | Nelson | David | North | $89,453 | $15,098 | $76,549 |
| 98678 | Pohle | Chester | North | $87,908 | $78,985 | $56,456 |
| 12345 | Lopez | Francesca | North | $10,876 | $12,990 | $15,887 |
| 76564 | Smith | Larry | South | $87,654 | $56,908 | $89,098 |
| 90786 | Suarez | Juan Miguel | South | $18,908 | $65,908 | $78,890 |
| 89076 | Carter | James | South | $89,654 | $89,098 | $56,897 |
| 23456 | Sperry | Margaret | South | $87,655 | $90,876 | $78,998 |
| 67890 | Jeffries | Janet | West | $78,965 | $56,987 | $66,789 |
| 56432 | Seals | Beverly | West | $28,765 | $56,432 | $45,321 |
| 67096 | Carracoa | Carla | West | $18,908 | $17,898 | $29,000 |
| | | | | $0 | $0 | $0 |

As you can see, this table contains the following fields:

- **Employee ID**: Contains the ID number of each sales representative
- **Last**: Contains the a last name of each sales representative
- **First**: Contains the first name of each sales representative
- **Region**: Identifies each sales representative's region
- **January**: Contains January sales for each sales representative
- **February**: Contains February sales for each sales representative
- **March**: Contains March sales for each sales representative

The application you will be building for InTouch must create a Word table from this data. The Word table should include all of the fields listed above, except for the Employee ID and Region fields. The completed Word table should look similar to the one in Figure 9-2.

**Figure 9-2** **WORD TABLE PRODUCED FROM THE ACCESS DATA**

Document1 - Microsoft Word

Quarter One Sales Table

| Last Name | First Name | January | February | March |
|---|---|---|---|---|
| **Lopez** | **Francesca** | **$10,876.00** | **$12,990.00** | **$15,887.00** |
| **Sperry** | **Margaret** | **$87,655.00** | **$90,876.00** | **$78,998.00** |
| **Pohle** | **Chester** | **$87,908.00** | **$78,985.00** | **$56,456.00** |
| **Nelson** | **David** | **$89,453.00** | **$15,098.00** | **$76,549.00** |
| **Carpenter** | **Candace** | **$18,907.00** | **$19,098.00** | **$78,986.00** |
| **Soderman** | **Pamela** | **$19,087.00** | **$27,890.00** | **$56,888.00** |
| **Carter** | **James** | **$89,654.00** | **$89,098.00** | **$56,897.00** |
| **Fuller** | **Steven** | **$89,765.00** | **$56,987.00** | **$67,543.00** |
| **Suarez** | **Juan Miguel** | **$18,908.00** | **$65,908.00** | **$78,890.00** |
| **Carracoa** | **Carla** | **$18,908.00** | **$17,898.00** | **$29,000.00** |
| **Sanchez** | **Frances** | **$78,987.00** | **$67,890.00** | **$55,876.00** |
| **Stockman** | **Bruce** | **$87,654.00** | **$76,345.00** | **$55,678.00** |
| **Smith** | **Larry** | **$87,654.00** | **$56,908.00** | **$89,098.00** |
| **Seals** | **Beverly** | **$28,765.00** | **$56,432.00** | **$45,321.00** |
| **Jeffries** | **Janet** | **$78,965.00** | **$56,987.00** | **$66,789.00** |

You will be writing the project code in an Access module. Within this Access module, you will need to use a program statement that will launch Word and create a new Word document.

Before you can do this, you need to specify that Word will be incorporated into your application. In programming terminology, you need to **set a reference** in the Access module that will make the Word object model available. Later in this tutorial, you will also have to write code that accesses the Excel object model. Thus, you also need to set a reference to the Excel object model within the Access code module. As a general rule, whenever you are writing a project that needs access to objects in other applications, you must set a reference to each of those applications.

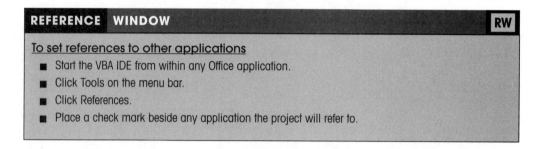

Gene has already set the references for this project. You will have a chance to view these references when you open the database that contains the first quarter sales data. Keep in mind that when you start your own projects from scratch, you must decide which references are required to meet the requirements of the project.

## To open the database containing the sales data and view the references set by Gene:

1. Use the Windows Explorer to make a copy of the Tutorial.09 folder from your Data Disk. Keep the copy as a backup, in case you want to repeat this tutorial later.

2. Verify that your original version of the Tutorial.09 folder is stored on your hard drive or your network drive.

3. Start Access and open the database named **InTouch**, located in the Tutorial.09 folder on your hard drive. Next, you need to open the Access Code Builder. In Tutorial 8, you did this by clicking an event in the property sheet. Because you will be writing a general procedure, rather than an event procedure, however, you can open the Code Builder just as you would open the VBA IDE in the other Office Applications, by pressing Alt+F11. You'll do that in the next step.

4. Press **Alt+F11**. The Access Code Builder opens.

5. Click **Tools** on the menu bar and then click **References**. The References – InTouch dialog box opens, as shown in Figure 9-3. Notice that several check boxes are selected, including the check boxes for the Word object model (Microsoft Word 9.0 Object Library) and the Excel object model (Microsoft Excel 9.0 Object Library). The list of items in your dialog box may differ from Figure 9-3, but you should definitely see the check boxes that are selected in Figure 9-3.

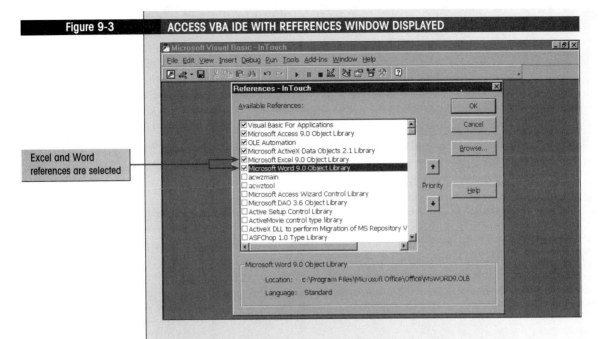

| Figure 9-3 | ACCESS VBA IDE WITH REFERENCES WINDOW DISPLAYED |

**Excel and Word references are selected**

**6.** Scroll through the remainder of the list and view the possible references for a project. Try to locate the PowerPoint object model. You do not need to select this object module to complete the InTouch project. But if you were going to create an Access application integrated with PowerPoint, you would need to select the PowerPoint object model.

**7.** Click **Cancel**. The References – InTouch dialog box closes, and you return to the VBA IDE.

**8.** Close the Code Builder. You return to the Database window.

Once you have set a reference to another application, all of its objects become available to the project. In this case, Gene has set references to the Excel and Word object models, so those objects will be available as you write the code for the InTouch application.

## Creating a New Word Document from Within Access

Now that you have verified that Gene has set the required references in the database file, you can begin writing the code that will perform the following tasks:

1. Start Word.

2. Create a new Word document.

3. Insert the Access data into the document as a Word table.

Your first task, then, is to write the code that will start, or launch, Word. While starting Word is a fairly simple matter from the user's point of view, it actually involves a number of steps from the VBA developer's point of view.

## Declaring a Variable as an Application Object

You must first declare a variable to be of the type `Word.Application`. This type of declaration is a little different from declarations you have used previously. So far, you have declared variables as Integers, Strings, and so on. But you probably didn't realize that you can declare a variable to be any kind of object. In this case, in order to start Word with a VBA statement, you need to declare a variable to be the Word application. When you declare a variable to be a Word.Application object, you are saying that this variable will refer to the Word Application. (Recall that the application itself, in each object model, sits at the top of the hierarchy.)

## Creating an Instance of an Application

After you declare the variable, you can write the statement that actually starts Word. To understand this statement, you need to be familiar with the concept of an instance of an application. Anytime you start an application, you are creating an **instance** of that application. When you start Word, you are creating an instance of the Word application. You can think of an instance as a copy of the application in your computer's memory. To create an instance of an application in VBA, you use the word **New**. While this might seem confusing, all you really need to remember is that the word New starts the application.

## Setting a Reference to an Object

In addition to understanding the concept of an instance of an application, you need to learn how to set a reference to an object in VBA code. When you **set a reference** to an object, you are establishing a name by which you can refer to a particular object. To set a reference, you use the `Set` statement. Its syntax is explained below:

| Syntax | Set objectvar = {(New) objectexpression \| Nothing} |
|---|---|
| **Explanation** | The `Set` statement assigns an object to the `objectvar` (object variable). **objectvar** is a variable that has been declared as an object. **New** is the word that indicates that you want to create a new instance of the object. **Objectexpression** is the name of the object to which you want to set a reference. **Nothing** sets `objectvar` so that it no longer refers to any object. |
| **Example** | `Set appWord = New Word.Application` This example sets the **appWord** variable so that it refers to a new instance of the Word application. `Set appWord = Nothing` This example sets the **appWord** variable so that it does not refer to any object. |

Thus, to declare Word as a variable and then start Word, you will need to use the following two VBA statements:

```
Dim appWord as Word.Application
Set appWord = New Word.Application
```

The first statement declares the variable `appWord` to be a Word application object, thus providing a reference to the application that will be started in the next statement. The second statement actually creates the new Word object and sets `appWord` to be a reference to the new application object. This is to say that any time you use the variable `appWord` in your code, you will be referring to the new instance of Word. After your project opens Word and sets the reference to the instance of Word, it must create a new document. In VBA terminology, it must add a document to the document collection and set a reference to the new document. The three VBA statements needed to perform this action are as follows:

```
Dim docWord As Word.Document
appWord.Documents.Add
Set docWord = appWord.Documents(1)
```

The first statement declares the variable, `docWord` to be a Word document object. The second statement adds a document to the Documents collection. (Just as if you clicked File on the Word menu bar and then clicked New.) Recall that `appWord` is the reference to the instance of Word. So `appWord.Documents` refers to the collection of documents in the application. Finally, the third statement sets a reference to the first document in the collection, the one with which you will be working. From this point on, you can reference the document simply by using the `docWord` variable.

## Making the Application Visible on the Screen

The final step in launching Word and creating a new document is to make the application visible on the screen. Note that this final step is not always necessary. Sometimes, you might want to create a project that launches an application (such as Word or Excel) and sends data to it, but never lets the user see the newly launched application. However, developers often choose to make the application visible in order to observe the newly launched application in action. In this case, making Word visible will allow you to observe the construction of the table. The following statement will make the application visible. Recall that `docWord` is a reference to the current document.

```
docWord.Application.Visible = True
```

You will now create the module that will launch Word from Access, create the new document, and make the application visible. Because you are currently testing your application, you will not save the document created by the application; rather, you will delete the new document each time you run a test.

*To create the module that will start Word and create a new document:*

1. In the Database window, click **Modules** on the Objects bar (if necessary) and then click **New** on the Database toolbar. The Code window opens in the Code Builder.

2. Click **Insert** on the menu bar and then click **Procedure**. The Add Procedure dialog box opens.

3. In the Name text box, type **CreateWordTable** and then click **OK**.

4. Within the procedure, type the following code:

```
Dim appWord As Word.Application
Dim docWord As Word.Document
```

```
'Launch Word, add a document, and
'set a reference to the new document
Set appWord = New Word.Application
appWord.Documents.Add
Set docWord = appWord.Documents(1)
docWord.Application.Visible = True
```

**5.** Compare your screen with Figure 9-4 and make any necessary changes.

| Figure 9-4 | NEW CODE IN CREATEWORDTABLE PROCEDURE |
| --- | --- |

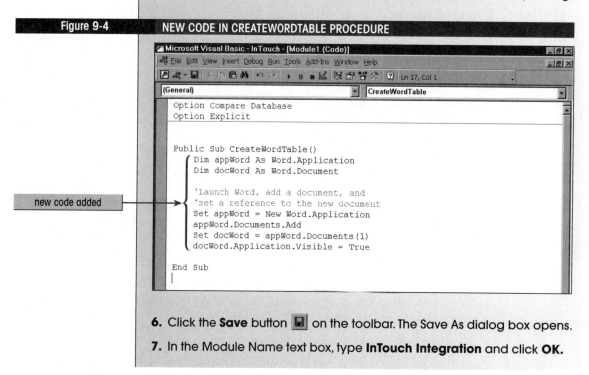

new code added

**6.** Click the **Save** button 🖫 on the toolbar. The Save As dialog box opens.

**7.** In the Module Name text box, type **InTouch Integration** and click **OK.**

Now that you have created the module, you can test it.

## To test the new procedure:

**1.** With your cursor anywhere inside the procedure, press **F5** to run the procedure. Word opens, displaying a new, blank document. Next, you need to return to Access to continue developing the new application. You must first close Word, however, so that the application can open it again later, when you retest your code.

**2.** Close the Word window. If you are asked if you want to save the document, click **No.** You return to the Access VBA IDE, with the Code window open.

Your code, so far, creates a new instance of Word and a new document. In the next session, you will learn how to write statements that will start Excel. Of course, you can use these same techniques to start any of the Office applications. Next, you will need to write code that will create a table and add a heading to the columns in the table.

# Inserting **Access Data** into a **Word Document**

Now that your application can create a new instance of Word and a new document, you can add code that will add a table to the document. Before you add the table, you will first add a descriptive title in the first paragraph of the document.

## Inserting a Title into a Word Document

The next section of VBA code will set a reference to the first paragraph in the document, add a title in the first paragraph, and then add a new paragraph. (The code you write later will then insert the table into this new paragraph.) The following code will accomplish these tasks:

```
'Add a title for the table and create a new paragraph
Set rngInsertionPoint = docWord.Paragraphs(1).Range
rngInsertionPoint.Text = "Quarter One Sales Table"
docWord.Paragraphs.Add
Set rngInsertionPoint = docWord.Paragraphs(2).Range
```

The first line, of course, is just a comment. The second line sets the reference to the first paragraph. Once the reference has been made, the variable `rngInsertionPoint` will refer to the first paragraph in the document. (You will need to declare this variable as a range in the variable declarations portion of the procedure.) The third line inserts the title "Quarter One Sales Table" in the first paragraph. The fourth line adds a new paragraph to the document. Finally, the fifth line sets a reference to the second paragraph, which is where you will insert the table in the next section of code. You will now add this code to the module you have already started.

---

### To add the VBA code that will add a title and a new paragraph to the Word document:

1. Type the following code into the module just below the code you typed previously:

```
'Add a title for the table and create a new paragraph
Set rngInsertionPoint = docWord.Paragraphs(1).Range
rngInsertionPoint.Text = "Quarter One Sales Table"
docWord.Paragraphs.Add
Set rngInsertionPoint = docWord.Paragraphs(2).Range
```

2. To declare the `rngInsertionPoint` variable move the cursor to the end of the other declarations in the `CreatedWordTable` procedure, and add the following statement:

```
Dim rngInsertionPoint As Word.Range
```

3. Compare your screen with Figure 9-5 and make any necessary changes.

**Figure 9-5**  **NEW DECLARATION AND CODE IN CREATEWORDTABLE PROCEDURE**

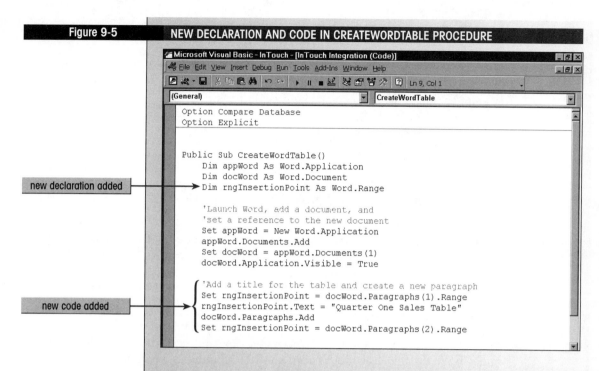

new declaration added →

new code added →

```
Option Compare Database
Option Explicit


Public Sub CreateWordTable()
    Dim appWord As Word.Application
    Dim docWord As Word.Document
    Dim rngInsertionPoint As Word.Range

    'Launch Word, add a document, and
    'set a reference to the new document
    Set appWord = New Word.Application
    appWord.Documents.Add
    Set docWord = appWord.Documents(1)
    docWord.Application.Visible = True

    'Add a title for the table and create a new paragraph
    Set rngInsertionPoint = docWord.Paragraphs(1).Range
    rngInsertionPoint.Text = "Quarter One Sales Table"
    docWord.Paragraphs.Add
    Set rngInsertionPoint = docWord.Paragraphs(2).Range
```

**4.** Save your work and run the program. This time, your application launches Word and inserts the title "Quarter One Sales Table" in the Word document, as shown in Figure 9-6. In Figure 9-6, the paragraph mark below the title indicates that the application also inserted a second paragraph. (The nonprinting characters are displayed in the figure to illustrate this point; they might not be displayed on your computer.)

**Figure 9-6**  **WORD DOCUMENT CREATED WITH VBA STATEMENTS**

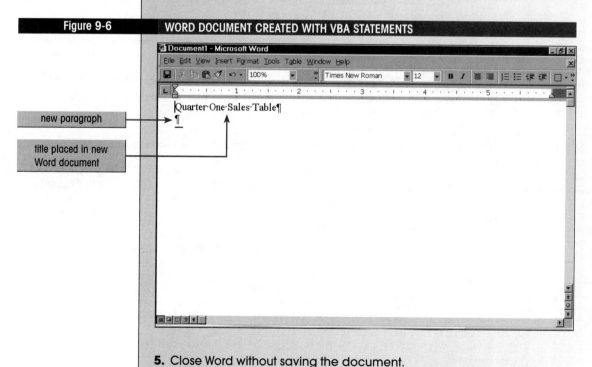

new paragraph →

title placed in new
Word document →

Quarter·One·Sales·Table¶
¶

**5.** Close Word without saving the document.

So far, your code adds a title to the Word document and inserts a new paragraph. The title will serve as the title for the table. Next you need to write the code that will actually add the table to the document and then add the column headings to the table.

## Inserting a Word Table into a Document

In programming terminology, in order to insert a table in a Word document, you need to add a table to the document's Tables collection. Figure 9-7 illustrates how the Tables collection fits into the Word object model. Note that this view of the object model shows more detail than the model introduced in Tutorial 5. However, now that you need to work with a table, it is important for you to see how the Tables collection fits into the Word object model. (The Tables collection is circled in the figure to draw attention to it.)

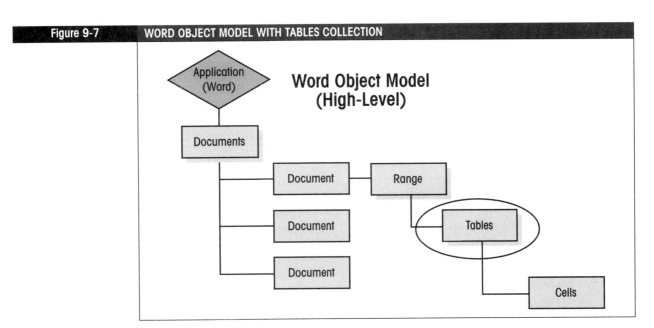

**Figure 9-7**    WORD OBJECT MODEL WITH TABLES COLLECTION

By default, the new document created by your application contains no tables. To be more precise, its Tables collection contains zero tables. It's your job to write the code that will add one table to this collection.

Recall that to reference a particular object in a collection of objects you use the name of the collection and the object's index. For example, `Documents(1)` refers to the first document in the Documents collection, whereas `Documents(2)` refers to the second document in the Documents collection. In the code you will write next, you will use an index number to specify with which table you are working. This might seem a little odd to you, since the new document will ultimately contain only one table, but the index is required by VBA, so you must supply it. To reference the first table in the Tables collection you would use this reference: `Tables(1)`.

In the previous steps, you set this reference to the second paragraph in the document: `rngInsertionPoint`. The following code will add the new table to this new paragraph:

```
With rngInsertionPoint
    .Collapse Direction:=wdCollapseEnd
    .Tables.Add rngInsertionPoint, 1, 5
End With
```

As you learned in Tutorial 5, the `With` statement allows you to consolidate your code. The first statement within the `With` statement simply places the cursor at the end of the current paragraph. The second statement adds a table to the Tables collection at the location of `rngInsertionPoint` (the second paragraph). This statement also specifies that the table will be one row by five columns. The reason you are initially setting up the table with only one row is so that you can let the table "grow" to accommodate the number of records in the Access table (which will provide the data for the Word table). The Word table will consist of five columns in order to accommodate InTouch's request that the table contain the last name, first name, and each of the three monthly sales amounts for each sales representative.

Next, your program must insert headings for the columns in the cells of the newly added table. You will set the font properties for the headings so that they stand out from the rest of the data you will be placing in the table. The following code will place appropriate headings in the one and only row currently in the table. The code also sets the font characteristics for the headings.

```
'Add headings to the first row of the table and set their font
With rngInsertionPoint.Tables(1).Rows.Last
        .Cells(1).Range.Text = "Last Name"
        .Cells(2).Range.Text = "First Name"
        .Cells(3).Range.Text = "January"
        .Cells(4).Range.Text = "February"
        .Cells(5).Range.Text = "March"
End With
'Modify the font properties for the first row
With rngInsertionPoint.Tables(1).Rows(1)
        .Range.Bold = True
        .Range.Font.Size = 12
End With
```

You can now add all of this code to your module to create the table and the first-row headings.

### To add the VBA code to create the table and add headings:

1. Make sure your cursor is just below the code you entered in the previous steps.

2. Type the following code:

```
'Add a table to the tables collection
With rngInsertionPoint
        .Collapse Direction:=wdCollapseEnd
        .Tables.Add rngInsertionPoint, 1, 5
End With


'Add headings to the first row of the table and set
their font
With rngInsertionPoint.Tables(1).Rows.Last
        .Cells(1).Range.Text = "Last Name"
        .Cells(2).Range.Text = "First Name"
        .Cells(3).Range.Text = "January"
        .Cells(4).Range.Text = "February"
        .Cells(5).Range.Text = "March"
End With


'Modify the font properties for the first row
With rngInsertionPoint.Tables(1).Rows(1)
        .Range.Bold = True
        .Range.Font.Size = 12
End With
```

**3.** Compare your module with Figure 9-8 and make any necessary corrections:

**CODE THAT ADDS HEADINGS ENTERED IN CREATEWORDTABLE PROCEDURE**

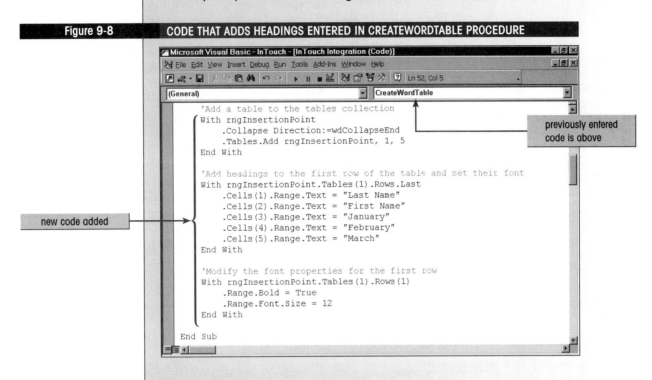

```
'Add a table to the tables collection
With rngInsertionPoint
    .Collapse Direction:=wdCollapseEnd
    .Tables.Add rngInsertionPoint, 1, 5
End With

'Add headings to the first row of the table and set their font
With rngInsertionPoint.Tables(1).Rows.Last
    .Cells(1).Range.Text = "Last Name"
    .Cells(2).Range.Text = "First Name"
    .Cells(3).Range.Text = "January"
    .Cells(4).Range.Text = "February"
    .Cells(5).Range.Text = "March"
End With

'Modify the font properties for the first row
With rngInsertionPoint.Tables(1).Rows(1)
    .Range.Bold = True
    .Range.Font.Size = 12
End With

End Sub
```

previously entered code is above

new code added

**4.** Save your work and run the program. After the program runs, you should see the table's title in the first paragraph of a Word document, followed by a table consisting of one row of formatted headings. Compare your Word document with Figure 9-9.

Figure 9-9   **WORD DOCUMENT WITH TABLE ADDED**

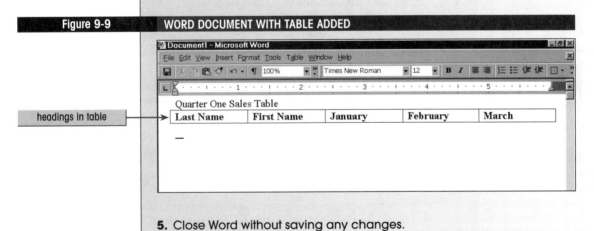

headings in table

Quarter One Sales Table

| Last Name | First Name | January | February | March |
|-----------|------------|---------|----------|-------|
|           |            |         |          |       |

**5.** Close Word without saving any changes.

You have finished writing the code that inserts the title, the table, and the table headings. Now you need to write the code that will take the data from the QuarterOneSales table and insert it into the Word Document. In order to retrieve the data from the Access table, you need to set up a recordset. In the next section you will learn to set up the recordset and move through each of the records in the recordset.

## Establishing an Access Recordset

The data that you want to insert in the Word table is currently in an Access table named QuarterOneSales. In order to transfer the data to Word, you must write code that creates a **recordset,** which is a collection of records. While you may not realize it, you actually have experience working with recordsets; anytime you open an Access table, you are viewing a recordset (a collection of records).

Within VBA, the topic of creating recordsets is a very large one. To keep the InTouch application simple, the program will create a recordset that contains all the fields and all the records in the table. When you become a more experienced programmer, you can create recordsets that contain only selected records or selected fields (or both).

The creation of the recordset is a two-step process. First, you must declare a variable that will serve as a reference to the new recordset. To do this, you need to take advantage of a technology known as ActiveX Data Objects (ADO), which Access 2000 uses to access its data. ADO incorporates a set of standard operations that allow you to work with data stored in different types of files or databases. Thanks to ADO, an application can connect to just about any kind of data source and retrieve information as data records. The data source could be an Access database, an Excel worksheet, a text file, or many other types of data files.

There are entire books dedicated to the topic of ADO; the details of it are beyond the scope of this one. However, this does not mean that you cannot use ADO in your application. In the case of the InTouch application, and for most simple uses of recordsets, you declare a recordset variable as follows:

```
Dim rstQuarterSales As New ADODB.Recordset
```

This statement declares the variable, `rstQuarterSales` to be a new ADODB recordset. The word "ADODB" indicates that `rstQuarterSales` will refer to an ADO database recordset.

After you declare the recordset variable, you need to open the recordset. The opening of a recordset has the same effect as opening a query or a table in Access; once it is open, the recordset becomes available for viewing and manipulating. In the case of the InTouch application, you want to open the database as a static database. A **static database** is one that cannot be opened or altered by other users, for example, in a networked environment.

Like most other objects, recordsets have methods. To open a recordset, you need to use its **Open method**. The syntax of the Open method is explained below.

| | |
|---|---|
| **Syntax** | recordset.**Open Source, ActiveConnection, CursorType, LockType, Options** |
| **Explanation** | The Open method allows you to open a recordset. The Open method will determine how the recordset is opened and how it can be used. The `CursorType` specifies whether the database will be opened as a static recordset. In the example below, the cursor type is static (using the constant: `adOpenStatic`) meaning that the records will be a static (unchanging) view of the data in the table. The `LockType` specifies what kind of locking will be set on the recordset. For example, you can specify that the recordset be read-only, meaning that the values in the recordset cannot be changed. You can use the `Options` portion of the syntax to specify a number of things, which are not discussed here, but you can read about them in the Help files. |
| **Example** | `rstQuarterSales.Open "QuarterOneSales", _`<br>`        CurrentProject.Connection, adOpenStatic` |

This example will establish a connection to the QuarterOneSales table, and while the connection is established no other user can alter it. More simply stated, this statement will open the QuarterOneSales table; while it is open, no other user will be able to access it.

You will now add these two statements (the declaration and the `Open` statement) to your project.

## To establish the recordset reference in your project:

**1.** Make sure you still have the Code window open.

**2.** Place the cursor near the top of the `CreateWordTable` module procedure, just below the declaration of the `rngInsertionPoint` variable, as shown in Figure 9-10.

| Figure 9-10 | CORRECT POSITION OF CURSOR IN CREATEWORDTABLE PROCEDURE |
| --- | --- |

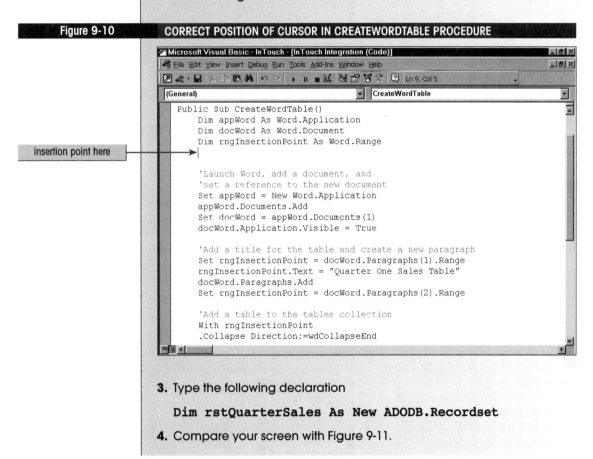

insertion point here

```
Public Sub CreateWordTable()
    Dim appWord As Word.Application
    Dim docWord As Word.Document
    Dim rngInsertionPoint As Word.Range
    |

    'Launch Word, add a document, and
    'set a reference to the new document
    Set appWord = New Word.Application
    appWord.Documents.Add
    Set docWord = appWord.Documents(1)
    docWord.Application.Visible = True

    'Add a title for the table and create a new paragraph
    Set rngInsertionPoint = docWord.Paragraphs(1).Range
    rngInsertionPoint.Text = "Quarter One Sales Table"
    docWord.Paragraphs.Add
    Set rngInsertionPoint = docWord.Paragraphs(2).Range

    'Add a table to the tables collection
    With rngInsertionPoint
    .Collapse Direction:=wdCollapseEnd
```

**3.** Type the following declaration

```
Dim rstQuarterSales As New ADODB.Recordset
```

**4.** Compare your screen with Figure 9-11.

| Figure 9-11 | VARIABLE DECLARED IN CREATEWORDTABLE PROCEDURE |
| --- | --- |

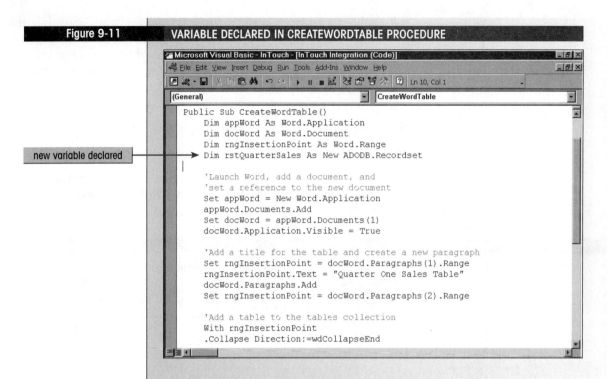

new variable declared

```
Public Sub CreateWordTable()
    Dim appWord As Word.Application
    Dim docWord As Word.Document
    Dim rngInsertionPoint As Word.Range
    Dim rstQuarterSales As New ADODB.Recordset

    'Launch Word, add a document, and
    'set a reference to the new document
    Set appWord = New Word.Application
    appWord.Documents.Add
    Set docWord = appWord.Documents(1)
    docWord.Application.Visible = True

    'Add a title for the table and create a new paragraph
    Set rngInsertionPoint = docWord.Paragraphs(1).Range
    rngInsertionPoint.Text = "Quarter One Sales Table"
    docWord.Paragraphs.Add
    Set rngInsertionPoint = docWord.Paragraphs(2).Range

    'Add a table to the tables collection
    With rngInsertionPoint
    .Collapse Direction:=wdCollapseEnd
```

**5.** Move your cursor down to just above the End  Sub statement, as shown in Figure 9-12.

| Figure 9-12 | CREATEWORDTABLE PROCEDURE |
| --- | --- |

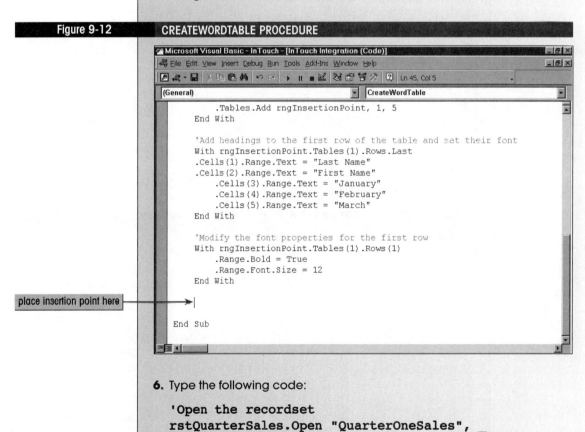

place insertion point here

```
        .Tables.Add rngInsertionPoint, 1, 5
    End With

    'Add headings to the first row of the table and set their font
    With rngInsertionPoint.Tables(1).Rows.Last
    .Cells(1).Range.Text = "Last Name"
    .Cells(2).Range.Text = "First Name"
        .Cells(3).Range.Text = "January"
        .Cells(4).Range.Text = "February"
        .Cells(5).Range.Text = "March"
    End With

    'Modify the font properties for the first row
    With rngInsertionPoint.Tables(1).Rows(1)
        .Range.Bold = True
        .Range.Font.Size = 12
    End With




End Sub
```

**6.** Type the following code:

```
'Open the recordset
rstQuarterSales.Open "QuarterOneSales", _
        CurrentProject.Connection, adOpenStatic
```

**7.** Compare your screen with Figure 9-13 and make any necessary corrections. Next, you can test the code to make sure it doesn't contain any errors. The new code will show no visible results on the screen.

| Figure 9-13 | CREATEWORDTABLE PROCEDURE WITH NEW CODE ADDED |

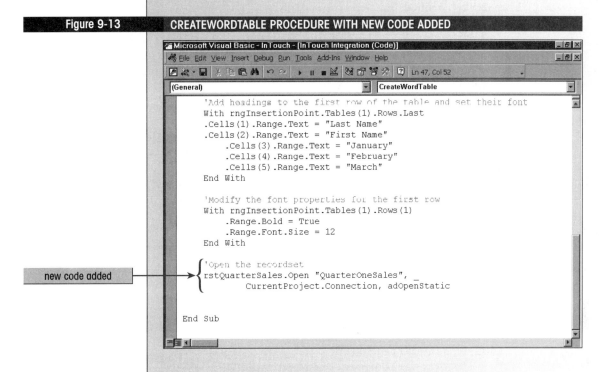

new code added

```
'Add headings to the first row of the table and set their font
With rngInsertionPoint.Tables(1).Rows.Last
.Cells(1).Range.Text = "Last Name"
.Cells(2).Range.Text = "First Name"
        .Cells(3).Range.Text = "January"
        .Cells(4).Range.Text = "February"
        .Cells(5).Range.Text = "March"
End With

'Modify the font properties for the first row
With rngInsertionPoint.Tables(1).Rows(1)
        .Range.Bold = True
        .Range.Font.Size = 12
End With

'Open the recordset
rstQuarterSales.Open "QuarterOneSales", _
        CurrentProject.Connection, adOpenStatic


End Sub
```

**8.** Save your work and run the program. The program inserts the table title, the table, and headings, just as it did the last time you ran it. But internally, the new code has established a connection with the database table.

TROUBLE? If you see an error message, you probably made a typing mistake. Check your code against Figure 9-13, make any necessary corrections, and run the program again.

**9.** Close Word without saving any changes.

So far you have written code that creates a new document and places a title in the document. The application then adds a table consisting of one row to the document. Within that row, the application inserts and formats column headings. Finally, the application establishes a connection with the database table from which you will draw records to place in the table.

In the next section, you will use the records in the database table to fill the Word table in your document.

## Adding the Recordset Data to the Word Table

You have written the code that creates and opens the recordset. Now that the recordset is open, you can write the code that will access the records in the recordset. The reference rstQuarterSales refers to the recordset, which includes the records in the QuarterOneSales table. The code you will write will access each record one at a time and assign its field values to variables. The code will then move the values of the variables to the table in the Word document.

In order to write the necessary statements, you need to take a moment to learn how to refer to an Access field in VBA. Each field has a name, and you can reference each field by using the name of the recordset, followed by the word "Fields," followed by the name of the field in parentheses and quotation marks. For example, the following statement refers to the field named "Last":

```
rstQuarterSales.Fields("Last")
```

In order to assign the value of the "Last" field to a variable, you must declare a variable as a `String` variable. (String is the appropriate type because the Last field contains only names.) Thus, you must type this statement:

```
strLastName = rstQuarterSales.Fields("Last")
```

Recall that in your project, you will be adding the fields `Last`, `First`, `January`, `February`, and `March` to your table. The fields `Last` and `First` contain characters, so for these fields String is the appropriate data type. However, the `January`, `February`, and `March` fields contain currency values (i.e. the sales figures), and so these variables require the Currency data type. Thus, you would declare the necessary variables as follows:

```
Dim strLastName As String
Dim strFirstName As String
Dim curJanuary As Currency
Dim curFebruary As Currency
Dim curMarch As Currency
```

To assign the values of the recordset's fields to the variable, you would use the following code, which incorporates the `With` statement for the sake of brevity:

```
With rstQuarterSales
        strLastName =.Fields("Last")
        strFirstName =.Fields("First")
        curJanuary =.Fields("January")
        curFebruary =.Fields("February")
        curMarch =.Fields("March")
End with
```

If you had chosen not to use the `With` statement, you would have to repeat `rstQuarterSales` in each reference to the Fields collection. Thus, the previous statements, without the `With` statement, would look like this:

```
strLastName = rstQuarterSales.Fields("Last")
strFirstName = rstQuarterSales.Fields("First")
curJanuary = rstQuarterSales.Fields("January")
curFebruary = rstQuarterSales.Fields("February")
curMarch = rstQuarterSales.Fields("March")
```

Now that you have the field values stored in the respective variables, you can place the values into the cells of the Word table that you created earlier. Recall that when you created the table, you inserted the column headings in the last row in the table, which was actually the *only* row. So in order to add a record to the table, you first need to add a row in which the record can be stored. The *new* row will actually become the new *last* row in the table. Once you have added the row, you can use the Last property to refer to the last row in the table. (The **Last property** represents the last item in a collection.) Thus, the following code will move the data stored in the variables to the cells in the table:

```
'Add a row to the table
rngInsertionPoint.Tables(1).Rows.Add
'Place values in the last row of the table
```

```
With rngInsertionPoint.Tables(1).Rows.Last
    .Cells(1).Range.Text = strLastName
    .Cells(2).Range.Text = strFirstName
    .Cells(3).Range.Text = Format(curJanuary, "currency")
    .Cells(4).Range.Text = Format(curFebruary, "currency")
    .Cells(5).Range.Text = Format(curMarch, "currency")
End With
```

The With statement establishes the fact that you are referencing the last row of the table (the new row created with the statement rngInsertionPoint.Tables(1).Rows.Add). The With statement states the cell in which the data is to be placed. The last name is placed in the first column -(Cells(1)-, the first name is placed in the second column -Cells(2)-, etc. You will now insert these two sections of code into the module.

## To add the code that inserts the data into the Word table:

1. Place your cursor at the top of the procedure just after the last variable you declared, as shown in Figure 9-14.

**Figure 9-14**    **CURSOR POSITIONED IN CREATEWORDTABLE PROCEDURE**

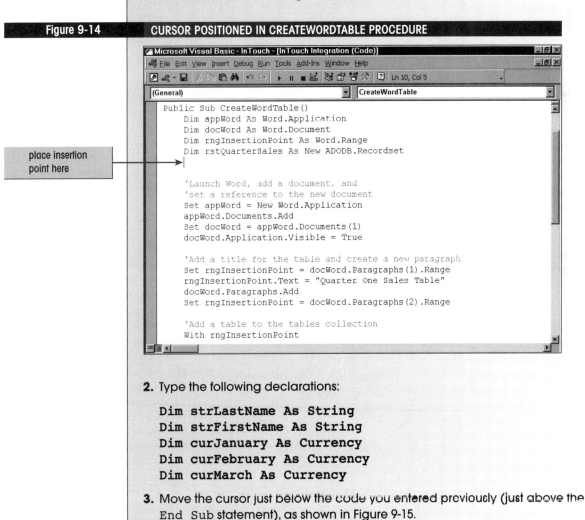

place insertion point here

2. Type the following declarations:

```
Dim strLastName As String
Dim strFirstName As String
Dim curJanuary As Currency
Dim curFebruary As Currency
Dim curMarch As Currency
```

3. Move the cursor just below the code you entered previously (just above the End Sub statement), as shown in Figure 9-15.

Figure 9-15    CORRECT CURSOR POSITION IN CREATEWORDTABLE PROCEDURE

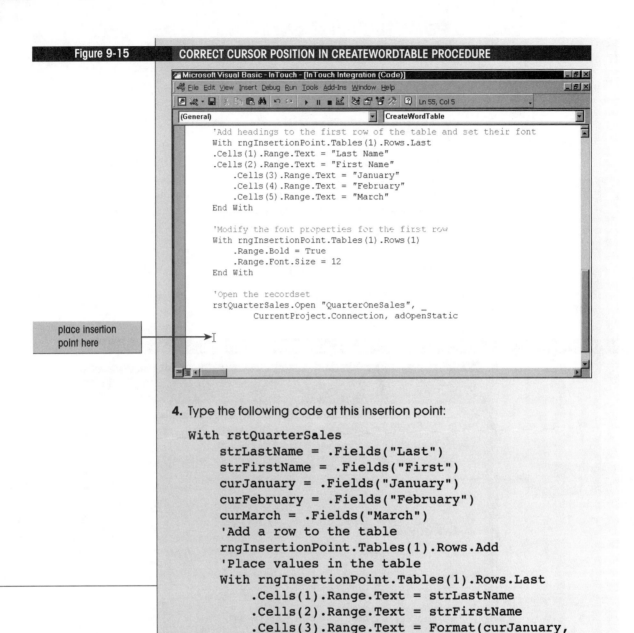

place insertion
point here

4. Type the following code at this insertion point:

```
With rstQuarterSales
    strLastName = .Fields("Last")
    strFirstName = .Fields("First")
    curJanuary = .Fields("January")
    curFebruary = .Fields("February")
    curMarch = .Fields("March")
    'Add a row to the table
    rngInsertionPoint.Tables(1).Rows.Add
    'Place values in the table
    With rngInsertionPoint.Tables(1).Rows.Last
        .Cells(1).Range.Text = strLastName
        .Cells(2).Range.Text = strFirstName
        .Cells(3).Range.Text = Format(curJanuary,
        "currency")
        .Cells(4).Range.Text = Format(curFebruary,
        "currency")
        .Cells(5).Range.Text = Format(curMarch,
        "currency")
    End With
End With
```

5. Compare your screen with Figure 9-16 and make any necessary corrections.

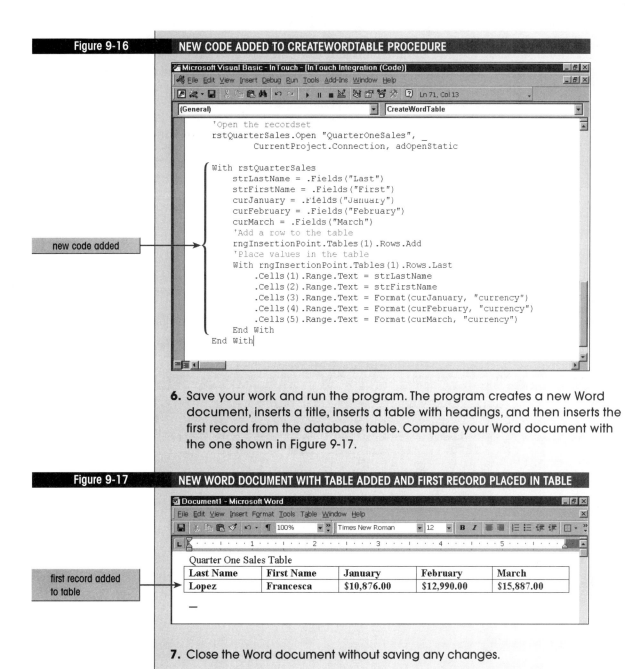

**Figure 9-16** — NEW CODE ADDED TO CREATEWORDTABLE PROCEDURE

new code added

```
'Open the recordset
rstQuarterSales.Open "QuarterOneSales", _
        CurrentProject.Connection, adOpenStatic

With rstQuarterSales
    strLastName = .Fields("Last")
    strFirstName = .Fields("First")
    curJanuary = .Fields("January")
    curFebruary = .Fields("February")
    curMarch = .Fields("March")
    'Add a row to the table
    rngInsertionPoint.Tables(1).Rows.Add
    'Place values in the table
    With rngInsertionPoint.Tables(1).Rows.Last
        .Cells(1).Range.Text = strLastName
        .Cells(2).Range.Text = strFirstName
        .Cells(3).Range.Text = Format(curJanuary, "currency")
        .Cells(4).Range.Text = Format(curFebruary, "currency")
        .Cells(5).Range.Text = Format(curMarch, "currency")
    End With
End With
```

6. Save your work and run the program. The program creates a new Word document, inserts a title, inserts a table with headings, and then inserts the first record from the database table. Compare your Word document with the one shown in Figure 9-17.

**Figure 9-17** — NEW WORD DOCUMENT WITH TABLE ADDED AND FIRST RECORD PLACED IN TABLE

first record added to table

Quarter One Sales Table

| Last Name | First Name | January | February | March |
|-----------|-----------|---------|----------|-------|
| Lopez | Francesca | $10,876.00 | $12,990.00 | $15,887.00 |

7. Close the Word document without saving any changes.

So far your application has created a new Word document, added a title to the document, added a table to the document with headings in the first row, and added data to the table from a single record in the recordset. Now you need to write the code that will insert the rest of the Access records into the Word table. In other words, you must write code that will iterate through the records in the recordset and move each record's data to the table.

## Iterating Through the Records in the Access Data Table

In order to write the code that will add the rest of the Access records to the Word table, you need to add a loop. The loop should continue until all the records have been placed in the table, a process known as **iterating** through the records. This loop will incorporate the **EOF property**, which indicates whether or not the cursor is positioned at the end of a file (or data table). If the EOF property is false, the program has not yet accessed the end of the file; if it is true, the program has reached the end of the file (or table). Thus, you can use the EOF property to control when the loop stops processing. In the case of the InTouch application, you want the loop to continue until the EOF property becomes true (that is, when the cursor has reached the end of the Access data table).

Within the loop, you also need some means of accessing the next record in the database. In other words, you need to use the recordset's MoveNext method. As you learned in Tutorial 8, this method simply makes the next record in the database the current record. Thus, the complete loop should look like this:

```
Do While .EOF = False
        {Statements entered in the preceding section go here.}
        .MoveNext
Loop
```

Note that the loop will incorporate the statements that add the recordset data to the table, which you entered in the preceding section. You will now add the loop statements to the procedure.

## To enter the loop statements into the procedure:

**1.** Place your cursor in the Code window in the location shown in Figure 9-18.

| Figure 9-18 | CURSOR POSITIONED IN CREATEWORDTABLE PROCEDURE |

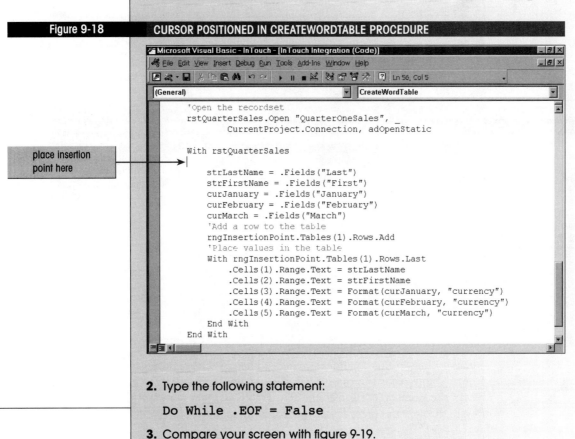

**2.** Type the following statement:

```
Do While .EOF = False
```

**3.** Compare your screen with figure 9-19.

Figure 9-19

**CREATEWORDTABLE PROCEDURE WITH LOOP STATEMENT ADDED**

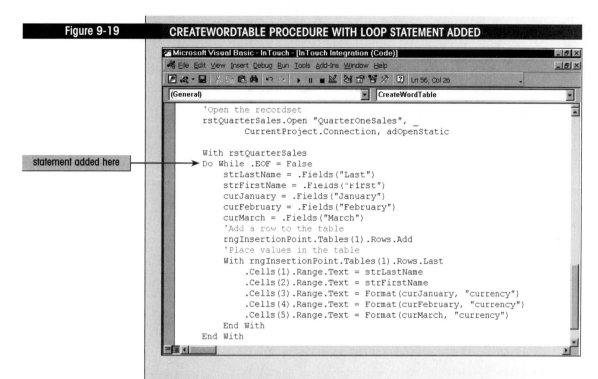

statement added here

4. Move your cursor to the location indicated in Figure 9-20 (between the two End With statements).

Figure 9-20

**CURSOR POSITIONED IN CREATEWORDTABLE PROCEDURE**

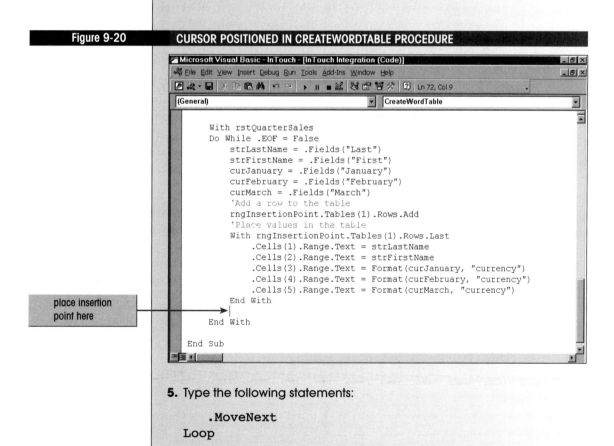

place insertion point here

5. Type the following statements:

```
    .MoveNext
Loop
```

**6.** Compare your code with Figure 9-21 and make any necessary corrections.

| Figure 9-21 | CREATEWORDTABLE PROCEDURE WITH COMPLETE LOOP STATEMENT |

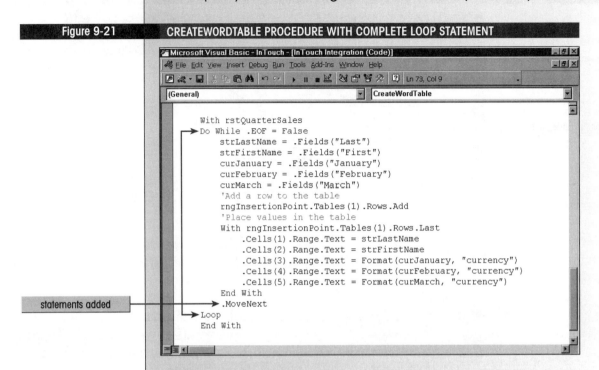

statements added

**7.** Save your work and run the program. This time all the records from the Access table are inserted into the Word table, as shown in Figure 9-22.

| Figure 9-22 | WORD TABLE CREATED |

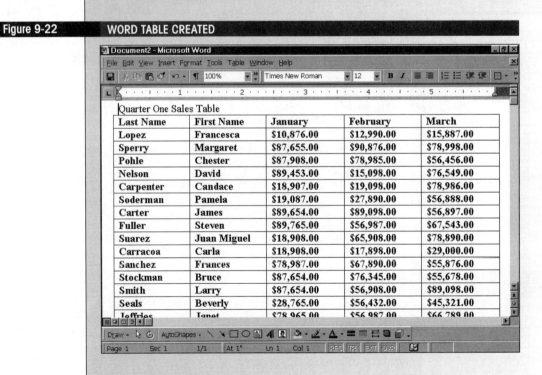

**8.** Save the document in the Tutorial .09 folder as **First Quarter Sales Data** and then close Word.

You have now successfully inserted the data into the Word table. As you show your results to Gene, he explains that this skill will be invaluable to you as you continue to work with VBA. He encourages you to learn more about ADO either by taking a course or by researching the topic in VBA help. He also explains that much of the code required to create the Excel worksheet will be similar to the code you just created. The major difference is that you will be working with the cells of a worksheet rather than the cells of a Word table.

## Session 9.1 QUICK CHECK

1. Write the statements needed to launch Word from Access.

2. Write the statement that will add a table at the range referenced by the variable `rngInsertionPoint`. The table should have five rows and two columns.

3. ADO stands for _____

4. You use the _____ method to make a recordset accessible.

5. The _____ property is set to true when the cursor is in the last record in a recordset.

## SESSION 9.2

In this session you import code into a module, and then test and examine this code. As you will see, this code is in many ways identical to the code you used in the preceding section, except that it involves Excel objects. Finally, you will write code that will create a 3-D column chart in Excel.

## Importing Code into a Module

The next part of your project for InTouch is to write code that creates an Excel worksheet from the QuarterOneSales table and then illustrates the sales data in a chart. Specifically, the application should perform the following tasks:

1. Start Excel and open a new, blank workbook.

2. Insert the data from the QuarterOneSales table into the workbook.

3. Add a column in the Excel worksheet that indicates each sales representative's total sales for the quarter.

4. Illustrate the total sales data in a 3-D column chart.

In your conversations with Gene, he explains that much of the code you will use in this portion of your project is very similar to the code you wrote for the creation of the Word document.

To save time, he has already created the code and saved it in a text file. You simply need to import the code into your code module and then run it to see how it works. Importing code into a module is similar to importing a text file into a Word document. You simply place your cursor in the module in the position where you want the file to be placed and then use the File command on the Insert menu.

**To import a file into a code module**
- Place your cursor in the module at the position where you want to insert the file.
- Click Insert on the menu bar.
- Click File.
- Select the file.
- Click Open.

Gene wrote the code you need in a procedure named the `CreateExcel`. He then saved the procedure in a file named Excel.txt. You will import this file now.

### To import the Excel.txt file into the current module:

1. If you took a break after the last session, open the **InTouch** database in Access, and then open the **InTouch Integration** module.

2. Move the cursor to the very end of the module, after the `End Sub` statement.

3. Click **Insert** on the menu bar and then click **File**.

4. Use the Look in arrow to change to the Tutorial.09 folder on your hard drive (or network drive, depending on where you copied the files), click the file named **Excel** and then click **Open**. The `CreateExcel` procedure is inserted into the Code window, immediately following the code you typed earlier. You will need to scroll through the Code window in order to see the entire procedure.

5. Read the code, paying special attention to the comments, which should help you understand what each section of code does. You'll learn more about the details of this code in the next section.

6. Save your work.

You have successfully imported the code into the existing module. In the next section you will test the code, and then examine it in detail.

## Testing **Imported Code**

You have just imported the code that will set up the Excel portion of the InTouch application. The code creates an Excel worksheet using the Access data as the source of the information. You will now test the code to make sure that it works correctly.

### To test the new procedure:

1. Verify that the cursor is located anywhere within the `CreateExcel` procedure, and then press **F5**. The procedure creates an Excel worksheet with data contained in the QuarterOneSales Access table. Figure 9-23 shows the worksheet with the data inserted.

Figure 9-23 | WORKSHEET CREATED IN EXCEL

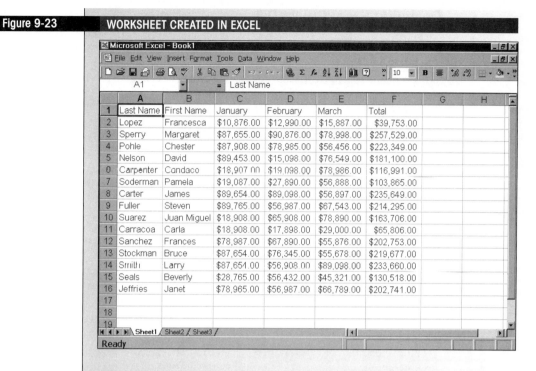

**2.** Examine the worksheet created by the program. Notice that the five columns of sales data from the Access table have been inserted into the worksheet. Notice also that the worksheet contains an additional column that sums the data for each row.

**3.** Close Excel without saving the workbook.

## Examining the Imported Code

Now that you have observed how the procedure works, you need to examine the code. As you scanned the code, you probably observed many similarities between this code and the code that creates the Word document. The Word portion of the module inserted the Access data into a Word table, which consists of columns and rows. The Excel portion of the program inserts the Access data into a worksheet, which also consists of rows and columns. In fact, the portion of code that inserts the Access data into the worksheet is almost identical to the code that inserts the data into the Word table.

Specifically, the `CreateExcel` procedure performs the following steps:

1. Starts Excel and creates a new workbook.

2. Places headings in the first row of the first worksheet in the new workbook.

3. Establishes a connection with the Access table "QuarterOneSales."

4. Copies the data from the Access table to the Excel worksheet.

5. Creates a column that sums the data in each row.

In the next several sections, you will examine the code in the `CreateExcel` procedure. Leave your Code window open as you read through the following explanation of each section of code.

## Declaring Excel Object Reference Variables

The first section in the procedure creates the variables required throughout the module. These require little explanation because they are all very similar to those used to create the Word document. The difference relates to the types of object in Excel as opposed to Word. For example, examine the following section, which declares the necessary variables for the Excel objects:

```
'Declare Excel object variables
Dim appExcel As Excel.Application
Dim xlBook As Excel.Workbook
Dim xlSheet As Excel.Worksheet
Dim chSales As Excel.Chart
```

The first statement declares a variable reference to an instance of Excel. Just as the `CreateWordTable` procedure launched Word by creating a new instance of Word, the `CreateExcel` procedure must launch Excel by creating a new instance of Excel. The second reference variable, `xlBook`, serves as a reference to the new workbook that the VBA program will add to the Excel application. The third reference variable, `xlSheet`, refers to the first worksheet in the new workbook. The data from the Access table will be placed in the first worksheet in the workbook. Finally, the last reference variable, `chSales`, will serve as a reference to the sales data chart.

The remainder of the variables declared at the top of the procedures relates to the column headings, and these are identical to those used in the creation of the Word document, with the exception of the variable named `lngRecordNumber`. This variable is used later in the program to establish the row in which data should be inserted. You will learn more about this variable later in this tutorial.

## Launching Excel and Setting up the Workbook and Worksheet

Recall that the `CreateWordTable` procedure had to create a new instance of Word, create a new document, and then make the application visible. These steps are identical for Excel, except that they apply to Excel objects rather than Word objects. The relevant code is as follows:

```
'Launch Excel and set up a Workbook and Worksheet
Set appExcel = New Excel.Application
appExcel.Workbooks.Add
Set xlBook = appExcel.Workbooks(1)
Set xlSheet = xlBook.Worksheets(1)
appExcel.Visible = True
```

The first statement creates a new instance of Excel—or you can say it launches Excel. The second and third statements add a new workbook to the Workbooks collection and set a reference to the new workbook. (As you know, Excel usually opens a new workbook automatically, as soon as Excel itself is started. However, Gene included this statement to prevent any errors that would occur if the user configured Excel to launch without opening a workbook.) The fourth statement sets a reference to the first worksheet in the workbook. Finally, the last statement makes this new instance of Excel visible. Recall that you want the application visible at this point so that you can observe the operation of your procedure as it is processed. In many situations, however, you might not make the application visible until the procedure had completed its work. In that case, you could move this statement to the bottom of the procedure to make the application visible after the procedure had been completed.

## Adding Column Headings to the Worksheet

The next part of the code inserts column headings to indicate what data is stored in each column. (Likewise, the `CreateWordTable` procedure also inserted column headings into the Word table.) As you learned in Tutorial 6, you reference a cell in VBA code by combining the relevant row number and column number. For example, to refer to cell A1, you would type `cells(1,1)`. Since you will be placing the column headings in row one, you can use a `With` statement that establishes the row number. Then, in the cell reference, you need only reference the column number. The code that places the headings in the worksheet is as follows:

```
'Add headings to the first row of the sheet
With xlSheet.Rows(1)
        .Cells(, 1).Value = "Last Name"
        .Cells(, 2).Value = "First Name"
        .Cells(, 3).Value = "January"
        .Cells(, 4).Value = "February"
        .Cells(, 5).Value = "March"
        .Cells(, 6).Value = "Total"
End With
```

Notice that the code adds a sixth column to the worksheet for the total sales for each salesperson. The total column will be used to create the chart later in the procedure.

## Establishing the Access Recordset

The next statement in the procedure is the same statement that you used in the Word document procedure.

```
'Establish the recordset of the Access table
rstQuarterSales.Open "QuarterOneSales", _
                     CurrentProject.Connection, adOpenStatic
```

Once again, this statement establishes a connection to the QuarterOneSales table. The `rstQuarterSales` reference variable will refer to this recordset throughout the remainder of the procedure.

## Inserting the Access Table Data into the Excel Worksheet

The code that actually inserts the Access Table data into the Excel worksheet is almost identical to the code that inserts the Access data into the Word table. This section of code is shown on the following page in Figure 9-24. Only the highlighted code differs from the code used in the `CreateWordTable` procedure.

| Figure 9-24 | CODE FOR ENTERING THE ACCESS TABLE DATA INTO THE EXCEL WORKSHEET |
| --- | --- |

```
                         'Loop through the records placing their values in the sheet
                             With rstQuarterSales
                                 Do While (Not .EOF)
                                     'Place values into variables
                                     strLastName = .Fields("Last")
                                     strFirstName = .Fields("First")
                                     curJanuary = .Fields("January")
                                     curFebruary = .Fields("February")
                                     curMarch = .Fields("March")

                                     'Determine the row to place the data
                                     lngRecordNumber = .AbsolutePosition
                                     lngRecordNumber = lngRecordNumber + 1
                                     With xlSheet.Rows(lngRecordNumber)
                                         .Cells(, 1).Value = strLastName
                                         .Cells(, 2).Value = strFirstName
                                         .Cells(, 3).Value = Format(curJanuary, "currency")
                                         .Cells(, 4).Value = Format(curFebruary, "currency")
                                         .Cells(, 5).Value = Format(curMarch, "currency")
                                         'Calculate total value and place it in the 6th column
                                         .Cells(, 6).Value = _
                                             .Cells(, 3) + _
                                             .Cells(, 4) + _
                                             .Cells(, 5)
                                     End With

                                     .MoveNext
                                 Loop
                                 'Set column sizes to fit the data
                                 xlSheet.Columns("A:I").AutoFit

                             End With
```

**1. determines the row in which data will be placed**

**2. references a particular cell in the Cells collection**

**3. sums quarterly sales for each record**

**4. sizes the column to fit the data**

The first set of highlighted statements (Number 1 in Figure 9-24) contains two statements that determine the row in which the data is to be placed. These statements are inside the `With rstQuarter Sales` statement. Thus, the statement:

```
lngRecordNumber = .AbsolutePosition
```

is the same as:

```
lngRecordNumber = rstQuarterSales.AbsolutePosition
```

In order to understand how this code works, you need to understand the concept of **absolute position,** which is the number of the record as it was entered into the table. The first record entered would have an absolute position of one, the second record entered would have an absolute position of two, and so on. Even if the records are reordered by sorting or by placing an index (Primary Key) on the table, the absolute position for each record will not change. As you might expect, then, the **AbsolutePosition property** returns the absolute position of the current record. The code above assigns the recordset's AbsolutePosition property to the variable `lngRecordNumber`.

Within the InTouch application, the AbsolutePosition property is used to determine in which row of the worksheet each record will be placed. The application will insert the records into the worksheet in the same order that they were entered into the Access table in the first place. Of course, you might choose to sort the worksheet data later according to one or more columns.

The first row in the worksheet contains headings. Thus, the first record in the Access table will be inserted into the second row of the worksheet. To generalize, then, the correct row number for each record is the record's AbsolutePosition property plus 1.

Note that the `With` statement eliminates the need to include the variable `lngRecordNumber` in the cell references. In fact, statements within this `With` statement require no references to the row number at all.

The second highlighted segment (Number 2 in Figure 9-24) contains an example of a reference to a particular cell in the Cells collection. Because this statement is included within the `With` statement, the statement:

```
.Cells(,1).value = strLastName
```

is equivalent to:

```
.Cells(lngRecordNumber,1).value = strLastName
```

Both statements place the value of the `strLastName` variable into the first row and first column of the worksheet. The remainder of the statements in this segment of code place appropriate values in the corresponding cells.

The third section of highlighted code (Number 3 in Figure 9-24) contains a statement that sums each month's sales figures for a given salesperson and places that value in the sixth column of the current row.

The final section of highlighted code (Number 4) uses the AutoFit method to make sure that all the columns containing data are sized appropriately. In Tutorial 6, you learned how to use the Autofit method to adjust the size of the worksheet's columns to fit the data stored within them.

# Creating an Excel Chart with VBA Statements

To complete the `CreateExcel` procedure, Gene wants you to add the code that creates a 3-D Column chart illustrating the sales data. Specifically, the code you write must perform the following tasks:

1. Add a chart to the Charts collection.

2. Set a reference to the new chart.

3. Establish the type of chart you want to create.

4. Establish the data source for the chart and specify how the chart should be plotted.

5. Establish the location for the new chart.

To complete the first task, you must use the Charts collection's Add method. The **Add method** will add a chart to the charts collection. Once again, you will use the `Set` statement to establish a reference to this new object (i.e., the new chart), as follows:

```
Set chSales = xlBook.Charts.Add
```

This statement sets the variable `chSales` as a reference to a new chart added to the Charts collection. From this point on, any mention of `chSales` refers to the new chart. Next, you need to write the following `With` statement:

```
With chSales
```

This statement simply specifies that the statements within the `With` statement refer to the chart referenced by `chSales`. Of course, in this case, one chart is involved. Nevertheless, you must still establish which chart in the Charts collection you are referring to. Next, you need to use the following statement to establish the chart's type:

```
.ChartType = xl3DColumn
```

From your previous experience with Excel, you know that you can create several different types of charts. In addition to a 3-D column chart, you could choose to create a 3-D area chart, a pie chart, a 3-D pie chart, and so on. Figure 9-25 lists some commonly used Excel chart types, and provides the appropriate VBA reference.

| Figure 9-25 | SOME VBA CHART REFERENCES |
| --- | --- |

| VBA REFERENCE | CHART TYPE |
| --- | --- |
| xl3Darea | 3-D area chart |
| Xl3Dcolumn | 3-D column chart |
| Xl3Dpie | 3-D pie chart |
| XlArea | Area chart |
| XlPie | Pie chart |
| XlLine | Line graph |

This is certainly not an exhaustive list of chart types. For a complete list, see VBA Help.

After specifying the chart type, you need to indicate where the data for the chart can be found. This requires the use of the chart's **SetSourceData method**, which specifies what data will be used to create the chart.

The necessary code looks like this:

```
.SetSourceData _
        Source:=xlSheet.Range("A2:A16,F2:F16"),
        PlotBy:=xlRows
```

This code will chart the data in two ranges, A2:A16 (which contains the worksheet headings) and F2:F16 (which contains the sales data you want to chart). Notice that in this statement, the ranges are within quotes.

The next part of the statement determines how the chart will be plotted—by rows or by columns. In this case, you will plot the chart by rows. Finally, the last statement in the procedure must specify where you want the chart to be located within the workbook. In this case, you want the chart to be placed on a new worksheet and you want to name that new sheet "Quarter Chart." Thus, you need to add the following statement:

```
.Location xlLocationAsNewSheet, Name:="Quarter Chart"
```

You will now enter this code in the `CreateExcel` procedure.

## To enter the code that creates the chart:

**1.** Place your cursor in the `CreateExcel` procedure just below the `End With` statement and just above the `End Sub` statement, as shown in Figure 9-26.

**Figure 9-26**  **CREATEEXCEL PROCEDURE IN THE INTOUCH INTEGRATION MODULE**

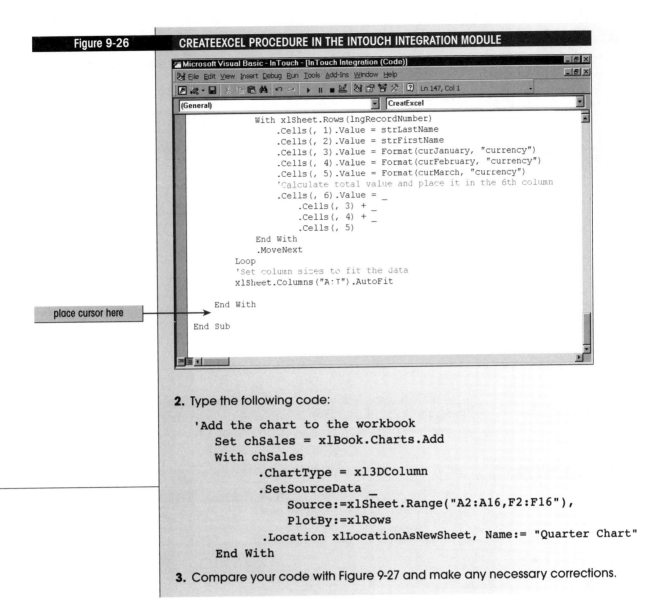

```
            With xlSheet.Rows(lngRecordNumber)
                .Cells(, 1).Value = strLastName
                .Cells(, 2).Value = strFirstName
                .Cells(, 3).Value = Format(curJanuary, "currency")
                .Cells(, 4).Value = Format(curFebruary, "currency")
                .Cells(, 5).Value = Format(curMarch, "currency")
                'Calculate total value and place it in the 6th column
                .Cells(, 6).Value = _
                    .Cells(, 3) + _
                    .Cells(, 4) + _
                    .Cells(, 5)
            End With
            .MoveNext
        Loop
        'Set column sizes to fit the data
        xlSheet.Columns("A:T").AutoFit

    End With

End Sub
```

place cursor here

2. Type the following code:

```
'Add the chart to the workbook
    Set chSales = xlBook.Charts.Add
    With chSales
        .ChartType = xl3DColumn
        .SetSourceData _
            Source:=xlSheet.Range("A2:A16,F2:F16"),
            PlotBy:=xlRows
        .Location xlLocationAsNewSheet, Name:= "Quarter Chart"
    End With
```

3. Compare your code with Figure 9-27 and make any necessary corrections.

Figure 9-27 CREATEEXCEL PROCEDURE

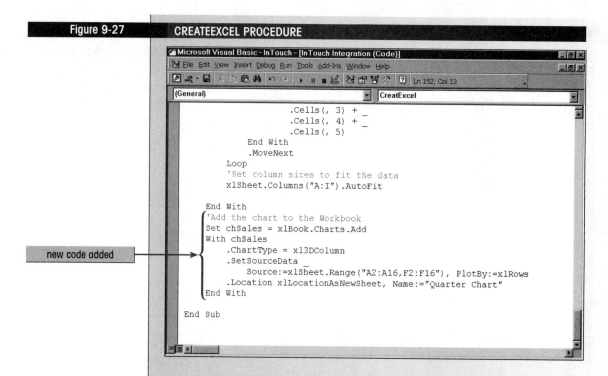

new code added

```
                    .Cells(, 3) + _
                    .Cells(, 4) + _
                    .Cells(, 5)
            End With
            .MoveNext
        Loop
        'Set column sizes to fit the data
        xlSheet.Columns("A:I").AutoFit

    End With
    'Add the chart to the Workbook
    Set chSales = xlBook.Charts.Add
    With chSales
        .ChartType = xl3DColumn
        .SetSourceData _
            Source:=xlSheet.Range("A2:A16,F2:F16"), PlotBy:=xlRows
        .Location xlLocationAsNewSheet, Name:="Quarter Chart"
    End With

End Sub
```

4. Save your work and run the program. The program creates a new worksheet, called Quarter Chart, and then inserts a 3-D column chart that illustrates the quarterly sales data. Compare your screen with Figure 9-28.

Figure 9-28 CHART CREATED IN EXCEL FROM ACCESS DATA

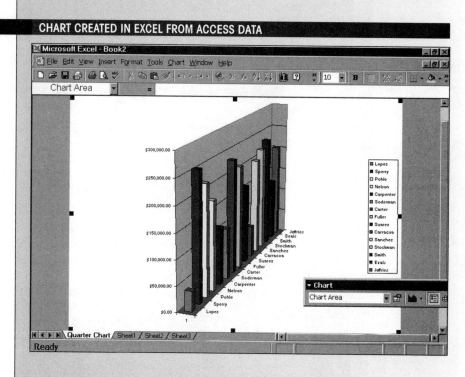

5. Save the workbook as **First Quarter Chart** in the Tutorial .09 folder, and then close Excel.

6. Close Access.

Gene Cox has reviewed your work on the Excel worksheet. He feels that this is exactly what InTouch was looking for on the worksheet. He explains that when he demonstrates this portion of the project, he will probably show Alexander, the sales manager at InTouch, some other types of charts produced with the same data and let him choose which type of chart he wants the final version of the project to create.

This completes the portion of the InTouch project assigned to you. Gene suggests that you use VBA Help to learn more about the topics related to the InTouch application. In particular, he suggests that you investigate the topic of ADO. He says it is an important part of working with data in all of the Office applications.

## Session 9.2 QUICK CHECK

1. To import a file into a module, click _____ on the menu bar and then click _____ .

2. Write the statements that will declare variables to reference an Excel Application, a workbook, a worksheet, and a chart.

3. When you want to reference a cell in Excel, you must reference the _____ number and the _____ number.

4. The _____ property returns the record number of the current record.

5. Use the _____ method to establish the location of the data that will be the source of an Excel chart.

## REVIEW ASSIGNMENTS

Judy Lynn Carter is a professor at a local college who recently began a mentoring program designed to help students succeed in computer-related fields. She created an Access table containing information about her advisees (that is, the students in the program). Her advisees are in the Business Department and are majoring in one of the following: Accounting, Business, CIS, or Management. Professor Carter regularly needs to send a memo to the dean that lists her advisees for the semester, and describes the current status of her program. Rather than repeatedly creating this list in Word, she has hired TnT to create an application that will automatically transfer the data from her Access database to a Word table. She would also like the application to create an Excel chart that compares the GPAs of all of her advisees.

Finally, she wants the application to create a PowerPoint presentation that she can use when discussing the mentoring program at academic seminars. The PowerPoint presentation should summarize her data. She would like the project to create a title slide and then a second slide that indicates the total number of advisees in each major along with the average GPA for each major. She suggests that this data would best be presented in a table.

1. Verify that you have created a backup copy of the Tutorial.09 folder.

2. Start Access and open the database named **Carter**, from the Review folder for Tutorial 9.

3. Open the table named Advisees and become familiar with the data stored in the table. Make a note of the correct field names so that you can use them in your VBA code.

4. If necessary, set references to the Word object library, the Excel object library, and the PowerPoint object library.

5. Open the VBA IDE, insert a new module, Save the new module, and name it Carter Integration.

6. Write a procedure that uses the data in the Advisees table to create a table in a new Word document. Format the data with the font and font size you feel is appropriate.

7. Write a new procedure that uses the data in the Advisees table to create a chart in Excel. The chart should be a column chart, with a row for each advisee.

8. Print the Excel Chart.

*Explore* ▶ 9. Edit the code for Step 6 so that it uses the same data but a different type of chart. You may choose any of the charts that were presented in the tutorial, or choose one listed in the VBA Help.

10. Print the second chart.

*Explore* ▶ 11. The code that creates the PowerPoint presentation is saved in a text file named **Ppoint**. Insert this file into the module. Save and test the module to make sure that it creates the presentation properly. After you have tested the module, name the presentation created by the module **Advisee Presentation**, print the presentation, and then close PowerPoint. Study the VBA code carefully, and try to interpret its various parts. Use VBA Help to learn about features that are unfamiliar to you.

12. Add comments describing each procedure. Add your name and the current date in comments at the top of the module.

13. Save the module and then print it.

*Explore* ▶ 14. On the printed module locate the procedure that creates the PowerPoint presentation. Read the sections that calculate the summary data and the averages. Write a short paragraph that explains how this code calculates the average.

*Explore* ▶ 15. In the Access VBA IDE, locate the code in the PowerPoint procedure that places the data into the table. Add the Format function to the statement so that the averages are formatted with two decimal places when placed into the table. (*Hint*: Use the #0.00 format so that each value displays two decimal places.)

16. Save your work and run the PowerPoint procedure.

17. Print the presentation again. Close PowerPoint without saving changes this time.

18. Close Access.

## CASE PROBLEMS

*Case 1. Renault High Computer Club* Mark Anthony is the president of the Renault High computer club. The club has annual membership dues of $20.00. The money is used to buy software and equipment and to provide refreshments at club meetings. Mark keeps the club roster in a Microsoft Access database. He stores the names of the students and the amount that each student owes for club dues in the database. As president, he is responsible for notifying club members when they haven't paid their dues. He has asked you to help him create a VBA application that will create a list of all club members and the dues owed (if any) as a Microsoft Word document.

1. Verify that you have created a backup copy of the Tutorial.09 folder.

2. Start Access and open the database named **CompClb**, located in the Cases folder for Tutorial 9.

3. Open the form named **Members** in Design View.

4. Familiarize yourself with the form. Check the names of each control in the property sheet.

5. Add a command button that will close the form. Set the button text to "Close" and name the button `cmdClose`.

6. Select the form and display the form's property sheet. Click on the Event tab in the form's property sheet.

7. Review the code for the Close button's `On Click` event.

8. Add comments at the top of the code that include your name and today's date.

9. Save your work and close the Code window.

10. Close the property sheet and save the form.

11. Select the Report button. Use the Code Builder for the `On Click` event to add code that will do the following:

   - Open a Microsoft Word document.
   - Build a table in the Word document. The table should have three columns, with Column 1 titled "First Name", Column 2 titled "Last Name", and Column 3 titled "Dues Owed".
   - Copy the information from the Access table called Members to the table you created in the Word document.
   - Make sure that the table columns are wide enough to display the information without the text wrapping to the next line.

12. Remember to add a reference to the Microsoft Word object library, using the References command on the Tools menu.

13. Add comments at the top of the code that include your name and today's date.

14. Save the procedure. Switch to Form View to test the code.

15. Use the Report button to create a Word document containing the club membership roster.

16. Insert your name and date at the top of the document.

17. Print the project's code.

18. Print the Word document.

19. Close Word without saving the document.

20. Close the VBA IDE and then close Access.

**Case 2. Preparing a Flyer for Middletown Animal Adoption Agency** Each week the Middletown Animal Adoption Agency prepares a flyer that is distributed to veterinarians around town. The flyer lists new animals that are available for adoption. William Woo, who is responsible for preparing the flyer and sending it to the veterinary clinics, stores information about each animal in an Access database. The database contains the animal's name, the type of animal, the animal's size, and a brief description of it. William would like you to create a VBA application that will copy the animal information into a Word document that he could then use as the flyer.

1. Verify that you have created a backup copy of the Tutorial.09 folder.

2. Start Microsoft Access and open the database named **Animals** located in the Cases folder for Tutorial 9.

3. Open the form named Pets in Design View.

4. Familiarize yourself with the form. Check the names of each control in the property sheet.

5. Add a command button that will close the form. Set the button text to "Close" and name the button cmdClose.

6. Select the form and display the form's property sheet. Click the Event tab in the property sheet.

7. Review the code for the Close button.

8. Add comments at the top of the code that include your name and today's date.

9. Save the procedure. Switch to Design View.

10. Save the form.

11. Select the Make Flyer button. Use the Code Builder for the On Click event to add code that will do the following:

   - Open a Microsoft Word document.
   - Build a table in the Word document. The table should have four columns, with Column 1 titled "Name", Column 2 titled "Type", Column 3 titled "Size", and Column 4 titled "Description".
   - Copy the information from the Access table called Animals to the table you created in the Word document.
   - Make sure that the table columns are wide enough to display the information without the lines wrapping.

12. Remember to add a reference to the Microsoft Word object library using the Tools, References menu dialog box.

13. Add comments at the top of the code that include your name and today's date.

14. Save the procedure. Switch to Form View to test the code.

15. Use the Make Flyer button to create a Word document containing the animal adoption information.

16. Insert your name and date at the top of the document.

17. Save your work.

18. Print the project's code.

19. Print the document.

20. Close Word without saving the document.

21. Close the VBA IDE and close Access.

*Case 3. Big Blue Memories*  Mark Delong owns and operates Big Blue Memories, a sports memorabilia store for the fans and supporters of Valley State College. The company has been in operation for 10 years and has seen a steady increase in business every year. Mark uses Microsoft Access to maintain his inventory and sales information. He likes using Access because it is easy to look up various items in his sales catalog. However, he would like to be able to create a chart of the store's sales for the last 10 years. You agree to develop a VBA program that will transfer his sales information to an Excel worksheet and then create a line chart illustrating the store's sales information.

1. Verify that you have created a backup copy of the Tutorial.09 folder.

2. Start Microsoft Access and open the database named **BigBlue** located in the Cases folder for Tutorial 9.

3. Select the form named Sales. Open the form in Design View.

4. Familiarize yourself with the form. Check the names of each control in the property sheet.

5. Add a command button that will close the form. Set the button text to "Close" and name the button `cmdClose`.

6. Select the form and display the form's property sheet. Click the Event tab in the Form's property sheet.

7. Review the code for the Close button.

8. Save the procedure. Switch to the Design View.

9. Save the form.

10. Select the Chart button. Use the Code Builder for the On Click event to add code that will do the following:

   - Open a Microsoft Excel Worksheet.
   - Copy the information from the Access **Sales** table to the worksheet. The worksheet should have two columns, with Column 1 titled "Year" and Column 2 titled "Sales".
   - Make sure that the table columns are wide enough to display the information without the text wrapping to the next line.
   - Use the Year and Sales columns from the worksheet to create a 3-D column chart.

11. Add a reference to the Microsoft Excel object library using the References command on the Tools menu.

12. Add comments at the top of the code that include your name and today's date.

13. Save the procedure. Switch to Form View to test the code.

14. Use the Chart button to create an Excel worksheet and a chart.

15. Save the workbook as **Big Blue Memories**.

16. Print the project's code. Print the worksheet and chart.

17. Close Excel without saving the workbook.

18. Close the VBA IDE.

**Case 4. *Training Mileage*** Darla Wilson is a personal trainer who works with runners to improve their speed and endurance. She creates a personalized training program for each of her clients. Darla uses Microsoft Access to record each client's training schedule. Using this database, she tracks the number of miles that a client runs and the date of the run. She asks you to create a VBA macro that will use Microsoft Excel to provide her clients with a chart of their weekly mileage.

1. Verify that you have made a backup copy of the Tutorial.09 folder.

2. Start Microsoft Access and open the database named **Runner** located in the Cases folder for Tutorial 9.

3. Select the form named Runners Log. Open the form in Design View.

4. Familiarize yourself with the form. Check the names of each control in the Properties pages.

5. Add a command button to close the form. Set the button text to "Close" and name the button `cmdClose`.

6. Select the form and display the form properties dialog box. Click the Event tab in the Form's properties pages.

7. Add comments at the top of the code that include your name and today's date.

8. Save the procedure. Switch to the design view.

9. Save the form.

10. Select the "Chart" button. Use the Code Builder for the On Click event to add code that will do the following:

   ■ Open a Microsoft Excel Worksheet.

   ■ Copy the information from the Access table named Log to the worksheet. The worksheet should have two columns, with Column 1 titled "Date" and Column 2 titled "Distance."

   ■ Make sure that the table columns are wide enough to display the information without the text wrapping to the next line.

   ■ Use the Date and Distance columns in the worksheet to create a chart.

11. Add a reference to the Microsoft Excel object library using the References command on the Tools menu.

12. Add comments at the top of the code that include your name and today's date.

13. Save the procedure. Switch to Form View to test the code.

14. Use the Chart button to create an Excel worksheet and a chart.

15. Save the workbook as Runners Log.

16. Print the project's code and print the chart.

17. Close Excel.

18. Close the VBA IDE and close Access.

## QUICK CHECK ANSWERS

### Session 9.1

1. ```
   Dim appWord as Word.Application
   Set appWord = New Word.Application
   ```

2. ```
   rngInsertionPoint.Tables.Add rngInsertionPoint 5, 2
   ```

3. ActiveX Data Objects

4. `Set`

5. `.EOF`

### Session 9.2

1. Insert, File

2. ```
   Dim appExcel As Excel.Application
   Dim xlBook As Excel.Workbook
   Dim xlSheet As Excel.Worksheet
   Dim xlChart As Excel.Chart
   ```

3. row, column

4. `AbsolutePosition`

5. `SetSourceData`
   ```

## A

**AbsolutePosition property**

When applied to a recordset, a property that indicates the actual record number of a record in the recordset or the number assigned to the record when it was entered into the database.

**Activate Method**

A method that will activate a specified object. In Excel, this method makes the specified worksheet the Active Worksheet.

**Active Window Object**

The window that is currently active in the Windows environment.

**Active Worksheet**

The worksheet in the Worksheets collection that is currently active.

**ActiveDocument**

The document in the Documents collection that is currently active.

**Add Method**

A method that adds an object to a collection such as the TabStops collection. When applied to Excel's Charts collection, a method that will add a chart to the charts collection.

**Application Object**

The actual application being accessed by VBA. Word, Excel, PowerPoint and Access are all application objects.

**Applications**

A program designed to perform specific tasks (for example, Word).

**ApplyTemplate Method**

A method that will apply a template to a PowerPoint presentation.

**Assignment Statement**

A program statement that assigns a single value to a variable.

**Autofit**

A menu command in Excel that allows you to size a column to accommodate the size of the data stored in that column.

**Autofit Method**

A VBA method used to size a column to accommodate the size of the data stored in the specified column. This method performs the same task as the Autofit command in Excel.

## B

**Breakpoint**

A statement marked in a way that tells VBA to process all the statements preceding it, and then stop.

## C

**Call Statement**

A statement that will invoke a specified procedure.

**Caption**

A property that specifies the text that appears on a control.

**Cells Collection**

As related to the Excel object model, the collection of cells in an Excel worksheet.

**ClearAll Method**

A method that will delete all tabs in a paragraph or document.

**Click Event**

The event that is triggered when the user clicks an object.

**Click Event Procedure**

The complete set of statements that make up the program to be triggered when an event takes place.

**Close Action**

An Access macro action that will close a particular object.

**Code Builder**

The Visual Basic Integrated Development Environment (VBA IDE) for Access.

**Code**

Program statements

**Collapse a Range**

As applied to the range object, the act of eliminating a range.

**Collapse Method**

A method that will collapse a selected range.

**Columns Collection**

As related to the Excel object model, the collection of columns in an Excel worksheet.

**Command Button Control**

A control used to provide a way for the user to execute some action.

**Comments**

Statements that provide documentation for your projects.

**Compound Condition**

A condition made up of multiple conditions combined using logical operators.

**Concatenation**

The process of combining strings.

**Continuation Character**

A character (underscore) that indicates that the current statement continues on to the next line.

**Control Objects (or controls)**

The various parts of a Graphical User Interface that allow the user to interact with the project.

**Control Structure**

A logical arrangement of statements.

**Control Variable (counter)**

A variable used with the For... Next loop that is responsible for counting the number of times VBA will process the loop.

**Count Property**

As related to PowerPoint slides, property that indicates the number of slides currently in the Slides collection.

**Current Event**

An event that is triggered when a new record is entered into a form.

## D

**Data Object**

An object that is associated with data.

**Debugging**

The process of handling errors in a program.

**Debugging Tools**

A set of tools included with VBA that are designed to make the process of finding errors as simple as possible.

**Decision Control Structure**

*See* Selection control structure.

**Declare a variable**

To define a variable in a project.

**Defensive Programming**

The process of anticipating and attempting to prevent errors.

**Delete Method**

A method that will delete selected text. As related to PowerPoint slides, the delete method will delete a specified slide in the Slides collection.

**Design Mode**

The program is in design mode when it is not running and the VBA IDE has all the tools available for altering the program.

**Developer**

A person who creates a computer program.

**Dim Statement**

The statement used to declare (define) a variable.

**Do Loop**

A set of statement that is continually processed until a condition results in either true or false as specified.

**Do...Until Loop**

A repetition control structure that repeats statements until a condition becomes true.

**Do...While Loop**

A repetition control structure that repeats statements while a condition remains true.

**Docked Window**

A window that is anchored to the edge of another window.

**DoCmd Object**

An Access object used to run Access actions.

**Document**

The process of adding documentation to a project (in comments).

**Documents Collection**

All the Word documents currently opened.

## E

**Empty String**

A string that contains no characters.

**EOF property**

As applied to a recordset, a property that indicates whether the last record in the recordset has been accessed.

**Event Driven**

Term used to refer to programs that are not triggered until a particular event takes place.

**Execute**

The process by which a computer reads a program, interprets it, and performs the actions specified in each line of code. Developers often use the term "run" instead, as in "run the procedure."

**Exit Sub statement**

A statement that causes a procedure to end.

**Expression**

The value to be assigned to a target variable.

## F

**Floating window**

A window that is unanchored so that it can be moved and sized as desired.

**Flowchart**

A diagram that illustrates the order in which statements are processed.

**Focus**

The state in which an object can receive mouse clicks or keyboard input. Developers commonly say that an object "has focus."

**Font**

A property that specifies the font in which text will be displayed.

**For...Next Loop**

A repetition control structure that implements an iterative loop.

**Form Module**

The code written for a particular form.

**Format function**

A function that converts a numeric value into a specified format.

**Formatting**

The way in a which a value or string appears in output.

**Frame Control Object**

A control into which you can insert other control objects in a form.

**Function**

A kind of VBA procedure that returns a single value.

**Functionality**

All the tasks a specific application can perform.

### General Procedure

A procedure that is not associated with a particular object's events. General procedures are often executed by a Call statement located within an event procedure.

### Global Variable

A variable that is available to all the modules and procedures in a project. Also called a public variable.

### Graphical User Interface (GUI)

An interface that includes images and text.

### Hardware

The computer itself, including the keyboard, the monitor, the processor, and so on.

### HeadersFooters Collection

As related to PowerPoint slides, a collection of all headers and footers of the Title Master.

### Hide Method

A method that removes the UserForm from the screen.

### Horizontal Applications

Applications that can be employed by many different kinds of organizations for many different kinds of tasks.

### Host Application

The application for which a VBA program has been written.

### Icon

Pictures on the interface that represent something else.

### If...Then...Else Statement

The VBA implementation of the Decision control structure.

### Image Control

A control used to display an image on a form.

### Immediate Window

A window that allows you to see the value of a variable at runtime.

### Index Number

As related to PowerPoint slides, the number of the slide in the slide collection.

### Initialize Event

An event that is triggered when the form is loaded.

### Input

The values or text that the user types in a text box. Sometimes referred to as "user input."

### Inputbox Function

A function that provides an easy way to retrieve a single item of data from the user.

### InsertAfter Method

A method that inserts text in a document after the current selection.

### InsertDateTime Method

A method that will insert the current data and time in a specified format.

### InsertFromFile Method

As related to PowerPoint slides, the method that will insert slides from a file into the current presentation.

### InsertParagraphAfter Method

A method that inserts a paragraph mark after the current selection.

### Instance

An application that is currently running.

### Interface

The means by which the user interacts with a program.

### Intrinsic Function

A predefined procedure that is provided along with VBA. Sometimes called a built-in function.

### IsDate Function

A function that receives a value and determines whether the value is a valid date.

### IsNull Function

A function that checks to see if a value is null (or empty).

### IsNumeric Function

A function that receives a value and determines whether the value is a valid number.

### Iterate

As applied to a recordset, the process of looping through the records in a recordset.

### Iterative Loop

A loop that processes a series of statements a certain number of times.

### Label Control

A control used to place some text on the screen for documentation purposes.

### Last Property

Property that indicates the last item in a collection.

### Layout Property

As related to PowerPoint slides, the layout of a particular slide or collection of slides.

### Len Function

A function that determines the length of text.

### Lines Collection

A collection of all the lines within a TextRange object.

### Logical Operators

Special words (AND, OR, and NOT) used to form compound conditions.

### Loop

A structure that continually repeats a series of statements as long as a particular condition remains true. Also known as a Repetition control structure.

## M

**Macro Module File**

The location where macro code is saved.

**Methods**

The set of actions that an object can perform.

**Module**

The part of a VBA project in which VBA code is saved.

**MsgBox Function**

An intrinsic function used to display a message to the user.

**Name Property**

As applied to an object, the property that specifies the name of an object. As related to the Font property, a property that specifies the name of a font.

## N

**Navigation Buttons**

Command buttons used to navigate through the records in a database.

**Null Value**

An empty value, or no value at all.

**Numeric Data Types**

Data types used for storing numeric data that will be used in calculations.

## O

**Object**

A thing that is defined by its characteristics and by what it can do.

**Object Model**

The various objects and collections of object included with an application.

**Object-Based Programming Language**

A language that works very closely with the objects available within an application such as Word or Excel.

**Open Method**

As related to a recordset, a method that opens a recordset.

**Option Explicit**

A statement that prevents the use of variables that have not been declared.

**Order of Precedence**

The rules governing the order in which mathematical operations will be performed.

**Output**

The result of one or more statements displayed either on the screen or on a printed page. Also known as "program output."

## P

**Paragraphs Collection**

A collection of all the paragraphs in a document.

**Presentations Collection**

A collection of all PowerPoint presentations currently open.

**Print Statement**

A statement that will display the result of a statement in the Immediate window.

**Private Sub — End Sub**

The statements that indicate the beginning and ending of a procedure.

**Private Variable**

A variable that is only available to the module or procedure in which it is declared.

**Programmatically**

A term used to indicate actions being carried out via program statements.

**Programming Constructs**

Another name for Control Structures.

**Programming Environment**

A special program used to develop computer programs. In VBA, developers use the VBA IDE programming environment.

**Programming Language**

A collection of words or commands that a developer can use to communicate with the computer.

**Programming an Object**

The process of assigning an event to a particular object and then writing the program statements that the event will trigger.

**Programs**

Instructions that tell the computer what to do.

**Project**

A collection of VBA files.

**Properties**

The characteristics that define a particular object.

**Property Sheet**

In Access, a dialog box that contains the properties for a particular object.

**Public Variable**

*See* global variable.

## Q

**Quit Action**

An Access macro action that will close an application.

## R

**Range Object**

A contiguous portion (block) of a document.

**Reference**

A VBA setting indicating that some code in a module will refer to an application other than the host application. The process of selecting which applications the code will refer to is sometimes called "setting references."

**Referring to a variable**

Using a variable's name within a program statement.

**Repetition Control Structure**

*See* loop.

**RGB Function**

A function that applies color to an object.

**Run**

*See* execute.

**Run mode**

The state in which a program is running (or executing).

**S**

**Selection Control Structure**

A structure that "decides" between two alternatives based on the results of a condition. Also called a decision control structure.

**Selection Object**

The items that are selected within the active window.

**SelLength Property**

A property that specifies the length of a selection.

**SelStart**

A statement that specifies where a selection (highlight) will begin.

**Sequence Control Structure**

A structure that processes one statement after the other.

**Set Statement**

A statement that establishes a reference to an object variable.

**SetFocus Method**

A method that will move the cursor to the specified object.

**SetSourceData Method**

As applied to Excel's Charts collection, a method that will establish the source of data for a chart in the Charts collection.

**Shape Object**

An object on the drawing layer of a slide.

**Shapes Collection**

A collection of all the shape objects on a particular slide.

**Size Property**

As applied to the Font property, a property that specifies the size of a font.

**Software**

Programs such as Word, Excel, Access, or PowerPoint.

**Sort Method**

As related to Excel, a method of the range object that will sort data according to specifications.

**Standard Module**

A module that contains only procedure and variable declarations that are not associated with a particular form.

**Static Database**

A database that cannot be opened or altered by other users of the same database.

**Story**

Term used by developers to refer to a Word document. *See* WholeStory method.

**String**

A collection of alphanumeric characters.

**Syntax**

The basic structure of a statement.

**T**

**TabStops Collection**

Consists of all the tabs set in a document.

**Target**

The variable or property to which you want to assign a value.

**Text Property**

The property that contains the actual text in a range.

**Textbox Control**

A control used to obtain data from the user.

**TextFrame Object**

The part of a shape object that can contain text.

**TextRange Object**

The text within a shape.

**Title Master**

As related to PowerPoint slides, the part of a presentation that maintains elements common to the entire slides collection.

**Toggle**

The process of turning a feature or setting off or on.

**U**

**Ucase Function**

A function that converts a value to all uppercase.

**Unload Method**

A method that removes the UserForm from the screen and from memory as well.

**UserForm**

A container for control object that serves as the background for the form. Commonly called a "form."

**V**

**Validate**

To check data for validity.

**Value**

The setting for a particular property.

**Variable**

A location in memory where data is temporarily stored at runtime.

**VBA Integrated Development Environment (VBA IDE)**

The VBA programming environment. Sometimes called the Visual Basic Editor.

**Vertical Market Applications**

Office applications that have been customized to satisfy the unique needs of an organization.

**Visible Property**

A property used to either display or hide an object.

**Visual Basic for Applications (VBA)**

A powerful programming language included with the Office suite. VBA allows you to create customs solutions for specific business needs.

**Visual Basic Editor**

*See* VBA Integrated Development Environment (VBA IDE).

**WholeStory Method**

A method that returns the entire text in a document. *See* Story.

**With Statement**

A statement that allows you to specify an object that will apply to all the statements between the `With` Statement and the `End With` statement.

**Workbook Object**

A particular workbook within the Workbooks collection.

**Workbooks Collection**

The collection of all Excel workbooks currently open.

**Special Characters**

\~(back slash), VBA 122

\> (greater than operator), VBA 138

< (less than operator), VBA 138

' (apostrophe), VBA 95

* (asterisk), VBA 121, VBA 122

+ (plus sign), VBA 121, VBA 122

- (minus sign), VBA 121, VBA 122

/ (slash), VBA 121, VBA 122

= (equal sign), VBA 138

>= (greater than or equal to operator), VBA 138

<= (less than or equal to operator), VBA 138

<> (not equal to operator), VBA 138

^ (caret), VBA 122

**A**

**absolute position, VBA 434**

**AbsolutePosition property, VBA 434**

**Access**

creating Word documents within, VBA 409–413

forms. *See* Access forms.

inserting Access table data into Excel worksheets, VBA 433–435

inserting Word documents, VBA 413–419

iterating through records in Access data tables, VBA 425–429

macros. *See* Access macros.

objects, VBA 356–357

recordsets. *See* Access recordsets.

**Access application, VBA 355–398**

database, VBA 358–360

macros. *See* Access macros.

Main Menu form, VBA 361–362

object property sheets, VBA 362–364

testing Main Menu, VBA 371

**Access forms, VBA 386–397**

conditionally altering appearance of controls, VBA 393–395

conditionally enabling and disabling text boxes, VBA 395–397

inserting labels, VBA 387–388

Main Menu form, VBA 361–362

programming labels, VBA 388–393

**Access macros, VBA 364–370**

attaching to command buttons, VBA 365–369

building using Quit action, VBA 369–370

testing, VBA 369

**Access recordsets**

adding to Word tables, VBA 421–425

establishing, VBA 418–421, VBA 433

**Access tables**

inserting data into Excel worksheets, VBA 433–435

iterating through records, VBA 425–429

**Activate method, VBA 279**

activating worksheets, VBA 196–197

**activating worksheets, VBA 279**

Activate method, VBA 196–197

**ActiveDocument, VBA 231**

**active presentation(s), referring to, VBA 318**

**ActivePresentation property, VBA 318**

**Active Window object, VBA 232**

**active worksheets, VBA 196**

**adding control objects to UserForms, VBA 67–69, VBA 78–90**

adjusting properties, VBA 79–80

command buttons, VBA 83–87

dragging pointer, VBA 78–79

Image controls, VBA 87–90

viewing projects in runtime, VBA 80–81

**addition operator (+), VBA 121, VBA 122**

**Add method, adding tabs, VBA 234–235**

**aligning command buttons, VBA 86–87**

**apostrophe ('), indicating comments, VBA 95**

**application(s), VBA 4**

creating instances, VBA 410

functionality, VBA 4

horizontal, VBA 4

host, VBA 5

making visible on screen, VBA 411–412

vertical market, VBA 5

Word. *See* Word applications.

**application objects, VBA 190**

**ApplyTemplate method, VBA 334–336**

**assignment statements, VBA 120–123**

altering object properties, VBA 191–192

**asterisk (*), multiplication operator, VBA 121, VBA 122**

**AutoFit method, VBA 283–284**

**B**

**BackColor property, changing, VBA 64–65**

**back slash integer division operator, VBA 122**

**BackStyle property, VBA 73–74**

**blank rows, finding using Do...Until loops, VBA 202–203**

**boldface, applying to fonts, VBA 286–288**

**Bold property, Range object, VBA 242**

**Boolean expressions, VBA 135.** *See also* If...Then...Else statements.

**breakpoints, setting in programs, VBA 145–148**

**built-in functions, VBA 132**

## C

Call statements, VBA 323–326
calling procedures, VBA 208–212, VBA 323–326
Caption property, VBA 65–66
    changing, VBA 66, VBA 70–73
caret (^), exponentiation operator, VBA 122
Cells collection, VBA 274, VBA 279
Cells property
    inserting data in worksheet, VBA 206–208
    worksheets, altering, VBA 195–196
changing object properties, VBA 64–65, VBA 66, VBA 79–80
    assignment statements, VBA 191–192
    controls, VBA 70–73
    multiple properties simultaneously, VBA 73–76
    title slides, VBA 345–347
    worksheets, VBA 191–194, VBA 195–196, VBA 197–199
charts, Excel, creating with VBA statements, VBA 435–439
Check Register project, VBA 153–159
    testing, VBA 200–208
    validating data, VBA 156–159
ClearAll method, clearing tabs, VBA 234
Click event procedures, VBA 48, VBA 91–95, VBA 93
    adding VBA code, VBA 91 95
Close action, Access, VBA 365
closing VBA IDE windows, VBA 12
code, VBA 5, VBA 19
    documenting, VBA 95–96
    imported. See imported code.
    modules. See modules.
    printing, VBA 32–33, VBA 96–97
    saving, VBA 27
    testing, VBA 24–26
    typing, VBA 21–23
CodeBuilder, VBA 378–379
Collapse method, Range object, VBA 244
collapsing ranges, VBA 244
collections, VBA 47
color, worksheet cells, VBA 285–286
Columns collection, VBA 274
command buttons, VBA 57
    adding to UserForms, VBA 83–85
    adding VBA code to Click events, VBA 91–95
    aligning, VBA 86–87
    attaching macros, VBA 365–369
    programming, VBA 92–95
    sizing, VBA 85–87
    spacing, VBA 86–87
comments, VBA 95
comparison operators
    If...Then...Else statements, VBA 138
    multiple, in compound conditions, VBA 138–139

compound conditions, multiple comparison operators, VBA 138–139
concatenating strings, VBA 245
conditions, VBA 135
    compound, using multiple comparison operators, VBA 138–139
conjunction, logical, VBA 139
continuation character, VBA 235–236
control objects (controls), VBA 55, VBA 56–57, VBA 67–77
    Access forms. See Access forms.
    adding to UserForms. See adding control objects to UserForms.
    conditionally altering appearance, VBA 393–395
    moving, VBA 87–88
    naming, VBA 69–70
    properties. See object properties.
    sizing, VBA 76–77
control structures, VBA 134–139
    adding Do...Until loops, VBA 281–283
    appropriate use, VBA 274–283
    avoiding null values with If statements, VBA 275–278
    Decision, VBA 134
    Do...Until and Do...While loops compared, VBA 280
    examining Do...Until loops, VBA 279–280
    finding first empty row using Do...Until loops, VBA 278–279
    inserting data into appropriate row, VBA 280
    Repetition. See Repetition control structures.
    Selection. See Selection control structures.
    Sequence, VBA 134, VBA 135
control variables, VBA 186
cursor, moving with SetFocus method, VBA 276

## D

data objects, VBA 49
data types, VBA 116–117
databases, static, VBA 418
dates, InsertDateTime method, VBA 338–339
debugging programs, VBA 141–152
    Immediate window, VBA 148–152
    setting breakpoints in procedures, VBA 145 148
    stepping through programs, VBA 141–145
debugging tools, VBA 141
Decision control structure, VBA 134
declaring variables, VBA 115–116
    as application objects, VBA 410
defensive programming, VBA 133
Delete method, VBA 232, VBA 319–320
deleting
    slides using Delete method, VBA 319–320
    tabs, VBA 233–234
design mode, VBA 20

developers, VBA 5
Dim statements, VBA 115–116
  valid and invalid variable names, VBA 118
disabling navigation buttons, VBA 382–385
displaying. *See also* viewing.
  frames, VBA 225–227
  messages using MsgBox function, VBA 137
division operator (/), VBA 121, VBA 122
docked windows, VBA IDE, VBA 11–13
DoCmd object, VBA 375–377
documenting your work, VBA 95–96
Documents collection, VBA 231
Do loops, VBA 172, VBA 173–185
  Do...Until. *See* Do...Until loops.
  Do...While. *See* Do...While loops.
Do...Until loops, VBA 173, VBA 179–182,
  VBA 278–280
  adding to project, VBA 281–283
  coding, VBA 180–181
  Do...While loops compared, VBA 182–185
  finding blank rows, VBA 202–203
  finding first empty row, VBA 278–279
  observing with Step Into feature, VBA 181–182,
    VBA 203–206
  stepping through, VBA 203–206
Do...While loops, VBA 173–179
  coding, VBA 174–176
  Do...Until loops compared, VBA 182–185, VBA 280
  observing with Step Into feature, VBA 177–179
dysjunction, logical, VBA 139


**E**

empty rows, finding using Do...Until loop,
  VBA 278–279
empty strings, VBA 92
EOF property, VBA 425–426
equal to operator (=), VBA 138
errors, debugging programs. *See* debugging
  programs.
event(s), VBA 47–48
event-driven programs, VBA 48
event procedures. *See* procedures.
Excel
  adding column headings to worksheets, VBA 433
  creating charts with VBA statements, VBA 435–439
  declaring object reference variables, VBA 432
  inserting Access table data into Excel worksheets,
    VBA 433–435
Excel object models, VBA 189–199, VBA 273–274
  activating worksheets using Activate method,
    VBA 196–197

altering properties, VBA 191–194, VBA 195–196,
    VBA 197–199
  default values in object references, VBA 194
  specific, referring to, VBA 190–191
Excel VBA IDE, VBA 49–55
  changing project names, VBA 52–55
  opening, VBA 49–50
  Project Explorer, VBA 50–52
executing programs, VBA 24–26
ExitSub statement, VBA 159
  ending procedures, VBA 276–278
exponentiation operator (^), VBA 122
expressions
  assignment statements, VBA 120–123
  Boolean, VBA 135. *See also* If...Then...Else statements.
  order of precedence, VBA 122–123


**F**

floating windows, VBA IDE, VBA 11
flowcharts, VBA 134
flow of control, VBA 134
focus, VBA 231
font(s), applying color and boldface, VBA 286–288
Font property, VBA 73
  Range object, VBA 241
footers, applying to title master, VBA 328–329
form(s). *See also* UserForm(s).
  Access. *See* Access forms.
  frame controls, VBA 224–225
  removing from screen, VBA 228–230
Format function, VBA 128
  adding to code, VBA 128–129
  formatting user input, VBA 129–131
  formatting values, VBA 127–128
form modules, VBA 168
formatting
  definition, VBA 128
  text, Range object, VBA 241–243
For-Next statements, VBA 185–187
  coding and observing, VBA 187–188
frame(s), hiding and displaying, VBA 225–227
frame control objects, VBA 224–225
functionality, VBA 4
functions, VBA 127–132
  built-in, VBA 132
  Format. *See* Format function.
  intrinsic, VBA 131–132
  MsgBox, VBA 137
  sub procedures versus, VBA 131–132

## G

**general procedures, VBA 320–326**
  calling, VBA 323–326
  coding, VBA 322–323
  integrating applications, VBA 406
**global variables, VBA 311**
**GoToRecord method, VBA 377**
**Gradebook application, VBA 258–273**
  grade assignment, VBA 267–273
  planning, VBA 261–262
  previewing, VBA 258–261
  viewing code, VBA 262–266
**graphical user interfaces (GUIs), VBA 55**
**greater than operator (>), VBA 138**
**greater than or equal to operator (>=), VBA 138**

## H

**hardware, VBA 4**
**HeadersFooters collection, VBA 328–329**
**Help system, VBA 34–37**
  starting from Immediate window, VBA 151–152
**Hide method, VBA 95**
**hiding frames, VBA 225–227**
**horizontal applications, VBA 4**
**host applications, VBA 5**

## I

**icons, interfaces, VBA 55**
**If statements, avoiding null values, VBA 275–278**
**If...Then...Else statements**
  adding to code, VBA 139–141
  building, VBA 135–137
  comparison operators, VBA 138
**image controls, VBA 57**
  adding to UserForms, VBA 88
  adjusting, VBA 89–90
**Immediate window, VBA 148–152**
  starting Help, VBA 151–152
**imported code, VBA 430–435**
  adding column headings to worksheets, VBA 433
  declaring Excel object reference variables, VBA 432
  establishing Access recordsets, VBA 433
  importing code into modules, VBA 429–430
  inserting Access table data into Excel worksheets, VBA 433–435
  testing, VBA 430–431
**index number, VBA 318**

**Initialize event, frames, VBA 225–227**
**input, VBA 19.** *See also* user input.
**InputBox function, VBA 337–338**
**InsertAfter method, VBA 238**
**InsertDateTime method, VBA 338–339**
**InsertFromFile method, VBA 326–328**
**inserting**
  Access table data into Excel worksheets, VBA 433–435
  data into worksheets, VBA 280
  data into worksheets via Cells property, VBA 206–208
  tabbed lists in documents, VBA 246–247
  text in Word documents. *See* inserting text in Word documents.
  titles in Word documents, VBA 413–415
**inserting text in Word documents, VBA 237–241**
  adding code, VBA 239–241
  Range object, VBA 238
  referring to objects multiple times in With statements, VBA 239
**InsertParagraphAfter method, VBA 238**
**Integer data type, VBA 116, VBA 117**
  prefix, VBA 118
**integer division operator (, VBA 122**
**Integrated Development Environment.** *See* **VBA Integrated Development Environment (VBA IDE).**
**integrating applications, VBA 405–439.** *See also specific applications.*
  general procedures, VBA 406
  setting references to other applications, VBA 406–409
**interfaces, VBA 48–49, VBA 55–58**
  control objects. *See* control objects (controls).
  GUIs, VBA 55
  planning, VBA 57–58
  UserForms. *See* UserForm(s).
**intrinsic functions, VBA 131–132**
**invalid data, VBA 116**
**IsNull function, VBA 383**
**iterating through records in Access data tables, VBA 425–429**
**Iterative loops, VBA 172, VBA 185–188**
  coding and observing For-Next statements, VBA 187–188

## L

**label controls, VBA 57**
  adding to UserForms, VBA 68–69, VBA 81–83
  changing properties, VBA 70–73, VBA 79–80
  spacing, VBA 77
**label objects, Access forms.** *See* **Access forms.**
**Last property, VBA 422**

**Layout property, VBA 330–334**

**layouts, applying to slides using layout property,**
   **VBA 330–334**

**Len function, VBA 158**

**less than operator (<), VBA 138**

**less than or equal to operator (<=), VBA 138**

**Lines collection, VBA 341–342**

**lists, tabbed, inserting in documents, VBA 246–247**

**logical conjunction, VBA 139**

**logical dysjunction, VBA 139**

**logical negation, VBA 139**

**Long integer data type, VBA 116**
   prefix, VBA 118

**loops (looping mechanisms).** *See* **Do loops; Do...Until**
   **loops; Do...While loops; Iterative loops; Repetition**
   **control structures.**

## M

**macro(s), VBA 28–34**
   Access. *See* Access macros.
   printing code modules, VBA 32–33
   recording, VBA 28–30
   running, VBA 30–31
   saving, VBA 33–34
   VBA compared, VBA 5–6, VBA 374–375
   viewing code, VBA 31–32

**macro module files, VBA 28**

**Main Menu form, Access, VBA 361–362, VBA 371**

**mathematical expressions.** *See* **expressions.**

**mathematical operators, VBA 121–122**
   order of precedence, VBA 121–123

**methods, VBA 47.** *See also* specific methods.

**Microsoft Office 2000, VBA 4**

**minus sign (-), subtraction operator, VBA 121,**
   **VBA 122**

**Mod (modulus arithmetic operator), VBA 122**

**modules, VBA 27**
   form, VBA 168
   importing code, VBA 429–430
   printing, VBA 32–33
   saving, VBA 27
   standard. *See* standard modules.

**mouse pointer, adding control objects, VBA 78–79**

**moving**
   controls, VBA 87–88
   VBA IDE windows, VBA 13–14

**MsgBox function, VBA 137**

**multiplication operator (*), VBA 121, VBA 122**

## N

**name(s)**
   objects within projects, VBA 69–70
   projects, changing, VBA 52–55
   variables, VBA 117–118

**Name property, VBA 65**
   changing, VBA 62–63
   Range object, VBA 241–242
   worksheets, altering, VBA 192–194

**navigation buttons, VBA 371–385**
   disabling, VBA 382–385
   DoCmd object, VBA 375–377
   programming, VBA 377–382
   VBA code versus macro actions, VBA 374–375

**negation, logical, VBA 139**

**not equal to operator (<>), VBA 138**

**null value, VBA 91**
   avoiding with If statements, VBA 275–278

**numeric data types, VBA 117**

## O

**object(s), VBA 46–49**
   Access, VBA 356–357
   application, VBA 190
   collections, VBA 47
   control. *See* control objects (controls).
   data, VBA 49
   events, VBA 47–48
   interfaces, VBA 48–49
   methods, VBA 47
   programming, VBA 91
   properties. *See* changing object properties; object
      properties.

**object-based programming languages, VBA 46.**
   *See also* **Visual Basic for Applications (VBA).**

**object models, VBA 189–199**
   Excel. *See* Excel object models.
   PowerPoint. *See* PowerPoint object model.
   Windows, VBA 232
   Word, VBA 230–232

**object properties**
   changing. *See* changing object properties.
   default, in object references, VBA 194
   values, VBA 47

**object references**
   abbreviating with Set statement, VBA 337
   setting, VBA 410–411

**object reference variables, Excel, declaring, VBA 432**
**Office 2000, VBA 4**
**opening**
  Excel VBA IDE, VBA 49–50
  UserForms, VBA 59
  VBA IDE in PowerPoint, VBA 15–17
**Open method, VBA 418**
**Option Explicit statements, VBA 119–120**
**order of precedence, VBA 121–123**
**outlines, PowerPoint presentations, VBA 302–303**
**output, VBA 127**

## P

**Paragraphs collection, VBA 231**
**plus sign (+), addition operator, VBA 121, VBA 122**
**PowerPoint object model, VBA 317–319**
  ActivePresentation property, VBA 318
  referring to specific slides in Slides collection,
    VBA 318–319
**PowerPoint presentations.** *See also* **Presentation**
  **Builder project.**
  active, referring to, VBA 318
  adding footers to title master, VBA 328–329
  applying layouts using Layout property, VBA 330–334
  applying templates with ApplyTemplate method,
    VBA 334–336
  inserting slides using InsertFromFile method,
    VBA 326–328
  slides. *See* slides.
**PowerPoint VBA IDE**
  macros, VBA 28–34
  opening, VBA 15–17
**prefixes, variables, VBA 118**
**Presentation Builder project, VBA 302–311**
  planning, VBA 307–311
  previewing, VBA 303–307
  Word outline, VBA 302–303
**Presentations collection, VBA 318**
**printing code, VBA 32–33, VBA 96–97**
**private variables, VBA 311**
**procedures**
  calling, VBA 208–212, VBA 323–326
  ending with Exit Sub statement, VBA 276–278
  general. *See* general procedures.
  inserting in standard modules, VBA 170–172
**program(s), VBA 4**
  debugging. *See* debugging programs.
  event-driven, VBA 48
  executing, VBA 24–26
  setting breakpoints, VBA 145–148

  stepping through, VBA 141–145
  storing data. *See* storing data within programs.
**program output, VBA 127**
**programming, VBA 4–5**
  command buttons, VBA 92–95
  defensive, VBA 133
  label objects in Access forms, VBA 388–393
  navigation buttons, VBA 377–382
**programming environments, VBA 5**
**programming languages, VBA 4–5**
  object-based, VBA 46. *See also* Visual Basic for
    Applications (VBA).
  syntax, VBA 4
**programming the object, VBA 91**
**project(s), VBA 50**
  changing name, VBA 52–55
  naming objects, VBA 69–70
  saving, VBA 66–67
**Project Explorer, VBA 50–52**
**properties, objects.** *See* **changing object properties;**
  **object properties.**
**property sheets, Access objects, VBA 362–364**
**public variables, VBA 311–317**
  declaring, VBA 311–313
  referring to in statements, VBA 313

## Q

**Quit action, building macros, VBA 369–370**

## R

**Range object, VBA 238–239**
  establishing new ranges, VBA 244
  formatting text, VBA 241–243
  methods, VBA 238–239
**recording macros, PowerPoint, VBA 28–30**
**references, setting.** *See* **setting references.**
**referring to variables, VBA 120**
**Repetition control structures, VBA 134,**
  **VBA 172–188**
  Do loops. *See* Do loops.
  Iterative loops. *See* Iterative loops.
**resizing.** *See* **sizing.**
**RGB function, VBA 285–286**
**rows, worksheets, sorting using Sort method,**
  **VBA 288–290**
**Run mode, VBA 24**
**running macros, PowerPoint, VBA 30–31**
**runtime, viewing projects, VBA 80–81**

## S

**salary calculator program, VBA 111–153**
 assignment statements, VBA 120–123
 control structures, VBA 134–139
 debugging programs, VBA 141–152
 functions, VBA 127–132
 If...Then...Else statements, VBA 139–141
 preview, VBA 113-114
 preview of code, VBA 123–124
 programming Calculate button Click event,
  VBA 124–127
 storing data within programs, VBA 114–120
 subprocedures versus functions, VBA 131–132
 validating data, VBA 133–134
**saving**
 macros in PowerPoint, VBA 33–34
 projects, VBA 66–67
 Word VBA documents and associated modules, VBA 27
**screen**
 making applications visible, VBA 411–412
 removing forms, VBA 228–230
**Select Case statement, VBA 267–273**
 adding to project, VBA 269–271
 observing with Step Into, VBA 271–273
 syntax, VBA 268–269
**selecting text using Selection object, VBA 232**
**Selection control structures, VBA 134, VBA 135–139**
 displaying messages with MsgBox function, VBA 137
 *See* If...Then...Else statements.
**Selection object, VBA 232–233**
**SelLength property value, VBA 158**
**SelStart statement, VBA 158**
**Sequence control structure, VBA 134, VBA 135**
**Session Listing project, planning, VBA 228**
**SetFocus method, VBA 158**
 moving cursor, VBA 276
**SetSourceData method, VBA 436**
**Set statement, abbreviating object references,
 VBA 337**
**setting references**
 to objects, VBA 410–411
 to other applications, VBA 406–409
**Shape objects, VBA 339**
**Shapes collection, VBA 339–345**
**Single data type, VBA 116**
 prefix, VBA 118
**Size property, Range object, VBA 242**
**sizing**
 command buttons, VBA 85–87

 label controls, VBA 76–77
 UserForms, VBA 60
 VBA IDE windows, VBA 13–14
**slash (/), division operator, VBA 121, VBA 122**
**slides**
 deleting using Delete method, VBA 319–320
 inserting in presentations using InsertFromFile
  method, VBA 326–328
 specific, referring to, VBA 318–319
 title, altering properties, VBA 345–347
**Slides collection, VBA 318**
 referring to specific slides, VBA 318–319
**software, VBA 4.** *See also* **application(s); program(s).**
**Sort method, sorting worksheet rows, VBA 288–290**
**spacing**
 command buttons, VBA 86–87
 label controls, VBA 77
**Speaker Listing project, VBA 220–227**
 Session Listing form, VBA 223–224
**standard modules**
 creating, VBA 169–170
 inserting procedures, VBA 170–172
**starting**
 Help system from Immediate window, VBA 151–152
 VBA IDE, VBA 7–8
**static databases, VBA 418**
**Step Into feature**
 debugging programs, VBA 141–145
 observing Do...Until loops, VBA 181–182,
  VBA 203–206
 observing Do...While statements, VBA 177–179
 observing Select Case statement, VBA 271–273
**stepping through programs, VBA 141–145**
**stories, VBA 232**
**storing data within programs, VBA 114–120**
 assigning data types, VBA 116–117
 declaring variables, VBA 115–116
 naming variables, VBA 117–118
 preventing undeclared variables, VBA 119–120
**string(s), VBA 92**
 concatenating, VBA 245
 empty, VBA 92
**String data type, VBA 116**
 prefix, VBA 118
**sub procedures, functions versus, VBA 131–132**
**subtraction operator (-), VBA 121, VBA 122**
**switching between IDEs, VBA 18**
**syntax, VBA 4**
 typographical conventions, VBA 112

## T

tab(s). *See* TabStops collection.
tables. *See* Access tables; Word tables.
TabStops collection, VBA 231, VBA 233–237
    adding tabs with Add method, VBA 234–235
    clearing tabs with ClearAll method, VBA 234
    continuation character, VBA 235–236
    viewing tab code, VBA 236–237
targets, assignment statements, VBA 120
templates, applying to presentations using
    ApplyTemplate method, VBA 334–336
testing
    Access macros, VBA 369
    Access Main Menu, VBA 371
    code, VBA 24–26
    imported code, VBA 430–431
text
    formatting using Range object, VBA 241–243
    inserting in Word documents. *See* inserting text in
        Word documents.
    selecting using Selection object, VBA 232
text boxes, VBA 57
    adding to UserForms, VBA 81–83
    conditionally enabling and disabling, VBA 395–397
TextFrame object, VBA 341
Text property, VBA 238
    TextRange objects, VBA 341
TextRange objects, VBA 341
title master, applying footers, VBA 328–329
titles, inserting in Word documents, VBA 413–415
title slides, altering properties, VBA 345–347
toggles, VBA 148
typographical conventions, syntax, VBA 112

## U

Ucase function, VBA 393
undocking, VBA IDE windows, VBA 13
Unload method, VBA 95
UserForm(s), VBA 55, VBA 56, VBA 58–67
    control objects. *See* control objects (controls).
    opening, VBA 59
    properties. *See* UserForm properties.
    sizing, VBA 60
UserForm properties, VBA 60–66
    changing, VBA 62–66
user input, VBA 19, VBA 127
    formatting, VBA 129–131
    obtaining using InputBox function, VBA 337–338

## V

validating data, VBA 133–134, VBA 156–159
    IsDate function, VBA 156
    IsNumeric function, VBA 156
    viewing code, VBA 157–158
valid data, VBA 116
values
    formatting with Format function, VBA 127–128
    null, VBA 91
    object properties, VBA 47
variables, VBA 115
    assigning with assignment statements, VBA 120–123
    control, VBA 186
    declaring. *See* declaring variables.
    global, VBA 311
    naming, VBA 117–118
    private, VBA 311
    public. *See* public variables.
    referring to, VBA 120
    undeclared, preventing, VBA 119–120
VBA IDE windows
    closing, VBA 12
    docking and undocking, VBA 11–13
    floating, VBA 11
    moving and sizing, VBA 13–14
    windows, VBA 9–11
VBA Integrated Development Environment
    (VBA IDE), VBA 5, VBA 6–18
    Excel. *See* Excel VBA IDE.
    opening in PowerPoint, VBA 15–17
    starting, VBA 7–8
    switching between IDEs, VBA 18
    windows. *See* VBA IDE windows.
VBAProject Properties dialog box, VBA 53–54
vbTab constant, VBA 245
vertical market applications, VBA 5
viewing. *See also* displaying.
    macro code, VBA 31–32
    projects in runtime, VBA 80–81
    tab code, VBA 236–237
visibility, applications, VBA 411–412
Visible property, frames, VBA 225–227
Visual Basic Editor. *See* VBA Integrated Development
    Environment (VBA IDE).
Visual Basic for Applications (VBA), VBA 4, VBA 5–6,
    VBA 46
    benefits, VBA 6
    IDE. *See* VBA Integrated Development Environment
        (VBA IDE).
    macros compared, VBA 5–6

## W

**WholeStory method, VBA 232**
**Window menu, PowerPoint VBA IDE, VBA 16–17**
**windows**
opening in VBA IDE, VBA 9–11
VBA IDE. *See* VBA IDE windows.
**Windows object model, VBA 232**
**With statements, referring to objects multiple times, VBA 239**
**Word applications, Speaker Listing project, VBA 220–227**
**Word documents**
adding Access recordset to Word tables, VBA 421–425
creating from within Access, VBA 409–413
inserting Access data, VBA 413–419
inserting tabbed lists, VBA 246–247
inserting text. *See* inserting text in Word documents.
inserting titles, VBA 413–415
inserting Word tables, VBA 415–417
iterating through records in Access data tables, VBA 425–429
**Word object model, VBA 230–232**
**Word tables**
adding recordset data, VBA 421–425
inserting into documents, VBA 415–417

**Word VBA IDE, VBA 19–27**
creating applications, VBA 19–23
executing applications, VBA 24–26
saving code and associated modules, VBA 27
understanding code, VBA 26–27
**Workbook object, VBA 190**
**Workbooks collection, VBA 190**
**worksheet(s)**
activating, VBA 279
activating using Activate method, VBA 196–197
active, VBA 196
adding column headings, VBA 433
AutoFit method, VBA 283–284
cells. *See* worksheet cells.
changing object properties, VBA 191–194, VBA 195–196, VBA 197–199
inserting data, VBA 280
inserting data via Cells property, VBA 206–208
sorting rows using Sort method, VBA 288–290
**worksheet cells, VBA 285–288**
applying boldface and color to fonts, VBA 286–288
color, VBA 285–286

# TASK REFERENCE

| TASK | PAGE # | RECOMMENDED METHOD |
|------|--------|--------------------|
| Actions, attaching to a control in Access | 365 | See "Macros, creating in Access". |
| Breakpoint, set | 145 | Click in the left margin beside the line that you want to specify as a breakpoint. Press Enter.<br>To remove a breakpoint, click the breakpoint icon in the margin and press Enter. |
| VBA IDE windows, cascade | 17 | Click Window, click Cascade. |
| Code Builder, Open in Access | 378 | To use the Code Builder to create an event procedure, open the form's Property Pages, click the ellipse button for the event whose procedure you want to program, click Code Builder, then click OK.<br>To use the Code Builder to create a general procedure, press Alt+F11. |
| VBA code, print | 32 | Open the VBA IDE (or the Code Builder in Access), open the code module, click File, click Print. |
| Code window, open for a form | 92 | In Word, Excel or Power Point, open the Project Explorer window, display the icon for the form whose code window you want to open, and double-click the form.<br>To open a Code window in Access, see "Code Builder, Open in Access." |
| Comments, add to a program | 95 | Type an apostrophe followed by the comment. Include an apostrophe at the beginning of every comment line. |
| Continuation Characters, use | 235 | Type a portion of a statement, add a space, add an underscore ( _ ), press Enter, type the rest of the statement. |
| Control Objects, insert into a form | 68 | In the Toolbox, click the button for the control you want to insert. Click the desired location on the form or drag the pointer on the form. |
| Control Objects, select | 73 | Click a control object in a form. To select multiple control objects, click one object, press and hold the Shift key, click additional objects. |
| Control Objects, programming | 91 | Double-click the control object. Type the code in the appropriate event procedure. |
| File, import into a module | 30 | Click in the module, click Insert, click File, select the file, click Open. |
| Form, print with code | 97 | Click File, click Print, select Code and Form Image. Click OK. |
| Frame, add to a form | 224 | Click the Frame control in the toolbox. Draw the frame on the form. |
| General Procedure, create | 321 | Click in a code module. Click Insert, click Procedure, type the name of the procedure in the text box, click OK. |
| Help, display | 35 | Click Help, click Microsoft Visual Basic Help. |
| Macro Builder, open in Access | 364 | In the Properties pages, click the ellipse button for the event you want to program, click Macro Builder, click OK. |
| Macro, record in Word, Excel or PowerPoint | 28 | Click Tools, point to Macro, click Record New Macro. When finished recording, click ■. |

| TASK | PAGE # | RECOMMENDED METHOD |
|------|--------|--------------------|
| Macros, create in Access | 364 | In the Macro Builder, click the list arrow in the action column. Click on an action. Alter options as needed. |
| Option Explicit, configure | 119 | Click Tools, click Options, click the Editor tab, check the Require Variable Declaration check box. |
| Printing Code | 32 | Click a code module. Click File and then click Print. Verify the Current Module option is selected. Click OK. |
| Project Explorer, open | 9 | Click ▨ |
| Project Name, changing | 52 | Select Project in Project Explorer. Click Tools then click Properties. Select General Tab. Type a new project name and description. |
| Property Sheet, display in Access | 362 | Right-click the object, click Properties. |
| Properties Window, display | 9 | Click ▤ |
| Property, change value of | 63 | Select the object (or objects) whose property you want to change. In the Properties window, click to the right of the property you want to change, enter a new property value. |
| References, set for other applications | 408 | In the VBA IDE (or the Code Builder), click Tools, click References, check any application to which you will refer in your project. |
| Step Into mode, debug a program with | 141 | Position cursor inside procedure to be debugged, click Debug, click Step Into. Press F8 to move forward one step at a time. To end debugging, click Reset. |
| Userform, insert | 58 | In the VBA IDE, click Insert, click UserForm. |
| Userform, size | 58 | Position pointer over any edge of the form and drag border to desired size. |
| VBA IDE windows, tile | 17 | Click Window, click Tile Horizontally or Tile Vertically. |
| VBA IDE Windows, undock | 13 | Click Tools, click Options, click the Docking tab. Deselect the check boxes for all windows you want undocked. |
| VBA IDE, start | 7 | Start an Office application, press Alt+F11. |
| VBA Program, run | 24 | In the VBA IDE, position the cursor in the procedure you want to run, then click ▶. |
| VBA Project, save | 66 | Click 🖫. |

# File Finder

| Location in Tutorial | Name and Location of Data File | Student Saves File As... | Student Creates New File |
|---|---|---|---|
| **Tutorial 1** | | | |
| Session 1.1 | | | |
| Session 1.2 | | | Tutorial.01\First Word VBA Program.doc |
| Session 1.3 | | | Tutorial.01\First PP Macro.doc |
| Review Assignments | Tutorial.01\Review\VBA Program.doc | Tutorial.01\Review\Edited VBA Program.doc | |
| Case Problem 1 | | | Tutorial.01\FirstExcelVBA.xls |
| Case Problem 2 | | | Tutorial.01\StoneWater Bookstore Macro.doc |
| Case Problem 3 | | | Tutorial.01\GatewayMacro.ppt |
| Case Problem 4 | | | |
| **Tutorial 2** | | | Tutorial.02\Checkbook.xls |
| Session 2.1 | | | |
| Session 2.2 | Tutorial.02\Checkbook.xls (continued from Session 2.1) | | |
| Session 2.3 | | Tutorial.02\Checkbook.xls | |
| Review Assignments | Logo.gif Tutorial.02\Review\Deposit.xls | Tutorial.02\Deposit Form.xls | |
| Case Problem 1 | | | Tutorial.02\Cases\STP Personnel Management.xls |
| Case Problem 2 | | | Tutorial.02\Cases\Cheryl's Kids.xls |
| Case Problem 3 | | | Tutorial.02\Cases\Sutherland Expenses.xls |
| Case Problem 4 | | | Tutorial.02\Cases\C&B construction.xls |
| **Tutorial 3** | | | |
| Session 3.1 | Tutorial.03\Salary.xls | Tutorial.03\Salary Calculator.xls | |
| Session 3.2 | Tutorial.03\Salary Calculator.xls (saved in session 1) | | |
| Session 3.3 | Tutorial.03\TnTChk.xls | Tutorial.03\TnT Checkbook.xls | |
| Review Assignments | Tutorial.03\Review\Tickets.xls | Tutorial.03\Review\Magnolia Playhouse.xls | |
| Case Problem 1 | Tutorial.03\Cases\Potter.xls | Tutorial.03\Cases\Potters Grades | |
| Case Problem 2 | Tutorial.03\Cases\Hours.xls | Tutorial.03\Cases\Hours Recorder.xls | |
| Case Problem 3 | Tutorial.03\Cases\Whitman.xls | Tutorial.03\Cases\Whitman Lumber.xls | |
| Case Problem 4 | Tutorial.03\Cases\OnTrack.xls | Tutorial.03\Cases\OnTrack Bicycles | |
| **Tutorial 4** | | | |
| Session 4.1 | | | Tutorial.04\Practice Loops.xls |
| Session 4.2 | | | |
| Session 4.3 | Tutorial.04\TnTChk.xls | Tutorial.04\TnT Check Register | |
| Review Assignments | Tutorial.04\CheckBk.xls | Tutorial.04\Review\TnT Deposit.xls | |
| Case Problem 1 | Tutorial.04\Cases\Grdbk.xls | Tutorial.04\CasesPotter Gradebook.xls | |
| Case Problem 2 | Tutorial.04\Cases\Flower.xls | Tutorial.04\Cases\Flower List.xls | |
| Case Problem 3 | Tutorial.04\Cases\Invoice.xls | Tutorial.04\Cases\Whitman Invoices.xls | |
| Case Problem 4 | Tutorial.04\Cases\Project.xls | Tutorial.04\Cases\C&B Projects | |

## File Finder

| Location in Tutorial | Name and Location of Data File | Student Saves File As... | Student Creates New File |
|---|---|---|---|
| **Tutorial 5** | | | |
| Session 5.1 | Tutorial.05\Speaker.doc<br>Tutorial.05\Listing.doc | Tutorial.05\Speaker Listing Preview.doc<br>Tutorial.05\Speaker Listing.doc | |
| Session 5.2 | | | |
| Session 5.3 | | | |
| Review Assignments | Tutorial.05\Review\Phone.doc | Tutorial.05\Review\Phone List.doc | |
| Case Problem 1 | Tutorial.05\Cases\Valley.doc | Tutorial.05\Valley Community College.doc | |
| Case Problem 2 | Tutorial.05\Cases\Whitman.doc | Tutorial.05\Cases\Whitman client Heading.doc | |
| Case Problem 3 | Tutorial.05\Cases\Write.doc | Tutorial.05\Cases\Write Word.doc | |
| Case Problem 4 | Tutorial.05\Cases\C&B.doc | Tutorial.05\Cases\Construction Footer.doc | |
| **Tutorial 6** | | | |
| Session 6.1 | Tutorial.06\GrdPrev.xls<br>Tutorial.06\GdStart.xls | Tutorial.06\Gradebook Complete.xls | |
| Session 6.2 | | | |
| Session 6.3 | | | |
| Review Assignments | Tutorial.06\Pool.xls | Tutorial.06\Review\Martindale.xls | |
| Case Problem 1 | Tutorial.06\Cases\Nursery.xls | Tutorial.06\Cases\Laurel Nursery Plant Information.xls | |
| Case Problem 2 | Tutorial.06\Cases\Dynamic.xls | Tutorial.06\Cases\Dynamic Accounts.xls | |
| Case Problem 3 | Tutorial.06\Cases\BkStore.xls | Tutorial.06\Cases\Griffith Bookstore Hours.xls | |
| Case Problem 4 | Tutorial.06\Cases\AftSchool.xls | Tutorial.06\Cases\Jane's After School Program.xls | |
| **Tutorial 7** | | | |
| Session 7.1 | Tutorial.07\Outline.doc<br>Tutorial.07\Preview.ppt<br>Tutorial.07\Builder | Tutorial.07\Presentation Preview.ppt<br>Tutorial.07\Presentation Builder.ppt | |
| Session 7.2 | | | |
| Session 7.3 | | | |
| Review Assignments | Tutorial.07\Review\Build.ppt<br>Tutorial.07\Review\Outline2.doc | Tutorial.07\Review\TnT Presentation Builder Final.ppt | |
| Case Problem 1 | Tutorial.07\Cases\Nurses.ppt | Tutorial.07\Nurses Training Seminar | |
| Case Problem 2 | Tutorial.07\Cases\Treats.ppt | Tutorial.07\Cases\Delightful Treats.ppt | |
| Case Problem 3 | Tutorial.07\Cases\Century.ppt | Tutorial.07\Cases\Century Brokers.ppt | |
| Case Problem 4 | Tutorial.07\Cases\Newman.ppt | Tutorial.07\Cases\Newman Student Organizations.ppt | |
| **Tutorial 8** Note: Students should be working with a copy of these files databases | | | |
| Session 8.1 | Tutorial.08\Library.mdb | | |
| Session 8.2 | | | |
| Session 8.3 | | | |
| Review Assignments | Tutorial.08\Review\Potters.mdb | | |
| Case Problem 1 | Tutorial.08\Cases\MVPlants.mdb | | |
| Case Problem 2 | Tutorial.08\Cases\Skates.mdb | | |
| Case Problem 3 | Tutorial.08\Cases\Masters.mdb | | |
| Case Problem 4 | Tutorial.08\Cases\EZClean.mdb | | |

## File Finder

| Location in Tutorial | Name and Location of Data File | Student Saves File As... | Student Creates New File |
|---|---|---|---|
| **Tutorial 9** Note: Student should work with a copy of these files | | | |
| Session 9.1 | Tutorial.09\InTouch.mdb | Tutorial.09\First Quarter Sales Data.doc | |
| Session 9.2 | | | |
| Session 9.3 | | Tutorial.09\First Quarter Chart.xls | |
| Review Assignments | Tutorial.09\Carter.mdb | | |
| Case Problem 1 | Tutorial.09\Cases\CompClub.mdb | Tutorial.09\Cases\Computer Club.mdb | |
| Case Problem 2 | Tutorial.09\Cases\Animals.mdb | Tutorial.09\Cases\Middletown Animal Adoption Flyer.mdb | |
| Case Problem 3 | Tutorial.09\Cases\BigBlue.mdb | Tutorial.09\Cases\Big Blue Memories.mdb | |
| Case Problem 4 | Tutorial.09\Cases\Runner.mdb | Tutorial.09\Cases\Runners Log.mdb | |